Eye on the Future

EYE ON THE FUTURE

Business People in Calgary and the Bow Valley, 1870–1900

Henry C. Klassen

UNIVERSITY OF
CALGARY
PRESS

© 2002 Henry C. Klassen. All rights reserved.

University of Calgary Press
2500 University Drive NW
Calgary, Alberta
Canada T2N 1N4
www.uofcpress.com

National Library of Canada Cataloguing in Publication Data

Klassen, Henry C. (Henry Cornelius), 1931–
   Eye on the future
   Includes bibliographical references and index.
   ISBN 1-55238-078-5 (pbk.).--ISBN 1-55238-086-6 (bound)

1. Business enterprises—Alberta—Calgary—History—19th century.
2. Business enterprises—Alberta—Bow River Region—History—19th century.
3. Businesspeople—Alberta—Calgary—Biography.
4. Businesspeople—Alberta—Bow River Region—Biography.
5. Alberta—Economic conditions—To 1905. I. Title.

HF3230.C35K52 2002   338.097123'38   C2002-910896-9

We acknowledge the financial support of the Government of Canada through the Book Publishing Industry Development Program (BPIDP) for our publishing activities.

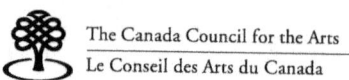

The Canada Council for the Arts
Le Conseil des Arts du Canada

No part of this publication may be reproduced, stored in a retrieval system or transmitted, in any form or by any means, without the prior written consent of the publisher or a licence from The Canadian Copyright Licensing Agency (Access Copyright). For an Access Copyright licence, visit www.accesscopyright.ca or call toll free to 1-800-893-5777.

Page, cover design, and typesetting by Kristina Schuring.

This book is dedicated to my beloved and loving family.

List of Tables		xii
List of Illustrations		xii
Preface		xv
Acknowledgments		xxii
Introduction		xxiv

1 The Meeting Place — 1

The Blackfoot — 1
The Coming of Montana Traders — 2
Hamilton and Healy's Trading Post — 3
Calgary's Changing Business System — 6

2 I. G. Baker & Co.: American Enterprise in the Wagon-Road Era — 9

I. G. Baker & Co. and its Networks of Stores — 10
Isaac Gilbert Baker and the Founding of a Trading Company — 11
Expansion in Montana — 13
Trading in the Canadian Prairies Begins — 14
Establishing a General Store in Calgary — 17
Survival and Expansion — 21
Responding to the Needs of the Mounted Police — 24
Achieving Growth through Ties to Native People — 25
Changing Natural Environment — 27
Prosperity in the Mid- and Late 1870s — 28
I. G. Baker & Co.'s Relationship with its Main Competitor, Power & Bro. — 30
Ongoing Commitment to Banking — 31
Expanding Merchandise Sales — 32
New Management at the Calgary Store — 33
Sources of Beef — 35
I. G. Baker & Co. and Capitalism — 36

3 Hudson's Bay Company:
British Enterprise in the Wagon-Road Era 39
Network of Trading Posts and Stores in Alberta 40
John Bunn and the Establishment of a Store in Calgary 43
Conflict between Richard Hardisty and Robert Hamilton 47
John Bunn and the Continuing Quest for Business 49
James A. Grahame and Calgary Business 51
Angus Fraser: New Manager 54
Charles J. Brydges and New Business Opportunities 55
An Uncertain Future 58
Charles J. Brydges' Visit to Calgary 60

4 Rails and Marketing
Impact of the Canadian Pacific Railway 65
Overcoming Barriers to Inland Transportation 67
Richard Hardisty Responds to the Canadian Pacific 68
I. G. Baker & Co. and the Canadian Pacific 71
Canadian Pacific and the Calgary Townsite 73
Business in Calgary after the Arrival of the Canadian Pacific 75
Coping with the Depression in the Mid-1880s 78
Business Opportunities during the Saskatchewan Rebellion 83
Peacetime Business 87

5 The Emergence of the Town of Calgary 93
Natural Advantages of Calgary 93
The Grid 94
George Murdoch: Harness and Saddle Maker 95
Isaac S. Freeze: A General Merchant 100
Specialization in Commerce 105
Rankin & Allan: Dry Goods Merchants 105
The Movement for Incorporation 107
Calgary's Early Government 110
Hamlets, Villages, and Settlers in the Bow Valley 113

6 Creating Banking Services — 119
Informal Private Credit Networks — 120
Private Banks — 121
Lafferty & Smith — 122
LeJeune, Smith & Co. — 128
Lafferty & Moore: Women in the Banking Business — 130
Chartered Banks — 133
Imperial Bank of Canada — 133
Bank of Montreal — 138
Responding to the Calgary Government's Financial Needs — 146
Financial Environment — 147

7 Building the Ranching Community — 149
Canadian Pacific Stockyards — 149
Land and the Rise of Big Ranch Companies in the Bow Valley — 151
American Roots — 152
Severe Winter of 1886-1887 — 153
Livestock Raising and the Natural Environment — 154
Ranching in the Bow Valley: The Conrads, I. G. Baker, and the Harris Brothers — 155
Cochrane Ranche Company — 159
British American Ranche Company — 161
Quorn Ranche Company — 167
Small Ranches — 171
Osborne E. Brown: Elbow River Rancher — 173
Arthur G. Wolley-Dod: Pine Creek Rancher — 176
John Quirk and his Medium-Sized Ranch — 180
Improving the Canadian Pacific Stockyards — 183

8 Maintaining the Family Farm — 185
The Banister Family Farm at Davisburg — 185
Farm Protest Movement in the Bow Valley — 188
Emergence of the Calgary Market — 190
Shattered and Fulfilled Dreams — 192
Robert Findlay: Homesteader at High River — 193
The Andrews Family Farm at Davisburg — 199
James F. McKevitt: Midnapore Farmer — 206
Farming at Davisburg: The David Suitor Family — 210
Informal Economic Networks — 214
Agricultural Societies and Fairs — 215
Voluntary Associations in the Bow Valley — 218
Farmers and the Natural Environment — 219
Financial Problems — 220
Kenneth Cameron: Okotoks Farmer — 220
Politics and Progress — 222

9 From Town to City — 225
- A Promising Place — 225
- Calgary: Southern Alberta's Railway Hub — 227
- Making Funds Available to Settlers — 234
- The Great Fire — 235
- Postfire Calgary's Builders — 240
- Canadian Pacific Station — 242
- Business and Hotels — 243
- Sandstone City — 244
- Turning Business Ideas into Business Organizations — 245
- George Alexander and the Alexander Block — 246
- William Roper Hull: Meat Packer and Rancher — 247
- Peter A. Prince and the Eau Claire & Bow River Lumber Co. — 251
- Hutchings & Riley: Harness and Saddle Makers — 255
- Environmental Problems — 259
- Alexander Lucas and Alberta's First City — 260
- Wesley F. Orr and a Young and Ambitious City — 261

10 Department Stores and Mass Distribution — 263
- Recovering from the Great Fire — 263
- Mass Distribution in Fort Benton — 264
- Calgary's First Department Store: I. G. Baker & Co. — 265
- Credit and Cash Sales — 267
- Wholesale Division — 269
- Retail Division — 269
- Competition — 271
- Sale of I. G. Baker & Co.'s Stores — 272
- A New Era in Department Store Business: Hudson's Bay Company — 275
- Grand Opening — 276
- New Sandstone Department Store — 278
- Labour Relations — 283
- Rewarding James Thomson — 284
- Edmund Taylor: New Manager — 285
- Expansion — 287

11 Women in Business — 293
- Gender and Workforce — 294
- Entrepreneurship — 299
- Janet Dewar and Dressmaking — 301
- Mary Macleod: Dressmaker — 301
- Margaret Leishman: Milliner — 302
- Annie A. Milner and the Millinery Trade — 303
- Frances Marie Carr: Boardinghousekeeper — 304
- Agnes K. Bedingfeld: Pekisko Rancher — 305
- Adela Cochrane: Mitford Entrepreneur — 310
- Agnes Carroll and the Holy Cross Hospital — 317
- Annie and Jean Mollison and Braemar Lodge — 324

12 Financing the Canadian Dream — 329
- The Canadian Dream — 329
- James A. Lougheed: Lawyer, Real Estate Entrepreneur, and Senator — 331
- Christina Kinnisten: Calgary Confectioner — 339
- Luey Dofoo and the Restaurant Business — 340
- Samuel and Helen Shaw: Midnapore Entrepreneurs — 343
- Sandy Watson: Pine Creek Farmer — 348
- Meopham Gardner: Ranching in the Bragg Creek Area — 350
- James C. Linton and Books — 354
- William Hanson Boorne and the Rise of his Photography Studio — 357
- James S. Mackie: Gunsmith and Bookseller — 362
- Service Businesses — 365

Conclusion:
Themes of an Era, 1870–1900 — 369
- New Technologies in Transportation and Communication — 369
- New Goods for Consumers — 370
- Business by Economic Sector — 371

Chronology — 374
Notes — 377
Bibliography — 421
Index — 435

List of Tables

1. Population in Calgary and the Bow Valley, 1891 — xxxii
2. Calgary and Bow Valley Population by Age Group and Gender, 1891 — xxxiii
3. Settlers in the Calgary District, 1875-1883 — 21
4. Leading Products at I. G. Baker & Co.'s Calgary Store, 1875-1891 — 22
5. Profits at I. G. Baker & Co.'s Calgary Store, 1880-1882 — 37
6. Demographic Structure of the Cowboy Culture in the Bow Valley, 1891-1901 — 152
7. Ranching Statistics for the Bow Valley, 1891-1901 — 171
8. Farming Statistics for the Bow Valley, 1891-1901 — 192
9. Sales and Profits at the Hudson's Bay Company's Calgary Store, 1892-1894 — 287
10. Sales and Profits at the Hudson's Bay Company's Calgary Store, 1899-1903 — 290
11. Women in the Out-of-Home Workforce in Calgary and the Bow Valley, 1891-1901 — 294
12. Women in the Clerical Workforce in Calgary and the Bow Valley, 1891-1901 — 295
13. Women-Owned Businesses in Calgary and the Bow Valley, 1891-1901 — 299

List of Illustrations

Map of the Bow Valley in 1900	xxvii
Map of Calgary in 1895	xxviii
North West Mounted Police March to the Bow Valley, 1874	5
Map of Calgary in 1883	8
Isaac G. Baker in 1885	10
Charles E. Conrad in 1885	11
William G. Conrad in 1885	12
I. G. Baker & Co.'s store in Calgary Bottom in 1882	18
I. G. Baker & Co.'s wagon train in Fort Macleod in 1887	19
Donald W. Davis in the 1880s	20
Hudson's Bay Company store in Calgary before 1884	42
Richard Hardisty in the 1880s	44
Charles J. Brydges in 1870	56
Canadian Pacific Railway passenger train in Calgary in 1884	63
George Murdoch in 1883	96
Isaac S. Freeze in late middle age	101
I. S. Freeze Block in 1890	104
Rankin & Allan Block, c. 1888	106
Sam Livingston in the 1890s	114
Operating Sam Livingston's threshing machine in the late 1880s	115
LeJeune, Smith & Co. in 1890	129
Lafferty & Moore in 1889	131
Imperial Bank of Canada's Calgary branch in 1890	137
Bank of Montreal's Calgary branch, c. 1890	144
Canadian Pacific Stockyards, c. 1890s	150
I. G. Baker & Co. warehouse, barns, corrals, and horses in 1884.	153
Circle Ranch round-up crew, c. 1890.	158
Matthew H. Cochrane, c. 1870s	160
William D. Kerfoot, c. 1890	162
Brood mares on the Quorn Ranche, c. 1893	168
Interior of Osborne E. Brown's log ranch house, c. 1890	174
Arthur G. Wolley-Dod in middle age	177
Map of John Quirk's ranch land and John Ware's ranch land in 1894	181
Albert E. Banister and his wife, Helen, in 1894	186
Robert Findlay in late middle age	194
Gavin Findlay and his wife, Caroline, and their son, Tom	198
The Findlay Farm	199
William J. Andrews and his Clydesdale stallion, c. 1917	200
Kate Andrews and her daughter Laura, c. 1902	201
Stacking oats sheaves on the Andrews family farm, c. 1903	205

James Francis and Julia McKevitt family, c. 1920	207
Albert and Blanche Herr's original homestead and farm, c. 1925	212
Albert and Blanche Herr's sons hauling grain to the elevators in DeWinton, c. 1925	213
Map of Calgary and its surrounding area 1895	231
Great Fire of 7 November 1886	236
T. C. Power & Bro. in 1888	241
Alberta Hotel in 1890	244
Alexander Block, c. 1890s	245
Hull Bros. & Co. float in Calgary parade in 1901	248
Peter A. Prince, c. 1918	252
Eau Claire & Bow River Lumber Co. in 1899	253
Hutchings & Riley in 1890	257
I. G. Baker & Co. department store in 1888	264
Hudson's Bay Company department store, c. 1904	280
Helen Rothney Macleod dressed for her marriage to A. E. Cross in 1809	296
Mrs. R. S. Knight (Susan Harris) in 1911	297
Women working at typewriters, C.P.R. land department, Calgary, in 1915	300
Mary Macleod, c. 1880s	301
Agnes K. Bedingfeld at her ranch house, c. early 1900s	306
Agnes K. Bedingfeld and her son Frank at their ranch, c. early 1900s	307
Adela Cochrane c. 1890s, Mitford entrepreneur	311
Agnes Carroll c. 1890s, founder of the Holy Cross Hospital	318
Holy Cross Hospital as it appeared, c. early 1900s	321
Braemar Lodge as it appeared, c. 1910	325
Sir James A. Lougheed, c. 1890s	332
The Clarence Block, c. 1890s	336
Luey Dofoo in late middle age	341
Samuel and Helen Shaw, c. early 1880s	344
Midnapore Woollen Mills, c. 1896	346
Sandy Watson's stopping house, c. 1920	349
Meopham Gardner, c. 1901	351
Clem Gardner roping a steer, Calgary Stampede, in 1919	352
Linton's Book Store in 1884	355
William Hanson Boorne in 1884	358
James S. Mackie in 1901	363

Preface

In this book, business in Calgary and the Bow Valley is defined very broadly. By business, I mean any economic activity in a market for profit, so that ranchers, farmers, real estate speculators, and other individuals like boardinghousekeepers are also seen to have been in business, along with those economic actors traditionally thought of as business people such as merchants, retailers, wholesalers, manufacturers, and bankers. Between 1870 and 1900, business activity became the preoccupation of many Calgary and Bow Valley households. The triumph of an orientation to the market was an early and pervasive phenomenon in the city and its region.

During these years, many Calgarians and Bow Valley people were in business for themselves. In this study, small farmers and small ranchers and small city entrepreneurs receive considerable attention. There is a stress on the contributions of agriculture to business; arable land became one of the greatest resources of Calgary and the Bow Valley. At the same time, I set out to tell the story of the economic actors conventionally thought of as business people, all of whom, like those in agriculture, operated in a market for profit. Thus, any economic activity in a market for profit is a defining characteristic of businesses in the city and the surrounding area in the late nineteenth century.

This book is a work of urban and regional business history. It should appeal to students of history, business administration students, and general readers alike. Students of history will, I hope, find business history important for understanding the late nineteenth century. Business history is a vital key to comprehending the past, and urban and regional business history, with its emphasis on the relationships between businesses in the city and the countryside, can be especially helpful. Business administration students, particularly those in urban and regional business viewed against the backdrop of national and international developments, will, I think, also find this study useful. From one significant vantage point, the business world of today is a regional one within the broader national and global spheres, and to operate effectively in it business people need to understand business practices in the city and in the surrounding area. Even in our increasingly globalized universe, urban and regional business history is a valuable subject. Within Alberta, it was in Calgary and the Bow Valley that many new business structures and management methods were first developed, and a number of these were later adopted by other communities in the province. This volume should also be of special interest to general readers because it provides a historical perspective on the roots of our current situation and locates late nineteenth-century business in its cultural and political setting as well as its economic and technological environment.

Preface

During the period from 1870 to 1900, business in Calgary and the Bow Valley experienced profound changes. *Eye on the Future* trains its lens on those changes and the capitalist pioneers who played such a major role in them. It explores the life and work of a number of forward-looking men and women who were both pioneers and capitalists – for example, Isaac G. Baker, Agnes K. Bedingfeld, and James A. Lougheed – and the institutions they helped build. "Capitalists," it has been observed, "are people who make bets on the future. The essence of capitalism is a psychological orientation toward the pursuit of future wealth and property."[1] This book, then, is a history of people who, knowing that change was in the very nature of things, kept their eye on the future.

Vision is a theme that linked the lives of these men and women. Not only did they see things others did not, they also made the most of their insights. Where others saw only constraints, they sensed opportunities and seized them. They were all risk takers, and many were experimenters and innovators as well. They were individuals of great self-confidence. Products of Canadian culture and institutions, they left their mark on business in Calgary and the Bow Valley as they assaulted the new frontiers. Among the things they had in common was their willingness to change with the times.

In 1870, people in Calgary and the Bow Valley lacked railway tracks to connect them with the rest of the nation. Most individuals enjoyed the thrill of riding a horse, and at least as many travelled by ox- or horse-drawn wagon. Travel conditions true for people in the region in 1870 still existed for many in 1900, but by then the region was linked to other parts of Canada by a railway and telegraph network. This formed the basis for a revolution in transportation and communications. The coming of rails opened the area to settlement, which helped to stimulate business development.

Business in 1870 primarily revolved around commerce. In the second half of the 1870s and the 1880s, this traditional activity of business leaders began to undergo enormous growth in scale. Merchants in Calgary increasingly became engaged in far-flung national and international ventures, which significantly expanded their influence and the potential for profits. Changes in transportation and communications helped bring about developments in ranching, farming, manufacturing, and banking. By 1900, the Bow Valley was producing more agricultural and industrial goods than any other region in Alberta.

Even more dramatic was the transformation of Calgary from a town to a city. This place had its origins as a town in 1883, when the arrival of the Canadian Pacific Railway fuelled the development of business. Benefiting from lower transportation costs, agricultural progress, and electricity, Calgarians went on a growth binge. The business culture of the late 1880s and early 1890s spawned a city that dominated the Bow Valley and southern Alberta. Some businesses did not advance rapidly during this period, but, in the euphoria of these years, few seemed to notice.

The entrepreneurial spirit displayed by so many people in Calgary and the Bow Valley grew out of the hope that hard work could bring prosperity to them. Great potential for business success existed in the region, and huge amounts of economic energy sprang from the widespread perception of real opportunity. Despite the failure of many individuals and business firms, business in Calgary and the Bow Valley was still often successful. The majority of merchants, ranchers, farmers, manufacturers, and bankers in the region had an entrepreneurial outlook. Entrepreneurs sought economic gain by introducing new goods, services, and techniques, and the creation of new enterprises called for entrepreneurial skills of the first order in the late nineteenth century.

This book posits entrepreneurial capitalism as a paradigm for interpreting the emergence of businesses in Calgary and the Bow Valley between 1870 and 1900. It introduces our generation to a number of business firm leaders, both men and women, who lived and worked in the city and its region during these years. Through profiles of these forward-thinking individuals, it reveals a dynamic relationship between turbulent economic life, consumer priorities, and firm strategy that holds significant lessons for today's business institution builders. These entrepreneurial visionaries in a variety of businesses, including retailing, ranching, farming, manufacturing, and banking, all worked to create markets for their products. They understood that economic and social change played a significant part in what customers wanted and what businesses made available, and they often succeeded in exploiting business opportunities produced by such change.

Everything, however, remained in flux, and success could not be predicted with any precision. The kind of "creative destruction" described by Harvard economist Joseph Schumpeter half a century ago was characteristic of the Calgary and Bow Valley economies between 1870 and 1900. Capitalism in the region was a process of transformation that destroyed old businesses and created new ones. Pressures of competition in the capitalist society bred continuous turmoil that, on balance, led to greater efficiency in the production of goods and services and enhanced the standard of living in Calgary and the surrounding area. The capitalist system was designed to tear down the obsolete and build something more advanced in its place. All of this was "creative destruction" in action in the last thirty years of the nineteenth century. Some business firms fell victim to their own missteps or to hard times, but the region as a whole moved forward.

Preface

Operating through business firms, entrepreneurs in Calgary and the Bow Valley carried out the turbulent process of creative destruction. Their triumphs frequently upset existing economic arrangements, transferring wealth and power from traditional to new sectors of the economy. In seeking profits in retail, agricultural, manufacturing, and financial industries, many of them built up their businesses while at the same time making positive impacts on the region's economic life. Observers were amazed at the ability of the flexible business system to take advantage of new technologies in ways that helped to raise productive capacity and to generate larger assets and more social benefits.

The inner workings of the business system in Calgary and the Bow Valley are at the heart of this book. It focuses on entrepreneurs, business firms, and industries. The study places more emphasis on individuals working within businesses than on the external perspectives of customers, governments, and competitors. From the inside, it shows how business firms came into being and operated.

I hope that anyone who reads this book will be rewarded with insight into how people pioneered in the development of business in a western Canadian city and its region in the late nineteenth century. My goal is to analyze the capitalist business world they created in Alberta's settlement era. From the outset, the settlement of Calgary and the Bow Valley was the product of urban and rural forces. This study shows how human beings in urban and rural settings seized business opportunities, helped to integrate the Calgary and Bow Valley economies, and worked to improve their surroundings as they bettered themselves in Canadian society. In doing so, they played a crucial part in Calgary's emergence as a city and in the Bow Valley's growth into an important agricultural region. Throughout the period from the 1870s to 1890s, the valley occupied a prominent place in the city's business life. Business enterprises in the city and ranching and farming businesses in the valley literally grew up together.

Although my primary aim is to examine the actors' roles in the rise of Calgary as the main centre of trade and in the development of its region, I have tried throughout to set this story within the broader framework of the economic, political, and cultural environments of the day. Business and civic leaders faced a series of urgent challenges: how to promote the economic growth of the city and the surrounding area; how to create demand for goods and services; how to finance transportation improvements – streets, bridges, roads, and railways; and how to assimilate substantial political and social change. These challenges were, as for other cities at other times, closely intertwined. Because Calgary was the first Alberta urban centre to become a city, these stimulating tasks have some of the fascination common to firsts of any type.

Preface

During the last three decades of the nineteenth century, Calgary and Bow Valley society witnessed the beginnings of industrialization and an early stage of consumerism. In the process, the economic requirements of the region changed. Initially, there was a need to establish a basic economy – transportation and communication systems, homes, sources of energy, commercial firms, ranches, farms, industrial enterprises, banks, and public buildings. Over the long term, while this was taking place, investment was particularly in land and capital equipment rather than heavy private consumption across the region. Aside from essential goods such as food, clothing, footwear, and furniture, the emphasis was on real estate, agriculture, commerce, industry, and public services.

The opening of the Bow Valley to settlement dramatically altered the distribution pattern for the goods needed by the region's citizens. In the 1870s and early 1880s, ox-drawn wagons dominated the long-distance freight and passenger transport. Freighters and wagoners – the men who held the locomotive power – met the personal and commercial needs of a gradually expanding population. Regardless of weather or road conditions, freight, supplies, and mail moved with a fair degree of certainty. Ox, mule, and horsepower made possible the delivery of hundreds of tons of goods to Mounted Police forts, hamlets, ranches, and farms. Wagon roads and trails were the only means of commercial activity. Attracting, encouraging, and sustaining come-to-stay people, trails helped to give direction to settlement in the Bow Valley. By the mid-1880s and even more so by the early 1890s, the railway network not only greatly accelerated the movement of long-distance freight and passengers, but also gave orientation to settlement, often reinforcing the influence of old trails.

The years from the 1870s to the 1890s spanned an era of amazing economic growth in Calgary and the Bow Valley. In these three decades, the region's agricultural, commercial, and industrial wealth increased significantly. Contributions by pioneers – merchants, manufacturers, farmers, ranchers, and bankers – became crucial to the evolution of this part of Alberta. Those who remained as permanent settlers left the imprint of their work upon a region once devoted to the buffalo hunt and the fur trade, transforming the structure of the economy almost beyond recognition. These changes were the result of great developments both within and outside the Bow Valley, the product of the ambitions and abilities of many people. In 1901, the population of Calgary and the Bow Valley rose to over eight thousand, while that of the district of Alberta increased to seventy-three thousand and that of Canada climbed to more than five million. When the 1901 census was taken, the frontier in the Bow Valley had not disappeared and the region had not been declared fully settled. Nevertheless, numerous

Preface

ranches, farms, and city business enterprises had become prosperous. Calgary, still the principal source of trade and contact with the outside world, was beginning to grow rapidly.

The natural resource endowment of the Bow Valley provided people with necessary opportunities to embark on careers in commerce, manufacturing, ranching, and farming. It is easy to imagine that during most of the last third of the nineteenth century the Bow Valley was a place swarming with business activity, intimately involved in the agricultural development of Alberta. Ranched and farmed, the rich land gave a reasonable living. The region contained strong landscape features, including the Bow River and its many tributaries, as well as rolling hills and wooded valleys. The Bow River system was favourably located to serve the needs of the extensive pioneer country lying within and beyond its basin with food, lumber, and other resources such as hydroelectric power. In the Bow Valley, potential wealth lay on the surface, especially in fertile soils, and below it, notably in oil and gas reserves and coal. So effectively were the oil and gas reserves developed later, in the twentieth century, that the valley's population eventually became large.

An important context for this study is the business ethos in Calgary and the Bow Valley in the late nineteenth century. For most of the period, many people were optimistic about the future state of the economy and believed that progress could best be secured by hard work. Constant striving might produce material well-being and increase human happiness. Businesses were also sensitive to the social responsibility concerns of the Calgary and Bow Valley public. Social, cultural, and charitable undertakings, including the General Hospital and the Holy Cross Hospital in Calgary as well as churches in the city and rural communities, drew considerable support from private contributions, many of them donated by the region's business leaders. Despite all the uncertainties and hardships associated with the opening of the area to settlement, there was a conviction that those who showed enterprise stood a good chance of receiving substantial reward.

Fundamental changes occurred in the business environment during the 1870–1900 period. At the beginning, in Calgary there were no banks to extend credit to business people. For the most part, small borrowers were dependent upon informal private networks of credit. A turning point came in 1885, when the advent of private banks expanded the money supply in Calgary and the Bow Valley. However, many inhabitants of the town and the valley became convinced that the region also needed branches of chartered banks. A year later, the coming of chartered bank branches made a great deal more bank credit available to finance commercial, agricultural, and industrial projects.

Preface

My examination of business in Calgary and the Bow Valley employs an integrated approach, one that recreates the efforts of various business firms as well as the dynamic between them. Far from existing in isolation, these forces interacted and were interrelated parts of the overall economic and social picture. Founded on opportunity, diligence, and a willingness to assume risks and responsibilities, business success in the city and its rural hinterland stimulated capital formation and urbanization and bred political change and economic and social mobility. In reconstructing the connections between urban and rural business enterprises, this book combines business history with political and cultural history.

Acknowledgments

Numerous individuals and institutions have helped me along in making this journey, offering guidance and support to complete this book. During many years of teaching in the Department of History, University of Calgary, I have benefited from the insights of my colleagues in Canadian history. I very much appreciate the interest they have taken in my work. For encouragement I am grateful to David Bercuson, Pat Brennan, Sarah Carter, Warren Elofson, Doug Francis, Herman Ganzevoort, Louis Knafla, David Marshall, Tony Rasporich, and Don Smith. Others in the Department of History also helped me. My thanks to Dorothy Harty, Karen McDermid, Carol Murray, Marjory McLean, Olga Leskiw, Brenda Oslawsky, Kelly Morris, and Laurel Halladay for splendid typing.

Over the years, many people provided a great deal of information by participating in interviews about their ancestors' business activities in Calgary and the Bow Valley in the late nineteenth century. These people's names are included in the bibliography. They went out of their way to aid my research, talking frankly about the business careers of their relatives and supporting this project in countless ways. Without their help, there would have been no book. I am thankful for their generous assistance.

It is worth emphasizing that this book is a work of urban and regional business history. As the individuals analyzed here well understood, there was a close relationship between Calgary and its region. They pursued new business opportunities relentlessly in the city and the surrounding area, always keeping their eye on the future. I owe a debt to historians Walter L. Buenger and Joseph A. Pratt. Their work, *But Also Good Business: Texas Commerce Banks and the Financing of Houston and Texas, 1886-1986*, helped to inspire my approach. To these scholars, I am grateful for example and inspiration.

A number of archivists and librarians in Canada and the United States enriched my research efforts, helping me to examine important collections. I am grateful for the dedication and patience of the staffs at the Glenbow Archives and Library, the Provincial Archives of Alberta, the University of Calgary Library, the Calgary Land Titles Office, the Calgary Court House, the City of Calgary Public Library, the City of Calgary Archives, the Corporate Registry Archives in Edmonton, the Hudson's Bay Company Archives in Winnipeg, the Montana Historical Society Archives in Helena, Montana, the National Archives of Canada, the National Archives in Washington, D.C., the Canadian Pacific Archives in Montreal, the Bank of Montreal Archives, the Canadian Imperial Bank of Commerce Archives in Toronto, the Royal Bank of Canada Archives in Mississauga, Ontario, the Baker Library at Harvard University, the Saskatchewan Archives Board in Regina, the K. Ross Toole Archives at the University of Montana Library in Missoula, the State of Montana Archives in Helena, the Missouri

Acknowledgments

Historical Society Archives, the Duke University Library, the Grey Nuns of Montreal Archives, and the Grey Nuns Regional Centre Archives in Edmonton. With efficiency and courtesy, these people offered their expertise and time in full measure.

I extend my gratitude to Doug Cass, Tony Rees, Lynette Walton, Lindsay Moir, Jennifer Hamblin, Catherine Myhr, Hugh A. Dempsey, Sheilagh S. Jameson, Pat Molesky-Brar, Susan Kooyman, Antonella Fanella, Jim Bowman, Brian Hanning, Yolaine Toussaint, Freeman Clowery, K. A. Hunking, Neil Forsyth, Brian O'Brien, Gord Rabchuk, Kathy Minorgan, Barbara R. Dailey, Lizz Frost, Ron Todoruk, Diane Thomas, Jennifer Bobrovitz, Dave Leonard, Robyn Herrington, Alex Wackett, Apollonia Steele, Saundra Lipton, Dave Walter, Anne Morton, Stephen Lyons, Jo-Anne Colby, Robert Stacey, Debbie Brentnell, Isabelle Ringuet, and Dale Johnson. They helped me locate hundreds of business records, newspapers, maps, photographs, and other materials for this book. Frequently they anticipated my needs.

I want to say a special word of appreciation to friends who contributed to the book with conversation: Don Clay, Jim Mackie, Jack Cooper, Larry Purdy, Joel Overholser, Charles McCulloch, Ken Grogan, Ron Martin, Doug Walker, Bill Cruikshanks, James E. Murphy, George Dunlap, Curly Galbraith, Simon Evans, Martin Blake, Jack Willison, Birnie Burnand, Bob Ermter, Norbert MacDonald, Bob Cooper, Alan V. M. White, Alastair Stewart, Bob Gregory, Salim P. Sumar, Clarence Richards, Stan Corry, Bill Lass, Jim Nichol, Bob Walker, Harry Sanders, Harland Bell, Michael Tarrant, Hugh Dixon, Harry Young, John Fox, Max Foran, Ken Cole, Paul F. Sharp, Tom Isern, John A. Eagle, David Breen, and John W. Bennett. I am grateful to them for their insights. They helped me test my ideas about entrepreneurial activity, expanding my understanding of how business leaders think and how businesses operate.

The team at the University of Calgary Press helped me complete this fascinating intellectual expedition. I was fortunate to work with director Walter Hildebrandt, whose valuable feedback and sustaining interest in this book helped me bring it to publication. I am grateful to several anonymous readers, who read an earlier version of this work for the University of Calgary Press and offered useful suggestions. I thank Joan Barton, Sharon Boyle, Joan Eadie, Peter Enman, Sona Khosla, John King, Kristina Schuring, Wendy Stephens, and Mieka West, all of whom brought their talents to bear on this project.

I am grateful to Tony Comper, Orde Morton, John Hunkin, and Jill ten Cate for their help. To Robin Poitras, cartographic technician in the Department of Geography at the University of Calgary, go my thanks for the preparation of the maps.

A final special note of thanks is due my family for enriching my life and sharing with me the joys of embarking on new journeys.

Introduction

The settling of the Bow Valley, from the prairies to the foothills of the Rocky Mountains, was an entrepreneurial adventure. In its origins and evolution, this society of white newcomers was market-oriented. The fortunes of Canadians in Calgary and the surrounding area were often derived from the increase in real estate values in the late nineteenth century. There was more to the story of capitalism in the Bow Valley than land, however. This tale, like the business histories of most other Canadian communities, was one of never-ending competition in the marketplace. It is remarkable with what persistence pioneers in Calgary and the Bow Valley pursued market forces in this period.

In Calgary and the Bow Valley, as in other parts of Canada, the capitalist system was organized around a market economy that stressed a number of essentials, such as ownership of private property, the rule of law, entrepreneurial opportunities, access to credit, and jobs that paid cash wages. By the early and mid-1870s, the forces of capitalism were beginning to gain momentum. Settlers in the region showed themselves ready to toil strenuously to achieve economic progress. They believed that economic advancement was possible and desirable, for individuals and families as well as for business enterprises and industries. The early capitalist era in Calgary and the Bow Valley – the last three decades of the nineteenth century – was a time of significant economic growth.

My book examines this growth especially in terms of the contributions that business firms, including retailers, ranchers, farmers, manufacturers, and bankers, made to it during the period from the 1870s to the 1890s. *Eye on the Future* tells the story of their accomplishments, without overlooking their shortcomings, inconsistencies, and failures. Reaching deep into the Canadian past – to early Calgary and its region – to retrace the origins of western capitalism, it is a story rich in drama and peopled with memorable personalities.

Introduction

Between 1870 and 1900, three misfortunes were visited upon the people in Calgary and the Bow Valley as the business cycle moved up and down: the major depression of 1873–79, the sobering depression of 1883–88, and the very severe depression of 1893–97. This study is about how people in the region endured, and ultimately prevailed, in the face of those adversities.

Eye on the Future is divided into twelve chapters. Chapter One introduces us to Calgary as a meeting place, for Native Canadians and entrepreneurs. The next three chapters present an extended analysis of business in Calgary and the surrounding area, with accounts of several entrepreneurs and two companies. Chapter Two deals with American enterprise in Calgary, the activities of I. G. Baker & Co. in the wagon-road era. In Chapter Three, we review British enterprise in Calgary, the operations of the Hudson's Bay Company in the wagon-road period. From these operations, we turn to the question of how Baker & Co. and the Hudson's Bay Company responded to the coming of the Canadian Pacific Railway in Chapter Four. Chapter Five focuses on the link between business development and the emergence of the town of Calgary and the appearance of hamlets and villages in the Bow Valley. The sixth chapter investigates banking services and how they shaped the growth of agricultural, commercial, and industrial enterprises. Chapter Seven contains key findings from my examination of the ranching business in the Bow Valley. The creation and evolution of Bow Valley family farms are explored in Chapter Eight. Chapter Nine reconstitutes the parts that entrepreneurs and businesses played in Calgary's transition from town to city. Chapter Ten analyzes the role department stores in Calgary occupied in the distribution process. In Chapter Eleven, we document the business experiences of women. The final chapter reconstructs the ways in which people in Calgary and the Bow Valley financed their dreams.

The chief benefits that came from the capitalist enterprise of individuals were a broadening of business opportunity and a rise in incomes. Despite the negative elements of capitalism in Calgary and the Bow Valley – such as extravagant profits that some business owners made and the high premium citizens sometimes placed on material things – it produced considerable employment and helped to improve the living standards of common people.

One of the most remarkable features of capitalism in the Bow Valley was the gradual development of the abundant natural resources of the region. Before resource endowments could produce long-term advantages, however, value had to be added to the raw materials discovered by the settlers. A lot of time and energy was spent on turning raw materials into final products: trees into lumber; coal seams into coal supplies; waterpower into electricity. As entrepreneurs moved into manufacturing, mining, and services, the economy became more diversified. Like the Canadian business system as a whole, capitalism in the Bow Valley added immense value to the natural resources of the area.

Over the years, gradual development also came to characterize Bow Valley agriculture. Many of the region's inhabitants worked on farms and ranches. Ranchers raised cattle primarily for beef markets. While farmers and their families grew grain crops and produced livestock partly for their own consumption, they sold substantial quantities of farm produce. From the increasing productivity of agriculture, including the prosperous cattle ranches and mixed farms, came the explosion of growth that led to the spread of capitalism across the Bow Valley. Soon the region was producing at a volume beyond its own needs. It was exporting cattle, horses, sheep, and wheat of considerable value. Agricultural expansion in the late nineteenth century also became vital to capitalist development elsewhere, for example in the Portage la Prairie area in Manitoba, as well as in the Billings region in Montana.[1]

In Calgary and the Bow Valley, capitalism relied heavily on credit as a way to finance growth in business. Desiring to retain control of their enterprises, some business owners tried to maintain their independence from creditors. Therefore, their businesses were largely self-financed, through reinvested profits and from their personal fortunes. But in numerous instances, self-finance was insufficient to stay in business – credit was needed. Thus, besides employing accumulated wealth, many business owners looked to family, friends, merchants, wholesalers, manufacturers, banks, and loan companies for credit. Often creditors lent short for three or six months, but then sometimes found that they could not get their money back at the due date. If the business was sound, the creditor's interests were usually best served by renewing the loan rather than by foreclosing a mortgage. Loans to such businesses, even if frequently renewed, could help to preserve the mutually beneficial ties between creditors and borrowers. For business owners in Calgary and the Bow Valley, short-term borrowing was extremely important. Several of them, however, were able to obtain loans of one or more years.

The prevailing view among Calgary and Bow Valley capitalists was that local and regional prosperity depended mostly on the zeal of individual entrepreneurs. Entrepreneurial success for individuals frequently came from a careful assessment of opportunities in commerce or industry or agriculture or banking. By trying to understand the wide range of successes and failures of others, business owners could develop entrepreneurial skills. Entrepreneurship embraced a variety of economic functions: starting a new venture, bearing risk, and innovative activity. By virtually any reckoning, entrepreneurs in Calgary and the Bow Valley were in the forefront of those who created a business culture in the region. Although there were many more male than female entrepreneurs, women made significant progress in business. Unfortunately for regional capitalists, whether men or women, they often lacked the financial resources to get ahead.

In the end, they usually could not hope to win the struggle to maintain their businesses in Calgary and the Bow Valley without some government intervention in the economy, including federal governmental assistance in the financing and construction of railways to open new entrepreneurial opportunities. Most striking was the evolution of the Canadian Pacific Railway system supported by public funds – its early promise as a unifier and developer of the Canadian nation had been fulfilled by 1885 beyond the dreams of the wildest optimist among federal officials. Many people saw in this development nothing less than the march of progress across an inviting landscape to aid business enterprise as well as to promote nationhood. Then, too, the federal tariff law both raised revenue for the national treasury and protected manufacturers from competitors abroad, thus providing individuals in Calgary and the Bow Valley with greater opportunities to invest their resources in manufacturing businesses. Federal legislation created a banking system that permitted nationwide branching, thereby ensuring the rise of large central Canadian-based banks capable of directing the flow of funds to their branches in Calgary and increasing the credit available in the city and the surrounding area.

The foundations of Calgary's business system date back to the 1870s, when the most important category of business leader was the general merchant, who increasingly found himself engaged in far-flung international ventures. Impressive fortunes were made in these entrepreneurial undertakings, powerful mercantile institutions were founded, and the basis was laid for a group of capitalists who did much to fuel greater expansion and change in the late nineteenth century. Agriculture began in the Calgary area in 1875, when the first farmers and ranchers started operations. Calgary was then a small dot on the map of the prairie West. The community was a mixture of Native, Canadian, and American cultures linked to a vast trading network. Before the city, there was the flat land along the Bow River that served as a meeting place. The Blackfoot still controlled most of the land around the centre, where they met those with whom they traded – Stoneys, Sarcees, Peigans, Bloods, Canadians, and Americans. Native people had been trading at this meeting place for centuries.

By the 1870s, there were signs of change. Local, regional, national, and international trade led to profound alterations in the economic and social structures of Bow Valley society. The year 1870 marked a turning point in the evolution of government in the western interior of Canada between Hudson Bay and the Rocky Mountains. The previous two hundred years had seen the development of the Hudson's Bay Company in Rupert's Land, as the western interior was called. Since 1670, the company had governed Rupert's Land in the name of the British crown and had dominated the fur trade in the region as well. The growth of the company's commerce added to the power of the imperial government. By the middle of the nineteenth century, the fur trade had grown sufficiently attractive that individual merchants began to challenge the Hudson's Bay Company's dominance. The exclusivity of commerce enjoyed by the company, therefore, declined steadily over the next few decades. In 1870, Rupert's Land was transferred to the Dominion of Canada, leaving the federal government in full command of the region. Manitoba became a province in that year, while the rest of the western interior was established as the Canadian Northwest Territories by the federal government.

This political changeover of 1870 had a profound impact on the economic and social order in the Northwest Territories. Once the Canadian government had assumed control of the Northwest Territories, it encouraged the settlement of the region. Seeking greener pastures, people in central and eastern Canada, the United States, and Great Britain began their migrations to Calgary and the Bow Valley. Migrants were not just looking for land to raise livestock and to farm, but also for opportunities to engage in merchandising and manufacturing. Early migrations usually followed Native trails. The river city provided a market where ranchers and farmers could purchase manufactured goods and sell agricultural produce. No matter how far the farmers and ranchers had to travel in order to reach the city, they kept in touch with the commercial centre to exchange their surplus products for vital manufactured tools and household items.

Winding eastward out of the Rocky Mountains, the Bow River possessed a stunning beauty and charm. Magnificent mountains towered over the riverbanks at the western end before the summits receded into the background and the river valley gradually flattened out and broadened, sprinkled with poplar trees as other waterways, like the Kananaskis River, the Ghost River, the Elbow River, Nose Creek, Fish Creek, and the Highwood River, emptied into the Bow River. Water was life. The Rockies captured and held the winter snow, releasing it in the spring to the foothills and prairies below. At the Bow's junctions with the Elbow River and Nose Creek, a flat plain dominated the landscape, offering a site where Calgary began. The Bow was not suited to steamboats, but it impressed people with its fresh, clean, and cold

Introduction

water, its ability to attract fish, and its great potential as a source of water for irrigating the land in the Bow Valley.

The Bow Valley, then as today, was an area of rolling hills and miniature river valleys between Canmore on its western edge and Gleichen on its eastern edge, about halfway between Vancouver and Winnipeg. In a land much written about, painted, and photographed, the prairies were covered with grasses and the foothills of the Rockies were dotted with groves of trees, some of which were created by early ranchers and farmers.

Calgary was a major beneficiary of the wealth generated by the Bow Valley. Besides drawing income from handling regional products, the burgeoning city controlled the import and export trade. The control of the region's money supply became centralized in Calgary through regional private banks and branches of national chartered banks. Local boosters, all of whom considered the Bow Valley the most promising area in southern Alberta, heralded the growth of the region as an assurance of the city's future prosperity. "The country," they reported in 1892, "is rolling prairie, with never-failing springs, brooks and rivers of pure water.... Cattle and horses feed and fatten on the prairie all the year round.... The native grasses never die, but cure on the root."[2] The Bow Valley, with its moderate climate, its 110 to 120-day growing season, and its fertile soil, was also ideal for the cultivation of wheat, oats, barley, and rye. Over the years, the rich ranching and farming country remained a significant underpinning in Calgary's growth. The city, in turn, was supremely important in the development of the Bow Valley; its businesses acted as a catalyst, helping to transform the surrounding area into a settled region.

The region served by Calgary businesses did not remain static between the early 1870s and 1900. During this time, the city grew significantly as improvements in transportation and communications integrated more and more of the surrounding area into its economic life. As part of a region that was underdeveloped relative to industrial central Canada, Calgary was a small city with huge aspirations. Its wealth flowed from a vigorous commercial sector, a productive agricultural sector, and an emerging industrial sector. A substantial portion of its industrial sector was composed of a national corporation headquartered in Montreal – the Canadian Pacific Railway. In transportation, banking, farm implements, insurance, and other industries, central Canadian companies exerted a tremendous influence over the Calgary and Bow Valley economies. The city's merchants, bankers, and manufacturers also steadily extended their influence over the commerce of a broad section of the Bow Valley. Through their control of local commerce and trade, Calgary entrepreneurs were able to achieve dominance over their rivals in nearby communities – Canmore, Morley, Cochrane, Springbank, Nose Creek, Millarville, High River, Okotoks, Gladys, Davisburg, Pine Creek, Midnapore, Namaka, Queenstown, Gleichen – boosting their city to a position of regional power. Some of the region's products, especially cattle but also wheat, entered national and international markets. As businesses based in Calgary became more involved in this wider economy, some of them grew from small enterprises into larger concerns active throughout the Bow Valley and in other parts of western Canada.

Calgary retailers who extended their sales routes to include hamlets in the Bow Valley watched railway building and capital investment increase. Railway construction, interrupted by the economic depression of the mid-1880s, began again in earnest in the early 1890s. In a few years, more than 350 miles of new road were opened in Alberta, including the Calgary and Edmonton Railway, completed in 1892.

Across the border, in the United States, a burgeoning railroad and telegraph network, as American historian Alfred D. Chandler, Jr. has written, "provided the fast, regular, and dependable transportation and communication so essential to high-volume production and distribution."[3] In Calgary and the Bow Valley, new business enterprises sprang up to exploit the substantial economies of scale and scope made possible by a new, large-scale railway and telegraph network.[4] For instance, William Roper Hull's success in meat production and distribution was predicated on the development of the new technologies.

Any effort to assess the Bow Valley based only on its geography – that is to say, its apparently remote location on the periphery of Canadian civilization in the late nineteenth century – is inappropriate. Despite its remoteness, the Bow Valley was tied to the Victorian culture of central and eastern Canada and Great Britain. The region was greatly influenced by Canadian Victorianism from the 1870s, and, by 1900, most of its residents embraced the cultural values of the national norm in this period, including a strong belief in progress and the power of technology, the importance of being responsible at home and in business, and the need for education. There was, however, a minority in the Bow Valley caught in a different lifestyle. The Calgary saloons were notorious for their rowdyism, and the police court was often the habitat of petty crooks, drunks, prostitutes, gamblers, and shady underworld characters. The inflow of transients, many of them single men of the roughest type, and the visits of boisterous cowboys sometimes made Calgary a "Wild West" frontier town in these years. Life on the range was rugged and occasionally violent. All this reflected the unrestricted, freewheeling nature of the region. Nevertheless, most Bow Valley people measured their achievements by the standards of Victorian Canada.

Introduction

Table 1. Population in Calgary and the Bow Valley, 1891

	Calgary	Bow Valley
Population	3881	2983
Percent born in Canada	62	54
Percent born in Britain	28	35
Percent born in USA	5	6

Source: Manuscript Census of 1891 for Calgary, Canmore, Gleichen, High River, Davisburg, Fish Creek, Pine Creek, Namaka, and Morley.

Calgary and Bow Valley Victorians were increasingly better educated. An important measure for this is provided by the rising expenditures for formal education, suggested in the growing number of public and private schools in the city and its region in the late nineteenth and early twentieth centuries. In 1885, there were one public elementary school and one private elementary girls' school in Calgary, with academies in other parts of Canada satisfying the appetites of those who desired and could afford further studies. By 1904, while the city boasted three public schools, with one of them (Central School) offering both elementary and high school courses, as well as two private girls' schools (Sacred Heart Convent and St. Hilda's Ladies' College) and one private boys' school (Western Canada College), rural Bow Valley had several public elementary schools, including Midnapore School, Priddis School, and Montrose School.[5] Thus, the investment in education was increasing, and skills imparted by education contributed to economic growth in the city and its region.

The population of Calgary and the Bow Valley was mostly of British descent and, therefore, ethnically homogeneous. The region's ethnic makeup included a number of French Canadians, quite a few Native Canadians, as well as some mixed-blood individuals, the offspring of Natives and French-speaking or English-speaking persons. But what stood out most was the cultural homogeneity of the people, which was revealed in the 1891 manuscript census statistics.

Table 1 shows that, by this time, the head count for Calgary was 3,881, and for rural Bow Valley 2,983. Individuals born in Canada, particularly in Ontario and the Northwest Territories, made up 62 percent of Calgary's population and 54 percent of rural Bow Valley's population. The overwhelming majority of these were both white and the children of British-born parents. Twenty-eight percent of Calgary's citizens, and 35 percent of rural Bow Valley people, were immigrants from Great Britain. The next largest immigrant group – Americans – accounted for 5 percent of Calgary's population and 6 percent of rural Bow Valley's population. Most of the immigrants from the United States were of British descent.

Table 2. Calgary and Bow Valley Population by Age Group and Gender, 1891

	Population	Percent of Total
Calgary Bow Valley Total	6,864	
Men age 20–39	2,484	36
Women age 20–39	874	13
Children under age 15	1,991	29

Source: Manuscript Census of 1891 for Calgary, Canmore, Gleichen, High River, Davisburg, Fish Creek, Pine Creek, Namaka, and Morley

Neither immigrants nor people from Ontario and other provinces, like Quebec, New Brunswick, Nova Scotia, and Prince Edward Island, would have continued to flow into the region had the economy stopped growing. At the same time, the coming of Canadians from central and eastern Canada and the arrival of immigrants, most of whom were hard working and vigorous young adults, speeded economic growth in Calgary and the Bow Valley. The story was much the same in many other frontier communities, not only in the Canadian West but also in the American West, where most people were young and healthy.[6]

Despite the imbalance of age and gender on the Bow Valley frontier, the pioneers were an energetic lot. As Table 2 shows, young men in their twenties and thirties made up about one third of Calgary's and the Bow Valley's population – 2,484 citizens represented 36 percent of all the people in the entire region. When the 874 young women of the same age group were added, about 49 percent of the region's population fell into the 20–39 age bracket. In turn, the significant number of young married couples explained the many children under the age of fifteen. While their numbers were considerably higher than half of the 20–39 age group, children under fifteen accounted for 29 percent of the region's population.

The ethnic makeup that resulted from immigration and the inflow of Canadians paid off economically because of the willingness of Calgary and Bow Valley society to absorb and make the best of what each contributing culture had to offer to the region. Some of those listed in the census as foreign-born came from continental Europe, with the largest number coming from Russia, Norway, Germany, Sweden, and France. Calgary and the Bow Valley also attracted a number of people from Iceland and China. On the Bow Valley Native reserves, created by Treaty 7 in 1877, lived many Native Canadians, some of whom were engaged in farming or ranching, while all of them together provided significant markets for entrepreneurs' goods as they had before that date. The region thus had a multicultural dimension; however, this

Introduction

did not lead to fatally divisive ethnic clashes. Although the acceptance of each culture was a slow, and sometimes painful, process, it constituted one of the remarkable triumphs of Calgary and Bow Valley society.

The relative openness of Canadian social structures and the legitimacy of the democratic Canadian state allowed Calgary and the Bow Valley to experience widespread economic and political change without massive unrest. Between the 1870s and 1890s, a capitalist ideology dedicated to reforming the political and legal system in Alberta and the Northwest Territories steadily gained influence in Canada. The Northwest Territories were ruled by a constitution – the Northwest Territories Act passed by the Canadian Parliament in 1875 – which granted to territorial citizens an array of rights, including the right to own private property, the cornerstone of capitalism. In 1882, Parliament approved an Order-in-Council dividing the Northwest Territories into districts: Alberta, Saskatchewan, Assiniboia, and Athabasca, under the territorial government in Regina headed by a lieutenant-governor. But members of the territorial government were not chosen by election. By the mid-1880s, the territorial government was under attack for being undemocratic. In 1886, Parliament granted representation to the Northwest Territories, with the district of Alberta receiving one seat in the House of Commons. Parliament established a legislative assembly for the Northwest Territories in Regina two years later, to which the Calgary electoral district elected two of Alberta's six members.[7] In 1897, Parliament passed a law that gave the Northwest Territories responsible government. The territorial lieutenant-governor henceforth had to choose policies and ministers approved by a legislative majority. This gradual move toward democracy in the Northwest Territories was calculated to preserve Canada's political, social, and economic stability, and it succeeded despite the Saskatchewan Rebellion of 1885.

During the last three decades of the nineteenth century, business interests in Calgary and the Bow Valley had an uneven impact on federal, territorial, and local government policymaking. But by the end of that century, they were being heard in city meetings, agricultural fairs, and the halls of territorial and federal governments. In this context, influential territorial statesmen, such as Frederick W. G. Haultain, began to acknowledge the growing importance of business interests. The territorial legislature in Regina, inspired by Haultain, now passed a series of laws which helped to strengthen the spirit of capitalism across the Northwest Territories, including Calgary and the Bow Valley. Legislation made possible the organization of partnerships for any legitimate business purpose. In Calgary, most businesses were conducted as single proprietorships or partnerships. Between the 1870s and 1890s, Calgary commercial and industrial firms, like Bow Valley ranching and farming businesses, tended to be relatively small, but they did stimulate economic development. Almost all such enterprises were family-owned and managed. Investors were responsible for paying 100 percent of an enterprise's debts, even if this required all of their personal assets. Given the heavy personal risks involved in owning a business during this period, a strong argument could be made for close, hands-on management by business owners.

Territorial law helped to accelerate economic growth in still other ways. Legislation encouraged the corporate form of business organization – grounded in the legal principle of limited liability – to spread in Calgary and the Bow Valley. This development was critical for the early stages of industrialization and the advent of big ranches, when large new companies needed substantial amounts of capital. Joint-stock companies established under British or American law developed operations in Calgary and the Bow Valley. In doing so, they became conduits for capital export to the region. The region was a popular site especially for British investors. By the closing years of the nineteenth century, Great Britain's accumulated pool of savings had grown so immense that it was able to export huge amounts of capital. At the same time, local and regional joint-stock companies formed under territorial law actively participated in business at home. The total capital raised by these companies was equal to only a small fraction of the capital imported from Great Britain and the United States. Nevertheless, they contributed to economic progress. Overall, corporate effort played a significant role in the regional economy.

From the start, Canadian capitalism in Calgary and the Bow Valley displayed many elements of a mixed economy. Federal, territorial, and city governments joined hands with business to raise economic activity in the region to new heights in the late nineteenth century. The appeal of a mixed economy was reinforced by fears among entrepreneurs that unrestrained market forces, which were usually their ally, might turn against them, particularly during the business downturn in the mid-1880s and the economic depression of the mid-1890s. Government activity, especially at the federal level but also at the city and territorial levels, was energetic, though frequently muddled. The policies followed by federal, city, and territorial governments toward business in Calgary and the Bow Valley were uncoordinated and haphazard. Collectively, however, they constituted an entrepreneurially oriented strategy for rapid economic growth in a developing region. Federal law, the keystone of the Canadian system, provided aid to business in the city and the surrounding area in the form of substantial land grants to railways, the protective tariff, and legislation that facilitated the establishment of limited liability corporations for any legitimate business purpose.

Introduction

In Canada, as in the United States, hospitality toward business was a major feature of federal law.[8]

Entrepreneurs working in Calgary and the Bow Valley in the late nineteenth century took pride in their participation in what has been called the world's Second Industrial Revolution. They knew that the First Industrial Revolution, led by Great Britain, had occurred between the 1760s and the 1840s. They also understood that the United States, Great Britain, and several European nations, particularly Germany, France, and the Low Countries led the Second Industrial Revolution, beginning in the 1840s. Two Calgary manufacturers, Robert J. Hutchings and William J. Riley, won a gold medal for their saddles and harnesses at the World's Fair in Chicago in 1893 during the heyday of the Second Industrial Revolution. Through their prize-winning exhibit, Hutchings and Riley demonstrated significant progress in manufacturing in Calgary.

In Calgary and the Bow Valley, capitalist economic progress and technological advance were closely related. As the region moved through the Second Industrial Revolution, transportation and communication were revolutionized, first by the railway and telegraph, and then by the telephone. Coal in the Bow Valley and in other parts of Alberta provided the critical energy for the railway locomotive. Manufacturing in Calgary was powered at first by steam generated by coal, and then also by electric motors. Traditional small shops persisted alongside medium-sized factories, and that pattern endured to the 1890s and beyond. Typical products included an array of consumer goods such as flour, saddles, harnesses, blankets, and shirts, and producers' goods such as farm tools and guns. As department stores emerged with a well-known name, made large capital investments, and developed a broad market reach, mass marketing began in Calgary.

Among many citizens of Calgary and the Bow Valley, there was an altruistic desire to share the Canadian way of life. Rooted in central and eastern Canadian traditions, this way of life was based on a blending of democracy with capitalism, a fusion of freedom with a mostly open marketplace. Merchants, manufacturers, farmers, and ranchers all sought material gain in the closing years of the nineteenth century, but more than merely a passion to get ahead economically as individuals motivated them. Many business leaders in the city and the country became a reliable mainstay of cultural and charitable activities. They saw in their businesses not only a vehicle for personal advancement, but also a route to family security and strong social relationships in the community. A great deal of it was symbolized by the Canadian dream of security for families, individual prosperity, a higher standard of living, home ownership, and the freedom of passing on material and cultural benefits to the next generation.

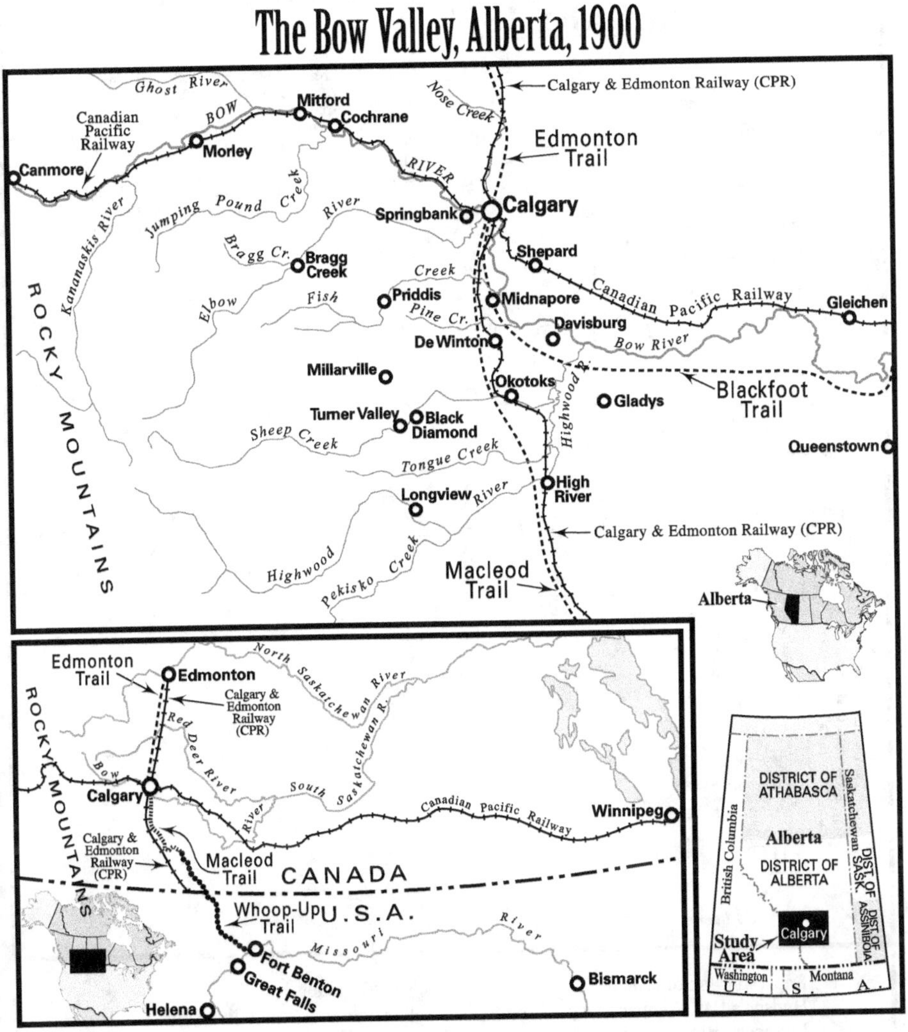

Introduction

Map 1. The Bow Valley, Alberta, 1900

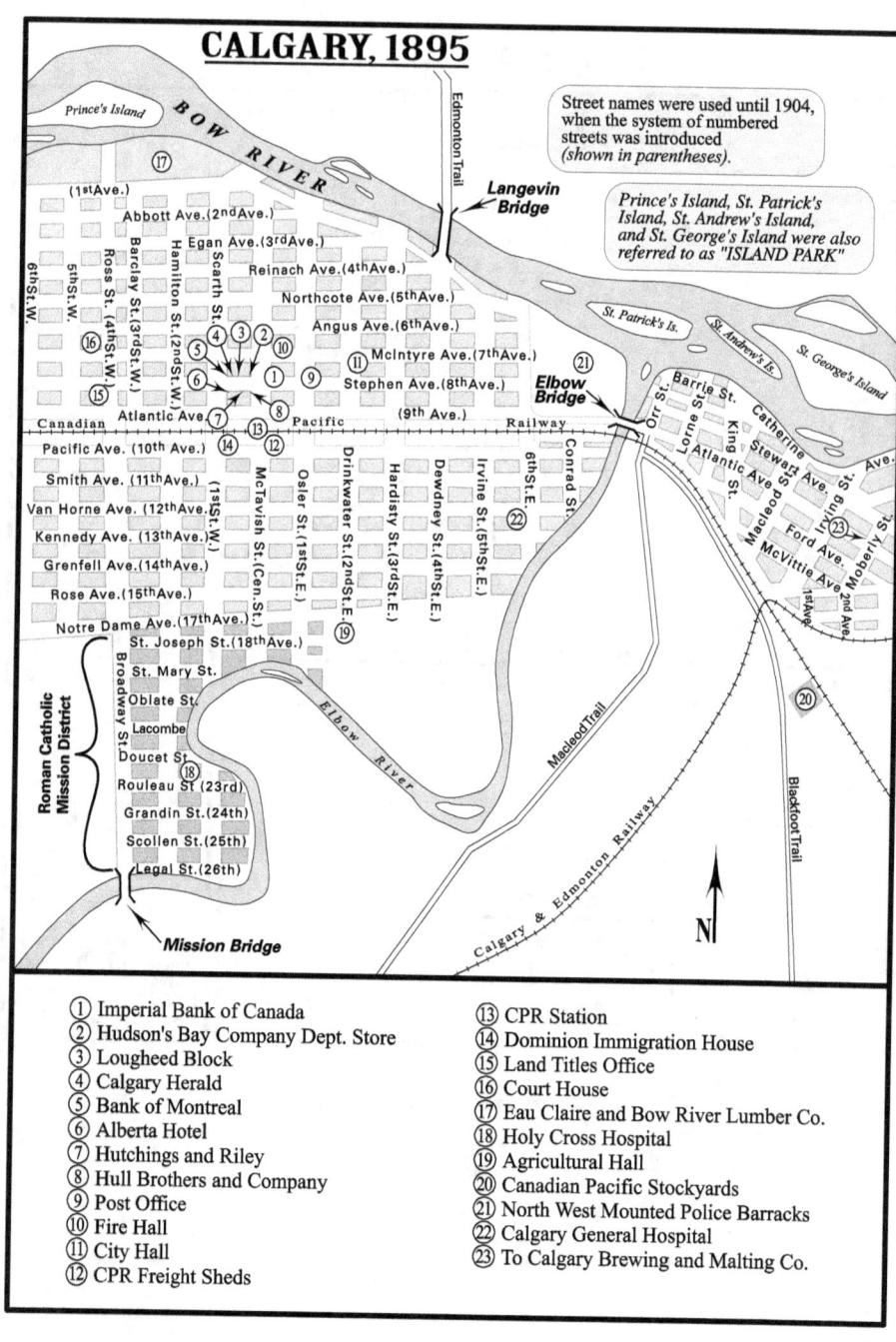

Map 2. Calgary in 1895

I

The Meeting Place

The Blackfoot

Calgary had been a meeting place long before it became a city. Its inhabitants, the Blackfoot, gained their living by a mixture of Native and Eurocanadian practices: hunting buffalo and beaver, fishing in the Bow and Elbow rivers, and gathering wild plants. They also traded at the Hudson's Bay Company's Edmonton House on the North Saskatchewan River, exchanging buffalo robes, beaver skins, dried meat, and fish for guns, ammunition, brandy, tobacco, hatchets, copper kettles, and ice chisels. In Calgary itself, the Blackfoot still controlled much of the land around their campsite, where they traded with the other tribes of the Blackfoot Confederacy – Stoneys, Sarcees, Peigans, and Bloods.[1]

Before the coming of white pioneers, the Blackfoot tapped the resources of two broad ecosystems: the Bow and Elbow and their floodplains, and the bluffs and several regions beyond the bluffs. Streams, floodplains, woods, bluffs, ponds, marshes, sloughs, prairies, and willowbrush provided complementary resources. These resources encouraged settlement by the Blackfoot along the boundaries of the two ecosystems from time to time, a practical way of achieving access to the resources of each and benefiting from them. With the arrival of white newcomers in later times, this settlement pattern continued. Pioneers often settled on the waterways beside prairies, gaining resources of both at the same time in order to build a new life.

Chapter 1: The Meeting Place

The Coming of Montana Traders

Signs of change loomed from the South. In 1864, Montana Territory was created, complete with a U.S. marshal and deputies, who before long tried to enforce the thirty-two-year-old law that prohibited the sale of liquor to Native Americans. In Fort Benton, at the head of navigation on the Upper Missouri River, and in Sun River the illegal sale of whiskey to Natives was the natural order of things. But on the whole, whiskey traders found it difficult to operate where there was effective legal prosecution. In the spring of 1869, whiskey traders John J. Healy and Alfred B. Hamilton of Sun River took their operations north of the border, to the confluence of the Belly and St. Mary rivers in Alberta, where they set up a whiskey post, Fort Hamilton, soon known as Fort Whoop-Up.[2]

By this time, the sale of liquor to Natives in the Canadian prairies was also prohibited by law, but whiskey traders in Alberta could and did escape punishment because the nearest law officers in Winnipeg could not easily bring them to justice. It was a tumultuous life, a long way from the seats of government and the niceties of Canadian society. Bartering their whiskey for buffalo robes from the Blackfoot, Healy and Hamilton hoped to make large and quick profits. Initially, financing for the Fort Whoop-Up trade came from credit supplied by Isaac G. Baker, an uncle of Hamilton and a prominent Fort Benton entrepreneur, although he soon severed his connection with the illegal whiskey trade.[3] Hamilton and Healy developed a trading network with the Blackfoot and other Natives north of the border, and their net profits from this trade soared to about $50,000 a year later.[4]

Healy and Hamilton's continuing success in the whiskey trade at Fort Whoop-Up lured other Montana traders into this business, particularly those from Fort Benton. In the next few years, Montana whiskey traders greatly increased their presence in southern Alberta. Whiskey became the most profitable trade item in the region during this period, but the traders also provided the Natives with other manufactured goods like guns, ammunition, flour, and blankets. Establishing whiskey posts at places such as Slideout, Standoff, Blackfoot Crossing, Elbow River, and Highwood River, they traded whiskey of inferior quality, much of which came from Chicago and St. Louis, Missouri.[5] In return, they received thousands of buffalo robes, especially from the Blackfoot, including those who camped at

Calgary from time to time. Most of these robes were sent by wagons south along the Whoop-Up Trail to Fort Benton, for shipment to New York City and other major American urban centres. The traders who came to southern Alberta were expected to know how to use a gun and were quick to defend themselves with it.

Whiskey traders lived a rough and vicious life at their posts in southern Alberta; suspicion and hostility often erupted into open conflict between them and the Native Canadians. The Blackfoot turned increasingly to whiskey, becoming dependent on trade with white people and craving manufactured goods. This injection of products from the industrialized world into Blackfoot culture altered society, undermining Native life. Important Blackfoot figures bore witness to the harm done by whiskey and talked and wrote about it in stinging, uncompromising terms. Complained Chief Crowfoot:

> The whiskey brought among us by the Traders is fast killing us off and we are powerless before the evil. [We are] totally unable to resist the temptation to drink when brought in contact with the white man's water. We are also unable to pitch anywhere that the Trader cannot follow us.[6]

The effects of the whiskey on the Blackfoot and other Alberta Natives were also described by Isaac G. Baker: "The Indians collect at the trading posts and are continually fighting among themselves and also with the white traders."[7] The incidence of crime on both sides was apparently high regarding murder and assault with a deadly weapon. In this atmosphere, the law tended to become what the traders wished to see it be – they often sought safety behind inner cabin walls. As Baker reported, "the trading posts are small cabins, divided into two rooms, with an opening in the division wall to pass the whiskey through. One pint is the usual price given for a buffalo robe worth $5.00."[8]

Hamilton and Healy's Trading Post

Growth in the whiskey trade in southern Alberta led Hamilton and Healy to set up a trading post at Calgary on the Elbow River in 1871 as a branch of Fort Whoop-Up as they sought to get closer to their Blackfoot markets. In doing so, they were in step with other

Chapter 1: The Meeting Place

Montana whiskey traders north of the border. Montana traders dominated the Calgary area in the early 1870s. The region lacked any capacity to respond to widespread and growing lawlessness. Anyone could set himself up as a whiskey trader. Run by Hamilton and Healy's manager Fred Kanouse of Fort Benton, the Calgary post was designed to produce substantial profits. But problems soon surfaced as Kanouse found himself caught up in a damaging situation. He ran into trouble when a band of Bloods visited the post to trade. Dissatisfied with the way the bartering in buffalo robes and whiskey was going, the Bloods turned on him with their Winchester repeating rifles, wounding him in his arm. Kanouse returned the fire, killing the Bloods' leader, White Eagle.[9] With assistance from a Blackfoot friend and others, Kanouse emerged victorious at the end of the fight, eventually recovered from his wound, abandoned the Calgary post in the spring of 1872, and then hauled the buffalo robes he had collected for Healy and Hamilton through Fort Whoop-Up down the Whoop-Up Trail to Fort Benton. For several months Calgary was again mostly a meeting place, where the Blackfoot and other Natives camped to trade.

The future of the Calgary post lay with the prospect of a new manager. Toward the end of 1872, Healy and Hamilton hired Donald Watson Davis, and immediately sent him to Calgary to manage the post. Born in 1849 on a farm in Londonderry Township in Windham County in southern Vermont, Davis was the son of Daniel and Laura Davis. Donald Davis as a boy did chores on his family's farm and attended the local school. Like many other Americans in the North as well as in the South, Davis found that the Civil War disrupted his life. During the conflict, he joined a Vermont regiment. In 1863, when he was only thirteen, Davis was in the Union lines that triumphed over the Confederates at the battle of Gettysburg, Pennsylvania, where he was wounded.[10] After the war, in 1866, he enrolled in the highly regarded Poughkeepsie Business College, from which he graduated the next year.[11] In mid-1867 he travelled to Cleveland, Ohio, where he enlisted as a private in the U.S. Army 13th Infantry.[12] Davis served as a military storekeeper at Fort Shaw on the Sun River in Montana for three years, handling the business side of the 13th Infantry and rising to the rank of quartermaster sergeant. At Fort Shaw, he also became friends with Sun River trader John J. Healy, and this set the stage for Davis's career change and his entrance into the whiskey trading business.

Chapter 1: The Meeting Place

March of the North West Mounted Police Across the Prairies to the Bow Valley 1874, as shown here in a painting by Charles William Jefferys. The arrival of the Mounted Police in Calgary in 1875 ushered in a new political and economic order that protected private property, thereby allowing people in Calgary and the Bow Valley to do business in an environment in which their property was safeguarded. (Courtesy of National Archives of Canada, C-073713, reproduced with permission of the C. W. Jefferys Estate Archive).

Chapter 1: The Meeting Place

At the end of 1870, after receiving his discharge from the U.S. Army, Davis acquired a new base, at Fort Whoop-Up in southern Alberta, where he could pursue his interest in business. At this point, through his personal connections with Healy, he got a job as a clerk.[13] During his two years at Fort Whoop-Up, Davis earned a reputation as an astute businessman, establishing himself as future management material.

By December 1872, Davis was managing Healy and Hamilton's whiskey post at Calgary. Healy once said that Davis "was my best man."[14] He was paid $150 a month, plus board and room.[15] But the Calgary post, suffering from neglect, was found by Davis to be in bad shape physically. To protect Healy and Hamilton's investment, Davis renovated the log post, and took charge of the trade with the Natives.[16] He exchanged mostly whiskey, but also ammunition, cloth, and other manufactured goods, for buffalo robes. Problems, however, continued to hurt the post: cold weather and ever-present whiskey-related violence among Montana traders and Native people.[17] Perceiving better opportunities south of Calgary, Davis closed the post and moved to Fort Whoop-Up in the spring of 1873. Still, he took two thousand buffalo robes worth about $12,000 with him from the Calgary post to Fort Whoop-Up.[18]

Calgary's Changing Business System

The business system at Calgary underwent great changes in the mid-1870s. With the closing of Healy and Hamilton's post there, the centre again became primarily what it had originally been – a meeting place for the Blackfoot and other Natives. Before long, however, new capitalist businesses of great significance were making their appearance. At about the same time came important developments in law and order, with the arrival of the North West Mounted Police. John Bunn, an enterprising Hudson's Bay Company trader on the Bow River near the Rocky Mountains, spent part of 1874 seeking a new location for trading with Native people, eventually choosing Calgary.[19] The coming of the Mounted Police to Calgary in August 1875 convinced him that he had made a good choice. In September, I. G. Baker & Co. of Fort Benton, the firm that had landed the contract to build the Mounted Police barracks in Calgary, erected a new general store there, on the west side of the Elbow River just at its junction with the Bow. By the end of that month, John Bunn had begun the construction of a Hudson's Bay Company trading post on the east side of the Elbow, and it was in these premises that he was soon doing business with the Natives.

The transfer of Rupert's Land, Hudson's Bay Company territory drained by rivers flowing into Hudson Bay, to the new Dominion of Canada in 1870 ensured that Calgary and the Bow Valley would be under the authority of the Canadian government. In Calgary and its region, the federal government was the law. Legally and practically, the government used the apparatus of the state to exploit the material resources of the Canadian West, including Calgary and the surrounding area. The whiskey trade was malignancy, a curse to Canada's existence as a nation. It had to be eradicated swiftly. The arrival of the Mounted Police, a federal force, ended the whiskey trade and contributed significantly to the protection of private property. Other main economic effects of the coming of the Mounted Police were the integration of Calgary and the Bow Valley into the business system of central Canada, and the direct promotion of mercantile development by the federal government. I. G. Baker & Co. and the Hudson's Bay Company took a steadily increasing role in economic life, and the nation benefited commensurately.

Calgary had much to offer firms like the Hudson's Bay Company and I. G. Baker & Co. As Hudson's Bay Company land commissioner Charles J. Brydges boasted:

> Calgary is the most charming spot I have seen in the North West so far, being a beautiful valley with the Rocky Mountains, with their snow capped peaks, as a background. The land is excellent – the grasses rich and thick – ample water – and wood not far off. The difficulty is early frosts, but I think early sowing and reaping will largely remove this objection.[20]

Sitting astride the confluence of the Bow and the Elbow Rivers, Calgary possessed another key asset as well: links to Native communities such as the Blackfoot, Stoneys, Sarcees, Bloods, and Peigans. These people soon provided important markets for the Hudson's Bay Company and I. G. Baker & Co.'s nascent trading ventures in Calgary. As growing numbers of Natives depended on them for various goods, their stores' concerns about product quality

Chapter 1: The Meeting Place

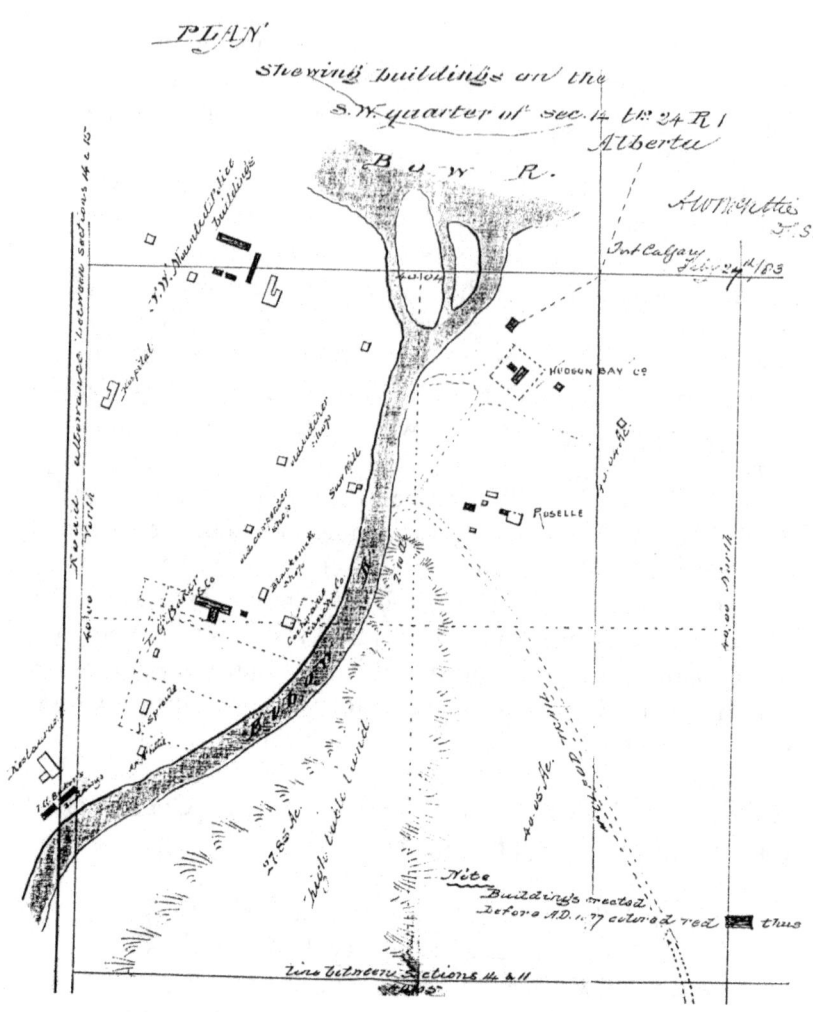

Map 3. Township 24 Range 1 W5M. Calgary in 1883, about six months before the coming of the Canadian Pacific Railway. (Courtesy of National Archives of Canada).

intensified. Over the years, the two companies achieved iconic status, not only within business but also in the popular culture of the day. Their names became familiar all over the Bow Valley and beyond.

2

I. G. Baker & Co.
American Enterprise in the Wagon-Road Era

During the last half of the 1870s and the early 1880s, I. G. Baker & Co. of Fort Benton, Montana was unquestionably Calgary's leading business enterprise. But in its local business activities this American firm was hardly alone. The Hudson's Bay Company's trading post, supported by the company's Edmonton and Winnipeg posts and the London head office, was a significant competitor. Other businesses in the Calgary area also challenged Baker & Co., but it outdistanced them all, in number of customers and volume of trade. Foreign direct investment – investment involving Baker & Co.'s active control of its decision-making – was a central and rapidly growing element in the growth and development of the Calgary and Bow Valley economies.

A great deal of Calgary commerce, largely river- and wagon-borne, was organized and directed by entrepreneurs residing in Fort Benton and St. Louis, Missouri – I. G. Baker and Charles and William Conrad, partners in Baker & Co. and men of extraordinary self-confidence. In this unincorporated American company, the partners and their families who built the firm controlled all the capital. It was an entrepreneurial or family enterprise. Throughout the early history of capitalism in the Bow Valley, this American firm was heavily involved in international trade. In commercial terms, some individuals and enterprises in Fort Benton, including the Baker & Co. partners and their company, were remarkably successful. Trade was often quite profitable for entrepreneurs and individual investors. Briskly moving commerce in and around Fort Benton stimulated demand for goods and services within Montana and enabled the town and its leading businesses to trade

Chapter 2: I. G. Baker & Co.

Isaac G. Baker in 1885, founder of I. G. Baker & Co. (Courtesy of Glenbow Archives, NA-568-5).

on an international scale. In this period, the Calgary economy can best be described as commercial in character. People depended on the technology of wagon transport to overcome long distances. Wagon lines, carrying freight, were mostly unscheduled. Passengers and mail moved by stagecoaches, which ran on very informal schedules. In Calgary and the Bow Valley, only a wave of technical changes in transportation and communication would make possible the beginnings of industrial development which occurred in the later years of the nineteenth century.

I. G. Baker & Co. and its Network of Stores

In the mid-1870s, I. G. Baker & Co., a pioneer of entrepreneurial capitalism, expanded from Fort Benton into the Canadian prairies by creating a network of stores in Fort Macleod, Calgary, and Fort Walsh comparable to the firm's network of stores and trading posts in Montana. The company's expansion was facilitated by the development of complex, loosely integrated personal and institutional networks that were international in scope and fostered business enterprise in Calgary and other prairie centres. Relevant institutions in these networks included the Canadian and American governments, the North West Mounted Police, and Canadian and American banks.

Calgary has had a long history of boom and bust, but in 1875 it was an amicable host on the rise. Baker & Co. men from Fort Benton walked the Calgary streets with as much of a sense of belonging as Canadian merchants. The place was a key point on Alberta trails. Calgary was situated in the northwestern corner of southern Alberta, with two trails – the Edmonton Trail and the Macleod Trail – converging on the centre to give the spot its pre-eminence. For at least eight years Calgary capitalized on the Macleod

Chapter 2: I. G. Baker & Co.

Trail, which was linked to the Whoop-Up Trail, to bring in the bulk of the required supplies from Fort Benton. From 1875 forward, these trails were freighting roads, created for commercial purposes. A year-round population of about one hundred people at Calgary occasionally increased significantly with the arrival of dozens of transients, especially freighters and bull whackers who brought supplies. The streets of the town bustled with commercial activity: they were full of ox-teams and wagon-masters loading up to start on trips. Trains of wagons pulled by oxen hauled buffalo robes and furs, heading out usually for Fort Benton but sometimes also for Edmonton. Connected to Fort Benton and Edmonton by a north-south network of freighting trails, Calgary became the essential hub as the wagon-road economy developed. From the last half of the 1870s to the 1880s, the trails served as a major freighting highway while southwestern Alberta changed from a culture based on buffalo hunting to one squarely based on ranching and farming.

Charles E. Conrad in 1885, partner in I. G. Baker & Co. (Courtesy of Glenbow Archives, NA-568-3).

Isaac Gilbert Baker and the Founding of a Trading Company

I. G. Baker & Co. was well established in Fort Benton before the firm extended its operations to Calgary in 1875. The founder of the business, Isaac Gilbert Baker, was a true representative of the Great Plains pioneer merchants of the post-Civil War era. His business life encompassed much of the plains experience. An energetic entrepreneur, he was at one time or another a fur trader, freighter, merchant, steamboat operator, banker, and rancher. Coming to the region when there were few settled communities, he lived to see settlement spread across the area. Born in 1819 at Ridgefield, Connecticut, Baker was the son of Amos Baker, a direct descendant of Sir Mathew Gilbert, deputy governor of Connecticut and a half-brother of Sir Walter Raleigh.[1] A graduate of Ridgefield

Chapter 2: I. G. Baker & Co.

Charles's older brother and partner, William G. Conrad, in 1885. (Courtesy of Glenbow Archives, NA-568-4).

High School, I. G. Baker had a keen mathematical brain and an amazing facility for writing letters well. In 1837, he went to Burlington, Iowa, where he hired out to Petridge and Company to trade with Native Americans for furs. He became a familiar figure in the fur trade over the following three decades. A fast worker with a natural aptitude for business, Baker moved to Fort Benton in 1864 to become the manager of the fur-trading firm Pierre Chouteau Jr. & Co. of St. Louis, Missouri.[2] With the confidence and zest of a man on the make, Baker struck out on his own at the first opportunity. Sometime in 1866 he and his younger brother George A., who also had a good head for figures and a gift for letter writing, set up the partnership I. G. Baker & Brother to establish a general store and engage in trading with Natives for buffalo robes and furs. As the most experienced trader, I. G. Baker became the senior partner. He contributed the bulk of the capital to the partnership in the form of merchandise.[3] A consistent and determined commitment to merchandising and buffalo robe and fur trading helped propel Baker & Brother ahead of most of its Fort Benton competitors as it earned a sound reputation for reliability and efficiency.

I. G. Baker's abilities clearly lay in in the practical organization and running of a major firm. He had the personality and contacts needed to maintain established ties and acquire new customers, combined with the attention to detail and toughness to ensure efficient operations.[4] He took pleasure from encouraging his brother George as well the clerks they hired. I. G. Baker was well liked and trusted by the partnership's staff. The long-term prosperity of the firm derived in part from the recruitment of talented clerks.

Such clerks included especially the two brothers, William G. and Charles E. Conrad, who began working for the firm in Fort Benton in 1868. They hailed originally from Wapping Plantation at Front Royal, Virginia, where William was born in 1848 and Charles in

1850, the sons of Southern aristocratic parents. As was the case with so many other youths of the day, their education in the local school was disrupted by the Civil War. During the conflict, they served as Confederate soldiers. As Civil War veterans, they had few options; certainly, they had no post-war job prospects at home. So they found employment in New York City business firms before moving to Fort Benton. Young men of vigour and enthusiasm, the Conrad brothers manifested many of the qualities of Southern gentlemen, but they had only one silver dollar between them when they arrived at the river port on the Upper Missouri.[5] At Baker & Brother, William and Charles worked hard, developed "good business habits," and proved to be wizards with numbers.[6] In 1873, they were admitted to the firm as partners, and a year later they bought George Baker's share in it.

The firm was now reorganized as I. G. Baker & Co., with I. G. Baker as its senior partner and William and Charles Conrad as its junior partners. Charles had considerable charm and was ideally suited to liaising with customers, while William was adept at doing office work. As head of the new partnership, I. G. Baker matured into an imaginative and dynamic leader. Ever since the late 1860s, when he had opened an office in St. Louis to establish warehouse facilities in that city, he had guided the firm to larger merchandise sales and higher profits. Around 1873, he moved to St. Louis to take charge of the firm's office there, while remaining in close contact with the Fort Benton office through correspondence and frequent visits. His brother George followed him to St. Louis a year later to become his salaried assistant and, by the early 1880s, was serving as president of the Continental Bank of St. Louis, an important source of credit for Baker & Co. All three Baker & Co. partners, I. G. Baker and Charles and William Conrad, understood the realities of the American business environment, and the importance of being able to operate competitively. To become competitive, it was essential to build up a network of branch trading posts and develop new trading connections.[7]

Expansion in Montana

Back in 1868, I. G. Baker's first step toward geographical expansion in Montana had been to open a trading post on the Milk River, three miles above Fort Browning. About the same time, he set up another trading post at the confluence of the Milk River and Porcupine Creek. At these two posts, Baker collected buffalo robes and furs from the Gros Ventres, Assiniboine, and Crows.[8] Initially, he secured the furs and buffalo robes by including whiskey in the trade goods he offered. But constant pressure from federal government officials forced him to stop his illicit whiskey trade in December 1870.[9]

In its main operations, collecting buffalo robes and furs for the American market in St. Louis and New York City, Baker & Co. faced the challenge of working in an increasingly competitive industry. There were many competitors, but the firm's principal rival was T. C. Power & Bro. of Fort Benton. Baker & Co.'s response to this situation proved adequate in the long run. Developing a network of branch trading posts was a deliberate strategy, part of an effort to offset the impact of competition in the buffalo robe and fur trade. In opting for a growth strategy through branching, I. G. Baker and his partners helped bring greater financial stability to their firm. Business connections also provided them with resources they often tapped to get over the difficult spots in their firm's early years. They used their ties to Donnell Lawson & Co., New York City bankers, to secure financial support. In addition, they were connected with Buckley Welling & Co., New York City dry goods merchants, and obtained supplies and credit from them.[10] As it grew, Baker & Co. diversified by securing Office of Indian Affairs supply contracts for the Blackfoot and Crow reservations in the Montana Territory.[11] Like the buffalo robe and fur trade, these contracts to supply the Native reservations with goods brought substantial profits to the firm.

Trading in the Canadian Prairies Begins

Baker & Co.'s prosperous operations allowed it to extend its network of trading posts into the isolated regions of the Canadian prairies. Over the years, the inflow of foreign direct investment into the prairies through this American firm became very important to the host region. Canadian markets first attracted attention from the enterprise in the 1870s. In 1873, the Baker & Co. partners opened a trading post at Fort Whoop-Up and another one on the St. Mary River a short distance from Fort Whoop-Up. However, "the whiskey traders so annoyed them and demoralised the Indians that they" felt compelled to close these two Canadian posts the following year.[12]

The arrival of the North West Mounted Police in southern Alberta in 1874 provided some guarantee against the continuation of the whiskey trade. As the political history of this region was very unstable, the idea that Baker & Co. needed political support, especially from the Mounted Police, was entirely reasonable. Charles Conrad, as a partner in Baker & Co., made an important contribution to the ending of the whiskey trade and the establishment of personal ties with the Mounted Police. In October of that year he heard that they were lost, extremely short of food, and facing starvation near the Sweet Grass Hills. Relief came in that same month when Conrad personally brought them wagon trains of supplies and killed buffalo to provide them with fresh meat, a move that helped the Mounted Police survive, reach Fort Whoop-Up, and gradually stamp out the whiskey trade.[13]

I. G. Baker solidified his firm's connections with the Mounted Police by inviting commissioner George French, assistant commissioner Colonel James F. Macleod, and assistant surgeon Richard Nevitt to stay in his home when they visited Fort Benton to secure additional supplies. "He fed us most royally, treating us in the most hospitable manner," reported Nevitt.[14] At this point, French outlined his plans to obtain supplies: he hoped that Baker & Co. would become the supplier of the Mounted Police because they faced the problem of a long, inefficient supply route from Winnipeg across the Canadian prairies to southern Alberta. They could not afford the costs of setting up their own national supply network. However, they needed to secure adequate supplies to ensure that they would be able to establish law and order in southern Alberta. I. G. Baker responded enthusiastically; he immediately contracted to supply groceries, hardware, clothing, medical supplies, and other goods for the Mounted Police in the region for the balance of the fiscal year ending 30 June 1875. Baker & Co. continued to serve the Mounted Police in this capacity for many years.

Baker & Co.'s enduring business relationship with the Mounted Police meant more to I. G. Baker and the Conrad brothers than money. From the beginning, they also derived personal satisfaction from their contact with Mounted Police officers such as Colonel James F. Macleod. Like him, they were clearly Victorian in character, stressing superior customer service and expecting hard work to

Chapter 2: I. G. Baker & Co.

translate into an improved standard of living someday. Just as Macleod's lifestyle reflected the Victorian culture of Canada, so theirs incorporated much of American Victorianism in the late nineteenth century. Crossing national boundaries, Victorianism emerged as an international culture – values and attitudes shared by English-speaking people in Canada, the United States, and Great Britain in this era. Cultural ties provided the Baker & Co. partners with resources they often tapped to smooth over rough spots in providing the Mounted Police with supplies.

Baker & Co., of course, already had valuable experience as a supplier. Like I. G. Baker, Charles and William Conrad had learned a great deal while their firm had served the American Office of Indian Affairs as a supplier of goods for the Blackfoot and Crow reservations. To deliver these goods to the Crows and Blackfoot, the three partners had organized their own overland freighting operation, which required trains of wagons pulled by oxen or mules. The arrival of the Chicago & North Western Railroad in Sioux City in 1868, followed by the Northern Pacific Railroad in Bismarck five years later, drove a transportation system into the heart of the Great Plains. They helped make marketing more effective for Baker & Co. as the cost of transportation dropped. Initially, sources outside the firm provided shipping services for it on the Missouri from St. Louis or Sioux City or Bismarck to Fort Benton, but in 1877 it acquired its own steamboat, the *Red Cloud*. Baker & Co. purchased its second steamboat a year later, appropriately christened the *Colonel Macleod*.[15] Perhaps most important in explaining the naming of the steamboat was Charles Conrad's desire to strengthen the firm's relationship with Colonel James F. Macleod, who was in charge of the Mounted Police in southern Alberta. A man of great energy and the partner destined to play the most significant role in the firm's southern Alberta operations, Charles Conrad got along well with Macleod from the start, and so it was natural to name the steamboat for him.

Charles Conrad and his associates successfully met the requirements of the first contract for supplies for the Mounted Police in southern Alberta. Their train of wagons, filled with 40,000 pounds of supplies, was sent north from Fort Benton along the Whoop-Up Trail to Fort Macleod on the Oldman River, the Mounted Police post. After delivering the goods in excellent condition, they pocketed a handsome profit. Colonel Macleod was impressed by their service. "I have every reason to be thankful to them for the prompt and satisfactory manner in which they carried out their contract with me and for the kind attention they paid to all I required of them," he wrote to the department of justice in the Canadian government in Ottawa, which was responsible for the Mounted Police.[16]

Then Colonel Macleod, who had come to Fort Macleod to establish a large Mounted Police presence there, gave Conrad a letter of introduction to Hewitt Bernard, deputy minister of justice. On his visit to Ottawa in February 1875 Baker, eager to repeat his success of the year before, sought a contract to continue to supply the Mounted Police with the goods they needed. The Canadian government and Baker felt comfortable working together, and so it gave him the contract he desired and later renewed it year after year. While Baker & Co. had received a government Mounted Police contract valued at $23,395 in 1874–75, the firm's profitable Mounted Police business grew over the next two years, with $244,828 in contracts.[17] By the end of the 1870s, they were among Baker & Co.'s biggest and most favoured Canadian customers. The Mounted Police desperately needed supplies, and firm had the capital and the transportation system to provide them. Its steamboats were often seen on the Missouri carrying the supplies up to Fort Benton, from where its wagon trains took them overland to Fort Macleod.

In order to service this rapidly growing Canadian market, Baker & Co. established a general store in Fort Macleod at the end of 1874 with Charles Conrad as its manager.[18] With the success of his business there, Conrad decided to expand the firm's operations north of the border. In early 1875, he began planning to open stores at Calgary and Fort Walsh in the Cypress Hills, where the Mounted Police also had set up posts. One of Conrad's earliest customers at the Fort Macleod store was Mounted Police surgeon Richard Nevitt, who purchased twenty-five yards of factory cotton and some dark blue cloth for the ceiling of his room to keep out the cold in the winter. Enjoying a reputation as an open, accessible man who valued good relations with customers, Conrad attracted much business at Fort Macleod.

Establishing a General Store in Calgary

Charles Conrad had an unerring sense of the principal market he was trying to reach in Calgary. His plan was simple: he would

Chapter 2: I. G. Baker & Co.

I. G. Baker & Co.'s store in Calgary Bottom in 1882. To facilitate business with the North West Mounted Police, the store was built close to the North West Mounted Police barracks just west of the Elbow River. From 1875 to 1883, Baker & Co. sold goods here (the company later used the building as a warehouse). (Courtesy of Glenbow Archives, NA-345-18).

open a Baker & Co. general store especially for the Mounted Police shopper and bring in goods by wagon train. He chose D. W. Davis, whom he had hired earlier to work for him at Fort Macleod, to supervise the construction of the Mounted Police post in Calgary and, at the same time, instructed him to establish a general store for the firm right beside the post. Arriving in Calgary in mid-September 1875, Davis occupied about thirteen hundred acres in Calgary Bottom, land that was located at the junction of the Bow and Elbow rivers and on the west side of the Elbow, just south of the site chosen for the Mounted Police. Pine and cottonwood trees a few miles up the Elbow offered logs for the construction of buildings. Within several weeks, besides having erected a small dwelling house for himself and the other Baker & Co. employees, Davis had begun the construction of the Mounted Police barracks as part of Fort Calgary.[19] By the end of the year, he also had built a store and become its first manager. By this time, the firm had set up a general store at Fort Walsh as well.

Achieving success in its general store business, Baker & Co. also planned to go into the mail service. From 1867 to 1869, I. G. Baker had been postmaster in Fort Benton and now, in 1875, he used his connections to government officials in Ottawa to secure

Chapter 2: I. G. Baker & Co.

I. G. Baker & Co.'s wagon train in Fort Macleod in 1887. This train ran from Fort Benton to Calgary, with a stop at Fort Macleod. (Courtesy of Glenbow Archives, NA-936-38).

the contract to provide mail service between Fort Benton and Fort Macleod, Calgary, and Fort Walsh.[20] Baker & Co. served the Canadian government in this capacity until the early 1880s. The mail came in to Calgary by wagon twice a month from Fort Benton, but the natural hazards of the trail and the weather made this communication difficult. Despite these problems, the coming of mail service provided Baker & Co.'s Calgary store with vital ties not only to Fort Benton, St. Louis, and other American urban centres but also to Canadian cities such as Ottawa and Montreal.

Baker & Co.'s store in Calgary was devoted to the storage and sale of merchandise, but the building also served as a meeting place for residents of the community. The Mounted Police – some fifty men – and settlers in Calgary Bottom such as John Monroe and Baptiste Annouse, as well as John Glenn, a farmer at Fish Creek, and David McDougall, a trader at Morley up the Bow, often combined shopping with visiting.[21] A social necessity for these sometimes lonely people, visiting probably helped increase the sales at the store. As growth occurred, Baker & Co. hired Mr. Kinghorn, a former Mounted Policeman, as a clerk to assist D. W. Davis.

Davis's entrepreneurial leadership spurred the firm to development in Calgary. He was willing to take risks and never lost heart, even

Chapter 2: I. G. Baker & Co.

Donald W. Davis, manager of I. G. Baker & Co.'s Fort Macleod store and of its Canadian operations, on his horse in the Fort Macleod area in the 1880s. (Courtesy of Glenbow Archives, NA-659-58).

during the difficult times of the mid-1870s. Davis proved flexible in his approach to business. He aimed at selling high-quality goods, whether those products were clothing, groceries, or hardware. While committed to marketing a wide variety of goods, he was flexible in the mix of items he offered. Even as he competed with the Hudson's Bay Company in distributing merchandise, Davis was eager to take the lead in selling new products as soon as markets existed for them in the Calgary area. He was an adventurous businessman, seeking out opportunities among the Mounted Police at Fort Calgary, the Blackfoot, Sarcees, Peigans, and Stoneys who visited Calgary Bottom and, increasingly in the mid- and late 1870s, the ranchers and settlers in the surrounding countryside. The social and economic environments within which Baker & Co. operated also aided the development of the firm. Davis's acceptance by the Mounted Police, Natives, settlers, and ranchers was particularly important. They supported the enterprise of Baker & Co. as a way of enhancing their own fortunes.

Table 3. Settlers in the Calgary District, 1875-1883

Year	Number of Settlers
1875	2
1883	46

Source: Provincial Archives of Alberta, Homestead Records, reel 2002, file 86751, statement made by Samuel H. Livingston, 8 May 1885; reel 2002, file 89165, statement made by John Glenn, 8 May 1885; reel 2000, file 43503, Settlers in Township 24, Range 1, West of the Fifth Meridian, October 1883.

The rich grasslands of Calgary Bottom and the Bow Valley provided the physical basis for the rise of ranching and farming. "The country beyond the Missouri Plateau from Edmonton south and west to the Rocky Mountains is excellent for grazing. The Blackfoot Indians used to breed great numbers of horses there before the whites came," observed I. G. Baker.[22] Although southwestern Alberta was potentially rich as an agricultural region, only in the Calgary area had a few farms been established by 1875. These were Sam Livingston's farm along the Elbow River near Calgary and John Glenn's farm at Midnapore, which they started in that year. By the summer of 1883, as Table 3 shows, there were about forty-six settlers in the Calgary district. The foundations of ranching lay in Montana herds that were the offspring of cattle brought to the Montana Territory from Texas, Washington, and Oregon. As early as 1874, drovers had delivered cattle to Morley on the Bow River. To fatten them, cattlemen relied on the nutritious grasses on the open range. In 1875, Baker & Co. diversified into ranching, establishing range rights on the pasturelands in Calgary Bottom by grazing work oxen on them.

Survival and Expansion

Baker & Co. developed what was, in effect, a general store and ranching business. It was an auspicious moment. The late nineteenth century was a period of great expansion for southwestern Alberta business, as the region became a predominantly ranching and farming area. From a land based on the buffalo robe and fur trades before 1875, southwestern Alberta became a region of ranches,

Chapter 2: I. G. Baker & Co.

Table 4. Leading Products at I. G. Baker & Co.'s Calgary Store, 1875-1891
Groceries
Beef
Dry Goods
Hardware
Farm Implements
Saddles and Harnesses
Wagons

Source: Glenbow-Alberta Institute Archives, Richard Hardisty Papers, Bow River, 14 December 1875, John Bunn to Richard Hardisty; Spitsea, 15 December 1875, Wm. Leslie Wood to Richard Hardisty; *Calgary Herald*, 31 August 1883; 1 February 1888; 3 March 1891.

farms, and small towns, villages, and hamlets by 1900. Between 1875 and the turn of the century, for the first time, more people worked in agricultural jobs than in hunting buffalo. Agricultural output rose significantly. The sales of leading products at Baker & Co.'s Calgary store (see Table 4) for much of this period – groceries, beef, dry goods, hardware, farm implements, saddles and harnesses, and wagons – benefited tremendously from this growth.

But the late nineteenth century was also a hazardous period for Alberta business, a time characterized by dramatic ups and downs in the business cycle of Canada. In the mid-1870s, a severe economic depression hurt many businesses, and a decade later a recession shut down many enterprises. In the playing out of Canada's business cycle there were successes and failures. With the persistent entrepreneurship of I. G. Baker and the Conrad brothers, their firm survived the 1870s and grew during the 1880s to become a regional mercantile company of considerable repute.

Initially, Baker & Co. purchased merchandise from wholesalers and manufacturers in eastern American cities such as New York City and Boston, which was then shipped to Fort Benton by railroad and steamboat and hauled about three hundred miles from Fort Benton's harbour to the Calgary store by ox-drawn wagons. D. W. Davis's trade at the store occurred especially with Native Canadians, while merchandise sales to the Mounted Police also remained important.

One item dominated the Native offerings to Baker & Co. in the mid-1870s: buffalo robes. "In 1876 as many as 15,000 buffalo robes were shipped south by this store alone, costing them in trade about 50 cents each, and fetching in Benton $5 to $10, according to quality," reported Mounted Police Captain Cecil Denny.[23] So numerous were the buffalo that for the next few years Baker & Co.'s Calgary store made substantial profits from its buffalo robe trade. In exchange for buffalo robes, Davis provided the Natives especially with flour, molasses, horses, saddles, Winchester repeating rifles, revolvers, cartridges, and blankets.[24]

Although Baker & Co. continued to grow in Calgary, problems emerged in the mid-1870s. One was that the United States imposed a 40 percent ad valorem duty on imported buffalo robes and furs in 1876. Reacting to this high tariff, which he knew would cost his firm dearly, I. G. Baker tried to minimize costs wherever possible. Like T. C. Power & Bro., his main competitor in the trade north of the border, he sought and immediately obtained a permit from the U.S. government to ship buffalo robes and furs from the Canadian prairies through Fort Benton to Montreal or London, England in bond, thus avoiding the payment of customs duties.[25] According to the Hudson's Bay Company, Baker & Co. and Power & Bro. together sold twelve thousand buffalo robes in Montreal each year in 1877 and 1879.[26] The permit also allowed Baker & Co. to ship bonded re-exports – manufactured goods – from central Canadian cities such as Montreal through Fort Benton to its stores in Calgary, Fort Macleod, and Fort Walsh. As a result, the bulk of the merchandise on the shelves of these stores consisted of duty free Canadian goods, while the rest was made up of American commodities on which customs duties had to be paid. In 1877, for example, the firm's merchandise purchases in central Canada, mostly in Montreal, came to over $300,000.[27] From I. G. Baker's perspective, the long-term goal of his move to bonded commerce was to facilitate increasing efficiencies, reduce prices to consumers such as the Mounted Police and Natives, and become more competitive in the Canadian market. To a large degree, this was achieved, and it helped give his firm immense market power in Calgary and elsewhere in the Canadian prairies.

Chapter 2: I. G. Baker & Co.

Responding to the Needs of the Mounted Police

In Calgary, Baker & Co. performed a wide spectrum of functions ranging from the import and export business to banking. The only banker in the centre until the mid-1880s, the firm played a critical role in providing financial services. Profits from banking became one of the important sources of income for its Calgary store. In response to a request from the department of justice in Ottawa in 1875, I. G. Baker immediately agreed to supply the Mounted Police in Calgary, Fort Macleod, and Fort Walsh with funds to pay their men at the start of each month.[28] Through the Ottawa branch of the Bank of Montreal and the First National Bank of Helena, Montana, he arranged to provide the Mounted Police with the Canadian dollars they needed. Baker & Co. received a commission of 2½ percent for this financial service.

But not very long after he began providing funds for the Mounted Police, Baker faced problems. He had difficulty in meeting the monthly Mounted Police payroll because the department of justice did not act quickly enough to ensure that sufficient Canadian government funds flowed from the Bank of Montreal to the First National Bank in Helena to Baker & Co.[29] To make things worse, in Calgary, inspector Ephrem Brisebois fell behind in giving Baker & Co. receipts for the payroll money it delivered to him.[30] In an effort to make the payroll process more efficient, I. G. Baker travelled to Ottawa in November 1876 to see Fred White, the justice department's clerk responsible for the Mounted Police. When he met with White, he asked him to improve co-ordination between Ottawa and his firm in the Canadian prairies. Baker's appeal evoked a positive response. On White's recommendation, the Liberal government of Alexander Mackenzie agreed to deposit $5,000 in Baker & Co.'s account at the Bank of Montreal each month.[31] The availability of an adequate supply of Canadian money allowed Baker to improve payroll operations.

Even as payroll operations were being revamped, Baker & Co. continued to deliver money on a regular basis to pay the Mounted Police. In Calgary, inspector Brisebois received the total sum of $4,624 for his men between March and July 1876.[32] Most of this money remained in the community, and much of it was spent in Baker & Co.'s store. Thus, in establishing financial services, the firm expanded its merchandise sales.

Chapter 2: I. G. Baker & Co.

Achieving Growth through Ties to Native People

Baker & Co. also achieved growth though its increasingly stronger ties to Native people. By this time, in order to secure large expanses of land for settlement, the Canadian government proposed creating separate reserves for each Native tribe in Alberta. In an effort to sweeten the offer, it also promised to provide annuities of food and supplies through suppliers such as Baker & Co. to Natives who ceded part of their land and accepted the restricted life of a reserve.[33] The government hoped that the reserve system would give the Natives an opportunity to start becoming Canadianized. Although the Natives disliked this approach to frontier planning, they negotiated treaties surrendering a great deal of the land they held in Alberta. Treaty 6 and Treaty 7 – the first pertaining to Cree land in central Alberta and central Saskatchewan and the second covering Blackfoot, Stoney, Sarcee, Blood, and Peigan land in southern Alberta – were signed on 23 August 1876 and on 22 September 1877 respectively.[34] All that remained to the Natives were reserves – tracts of land of various sizes – and the promise from the federal government that it would provide them with annual treaty payments to be used to obtain food and other supplies, farming assistance, and education and health services. I. G. Baker hoped to secure many of the government supply contracts to meet the needs of the Natives, and his hopes were largely realized. Like his other Canadian stores, Baker's store in Calgary eventually helped him to move more deeply into the Native market.

Native reserve markets in Alberta first attracted attention from Baker & Co. in 1876. In April of that year, I. G. Baker made a trip to Ottawa to look into marketing possibilities on Native reserves.[35] Because of his firm's reputation as a reliable supplier, David Laird, minister of the interior, warmly welcomed him. The department of the interior usually awarded supply contracts to the lowest bidders. From the start, I. G. Baker's strategy was to keep his bids low and seek to make money on volume. Much came of his trip, for his firm soon won a Canadian government contract to deliver 224,000 pounds of beef in the form of live cattle to Battleford, at the junction of the North Saskatchewan and Battle rivers.[36] The cattle were driven from Fort Benton up the wagon trail to Fort Walsh and from there over Saskatchewan prairie lands to Battleford. They arrived in good shape in Battleford on 24 July in readiness for slaughter and consumption by the Cree at the Treaty 6 negotiations. The department of the interior's agent then took charge of the cattle, driving them to Fort Carlton and Fort Pitt, where the negotiations took place. Thus, the whole beef venture was successful.

Baker & Co. had, however, been late in getting the cattle to Battleford: for a variety of reasons, they were delivered there eight days after the contract deadline. Consequently, the department of the interior imposed a penalty of $400 on the firm, leaving it with a reduced payment of $6,923 for the cattle. Baker & Co. received the payment through the Bank of Montreal, which became an increasingly significant institution in the firm's life. But when I. G. Baker explained that the department of the interior's agent had only reached Battleford on 24 July, the same day on which the cattle were delivered, the sum of $400 was added back to the payment.[37] Confident that Baker & Co. would continue to serve the Canadian government as an important resource, the department of the interior promoted the firm's stature as a responsible supplier.

Baker & Co. also took full advantage of the opportunities that grew out of Treaty 7 at Blackfoot Crossing on the Bow River below Calgary in September 1877. Charles Conrad, who was present at the signing of the treaty, oversaw Baker & Co.'s activities at this significant event.[38] The contract the firm won led to its delivery of over 36,000 pounds of beef and over 35,000 pounds of flour to the Blackfoot, Stoneys, Bloods, Peigans, and Sarcees at Blackfoot Crossing. In its role as banker, Baker & Co. delivered $62,292 to Colonel Macleod, the treaty commissioner, enabling him to provide the Natives with treaty money.[39] The firm received $10,074 for all the services it rendered at Blackfoot Crossing. At the time of Treaty 7, Baker & Co.'s store in Calgary earned profits through its sale of goods to the Blackfoot, Sarcees, and Stoneys who had treaty money to spend. Besides purchasing clothing and food, the Natives now also bought agricultural equipment as they began to farm on the reserves. Similarly, the firm's Fort Macleod store benefited from providing the Bloods and Peigans with merchandise.

The Natives in the Bow Valley – Stoneys, Sarcees, and Blackfoot – had surrendered thousands of acres of their traditional territories, but most of them found it difficult to put down roots and become settled farmers on the reserves. They received instruction in farming and other ways of white society, but they were reluctant to accept life within the assigned boundaries. No longer able to hunt and ride as freely as they had in the past, they had to rely increasingly on the federal government annuities of food and supplies to survive. Conditions for the Natives were certainly discouraging: the challenge of starting to farm was daunting enough, but also disturbing was the decline of the buffalo population. As recently as the early 1870s, buffalo had numbered in the tens of thousands, and the large herds that roamed across Alberta had provided vital sources of sustenance for Native people. They derived much from the buffalo: food, clothing, shelter, and tools.

Of course, the Natives knew that white people such as I. G. Baker and his associates also valued the buffalo; for several years they themselves had exchanged buffalo robes for guns, ammunition, and other goods with these white traders. But they had no conception of how destructive the demand for the buffalo would become eventually. By 1879, the great herds of Alberta buffalo were nearly destroyed. Although no Native chief could have predicted at the time of the treaty-making how terrifying the future would be, some obviously felt that they would have to find an additional way to supply the needs of their people. Facing extremely limited alternatives, they saw the federal government's promise of provisions through suppliers like Baker & Co. as an acceptable strategy for survival on the reserves. The Natives who stayed on reserves in the Bow Valley found that the government provisions promised came to them, often through Baker & Co., on schedule and usually in sufficient quantity during the late 1870s.

Changing Natural Environment

Killing almost the last buffalo marked a major change in the Bow Valley's natural environment. Native Canadians hunting the buffalo as much for trade as for food, Baker & Co. and other commercial businesses shipping robes to robe dealers, and the demand by tanners for attractive leather meant rapid extinction for the buffalo. Some people defended profligate use of this resource, arguing that so long as these animals seemed to exist in inexhaustible numbers there need be no concern about them. But sensitive and intelligent observers lamented the indiscriminate slaughter of the buffalo in the region. Visitors to the Bow Valley in 1879 noted that the buffalo were virtually extinct.

Chapter 2: I. G. Baker & Co.

Although the buffalo became rare, game remained plentiful in the Bow Valley. Travellers found prairie chickens, partridges, rabbits, and deer in abundant quantities. Rivers and creeks yielded several varieties of fish. In winter as well as in summer, a portion of the food consumed by most Natives and some settlers came from hunting and fishing.

Prosperity in the Mid- and Late 1870s

The mid- and late 1870s were prosperous years for Baker & Co. at the Calgary store. Merchandise sales came to tens of thousands of dollars, an amount larger than that expected by I. G. Baker, especially during the depression in the middle of that decade.[40] The federal government contracts for the supply of goods required by the Natives and the Mounted Police were crucial to the firm's success. Prosperity brought staff growth to Baker & Co. By mid-1877, the firm had increased the size of its Calgary staff by hiring a new clerk, George C. King, a former Mounted Policeman who knew Calgary well through his work in the Force there.[41] Born in 1848 in Chelmsford, England, King attended Hunt's School in Springfield. Business attracted him. He first worked as a clerk in a British mercantile firm, and then in early 1874 moved to Toronto to take a job with James Lumbers, a wholesaler. Later that same year, King joined the North West Mounted Police, in which he became a member of the detachment stationed in Calgary. After leaving the Force in mid-1877, he began to work for Baker & Co. as a clerk. Under D. W. Davis's guidance, King quickly learned the general store business. The position was instrumental in King's advancement. In 1878, I. G. Baker made King manager of the Calgary store, and Davis became manager of the firm's store in Fort Macleod. At the same time, Davis succeeded Charles Conrad as head of Baker & Co.'s Canadian operations, while Charles joined his brother William in carrying out the overall administration of the firm at headquarters in Fort Benton.

I. G. Baker's knowledge of the operations of all the stores at home and abroad earned him the respect of the managers and permitted him to plan for the future. His strategy – a wide range of goods and an emphasis on quality – led to substantial profits and an expanding concern. Affable, but hard driving, he often travelled to the Fort Benton headquarters from his St. Louis office to discuss the far-flung mercantile venture with his partners. Working closely together with William and Charles Conrad, he delegated increasing responsibility for operations to them. At the same time, he allowed them to buy additional shares in the firm. By 1878, according to an R. G. Dun & Co. credit report, Charles and William's investment in the partnership had grown to $65,000, while I. G. Baker's share in it was $100,000.[42] As the firm expanded and became more complex in its activities in the United States and Canada, information flow between the managers of the individual stores and the Conrads grew in importance. To keep track of Baker & Co.'s operations, a thorough accounting system was set up.

Like the other Baker & Co. stores, the one in Calgary relied on the time-honoured double-entry bookkeeping system, using the journal to record the many daily transactions and the ledger to show monthly and annual balances.[43] Accounts of the Calgary store provided a historical record of its financial transactions, along with information necessary for the orderly conduct of business. Seeing the need for general administrative control, I. G. Baker and the Conrad brothers expected store managers to work with standardized accounting procedures in order that accurate information on costs, profits, and losses could be developed. By and large, the store in Calgary did this in a systematic and rational way. Through regular correspondence, it helped build channels of communication with head office that assured effective administration.

But Baker & Co.'s Calgary store faced problems. For instance, the hay the firm delivered to the Mounted Police in Calgary, as well as in Fort Macleod and Fort Walsh, in the fall of 1876 was of poor quality. I. G. Baker had agreed to provide "good well cured blue joint prairie hay," but Colonel Macleod complained that what the Mounted Police received was hay that "was not cut early enough and that a great part of it was cut after it had got bleached and injured by the frost." Macleod went on to say "it is an unpleasant fact that at all our posts outsiders have secured for themselves better hay than we got from you."[44]

Despite this problem, the staff at the Calgary store worked hard to ensure that it could offer high-quality products. To support its expanding operations, as William Conrad pointed out, Baker & Co. developed the land it occupied in Calgary Bottom, cultivating "portions thereof, raising crops of oats, potatoes and other vegetables thereon annually." As well, the firm "partly fenced in [the] "land, and placed a number of substantial buildings on [it].[45]

Chapter 2: I. G. Baker & Co.

I. G. Baker & Co.'s Relationship with its Main Competitor, Power & Bro.

As Baker & Co.'s operations grew in size and complexity, so did the firm's relationships with its rivals, especially its main competitor, T. C. Power & Bro. of Fort Benton. The business of delivering supplies to the Natives and the Mounted Police through Canadian government supply contracts became increasingly competitive in the late 1870s. In fact, fierce competition in securing government supply contracts would grow even more pronounced in the early and mid-1880s. During these years, the Baker & Co. partners tried to limit that competition to protect their firm's earnings. Through co-operative efforts, they sought to stop price cuts by their rivals, but they were only partially successful in this tactic. Baker & Co. and Power & Bro. shared price lists and divided markets. On one occasion in January 1881, Power & Bro. went after all the Native supply contract trade in the Montana Territory, while Baker & Co. sought the Mounted Police and Native supply contract business in the Canadian prairies.[46]

At the same time, Baker & Co. derived much of the support for securing the Native and Mounted Police supply contract trade in the Canadian prairies from personal and business connections. Personal trust was essential in capturing the government supply contract business. Through their satisfactory performance, the Baker & Co. partners won the confidence of John A. Macdonald's Conservative government. Ties to influential Mounted Policemen were also important to Baker & Co.'s success. In 1881, Charles Conrad married Alicia Stanford, whose brother James had served as a Mounted Policeman before becoming Baker & Co.'s bookkeeper at Fort Benton. Conrad reached beyond his family circle to tap additional sources of support in the Canadian prairies. The key lay in his relations with Colonel James F. Macleod, the Mounted Police officer whose life became increasingly intertwined with the development of Baker & Co. "Col. Macleod," wrote his wife Mary to Alicia Conrad, "joins me in wishing you and Mr. Conrad a long, happy life together. I know that Mr. Conrad, who is a great favourite of ours, will make the very best of husbands."[47] The gifts Charles Conrad had given the Macleods' daughter and son were gratefully recalled by Macleod in a letter to him: "Both Mrs. Macleod and I are very much obliged to you for the nice presents you sent to our girl and boy."[48]

Besides maintaining good relations with Macleod, Baker & Co. continued to co-operate with rival firms like Power & Bro. to try to end competition and price wars. In the Mounted Police and Native beef markets in the Canadian prairies, where Baker & Co. had historically been stronger, profits were reduced by almost continuous price cuts. Increasing competition hurt Baker & Co. To limit competition, Baker & Co. hammered out individual agreements with Power & Bro. In September 1881, Baker & Co. sold its store in Fort Walsh to Power & Bro. and bought Power & Bro.'s store in Fort Macleod. A little more than a year later, in February 1883, Baker & Co. promised not to reopen in Fort Walsh and Power & Bro. agreed not to open new stores in Fort Macleod and Calgary and their regions before 30 June 1884.[49] Baker & Co.'s efforts were only partially successful. The firm's share of the merchandise market in Fort Macleod rose to some extent; at the same time, its strategy of co-operation helped to protect its profits in Calgary and Fort Macleod. Even so, Baker & Co. faced growing competition from the Hudson's Bay Company in Calgary, a situation that would continue to present a challenge.

Ongoing Commitment to Banking

In their response to this problem, the Baker & Co. partners reaffirmed a theme growing out of the firm's earlier development. Behind some of their actions was an ongoing commitment to banking, and this strategy helped to protect the firm. Baker & Co. had to fund its growth internally through retained profits, but its owners sought to broaden its financial base through loans from banks. Drawing on their banking experience at Baker & Co., William Conrad and I. G. Baker played an important role in founding the First National Bank of Fort Benton in 1880. When Conrad visited St. Louis in mid-April of that year, he immediately went to Baker's office. Baker set up a meeting at which Conrad successfully presented his idea on a new bank in Fort Benton to several businessmen: Helena entrepreneurs S. T. Hauser and T. C. Power; Edgar G. Maclay, a Fort Benton merchant; and I. G. Baker's brother, George.[50] After making his presentation, Conrad called on the men at the gathering for support; they accepted his initiative. Soon thereafter, all these entrepreneurs incorporated the

First National Bank of Fort Benton under the laws of the United States.

Capitalized at $50,000 (500 shares of stock valued at $100 apiece), the bank had several original stockholders. Hauser received 240 shares. Power held 125 shares, while William Conrad received 105 shares.[51] I. G. Baker, Edgar Maclay, and George Baker held 10 shares each. Headed by William Conrad as president, the First National Bank of Fort Benton raised its authorized capitalization to $100,000 in early 1882 and brought new investors into the picture, among them Edgar Dewdney, lieutenant-governor of the Canadian Northwest Territories, who received 50 shares.

Certainly one reason for including Dewdney as a stockholder was William Conrad's desire for securing a great deal of business with the Canadian government. "I issued the fifty shares in Dewdney's name," Conrad wrote to Hauser, "hoping to get a deposit by it of $100,000 or $200,000 from the Canadian Gov't if he recommends it. I think there is but little doubt about it."[52] The First National Bank of Fort Benton became a depository for Canadian Mounted Police and Native funds. These funds served as an income earner, for the bank received a 1½ percent rate of exchange on them.[53] At its inception the First National Bank of Fort Benton resembled most new American national banks: it vied with other banks for the acquisition of deposit accounts. As deposits grew, the size of loans also expanded. The First National Bank of Fort Benton focused its attention on local borrowers and local businesses, especially enterprises such as Baker & Co. During the 1880s, it supported this firm, extending loans to it and thus helping it to develop its business in Montana as well as in the Canadian prairies, particularly in Fort Macleod and Calgary.[54]

Expanding Merchandise Sales

Baker & Co.'s branch stores in Calgary and Fort Macleod accounted for a substantial part of the total value of the firm's expanding merchandise sales in the early 1880s. As was the case with many late-nineteenth-century Montana mercantile houses, Baker & Co. continued to achieve growth by developing its branch stores. The firm's partners, recognizing the importance of a large and diverse stock of goods to successful merchandise operations, continued to rely mostly on their own transportation system to keep the shelves and barrels in their stores filled.

In early November 1879, Baker & Co.'s steamer *Colonel Macleod* arrived in Fort Benton with seventy tons of freight, some of which was then hauled by the firm's wagon trains to its stores in Fort Macleod and Calgary.[55] Landing at Fort Benton in July 1880, the firm's steamer *Red Cloud* carried 149 packages destined for its Calgary and Fort Macleod stores.[56] Sometimes, however, Baker & Co. depended on other steamboat lines to deliver its goods to Fort Benton. For example, in May of that year the *Far West* of the Yankton-based Coulson Line brought in 1,852 packages for Baker & Co., including 180 sacks of potatoes.[57] In an effort to control overland transportation costs, Baker & Co. usually shipped its goods to southern Alberta by its own wagon trains. The Native reserves in the Fort Macleod and Calgary areas relied on Baker & Co.'s wagon trains to carry up six thousand sacks of flour for them in 1880, as required by the firm's contract with the Canadian government.[58] Hired wagon masters served the firm well. For instance, at the height of the summer freighting season in mid-July 1882, wagon master W. H. Patrick carefully loaded Baker & Co.'s wagon train with merchandise in Fort Benton to meet the demands of the market in southern Alberta.[59] With the arrival of the merchandise at the firm's Fort Macleod and Calgary stores several weeks later, they were once more in a position to satisfy the needs of consumers and grow. By the end 1882, Baker & Co.'s Calgary store had earned profits of $20,317 and its Fort Macleod store, $41,613.[60]

New Management at the Calgary Store

The expansion of Baker & Co.'s operations and new commercial opportunities brought new management to the Calgary store. When George C. King resigned as manager of the store in early September 1882 to start his own general store business in Calgary, he was replaced by John Lee Bowen.[61] Born in Virginia in 1859 and a brother-in-law of William Conrad, Bowen began in Baker & Co.'s store in Fort Benton around 1879, where he served as a clerk for three years. He joined the firm's store in Fort Macleod as a clerk in June 1882, a position he held until his appointment as manager of its Calgary store three months later.[62]

Chapter 2: I. G. Baker & Co.

In mid-September 1882, the *Macleod Gazette* noted that George C. King, the previous manager, could justifiably be proud of his accomplishments in the Calgary store:

> I. G. Baker & Co. have a splendid appearing store. Everything is arranged in most excellent taste and looks ship-shape and business-like. The office is roomy and nicely fitted up. Mr. King deserves much credit for the way in which this store has been kept.[63]

John Bowen, the new manager, continued the improvements made by King. Assisted by a new clerk, Ontario-born Norman T. Macleod, a nephew of Colonel James F. Macleod, Bowen moved quickly to further increase the attractiveness of the display of the store's goods.[64] Toward the end of September, a new bookkeeper, Frank Crosby, who came from Boston, began working at the store.[65]

At the heart of Baker & Co.'s Calgary business lay personal trust. In running the firm's store, Bowen often had to rely on friends and relatives. He conducted the business with the aid of Frank Crosby and Norman Macleod, both of whom he found trustworthy and competent. By writing letters, Bowen stayed in close contact with D. W. Davis, the Fort Macleod store's manager, who also continued to oversee Baker & Co.'s entire Canadian business, including its Calgary store, as well as with William and Charles Conrad in the firm's Fort Benton head office. Traditional business methods remained in vogue at the store in Calgary: the use of double-entry bookkeeping and promissory notes.[66]

At Baker & Co.'s Calgary store, Bowen engaged in several types of trade, importing merchandise from the United States and, more importantly, bringing in Canadian bonded goods such as groceries from the Montreal firm of Tees, Costigan & Wilson through the United States.[67] He also shipped furs and wolf skins in bond through the United States to Montreal, besides exporting some of these items to New York City. In addition, Bowen sold merchandise at retail to local farmers, ranchers, and Natives and at wholesale to local and regional traders. The Calgary store carried a broad assortment of goods, everything from groceries, boots and shoes, and hardware to agricultural implements, harnesses and saddles, wagons, and barbed wire.[68]

The mark-up on goods arriving at the Calgary store from places such as Montreal and New York City was high, but Baker & Co. incurred high transportation and storage costs and faced fluctuating markets, causing the firm to sputter at times. Even so, Baker & Co.'s capital and organizing skills put goods onto the store's shelves.

With cash in short supply in Calgary and its region, Bowen often found himself extending credit to his customers. Baker & Co. allowed him to offer liberal credit terms to customers, usually as long as three months.[69] Sometimes he sold merchandise on a barter basis, accepting furs from Natives and cattle from ranchers and farmers in payment. The furs were sent east to pay off debts to suppliers, while the cattle were fattened in Baker & Co.'s pastures in Calgary Bottom and used to provide beef for the firm's Native and Mounted Police supply contracts with the Canadian government.

Sources of Beef

Montana, however, continued to be the main source of beef for Baker & Co.'s Mounted Police and Native supply contracts in the Canadian prairies. Between 1881 and 1883, the Baker & Co. partners imported 6,195 head of cattle into Alberta from Montana.[70] In early 1882, Charles and William Conrad and I. G. Baker thought that the time had arrived to set up a new company devoted to cattle raising and, on 25 May, they formed a Montana-chartered corporation, the Benton & St. Louis Cattle Co.[71] Capitalized at $500,000, the company had a number of stockholders, with the Conrad brothers and Baker owning the majority of the shares. Charles Conrad was the company's president, Baker served as its vice-president, and William Conrad became its treasurer.

The Conrad brothers and Baker led the Benton & St. Louis Cattle Co. into a period of significant growth and prosperity. Between 1882 and 1893, the company's herd grew from 1,600 to 22,500 head of cattle, with 15,000 grazing in Montana and 7,500 in Alberta.[72] The company operated on large tracts of rangeland, raising its Alberta herd on the rich grasses between the Belly and the Bow rivers and its Montana herd on the pastures along the Marias River and in the Sweet Grass Hills. From its earliest days, the Benton & St. Louis Cattle Co. played an important role in

Baker & Co.'s evolution. Each year it produced hundreds of cattle in Montana and Alberta to provide beef for Baker & Co.'s Native and Mounted Police supply contract markets in the Canadian prairies, including those at Calgary.

In 1882, for example, Baker & Co. needed this beef to help complete its $450,000 contract with the Canadian government to provide supplies to the Natives and Mounted Police at Calgary, Fort Macleod, Fort Walsh, Battleford, Prince Albert, Qu'Appelle, and Wood Mountain.[73] At the same time, Baker & Co. proved useful in other matters, especially in delivering the Mounted Police payroll and the Native treaty money. In Calgary, as in the other centres, the Mounted Police and the Natives spent their money freely at the local stores. The Baker & Co. and Hudson's Bay Company stores in Calgary – the only two outlets in the place – shared this business, but the largest portion of it went to the Baker & Co. store.

A growing number of the Baker & Co. store's merchandise sales occurred through word-of-mouth to potential customers in the Calgary area, including ranchers and farmers. One of these customers was the Cochrane Ranche on the Bow River west of Calgary. In September 1882, the store was also instrumental in selling 550 steers to the Cochrane Ranche. Driving the steers up to the ranch from Fort Benton, Baker & Co. received $40 per head for them.[74] In addition, the ranch paid the firm $2,000 to cover all expenses of driving the steers to their destination.

I. G. Baker & Co. and Capitalism

In the last half of the 1870s and early 1880s, I. G. Baker and his partners, Charles and William Conrad, were the pre-eminent entrepreneurs in Calgary and the Bow Valley. With an orientation toward the future, they were market leaders in Fort Benton and major players in merchandising and ranching in Alberta. Their mounting commercial and agricultural success reinforced their belief in the logic of entrepreneurial capitalism. At Baker & Co.'s Calgary store, its average yearly sales from 1875 to the end of 1882 came to over $100,000, a respectable sum.[75] Table 4 shows that while the store's net profits fluctuated during the early 1880s, they increased considerably in this period. As the spring trading season approached in February 1883, I. G. Baker took the occasion to write a letter to

Table 5. Profits at I. G. Baker & Co.'s Calgary Store, 1880-1882

Year	Profits
1880	$ 2,143
1881	1,516
1882	20,317

Source: Hudson's Bay Company Archives, D20/63, f. 222, Winnipeg, 3 October 1890, W.H. Adams and E.K. Beeston to J. Wrigley.

his partners William and Charles Conrad that summarized the firm's accomplishments. Referring to the firm's profits on its operations in Montana and the Canadian prairies for 1882, Baker observed:

> If it was a showing of $40,000 or $50,000 of profit, I would say it was a splendid showing. So now when it is a quarter of a million, I don't know what to say. Such results must produce a very enjoyable feeling.... With such a start at your ages your possibilities are very great to rank high as capitalists.[76]

While Baker & Co.'s business in Calgary was progressing by leaps and bounds, the Hudson's Bay Company presented an increasing challenge by the spring of 1883. The British-owned Hudson's Bay Company persisted as an important part of Calgary's business system and proved capable of co-existing with Baker & Co.

3
Hudson's Bay Company
British Enterprise in the Wagon-Road Era

Southwestern Alberta – particularly Calgary – was an unlikely place for the British-owned Hudson's Bay Company, a pioneer of entrepreneurial capitalism, to set up a store. In fact, however, a store was established at Calgary in 1875 and continues in operation today. It was the only permanent Hudson's Bay Company store in southwestern Alberta until World War II, and has remained a major retail outlet for a regional market that encompasses the Bow Valley.

The early promoters of Calgary's Hudson's Bay Company store assumed that there was little opportunity for their enterprise to satisfy the needs of southwestern Alberta. Instead, they felt that geography granted to Fort Benton firms such as I. G. Baker & Co. a virtual monopoly in supplying the needs of the region. They saw a protected market for the products of Fort Benton businesses, because of the great distance that separated the region from the Hudson's Bay Company's prairie headquarters in Winnipeg. When compared to the 300-mile Fort Benton-Calgary route, the distance from Calgary to Winnipeg was truly long. The 830 miles of prairie between Winnipeg and Calgary did permit land communication, but ox-drawn carts or wagons seldom used this very long route. The 200-mile Calgary-Edmonton route and the North Saskatchewan River-Lake Winnipeg-Red River system became the main channel of trade for the Hudson's Bay Company, but did little to bring Winnipeg into a closer relationship with Calgary. While the Fort Benton-Calgary route invigorated Fort Benton's trade with Calgary, the high cost of transportation in the Canadian prairies placed severe restrictions on the trade between Calgary and Winnipeg.

The Hudson's Bay Company, nevertheless, built a store in Calgary in part as a defensive response to the need to protect its traditional opportunities for trade in central and northern Alberta's rich fur regions, notably the Edmonton and Lac La Biche areas. Through the Calgary store, the company sought to establish a presence in southern Alberta and thus create a barrier to competition from Fort Benton firms in the central and northern districts. The company's efforts were only partially successful.

Network of Trading Posts and Stores in Alberta

With the establishment of the store in Calgary, the Hudson's Bay Company did, however, enlarge its network of trading posts and stores in Alberta, of which the store in Edmonton on the North Saskatchewan River was the most important. The British contribution to all of this was vital. British investors, especially those in London, were captivated by the dream of riches which overseas trade generated in the late seventeenth century. In 1670, the British Crown granted exclusive trading rights in a vast tract of land between Hudson Bay and the Rocky Mountains – the drainage basin of Hudson Bay – to the Hudson's Bay Company, a joint-stock company incorporated that year in London by a royal charter, as a means of augmenting England's power overseas. It came to be known as Rupert's Land, for one of the principal investors in the company was Charles II's cousin, Prince Rupert. Englishmen wanted furs, and Rupert's Land had a great deal of value to offer to them. Before long, the Hudson's Bay Company became the entrenched British monopoly in Rupert's Land, maintaining trade in furs with the Natives at posts on the shores of Hudson Bay.

The key to the Hudson's Bay Company's success was London and its region. London hatter/felters and furriers purchased most of the furs from the beginning. Of all the furs the company sold, beaver was the most significant: top-quality wool felt hats were made from beaver pelts in response to the demand of high fashion. The fine garment trade provided a market for other furs such as marten, otter, wolf, and fox. London's region could supply the various commodities such as blankets, hardware, guns, and ammunition that the company needed to sell in Rupert's Land in order to buy furs. Trading and shipping were combined functions;

Chapter 3: Hudson's Bay Company

the company owned its own fleet of sailing ships to use in the trade. By 1718, it was posting profits and paying dividends. Initially incorporated for only £10,500, the company had its authorized capitalization raised to £103,950 in 1720.[1]

From a business viewpoint, the choice of that year to increase the capital seems unfortunate. But the Hudson's Bay Company, although hurt by the downturn in the market associated with the collapse of the South Sea Bubble in 1720, gradually recovered from the blow, remained profitable, and continued to pay dividends through the rest of that decade and beyond.

British capitalists thought that national prosperity depended in part upon the zeal of individual entrepreneurs, such as those who invested in the Hudson's Bay Company. In the history of capitalism, the British business experience is particularly important. Britain's reliance on individual entrepreneurship, its development of a business system that was clearly international in its orientation, its great emphasis on the rule of law and property rights, and its tendency to give monopoly rights to trading companies to sustain the British Empire were traditions that reappeared in Rupert's Land.

Despite the appearance of British patterns of doing business in Rupert's Land, Canadian traders from Montreal gradually undermined the Hudson's Bay Company's charter monopoly. To lessen competition from the Canadians, the company decided to adopt a new approach: starting in 1774, it set up a growing network of trading posts in the interior of Rupert's Land, including one at Edmonton in 1795, to collect furs from the Natives. The men the company sent to Edmonton and the other trading posts were expected not to reap much in the way of individual rewards but, rather, to work for the company and for the British Crown. Hudson's Bay Company executives in London came increasingly to believe that the possession of fur trading posts in the western portion of Rupert's Land would not only strengthen the company but also enhance the nation's wealth and security. The furs sent from Edmonton to England were valuable and helped the company to grow. From the 1790s onward, the company faced intense competition in Alberta from the Montreal-based Northwest Company, but this came to an end in 1821 when the two enterprises united to become a more powerful Hudson's Bay Company

However, when the Hudson's Bay Company sought new trading opportunities by opening the Peigan post in 1832 on the upper Bow

Chapter 3: Hudson's Bay Company

Hudson's Bay Company store in Calgary before 1884, located on the east side of the Elbow River. (Courtesy of Glenbow Archives, NA-2074-2).

River, thirty-five miles above future Calgary, it faced problems. The company expected the postmaster, John Edward Harriott, to collect many furs especially from the Peigans, but the history of the post was extremely short. Offering guns, ammunition, blankets, and a large volume of rum, Harriott obtained only a few furs from the Peigans for sale in England.[2] They did not become regular customers. The main difficulty was that they preferred to take their furs to American traders on the Missouri River, where they could obtain supplies at lower prices. Consequently, Harriott abandoned the Peigan post in 1834.

Within Rupert's Land, free traders began to compete openly with the Hudson's Bay Company for control of the fur trade in the mid-nineteenth century. The company's trade monopoly became an important grievance among the free traders. All indications were that the enterprise could no longer exercise the governmental functions once fulfilled by this great chartered concern. Britain still considered trade in Rupert's Land to be a national asset but was unwilling to defend it by military force in a sustained way. The brief British military effort to keep up the empire in Rupert's Land took a relatively small sum of money. Back home, however, many Britons felt that even this money could have been put to better use elsewhere. What had begun as a commercial venture in 1670 sponsored by British capitalists and protected by the imperial government became a state responsibility the nation could not afford as the costs of empire rose in other parts of the globe. Officially, the Hudson's Bay Company retained its exclusive trading rights in Rupert's Land until 1859, but the company actually lost its trade monopoly a decade before. The job of safeguarding Rupert's Land for British trade and for Canada within the British Empire was eventually taken over by the new Canadian nation.

The creation of the Dominion of Canada in 1867 greatly affected business opportunities for the Hudson's Bay Company and, with the transfer of Rupert's Land to Canada in 1870 and the coming of the Mounted Police to Alberta four years later, a new business system emerged. The arrival of the Mounted Police, besides making property rights secure and encouraging settlement, increased the demand for goods and allowed the company to develop new business activities, some of which proved to be very profitable. For instance, with the passage of time, the company built a network of general stores in southwestern Alberta as settlement spread across the region. Leading individuals in the company also established close ties with a number of emerging Canadian government institutions. These included the Mounted Police, the department of Indian affairs, and the department of the interior, all of which generated new opportunities for business enterprises.

John Bunn and the Establishment of a Store in Calgary

A dramatic new opportunity was the Calgary trade. In September 1875, after having collected buffalo robes for the Hudson's Bay Company from Natives for about a year at the confluence of the Bow and Ghost rivers in the rolling foothills of the Rockies, John Bunn moved downstream to establish a store for the company in Calgary, at the junction of the Bow and Elbow rivers on the east side of the Elbow. Besides building a store, or trading post as it was sometimes called, Bunn erected a dwelling house where he lived with his wife and daughter. A competent storekeeper who had served effectively as a clerk for the company on the North Saskatchewan River several years before, by mid-December Bunn had supplied the Blackfoot customers at the Calgary store with a variety of goods in exchange for five hundred buffalo robes. This was "something more than I had at the same date last winter," he reported.[3] Bunn sent the robes via Edmonton and the North Saskatchewan to Winnipeg for sale in the

Chapter 3: Hudson's Bay Company

Richard Hardisty, Hudson's Bay Company's chief factor in Edmonton and general manager of its Calgary store, in the 1880s. (Courtesy of Glenbow Archives, NA-1030-16).

London and Montreal markets. Company-owned ships crossing the Atlantic linked Hudson Bay and London. In Winnipeg, the company organized packs of robes, shipping some by York boats across Lake Winnipeg and down the Hayes River to York Factory on Hudson Bay for export to London and others in bond through the United States to Montreal.[4]

The opening of the Calgary trade was one of the most spectacular examples of new opportunities. But for John Bunn the road to further success was tortuous, and he did not tread it easily. The shortage of supplies presented a basic business problem. A great deal of the food needed in Calgary and the Bow Valley had to be brought in from elsewhere. Bunn could not keep up with I. G. Baker & Co. and the other Fort Benton traders in the Calgary area such as A. P. Samples, who was connected with T. C. Power & Bro., in supplying the Blackfoot with staples like flour and molasses. Nor could Bunn keep pace in supplying the Natives with horses and repeating rifles. By contrast, Fort Benton firms moved quickly to satisfy the Native demand for rifles and horses, exchanging them for buffalo robes and furs. "Our greatest drawback in trade," Bunn complained to Richard Hardisty, the Hudson's Bay Company's chief factor in Edmonton, "is the want of horses."[5]

Richard Hardisty had been assigned the general supervision of the Calgary store's operations; in the company's chain of command, he was accountable to its chief commissioner, James A. Grahame, in its prairie head office in Winnipeg. Born in Baie-du-Poste, Quebec, around 1832, Hardisty was educated at the Red River Academy in the Red River Settlement, Manitoba.[6] He joined the Hudson's Bay Company in Red River in 1849 as an apprentice trading postmaster. In 1872, after clerking for the company at Cumberland House,

Carlton House, and Rocky Mountain House, he became chief factor in Edmonton. A diligent and able man, Hardisty got along well with John Bunn. Given a fairly free hand by Hardisty, Bunn worked hard to develop the Calgary store's business. To lessen competition and exercise greater control over his trade with the Blackfoot, he requested more supplies from Winnipeg in his letters to Hardisty. Deploring the lack of sufficient goods for trading at the Calgary store, Hardisty wrote to James A. Grahame in Winnipeg supporting Bunn's request,[7] but Grahame was unwilling to invest more of the company's earnings in keeping the Calgary store supplied with the items the Blackfoot desired.

The problems of poor transportation facilities and long distances also hindered John Bunn's trade at the Calgary store. Hudson's Bay Company ox-drawn carts, as well as independent freighters' wagons pulled by oxen, linked Calgary to Edmonton; the company's steamboats on the North Saskatchewan River-Lake Winnipeg-Red River route provided a connection between Edmonton and Winnipeg.[8] The company successfully capitalized on the Edmonton Trail during the wagon-road era, even though rivers such as the Red Deer were anything but an easy crossing. But navigation on the North Saskatchewan, with its low waters and many rapids, was a particularly troublesome matter. The hazards on the North Saskatchewan meant that supplies moving from Winnipeg to Calgary were frequently delayed, and this made business transactions difficult. Given these circumstances, the company's effort to provide its Calgary store with supplies remained a monumental and very expensive undertaking. In 1876, in an attempt to overcome the transportation and supply problems and attract buffalo robes and furs such as beaver, wolf, and lynx from the Blackfoot, Stoneys, and Sarcees, Bunn purchased fifty sacks of flour from his main competitor, Baker & Co., for the trade, but he did not have enough cash to pay for flour.[9]

Hungry for success, Bunn wanted the Calgary store to become an enterprise of the first rank, but the shortage of supplies such as flour outraged him. What little flour arrived from the Hudson's Bay Company's Fort Garry warehouse in Winnipeg was extremely inferior. Robert Hamilton, the company's inspecting chief factor, sent James A. Grahame an assessment of the situation at the Calgary store:

> I would remark that the flour received from Fort Garry is of a very inferior quality and compares most unfavourably with that which is imported by many of our opponents. I am told that the Blackfeet on the Plains at once notice the difference, and will not take our flour when they can procure that brought from Benton.[10]

However, little was done to improve the quality of the flour that the Calgary store obtained from the company's Fort Garry warehouse.

John Bunn now also paid attention to the need for developing a new transportation route. He did not want to continue using the difficult North Saskatchewan to bring in supplies, because the high cost for delivery was causing losses at the Calgary store. Instead, he tried to persuade his superiors in the Hudson's Bay Company that small steamboats ascending the South Saskatchewan and Bow rivers were the best hope for improving the transportation of supplies to Calgary. Bunn told Hardisty,

> I can't help expressing my strong conviction ... that steamboat [transportation] on the South branch is the true inlet to this part of the country.... I am very sure that such a move & only such would turn the tide of trade from Benton to this way. The field is open. It remains to be seen whether the Co. will take it or leave it to others to take the lead. From all I can learn from Indians & others there does not seem to be any difficulty in the way of small steamers running up even to the Elbow during the summer months.[11]

Bunn attracted the support of Robert Hamilton. As a senior Hudson's Bay Company officer, Hamilton always sought to lower transportation costs and to make the Calgary store profitable. Since he was unable "to procure any reliable information as to the Bow River being navigable or not," he took the initiative in trying to make a careful investigation. "I authorised Mr. Hardisty," Hamilton reported to James A. Grahame,

> ... to instruct Mr. John Bunn to proceed next spring, after the close of his trade, with a skiff and a couple of men, and thoroughly examine the whole route as far as the junction of the North and South Saskatchewan. Should the route

Chapter 3: Hudson's Bay Company

be found practicable, it will be an easy matter to construct a few strong bateaux and float the returns down as far as the Forks, or LaCorne, where they could be stored till the steamer passed."[12]

Hardisty immediately got in touch with Bunn, instructing him "to go down the Bow River in spring ... to see if the river is navigable."[13] Apparently Bunn followed these instructions. The situation is by no means clear; it appears that Bunn's findings were discouraging. At any rate, the shallow Bow River was unusable for navigation and Hudson's Bay Company steamboats were not introduced on it. The North Saskatchewan, with its numerous rapids and low waters, remained the company's route to Calgary; its freight and supplies from Winnipeg continued to move along this river with uncertainty. Lack of adequate financial resources available to Bunn meant that in real terms he was even more isolated than the great distance from Winnipeg might suggest.

Despite the transportation problem, Bunn's unremitting attention to collecting buffalo robes and furs at the Calgary store yielded some results. But he shared Hardisty's view that the store should find ways to make more progress. Hardisty came to see the desirability, even the imperative, of setting up small, temporary Hudson's Bay Company outposts in the surrounding area during the winter to limit the competition from the American traders. Even before the opening of the store in Calgary, Hardisty wrote to Grahame: "As the country is much overrun with these traders, I can see no other way of getting our share of the plains trade than to have little outposts for the winter, where it would be convenient to haul in returns early in spring."[14] Grahame agreed and, at the start of 1875, threw his support behind this strategy. But differences of judgment regarding the idea of small, temporary outposts – differences rooted in conflicting economic theories – soon appeared.

Conflict between Richard Hardisty and Robert Hamilton

By the end of 1875, those differences centred on the personalities of Richard Hardisty and Robert Hamilton. In part, they involved a dispute over how the Hudson's Bay Company should best use its resources for the expansion of its business. "I still hold," Hamilton wrote Grahame,

> ... that the plan of establishing outposts at different points on the plains is an expensive way of conducting our business, both on account of the migratory habits of the buffalo, and also owing to the very great opposition with which we have to contend, for the whole country is now covered with petty traders.

These traders came not only from Montana but also from Manitoba. Hamilton believed that those from Manitoba, who were still called free traders by the Hudson's Bay Company as they had been before 1870, could be used as middlemen by the company. "I certainly do think," he added,

> ... that by judiciously availing ourselves of the services of many of the Free Traders, and employing them as our Middle Men instead of having them for opponents (and in consequence, see the bulk of the trade, as is now the case, pass into other hands) we might build up a large and profitable business."[15]

In the end, however, neither Hamilton's dream of middlemen nor Hardisty's vision of small, temporary outposts in the Calgary area was realized, because the Hudson's Bay Company's London and Winnipeg officers decided not to spend money on implementing either one of these proposals.

By this time, Hamilton thought that the success, even the very survival, of the Hudson's Bay Company's Calgary store depended on the company's willingness to act not only as a fur trader but also as a merchant committed to serving the needs of Mounted Policemen, ranchers, and farmers. He called for a vigorous mercantile program to enlarge business opportunities for the company.[16] Being a more cautious man than Hamilton, Hardisty at this time offered no program to help the company's store in Calgary reach out beyond the Native trade to other customers in the Calgary region.

John Bunn and the Continuing Quest for Business

Originally, John Bunn felt optimistic that the establishment of a Hudson's Bay Company store at Calgary would mean ample opportunities for the development of business with the Mounted Police.[17] But the assortment of goods he received from the company's Fort Garry warehouse was so limited that he could do little to serve the Mounted Policemen's needs. Bunn was seeking equilibrium among the Native, Mounted Police, and agricultural markets so that his store could grow. To him, it seemed that the senior Hudson's Bay Company officers in Winnipeg were terribly slow in reaching for business beyond the Native trade. Like others who knew Grahame, Bunn was aware that his boss in Winnipeg wanted him to devote most of his energies to collecting buffalo robes and furs from the Native people in the Calgary area.

Bunn responded by continuing to seek trade with the Natives, especially the Blackfoot, in 1876. But as a man who was willing to change with the times, he also broadened his contacts; as a result, he sold goods to others in Calgary and the surrounding region, including prominent farmer John Glenn and Mounted Policeman George C. King, as well as the Reverend John McDougall at Morley.[18] Sam Livingston, another important farmer in the Calgary area, often purchased goods at Bunn's trading post.[19] For Bunn, whose career until now had been shaped almost entirely by the buffalo robe and fur trade, this business represented a new level of activity. It was a new challenge: in selling goods to white customers, he was doing things he had never done before. But he was confident that he could meet this new challenge.

John Bunn obtained the services of independent freighters like George Washington Emerson, Louis Roselle, and Willie Whitford to haul merchandise, buffalo robes, and mail on their wagons between Calgary and Edmonton. As a freighting road, in spite of its difficult river crossings, the Edmonton Trail served the company well. Bunn appreciated the mail service, but he quickly discovered that the trips of the freighters were not frequent enough to get all his letters out soon after he wrote them. From time to time, he therefore asked individuals such as John McDougall, Joe Mallette, and Colonel James F. Macleod, all of whom occasionally had to travel to Edmonton, to take his letters with them. Most of Bunn's letters

Chapter 3: Hudson's Bay Company

were written to Richard Hardisty in Edmonton, although some of them were communications to senior Hudson's Bay Company officers and had to be forwarded to Winnipeg or Montreal.

Hardisty continued to support Bunn's efforts at the Calgary store to trade for buffalo robes. But in the winter of 1876-1877, Bunn's share of the Calgary robe market shrank drastically, as Baker & Co. collected nearly all the robes from the Blackfoot. "Up to now," Bunn wrote Hardisty in February 1877, "there has not been any robe trade at all." Baker & Co.'s broad assortment of goods and lower prices than those offered by Bunn also allowed the firm to dominate the cash sale of merchandise to the Mounted Police and farmers in Calgary. The Hudson's Bay Company had failed to prepare its Calgary store for much business with these people. "None of our goods seem to meet the requirements of those who want to buy for cash," complained Bunn to Hardisty.[20]

Even Bunn's trade with the Natives was a very demanding business and rife with uncertainties. In June 1877, on the eve of the Treaty 7 negotiations at Blackfoot Crossing, the key problem for Bunn was that he had very few supplies for the Natives. "I expect that at the treaties," he told Hardisty, "flour & provisions generally will be the great demand, in which case I don't see that we have much chance of doing much against the Yankees.... However, I suppose we ought to try our best."[21] As Bunn reminded Hardisty in July, "I. G. Baker & Co. are the only people who have" flour "here."[22] Working hard to protect the Hudson's Bay Company's interest, Bunn managed to obtain some new supplies from Edmonton in August. But at the treaty negotiations in September, Bunn had little success in his attempt to sell merchandise to the Blackfoot, for they generally preferred to buy Baker & Co.'s goods, which were better in quality and cheaper.[23] Because he was permitted to pay only $2 for a first-class buffalo robe while Baker & Co. offered as high as $4 for one, Bunn also fared badly in his efforts to attract buffalo robes from the Blackfoot.[24]

Difficulties with the Hudson's Bay Company's high-priced goods for white customers in Calgary also continued, and as a result Bunn was doubtful about the prospects of securing their business. "I must confess," he told Richard Hardisty in July 1877,

> ... that I am somewhat staggered about getting fancy goods, i.e. white man's goods, for to tell you the plain fact I. G. Baker

& Co. have got a stock of goods here & sell at such prices that put us completely to the block – tweed suits from $15 to $20; boots of all descriptions from $2 to $4.50. In fact they appear to have brought down their prices to the lowest possible figure. As they get all their goods bonded through from Canada, they have no duties to pay. Really, you would be surprised to see their store here.

For an expansion-minded merchant like Bunn a broader assortment of goods was undeniably essential. "If you have an ample supply," Bunn wrote Hardisty, "then I should say send us a small quantity but as great variety as you can so that we will have a better chance of selling."[25]

In his quest for a wider assortment of goods, Bunn hoped to make the Hudson's Bay Company's Calgary store more appealing especially to the Mounted Police. As always, they received pay for their work every month, and this meant that they had cash to spend. In June 1877, Bunn pressed Hardisty to ship attractive goods down to Calgary: "I hope you will send me as nice saleable articles as you can. When the troops get filled up again, then there will be lots of money floating round & some will come to our store if we only have the stuff."[26] Hardisty did what he could, but top Hudson's Bay Company officers in Winnipeg and in London, England were not prepared to significantly broaden the Calgary store's range of offerings. Becoming increasingly comfortable on good salaries, these officers failed to perceive the changes occurring beyond the company's traditional operations. They missed a golden opportunity to sell goods to white people in Calgary, the most rapidly expanding segment of the market in the late 1870s and early 1880s.

James A. Grahame and Calgary Business

In particular, James A. Grahame, the company's chief commissioner in Winnipeg, became too complacent, too content with the status quo. His willingness to keep the Calgary store open served the company well, but his unwillingness to invest as heavily in a broader range of goods as Baker & Co. hurt the Hudson's Bay Company. Born in 1825, Grahame had begun as an apprentice clerk in the Hudson's Bay Company in 1843. He became a chief factor in 1861, and the chief commissioner of the company in 1874, a position he held until his retirement in 1884. By the mid- and late 1870s, Grahame, while admirable in his loyalty to the company, lacked the vision needed to change with the times. For instance, in terms of customers he remained committed to the Natives, but he was reluctant to meet the challenge of supplying the Mounted Police with goods and services. In November 1876, the Canadian government wanted the Hudson's Bay Company to start handling the payroll for the Mounted Police throughout the Northwest Territories, including Calgary. But Grahame was not interested in venturing into this new field. "I confess," he wrote to the company's London head office, "I do not see how we can undertake this business. We have no safes at our stations.... Our clerks in the interior are not accustomed to the bank business."[27]

Grahame reacted in a similar way to the opportunity to compete for the Mounted Police supply contracts to meet the needs of the men in Calgary and elsewhere in the Northwest Territories. In the spring of 1877, the Canadian government approached the Hudson's Bay Company, hoping that it would be interested in the Mounted Police supply contract business. But Grahame did not like the idea of taking the risk to compete with Baker & Co. for supply contracts. Far from showing enthusiasm for the chance to provide the Mounted Police with supplies, Grahame's correspondence with the London head office reflected his reluctance to expand his operations:

> The amount of supplies necessary for furnishing the frontier Mounted Police stations would represent a considerable sum, and the pay of the Troops would tend to swell it.... We cannot possibly organize arrangements to compete with the parties importing by the Missouri River unless we import by the same route, and I am unable to find an officer qualified to superintend such an important enterprise....To enable us to compete with any hope of success for any of the government contracts which are annually issued ... we must be prepared to incur a heavy outlay of money to provide the necessary supplies.[28]

Obviously, high transportation costs in the prairie West continued to pose a particular challenge to the Hudson's Bay Company, but its London executives and Grahame did not respond by making substantial investments in arrangements for the use of steamboats on the Missouri and in Mounted Police supply contracts. While willing to invest modest sums in supplying the Mounted Police with some goods in Calgary, company officers lagged far behind Baker & Co. in investing in the Mounted Police business, a market that represented a significant change in the business environment. Content with current profits, Grahame and the London executives failed to prepare their company for the future as well as they might have.

Grahame's conservative, stand-pat outlook contributed to the decline of the Hudson's Bay Company Calgary store relative to the much more energetic competitor, Baker & Co. His failure to take advantage of the growing importance of the Mounted Police market made it impossible for John Bunn to seize a great opportunity in a new field.

Bunn's efforts to secure buffalo robes from the Blackfoot in 1876 and 1877 also bore poor results, in part because of Grahame's unwillingness to reinvest the Hudson's Bay Company's profits in new horses and repeating rifles for its Calgary trade. While many considerations lured the Blackfoot with their best robes to Baker & Co.'s store in Calgary, the most important was that they could exchange them for rifles and horses. Baker & Co.'s store was well known for its ample supply of horses and rifles, and the perception that they would be available there influenced the Blackfoot. Competition from Baker & Co. proved too powerful for John Bunn's Calgary store. After doing most of their business with Baker & Co.'s store, the Blackfoot offered what was left of their robes, usually the poorest ones, to John Bunn. Consequently, in Montreal, Hudson's Bay Company officer James Bissett, who had joined the company as a clerk in 1853 and who now played a major role in selling its robes in the city, complained about the poor quality of the robes he had received from Calgary. Not surprisingly, in his letter to Richard Hardisty in November 1877, Bunn recalled what he had said two years before:

> You will remember that ... I stated that unless we were supplied with certain items in our Outfit, a list of which I enclosed & the chief of which were horses & repeating carbines, we would not be prepared to meet the strong opposition that would surely be in the country another winter. We were *not* supplied with these items & the consequence was just what Mr. Bissett complains of.

Bunn emphasized that

> ... the largest & best robes went to the American traders for their horses & guns & we had to take the refuse or go without altogether. If we would have been supplied with those things as well as they, the result would have been very different.[29]

Angus Fraser

New Manager

By mid-1878, John Bunn had left the Hudson's Bay Company, and shortly thereafter Angus Fraser was placed in charge of the company's Calgary store. Fraser, an astute businessman who believed in himself and wanted to expand the store's operations, served as manager until he stepped down in 1885. Born in 1835 in Inverness, Scotland, Fraser worked as a railway conductor in his homeland.[30] In 1861 he came to Rocky Mountain House to take a job with the Hudson's Bay Company. He served as Bunn's assistant for about two years before assuming the duties of postmaster at the company's store in Calgary. Like Bunn, Fraser got along well with Richard Hardisty. Hardisty found Fraser to be "a trusty, reliable man."[31]

By this time, the collection of provisions, especially pemmican, from the Blackfoot in exchange for trade goods had become important in the development of the Hudson's Bay Company's Calgary store. Like John Bunn before him, Angus Fraser continued to try to obtain not only buffalo robes but also pemmican from the Blackfoot, an item that the company needed to ensure an adequate supply of food for its employees in Edmonton and the other northern posts.

For awhile, Fraser and Richard Hardisty followed a strategy of developing the provision trade as the most effective way to help offset the Hudson's Bay Company's Calgary store's failure to compete with Baker & Co. in attracting white customers. Baker & Co. continued to enjoy a unique combination of circumstances that sustained its substantial operations in Calgary. The firm's transportation system and communications were advanced, a necessity in the large, spread-out region in which it operated. A

Chapter 3: Hudson's Bay Company

crucial factor was that capital was available to Baker & Co. Large amounts of capital could be mobilised for the firm's promising investments in Montana and the Canadian prairies. The Hudson's Bay Company thus continued to face stiff competition from Baker & Co. in Calgary. As Richard Hardisty observed in June 1878:

> Baker and Company from Benton are gradually making inroads on us, and draw away a good deal of the custom of those around by underselling us in most of the essentials required by white settlers in a new country. This American firm having the contract from the Canadian Government to furnish all the supplies required by the Mounted Police, and a good part of the Indian Department, gives them a very strong hold in the country. It is under this disadvantage that our Post out on the Bow River labours, for Baker can throw in supplies, most part of the year, by Benton and undersell us. This Post would scarcely be worth keeping up if we did not have to depend on it in case of a failure [in Edmonton] for a provision trade.[32]

Important as the provision trade was in framing the Hudson's Bay Company's affairs in Calgary, however, tradition and business opportunities continued to shape and reshape its store there. The company sought to adhere to its tradition of devoting most of its energies to collecting buffalo robes from the Blackfoot and doing limited business with white customers. True to tradition, Hudson's Bay Company officers in Winnipeg made few funds available for store expansion in Calgary.

Charles J. Brydges and New Business Opportunities

London executives had a chance to reassess the future for their company through their choice of a new top officer in Winnipeg. It was an opportunity they did not miss. Charles J. Brydges, the new Hudson's Bay Company land commissioner recruited in June 1879, eventually helped the company to seize new business opportunities in Calgary in the burgeoning field of merchandise sales to white customers. Born in 1827 in London, England, Brydges was educated in a local boarding school. He joined the London and Southwestern

Chapter 3: Hudson's Bay Company

Charles J. Brydges in 1870, during his time as general manager of the Grand Trunk Railway of Canada. He became the Hudson's Bay Company's land commissioner in Winnipeg in 1879. (Courtesy of Glenbow Archives, NA-5201-5).

Railway as a clerk in 1843, and became the assistant secretary a number of years later. He came to Canada in 1853 as managing director of the Great Western Railway, and was appointed general manager of the Grand Trunk Railway in 1862. Leaving the Grand Trunk in 1874 to become general superintendent of government railways in the Canadian government, Brydges held this position until his appointment as Hudson's Bay Company land commissioner in 1879.[33]

Brydges had clear ideas about how to improve Hudson's Bay Company's prospects in the long run – ideas that came from his background as a railway executive and reflected views that were common among Canadian business executives of Brydges' generation. His vision of a freshly invigorated Hudson's Bay Company, expanding in the general store field and competing more successfully in merchandise sales to a wide spectrum of customers, was eventually realized. Brydges expressed the right notions about the prospects for improving the company. The notions he aired and the programs he initiated to revive the Hudson's Bay Company were but one expression of the general confidence felt in Canadian business circles during the late 1870s and early 1880s. Although a serious economic depression had plagued the Canadian economy during the mid-1870s, in general the nation was again becoming prosperous at the end of that decade. After John A. Macdonald became Prime Minister once more in 1878, there was even greater optimism. Macdonald exuded confidence and promoted economic policies, popular among leaders of large firms, that promised to counteract the impact of depressions and take the nation's economy to greater heights of prosperity.

Brydges was very much a part of this picture. In particular, he believed that he had the insight needed to ensure that the

Hudson's Bay Company would move steadily upwards and increase its influence. As the company's land commissioner in Winnipeg, Brydges travelled widely and visited many of the company's trading posts and stores, including those in Calgary and Edmonton. Soon after being appointed to this position, he set out a strategy for reinvigorating the Hudson's Bay Company. He sought to reorient the company so that it would invest more aggressively in retail stores for a broad range of local people than it had traditionally done.[34] He also wanted the company to compete vigorously for Canadian government supply contracts to meet the needs of the Mounted Police and Natives. Brydges established close ties with the department of Indian affairs, of which Prime Minister John A. Macdonald was the superintendent-general, the department of the interior, and the Mounted Police and contributed to the ability of this loosely integrated network to generate business opportunities for the Hudson's Bay Company.

The changes that Brydges inspired, however, occurred not rapidly but only gradually. In seeking to win contracts for supplying the Mounted Police and Native people, the Hudson's Bay Company as a corporation was still very cautious. In fact, in 1880 and 1881 no attempt was made to provide the Natives and Mounted Police at Calgary with supplies through Canadian government contracts. This, in addition to the disappearance of the buffalo from Alberta and the simultaneous loss of the buffalo robe trade in 1879, made it difficult for the company to stabilize the market for its products. With the exception of Brydges, Hudson's Bay Company officers in Winnipeg remained reluctant to invest the company's earnings in supplies in Calgary on a contract basis. Their hesitancy to move into the supply contract business in centres west of their trading post at Qu'Appelle grew, in part, out of their inability to handle the competition of the better-positioned Baker & Co. In their response to this problem, they reaffirmed a theme arising from the Hudson's Bay Company's earlier history. Behind their inaction was a continued commitment to protect their company from a substantial increase in transportation costs. In freighting goods overland from Fort Benton on the Missouri to Calgary, Baker & Co. continued to enjoy a comparative advantage; costs were so low as to permit successful competition with the Hudson's Bay Company. The advantage continued to rest largely on the shorter distance between Calgary and Fort Benton than between Winnipeg and

Calgary. Chief factor John H. McTavish wrote from Winnipeg in February 1881:

> On comparison of Baker & Co.'s tender of last year with our figures and what we might be able to accomplish the ensuing season, I see clearly it is useless for us to put in a tender for any of the Plain points beyond Qu'Appelle. With the uncertainty of navigation on the Saskatchewan River, we must base our transport on overland rates which are double what they appear to be from the Missouri.[35]

An Uncertain Future

The Hudson's Bay Company's decision to avoid launching into contracts to supply the Mounted Police and Natives at Calgary meant that its store there continued to lag far behind Baker & Co. in its trading capabilities. Baker & Co. continued to get the cream of the business in Calgary. By 1881, as Angus Fraser was coming to realize, the Hudson's Bay Company's store faced an uncertain future. In fact, he was surrounded by rumours that the store he was managing was about to be abandoned by the company. Captain Cecil Denny even offered to buy the company's buildings in Calgary for $1,000. But Richard Hardisty was quick to make clear that they were not for sale. "I took no notice of his offer," wrote Hardisty, "and nothing further was said or done about it."[36]

Nevertheless, the Hudson's Bay Company's store at Calgary, which was still trying to establish itself in the merchandise trade, led a shaky existence. By 1881, the store teetered on the brink of failure. This problem brought changes to the company. To improve the company's position, Hardisty and Fraser sought to secure its claim to the land that it occupied in Calgary at the confluence of the Bow and Elbow rivers on the east bank of the Elbow. Ever since 1875, the Hudson's Bay Company had been a squatter at Calgary. Before the Calgary area was surveyed in 1880, the Canadian government was sensitive to the rights of squatters. Long before that year, the government had recognized the rights squatters had acquired by living on and improving Dominion land. If a squatter living on Dominion land became a homesteader, he was entitled to the value of the improvements he had made before starting to homestead. Under the Dominion Lands Act, enacted in 1872, any bona fide settler was permitted to file claim to 160 acres of Dominion land as a homestead for a $10 fee. But the Hudson's Bay Company did not qualify as a settler, and so it could not homestead 160 acres.[37] There was no Hudson's Bay Company presence in Calgary in 1870, when the company had acquired 50,000 acres of land around its trading posts in Rupert's Land in exchange for the cession of its territory to Canada. Consequently, while the company claimed three thousand acres of land around its long-established Edmonton trading post, it could make no such claim around its newly opened trading post in Calgary.

A partial solution to these problems soon appeared. In the spring of 1881, Fraser, acting on Hardisty's advice, successfully homesteaded in his own name 160 acres of land around the Hudson's Bay Company store on the east bank of the Elbow. In this way Fraser, who was eventually to sell his homestead to the company, tried to protect its interests in Calgary. As Hardisty stated, "I … advised our man, Fraser, to take up the place in his own name in the meantime, till the Company would secure their claim, so as to prevent any parties building too near him."[38] By August 1882, Fraser had improved his homestead by breaking five acres on it.[39]

The improvement of the new homestead might have come to naught had the Hudson's Bay Company's marketing efforts not also met with some success. Sales of merchandise were, of course, essential for the company's growth and development in Calgary. The company continued to rely on Angus Fraser to sell its goods. In 1882, he was responsible for the sale of tea, sugar, flour, bacon, and other items to local customers such as James Walker, a former Mounted Policeman who had become a homesteader and a sawmill operator in Calgary.[40] Still, the shortage of goods at the Hudson's Bay Company's Calgary store hurt the company. Steamboat transportation problems on the North Saskatchewan, plus the hesitant participation of the company in the Calgary trade, meant that the store in Calgary received only a small fraction of the goods it needed. When the treaty payments were made at Blackfoot Crossing in 1882, Fraser could not keep up with Baker & Co. in selling merchandise to the Blackfoot. Had Fraser had an adequate supply of goods "he would have held his own with his Yankee neighbours," observed William McKay, a clerk at the Hudson's Bay

Company's Edmonton trading post. Fraser's "White Trade," for which he received only a few goods from Edmonton in the fall of 1882, was also discouraging. "As it is," noted McKay, "I can only send him some tobacco and gunpowder." By contrast, as McKay went on to report, there were "over 100 Bull Teams on the road between Benton and Macleod. Baker & Co. will have an immense assortment of goods this year" in Calgary.[41]

Charles J. Brydges' Visit to Calgary

Charles Brydges, always looking to the future, was now an enthusiastic advocate of the Hudson's Bay Company's interests in Calgary. In early September 1882, he visited Angus Fraser in the company's Calgary store. He quickly formed a high opinion of Fraser's business capacities. In his report to William Armit, secretary in the company's London head office, Brydges revealed the problems Fraser faced:

> Our man named Fraser, who is very highly spoken of all over the country, told me that he could sell a great quantity of goods at excellent prices, if he could only get them…. We have several small buildings, about a quarter the size of Baker's. Baker has a large supply of goods on hand, their present stock being worth about $25,000. We had to buy what we wanted there, owing to there being nothing at the H. B. store.

Then Brydges provided more details about the difficult situation. Fraser, he said,

> … received in Sept. 1881, a total weight of 3,300 pounds of goods. They were all sold out in less than a month. He got no more till late this spring when he received 600 pounds weight, all of which was sold out in 2 or 3 weeks. He says this occurs every year, and that for more than 10 months every year he has nothing to sell, whilst Baker is busy every day. On my way to Macleod I met 27 Red River carts and 6 large double wagons, laden with goods for Baker's store at Calgary.[42]

In this report to William Armit, Brydges promoted the image of Fraser as an effective leader in merchandising despite constantly being confronted with the problem of an acute shortage of goods. "There are about 1,000 Indians near Calgary who are known to & friendly with Fraser," wrote Brydges.

> They have so much confidence in him that they leave considerable amounts of their treaty money in his hands. They would prefer to deal with him if they could. He has also the confidence of all the white people who are now going in both as farmers & ranchmen. On the 6th Sept. I took an inventory of what was in his store. It was as follows: 4 suits of English clothes, 2 vests, 1 Great Coat, 2 pair cord trousers, 8 copper kettles (unsaleable), 1 piece cord cloth, 16 hats, 1 case old fashioned trading guns which the Indians will not now buy, and a small quantity of powder. There was no shot – no sugar, tea, bacon or flour or blankets. His whole stock, such as it was, was worth less than $500 whilst Baker's was worth from $25,000 to $30,000, besides large consignments on the way. Fraser had about $50 worth of furs – could not secure any having nothing to sell.[43]

Whether the Hudson's Bay Company's goods moved between Winnipeg and Calgary on steamboat or cart, transportation was always expensive, especially when it was compared to the transportation system used by Baker & Co. "It costs" Baker & Co. "2½ cents a pound to get their goods from Montreal via Duluth, Bismarck & the Missouri to Benton," wrote Brydges to Armit.

> They get cheaper than other people, owing to Baker owning steamers themselves and giving their own freight low rates. From Benton to Macleod they pay 2 cents a pound for teaming, making the cost 4½ cents a pound. It costs 1 cent a pound more to Calgary or 5½ cents.... Fraser told me we pay 3 cents a pound from Edmonton to Calgary, 200 miles. The boats on the Missouri River, where there is competition, charge 1 cent a pound average from Bismarck to Benton – sometimes a little less. The charge from Winnipeg to Edmonton is 6 ¼ cents a pound.

Chapter 3: Hudson's Bay Company

Thus, while it cost Baker & Co. 5½ cents a pound to move its merchandise from Montreal to Calgary, the Hudson's Bay Company paid 9¼ cents a pound to ship its goods from Winnipeg to Calgary.[44]

Despite these transportation and supply problems the Hudson's Bay Company faced at Calgary, the centre's proximity to agricultural country was a major asset. Brydges informed Armit:

> Calgary is the most charming spot I have seen in the Northwest so far, being in a beautiful valley with the Rocky Mountains, with their snow capped peaks, as a background. The land is excellent – the grasses rich and thick – ample water – and wood not far off. The difficulty is early frosts, but I think early sowing and reaping will largely remove this objection.... Calgary is a prominent point in the grazing country. It is splendid land – excellent grasses – and admirably fitted for first class ranches. This ranch country extends about 50 miles north of Calgary & south to the boundary. It is upwards of 50 miles deep, and about 200 long. This area contains from 6,500,000 to 7,000,000 acres and is capable of supporting from 600,000 to 700,000 head of cattle. It has now nearly 20,000 head, and to be increased by winter to about 30,000.[45]

Brydges felt confident that the soils, vegetation, and other features of the landscape in Calgary and the surrounding region all pointed toward a place that would become a great urban centre. He believed that the Hudson's Bay Company store would some day be a significant part of that urban greatness. As early as January 1882, Brydges had told James A. Grahame that the company had "a post at Fort Calgary, which is very likely to become an important post."[46] By mid-1883, Angus Fraser had taken advantage of opportunities to make valuable improvements in the company's establishment. Besides maintaining its four buildings, including the store, and the fence that surrounded them, he had created two vegetable gardens and built a fence around the pasture where the company's cattle grazed.[47] He was pressing ahead with trade, using the Edmonton Trail to bring in merchandise.

Prairie trails had been important arteries of commerce almost from the time in 1875 when the Hudson's Bay Company and Baker

Chapter 3: Hudson's Bay Company

Passengers in Calgary in 1884 on Canada's first transcontinental, the Canadian Pacific Railway. (Courtesy of Glenbow Archives, NA-967-12).

& Co. had come to Calgary. In mid-1883, goods such as flour and clothing were still rumbling slowly along trails to these firms' Calgary stores by wagon. But now from Montreal came the stirring news that the steam locomotive, running on iron rails, would soon move cargo and people to the West. Like Baker & Co., the Hudson's Bay Company expected that Calgary would rise to greatness on the proposed Canadian Pacific Railway between Montreal and Vancouver. The Hudson's Bay Company and Baker & Co. also were hopeful that the railway would greatly improve transportation for their enterprises.

4

Rails and Marketing

Impact of the Canadian Pacific Railway

Calgary's rapid development began when the town acquired rail connections to central Canada and the Pacific Coast. In August 1883, the first railway – the Canadian Pacific, a pioneer of entrepreneurial capitalism – reached Calgary. Only as Canadian Pacific leaders and administrators could identify themselves with the underlying economic and social impulses of their time could they plan and build a great institution. They had to be in accord not only with the interests of the stockholders and the desires of consumers, but also with the deep currents of opinion which were shaping Canadian society of the future. The railway was completed between Montreal and Vancouver two years later, just in time for Calgary to benefit from further developments in the mid-1880s. Continuing to demonstrate its great importance, the Canadian Pacific spurred the growth of ranching and farming near Calgary. The Canadian Pacific drew Calgary area cattle eastward to Winnipeg and southward to the American border, from where they went on American trackage and Canadian rails to central Canadian markets. Canada came to depend on Alberta for its beef, and Calgary helped supply that demand. By 1885, Calgary was a regional commercial centre with a population of about one thousand serving the needs of the Bow Valley's approximately two thousand residents, many of whom lived and worked on ranches and farms in the rural areas surrounding Calgary.

Before these rapid economic and social changes, Calgary had been something of an "island community," with few effective ties to the national economy. The rural residents in the Bow Valley raised

Chapter 4: Rails & Marketing

livestock, grew their own oats, barley, and wheat, and sometimes hunted to supply meat. Although the rich soil and grasses of the region were ideal for cattle and grain, few people produced a great deal of these potential money crops because of the lack of reliable transportation to national markets. Rather, local ranchers and farmers took their surplus products to Calgary and traded them for manufactured goods. Following prairie trails, they rode horses or horse- or ox-drawn wagons to the centre to do business. At a time when long-distance freighters hauling goods for merchants to Calgary by team and wagon needed at least a whole day to travel twenty-five miles, the Canadian Pacific represented a tremendous increase in speed. Making an average speed of thirty-five to forty miles an hour between stations, the railway brought the era of quick, all-weather, long-distance transport to Calgarians. The arrival of the Canadian Pacific forged stronger connections between Calgary and the outside world, enabling the once isolated centre to become more tightly integrated into the regional and national economies.

 The Canadian Pacific, whose importance to Calgary and the Bow Valley can hardly be overestimated, helped create industrial capitalism in the region. Although general merchants remained at the heart of Calgary's economy, there were the beginnings of new industries, which promised to provide jobs for many local people. The new industries, of which the most significant were lumber, meat, electricity, leather, and flour, had to compete vigorously with commercial and agricultural enterprises in order to participate in the Second Industrial Revolution, in which transportation and communication were revolutionized by the railway and telegraph. The corporate form now often proved to be a necessary device for marshalling the large amounts of capital required to develop the big industrial businesses. Developing the techniques of mobilizing the unprecedented amounts of capital needed to construct a large-scale road, the railway expanded its services and responded to the transportation demands of the new industries that grew up in Calgary over the next one and a half decades. A complex machine, spread out over vast distances, the Canadian Pacific played a major role in the marketing and distribution of products such as beef, lumber, flour, harnesses, and saddles. Stimulating production of coal and fuelling capital growth, the railway was vital to the gradual emergence of a small industrial society in the city in the late nineteenth century.

Chapter 4: Rails & Marketing

Overcoming Barriers to Inland Transportation

Surveying the Canadian Pacific helped trigger Calgary's real estate boom and stimulated the growth of the Hudson's Bay Company and I. G. Baker & Co. in Calgary in the early 1880s, though the railway itself took much longer to make significant progress. The Canadian Pacific's officers were among the Canadian leaders who recognized that overcoming the barriers to inland transportation was essential for the growth of the national market. The first company to undertake the railway's construction incorporated in 1872 and collapsed before its own stock could be sold. Even with enthusiastic support from leading Montrealers such as Hugh Allan, efforts to raise capital for this private railway company proved unsuccessful.[1] In 1874, the project became the responsibility of Alexander Mackenzie's Liberal government, which launched a scheme to build a publicly owned railway. Nearly twelve months passed before the first sod for the railway was turned at Fort William in 1875. A less favourable year to start construction would be difficult to imagine. As a nationwide economic depression in the mid-1870s shattered hopes for expansion, the fiscal condition of the government deteriorated. With the government's resources stretched to their limits, an isolated section of the railway was built in Ontario. But in 1878, the railway finished a line in Manitoba, from Winnipeg south to the American border. The St. Paul & Pacific Railroad reached the border from St. Paul, Minnesota. At long last, an all-rail link had been forged between Winnipeg and St. Paul, giving Manitoba wheat an outlet through American territory.

Inevitably, there were still problems, particularly for the Canadian Pacific – the government still had to find the money to proceed with construction. But the Canadian Pacific renewed itself as prosperity returned in the late 1870s and early 1880s. In 1881, responsibility for the project passed to a new Montreal-based company, which embarked on an ambitious private scheme of rapid construction. Montreal had the businessmen needed to back the road. The Conservative government under John A. Macdonald threw its support behind the new Canadian Pacific Railway, projected to run from Montreal through Winnipeg and Calgary to Vancouver, by giving it a cash subsidy of $25 million and a grant of twenty-five million acres of land in the prairie West.

Calgary's earliest railway thus began as a corporation managed and financed especially by Montreal businessmen, but also funded in large measure by the Canadian government. During 1881, two prominent Montreal citizens, George Stephen and his cousin, Donald A. Smith, each contributed $500,000 to the Canadian Pacific Railway – in total, a respectable 20 percent of the subscriptions up to that time.[2] Men like Stephen and Smith invested not only money but also tremendous entrepreneurial energy. They hoped to profit personally from their efforts, and in several ways. For Stephen, the president, and Smith, a director, the expected profits the road would produce in moving freight and passengers were attractive. As president of the Bank of Montreal, which backed the road, Stephen wanted to promote his bank's fortunes by investing in the railway. To Smith, who was a director of the Hudson's Bay Company and one of its major shareholders, the railway's expected effect on the company was appealing. He believed that the railway would be an ideal way for decreasing the difficulty and cost of transporting the company's goods to its Calgary store. The Canadian Pacific came to dominate the Calgary transportation and communication networks – networks that were essential for the coming of large-scale marketing.

Montrealers like Smith and Stephen shared the assumption that the central Canadian terminus of the Canadian Pacific Railway should naturally be Montreal. They realized that their city would have a special relationship to the road: it would augment Montreal's access to its prairie hinterland. In Montreal, the exchange of merchandise had already become an exercise in regional conversion. From the mid-1870s onward, its city streets had become places where hardware and dry goods had been turned into buffalo robes from Calgary. Stephen and Smith thought that the railway would reinforce Montreal's advantage: the road would increase the city's power to offer its prairie hinterland the best market in Canada.

Richard Hardisty Responds to the Canadian Pacific

Construction of the Canadian Pacific west of Winnipeg during 1881 amounted to about 161 miles, the railway nearly reaching Oak Lake, Manitoba. This prairie route provided a link to Montreal, principally via the Canadian Pacific's branch line between Winnipeg and Pembina on the Canadian-American border, the St. Paul, Minneapolis & Manitoba (successor to the St. Paul & Pacific), the Chicago, Milwaukee & St. Paul, and the Grand Trunk. The first regular freight and passenger service between Winnipeg and Oak Lake began on 11 June 1882, proving that 161 miles of rails were a big improvement over prairie trails.[3]

Within two weeks Richard Hardisty, the experienced Hudson's Bay Company chief factor in Edmonton, was delighted to learn that enterprising ranchers and farmers were arriving in Calgary expecting that the end of the line would soon reach the centre. He responded positively to the new technologies in transportation and communication. A knowledgeable entrepreneur, strong in his insights and commitment to the Edmonton-Calgary area, Hardisty was now eager to make his mark. "There appears to be a great change rapidly taking place in this part of the country," he reported to James A. Grahame, chief commissioner of the Hudson's Bay Company in Winnipeg. "People are flocking in in connection with the Canadian Pacific Railroad and cattle ranches, besides others going in for the purpose of settling down on farms." Hardisty urged Grahame to send a large supply of goods to the Hudson's Bay Company's Calgary store to enable it to compete with Baker & Co. The store, he wrote,

> would require a good supply of groceries & goods suited for the trade, sent in there at an early date. No doubt, I. G. Baker and Co. will have in a large supply of all kinds, and be able to undersell us in groceries, etc. on account of the present means of transport, but if the Railroad runs to Calgary, we can then be better able to compete with them.[4]

Grahame did not much heed this advice, but the westward extension of the Canadian Pacific into the prairies continued. By this time, William C. Van Horne was by far the most important addition to the railway's management. Born in 1843 in Illinois, Van Horne had extensive experience in building railways in the United States. He joined the Canadian Pacific on 1 January 1882, as general manager, a position he held until 1888, when he became the railway's president. Given a free hand by George Stephen, Van Horne pushed the line westward to Moose Jaw, Saskatchewan by the end of August 1882.[5] The Hudson's Bay Company's store in Calgary was not prepared for the many people who came to the centre, in anticipation of the arrival

Chapter 4: Rails & Marketing

of the railway in the near future. Lamenting the lack of goods at the Calgary store, William McKay, the Hudson's Bay Company's clerk in Edmonton, wrote: "I think it is high time that some measures were adopted to insure our interests being looked after in Winnipeg so that in future we will get our outfits at the proper time."[6]

Within six months, however, it seemed that things would begin to change. Everyone was aware of the Canadian Pacific's rapid westward extension. By April 1883, the line's rails were serving Maple Creek, Saskatchewan, about 230 miles east of Calgary.[7] Already in February, Richard Hardisty argued that the Canadian Pacific should become the preferred way to bring the Hudson's Bay Company's goods to Calgary from Winnipeg. As an innovative businessman, he understood railway freight charges and procedures. From Edmonton he wrote to Grahame, asking him to use the railway:

> I now enclose a requisition to be supplied for Calgary by the C.P.R. line, which can be freighted by carts [sent from] Calgary when the pieces reach the end of the line. If you decide to the have the pieces at the end of the track at a certain date, I can make arrangements when I go out to Calgary to have the carts there on that date.[8]

The strategy adopted by Hardisty of selling a diverse range of products eventually turned out to be an important formula for success. The goods he requested for the company's Calgary store included a wide variety of groceries, men's and women's and children's clothing, horse blankets, and axe handles.

But Hardisty's efforts to have the Hudson's Bay Company's goods sent to Calgary by cart from the end of track proved unsuccessful. In Winnipeg, Grahame continued to rely on steamboats on the Red River-Lake Winnipeg-North Saskatchewan River route and carts on the Edmonton Trail to ship goods to the Calgary store. The difficulties, expense, and uncertainty of such shipments greatly limited the prospects for the company's trade at Calgary. "It is to be regretted," complained Hardisty in June 1883, "that the Outfit for Calgary could not have been sent by the Railroad.... It will now be a month or more later in reaching its destination by Edmonton, and at a much heavier expense."[9]

I. G. Baker & Co. and the Canadian Pacific

By contrast, the Canadian Pacific attracted attention from I. G. Baker & Co. in the early 1880s. Charles Conrad, a Baker & Co. partner, was an entrepreneur who had a keen sense of what was feasible. In mid-March 1883, he made a trip to the Canadian Pacific's head office in Montreal to explore the possibility of having the railway bring Baker & Co.'s goods to the end of track for shipment by ox-drawn wagons to Calgary. Within a week, Conrad made arrangements to ship the goods from Montreal to Winnipeg by rail, using the Grand Trunk, the Chicago, Milwaukee & St. Paul, the St. Paul, Minneapolis & Manitoba, and the Canadian Pacific's Pembina-Winnipeg branch line. From Winnipeg the shipment would move west along the Canadian Pacific's main line to the end of track at Maple Creek, where Baker & Co.'s wagon trains would be waiting to take the goods to Calgary.[10] In this way the first shipment, including groceries from Tees, Costigan & Wilson in Montreal, reached Calgary in the spring of 1883.[11] The Canadian Pacific provided an efficient method of bulk transportation that dramatically lowered costs. The railway carried Baker & Co.'s goods at a fraction of the cost of transport by wagon.

The westward extension of the Canadian Pacific to Medicine Hat at the end of May and to Calgary in mid-August 1883 meant that more and more of Baker & Co.'s goods arrived in Calgary by rail.[12] The Canadian Pacific revolutionized Calgary's access to central Canada and the American Midwest and East. The coming of the railway and its ally, the telegraph system, put an end to distribution difficulties and the inefficient transmission of information. By the fall of 1883, Calgary had speedy rail communication with important North American cities, including Chicago, Toronto, Montreal, and New York. The greater power and speed of the Canadian Pacific enabled Calgary to break free from the environmental and economic constraints of Baker & Co.'s earlier transport system – ox-drawn wagons. Railway transportation to Calgary did not bring a sudden end to the overland freighting business between Calgary and Fort Macleod and Calgary and Edmonton, however. Commercial freighters' wagon trains could be seen on these routes until 1891-1892, when Canadian Pacific branch lines from Calgary reached Edmonton and Fort Macleod.

Baker & Co. had spent money renovating its store in Calgary in early and mid-1883 in order to prepare for the expected increase in business with the arrival of the Canadian Pacific. Even before the coming of the railway, the firm's store on the west bank of the Elbow was recognized as a landmark in the business centre of the place. John L. Bowen, the store's forward-looking manager, wanted a building that would provide the most up-to-date facilities for merchandising. The *Macleod Gazette* reported that "the new front and interior decorations" were the special features of the renovated building, and that the premises were "a striking comparison to anything that Calgary has yet produced."[13]

In the eight years of the store's existence, one location had been distinguished by its presence. It remained at the junction of the Bow and Elbow on the west side of the Elbow, on thirteen hundred acres of land in Calgary Bottom where it was first set up by I. G. Baker and his partners Charles and William Conrad. Their efforts at raising livestock on the land showed that cattle did well on the rich grasses. Throughout Calgary's earlier history, the site had been a Blackfoot path south to Montana and north to the waters of the Bow River and beyond to Edmonton. When Baker & Co. arrived in 1875, the firm adopted this route and the land around it for its own needs. Soon it became popularly known as the Edmonton Trail to the north and the Macleod Trail to the south. But Baker & Co. was only a squatter on the land. The firm's growing operations required it to secure the land as it was jockeying for position along the main road of commerce.

As early as March 1882, the Baker & Co. partners wrote to Prime Minister John A. Macdonald in his capacity as minister of the department of the interior, eagerly seeking to obtain 160 acres in the 1,300-acre site in Calgary Bottom as a homestead on the grounds that they had made valuable improvements over the years.[14] In addition to a number of buildings that had been erected, portions of the land had been cultivated and used to grow oats, potatoes, and other vegetables. The partners also offered to purchase the rest of the site. Macdonald considered the homestead application and the purchase offer but said nothing directly to the partners. However, they did not drop the matter as a lost cause. Ebullient about Calgary's future and the prospects for merchandising in the coming years, they persisted in their effort. "I think Calgary will be the big town of the Northwest.... Hope we will get the land we claim and have applied for," William Conrad wrote to Edgar Dewdney, lieutenant-governor of the Northwest Territories, in January 1883.[15] Three months later, Charles Conrad visited Macdonald in Ottawa and again applied for a homestead and for permission to purchase the balance of the 1,300-acre site Baker & Co. occupied in Calgary Bottom.[16] Charles Conrad's quest for a homestead failed because the department of the interior did not regard the Baker & Co. partners as agricultural settlers; but their firm was allowed to buy 16¼ acres in the Calgary Bottom site north of the Canadian Pacific and on the west bank of the Elbow.[17] Baker & Co. paid $50 per acre for the land.

Initially, the Baker & Co. partners hoped that Calgary would rise to greatness on the west bank of the Elbow and thereby increase the value of their firm's land holding and augment its commercial importance. For similar reasons, the Hudson's Bay Company officers hoped that Calgary would grow big on the Elbow's east bank. These two firms, each with its own ambitions for the future, tried to influence the Canadian Pacific's choice of the location of its station in Calgary. Baker & Co. naturally wanted the station on the Elbow's west bank, while the Hudson's Bay Company sought to have it placed on the east side of the Elbow. Calgary thus was not an economically united community. The Canadian Pacific, with its power to transform the landscape and determine the location of the new Calgary townsite, shared neither the Hudson's Bay Company's vision nor that of Baker & Co.

Canadian Pacific and the Calgary Townsite

The Canadian Pacific possessed a key asset: it owned Section 15, which lay about one mile west of the Elbow, beyond Calgary's settled area. When John M. Egan, the railway's general superintendent of the western region, visited Calgary in July 1883, he decided to build its station on Section 15 and have the townsite laid out around the station. "At Calgary on Section 15," Egan wrote William C. Van Horne, "there is a very good location for a Town site. No squatters on this Section, as the Mounted Police have kept them off there.... I have no doubt that when you see the place it will please you. It is West of the Elbow.... It is a natural Town site, and far ahead of any location that we have on the line of the Road." In part,

Chapter 4: Rails & Marketing

Egan's desire to unite the Calgary community economically and make quick profits for the Canadian Pacific through town lot sales prompted his decision. "As you are perhaps aware," he added,

> there is considerable strife between the people East of the Elbow and those West. The buildings of the Mounted Police, I. G. Baker, and several others are West of the Elbow, and the Hudson's Bay Co.'s stores, and a number of settlers are East. In locating the Station Grounds, I have placed them towards the West end of the Section as I think by that location, the strife between the places will be ended.[18]

About a year before the selection of the Calgary townsite, the Canadian Pacific had organized a subsidiary, the Canada Northwest Land Company, to develop townsites along the main line of the railway.[19] In the fall of 1883, the company appointed W. T. Ramsay as its agent in Calgary, directing him to supervise the surveying of the townsite and to organize the public sale of lots.[20] A real estate entrepreneur and an insurance agent, Ramsay promoted the townsite at every opportunity. Like other local people, he hoped to benefit from the development of Calgary. He hired A. W. McVittie, a Dominion land surveyor, to do the survey, and in January 1884 the land was opened for settlement.[21]

The initial sale of lots proved highly successful. Convinced that Calgary was a town that had a great future, buyers purchased nearly two hundred lots within two hours after the sale began for prices ranging from $300 to $450.[22] The terms were a down payment of $50 and a rebate of one-half of the purchase price if buildings were erected and occupied before 1 April. Calgary residents were offered the first opportunity to buy lots. As the months and years passed, many more lots were put up for sale.

The Calgary townsite plan contained 125 blocks, all separated by rather narrow streets and alleys. Some of the main arteries measured sixty-six feet in width.[23] Several streets running east-west, as well as some north-south streets, were named for Canadian Pacific officers. Stephen Avenue served as the major thoroughfare and the principal business street, while McTavish became the main cross street. The railway station was located alongside Atlantic Avenue, roughly in the middle of the townsite. In Calgary the station, along with the railway's nearby freight sheds, constituted the hub of activity in merchandise delivery. Profitable, and for the most part practical at the time, the Calgary plan reflected the traditional North American grid pattern. Originally, the town developed more on the north side of the railway than on the south side.

Most of the major commercial establishments were located along Stephen Avenue. In March 1884, Baker & Co. moved to the townsite. The firm began operations on four lots it purchased from the Canada Northwest Land Company on the corner of Stephen and McTavish, in central Calgary.[24] Located near the Canadian Pacific station, the site provided Baker & Co. the space needed to begin business. Several months later, the firm finished construction of a store building and moved in merchandise, while at the same time keeping some goods in its old warehouse on the Elbow. To satisfy the demands of its customers, Baker & Co. bought a fresh selection of goods especially from wholesalers and manufacturers in Montreal, which were then shipped to Calgary by railway and hauled from the railway station and freight sheds to the store by ox-drawn wagons. Parallel to the Canadian Pacific right of way was the telegraph; this communication, while essential for the railway's own traffic control, was critically important in permitting instant messages to flow between Baker & Co.'s Calgary store and its Montreal suppliers.

Business in Calgary after the Arrival of the Canadian Pacific

The Canadian Pacific greatly expanded business opportunities for Calgarians. For example, as manager of Baker & Co.'s store, John L. Bowen felt optimistic that the coming of the railway would mean new opportunities for the development of the enterprise. Although groceries and clothing were his leading products, he followed a policy of diversified sales. Continuing a strategy that had traditionally characterized Baker & Co. in Calgary, Bowen avoided too much specialization. At the store he carried whatever goods he thought would bring profits to the firm. In addition to clothing and groceries, he offered dry goods, boots and shoes, hats and caps, woollen blankets, stoves, tinware, harnesses, saddles, agricultural implements, and barbed wire.[25]

The year 1883 and the early months of 1884 were prosperous times for Baker & Co. in Calgary. With the arrival of the Canadian Pacific, the town's population rose rapidly to one thousand by the end of 1883. Consequently, the centre's people needed increasing quantities of goods. Sales expanded substantially. A significant portion of Baker & Co.'s sales at Calgary continued to come from the Mounted Police and Native supply contracts the firm won in these years.[26] As it grew, Baker & Co. also continued to benefit from its contract with the Canadian government to carry mail from Fort Benton to Fort Macleod to Calgary until the end of December 1883.[27]

The success of the Canadian Pacific helped spur economic growth and business development in Calgary. In July 1883, for instance, the Hudson's Bay Company made the important decision to move the headquarters of its trade in Alberta from Edmonton to its Calgary store.[28] Richard Hardisty, who was still responsible for the company's Alberta operations, moved to Calgary and continued his general supervision of the store, while Angus Fraser remained its manager. Calgary was a geographical node for regional commerce. On 14 August, the Hudson's Bay Company began to ship its goods to Calgary from Winnipeg by the Canadian Pacific.[29] The first shipment filled an entire car. It was clearly cheaper for the company to ship merchandise by rail than by the longer route on the Red River, Lake Winnipeg, and the North Saskatchewan, and the goods arrived in Calgary in better condition. Other advantages of the Canadian Pacific lay in its speed and all-season reliability. The railway rapidly emerged as the chief link connecting Winnipeg with Alberta, and it created fresh commercial opportunities for the Hudson's Bay Company in Calgary.

The Hudson's Bay Company's store no longer had to wait for months on end to receive merchandise from Winnipeg. Business at the store was picking up, as it offered a broader assortment of goods. Native people remained the principal market but, as Richard Hardisty reported, "the whites" were "gradually coming in." Progress, however, was slow. In Winnipeg, James A. Grahame was still averse to taking many risks, and he hesitated to commit fully to the trade with white customers. The appearance of inferior flour and poor-quality blankets in the store retarded business. "I am sorry to say," complained Hardisty, "that our flour is only taken when the traders run out, as they say it is inferior…. It is a great pity those…. blankets were ordered. The Indians won't look at them."[30] Hardisty noted that "I. G. Baker & Co. are getting in a very superior quality of flour from Montana which gets a much readier sale than ours."[31]

Chapter 4: Rails & Marketing

At a time when its competitors – principally Baker & Co., but also a number of small traders – made special efforts to display their small goods attractively in show cases, the Hudson's Company's store in Calgary had no such cases. "The show cases are required," explained Hardisty, "to have our smaller items that are easily stolen shown to the public, if we expect to do anything. Every petty store here has them, and we cannot expect to compete with them if we cannot make an equal show."[32] To handle the store's increasing business in small goods, show cases were soon installed.

Not even these improvements gave the Hudson's Bay Company's store in Calgary facilities and room enough to keep up with its growing business. To solve this problem, Hardisty persuaded Grahame to provide larger premises. In January 1884, Hardisty began looking for lots in the new Calgary townsite upon which the company could build a larger store. A month later, the company acquired four lots on the corner of Stephen Avenue and McTavish Street.[33] The land was across the street from Baker & Co.'s store and near the Post Office, in Calgary's downtown.[34] The Hudson's Bay Company's relocation was part of a general migration of business establishments out of the Elbow River area. This area was simply becoming too isolated for business, and by the end of 1884 most enterprises had moved to the emerging business district around Stephen Avenue and Atlantic Avenue.

Construction of the Hudson's Bay Company's new store proceeded smoothly, and the first goods were sold there in the summer of 1884. By the end of that year the store had become the centre of the company's operations in Calgary and had a value of $2,200.[35] The store building, measuring seventy-five by fifty feet, enclosed three sections: one for groceries, the second for dry goods, and the third for hardware. Angus Fraser, the store's popular manager, continued to attract the Blackfoot, while simultaneously developing his business with white customers.

By this time, the store in Calgary had gained a unique role in the Hudson's Bay Company's trade in Alberta. With the advent of the Canadian Pacific, a portion of the company's goods bound for northern Alberta points was carried by rail to Calgary, and then shipped north by ox-drawn carts along the Edmonton Trail. At the company's Calgary store, Angus Fraser was responsible for overseeing the transshipment of merchandise from the Canadian Pacific to the carts heading for the company's stores in Edmonton

Chapter 4: Rails & Marketing

and other northern places such as Lac la Biche. With Calgary as a linchpin for this transportation activity, the company's store there grew in importance.[36] The company's steamboats on the North Saskatchewan were dwindling in significance, although they were still used to carry some of its goods to Edmonton and other northern points. Still, Calgary's strategic position on the Canadian Pacific made the town a major shipping link for the Hudson's Bay Company's merchandise.

The appearance of a new Baker & Co. store at Battle River south of Edmonton, near a band of Stoney Indians, in March 1884, however, put the Hudson's Bay Company very much on the defensive.[37] With a growing willingness to make new investments, Baker & Co. was breaking into central Alberta, challenging the Hudson's Bay Company on its traditional home ground. Richard Hardisty responded by opening a new Hudson's Bay Company store at Battle River in May.[38] Even so, the company could not keep up with Baker & Co. in the market for Native trade goods there.

Baker & Co. could look upon its accomplishments in last half of the 1870s and the early 1880s with considerable satisfaction. Financially, the firm was in good shape. Baker & Co. was a more complex firm than ever before, with growing operations in Alberta and the rest of the prairie West. In the prairie region as a whole, during this period the firm made sales of $1 million to the Canadian government annually, and it earned profits of 20 to 25 percent on these sales.[39] By 1884, Baker & Co. controlled about $200,000 in total goods at its two stores in Fort Macleod and Calgary. In addition, the firm was active in merchandising at Battle River, as well as in Silver City, west of Calgary in the Rockies, where prospectors hoped to be successful in their search for silver.

Coping with the Depression in the Mid-1880s

A nation-wide economic depression in the mid-1880s temporarily crushed hopes for expansion. The slump slowed the development of Canada's businesses and caused unemployment. In the prairie West, relatively little economic growth occurred.

For Baker & Co., which was trying to hold its own in the general merchandise trade, the results of the depression were very discouraging. In Calgary, the firm's sales dropped. Its problems were not unusual. The depression put intense pressure on the profits of most of Calgary's businesses. By mid-1884, all merchants in the town faced hard times.

By this time, Baker & Co. wanted to sell its entire business in Calgary and the rest of the prairie West, even though it was still the market leader in general merchandise. From St. Louis, Missouri in August 1884, I. G. Baker wrote a long letter to the Hudson's Bay Company's committee in London, England, offering to sell the Canadian business. "We presume," Baker began,

> you are aware that we have been your greatest competitors in the Canadian Northwest both in the trade and securing the Government Contracts.... If you wish to buy us out, we will sell to you all our business in the Canadian Northwest, and turn our business over to you at once and after the expiration of the present Contracts will quit that Country and not compete with you any longer either for trade or Contracts.

Baker noted that

> ... we have on hand at our two stores [at Fort Macleod and Calgary] about $200,000 worth of goods which we will invoice to you at net cost laid down. We will sell you our stores, warehouses, corrals, etc. for $20,000. Our trains and land transportation consists of four or five hundred head of oxen, a number of horses, from fifty to one hundred wagons which we will invoice at value, about $40,000. The beef of the oxen is worth this, as they will weigh 1,600 lbs. each.

Turning to the customer accounts in the stores, Baker observed that "there is standing on our books to the credit of our customers about $75,000 which we can pay off or you assume as you wish. If you assumed this, there would be a balance due us of $250,000 or $275,000."[40] Baker proposed that, if the Hudson's Bay Company should be interested in his offer, he or Charles Conrad or William Conrad would be willing to meet the company's representative in New York City or Montreal or Winnipeg or Calgary or Fort Macleod to arrange the sale.

This seemed like a dangerous gamble to the Hudson's Bay Company. In its reply to I. G. Baker in September, the company's

London committee expressed the view that we "are unwilling at present to increase the trading establishments of the Company in the Northwest Territory." The close of the London Committee's letter, nonetheless, contained an interesting suggestion: "If however upon further consideration you decide upon withdrawing from the trade at Calgary where the Company are erecting new premises and some portion of your supplies are suitable both as to quality and price for the Company's trade next season it might be desirable for you to communicate with" Joseph Wrigley, who in July 1884 had succeeded James A. Grahame as the company's chief commissioner in Winnipeg.[41]

The thought of acquiring Baker & Co.'s Calgary business hardly excited Joseph Wrigley. In his opinion, Baker & Co. in Calgary was not an appealing prize to be coveted by the Hudson's Bay Company. Born in 1839 in Yorkshire, England, Wrigley graduated from Rugby College. He joined his father's textile manufacturing concern in Huddersfield, staying in this line of work until shortly after his father's death, at which time the business was sold.[42] Joseph Wrigley also served as president of the Huddersfield Chamber of Commerce. Leaving England for Canada, he took over as chief commissioner of the Hudson's Bay Company in Winnipeg in August 1884.

With the retirement of James A. Grahame, the Hudson's Bay Company's London committee had a chance to reassess the future of their company through their choice of a new chief commissioner. It was an opportunity partially missed. Although not satisfied with the company's current earnings and dividends, the committee chose Joseph Wrigley, who would to some degree perpetuate Grahame's strategies into the late 1880s. Grahame's unwillingness to invest as heavily in the Native and white markets in Calgary as Baker & Co. hurt the Hudson's Bay Company. His stand-pat outlook contributed to the company's decline relative to the much more energetic merchandiser Baker & Co.

In carrying out his responsibilities as the new chief commissioner, Joseph Wrigley was initially reluctant to invest the Hudson's Bay Company's earnings in new facilities in Calgary. But Richard Hardisty, known as a man who did not let grass grow under his feet when opportunity knocked, told Wrigley that it was "necessary that a building should be erected [in the town] to answer the purpose of a warehouse in connection with our store in Calgary, which is required as soon as possible. It is also necessary to have one at or near the [Canadian Pacific] station as a general warehouse as long as this remains the shipping point for the North and elsewhere."⁴³ Wrigley responded revealingly by arguing "that money expended in building is sunk and can no longer be profitably turned over."⁴⁴ His reluctance to build warehouses in Calgary was unfortunate for the Hudson's Bay Company. While recognizing the need to alter some ways of doing business – he took the company in new directions in sales to white customers – Wrigley did not radically change its strategy. Rather than thoroughly revamp the Calgary store complete with warehouse facilities so that it could become more competitive, Wrigley chose to limit the investment of profits in new facilities.

So it was as well with the opportunity to purchase Baker & Co.'s Calgary business. Wrigley was not on the lookout for new chances for investment; however, toward the end of September 1884 he asked Richard Hardisty to give him an assessment of Baker & Co. in Calgary. Hardisty reported that "I cannot say more than what I have heard regarding the firm of Baker and Company ... the branch of the firm here, I believe, is not doing much."⁴⁵ Wrigley opposed the idea of buying Baker & Co.'s business in Calgary, in part because he thought that it was unprofitable. After William Conrad visited Wrigley in Winnipeg in early October to discuss the matter, Wrigley outlined his attitude in a letter to the Hudson's Bay Company's London committee: "I think it would be well for us not to appear anxious or very interested in this matter, as it scarcely seems probable that Messrs. Baker & Co. would take this step if they found their trade in the Northwest profitable and proposed to remain in it."⁴⁶ Richard Hardisty supported Wrigley because the chief trade commissioner's ideas about Baker & Co. largely coincided with his own: "this buying out the interests of I. G. Baker & Co. is a matter, in my opinion, which requires to be gone into with great caution. To buy them out would be a great advantage to them and no benefit to us."⁴⁷

But William Conrad mounted a major effort to sell Baker & Co.'s business in Calgary, as well as in Battle River and Silver City, to the Hudson's Bay Company. In a letter in January 1885 from his winter home in Virginia, he informed Wrigley that the "inventory of our stock of goods at Calgary ... shows that there are $42,878.01 in goods, and our agent reports about $7,000 at Battle River, and at Silver City $7,500, making a total on hand $57,378.01. We are willing to sell our entire business there ... and I am satisfied

Chapter 4: Rails & Marketing

it will be to our mutual benefit that we trade in this way."[48] But even now, Wrigley saw no advantage in purchasing Baker & Co. in Calgary, Silver City, and Battle River. As a director of the Hudson's Bay Company, Donald A. Smith agreed with Wrigley's position. In March 1885, Smith remarked in a letter to the company's London committee, "it is not desirable to increase capital unless it can clearly be shown that it will be advantageous to do so.... We hardly think it will be in the interest of the Company to take over the stock which Messrs. Baker & Co. have on hand at Calgary."[49] Thus, the Hudson's Bay Company turned down Baker & Co.'s offer to sell its business in Calgary and continued to develop its own store there.[50] Its actions, however, were not enough to enable the company to catch up with competitors like Baker & Co. and G. C. King & Co., a rapidly expanding general merchandising firm in the town.

The depression of the summer and fall of 1884 had been hard on Baker & Co. in Calgary. But with some economic recovery in late 1884 and 1885, the firm increased its sales in groceries, dry goods, and hardware in the town. The growing sales revived flagging spirits among the firm's owners: Charles and William Conrad as well as I. G. Baker. They consciously kept their business diversified, being careful not to make it too dependent on the local market. Their diversified firm continued to benefit from their ability to win lucrative contracts from the Canadian government to provide the Natives and the Mounted Police with supplies. The most obvious way to secure these contracts was by submitting the lowest bid and providing the highest quality service in a prompt manner. Baker & Co. learned this lesson early in its history, and it established a reputation as a reliable, efficient supplier.

The firm also continued to take advantage of the presence of the Canadian Pacific to cut transportation costs. As early as the spring of 1883, the scale of Baker & Co.'s rail shipments allowed it to make savings and this in turn brought savings to its customers. Partly as a result of its falling transportation costs, the firm was able to push down the prices of its goods, thereby disciplining the retail industry as a whole. For example, the Hudson's Bay Company was forced to respond to Baker & Co.'s pressure by cutting its prices faster than it otherwise would have done. All this helped to bring goods more cheaply to more people in Calgary and the Bow Valley than otherwise would have been the case. As Charles Conrad explained to a potential customer, J. E. Chipman, a partner in the Halifax

Ranche Co. operating west of Fort Macleod, "Our facilities for freighting with the low rate we have with the CPR (owing to the large quantity of freight we will be able to give them) will enable us to sell you goods and make 20 % and still the goods will be cheaper than you possibly can deliver them for."[51]

Such success required adapting to new transportation realities. Baker & Co. typically made savings on the Canadian Pacific by shipping particular goods to Calgary by the carload: a carload of hardware, two carloads of flour, a carload of dry goods, and so on. In this way, the firm obtained lower freight rates. For instance, in November 1884 Baker & Co. secured low carload freight rates by bringing in three carloads of A1 flour by the Canadian Pacific.[52] At the same time, the business environment in the town was beginning to improve. "A month ago business in Calgary was considered dull," reported the *Calgary Herald* on 12 November, "but this month has brought a welcome revival. A large trade is being done every day by King & Co. and I. G. Baker & Co.... There is considerable money in circulation and buying is brisk."[53] A week later, Baker & Co. announced in the *Calgary Herald* that it would soon receive $10,000 worth of new goods.[54]

Competition in merchandise sales presented a major challenge to John L. Bowen, Baker & Co.'s manager in Calgary. In early 1885, G. C. King & Co. slashed its merchandise prices, setting off a price war that destroyed almost all profits. Bowen promptly responded by cutting his prices.[55] He also reacted to the competition by expanding the coverage of Baker & Co.'s Calgary store. The store increasingly served as a distributor to small merchants in the town, that is, it sold at wholesale as well as at retail. By mid-1885, a significant portion of Baker & Co.'s store sales were made at wholesale, as were those of G. C. King & Co.[56] Still, retailing remained at the core of the Baker & Co. store's activities, as it sold goods to townspeople, ranchers, farmers, and Natives. The firm adapted to changing conditions by being pragmatic and experimental – it tried anything that offered profit.

Business Opportunities during the Saskatchewan Rebellion

With the outbreak of rebellion in Saskatchewan in March 1885, Baker & Co. positioned its stores in Calgary and Fort Macleod to take advantage of military-related opportunities. The Canadian troops required supplies, and in large quantities. Soon the Canadian Pacific was doing all the federal government officials expected, straining the resources of its vast network to move supplies from central Canada to Calgary. Existing military transport could not carry the load beyond Calgary, and so local wagon trains became the only hope of keeping the supplies moving between Calgary and Edmonton and the military machine running in Alberta. In the process, Calgary became an important supply depot for the troops as they marched deeper into rebel territory. Baker & Co. proved that it could change to meet the conditions of the rebellion. The troops' demand for supplies grew significantly as the conflict progressed. Under the intense pressure of the rebellion, Baker & Co. financed the acquisition of additional supplies from its own resources. As the troops penetrated the northern Alberta and Saskatchewan prairies, long lines of wagons including those of Baker & Co. carried supplies to the fighting men. Everyone knew that the troops could penetrate rebel territory only as far as supply lines allowed.

Providing the troops with supplies, while maintaining its stores in Calgary and Fort Macleod for essential civilian purposes posed a major challenge to Baker & Co. The combination of rebellion-time conditions and having the Canadian military as a customer in the prairies presented unusual hazards, against which Baker & Co. sought to retain profits. Early in the rebellion, the firm learned that when the military cancelled an order, the supplier could be hurt. On 1 April 1885, at its Fort Macleod store Baker & Co. contracted to provide supplies to the Canadian troops in Swift Current. The firm's wagon train with supplies for the troops reached a point halfway between Fort Macleod and Medicine Hat only to learn that the military had cancelled the contract. Baker & Co. had to wait for seven months to receive compensation for the money it spent to move the supplies out into the prairies and back to Fort Macleod again.[57]

At the very beginning, Baker & Co. made a fundamental decision about its strategy during the rebellion: to focus on what it could do best – sell and transport essential supplies. Using the Canadian Pacific, the firm brought goods from central Canada to Calgary quickly. One of Baker & Co.'s proudest accomplishments was in arranging for the carriage of supplies from Calgary to Edmonton. For instance, on 30 May the firm's ox-drawn wagons left its Calgary store for Edmonton with seventy thousand pounds of ammunition for the troops.[58] Other northward shipments for the military included groceries, clothing, boots, saddles, blankets, and sacks. Even in July, after the fighting had stopped, the troops needed supplies, and Baker & Co. responded by using its wagon trains to ship sixty-three thousand pounds of goods from Calgary to Edmonton.[59]

The Hudson's Bay Company's store in Calgary also provided a link between the Canadian Pacific and the military in Alberta during the rebellion. With steamboat transportation on the North Saskatchewan disrupted by the rebellion, the company's reliance on the railway to move supplies from Winnipeg to Calgary was of critical importance. In mid-April 1885, the company brought a carload of oats from Winnipeg to its Calgary store by rail and then used its ox-drawn carts to deliver the oats as feed for the horses of the Canadian troops.[60] At the company's store in Calgary, Richard Hardisty worked hard to provide the troops in the Calgary and Edmonton areas with groceries, clothing, and other essential items such as medical supplies. On 17 April, he sent an urgent request for supplies to Joseph Wrigley, the company's chief commissioner in Winnipeg:

> ... under separate cover you will find a requisition for Calgary, which I would like to have filled as soon as possible. We are, at present, kept pretty busy, having orders at any moment, and many things asked for. I am obliged to buy elsewhere from not having them in stock. I am sending for what I consider will be asked for by freighters and others who are employed in the transport of the troops [to Edmonton].[61]

Hardisty exhibited considerable management skill in co-ordinating the movement of supplies by the Canadian Pacific from Winnipeg to Calgary, and then by the Hudson's Bay Company's ox-drawn carts to the military in the Edmonton area.

The company's store in Calgary made a further contribution during the rebellion by providing payroll funds for the military. In particular, funds were needed to pay the troops in Calgary under the command of Major-General T. B. Strange. On Friday, 17 April Strange asked Hardisty to bring in the necessary payroll funds from the Hudson's Bay Company's Winnipeg office. Hardisty promptly sent a letter to Joseph Wrigley requesting the money:

Chapter 4: Rails & Marketing

> The General has told me to be prepared to have the money on hand for paying the troops and others when called upon. He is most anxious to throw all the business into our hands, and he does pretty much as I advise him. He has implicit confidence in my acting fairly with him.... I expect to wire for the money before this reaches you, as I wish to have it sent up by next Tuesday's train, so that I can be prepared when called upon. I will require $20,000 to begin on, as there will be some heavy payments to be made about a month after the men have been on service.[62]

Apparently, all went according to plan: the Canadian Pacific brought the payroll funds to the Hudson's Bay Company's Calgary store the following Tuesday.

As the rebellion dragged on, the company needed more transport to deliver supplies to the troops in the Edmonton area. The lack of transport sometimes forced Hardisty to use Baker & Co.'s ox-drawn wagon trains or other freighters to move supplies to the fighting men, but this hampered his flexibility. In the fierce competition for military-related business, he wanted to be as self-sufficient as possible.[63] Consequently, on 3 June he wrote to Joseph Wrigley with a request to employ the services of the Canadian Pacific to ship carts and horses from Winnipeg to Calgary for his use in freighting to Edmonton:

> I wired you last night to send us 50 carts, horses, and harnesses so that we can do our own freighting. It is impossible to get men just now to do any freighting for us under 8 cents per pound. It would be cheaper in the end to have our own teams.... We cannot afford to pay 8 cents per pound to Edmonton.... If need be, I can send a man down to look after the horses up from Winnipeg.[64]

How successful Hardisty was in his quest for carts and horses is unknown, but it was difficult to reject his argument that the Hudson's Bay Company would be better off to operate its own cart trains.

By the end of the rebellion in late June 1885, the Hudson's Bay Company's Calgary store, under Richard Hardisty's direction, had achieved a great deal in meeting the needs of the troops and had begun the conversion to peacetime merchandising. During the early weeks of the rebellion, Hardisty had told Joseph Wrigley that,

> it will be better for us to do all we can [to provide the troops with supplies] successfully, and the quicker this is done, the sooner we will be able to attend to our own affairs. No one will be in a fit state to do any business as long as this excitement is kept up and the quicker we assist to put it down the better for ourselves.[65]

Important as the rebellion was in framing the Calgary store's affairs, however, the local management continued to shape the institution. Indeed, management's willingness to seize regular business opportunities led to the store's growth.

Peacetime Business

The expansion that occurred during the rebellion was a special impetus to reorganization at the Hudson's Bay Company's store in Calgary. At the start of June 1885, James W. Thomson succeeded Angus Fraser as the manager of the store. Born in 1860 in Scotland, Thomson was a dynamic entrepreneur and quickly earned the respect of Richard Hardisty, who continued to oversee the company's operations in Alberta, including those in Calgary. Besides knowing what would sell, Thomson possessed an instinct for developing good relations with customers.

But for Thomson the future must have seemed uncertain at this time, presenting both opportunities and hazards. Like the Hudson's Bay Company's competitors in town, he did not know what would happen at the conclusion of the rebellion. A principal hazard lay in economic conditions, as the profitability of the company's Calgary store depended heavily on the business cycle. No one could be certain of the impact of the disappearance of the military market. Some observers felt that Calgary might fall back into stagnation. Although the end of the rebellion brought great uncertainties for Thomson, peacetime also meant continued opportunity to revitalize the company's store at Calgary. Adjusting to new market realities, he hoped to increase merchandise sales to ranchers, farmers, Calgary residents, and Natives.

Chapter 4: Rails & Marketing

Thomson wanted the store to continue to sell a diversified range of goods for a variety of markets. One of the opportunities he saw was in products for Native people, with an emphasis on blankets. His basic strategy in building a relationship with Natives was to offer them goods they needed especially when they received their treaty payments. Like Angus Fraser before him, Thomson initially obtained merchandise from the Hudson's Bay Company's Winnipeg warehouse by ordering by mail, not by making a trip to Winnipeg by the Canadian Pacific and personally selecting his goods. He relied on Joseph Wrigley to select and assemble the order. "Blankets are required for the Indian treaty payments," Thomson wrote to Wrigley in mid-September 1885.

> The payments at Blackfoot Crossing commence next week and I am sending an outfit down. The stock of blankets will hardly be sufficient to meet the demand there.... There is about $20,000 paid to the Indians in this vicinity and by having a stock on hand suitable for the wants of the Indians I hope to be able to secure a considerable portion of this sum.

Not only the Blackfoot but also the Peigans and the Bloods were potential customers. "Our blankets," Thomson added, "are greatly in demand by the Indians – Bloods and Peigans coming all the way from Fort Macleod for them."[66]

The sale of goods to ranchers and small traders reaffirmed Thomson's commitment to diversification. Among these customers was David McDougall, trader and rancher in Morley. "The order to be shipped to Morley" by the Canadian Pacific, noted Thomson, "is for David McDougall, trader there who has a large cash credit balance in our books and who is also one of our best customers."[67] Sales such as this one were essential for the Hudson's Bay Company's Calgary store's growth and development.

By placing orders by mail, Thomson ran risks. Not only did he chance unsuitable merchandise, he also exposed himself to possible criticism from customers who could not find in the company's Calgary store the goods they wanted. To avoid these problems and to assure himself of a large and well-selected stock, Thomson sought and received Richard Hardisty's permission to make a trip by the Canadian Pacific to Winnipeg and personally select his goods. Joseph Wrigley's approval was also needed. Consequently, Thomson wrote to him:

Chapter 4: Rails & Marketing

> As our stock is getting very low in several lines, especially dry goods, I would ask your permission to go to Winnipeg to select what is necessary as soon as possible after arrival of fall goods at depot. I have spoken to Mr. Hardisty as to the advisability of doing so and he thinks it desirable that I should go. I should certainly not take more than what would be absolutely required. Business has been satisfactory and I should like always to meet the wants of the customers.[68]

Presumably, Wrigley granted Thomson's request. Thus, by making a personal trip to the Hudson's Bay Company's Winnipeg warehouse, Thomson tried to satisfy the requirements of the local markets.

Thomson also hoped that Joseph Wrigley would aggressively seek contracts with the Canadian government to provide the Mounted Police and Natives in the Calgary area with supplies. How much money the Hudson's Bay Company put into supplies delivered to the Mounted Police under contract is unknown. But between July 1885 and June 1886 the company received only $7,162 for supplies – especially farm implements and flour, but also bacon, tools, clothing, biscuits, and tobacco – delivered under contract through its Calgary store to the Blackfoot, Sarcees, Stoneys, Bloods, and Peigans, about one-fifth of previous year's sum.[69] As a result of this small revenue, the Hudson's Bay Company continued to compare unfavourably with its major competitor, Baker & Co.

Baker & Co. continued to pour substantial sums of money into Native and Mounted Police supply contracts. Between July 1885 and June 1886, the firm received $341,517 for supplies delivered under contract through its Calgary and Fort Macleod stores to the Blackfoot, Sarcees, Bloods, Peigans, and Stoneys, a marked increase over the previous year's revenue.[70] The firm's income from the Mounted Police supply contract was probably smaller but still significant. Among the goods Baker & Co. provided to the Natives were farm implements, tools, oats, hay, coal, beef, bacon, flour, tea, sugar, biscuits, clothing, and tobacco. Beef, however, remained by far the most important, accounting for about 97 percent of the value of the supplies. The bulk of the firm's beef came from its own ranch in the Fort Macleod area. Baker & Co. remained committed to raising its own cattle on this ranch as a way of lowering the cost of the supply of beef, but the firm's occasional cattle purchases at ranches such as the Walrond Ranche and the Maunsell Bros.' ranch also became important for success.[71]

Chapter 4: Rails & Marketing

At the Calgary store, manager John L. Bowen's practical knowledge of Baker & Co.'s various business activities afforded him significant opportunities in promoting the firm to the larger public. Like D. W. Davis, the firm's manager in Fort Macleod, Bowen was very much involved with public relations. He used Baker & Co.'s advertising resources to direct the image of the firm's store. Newspaper advertising became increasingly important as he tried to reach out to more customers. Just as Davis advertised in the *Macleod Gazette*, so Bowen placed eye-catching advertisements in the *Calgary Herald*. People in Calgary and the surrounding area could and should, the Baker & Co. store advertisements suggested, take advantage of the opportunity to purchase superior goods that had just arrived by Canadian Pacific from Montreal.[72] Bowen also made public appearances to keep Baker & Co. in the public's eye as a willing leader in the development of Calgary's economy. For instance, in July 1885, he became first vice-president of Calgary's newly established board of trade.[73] Bowen's attention to public relations and economic development served both the town and Baker & Co. well.

But although Bowen's favourable public relations helped give the American-owned Baker & Co.'s Calgary store a central presence in the marketplace, the firm's success in obtaining Native and Mounted Police supply contracts from the Canadian government generated a negative response in central Canadian newspapers. These unfriendly papers demanded "that the contracts be given exclusively to Canadian firms."[74] The decision lay with Prime Minister John A. Macdonald. He ignored the question of foreign ownership. The problem of Baker & Co.'s position as a foreign-owned firm in a nationalistic environment was relieved by Macdonald's decision to continue the government's policy of giving the Mounted Police and Native supply contracts to the lowest bidders.[75] Because Baker & Co. maintained its strategy of keeping its bids low and providing high-quality service, it continued to win supply contracts and to grow in strength in Alberta.

In Alberta, nationalistic pressures were offset by local support for Baker & Co. "I. G. Baker & Co.," wrote the *Macleod Gazette*,

> have always competed for these contracts with Canadian firms, but as their tenders have been lower than the others, they have been accepted. With regard to the carrying out of these contracts, as far as we have ever known they have given the best possible satisfaction.... There is no other firm in Canada which can put the transport on the road which they can.... There is still another thing. With the exception of some very few articles, I. G. Baker & Co. purchase all the goods for their several Canadian houses in Canada, and ship them over the Canadian Pacific road to their destinations.

Baker & Co.'s good relations with Alberta settlers was also an important factor. As the *Macleod Gazette* put it,

> ... to be sure the profits of the business go to the United States, but as far as we in the Northwest are concerned, that makes no difference. The money might as well go to Benton or St. Louis as to eastern Canada, and then no eastern firm would be as liberal with the settlers.[76]

The *Macleod Gazette*'s great confidence in Baker & Co. was vindicated: the firm did continue to provide excellent service. Among Canadian government officials as well as the people in the Calgary and Fort Macleod areas, the enterprise retained its reputation as a reliable, efficient supplier during the next half decade.

Above all, Baker & Co. helped Calgary become the pre-eminent commercial centre of southwestern Alberta. Of the business enterprises in Calgary, Baker & Co. was the most prominent, its activities the most complex, and its influence the most pervasive. The firm was one of the most important pioneers in building the foundation of the local economy – the economy that was so necessary for the emergence of the town of Calgary.

5

The Emergence of the Town of Calgary

Calgary emerged as an important Alberta town in the years 1883 through 1885. As late as the start of 1883, Calgary possessed only about one hundred inhabitants; but two years later it had become a commercial centre of one thousand, the largest town in the Bow Valley and southwestern Alberta. The arrival of the Canadian Pacific had changed the situation. When the line reached it in August 1883, Calgary possessed its first transcontinental rail connection. To increase traffic, the Canadian Pacific tried to attract settlers and mounted a nation-wide advertising campaign that portrayed southwestern Alberta as a Garden of Eden. Relatively cheap overland transportation became available. During the years 1883 to 1885, the cost of travelling from Winnipeg to Calgary was about $13.[1] Calgarians rejoiced in the Canadian Pacific. By far the greater number of Calgarians who were in the town by the time of the great fire of 1886 had arrived by the railway. The Canadian Pacific helped Calgary participate increasingly in far-flung networks of trade, investment, and finance.

Natural Advantages of Calgary

People came to Calgary and its region to take advantage of new opportunities. The possibilities of raising cattle and developing farms drew many into the Bow Valley. Initially, Calgary grew as a commercial centre exploiting natural resources in the surrounding area. The town owed its growth to many causes, but most importantly

Chapter 5: The Emergence of the Town of Calgary

to the control it exercised over the ranching and farming industries of the Bow Valley. Of great significance as well was the work of the Canadian Pacific. Through its control of the townsite – section fifteen – the railway both increased its private fortune and built up Calgary. A mini health boom attracted some people in the mid-1880s as they sought southwestern Alberta's relatively mild climate and natural beauty. With its chinook winds, Calgary had, its boosters observed, winters that were "not only agreeable but positively acceptable."[2]

The natural advantages of Calgary stressed repeatedly by local leaders were real. Calgary grew as a river valley town, at the confluence of the Bow and Elbow rivers. Although the rivers were not usable for navigation, they remained important as sources of fresh, clean water. The country directly south and north of the town was fairly easy of passage for wagons, and contemporary observers assumed that railways would eventually follow the wagon routes. The town's position on the Bow placed it on the path of the natural east-west line of communication in the area between the Blackfoot reserve and the foothills of the Rocky Mountains. As the editor of the *Calgary Herald* declared on 31 August 1883, shortly after the coming of the Canadian Pacific,

> Calgary has long been acknowledged as the great central point of the extensive fertile strip along the Rockies, extending from the Blackfoot reserve on the east to the mountains on the west…. But it will now assume a place of much more importance and become the greatest distributing point west of Winnipeg.[3]

The Grid

Early Calgary's physical design – the grid – provided for profits, speedy and efficient development, and urban growth. When the Dominion land surveyor W. F. King filed his plat for Calgary in January 1884, he determined the physical shape of the city for more than a century.[4] Making a city by laying out straight streets to cross at right angles and, in the process, creating a gridiron or checkerboard of fairly uniform urban blocks was not something new or unusual. Like the Greek and Roman planners of old, Canadian planners had long used the grid to design cities. As was the case with other prairie West towns, Calgary was gridded because that was seen as the most effective way to survey and divide urban land for rapid sale and gain.

In Calgary, the use of the grid delineated the transformation of Bow Valley land into real estate, a commodity whose main value was its market value. Very little land was removed from the market in the downtown area for public use. The only significant public space in Calgary in the 1890s was Island Park – Prince's Island, St. Patrick's Island, St. Andrew's Island, and St. George's Island – on the Bow River.[5] Rather than representing an environmentally sensitive approach, the grid was arbitrarily imposed on all kinds of topography in the city. For instance, it made no allowances for Calgary's meandering river topography. Stretching right to the riverbank, downtown streets then began again on the other side, a design that led to traffic difficulties. The grid reflected the freemarket economy, with no social regulations on land use.

Despite its social deficiencies, the grid provided for Calgary's physical growth. The drive for urban expansion was certainly expressed in the town's design. In adopting a strategy of urban growth, Calgary promoters were following in the footsteps of many late nineteenth-century prairie town builders. They did so in the hope of attracting the attention of outside investors, upon whom Calgary's future in part depended. Among the earliest outside investors were I. G. Baker & Co. and the Hudson's Bay Company. There were other investors and leading pioneers in the development of Calgary, each of whom played a significant entrepreneurial role: George Murdoch, harness and saddle maker; Isaac S. Freeze, general merchant; and Andrew D. Rankin and Alexander Allan, dry goods merchants.

George Murdoch

Harness and Saddle Maker

Believing that Calgary was about to become an important centre, many entrepreneurs flowed into town, buying lots and often acquiring land as well in the surrounding grasslands of the Bow Valley. Among those who purchased town lots and became early manufacturers was George Murdoch. An experienced harness and

Chapter 5: The Emergence of the Town of Calgary

George Murdoch (far right) at his tiny shop and home in 1883, harness and saddle maker who symbolized the transfer of technology from New Brunswick and Chicago to Calgary. (Courtesy of Glenbow Archives, NA-1728-1).

saddle maker, Murdoch symbolized the transfer of technology from New Brunswick and Chicago to Calgary in the early 1880s.

Born in 1850 in Paisley, Scotland, Murdoch at the age of four boarded a ship bound for New Brunswick. With his parents, he made the hazardous Atlantic crossing to Saint John.[6] After attending a local school, he learned the harness and saddle making trade in Chicago. Using what money he had saved from odd jobs, Murdoch started a small harness and saddle manufacturing business of his own in that city. A man with considerable technical skill, he emerged as a capable harness and saddle maker. Creative, and willing to accept risks in exchange for profits, he also demonstrated his entrepreneurial talent. But the Great Fire of 1871 destroyed his shop in Chicago.

Consequently, Murdoch re-evaluated his situation and returned to Saint John to begin again as a manufacturer of harnesses and saddles.[7] The financial rewards were meagre, but he was able to earn enough to support himself and his wife, Margaret Flood, whom he married in Saint John in January 1879. Because business over the next few years was poor, Murdoch decided to look for work

Chapter 5: The Emergence of the Town of Calgary

in western Canada. In March 1883, he left his wife Margaret and two children at home and departed for Winnipeg, where he went to work in a harnessmaking firm. But his low income made him restless and extremely anxious to strike out on his own once more. Leaving this firm at the end of April, he kept his eyes open for harness manufacturing opportunities farther west. Canada was a nation in motion, and the Bow Valley exerted a strong lure for many in search of a fresh start in life. In Winnipeg, Dr. Brunskill talked with George Murdoch and convinced him to visit Calgary. During this time, Margaret assisted her husband George. Having brought money into their marriage, she provided him with financial support as he continued to struggle for a foothold in the production of harnesses and saddles.

After travelling by train to Maple Creek, the end of track, Murdoch went on by ox-drawn wagon, reaching Calgary on 13 May, three months before the coming of the Canadian Pacific.[8] The move proved to be beneficial for him, for it meant better business opportunities. Making Calgary his lifelong home, he began harness and saddle making operations on a lot in Calgary Bottom west of the Elbow. Located near Baker & Co.'s original store, the site provided Murdoch with the space required to begin work. Starting in a tent, he immediately secured two jobs repairing harnesses and saddles. "Charge like the mischief," he wrote in his diary, "as a dollar is handled here like 25 cts at home."[9] The cost of living in Calgary was high – Murdoch paid one dollar for five loaves of bread. On 16 May he began construction of a harness and saddle manufacturing shop, using logs and boards he had purchased at Major James Walker's Bow River Mills, the town's first sawmill. The building, twelve by twelve feet, sheltered Murdoch's leather, sewing machines, and hand tools, as well as Murdoch himself before he built a house. Thus, he became the first harness and saddle maker in Calgary.

Calgary offered a budding manufacturer like Murdoch a great deal. "Calgary bottom," he noted, "is the finest natural town site I ever saw."[10] Virtually each day brought new discoveries. "The view of the Rockies," he wrote, "is beautiful tonight. They seemed about ten miles off. They are 45."[11] With the arrival of the Canadian Pacific in mid-August 1883, the town had railway connections to leather and other raw materials, as well as to regional markets for finished goods. Calgary and the surrounding area possessed another significant asset: ranchers, farmers, and local citizens who needed

Chapter 5: The Emergence of the Town of Calgary

Murdoch's manufacturing skills and were willing to buy his products. Besides continuing to do repair work, he made new saddles and harnesses. Murdoch's business was a success from the beginning. Even though the market for harnesses and saddles was small from time to time in late 1883 and early 1884, Murdoch's shop enjoyed modest but gradually rising profits. To handle his increasing business, he made an addition to the Calgary Bottom shop in October 1883.[12]

But not even this addition gave Murdoch room enough to keep up with his expanding trade. In mid-January 1884, he began looking for land upon which he could build a larger shop. Within a few days, Murdoch acquired two lots in section fifteen, on Atlantic Avenue opposite the Canadian Pacific's freight sheds.[13] In mid-March, he moved his shop from Calgary Bottom to his land on Atlantic Avenue and immediately started to enlarge it. Construction of the building proceeded quickly and, before the end of the month, Murdoch was manufacturing leather goods in the new shop.[14] He purchased tanned leather as well as finished goods from wholesale leather dealers in Winnipeg – C. H. Field & Co., W. N. Johnston, and E. J. Hutchings – who then shipped them to Calgary by the Canadian Pacific. While he usually sent his orders for raw materials and finished products through the mail to Winnipeg, Murdoch occasionally made a buying trip to the city.[15] In the absence of a bank in Calgary, he opened an account in the Bank of Nova Scotia in Winnipeg and wrote cheques on it. Perhaps he also borrowed money from the bank as the need arose; certainly, he could offer his shop and leather goods as collateral.

By this time, Murdoch was making a variety of leather goods, including harnesses, saddles, bridles, chaps, and whips. Using hand tools and sewing machines, he produced high-quality goods. Nearly all of these products were sold in Calgary and the surrounding region. Murdoch had numerous customers.[16] A number of these were farmers such as James Barwis. Others were ranchers, like Wilfred F. Rivers and Colonel Francis DeWinton. Murdoch sold many of his goods to Calgarians, ranging from J. H. Cummings, who owned a livery stable, to George C. King, the general merchant, to the Mounted Police. Reaching beyond Calgary to other communities, Murdoch sold his products to David McDougall in Morley and Dr. Robert G. Brett in Banff. Since Murdoch became heavily involved in selling goods to the Blackfoot, it is worth noting that he used a Blackfoot dictionary to learn their language. Murdoch succeeded in establishing control over his increasingly complex operations through the adoption of an adequate bookkeeping system.[17]

During the Saskatchewan Rebellion, Murdoch took advantage of new business opportunities. To fight the rebels, the Canadian troops required a variety of leather products, from saddles to harnesses to bridles. Murdoch's response – the manufacture of leather goods especially for military purposes – helped to supply the advancing troops. By the end of the first week in April 1885, he had provided Major George W. Hatton and his men in Calgary with three saddles as well as other leather products such as harnesses.[18] The rebellion-time demand for these goods continued, and Murdoch acted quickly to assist the military. "Working all day at military stuff … worked after supper a couple of hours," he wrote in his diary on 16 April.[19] Three days later, at nine o'clock in the evening, Sam Steele of the Mounted Police, who commanded Steele's Scouts during the rebellion, suddenly placed an order for bridles. "I went back to shop and made 3 bridles. House at 7 a.m.," wrote Murdoch next morning, after having toiled all night to produce them.[20] During the rest of April, as well as in May and June, Murdoch continued to seize rebellion-time opportunities in the burgeoning field of saddles, bridles, and harnesses.

Before long, Murdoch needed help in operating his shop, so he searched for trustworthy employees with experience in the harness and saddle making business. But skilled workers were not easy to find in Calgary. Jim Clute worked for Murdoch as a harness maker for a number of months in 1884 and 1885 before leaving Calgary for Idaho.[21] From his wide contacts in business circles, Murdoch learned that Henry Hutchinson might be available for the position of harness maker. By February 1885, Hutchinson was working in the shop, but at the end of April he left for Fort Macleod to start his own harness making business.[22] In early June, Murdoch filled the vacancy by hiring James Lambert.[23] With the expansion of his operations, Murdoch hired James Olding as a harness and saddle maker in the fall of 1885.[24] By now, Murdoch was well enough established to arrange for his wife Margaret and their two children to come from Saint John, New Brunswick to join him in their new home in Calgary.

Despite the growth of his business Murdoch, like many beginning businessmen, was cash-poor. The expansion of his shop came largely out of retained earnings – profits provided funds for development.

Chapter 5: The Emergence of the Town of Calgary

Anxious to continue to expand his operations, Murdoch sought more funds than retained profits alone could supply. He occasionally borrowed from friends and family, particularly as a way to obtain working capital. During the three years ending in January 1886, Murdoch borrowed a total of $1,730 from his wife.[25] This helped him to secure adequate financing to develop his harness and saddle making business.

Isaac S. Freeze
A General Merchant

While the manufacturing of such products as harnesses and saddles fuelled Calgary's early development, commerce remained the prime engine of economic growth. As more people moved into the town, many of them coming as immigrants and passing through the Dominion Immigration House near the Canadian Pacific station, commercial activity continued to be the most powerful force driving the Calgary economy. General merchants were the key group in the town's commercial world. Isaac S. Freeze's career was typical of those entrepreneurs who became early-day general merchants. Born in 1847 in Penobsquis, King's County, New Brunswick, Freeze attended a local school.[26] Later, he secured a job teaching school in the Moncton area.[27] About that time he married Evelyn Lewis, who was also a schoolteacher there. After leaving the teaching profession, the couple moved to Anagance, King's County, where Isaac Freeze opened a general store. But the economic depression of the mid-1880s in New Brunswick destroyed his hopes for growth in Anagance.

Seeking greener pastures, the energetic and venturesome Isaac Freeze sold his store in the spring of 1883 and headed off by train across the continent to the prairie West. The Canadian Pacific carried him from Pembina via Winnipeg to Medicine Hat, the end of track, from where he rode to Calgary on a horse-drawn wagon. Isaac kept in touch with his wife Evelyn back home by letters until she was able to join him a year later. Freeze persuaded John G. Vanwart, his friend from New Brunswick, to team up with him in starting a general store, on the east bank of the Elbow River, in mid-June.[28] No one knew exactly where the Canadian Pacific would

Chapter 5: The Emergence of the Town of Calgary

locate the townsite, but Freeze and Vanwart hoped it would be east of the Elbow. Each partner invested $1,000 in the small store. Isaac Freeze did not have much capital, but he had a good business head, lived modestly, and was confident. We "will build small store on as cheap a scale as possible," Isaac wrote Evelyn. "It is hard to tell how I will succeed out here but have hopes that I may succeed. At any rate shall work along safely. The town, wherever it will be, will soon be located and then will have better idea of matters."[29]

Within two weeks, Isaac Freeze returned to Winnipeg to purchase a general stock of goods worth about $3,000 on which the freight

Isaac S. Freeze in late middle age, the creative force behind the development of his general store. (Courtesy of Glenbow Archives, NA-4298-2).

charges came to nearly $1,000, while Vanwart erected the store. The cost of the store building, eighteen by twenty-four feet, was about $500. Freeze naturally hoped that the Canadian Pacific would soon be completed all the way to Calgary. Without the completion of the line between Medicine Hat and Calgary, the freight charges would remain very high. Isaac Freeze thought it best to become established in the general store trade before bringing Evelyn to Calgary, but he had no doubt that she would like the town. "If the business pays," he wrote his wife, "I will want you to come out in spring" to Calgary. "You would like this place. It is so nicely situated and cool even in the hottest of weather with plenty of shade trees along the river. Excellent fishing, so grand place for sports."[30]

Once back in Calgary, the cultured Isaac Freeze remained extremely optimistic about the future of the town and of his general store business. "Here we have the highest order of intelligence," Isaac told Evelyn. "Here most everyone is well educated and full of energy and push and mostly young men."[31] The coming of the Canadian Pacific all the way to Calgary in mid-August 1883 offered Isaac Freeze and other local businessmen a direct link to Winnipeg. Writing to Evelyn on 12 August, Isaac observed that "the C.P.R.

Chapter 5: The Emergence of the Town of Calgary

train came in yesterday afternoon about 5 p.m. There was a big crowd of men laying down the sleepers and rails. It looked very pretty to see so many of the steel sledges that they use driving in the spikes glistening in the sunshine.... There will be a big rush here in a few days, lots of ladies coming in now."[32] The men far outnumbered the women in Calgary, but with the arrival of the railway the imbalance of males and females became less pronounced. In order to accommodate the growing number of women and to maximize opportunities for sales, Freeze and Vanwart diversified their general store's product mix by offering a broader range of merchandise, including more lines of ladies' clothing.

By mid-August 1883, one of Freeze's dreams had come true. The completion of the Canadian Pacific to Calgary had created a foundation for more reasonable freight costs and further economic growth. The increasing demand for the goods Freeze and Vanwart's general store carried – a wide variety of groceries, hardware, and clothing – drove up its sales. Sales in August came to more than $2,300, an encouraging sum.[33] By the end of September, the partners were selling at retail as well as at wholesale. By this time, their total sales since they had started at the end of July amounted to over $4,000. For this period, the store posted profits of at least $1,000.[34] This allowed the partners to make improvements on their store, including a new wooden exterior.

Sometime in October 1883, Freeze and Vanwart decided to dissolve their partnership. Vanwart took his son into partnership with him and together they opened a new general store in Calgary, while Freeze stayed in the old store.[35] Isaac Freeze envisioned only success. Trying to anticipate future needs, he ordered a carload of flour from Winnipeg. "I will have a carload of flour in this week, retails at $4.50 per 100 lbs.," Isaac wrote Evelyn at the end of October.[36]

Calgary continued to function as the service centre of the Bow Valley. Already there were twenty stores, ten hotels, four billiard halls, as well as six lawyers and four medical doctors. Nonetheless, some clouds appeared on the horizon. Development in Calgary almost came to halt, in part because the townsite had as yet not been surveyed. "Times will be dull here this winter on account of our town not being surveyed," Isaac predicted in his letter to Evelyn.[37] "Sales for the past week were only $88, pretty low," he reported at the end of November 1883.[38]

Far from discouraged, however, Isaac Freeze continued to take

Chapter 5: The Emergence of the Town of Calgary

advantage of new opportunities in the general store business in Calgary. An enterprising merchant and ardent booster, Isaac linked his and Evelyn's future with that of the infant prairie town. "You will be charmed with Calgary," Isaac told Evelyn. "I can see you now feasting on the beautiful scenery and admiring Nature's townsite for the West."[39] He spent much of January 1884 seeking a new location for his store in the new townsite – Canadian Pacific's section fifteen. By this time, the survey of the townsite had been completed. Canadian Pacific "lots will be on the market this week," Isaac wrote Evelyn on 5 January. "I don't know where to buy my lot. Some lots in what will become the best business portion of the city will be worth a good deal in time. Others will not increase in value very much. Wish I knew what part would turn out best."[40] By the end of the month, Freeze had purchased a lot in the heart of downtown Calgary, on Atlantic Avenue near the Canadian Pacific station. At the beginning of March, with his merchandise sales rising significantly, he arranged to have his store moved from the Elbow River to his new lot, paying the movers $55 for the job. "Stephen Avenue is the main street, but Atlantic Avenue is a good stand for a store. My sales last week were over $250 and I have been out of a good many articles, but expect them by next freight," Isaac wrote Evelyn on 9 March.[41] Not long afterward, Freeze increased the size of his store and made it more efficient in order to handle his growing operations.[42]

Isaac Freeze also was quick to erect a house on Stephen Avenue, not far from his store. He had enough confidence in his store's future to move Evelyn and their infant children – son Dio and daughter Edna – to Calgary. Their arrival in the new family home on 16 April 1884 meant a happy reunion. Happiness in the family was mixed with sadness, however. Edna had fallen seriously ill on the train while travelling to Calgary.[43] Sitting up with his sick daughter night after night, Freeze was too tired to do much business in his store during the day. On 19 April Edna died. Both parents were devastated by grief.

At about the time of Edna's death the market for Freeze's products picked up dramatically, and he was able to sell more groceries, dry goods, and hardware. To keep up with the growing demand for his products, Freeze replenished his stock by purchasing merchandise from Winnipeg wholesalers, including $500 worth of clothing from the firm Sanford, Vail & Co.[44] Besides being able to secure these goods on credit, Freeze seems to have had access to

Chapter 5: The Emergence of the Town of Calgary

I. S. Freeze Block on Stephen Avenue in 1890. From *The Dominion Illustrated*, Calgary Special, 28 June 1890. (Courtesy of Glenbow Library).

credit at the Bank of Nova Scotia in Winnipeg.[45] In turn, Freeze offered credit accounts to many of his customers in Calgary and the Bow Valley. For instance, in January 1885, he sold $293 worth of goods to Neil Macleod, a Calgary hotelkeeper, on credit.[46] Most farmers had money when their crops came in during the autumn months, but they depended on credit the rest of the year. Money was generally scarce, and Freeze often exchanged his groceries, hardware, and dry goods for farmers' crops and livestock.[47] Thus, through barter, he managed to dispose of some of his wares to rural customers who lacked the ready cash with which to make purchases. Freeze also was busy in his store selling goods to Native people, especially the tobacco that many of them wanted.[48]

By the spring of 1885, Freeze had "established a snug little trade," observed T. S. Burns and George B. Elliott.[49] Freeze did business as far away as Silver City, in the Rockies west of Calgary. Travelling by the Canadian Pacific to Silver City, he sold almost everything imaginable to prospectors there, sometimes receiving payment in gold dust. But Freeze continued to build up his trade in Calgary and the Bow Valley. The ads he ran in the *Calgary Herald* in the summer and autumn of 1885 reminded customers that he was offering low-priced goods at wholesale and retail.[50]

Competition heated up, as the presence of the Canadian Pacific brought more general store operators to Calgary. In the mid-1880s, Freeze's enterprise was just one of a number general stores in town. By the autumn of 1885, there were eight other merchants in the general store business. As a rule, rivalry played out along several dimensions, including service and the availability of credit. Good service created a trusting relationship between Freeze and his customers, and credit accounts helped to tie them to his store. Despite fierce competition, Freeze's establishment was prospering.[51]

By 1890, expanding markets and increasing profits made it possible for Isaac Freeze to erect the Freeze Block on Stephen Avenue and use it for his general store trade.

Specialization in Commerce

The growth of commercial activities made possible by the arrival of the Canadian Pacific and the development of agriculture in the Bow Valley caused significant changes in the Calgary business system. A more complex network of business transactions emerged and presented some opportunities for specialization in business enterprise. By the mid-1880s, a number of specialized commercial establishments were operating in Calgary, including two hardware stores, two drug stores, three bookstores, one furniture store, and one dry goods store.[52]

Rankin & Allan
Dry Goods Merchants

Individual entrepreneurs in specific fields of endeavour, such as Andrew D. Rankin and Alexander Allan in dry goods, illustrated how merchants successfully entered the new world of specialization in Calgary. Almost nothing is known about Andrew Rankin's early years, except that he was born in 1860 in Scotland.[53] Born in 1859 in Bucksburn, Scotland, Alexander Allan was educated in the Dyce Public School.[54] Both Rankin and Allan served apprenticeships in dry goods stores in Aberdeen in the 1870s before crossing the Atlantic to take a series of jobs in dry goods firms in Montreal and in the United States in the early 1880's.[55] In 1882, the two men went to Winnipeg, where they got positions in the dry goods department of the Hudson's Bay Company store.[56] With their mercantile aptitude and broad knowledge of the dry goods trade, they did much to advance the store's business.

Both men were young and ambitious. After working for the Hudson's Bay Company store in Winnipeg for about two years, Rankin and Allan broke away to form their own dry goods firm in Calgary in April 1884.[57] As partners in the firm Rankin

105

Chapter 5: The Emergence of the Town of Calgary

Rankin & Allan Block on Stephen Avenue near McTavish Street, c. 1888. (Courtesy of Glenbow Archives, NA-789-76).

& Allan, they depended on the earnings and marketing skills they had acquired over the years to get started. The mercantile and personal friendship of the two men became one of the pillars of their fortune. Located on Stephen Avenue opposite the Royal Hotel, their dry goods store was the first business enterprise in this line of trade in Calgary. Immediately there were dire predictions that the store would be a failure.[58] Some people thought that the local and regional markets were too restricted to permit specialization. From the very beginning, however, the venture was a success.

Aggressive entrepreneurs, Rankin and Allan used advertising to expand sales beyond Calgary to most of the Bow Valley. Their creativity helped bring sparkle and zest to their advertising. Selling at wholesale and retail, they adopted the one-price system, with the prices plainly marked on the items. Price was not a matter for negotiation. The partners offered a wide array of high-quality goods: men's and boys' ready made clothing, fancy goods, bed and table linen, blankets, carpets, oilcloths, curtains, and blinds.[59] Besides importing goods from the United States, the store also relied on domestic products. Initially, Allan made trips to Winnipeg to purchase goods for the firm.[60] As the business grew, he usually made two buying trips to Montreal, Toronto, and New York City each year, one for the spring trade and one for the winter trade.[61] Now people thought that Rankin and Allan were in the right place at the right time with this venture. As Burns and Elliott put it in the spring of 1885,

> [Rankin & Allan] are specialists in their line and from an intimate knowledge of their business they are enabled to select their stock and buy to the best advantage which is a benefit to their customers. They are attentive to their business, courteous in their dealings and are building up a safe and flourishing trade.[62]

Rankin & Allan was an innovative enterprise. To attract female customers, the firm launched a millinery department. Through their well-established business contacts in central Canada, Allan and Rankin recruited an experienced milliner there to take charge of the new hat-making unit in their Calgary store.[63] By cultivating female customers, the partners were able to expand the store's sales volume. In all parts of the store, the stock was kept fresh and clean.[64] The partners conducted business on a personal, face-to-face basis – they knew their customers by name. By the end of 1885, Rankin & Allan had emerged as one of the most successful dry goods firms in the prairie West. The success of the firm, reflected in its handsome quarters in a sandstone block on Stephen Avenue by 1890, helped give Calgary an aura of permanence and stability appreciated by many citizens.

The Movement for Incorporation

Already in early 1884, residents frequently complained about the failure of the Canadian Pacific's subsidiary, the Canada Northwest Land Company, to handle the problems of growth in the community. An incorporated company, it depended for income upon the sale of lots in the Calgary townsite. Yet the company's agent, W. T. Ramsay, lacked sufficient funds to make needed improvements, such as the establishment of a police service, the development of streets, the construction of a water system and a sewer system, the creation of a public market, and, especially, the organization of a fire department for the protection of capitalistic ventures that benefited the public good. Many people seemed to be in the land business, but the real estate boom that Ramsay hoped for did not arrive. Great immediate success eluded him.

At the same time, there was land speculation in Calgary as moneyed interests, and even ordinary citizens, snapped up town lots. Speculation cut across class lines. All speculators, whether poor or wealthy, hoped to make killings in real estate. Calgary did not froth with speculation at this time, but people did compete for choice lots, believing that land prices would rise and allow them to realize big profits on the lots they planned to sell.

Land values in Calgary spurted considerably, transforming individuals who were usually prudent into people expecting to

Chapter 5: The Emergence of the Town of Calgary

become rich. For instance, in 1885 a man purchased a lot on Stephen Avenue for $200. Five years later, he refused an offer of $5,000 for the same lot, thinking he would soon be offered a larger sum.[65] The harsh economic depression in the mid-1890s shocked Calgary speculators. As property values plummeted, many a fortune evaporated. "Property is very stagnant here," wrote Wesley F. Orr, real estate entrepreneur.[66] A number of speculators accepted failure; earlier, they had seen opportunity and put money into land, but now they lost their investment and lived with the results.

All the while, citizens revelled in a fondness for community, in a sense of mission, and in involvement in larger society. In January 1884, they began to call for incorporation of the town, seeing it as essential for progress. As the *Calgary Herald*, founded in August 1883 and the first newspaper in Calgary, remarked in March 1884, "if Calgary is to be in a fit state to meet this season's exigency of development the municipal machinery should be at once put in place and in motion. Concerted measures should be at once taken to place the town before the outside public in the most favourable light."[67]

This was true booster talk, and most local leaders favoured incorporation as a way to advance the town's future prosperity. A booster group emerged, bearing the name Civic Committee. By promoting the idea of incorporation, this organization sought to attract newcomers and capital, elements that could contribute to Calgary's stability and permanence. The members of the Civic Committee, elected at a public meeting on 14 January 1884, included lumber manufacturer James Walker, George Murdoch, and George C. King.[68] These men and their colleagues eagerly discussed the question of incorporation with Edgar Dewdney, lieutenant-governor of the Northwest Territories, during his visit to Calgary.[69]

As entrepreneurs, Murdoch, Walker, and King helped establish the economic character of Calgary and in many respects were beginning to shape the quality of urban life. In Calgary, there was a close alliance of civic-spirited capitalists and cultural leaders. Newspaper writers, architects, and musicians mingled with entrepreneurs. Before long, the movement for incorporation gained momentum, and by the third week of January a petition was circulating among the citizens. George B. Elliott, editor of the *Nor'Wester* and a local promoter speaking for those who supported the change, observed that "the great necessity of fire protection is admitted on all sides, and this has been one of the chief reasons why incorporation is asked for."⁷⁰ Because the town's population at this time was approximately one thousand people, the petition noted that Calgary easily met the territorial government's requirement that a town had to have three hundred or more residents. A large number of Calgary property owners signed the petition for incorporation, and on 25 January 1884 they sent it to Edgar Dewdney in Regina.⁷¹

Things did not go well, however. For a while, opponents appeared to have a chance. Dominion land surveyor A. W. McVittie and other property owners, some of whom were absentee land owners, in section fourteen east of the Elbow River tried to stop the movement for incorporation. These critics, instead of taking a long-range view of town development, complained that the value of their property east of the Elbow and far from the central business district would not rise in the near future.

But the *Calgary Herald* responded by saying that "if incorporation is good for any of us, it must certainly be good for Mr. McVittie. His property will increase in value as the town increases."⁷² George Murdoch and James Walker reminded critics that the Civic Committee had acted "in accordance with the ordinances of the Northwest Territories."⁷³ These and other supporters of incorporation placed particular emphasis on the need for a fire department, and they defined this issue largely in terms of the protection of private property and of the town's future development.

Recognizing that at least two-thirds of Calgary's residents supported the petition for incorporation, Dewdney approved the request. On 7 November 1884, he issued a proclamation incorporating the town.⁷⁴ In the first municipal election, on 3 December, the citizens elected George Murdoch as mayor. The men elected as councillors were Isaac S. Freeze; S. J. Hogg, a lumber merchant; J. H. Millward, a painter; Neville James Lindsay, a medical doctor (a recreational facility bearing Lindsay's name—a park— appeared later in downtown Calgary) ; S. J. Clark, a hotelkeeper; A. Grant, a hardware merchant; and S. N. Jarrett, an architect and building contractor.⁷⁵

Like many urban promoters on the prairie frontier, Murdoch, a leading spirit in the development of Calgary in the mid-1880s, combined private interests with community interests. Since his arrival in Calgary in May 1883, Murdoch had been very much involved in the economic, social, and political life of the community. He became a justice of the peace, police magistrate, as well as secretary of the Turf Club.[76] In addition to remaining active as a harness and saddle maker, he built up a small ranching business in the Nose Creek area. Prairie leaders such as Murdoch had confidence in themselves and in their towns, and their boosterism frequently reflected the growth of a new settlement in the Canadian West. In Calgary, Murdoch and others established a centre for the ranching and farming interests of the Bow Valley and southern Alberta. At the end of 1884, after being hurt by an economic depression in the summer of that year, Calgary still had a population of about a thousand, but obstacles to progress remained, especially the lack of rail connections to Fort Macleod and Edmonton.[77] Still, incorporation had increased faith that the young town's future might well include railway extension to the south and north.

Calgary's Early Government

On 12 December 1884, at the meeting of town council, Mayor Murdoch undoubtedly informed his fellow councillors that there was no money in the treasury.[78] To develop a financial base for Calgary, the council acted on his recommendation to establish reasonable property and licence taxes.[79] It also passed a whole range of by-laws designed to protect the town and its people, including an early one that provided for fire protection.[80] Others involved provisions for things such as police service, water distribution, the creation of a public market, the impoundment of stray animals, and sanitary regulations to guard the health of residents.[81] Initially, local development was financed mainly through funds derived from property taxes. Licences for businesses provided additional money for the town treasury.

Civic pride, a desire that their town win recognition as a part of Canada's urban network, motivated the first mayor and councillors of Calgary. As mayor, Murdoch worked hard to unite his town's citizens and create public confidence in town government. He envisaged the development of an orderly Calgary in which the people would seek to make their town a better environment in which to live and work. In an attempt to provide some basic urban services, he led council in improving street surfaces, filling the potholes, and making other decisions about public safety that allowed the town to function. On looking back over the twelve months of his administration at the end of 1885, Murdoch noted: "surmounted and overcame the most difficult things, such as ... making rough places smooth on Stephen and Atlantic Avenues."[82]

Despite Murdoch's attitude and actions, however, there were critics who claimed that the town was not well governed. They grumbled especially about property taxes and civic expenditures. "Over $3,000 has been incurred already for maintaining chiefly a large staff of officers," complained the *Calgary Herald* in February 1885,

> ... and the citizens do feel extremely annoyed over it. There is not a man with taxable property in town who is not alarmed at the prospect before him, and with good reason. Putting the population of Calgary at 1,000 souls it means a tax of $3 a head for every man, woman, and child in town.... It wants very little to get this town to petition the lieutenant-governor to withdraw its charter.[83]

The complaints about property taxes continued, but the grumbling never developed into a movement for disincorporation.

Certain problems caused increasing concern among the people of Calgary, however. For instance, citizens complained that the licence fees for saloons were not high enough.[84] With the passage of time, critics called for lower licence fees for draymen and watermen.[85] Relations between the town council and livery stable keepers became strained, due to what they considered excessive licence fees.[86] Concerned about budgetary matters, some town dwellers thought that the arrangement to rent premises for the town council at $20 per month was too costly.[87]

Over time, however, Calgarians were content to be led in the town council by a small group of prominent citizens who decided what was in the best interests of the community. There was an underlying consensus in the community that the broad powers of the town council, which were identical to those of other town councils in the Northwest Territories, including the right to tax property owners and businesses and to borrow money in order to support internal improvements, should be used to promote economic progress and secure social harmony. In local politics, this general pattern of consensus reflected a concept of a cohesive corporate society in the mid-1880s. Public statements emphasizing Calgary's civic responsibilities and its particular advantages and hopes drew on the theme of opportunity that was common in the booster mentality of many towns in the Northwest Territories.

Town government in Calgary, as in other towns on the urban frontier in the prairie West, tended to deal best with problems after a crisis or a brush with disaster. The threat of destructive fires was one of the dangers of town life. On 5 January 1885, a $900 fire destroyed a house on Atlantic Avenue as well as some of the possessions of the tenant, W. R. Roberts, a jeweller, who occupied it. "If the house had not been so far away from every other building in town," observed the *Calgary Herald*, "it is hard to guess what the consequences would have been. With the west wind blowing as it was then, if it had been the Royal Hotel which had caught, the whole town east of the *Herald* office would have been in danger."[88] Mayor Murdoch's first instinct was to persuade the town council to establish a fire-fighting force. By September 1885, a volunteer fire department had been organized, several town wells had been dug at principal street intersections in downtown Calgary, and a hook, ladder, and bucket corps had been formed.[89] Soon some equipment, including a fire engine, was purchased.[90] Despite the efforts of Murdoch and other promoters, accumulating the funding necessary to place the fire department in a position to protect the town and its population proved difficult, but enough was secured to keep the project from collapsing. Yet observers noted that the fire-fighting force was a far cry from the efficient one they hoped would emerge in Calgary. The town continued to rely on a poorly funded fire department.

Fortunately for Calgarians, disasters did not have to occur before the town council addressed other community issues in the mid-1880s. For example, Calgary promoters worked hard to secure the construction of a town hall. Since December 1884, the town government had lacked adequate quarters to function effectively. In the summer of 1885, the town council, led by Murdoch, ordered the erection of a new town hall, on McIntyre Avenue.[91] The town hall tower, one of the taller structures in Calgary, became an object of local pride. In addition, Calgary's civic leadership had the foresight to undertake a program of providing adequate streets, as well as a bridge across the Elbow near Fort Calgary called the Elbow Bridge.[92] The federal government agreed to aid the town in constructing a bridge across the Bow at the ferry on the Edmonton Trail, named the Langevin Bridge after Hector Langevin, the federal minister of public works. Before long, another bridge – the

Chapter 5: The Emergence of the Town of Calgary

Mission Bridge – was built across the Elbow in the Roman Catholic mission district. With better transportation resulting from these improvements by the late 1880s, businessmen were able to increase the scope of their operations.

Entrepreneurs co-ordinated their private actions through the Calgary board of trade, which was formed in the summer of 1885.[93] At the first annual general meeting, on 8 July, citizens elected James Walker as president; I. S. Freeze, S. J. Hogg, T. W. Soules (produce merchant), A. Henderson (medical doctor), A. Ferland (general merchant), James A. Lougheed (lawyer), and Andrew D. Rankin as council members; John L. Bowen as first vice-president; and E. R. Rogers (hardware merchant) as secretary-treasurer. In keeping with the general desires of the business community, in 1885 the board helped obtain a bonded warehouse and attempted to secure a more functional railway yard in Calgary.[94] Collective activity through the town government and the board of trade aided the growth of Calgary as well as the development of the Bow Valley.

Hamlets, Villages, and Settlers in the Bow Valley

From its founding, Calgary served as the dominant urban centre in the Bow Valley, and over the decades its success inspired the development of farms and ranches in the region. At the same time, the founding of hamlets and villages, all of which had close economic ties to Calgary, reflected the spread of settlement across the Bow Valley. In the mid-1870s, a hamlet appeared to the west of Calgary. Thirty miles away, on the north side of the Bow River, a young Methodist missionary John McDougall and his brother David started a mission, a general store, and a cattle ranch among the Stoney people in 1873.[95] John McDougall, who soon established a Methodist church, named the hamlet Morley, after the prominent British Wesleyan Methodist preacher, W. Morley Punshon.[96] Fertile and rolling, the Morley district was brought under agricultural production. From this beginning, Morley and the surrounding area grew slowly and provided a market for Calgary. The dream of a railway for Morley was realized when the Canadian Pacific arrived in September 1883, an event that speeded settlement in the community.

Improved transportation also spurred settlement elsewhere in the Bow Valley. Canmore, sixty-seven miles west of Calgary,

Chapter 5: The Emergence of the Town of Calgary

Sam Livingston in the 1890s, first farmer in the Calgary area and innovator whose use of a mechanical reaper and a threshing machine on his farm helped to thrust farming technology forward in the Bow Valley in the late nineteenth century. (Courtesy of Glenbow Archives, NA-152-1).

on the north side of the Bow, obtained the Canadian Pacific in May 1884. With that, the hamlet sprang into active life, and many improvements began to be made.[97] As a divisional point on the railway, Canmore became the home of a number of men needed to service the trains on a regular basis. James Conroy, a local entrepreneur, established a hotel for the Canadian Pacific employees. Soon, Quebec-born Joseph Chenier started a general store, known as J. Chenier & Co., in the community. The coal mining industry came to lie at the core of Canmore's development around 1891, when H. W. McNeill & Co., headed by American-born H. W. McNeill, opened a coal mine at the hamlet and began supplying Canadian Pacific trains between Medicine Hat and Kamloops with bituminous coal.[98] Before long, Canmore had well-established trade connections with Calgary. The Canadian Pacific sped foodstuffs and other commodities from Calgary to Canmore consumers. Calgary tapped its growing hinterland, drawing coal from the Canmore colliery. Coal long remained at the heart of Canmore. The hamlet incorporated as a village in February 1965 and as a town eight months later.

In the early 1880s, two agricultural settlements sprang up to the east of Calgary. Thirty-one miles downriver from Calgary, on the north side of the Bow, Major-General Thomas B. Strange established the hamlet of Namaka on the Canadian Pacific. Aided by his central Canadian and English friends, Strange formed the Military Colonization Ranch Company in 1881. Within a few years, he was successfully operating a large cattle and horse ranch in the Namaka area.[99] In 1883, ten miles downriver from Namaka, Victor J. Beaupré opened a general store in the hamlet of Gleichen on the Canadian Pacific.[100] Like ranchers in the Namaka district,

Chapter 5: The Emergence of the Town of Calgary

Operating Sam Livingston's threshing machine complete with a horse-power attachment in the late 1880s. (Courtesy of Glenbow Archives, NA-3981-1).

ranchers in the Gleichen area, including Felix A. McHugh, regularly used the railway to ship livestock to Calgary. Gleichen incorporated as a village in 1899. Namaka never incorporated as a village or town, and became a part of the rural municipality of Bow Valley in 1913.

During the 1880s, the Bow Valley became known as a fertile and productive region. Since the 1870s, farming and ranching had expanded and contributed to the development of the valley and the rise of Calgary. Settlers followed a strategy of diversified production as the most effective way to achieve growth. For instance, Sam Livingston, who started his farm on Fish Creek in the spring of 1875, just south of Calgary in the present Glenmore Reservoir area, experimented with a variety of crops, from grains such as wheat, barley and oats to vegetables like potatoes, carrots, and beets.[101] Born in 1831 in the village of Blessington, County Wicklow, Ireland, Livingston moved to the United States at the age of sixteen.[102] His career as a gold prospector began in 1849, when he went to California, and later he also looked for gold in British Columbia, Saskatchewan, and Alberta. Then he was active in freighting and trading in Alberta for a number of years before he became a farmer at Calgary. By 1885, Livingston had sixty acres in crops on his farm.[103] An innovator, he soon relied on new technology, including a mechanical reaper and a threshing machine.

Chapter 5: The Emergence of the Town of Calgary

In the late 1870s, irrigated farms appeared. The first irrigator, John Glenn, is credited as the first to settle at the hamlet of Midnapore south of Calgary, arriving in July 1875. Born in 1833 in County Mayo, Ireland, Glenn immigrated to the United States in 1849, eventually finding work on a ranch at Waco, Texas.[104] In 1861, he enlisted as a Confederate soldier in the Civil War, but during the conflict he came to oppose slavery, left the Confederate army, and joined the Union army. In the decade that followed the war, he prospected for gold in the American West and western Canada before moving to Calgary in search of farming opportunities. Sensing the agricultural possibilities of the Bow Valley, Glenn settled on land at the confluence of Fish Creek and the Bow, where he began the cultivation of the rich soil. In 1879, after selling his farm to the Canadian government, the perceptive Glenn homesteaded land farther west along the south side of Fish Creek at Midnapore, constructed irrigation ditches, and planted wheat, oats, barley, and vegetables.[105] By August 1883, he was experimenting with three varieties of wheat: Australian white, Canadian club, and Champlain.[106]

Irrigated farms produced abundant crops. As a successful irrigator, in September 1884 Glenn said:

> I have never failed in raising a good crop of wheat, oats, barley and vegetables of all descriptions ... and have also raised tomatoes and cucumbers every year in the open air. Of wheat I have averaged 37 bushels; oats 57 bushels; barley 71 bushels to the acre; and have some this year not behind that standard. Average yield of potatoes, on eight acres last year, was 225 bushels to the acre.[107]

By 1885, Glenn had fenced two hundred acres and had ninety acres in crops.[108]

John Glenn was not, however, the only settler in the Midnapore community. Others who came and stayed included English-born Samuel W. Shaw, who, together with his wife Helen and their eight children, arrived in 1883. Shaw, Midnapore's most prominent landowner and entrepreneur, developed a farm, operated a woollen mill, ran a general store, and encouraged the growth of educational and religious organizations.[109] John Glenn's success and the availability of cheap, fertile land fed Samuel Shaw's dreams.

Chapter 5: The Emergence of the Town of Calgary

The example of John Glenn also inspired new settlers to discover the agricultural potential of nearby areas to the south such as Pine Creek, and their success attracted others. One of the earliest farmers at the Pine Creek settlement was M. McInnes, a native of Ontario who started his farm around 1882. A 160-acre homestead, the farm brought prosperity to its owner. As McInnes observed in September 1884,

> The land in this district is a deep black loam, with clay subsoil, and well adapted for agricultural purposes; and there are large tracts of it yet unoccupied. Water is easily accessible anywhere, either in rivers, creeks or springs, and contains no alkali. I consider the advantage I possess in having good water for my stock is a great source of wealth to me.

Like other settlers in the Pine Creek area, McInnes, besides raising livestock, followed a policy of diversified cropping. "I consider it pays best to engage in mixed farming," he noted.[110]

About eight miles south of the Pine Creek settlement, at Okotoks on Sheep Creek, farmers brought additional acres of arable land into cultivation. Okotoks began on the Macleod Trail as a hamlet in 1880, when Kenneth Cameron settled on his farm there.[111] In Okotoks, Cameron was the first individual to grasp the challenges and opportunities presented by the lodging industry, as he established a stopping house on his farm a few years later. By 1884, other farmers had appeared in the Okotoks area, including Hannibal Clark, who possessed two oxen and had eight acres in crops.[112] In September of that year, a visitor to the Okotoks district observed that it contained "a number of settlers" and emphasized that he was "pleased with the evidences of energy and thrift – the hillsides and valleys being dotted here and there with herds of cattle and flocks of sheep, peacefully enjoying the balmy air, and growing fat upon the luxuriant and luscious grasses."[113] In the early 1890s, Okotoks became the home of entrepreneur John Lineham's saw mill and lumber business, as well as his Lineham Block.[114] Okotoks incorporated as a village in 1899.

High River, another village in the Bow Valley, was founded in 1881 and incorporated in 1901. Located on the Highwood River thirty-five miles south of Calgary, the community at first contained only ranchers. John D. Norrish, rancher and former Mounted

Policeman, promoted the settlement of High River. Possessing one hundred head of cattle and six horses by 1885, Norrish encouraged ranchers as well as farmers seeking a future to move to the High River area.[115] Like Norrish, other ranchers such as James McDonough turned their land into prosperous ranching enterprises.[116] McDonough possessed forty head of cattle and twelve horses, and had forty acres under cultivation.

The sizes and functions of river settlements in the Bow Valley varied, but most were little more than primitive centres offering some basic services. Few were incorporated or platted in the late nineteenth century. But they represented the beginnings of the urban tradition in the Bow Valley outside Calgary. By the mid-1880s, Cochrane had begun to emerge on the north side of the Bow River twenty-three miles west of Calgary as a ranching centre. Named for Quebec Senator Matthew H. Cochrane, the hamlet of Cochrane lay on the main line of the Canadian Pacific Railway and was incorporated as a village in 1903.

Local ranchers such as E. G. Jenkins and G. E. Goddard, manager of the Bow River Horse Ranch, general storekeeper James Johnson, and the Canadian Pacific were committed to keeping the railway's station at Cochrane and successfully resisted Thomas B. H. Cochrane's attempt to have it moved three miles west to Mitford.[117] "At the present location [Cochrane], we are doing a considerable business with ranchers, and, as you know, this business is of a permanent nature and likely to increase," wrote J. Niblock, assistant superintendent of the Canadian Pacific's western lines.[118] As ranchers raised more cattle and horses and brought some land under cultivation to grow oat crops and feed them during the winter months, Cochrane grew.

All this economic growth was not accomplished without the help of creditors. The critical role of credit in financing economic development in Calgary and the Bow Valley gave rise to financial services. A diverse and responsive banking sector – private banks and chartered banks – was an important strength of the local and regional economies in the late nineteenth century.

6

Creating Banking Services

As Calgary and the Bow Valley moved through the Second Industrial Revolution, institutional rearrangements under Canadian capitalism reflected a complex blend of the old order with the new. Before 1885, commercial banks were non-existent in the region, and old, informal private credit networks made an extremely important impact on the local and regional economies. The historical record shows that these credit networks remained significant in financing business in the last half of the 1880s and 1890s and into the twentieth century. But with the advent of new commercial banks in 1885, businesses in Calgary and the Bow Valley came to depend heavily on bank credit.

Calgary developed as a banking centre for the next century and beyond. Banking success from the 1880s to 1900 nourished commerce and manufacturing in the city as well as agriculture in the countryside, all the while reinforcing the interconnections between the Calgary and Bow Valley economies. Broadly viewed, the emerging field of banking in the city – with its attendant risks, responsibilities, and rewards – was much the same as that in many other successful frontier communities in the Canadian West.

I. G. Baker & Co. as a banker, three private banks, and two chartered banks all were willing to risk fairly deep involvement in Calgary and the surrounding area. Carrying out their functions efficiently, these pioneers of banking did not withdraw their services on the first encounter with adverse conditions. Instead, they persisted for some time. But the two chartered banks – the Bank of Montreal and the Imperial Bank of Canada – stand out; they are still in Calgary today. There were a number of bad and doubtful

Chapter 6: Creating Banking Services

loans. The late nineteenth century was a risky time for Canadian banks as well as for other businesses, a period of striking ups and downs in the business cycle. Downturns in the economy increased the number of bad loans. An economic depression in the mid-1880s shut down a number of businesses in Calgary and the Bow Valley, and a very serious depression hurt many business enterprises in the region a decade later. With their persistent entrepreneurship and their large resources, however, the Calgary branches of the Imperial Bank of Canada and the Bank of Montreal survived the 1880s and expanded during the 1890s and beyond to become regional businesses of great repute.

In some other new western Canadian communities, the chartered banks did not do so well. For instance, for the Bank of Montreal's Portage la Prairie branch, which was still trying to establish itself, the results of the depression in the mid-1880s were disastrous. By June 1884, this branch was closed.[1] But in other new centres, such as Winnipeg and Regina, the Bank of Montreal's branches survived despite hard times.

Informal Private Credit Networks

In the pre-1885 Calgary and Bow Valley economy, many families struggled every day to make ends meet, often standing desperately in need of financial assistance. When unemployment, illness, or injury disturbed the balance between income and expenses, families were forced to look for money. In these circumstances, boarders could be taken in, children could work and bring home their earnings, and savings could be effected through smaller meals, but frequently it was impossible to purchase merchandise, acquire land and livestock, put in a crop, or start a new business without credit.

General merchants in Calgary, especially I. G. Baker & Co., but also G. C. King & Co., played a key part in the evolution of private credit networks. Between 1883 and 1885, Baker & Co. as a banker made short-term loans, usually for ninety days, to people such as George L. Fraser, a Calgary confectioner; Victor Beaupré, storekeeper at Gleichen; Sheep Creek farmer Henry J. Carroll; and the owners of the Mount Royal Ranche on the Ghost River.[2] These loans, usually carrying an annual interest rate of about 12 percent, were secured by chattel mortgages – mortgages on livestock in the case of ranchers and farmers. The size of the loans ranged from $100 to $300. The close ties between Baker & Co. and farmers and ranchers offer an excellent example of the importance of agriculture to Calgary's economy. As the Calgary and Bow Valley economies grew in size and complexity, the credit networks widened. In the mid-1880s, there were in Montreal, Toronto, and Winnipeg a number of wholesalers, part of whose business lay in supplying Baker & Co. and other Calgary firms with goods on credit.[3]

In a community with no banking system, informal private credit networks performed several valuable functions. They made a significant contribution to the funding of trade in Calgary and the Bow Valley in an era when money was scarce. Credit also helped to bring into use financial resources that otherwise might have remained idle. Finally, the availability of credit resulted in an increasing total production of goods and services in the town and the surrounding region.

Private Banks

Private and chartered banks came to represent an important new source of credit available to businesses in Calgary and the Bow Valley. In snowball fashion, the pools of money available to business enterprises grew larger year by year. One early milestone was the emergence of private banks, which began in 1885 and took small steps forward into the early 1890s. A second milestone was the appearance of chartered banks, which started in 1886, and then surged ahead over the next decade and a half. The private banks operated as unincorporated banks and possessed considerably less capital than the chartered banks, but they were at the same time connected to a network of chartered banking services. Organized as partnerships, three private banks appeared in Calgary in quick succession: Lafferty & Smith, LeJeune, Smith & Co., and Lafferty & Moore. Like the private banks in many other prairie West urban centres, the earliest one in Calgary established itself before the coming of chartered banks and played a pioneering role in supplying bank credit.

Chapter 6: Creating Banking Services

Lafferty & Smith

The first of the private banks, Lafferty & Smith, opened its doors to the public in Calgary in April 1885.[4] This business was a partnership of James D. Lafferty and Frederick G. Smith, the two driving forces in bringing commercial banking to the town. Recognized as entrepreneurial leaders in the town, Smith and Lafferty were risk takers and drawn to the challenge of extending credit to a wide range of urban and rural businesses. Smith was born in 1855 in Port Hope, Ontario, where he attended Trinity College School. In 1872, he began his career as a clerk in a branch of the Montreal-based Merchants Bank of Canada in Lindsay, Ontario.[5] He worked for this chartered bank for nine years in Ontario, serving as a teller in Berlin, Lindsay, and Toronto, and finally as an accountant in Owen Sound from 1879 to 1881. Striking out on his own, in 1882 Smith joined R. Hepburn and G. L. Irwin in opening a private bank in Regina. The new firm, Hepburn, Irwin & Smith, made only limited progress, and it disappeared at the end of 1883. Undaunted by his lack of success, Smith reorganized his firm as F. G. Smith & Co. at the beginning of 1884 and as Lafferty & Smith in early 1885 in Regina. In this latest venture, a new partner, James D. Lafferty, a medical doctor, joined Smith.

James Lafferty's background was remote from the banking field, but he was the most crucial person in convincing Smith to remain in the private banking sector. Born in 1849 in Perth, Ontario, Lafferty enrolled in the Royal College of Physicians and Surgeons of Queen's University, Kingston, from which he graduated in 1871.[6] In that year, he opened a medical office in Perth. Lafferty's initial foray into medicine proved encouraging. He continued his medical studies at the Ward Island Hospital in New York City in 1872 and 1873. After returning to Ontario, he practised in Pembroke until 1881, when he went to Winnipeg to serve as a surgeon in the Canadian Pacific Railway. The railway transferred him to Regina in 1883, and then to Calgary two years later.[7] In deciding to go into banking while maintaining his medical practice, Lafferty chose to commit his money and his managerial talents to Frederick Smith's fledgling bank. Believing that Smith was an astute businessman, he was optimistic about the bank's future.

In early March 1885, Frederick Smith travelled by train from

Chapter 6: Creating Banking Services

Regina to Calgary to set up a new branch for Lafferty & Smith.[8] Smith and Lafferty had a vision of creating a small bank in Calgary and realized that they would have an excellent opportunity to build a banking business as trade in the town expanded. They criss-crossed the town in search of new business, and their work involved not only greeting prospective customers but also offering an attractive package of services. After having established the Calgary branch, Smith returned home on 19 April to continue to run the bank's Regina office. Lafferty & Smith began operations in Calgary toward the end of April in rented quarters in a frame building next to the post office on Stephen Avenue.[9]

Thomas N. Christie, an experienced banker, became Lafferty & Smith's first manager in Calgary, a position he held until 1887. Born in 1855 in Melbourne, Ontario, Christie began as a clerk in the Toronto-based Royal Canadian Bank.[10] He worked his way up the ladder in this bank, and by 1882 he had moved on to join the staff of the Ontario Bank in Toronto. In that year, Christie left the Ontario Bank for Regina and, by early 1885, was working for Lafferty & Smith there. In March, Christie relocated to Calgary to take charge of Lafferty & Smith's daily operations. From the beginning, Christie got along well with James Lafferty and Frederick Smith, who had general supervision of the affairs of the firm in Calgary. Although Lafferty continued to give most of his time to his medical practice in Calgary, he devoted some of his energies to his banking business in the town.[11] Lafferty's wife Jessie, who was born in Carleton Place, Ontario in 1850 and who joined the firm in 1885 as a partner, shared the responsibility of running the bank, making her one of Calgary's earliest women in business.[12] How much capital Frederick Smith and James and Jessie Lafferty contributed to the partnership is unknown, but under the terms of the partnership agreement the three partners likely shared in the profits and losses of their firm in proportion to their respective investments.

With a good rail connection between Regina and Calgary, it was possible for Frederick Smith to pay a quick visit to the bank's Calgary office whenever necessary.[13] Strongly committed to its growth, he was the guiding hand for the branch in Calgary. In his lifetime, Smith was given credit for playing a major role in creating and developing the bank's business in the town and its region.[14] Indeed, he helped make Lafferty & Smith a force to be reckoned with.

Frederick Smith, James Lafferty, Jessie Lafferty, and Thomas

Chapter 6: Creating Banking Services

Christie led their private bank in Calgary into a period of significant growth and prosperity. By 1886, at the close of its first full year of operations, Lafferty & Smith, with its head office in Regina and a rising branch at Calgary, had set up new branches in Edmonton and Moosomin, Saskatchewan. In 1888 George Henry Ham, author of the book *The New West*, noted that Lafferty & Smith was among the banks in Canada that was "showing good profits."[15]

Lafferty & Smith was an institution whose historical rise to prominence in Calgary and other parts of the prairie West exemplified in microcosm the importance of private banks in the late nineteenth century. Its early founding, growth, and diversification took place in an era of private banking, when entrepreneurship could thrive. Lafferty & Smith experienced substantial growth in the mid- and late 1880s as it followed a policy of developing a diversified loan portfolio. The bank extended its interests beyond businesses in Calgary into diverse areas such as ranching and farming in the Bow Valley. Lafferty & Smith was the only bank in Calgary until October 1886, but after that date it faced competition from two chartered banks in the town: the Imperial Bank of Canada and the Bank of Montreal.[16] Making bank loans became an increasingly competitive business.

Lafferty & Smith, however, continued to act as an unincorporated private bank. Such institutions, operating without charters from the federal government, possessing no note issuing privileges and, unaffected by legislative control of interest rates, were fairly common in the prairie West before 1900.[17] Like other private banks, Lafferty & Smith had the advantage that no minimum capitalization was required for it to start business and the added advantage of no government restrictions on its loans and deposits. It could do a flourishing business, as long as it could maintain public confidence.

Thomas Christie took up his duties as manager in Calgary in the fourth week of April 1885, when he gathered the supplies needed by the bank.[18] By that time, the bank had moved into its quarters on Stephen Avenue. When Lafferty & Smith opened its doors to the public, it offered all the usual financial services: it provided a place of safekeeping for the deposits of its customers, made loans to them, and processed their cheques. To attract customers, the bank periodically ran advertisements in newspapers. From the beginning, a careful approach to the business of banking guided the conduct of Thomas Christie. This basic soundness served the bank well.

The new Lafferty & Smith bank benefited greatly from its ties to the Bank of Montreal from the time it opened for business in Calgary. Making loans to customers in Calgary and the Bow Valley demanded more money than Lafferty & Smith could provide. The bank sought local and regional deposits to finance its lending operations. But while it collected considerable sums by paying attractive interest rates to customers on their deposits, it was still short of funds. To ease capital shortage problems, the bank initially borrowed money from the Bank of Montreal's branch in Regina as well as from the Imperial Bank of Canada in Toronto. By the spring of 1887, it was securing funds from the Bank of Montreal's newly opened Calgary branch. At the same time, the Bank of Montreal in Calgary held a substantial deposit from Lafferty & Smith. R. G. Dun & Company, the credit-rating agency, considered Lafferty & Smith worth between $20,000 and $40,000, a relatively small amount, but this nevertheless helped to inspire confidence in this private bank's stability.[19]

A. D. Braithwaite, manager of the Bank of Montreal in Calgary, learned that in addition to the strength of Lafferty & Smith itself, its owners as individuals outside the business were in a good position. James Lafferty was worth $15,000, his wife Jessie $8,000, and Frederick Smith $5,000.[20] Braithwaite felt that a key to success for Lafferty & Smith lay in Frederick Smith and Thomas Christie's extensive previous experience with chartered banks in Ontario. Certainly, he believed that with this background Smith and Christie "had the requisite drilling in the everyday routine of banking." Most important for the future, Braithwaite wrote, "I have a very high opinion of Mr. Smith, who is a shrewd, close businessman and who I have always found very straightforward & honourable privately."[21] Prospects for Lafferty & Smith in Calgary were bright.

From the outset, Lafferty & Smith aided economic development in Calgary and the Bow Valley by increasing credit. The region served by the bank did not remain static in the mid- and late 1880s. During this time, Calgary grew significantly as improvements in transportation and communication integrated ever more of the surrounding area into the economic life of the town. The improved transportation provided by the Canadian Pacific stimulated business in general and thereby augmented deposits and demand for loans at Lafferty & Smith. At the same time, Calgary's trade area expanded. The town's merchants and manufacturers gradually extended their influence over the commerce of a broad section of the Bow Valley. Some of the region's products, especially cattle, entered national,

Chapter 6: Creating Banking Services

British, and American markets.[22] As business enterprises based in the town became more involved in this wider trade, Lafferty & Smith grew.

In the mid- and late 1880s, Lafferty & Smith was closely linked to the ranching industry. As the bank said in its newspaper advertisement, "Special attention given to advances to stockmen and ranchers."[23] Livestock raisers in the Bow Valley took advantage of the recent improvements in transportation and communication to steadily expand the production of cattle. While the growing volume of cattle produced larger profits, it also created a greater need for bank credit. Ranchers required much more capital to purchase and raise cattle. Lafferty & Smith took its first steps into the financing of the livestock industry by making loans to small borrowers. The ranks of the small livestock raisers who borrowed money from Lafferty & Smith included William B. Wyllie, who had a ranch in the Calgary area. Lafferty & Smith also pursued the business of larger ranchers, such as Thomas B. H. Cochrane at Mitford and Thomas Lynch at High River. The size of the short-term loans, which carried an annual interest rate of 24 percent for small ranchers and 12 percent for larger ones, varied from $300 to $10,000.[24] They were secured by livestock and ranch equipment.

Agriculture in the Bow Valley had begun to change by 1886. It was more diversified, and somewhat more dependent upon grain crops. By this time, it also was bringing greater prosperity to the region. The increase in farming was the most important example of this change. Like so many other things, the story of farming in the Bow Valley was tied to private banking. Farmers needed credit to buy equipment. Lafferty & Smith financed a number of farmers, including John F. McInnis, James W. Pickard, P. S. Hailand, and J. C. M. Davis.[25] Made against the collateral of a few cattle and horses, farm implements, and firewood and usually carrying an annual interest rate of 24 percent, these short-term loans to farmers were relatively small.

The economy of Calgary revolved around the growth of ranching and farming in the Bow Valley. Not only did ranchers and farmers need bank services, however, but so too did Calgary businessmen. Calgarians, such as hardware merchant E. E. Rogers, baker Frank J. Claxton, and Calgary Lumber Company owners, including Thomas B. H. Cochrane, increasingly turned to Lafferty & Smith for credit.[26] All of these short-term loans were protected by chattel mortgages.

Competition from the Imperial Bank of Canada and the Bank of Montreal, the two chartered banks that appeared in Calgary in October 1886, had a major impact upon Lafferty & Smith's interest rates. Rates on many of Lafferty & Smith's smaller loans fell from a prevailing 24 percent annual rate to the 18 percent level by December 1886.[27] Lower prices on loans helped increase credit and aided the economic development of Calgary and the Bow Valley.

Frederick Smith and James and Jessie Lafferty realized that developing their bank in the face of competition from the Bank of Montreal and the Imperial Bank of Canada would prove difficult. Convincing customers to offer deposits to build their accounts at Lafferty & Smith was an incredible challenge. The bank began to compete more vigorously for customers and their deposits, bidding aggressively in the rapidly developing local and regional markets for deposit funds. As before, newspaper advertising was used to attract new accounts, but now the power of this promotional technique became even more important. The bank's preference was to finance lending in Calgary and the Bow Valley largely by local and regional borrowing through the collection of deposits. With an insufficient level of deposits, however, the bank continued to borrow money from the Bank of Montreal to help fund its business.[28] As Lafferty & Smith's operations grew in size and scope, it was able to tap new resources. In March 1887, Lafferty & Smith borrowed $5,000 from the Regina branch of the Merchants Bank of Canada, a loan made possible by Frederick Smith's connections with this bank.[29]

With the growth of Lafferty & Smith's business in Calgary and the Bow Valley, the bank's head office was transferred from Regina to Calgary in June 1886.[30] In response to its increasing size and status in Calgary, the bank moved out of its tiny rented quarters on Stephen Avenue to its own new and more substantial building on the same avenue between McTavish and Osler streets.[31] At the same time, Frederick Smith moved to Calgary to manage headquarters operations, while Thomas Christie became manager of the Regina branch. In the spring of 1887, Christie made another move, this time to Moosomin to manage the bank's branch there. At this juncture, Henry LeJeune, a native of London, England who had been employed by the Merchants Bank of Canada in Ontario between 1869 and 1882 and by Lafferty & Smith's Regina office several years later, was appointed manager of that office.[32]

Throwing himself into the task in Calgary with great enthusiasm,

Chapter 6: Creating Banking Services

Frederick Smith remained the primary driving force behind the bank's growth over the next few years. The solid progress of Lafferty & Smith in the town and the Bow Valley was aided by the bank's ability to keep many of its traditional customers and attract new ones. Ranchers, farmers, and Calgary businessmen continued to be the principal sources of Lafferty & Smith's regional and local business.

Under Smith's management, Lafferty & Smith's Calgary office was a modest success, even though it was falling behind its competitors, the Imperial Bank of Canada and the Bank of Montreal.[33] The Calgary office of Lafferty & Smith made loans to substantial ranchers such as John Quirk in the Sheep Creek area, as well as to smaller ones like Bryce Wright in the Pine Creek district. Among the farmers to whom Lafferty & Smith lent money was Arthur Thompson in the Calgary area. The bank made an increasing number of advances to Calgary businessmen, including William H. Cushing, a sash and door manufacturer and building contractor; Samuel Parrish, a produce merchant; Charles F. Harris, a freighter; and S. J. Hogg & Co., lumber merchants.

LeJeune, Smith & Co.

Lafferty & Smith's Calgary operations were moderately profitable, but James Lafferty and Jessie Lafferty's desire to drop out of the partnership brought changes to the firm. On 23 February 1889, Lafferty & Smith was dissolved and the firm's business was purchased by Frederick Smith and Henry LeJeune, who formed a new private banking firm known as LeJeune, Smith & Co., with its head office in Regina and a network of branches in Calgary and Moosomin.[34] Henry LeJeune assumed direct supervision of the Regina headquarters; Frederick Smith served as manager in Calgary. At this time, Thomas Christie joined LeJeune, Smith & Co. as a partner in Regina, while his cousin A. E. Christie became manager of the Moosomin branch.

At LeJeune, Smith & Co.'s Calgary branch, Frederick Smith moved quickly to continue to provide loan and deposit services for his customers. The local branch of the Bank of Montreal was willing to lend money to LeJeune, Smith & Co. to help the private bank operate. Smith still enjoyed the confidence of the Bank of Montreal – that contact was crucial because it helped him obtain loans for his

Chapter 6: Creating Banking Services

Promissory note to be paid at LeJeune, Smith & Co.'s office in Calgary on 25 August 1890. From Supreme Court of the Northwest Territories, Calgary, Civil Cases Files. (Courtesy of Provincial Archives of Alberta).

bank.[35] LeJeune, Smith & Co. acted as a treasury especially for small ranchers and Calgary businessmen, taking deposits from them and providing them with funds for their operations. For instance, in the spring of 1889, LeJeune, Smith & Co. lent money to Springbank rancher Stephen Wilson, as well as to Calgary insurance agent Robert Ogburn.[36]

Just as LeJeune, Smith & Co. was on its way to building up its lending business, however, unforeseen circumstances caused changes in the firm. Quite unexpectedly, on 4 July 1889, Frederick Smith died at the age of thirty-four.[37] Smith had become fond of Thomas Christie and had much respect for his business sagacity. Not surprisingly, he named Christie as one of the executors of his estate, which consisted of some real estate holdings worth about $5,000. He appointed his brother, Bruce Smith, a Calgary lawyer, as his other executor. Frederick Smith left his entire estate to his wife, Mary.[38] They had two infant children, and in his will Frederick made it clear that after Mary's death the estate should be turned over to them in equal shares. Over the next two years, with their eyes on the well-being of Mary and her children, Thomas Christie and Bruce Smith wound up the affairs of Frederick Smith's estate.

When Frederick Smith died, Thomas Christie became responsible for managing the private banking firm LeJeune, Smith & Co. in Calgary.[39] Henry LeJeune was exceedingly pleased to see Christie serve as manager of the bank's Calgary branch because he had extensive banking experience and was well respected by business people in Calgary and the Bow Valley. The bank was a profitable firm with a promising future. But as things moved forward at LeJeune,

Chapter 6: Creating Banking Services

Smith & Co., it needed a new infusion of capital to invigorate its balance sheet. The decision of Henry C. Lawson, a Regina fire and life insurance agent and rancher, to join the bank as a partner in July 1889 provided the means to secure the desired additional capital.

In Calgary, Thomas Christie was quick to increase the size of LeJeune, Smith & Co.'s office and to make it more efficient. In August 1889, Christie moved the bank into spacious quarters in the Pettit & Ellis brick block on Stephen Avenue, just east of the *Calgary Herald* office.[40] Christie felt that Calgary businessmen and relatively small ranchers still constituted a fine market for loans.[41] He believed in aggressive extensions of credit to reliable firms in growth sectors of the Calgary and Bow Valley economies, but he wanted to avoid earning the reputation of a plunging lender – and treading that narrow line was a great challenge. During the next few years, LeJeune, Smith & Co. made loans to a number of ranchers in the Bow Valley, including J. D. Lynch, Albert E. Botterell, Charles and John Spalding, John Widdicombe, Joseph A. Miles, Bryce Wright, F. W. Frith, and William F. Bredin. In Calgary, LeJeune, Smith & Co funded the operations of businesses such as those of lawyer T. B. Lafferty and civil engineer E. C. Dawson.

Lafferty & Moore

Women in the Banking Business

Meanwhile, on 23 February 1889, the private banking firm Lafferty & Moore was formed in Calgary. This banking business, located on Stephen Avenue, was a partnership of Jessie Lafferty and Elizabeth Moore. These two women derived much of the support for the founding of Lafferty & Moore from Jessie's husband, Dr. James Lafferty, and Elizabeth's husband, James Stewart Moore, an Irish-born Calgarian who had a ranch in the Sheep Creek district. James Lafferty and James Moore each agreed to endorse the notes of the partnership to a total of $50,000, a move that helped the firm establish credit and prosperity. Believing that the firm was safe and responsible, the Calgary branch of the Bank of Montreal provided it with a line of credit of $100,000.[42]

Jessie Lafferty and Elizabeth Moore's entrepreneurial abilities matched their imagination and vision. By 1890, their private

Chapter 6: Creating Banking Services

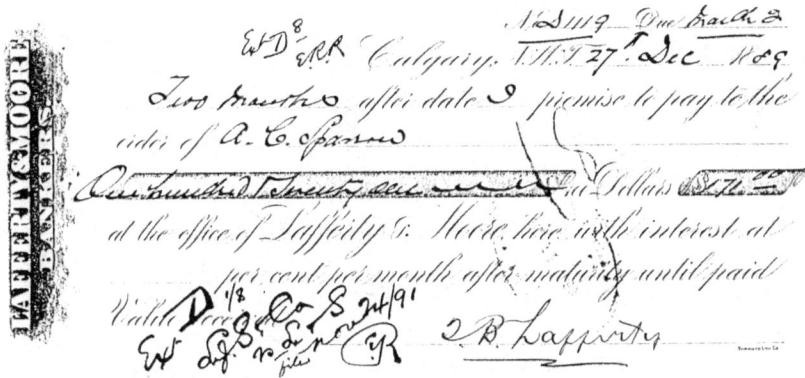

Promissory note to be paid at Lafferty & Moore's office in Calgary on 2 March 1890. From Supreme Court of the Northwest Territories, Calgary, Civil Cases Files. (Courtesy of Provincial Archives of Alberta).

bank, with its head office in Calgary, had branches in Edmonton, Regina, Moosomin, Moose Jaw, and Vancouver.[43] Jessie Lafferty and Elizabeth Moore assumed supervision of all the affairs of the bank, while P. G. Gray, who had previously managed the Edmonton branch of Lafferty & Smith, served as manager of the Calgary head office. By this time, Lafferty & Moore was worth from $20,000 to $40,000, reported the R. G. Dun & Company credit correspondent.[44] Under Jessie Lafferty and Elizabeth Moore's leadership, the bank established a reputation for soundness and reliability.

Between 1889 and the early 1890s, the economies of Calgary and the Bow Valley grew sufficiently to support two private banks – Lafferty & Moore and LeJeune, Smith & Co. – and three chartered banks: the Bank of Montreal, the Imperial Bank of Canada, and the Montreal-based Molson's Bank, which appeared in Calgary in 1891.[45] Despite the growing competition from chartered banks, private banks held their own and were especially welcome in small towns such as Calgary during this period. Private banks, through a reliance on funds from chartered banks, did increase the supply of money, expand credit facilities, and promote economic development in Calgary and the Bow Valley.

In the public mind in Calgary and the Bow Valley, Lafferty & Moore was not associated with economic exploitation. Rather, Calgarians and rural people maintained a positive attitude toward the financial services that the firm provided. Critics of large financial institutions might worry about the growing power of the big central Canadian-based chartered banks in the prairie West.[46] But

Chapter 6: Creating Banking Services

a local private bank like Lafferty & Moore that included among its customers small ranchers, Calgary business people, and some farmers and workers was not an institution that was perceived as a threat to society.

Lafferty & Moore established contact with many businesses in Calgary and the Bow Valley during the period from 1889 to the early 1890s.[47] As bankers, Jessie Lafferty and Elizabeth Moore were both careful and flexible – they did what they did extremely well and, over the years, made few mistakes. They had every right to take pride in their accomplishments. Their bank extended loans to farmers such as Duncan McArthur in the Pine Creek area, Samuel W. Shaw at Midnapore, and E. H. Matthias in the Nose Creek district, as well as to workers in Calgary such as Archibald Buie. Within the Bow Valley livestock raising community, Lafferty & Moore made advances especially to small ranchers such as John K. Rolls and John Cameron in the Sheep Creek district and Albert A. Greer in the Calgary area. Lafferty & Moore also had many loan customers among small-scale businessmen in Calgary, including Frank H. Armstrong, a livery stable keeper; William Carroll, a merchant tailor; Thomas Bunce, a carpenter; and lawyer T. B. Lafferty.

By the mid-1890s, Calgary and the Bow Valley had experienced almost a decade of private banking, and this was one means of assuring that many businesses in the town and its region would have ready access to credit facilities. By 1885, the importance of private banks in Calgary was inescapable. Much of their early dominance was based on the relative geographic isolation of the town and their ability to take advantage of their connections with chartered banks. But private banking's initial dominant position in the Alberta banking industry was steadily eroded by the establishment of branches of three of central Canada's chartered banks in Calgary – the Bank of Montreal, the Imperial Bank of Canada, and Molson's Bank. Gradually, the chartered banks eclipsed private banks in Calgary as a source of funds for expanding or new business enterprises. "Private banks were only an expedient. We knew they would not last when the chartered banks started coming in," recalled Thomas Christie.[48] The Bank of Montreal acquired Lafferty & Moore in 1893 and LeJeune, Smith & Co. a year later.[49] In Calgary, the era of private banking had passed.

Chartered Banks

The expanding market for capital in Calgary prompted the development of chartered banks' branches in the late nineteenth century. By 1898, Calgary had branches not only of the Imperial Bank of Canada, the Bank of Montreal, and the Molson's Bank, but also of the Quebec City-based Union Bank of Canada. In the town and its region, the constant need of business people for money outstripped the small resources of the private banks, forcing them to broaden their search to chartered banks, where they could usually obtain credit at better rates. As Canadian chartered banks followed the Canadian Pacific Railway westward and stitched regional networks of branch offices together to create national organizations, they altered the form of banking. A higher market share permitted them to continue pursuing economies of scale; at the same time, they took full advantage of the economies of scope offered by their networks of branches. Chartered bank branches in Calgary were a vital part of national networks.

At the top of Canada's system of credit structures and channels were the chartered banks. Whereas the private banking sector underwent many organizational changes, the chartered banks were a relatively stable sector in the late nineteenth century. The chartered banks' joint-stock, limited-liability status increased their resources and expanded their activities in providing short-term credit. The major figures in the chartered banks' head offices were their salaried general managers. Given their huge responsibility of making the banks' strategic decisions, their salaries were considerably higher than those of branch managers in Calgary. Acting on the instructions given them by the general managers, branch managers tried to build up branch business. On the client side, branch managers provided advice and credit facilities to local and regional borrowers.

Imperial Bank of Canada

In Calgary, the age of chartered banking began in early October 1886, when a branch of the Imperial Bank of Canada was opened in the town. Even prior to this date, Calgarians had sought to bring chartered banking into the town, but their efforts had met with no

Chapter 6: Creating Banking Services

success. Expectations were heightened in January 1884 by a plan to establish the Ranchers' Bank of Canada as a chartered bank, with its head office in Calgary.[50] This promotion failed to take off, however. Six months later, local citizens invited the Bank of Hamilton to set up a branch office in Calgary, but that bank was unwilling to take this step.[51] Finally, Peter McCarthy, a Calgary lawyer who was sure of his purpose and confident of his entrepreneurial ability to bring about change, turned to another bank. On 15 July 1886, McCarthy wrote to the board of directors in the Imperial Bank of Canada's head office in Toronto, strongly recommending that it establish a branch in Calgary. After carefully examining the situation, the board responded by opening a branch office in the town on 6 October.[52]

Establishing branch offices nation-wide was the conventional method of extending a chartered bank's business in Canada in the late nineteenth century. The crushing of the 1885 Saskatchewan Rebellion meant the growth of settlement, urbanization, immigration, and banking. Peace in the prairie West markedly accelerated the pace of economic development, stimulating the expansion of chartered banks. By October 1886, the Imperial Bank of Canada operated a network of fifteen branches across the nation, including three in the prairie West.[53] With the extension to Calgary, the bank hoped to increase its involvement in prairie business.

The Imperial Bank of Canada appointed its first manager of the Calgary branch, Samuel Barber, at a salary of $1,000 per year. Having recently served as accountant in the bank's branch in Brandon, Manitoba, Barber was well qualified for the job.[54] A dynamic and efficient banker, he was shaped by his faith in economic progress. The temporary space occupied by the bank's Calgary branch in a rented room in C. W. Peterson's law office on Stephen Avenue was relatively small.[55] Barber immediately made plans for more permanent facilities. Before long, the branch moved into considerably more commodious rented quarters in the Dunn & Lineham block on Stephen Avenue.

When the Imperial Bank of Canada opened its doors to the public in Calgary on 6 October 1886, it was the only chartered bank in the town – just eleven years after its founding. This corporation's founder, H. S. Howland, a prominent Toronto wholesale hardware merchant, leaped into the banking business with zest and championed nation-wide branch banking. The national Bank Act, passed in 1871, allowed branching. In 1880, the Imperial Bank of Canada acquired a toehold in the prairie West by establishing a branch office in Winnipeg; after that, it never looked back.[56] It expanded into Brandon in 1882, and then to Calgary four years later.[57]

The Imperial Bank of Canada, operating with a charter from the Canadian government and regulated by it, enjoyed substantial advantages. Like other chartered banks, the Imperial Bank of Canada could issue currency and, like them, it promised to redeem it in gold or gold in the form of Dominion notes. With Canada on the gold standard, Canadian bankers saw gold as the fundamental guarantor of value, a measure that was universally recognized by people in determining the worth of things. As elsewhere in the nation, in Calgary and the Bow Valley the bank's notes won immediate acceptance. Its relatively high capitalization – $1,500,000 in 1886 – inspired confidence in its stability, and federal government supervision helped assure the public of its financial soundness.[58] As in the case of other chartered banks, the Imperial Bank of Canada was relatively large compared with most private banks. Generally speaking, a regulated bank such as the Imperial Bank of Canada had come to be seen by Calgarians and other Canadians as a safe bank.

Before the Bank of Canada finally replaced the chartered banks as issuers of bank notes and became the exclusive source of paper money in 1945, the hallmark of Canadian currency was its diversity. But the currency was only as good as the chartered bank that issued it. Fortunately for Canadians, the Imperial Bank of Canada's notes, like those of the Bank of Montreal, the Molson's Bank, and the Union Bank of Canada, were good.

Still, during Samuel Barber's first few weeks as manager of the Imperial Bank of Canada's Calgary branch, business was extremely slow. "In a little 8 x 10 shop he and one clerk had patiently waited for business, and he began to be afraid that the predictions of a banker who visited the town at the time, that the Imperial Bank would withdraw from the town and the young men would lose their situations, would be verified," recalled Barber half a dozen years later.[59] But this did not happen. Instead, the Calgary branch grew gradually, taking deposits and providing credit for the town's businessmen as well as for ranchers in the surrounding region.

Managing the Calgary branch with a sense of vitality and dynamism, Samuel Barber made a significant contribution to its early development. In keeping with instructions from the Imperial Bank of Canada's general manager D. R. Wilkie in Toronto, who had

Chapter 6: Creating Banking Services

previously served as manager of the Quebec Bank's St. Catharines and Toronto branches, Barber followed a policy of developing a diversified loan portfolio.[60] In addition to making advances especially to medium-sized and large ranchers, the bank extended loans to a variety of Calgary businessmen. Credit for farmers in the Bow Valley was available at the bank only on a limited basis in the last half of the 1880s, however, for like most other chartered banks the Imperial Bank of Canada did not consider farms a very safe and profitable outlet for the use of its funds.

At the Toronto headquarters, Wilkie, with the directors' approval, made decisions regarding loan applications from large borrowers, leaving Barber to deal with the smaller loans. At the same time, Barber carefully read all the loan applications and passed on his assessment of them to the Toronto head office. While Wilkie was responsible for broad policy decisions and formulated the theoretical underpinnings of the bank, he never forgot that Barber and his staff were at the front line of the bank's financial services. In particular, Barber, as the Calgary branch manager, was competing with other banks to establish the Imperial Bank of Canada's reputation in the town and the Bow Valley as well as to secure new business. No one in the bank had a better appreciation of local and regional needs than he did. The many letters Barber wrote to head office, combined with head office's replies, strengthened corporate feeling and played an important part in the effective management at the Calgary branch.

Barber inspired his staff with his passion for excellent service. Between 1886 and the early 1890s, the Imperial Bank of Canada's Calgary branch extended loans to a number of substantial ranching businesses in Alberta, including the Quorn Ranche, the Glengarry Ranche, McHugh Bros. (Thomas, Felix, and John), and Addison McPherson in the Bow Valley, as well as the Little Bow Cattle Ranche and the Winder Ranche to the south.[61] These ranching enterprises needed extensive credit and were among the bank's major customers.

The terms of the financing offered to McHugh Bros. on the Bow River east of Calgary were fairly typical of the terms of the loans made to all these ranching concerns. For example, in March 1888, the bank lent $1,000 to McHugh Bros. and, during the next two years, their debt to the bank grew to $13,000 as they expanded their ranching operations. The loan, carrying an annual interest rate of 10

Chapter 6: Creating Banking Services

Imperial Bank of Canada's Calgary branch (centre left) on Stephen Avenue in 1890, with I. G. Baker & Co.'s department store to the left and John Field's drugstore and Rankin & Allan's dry goods store to the right. From *The Dominion Illustrated*, Calgary Special, 28 June 1890. (Courtesy of Glenbow Library).

percent, was secured by McHugh Bros.' promissory note, all their horses and cattle, and their real estate holdings in Calgary.[62]

National banking regulations at this time did not allow chartered banks to lend with real estate as security unless they accepted a land mortgage in addition to a promissory note and a chattel mortgage. Because the loan to McHugh Bros. met these requirements, the Imperial Bank of Canada had no problems with the federal regulators. In the late nineteenth century, real estate lending was not in the chartered banking mainstream, and it was closely regulated under the national Bank Act. Indeed, in the national banking system, lending against the collateral of land was virtually a taboo. An important objection to real estate collateral by itself was that whatever the value of a piece of land might be in theory, it was difficult to realize that value quickly. But McHugh Bros. were successful in the ranching business and were able to pay down the debt to the bank to $9,300 by the beginning of January 1891. At this point, the Imperial Bank of Canada made an additional $2,500 loan to assist in developing the ranch.

Chapter 6: Creating Banking Services

In addition to extending loans to ranching businesses, Samuel Barber courted new loan accounts among Calgary firms. He devoted a good portion of his energy to generating profitable actions for the Imperial Bank of Canada in Calgary, while simultaneously stressing the importance of the institution to the town and the Bow Valley. This emphasis reflected the boosterism that was characteristic of his approach. Barber's success in his branch office brought him to the attention of local businessmen, many of whom were able to secure loans from the bank. Between 1886 and the early 1890s, the bank's customers in Calgary included Archibald Grant, a hardware merchant; Soules & McGinnes, cattle dealers; A. E. Shelton, a furniture merchant; lumber manufacturer James Walker; John G. McCallum, a building contractor; the dry goods firm Rankin & Allan; Pat Burns, a meat packer; and the Eau Claire & Bow River Lumber Co.[63]

The Barber administration of the Imperial Bank of Canada's Calgary branch was one of expansion between 1886 and the early 1890s. Deposits and loans rose gradually. The staff at the branch grew steadily, rising from two at the time of the opening for business in October 1886 to six in July 1892. At the end of this period, besides Barber as manager, there were five other male employees: Murney Morris, accountant; J. S. Gibb, teller; J. M. Lay, ledgerkeeper; and M. C. Bernard and J. S. Douglas, who served as clerks.[64] Under the direction of the executives in the Toronto head office, Samuel Barber and his staff helped the Imperial Bank of Canada handle an increasing volume of business in Calgary and the Bow Valley. By providing vital financial services in a still developing and credit-hungry region, the bank made profits for its stockholders and aided the economic growth of the town and the surrounding area.

Bank of Montreal

The Bank of Montreal, with its head office in Montreal, was another chartered bank that benefited from and assisted in the development of the economies of Calgary and the Bow Valley. It is difficult to imagine the economic upsurge of the Calgary area without the presence of chartered banks. Chartered banks had an enormous influence on the town and its region, and it was no coincidence that a branch office of the Bank of Montreal emerged a few years after Calgary was integrated into a nation-wide railway system – the Canadian Pacific. The Canadian Pacific provided banks in the town with more customers and helped those customers increase their business activities. As the railway bridged the great gulf of land that separated Calgary and central Canadian cities, commerce flourished. So, too, in many ways, did the banking business.

The close ties between the Bank of Montreal and the Canadian Pacific were most evident during the first half of the 1880s, when the bank helped finance the building of this railway across the nation. Founded in 1817, the Bank of Montreal had a nation-wide network of twenty-eight branches in September 1886, including the Winnipeg and Regina offices in the prairie West.[65] With $12 million in capital stock, it was the largest bank in Canada and continued to provide the Canadian Pacific with an essential commodity – credit – even as it allowed more extensive and efficient transportation into and out of Calgary. This interaction of finance and railway with the development of Calgary is illustrated by Donald A. Smith's involvement in the Bank of Montreal and the Canadian Pacific. As vice-president of the Bank of Montreal and a Canadian Pacific director in 1886, Smith helped to fund the railway's operations in Calgary.[66] He also was a Hudson's Bay Company director and, through his connection with the Bank of Montreal, helped to fund the company's Calgary store.

Smith recognized that the Bank of Montreal, with its network of branches stretching across the nation, was attuned to the needs of the day. Indeed, he promoted the growth of such extensive branching. As Canadian Pacific Railway expansion gained momentum, populating western Canada and culminating in the completion of the first transcontinental railway in 1885, it produced an accompanying flurry of land deals, corporate charters, and banking developments. Entrepreneurial spirits were not stultified by tradition, and the democratic political system allowed businessmen to prosper. Bank credit, while still not plentiful, was becoming increasingly available through the national banking networks. The opportunity to make money was irresistible, whether in land or in banking.

Like Donald A. Smith, Charles F. Smithers, the Bank of Montreal's president, and Wentworth J. Buchanan, its general manager, favoured nation-wide branch banking.[67] All three men were ambitious, the embodiment of the dynamic, acquisitive spirit of the late nineteenth century. Born in 1822 in London, England,

Chapter 6: Creating Banking Services

Smithers devoted most of his career to the banking business. From 1847 to 1858, he worked for the Bank of British North America in Montreal. Then he spent most of the next twenty-one years with the Bank of Montreal, becoming its general manager in 1879. He filled this position for two years before serving as president of the bank from 1881 until his death in 1887. Buchanan was just as active in banking as Smithers, and he served the Bank of Montreal for thirty-eight years. Entering the bank in 1852, Buchanan rose several ranks to become manager of the bank's Montreal branch in 1874, assistant general manager of the bank in 1880, and general manager in 1881, a position he held until 1890, when ill health forced his retirement.

In the mid-1880s, as the market crisis of the economic depression was coming to an end, the future looked bright. The Bank of Montreal was now a $12 million enterprise and certainly expected to continue growing. Evidence of this expectation was shown in mid-August 1886, when Buchanan made a trip to Calgary to explore banking possibilities there. After returning to the Montreal head office, he recommended setting up a branch in Calgary.[68] He urged Bank of Montreal executives to consider moving more deeply into the prairie West banking market by extending its branch network. Much came from Buchanan's trip, for his journey laid the groundwork for the bank's expansion. At a board meeting on 7 September, Smithers and the other Bank of Montreal directors decided to open a branch office in Calgary.[69] By doing so, they demonstrated, as they had on many previous occasions through their decisions to set up new branches, that their roles at the Bank of Montreal extended well beyond the city limits of Montreal. Within the city as well as outside it, Smithers and Buchanan's personal reputations and the bank's good record helped retain public confidence in the institution.

With the full support of Smithers, Buchanan prepared the way for the opening of the bank's Calgary branch. He made arrangements with Dunn & Lineham in Calgary for the proposed new branch office to be located in their block on Stephen Avenue. Then the Bank of Montreal's board authorized Smithers to sign a one-year lease for these premises at $900 per annum, with the option of renewing the lease for two additional years.[70] On 5 October, Arthur D. Braithwaite was appointed manager of the Calgary branch office at a salary of $1,500 per year. Born in Isle of Wight in the English Channel, Braithwaite had worked for the Bank of Montreal in

Chapter 6: Creating Banking Services

central Canada and Winnipeg before serving as manager of its Regina branch from 1882 to 1886.[71]

Quick-witted and diligent, Braithwaite took up his duties on Monday, 25 October 1886, when the Bank of Montreal's Calgary branch opened for business. At this point, the branch's quarters in the newly built Dunn & Lineham block were still "in a very dirty & uncomfortable state. We shall hardly get the carpenters out by the end of the week," reported Braithwaite to Buchanan.[72] Soon, however, the construction of the handsome branch office was finished and Braithwaite was able to work efficiently.

When the Bank of Montreal's Calgary branch opened its doors to the public, it joined a small fraternity of Calgary banks. In October 1886, two other banks – the Imperial Bank of Canada and the private banking firm Lafferty & Smith – were competing with the Bank of Montreal, each trying to carve a place for itself in the business affairs of Calgary and the Bow Valley. The Bank of Montreal's Calgary branch enjoyed the advantage of having the federal government as one of its major customers in the town from the time it opened for business.[73] Before long, the Calgary branch was serving the local post office, Mounted Police detachment, and land titles office and holding substantial deposits from them. The Bank of Montreal's Calgary branch also had the advantage of serving Lafferty & Smith and holding a significant deposit from this private bank. The Bank of Montreal's notes, like those of the Imperial Bank of Canada, were met with high regard across the nation.

Being competitive and optimistic by nature, Braithwaite constantly sought to stimulate the Bank of Montreal's growth in Calgary by targeting a diverse market. In the last half of the 1880s, this market included relatively few Bow Valley farmers, however. Farmers had limited access to the bank's credit facilities. One of the Calgary branch's earliest customers in the commercial world was I. G. Baker & Co. This firm continued to do a large volume of business in its Calgary store, and Braithwaite was convinced that the Baker & Co. account "cannot but result to our advantage."[74] Within a week, Braithwaite had also garnered other important accounts, including those of the local Hudson's Bay Company store and Samuel Parrish, the flour and feed merchant.

Samuel Parrish needed a fair amount of capital to buy and store flour and feed. He had access to some credit advanced by Lafferty & Smith. Parrish also had well-established contacts with provision

Chapter 6: Creating Banking Services

merchants in Brandon, Manitoba which had led to a line of credit. But as trade in Calgary grew rapidly, Parrish's credit needs surged. At the end of October 1886, he turned to the Bank of Montreal for short-term credit. "Mr. Parrish has the character here of a straightforward, reliable man," observed Braithwaite.[75] This statement contributed to the decision by the bank's general manager and directors to approve Parrish's loan application. The Bank of Montreal lent him $3,000 on flour and feed secured by warehouse receipts. In May 1887, the bank made a further loan to Parrish with a chattel mortgage, a promissory note, and his real estate in Calgary as collateral.[76] Short-term credit at the bank's Calgary branch became a prerequisite for Parrish's prosperity.

Arthur Braithwaite also looked toward the industrial community in Calgary for his lending business. For example, in December 1886, he was quick to grasp the opportunity to supply the working capital requirements of the Eau Claire & Bow River Lumber Co. This company, with $500,000 in capital stock and a workforce of about fifty men, already had one million logs in the Bow River, and it expected to have three or four million more in the following spring. Peter A. Prince, the company's Quebec-born general manager, owned 10 percent of the stock. "The company are building a first class mill" in Calgary "estimated to cost $75,000," Braithwaite wrote to Buchanan. "They have been doing a great deal of work in cribbing the river, building dams. They have a splendid river to float their logs and large limits" in the Kananaskis country west of Calgary, "but the timber is very small. From what I can hear the Coy is a very strong one and I should like to make the advance."[77] Soon the Bank of Montreal's Calgary branch was making substantial loans to the Eau Claire & Bow River Lumber Co.

Always on the lookout for new business, Braithwaite wanted to broaden the Bank of Montreal's industrial commitments. An opportunity came in 1891, when the Bank of Montreal's Calgary branch made a loan of $3,250 to the Golden Mining & Smelting Co. of Canada in Golden, British Columbia. The entrepreneurs who played a key role in this company's evolution were two of Calgary's business leaders: Henry B. Alexander, who, together with his brother George, operated a ranch in the High River area; and local lawyer Peter McCarthy. Eager to develop their smelting business, McCarthy and Alexander applied to Braithwaite for a further loan of $4,000. Braithwaite's response was favourable. "I

Chapter 6: Creating Banking Services

anticipate repayment this fall, I am anxious to keep this smelting business & I think I am perfectly safe," Braithwaite wrote to Edward Clouston, the bank's new general manager, in June 1891.[78]

Meanwhile, Braithwaite continued to focus his attention on local borrowers and local ventures. One of these ventures was the Calgary Gas & Waterworks Co. Incorporated for $100,000 in the spring of 1890, this new company was set up for the purpose of supplying the town of Calgary with water.[79] Headed by George Alexander as president, the company brought new investors into the picture, among them his business friends in England. But the Calgary Gas & Waterworks Co. was still short of capital. The firm periodically had to borrow money for working capital from the Bank of Montreal's Calgary branch. After obtaining an initial loan of $10,000 for his company from the bank, Alexander requested a further advance of $10,000 in September 1890. Braithwaite saw Alexander as a "most valuable customer," with good personal and business connections in England, and, consequently, recommended that the bank's head office approve his loan application.[80] Within a week, Braithwaite received a telegram from the bank's general manager, telling him that "you may make advance of $10,000 to Geo. Alexander."[81] Ranchers also benefited from the bank's lending operations; for example, it made loans to George Alexander's Two Dot Ranch in the Nanton area.

In the late 1880s and early 1890s, the activities of the Bank of Montreal's Calgary branch were shaped by the growth of the Calgary and Bow Valley economies, the need to fund new enterprises such as the Calgary Gas & Waterworks Co., and the need to expand traditional services. Since its inception, the town of Calgary had been deeply involved in the trade of goods, and the public's growing demand for goods created a demand for more loans. Much of this expansion thus came in the traditional area of commerce with loans provided to the bank's long-time customers. The Calgary branch was a profitable venture and continued to be an important source of financing for merchants, especially the prominent ones.

The Calgary branch's close ties to old customers was perhaps best attested to by its relationship with G. C. King & Co., general merchants, a major firm in which former Mounted Policeman George C. King was the chief partner. In March 1887, the bank made a $7,000 loan to this firm. The loan carried an annual interest rate of 9 percent. No one understood better how valuable

143

Chapter 6: Creating Banking Services

Bank of Montreal's Calgary branch on the corner of Stephen Avenue and Scarth Street, c. 1890. (Courtesy of Glenbow Archives, NA-1075-8).

George C. King was as a customer than Arthur Braithwaite. As he told the bank's general manager Wentworth Buchanan, George C. King "has ever since we have opened done his best to throw business our way, and has given me valuable advice in regard to the character & standing of the people here. He is a straightforward thoroughly honourable man and has a good deal of influence all through this section."[82]

In the next few years, however, G. C. King & Co. began to experience serious financial problems, which were exacerbated by the hard winter of 1886-1887, in which most ranchers in the Bow Valley suffered severe losses. Many of their cattle were frozen to death. Although the better winters that followed provided some respite for the ranchers as their herds of cattle grew again, they still had great difficulty in keeping up with the payments for the goods they had purchased from G. C. King & Co. Faced with an astonishing number of customers with unpaid bills, the firm was forced to operate at a loss and went bankrupt. In February 1890, it made an assignment for the benefit of its creditors.[83]

Among G. C. King & Co.'s main creditors were the Bank of Montreal and several wholesale houses in Montreal and Toronto. The firm owed the Bank of Montreal's Calgary branch over $14,500.[84] Looming large as well among G. C. King & Co.'s debts were the sums it owed to individuals. For instance, Joseph Stimson, a High River rancher, held more than $11,400 of the firm's debts.[85] Thus, the creditor map of G. C. King & Co. stretched from High River to Calgary in the Bow Valley to Toronto and Montreal. As George C. King's principal creditor, the Bank of Montreal's Calgary branch still had faith in him and was willing to extend more credit to him, and thereby played a crucial role in helping his firm to recover from bad times and grow in the early 1890s.

Chapter 6: Creating Banking Services

The time had, of course, long since passed when the Calgary branch's functions could be accommodated in the relatively small quarters in the Dunn & Lineham block. In response to its increasing size and status in Calgary, the Bank of Montreal moved out of the Dunn & Lineham block into its own substantial building on the corner of Stephen Avenue and Scarth Street in December 1889. Having spent $50,000 on the new structure, the Bank of Montreal directors saw it as an impressive symbol of the importance the institution had achieved in the Calgary financial community.[86] "The new premises are a great improvement on the old, and it is to be hoped the business to be transacted there will be correspondingly increased," observed the *Calgary Herald* in a bit of boosterism.[87]

Meanwhile, the size of the Calgary branch's all-male staff had also grown. When Arthur Braithwaite had become manager in 1886, the number of bank employees was only two. By 1888, this had risen to four. In addition to Braithwaite as manager, there were W. H. Hogg, accountant; C. A. Lawford, teller; and L. Strachey, clerk. Quite naturally, all members of the staff got to know one another. In this family atmosphere, it also was possible to deal with problems on a one-to-one basis. In the fall of 1892, when Braithwaite left the Calgary branch to become acting manager of the Bank of Montreal's office in Hamilton, he was succeeded by W. B. Graveley, former manager at its branch in Almonte, Ontario.[88] At a farewell dinner for Arthur Braithwaite in Ingram's Restaurant, George C. King, still one of the bank's valued old customers, noted that the growth of the Calgary branch stood as a testament to the leadership of Braithwaite.[89]

But while service to traditional customers such as G. C. King & Co. remained an important part of the Calgary branch's loan portfolio, the economy of Calgary was beginning to undergo a transformation in the early 1890s. New industrial enterprises such as the Calgary Brewing & Malting Co. turned to the Bank of Montreal for support. Like Braithwaite before him, W. B. Graveley, the new manager of the Calgary branch, kept a watchful eye on the development of such enterprises. Persistent and effective, he brought in new business. Founded in 1892 by A. E. Cross, a Montreal-born entrepreneur who had started in the Bow Valley as a veterinarian on the Cochrane Ranche and was now operating his own ranch west of Nanton in the rolling foothills of the Rockies, the Calgary

Chapter 6: Creating Banking Services

Brewing & Malting Co. was incorporated for $100,000 and, by the mid-1890s, was producing beer for local markets.[90] Cross received backing not only from his father, Alexander Cross, a Montreal judge, but also from some of his friends who were involved in ranching. Short of funds from the outset, the Calgary Brewing & Malting Co. relied as well on the Bank of Montreal.

Graveley placed a high priority on acquiring this new industrial account because, as he told Edward Clouston, the general manager, he believed that "there is every prospect of" the company "becoming a large and profitable business."[91] Clouston and the Bank of Montreal directors warmly accepted Graveley's initiative. In September 1893, the Calgary branch made a $15,000 loan to the Calgary Brewing & Malting Co. What Graveley perceived was that the firm would grow and prosper – and his view proved well founded. Delighted by his ability to exert considerable influence with the senior executives at the Bank of Montreal, Graveley continued to make steady progress at the Calgary branch in terms of business volume and profitability. While the branch under his management made the majority of its loans to commercial and industrial firms, it also financed ranching enterprises, including George Lane's Willow Creek Ranche.

Responding to the Calgary Government's Financial Needs

While lending money to the private sector in Calgary and the Bow Valley was the core business of the chartered banks and their main source of earnings, they also responded to the Calgary government's financial needs. On 10 November 1886, three days after the great fire in downtown Calgary, the Bank of Montreal's Calgary branch lent $6,000 to the town, and branch manager Arthur Braithwaite became the town treasurer. The interest rate on the loan, payable in twelve months and secured by town taxes, was 8 percent per annum.[92] This loan enabled the town to purchase a new fire engine, new fire hoses, and new water tanks, deepen the town wells, and build a new fire hall.[93]

Through Braithwaite's efforts, the Bank of Montreal's Calgary branch also obtained the town account before long. In so doing, it provided a place for the town to deposit its funds. Braithwaite had already developed close ties with mayor George C. King, the general merchant. "King is the mayor of the town and has given us the town account," Braithwaite told the bank's general manager Wentworth Buchanan in February 1887.[94] At the same time, the bank's continuing loans to the town provided a profitable and relatively safe outlet for the use of the growing deposits generated by increasing prosperity in the Calgary and Bow Valley business world.

When Samuel Barber, manager of the Imperial Bank of Canada's Calgary branch, became the new town treasurer in early 1888 with the election of furniture dealer A. E. Shelton as the new mayor, Braithwaite sat on pins and needles, fearing that the town account would be transferred to the Imperial Bank of Canada. As Braithwaite wrote to Wentworth Buchanan,

> Mr. Barber, manager of the Imperial Bank, has been made treasurer of the town, so I presume we shall lose the town account. The mayor and five of the six councillors are customers of the Imperial which naturally accounts for the change.[95]

The transfer of the town account to the Imperial Bank of Canada solidified the ties between that bank and the town council.

The Imperial Bank of Canada's Calgary branch now functioned as the banker for the town government, keeping the town's funds on deposit. As the branch's manager, Barber made substantial loans to the town.[96] With Calgary's growth over the next few years, the town also continued to make use of the Bank of Montreal for financial needs. This situation engendered intense competition for the town account. By February 1892, Braithwaite had again secured the town account for the Bank of Montreal's Calgary branch.[97] In the process, he lowered the interest rate on the bank's loans to the town from the prevailing 8 percent annual rate to the 6 percent level. These loans were important in speeding up the orderly development of public services, including better sewage and water supply systems, in Calgary.

Financial Environment

From the mid-1880s to the end of the century, Calgary and the Bow Valley made significant progress in shaping a financial environment that provided stability and fostered economic advancement. After

Chapter 6: Creating Banking Services

Calgary achieved town status, the development and expansion of banking services was evident in every economic market. Private banks and branches of chartered banks were typically well managed. Mobilizing loans for commercial, agricultural, and industrial enterprises, they relied on estimates of creditworthiness, reputation, and trust. Like Calgary merchants and manufacturers, chartered banks and private banks demonstrated tremendous confidence in the agricultural economy of the Bow Valley by expanding substantially the volume of credit granted especially to the biggest ranchers but also to some farmers. In agriculture, funds devoted to financing the ranching industry were the largest but not the only part of the credit structure. Included as well was the credit that flowed particularly from the private banks into farming operations.

Farmers seeking land mortgage money for the purchase of farmland almost always had to rely on loan companies, however. In the Bow Valley, a number of farmers who needed land mortgage money obtained loans running one year or longer from the Glasgow-based North British Canadian Investment Company.[98] For instance, in November 1886 this company lent $700 to Samuel W. Shaw, a Midnapore farmer. The thirteen-month loan, carrying an annual interest rate of 10 per cent, was secured by Shaw's three lots in Calgary. In the spring of 1887, the company made a $500, one-year loan to William Byers, a farmer in the Calgary area, with real estate in the town as collateral. Bow Valley ranchers also borrowed money from the company. In May 1887, the North British Canadian Investment Company lent $1,500 to Thomas Lynch, a High River rancher. The one-year loan, carrying the usual annual interest rate of 10 percent, was secured by Lynch's four lots in Calgary. In extending credit to farms and ranches, the company contributed significantly to the region's growing economy.

At the same time, many ranchers and farmers maintained high savings rates and accumulated a fair amount of capital. In these early settlement years, agricultural wealth holders usually made direct investments in physical assets, such as land, machinery, and livestock. In general, however, capital was scarce. To attract a substantial number of new settlers to the Bow Valley, land prices had to be set relatively low. Despite capital shortages, the westward population movement continued and helped shape the Bow Valley's number one enterprise, agriculture.

7

Building the Ranching Community

Trade in the principal commodity bought and sold in Calgary – livestock – was given an impetus with the construction of Fort Benton-based T. C. Power & Bro.'s stockyards in 1884, the prairie town's first stockyards.[1] Located in east Calgary, the stockyards aided Power & Bro. in sending dressed beef and live cattle by the Canadian Pacific Railway to the end of track in the Rocky Mountains to feed its construction crews. Having purchased the cattle from big ranches in southern Alberta and the American West, Daniel Webster Marsh, Power & Bro.'s manager in Calgary, shipped two carloads of beef each week to the Canadian Pacific construction camps in June of that year.[2] By 1885, Marsh, seeking to make the most of the opportunities in commerce, was supplying the railway's construction crews with beef especially from southern Alberta ranches, thereby helping to open the region and link its development and destiny with Calgary. Meanwhile, in 1884, Marsh opened Power & Bro.'s general store on Stephen Avenue. In this way, Calgary became an increasingly important recipient of foreign direct investment by firms based in the United States.

Canadian Pacific Stockyards

With the rapid growth of the ranching industry in the Bow Valley and southern Alberta, there was a demand for larger stockyards.[3] In 1887, the Canadian Pacific responded to this demand by building new and bigger stockyards east of the Elbow River, situated on forty

Chapter 7: Building the Ranching Community

Canadian Pacific Stockyards in east Calgary, c. 1890s. (Courtesy of Glenbow Archives, NA-2407-5).

acres of land that the railway leased from the town of Calgary. When the stockyards opened, the sewer and drainage system carried away water and offal to the Elbow, which soon became polluted. Made of bridge material, telegraph poles, and railway ties, the cattle pens were capable of handling hundreds of animals.[4] The closing of the old stockyards cleared Calgary's streets of drovers and their cattle, but despite the prevailing northwesterly winds the smell of the Canadian Pacific Stockyards sometimes reached the town on strong prairie winds from the east. Town officials did not seem to worry about this very much, however, for it was the aroma of an expanding livestock trade that had become the key to Calgary's growth.

It was a *Calgary Herald* reporter who best described the life and spirit of the Canadian Pacific Stockyards. One day in August 1888 when a shipment of 255 beef cattle left Calgary for British markets, the stockyards gave the reporter something to write about:

> At 5 p.m., J. S. Feehan, station master, ran down from Calgary station to the stockyards with a train of 14 cattle cars. The cattle being already in the C.P.R. pens, the work of loading commenced at once.... There was a large lot of men on hand, and the work went on quite lively, considering that these cattle had never been in as close quarters before.... The loading was done in a short time occupying only an hour and thirty minutes.... Altogether this event promises great things for the future of the Calgary cattle business.[5]

Land and the Rise of Big Ranch Companies in the Bow Valley

The cattle economy linking Calgary and the Bow Valley was sustained by the vast stretches of accessible land in the region and the people who settled in it. In 1881, an order-in-council passed by John A. Macdonald's Conservative cabinet established the lease system, which enabled the government to grant to ranchers leases closed to settlement of up to a hundred thousand acres for a term of twenty-one years at the rate of 1 cent per acre per year.[6] With improvements in transportation and communication, especially the arrival of the Canadian Pacific Railway in 1883, came the rise of big ranch companies in the Bow Valley. They pioneered important livestock operations in the region. In the 1880s, aside from the Canadian Pacific, the chartered banks, and the Eau Claire & Bow River Lumber Co., these ranches were the largest businesses in the Bow Valley. The biggest ones were capitalized at $500,000 and ran more than five thousand head of cattle on their leases.

Big ranching enterprises developed especially when companies combined large-scale livestock production on the open range with mass distribution to become vertically integrated businesses controlling all or most of the stages of production and marketing of their products. Capitalism came to the Bow Valley ranching frontier with livestock destined for the marketplace. Raising livestock, mostly cattle but also horses and sheep, was an activity that contained a powerful element of capitalism, and this proved to be momentous for Calgary's and the Bow Valley's future. A big ranch company often helped provide employees with ranching skills that allowed them to move successfully to ownership of a small ranch, such as John Ware's undertaking, or a medium-sized ranch, such as A. E. Cross's venture. These connections between big, medium-sized, and small livestock raisers helped build the ranching community in the Bow Valley. The trade in cattle and horses between small, large, and medium-sized ranchers, coupled with work exchanges and visiting, reinforced the ties that bound the livestock raising community.

Fairly good prices for beef in the 1880s and 1890s stimulated the cattle industry in the Bow Valley. Choice steers brought ranchers from $40 to $45 a head in Calgary, as well as in Liverpool, England, in the process generating reports of substantial profits.[7] The possibilities of making money in the livestock business drew

Chapter 7: Building the Ranching Community

Table 6. Demographic Structure of the Cowboy Culture in the Bow Valley, 1891-1901

Year	1891	1901
Cowboy Population	26	59
Percent Born in Canada	38	46
Percent Born in USA	31	20
Percent Born in Britain	31	31

Source: Manuscript Census of 1891 for Calgary, Canmore, Gleichen, High River, Davisburg, Fish Creek, Pine Creek, Namaka, and Morley; Manuscript Census of 1901 for Calgary, Canmore, Gleichen, High River, Davisburg, Pine Creek, Morley, Queenstown, Shepard, Nose Creek, Springbank, Cochrane, Jumping Pound, Okotoks, Millarville, Priddis, and Pekisko.

favourable comments from visitors to the region. "If I were not the governor general of Canada, I would be a cattle rancher in Alberta," declared Canada's governor general, the Marquis of Lorne, in 1881.[8] Such statements did not go unnoticed. From 1881 to the mid-1880s, the ranges in the Bow Valley became increasingly stocked with cattle, the trend toward big companies grew, and more and more capital flowed in from central Canadian, British, and American investors.

American Roots

The roots of Bow Valley ranching practices lie deep in American soil. During the 1870s and 1880s, the early Bow Valley ranchers used livestock raising methods that had been developed in the American Great Plains. American ranching techniques, such as open-range herding, rounding up scattered cattle, weaning and branding calves, and culling old cows, enabled Bow Valley ranchers to handle the growing livestock trade. Ranchers and cowboys from the United States played a key role in fashioning practices capable of enlarging and shaping ranching opportunities on the open range. The American-born cowboys were a minority, but their methods greatly influenced both Bow Valley society and the course of Alberta history, for they meshed beautifully with the needs of a vital, growing region and thus became part of the Alberta culture.

Table 6 shows the demographic structure of the cowboy culture in the Bow Valley. Of the twenty-six cowboys in the region's ranching work force in 1891, eight, or 31 percent, came from the United

Chapter 7: Building the Ranching Community

I. G. Baker & Co. warehouse, barns, corrals, and horses (foreground) in Calgary Bottom on west side of the Elbow River in 1884. (Courtesy of Glenbow Archives, NA-1406-163).

States. The largest group, with ten men representing 38 percent of the work force, came from other parts of Canada, especially Ontario. British-born men, eight in number, accounted for 31 percent of the cowboy population. However, changes had occurred by 1901. As the cowboy population in the Bow Valley grew to fifty-nine in that year, the American-born segment dropped to 20 percent and the group from elsewhere in Canada rose to 46 percent, while the British-born component remained at 31 percent. Only one man from Denmark and one from Sweden represented western continental Europe.[9] By this time, the ranching techniques of ranchers and cowboys from the United States were well established in the Bow Valley. In seizing new ranching opportunities, Bow Valley livestock raisers continued to follow American ranching practices.

Severe Winter of 1886-1887

However, a crucial fact affected the development of ranching. Lethal, legendary snowstorms punctuated the winter of 1886-1887. After heavy downpours, deep, unyielding snow covered the Bow Valley, killing many cattle and etching itself in the personal and collective memories of ranchers. The severe winter struck a deadly blow to the open-range livestock industry, with numerous ranches sustaining large losses.

Those cattle "that came in early in the season and got well fattened up before the winter set in have done fairly well, and there won't be more than from 15 to 18 percent of loss among them, but those cattle that came in poor in the fall will suffer severely, the

153

Chapter 7: Building the Ranching Community

loss amounting to probably 25 to 30 percent," observed the *Calgary Tribune*.[10] A substantial part of the cattle kingdom in the Bow Valley lay in ruins. There was, however, a legacy of improvement, stemming in part from the technology of barbed-wire fencing, an American invention. With the increasing use of barbed-wire fences to enclose pastures and the growing trend toward feeding hay in the winter, it became possible for many Bow Valley ranchers to survive and to enhance the quality of beef over the next two decades. The utilization of enclosed pastures also aided livestock raisers in improving the bloodlines in their herds. Much as they appreciated access to the grass on the open range, they realized that open-range herding often led to the problem of their purebred Shorthorns or Herefords breeding with inferior cattle.

Livestock Raising and the Natural Environment

Between the 1870s and 1890s, Bow Valley ranchers tapped grass, soil, and water on leased lands and on lands they owned. Occasional misuse of these resources was not overlooked, but it was usually tolerated. Nature's bounty greatly impressed people in frontier Bow Valley. The region sported many streams, the plentiful soil was fertile – amazingly fertile to those who came from sandy or rocky stretches of land – and the growing season was fairly long. Then, too, the area enjoyed both good drainage and adequate shelter. Although precipitation was not always sufficient in this period, irrigation was feasible on a number of ranches. A lively sense of expectation, the thrill of starting a new livestock-raising business, and the moderate climate lifted spirits for many individuals.

No snowstorms in the late nineteenth century were as terrible as those in the winter of 1886-1887, but other snowstorms also resulted in deaths among ranchers' cattle and sheep. Some livestock raisers who came with high hopes found the winters not to their liking, and left the Bow Valley in disappointment. Many of the ranchers who went to the region failed to strike it rich in cattle or sheep or do well in their horse-raising ventures. Livestock raisers nervously pondered the direction of future ranching developments, but many of them learned how to cope with Bow Valley winters and remained in the region to become prosperous.

Chapter 7: Building the Ranching Community

Ranching in the Bow Valley
The Conrads, I. G. Baker, and the Harris Brothers

From the beginning, Canadians assumed that Alberta could support ranching in the Bow Valley. Adaptations of techniques commonly practised in the American Great Plains were essential, but the example of John McDougall at Morley in 1873 and I. G. Baker & Co. at Calgary two years later proved that experimentation could succeed. Baker & Co. borrowed many of the techniques and tools of the Montana ranchers and, as Calgary emerged as a trading centre in 1875, the firm also began to adopt the American open-range approach to livestock raising. The ranching concern of Baker & Co., the well-established partnership of Charles and William Conrad and I. G. Baker, was the first ranch in the Calgary area, and the pasturage for its cattle was free for the taking. The firm was an important element in placing the early, strong capitalistic imprint on the culture of the Bow Valley, and it reflected the growing flow of foreign direct investment from the United States into the region. Eventually, the firm expanded its operations in the Bow Valley, creating a large, low-cost ranching enterprise organized to take advantage of open-range herding, rationalization of management, and tremendous economies of scale.

In the mid-1870s, the Canadian government tolerated, and even encouraged, the settlement of squatters in the Bow Valley. Land was easy to come by. With its great entrepreneurial drive, Baker & Co. simply took over an unclaimed area of about thirteen hundred acres at the confluence of the Bow and Elbow rivers, near its trading post.[11] As a ranching enterprise, the firm did not have to own any land at this time, since all the Dominion land in the Bow Valley was generally seen as open range. The trading post, other buildings, and the corrals that Baker & Co. erected served as its ranch headquarters. On its ranch along the Bow and Elbow, the firm had several miles of running water for its cattle. In this stretch of range, it gained a monopoly not only on water but also on grass.

Finding markets for its stock was not difficult for Baker & Co. The presence of the Mounted Police and Native Canadians – Blackfoot, Sarcee, and Stoney – created a demand for beef in and around the river town of Calgary. The firm was soon driving its

Chapter 7: Building the Ranching Community

cattle from Montana to its Calgary range, where they were fattened on grass and sold to the Canadian government to provide beef for the Natives and Mounted Police. For awhile, William and Charles Conrad of Fort Benton, the chief owners of Baker & Co. by the early 1880s, thought that the range might always be open and free, but gradually they came to recognize that complete ownership of the land was the only way to assure full control of the water and grass for their livestock. Before long, in addition to using barbed-wire fences to control their cattle and to keep out trespassers, they grew oats for winter feed. In 1882, they purchased parcels of land in Calgary Bottom along the Elbow and Bow rivers from Baptiste Annouse and John Monroe.[12] Two years later, the Canadian government sold the Conrads 16¼ acres in Calgary Bottom for $638, as well as 640 acres near Calgary at $2.50 an acre.[13]

The Conrads followed a general strategy of expanding geographically to other areas in the Bow Valley as the best way to grow. As opportunities for using new ranch lands opened up, they took advantage of them. The essential first step in exploiting new areas was their decision to join their friends, especially I. G. Baker of St. Louis, Missouri and Fort Benton rancher John Harris, in creating the Benton & St. Louis Cattle Co. in 1882, a Montana firm that was capitalized at $500,000 and operated in both Montana and Alberta. A centralized management control was quickly established in Fort Benton, and the facilities and personnel for the production of cattle were rationalized to achieve economies of scale and scope. Under the Conrads' leadership, in the spring of 1886 this company leased from the Canadian government a large portion of the range in the vicinity of Kipp, between the Belly and Bow rivers, as pastureland. This lease, together with another lease, gave them control of a total of more than 130,000 acres of land. For the most part, the Conrads' great strengths – low-cost production of cattle on the open range and centralized administrative control – resulted in handsome profits and a growing enterprise. But problems plagued the Benton & St. Louis Cattle Co. The severe blizzard in the winter of 1886-1887 killed many of the company's cattle in Alberta and Montana. Fierce competition from settlers bent on farming instead of ranching forced a transition from open-range to closed-range ranching in Alberta. In 1892, the Canadian government cancelled the Conrads' big leases. They responded to this situation by purchasing about eight thousand acres of land at $3 per acre between 1893 and 1902: five hundred acres at the junction of the Belly and Little Bow rivers and, most importantly, seventy-five hundred acres in the Bow Valley at Queenstown, eighteen miles south of the main line of the Canadian Pacific Railway and bounded on the north by the Blackfoot reserve.[14]

Their Queenstown ranch in the Bow Valley, also known as the Circle ranch from the "O" brand on their cattle, gave the Conrads and their associates valuable pastureland.[15] "It looks to me," wrote I. G. Baker to John Harris, "that the acquisition of the Queenstown lands was very desirable. You know it is sort of a craze with me to own good hay and grazing land."[16] The ranch possessed other key assets as well. As the Conrads boasted, it embraced the Buffalo Hills, which provided much-needed shelter for their cattle on the range and for the corrals and ranch buildings. The Queenstown also lay in the path of a six-mile-wide strip of Chinook wind, which helped compensate for the harder winters in this eastern part of the Bow Valley.

Even more importantly, the Queenstown offered the Conrads control of several springs of pure water.[17] Copious supplies of water were needed for their herd of about fourteen thousand head of cattle. The Conrads' influence in Canadian government circles had allowed them to purchase the most prized quarter section within the ranch, one which contained the best of these springs, despite Ottawa's original decision to set aside this land as a stock-watering reserve for all the local cattlemen. Not surprisingly, other ranchers in the area, especially Thomas P. McHugh, who had earlier failed in his attempt to acquire this quarter section, harboured resentment about the Canadian government's willingness to tilt its land policy in the Conrads' favour. Engaging the services of James A. Lougheed and R. B. Bennett, two distinguished Calgary lawyers, Hughes attacked the Conrads, but his attack produced nothing but more animosity. The Conrads, however, continued to pasture most of their Alberta cattle on the Queenstown, relying on its magnificent springs as their principal source of water.

The Conrads produced for the market in Calgary and beyond, sending their cattle from their Queenstown ranch to the Canadian Pacific Stockyards in Calgary for local consumption, as well as for shipment directly to British Columbia and Chicago and, indirectly, through Calgary and Winnipeg cattle dealers, to Great Britain.[18] They also participated in the market economy by supplying beef to the Natives on the Blackfoot, Sarcee, and Stoney reserves.

Chapter 7: Building the Ranching Community

Circle Ranch round-up crew in the Lethbridge area, c. 1890. Circle manager Howell Harris (far left) is standing behind a wagon. (Courtesy of Glenbow Archives, NA-118-1).

As the Conrads tried to improve the quality of their Queenstown cattle through breeding programs, confining and controlling their stock became increasingly necessary. Like other ranchers in the Bow Valley, they turned more and more to using barbed wire. Their manager, Howell Harris, brother of John Harris and a successful experimenter, moved quickly to acquire purebred Hereford bulls and to pasture them with breeding stock in fenced fields. Howell Harris also established a spring-based irrigation system, produced hay, oats and barley in irrigated, fenced fields, and stored the crops for winter-feeding. As the years rolled by, in an effort to keep down costs, he introduced relatively cheap Mexican cows into the Queenstown herd, blending them with splendid Hereford, Shorthorn, Galloway, and Polled Angus bulls. Hazards of drought, blizzards, fire, heel flies, wolves, cattle rustlers, and disease such as black leg and mange were all part of Harris's daily life. The stress of these hazards could shake him, but it was offset in part by his willingness to exchange work with neighbouring ranchers, including control of mange among cattle through the use of dipping vats. Besides knowing a great deal about cattle and saddle horses, he took pride in his ranch records, committing to paper the number of cattle he turned into or removed from each pasture on the Queenstown, how many calves he branded, and their shipping weights and sales.[19] Harris's careful records and efficient management helped the Queenstown operation with its well-known Circle cattle to remain viable during the 1890s and beyond.

The experience of the Conrads revealed that the Bow Valley was hospitable to Montana ranching techniques. Old American traditions of raising cattle did fit the conditions north of the border, even when the leaders resided far away. Having invested a great deal of money in the Bow Valley, the Conrads' aim was to make profits from the land they worked in the region as a firm and as individuals.[20] It was especially the promise of individual reward that helped ensure the success of their enterprise.

Cochrane Ranche Company

All the conditions true for Americans like the Conrads also existed for Canadians such as those associated with the large Cochrane Ranche Company. John A. Macdonald, recognized in his own day as a Conservative Prime Minister with a broad vision, did much to encourage this and other companies in building their ranching businesses. Interested in strengthening the nation through the promotion of business enterprise, he established a program that granted generous terms to big ranchers. By 1881, Macdonald's government was offering large leases to companies to entice private entrepreneurs to invest money in Alberta ranching ventures and thereby further Canadian interests. These companies were businesses in which individual investors spread their risk by sharing ownership. To stimulate the growth of ranching, the lease typically granted the companies exclusive grazing rights in particular areas in the Bow Valley and Alberta. Incorporated on 5 May 1881 and with its head office in Montreal, the Cochrane Ranche Company was the first venture in which central Canadian entrepreneurs, with the support of the federal government, sought new ranching opportunities in the Bow Valley.[21] The company's lease of a hundred thousand acres gave it the right to graze its cattle on the Bow River west of Calgary.

Capitalized at $500,000 (five thousand shares of stock valued at $100 apiece), the Cochrane Ranche Company had several stockholders. Matthew H. Cochrane, the company's founder,

Chapter 7: Building the Ranching Community

Matthew H. Cochrane, c. 1870s, founder of the Cochrane Ranche Company. (Courtesy of Glenbow Archives, NA-239-25).

who was a farmer and an award-winning Shorthorn cattle breeder of Hillhurst, Quebec, a Montreal boot and shoe manufacturer, and a Conservative member of the Canadian Senate, received a thousand shares. A man of considerable inner strength, Cochrane had imagination and was capable of conceiving great schemes for development; it became his dream to be as successful in Alberta as he was Quebec. He developed a network of information and influence in Ottawa, the most visible member of this network being John A. Macdonald. Duncan McEachran, a veterinarian surgeon of Compton, Quebec, held a thousand shares as well. James A. Cochrane, a son of Cochrane and active on his father's Hillhurst Farm, obtained five hundred shares. In addition, Major James Walker, the former Galt, Ontario farmer and one-time Mounted Policeman, and John M. Browning, a farmer of Longueuil, Quebec, received a hundred shares each. At that time, the remaining twenty-three hundred shares were not distributed. The Canadian Bank of Commerce in Montreal served as the company's banker.[22]

The management of the Cochrane Ranche was fairly standard. Each year in Montreal, stockholders elected a board of directors who, in turn, chose the officers of the company: president, managing director, treasurer, and resident ranch manager. Power, on a daily basis, rested with the president, who was assigned the general supervision of all the affairs of the company, and the managing director, who was given general oversight of the ranch. Matthew Cochrane was the company's president, while McEachran served as managing director and Browning as secretary-treasurer. James Walker became the resident manager at the Big Hill, the ranch's headquarters west of Calgary in the Bow Valley.[23] Later, Walker took over the sawmill that the company established in Calgary.

The Cochrane Ranche did not start out grandly, however. Its first years in Alberta were thoroughly miserable. Matthew Cochrane as president and McEachran as managing director may have controlled the ranch from Montreal, but they did not really administer it. They had a powerful voice in how many head of cattle to purchase and at what price, but they knew little about the actual conditions under which the ranch operated. There was almost no co-ordination between the Big Hill and Montreal parts of the administration. Effective management of the ranch was impossible because neither the Montreal management nor James Walker had the information or methods to ensure an efficient use of available resources and so to keep down ranching costs. The Cochrane Ranche experienced major problems with the herd of 6,700 Hereford cows, calves, and steers that was purchased in Montana and driven north to the Big Hill in the fall of 1881.[24] The drive was marked by its emphasis on rapid delivery. Greatly weakened by the fast pace at which it was forced to travel, the herd was in poor shape when it arrived at the Big Hill. In this condition, hundreds of calves, steers, and cows died on the open range as they faced a raging blizzard in October. Then, in the summer and fall of 1882, without seeking better ways to organize the second cattle drive, the Montreal management brought in five thousand head of cattle from Montana. As a severe snowstorm blanketed this herd at Fish Creek near Calgary on 28 September, and as it was hit by an extremely cold winter soon after it reached the Big Hill, the Cochrane Ranche's owners were beleaguered. Unlike other ranchers, they did not allow their cattle to roam eastward beyond their lease to more sheltered areas in the Bow Valley. Thousands of head of Cochrane Ranche cattle had perished by the spring of 1883, and the company reported crippling financial losses.

British American Ranche Company

These losses permanently killed the Cochrane Ranche Company's aspirations of developing a profitable position in cattle at the Big Hill. Perhaps a more southerly location, its owners thought, would provide more favourable conditions for cattle raising.[25] After transferring their Cochrane Ranche cattle operations south – outside the Bow Valley – to their new lease between the Waterton and Belly rivers in the summer of 1883, Matthew Cochrane and some

Chapter 7: Building the Ranching Community

William D. Kerfoot, c. 1890, manager of the British American Ranche. (Courtesy of Glenbow Archives, NA-1697-1).

of his associates formed a new firm, the British American Ranche Company, to transform the Big Hill into a sheep-raising venture.

For reasons not fully clear, Matthew Cochrane and his colleagues concluded that their chances of succeeding with sheep at the Big Hill were fairly good. Perhaps they believed that sheep might make the lease economically salvageable, if not very profitable. Cochrane, who incorporated his new enterprise on 5 February 1884, was again to be president and responsible for over-all company policy and performance.[26] Montrealer William Cassils, president of the Canadian District Telegraph Co., became vice-president. John M. Browning again became secretary-treasurer. From the company's head office in Montreal, Browning was to oversee operations as well as sales at the British American Ranche. The company's officers secured financing for the enterprise by occasionally borrowing from the Bank of Montreal.

In April, Cochrane placed a new manager in charge of the sheep ranch on the north side of the Bow at the Big Hill – William D. Kerfoot. Cochrane had made a good choice, for Kerfoot proved to be a clear-headed manager. Born in 1857 in Virginia, Kerfoot had lived and worked on a ranch in Montana as a young man.[27] In 1883, he came to Calgary to obtain a position as a cowboy at the Cochrane Ranche, in which his ability soon made him foreman.[28] In the summer of 1884, just about two months after he had become manager of the British American Ranche, Kerfoot, together with Cochrane, visited Sun

Chapter 7: Building the Ranching Community

River, Montana to purchase eight thousand sheep. How much previous experience Kerfoot had with sheep is unknown, but he did a creditable job. He was highly competent in supervising personally the work of driving the herd north into the Bow Valley. The sheep consisted of Merinos and Shropshires as well as a cross of the two breeds. Travelling about six miles a day, they arrived at the Big Hill in the fourth week of September "with scarcely any loss" and were "as fat as butter."[29]

Kerfoot moved quickly to erect sheds for the sheep at the Big Hill and to put up hay for winter-feeding. To provide veterinary care, Cochrane recruited A. E. Cross, who had recently graduated from the Montreal Veterinary College.[30] A man who excelled at anything he put his mind to, Cross learned to maximize his skills in meeting the health needs of the sheep. But by October 1885, at the close of its first full year of operations, the British American Ranche had made no progress in terms of growth and profitability. There were problems in venturing into raising sheep on the open range. Although the sheep drive from Montana over land and across many streams had generally been successful, "crossing the very high waters" had placed a strain upon the herd and left Kerfoot with "a number of weak little lambs" that died in the winter of 1884-1885. Then, in the spring, "a prairie fire" passed "over the lamb band causing ... great loss." A few weeks later, another prairie fire drove the herd "into a slough, smothering and drowning about 200 of the band." In the shearing season, Kerfoot discovered to his dismay that the wool on the remaining sheep had been damaged by the fires and was "not very good."[31]

A basic problem that made matters even worse was that the British American Ranche depended on a few inexperienced shepherds to look after the sheep. Kerfoot asked Cochrane for three more shepherds, especially men who had demonstrated their ability to work effectively with a large herd. While willing to redress the ranch's big disadvantage, Cochrane brought in only two experienced shepherds from Aberdeen, Scotland.[32] The lack of a sufficient number of skilled shepherds caused no end of headaches. Cochrane had some very positive business qualities, including a strong will in steering toward the goals he set himself, but he did not have enough personal contact with operations at the British American Ranche.

Despite the work force's shortage of expertise in herding, Kerfoot

Chapter 7: Building the Ranching Community

remained a solid everyday leader at the British American Ranche, seeking to raise and sell quality sheep. The market for mutton in the growing town of Calgary was picking up, and Kerfoot was able to make some local sheep sales. For example, in the summer of 1885 he sold 150 sheep at $7 each to Angus C. Sparrow's butcher shop.[33] The butcher shop took another 125 sheep at $6.50 each in January 1886. Having obtained a special freight rate from the Canadian Pacific, Kerfoot shipped several carloads of wool from the hamlet of Cochrane to Montreal in mid-September.[34] By this time, he had put up enough hay on the British American Ranche to feed all the sheep through the next winter.

Although wool and mutton were their leading products, the British American Ranche's owners followed a policy of diversified production and sales. Reluctant to tie their ranch's future too closely to any one or two products, they ran about 450 horses on the open range on the south side of the Bow at the Big Hill from the beginning.[35] During the Rebellion of 1885, his horses at the Big Hill became Cochrane's primary focus of attention as the Canadian troops required horses. "I imagine there will be a sharp and quick demand for horses suitable for saddle," Cochrane wrote Kerfoot,

> ... and if you have not already commenced think you should get all that are fit in the band broken so as to take advantage of the demand. I presume you are alive to the situation, and very likely you are doing just what I suggest. If you could clean out a good lot of the old band, it would enable the Co. to put in some good brood mares.[36]

Using his contacts in Ottawa, Cochrane was able to secure orders for horses from the Canadian government. The British American Ranche emerged as an important supplier to the Canadian troops; driving a number of saddle horses from the ranch to Calgary, Kerfoot sold them to the government at what he considered "very good figures."[37] Although afflicted by diseases such as distemper, the remaining horses survived and generally prospered on the Big Hill grasses. In the summer of 1886, Kerfoot bought over seven hundred horses in British Columbia, mostly brood mares but also some stallions. With this purchase, the herd of horses at the British American Ranche continued to grow in strength.[38]

Sharply in contrast was the sheep business, with John M.

Browning's insistence that Kerfoot was responsible for the disappearance of 771 sheep. The problem of the missing sheep took Kerfoot by surprise.[39] He was stunned, but he defended the shepherd who had been looking after the sheep. All of this cost Kerfoot his job. When Matthew Cochrane dismissed him on 28 October 1886, Kerfoot sued the British American Ranche.[40] At the hearing before Judge Charles B. Rouleau in Calgary, James A. Lougheed argued Kerfoot's case, pointing out that his dismissal was unreasonable. The court returned a verdict in Kerfoot's favour, awarding him $1,650 in damages.[41]

Kerfoot had in a scant eighteen months helped to build up one of the Bow Valley's leading ranches, an enterprise known throughout Alberta especially for its herd of twelve thousand sheep.[42] It was truly a big ranch. But the sheep business was not a profitable operation. In August 1886, just two months before he was dismissed, Kerfoot asked Matthew Cochrane to bring in three more experienced shepherds from Aberdeen, Scotland to augment the workforce and bolster the sheep herding skills at the British American Ranche. The three shepherds – Alexander Stuart, William Martin, and Alexander P. Stewart – arrived at the Big Hill in mid-October 1886.[43] These gifted men played an important role in holding the economically precarious ranch together, as Ernest B. Cochrane, one of Matthew Cochrane's sons, became manager, replacing Kerfoot, who now struck out on his own in horse and cattle ranching on Grand Valley Creek a few miles west of Cochrane.[44]

Over the next two years, the British American Ranche's operations were generally unsatisfactory. Still, Stewart, Martin, and Stuart helped watch over the sheep grazing on the open range, making effective use of the sheep dogs which they had brought with them from Scotland. Two dogs had accompanied each of the new shepherds: one mature and well trained in the ways of herding sheep and the second a young dog.[45] Besides responding to the opportunity to earn some money, the men came because they believed the ranch offered a chance to be creative; they were clearly interested in guiding the herd of sheep along a viable course of future development. Yet they found the bands of sheep within the herd working in an uncoordinated manner. Acting on their sense of responsibility to the ranch, they sought to improve communications between the sheepherders and to combine the bands into a cohesive unit.

Acrimonious labour relations, however, hindered their efforts. As

Chapter 7: Building the Ranching Community

Stuart, Martin, and Stewart arrived at the British American Ranche, labour matters at the Big Hill became more complex. In this sphere of activity, the ranch's owners hardly tried to make improvements. But there was room for change, especially in wages. For their long shifts, sunrise to sunset, the three new shepherds received wages that were perhaps somewhat below average for sheepherders on ranches. In the years 1886 to 1888, they received $32 per month plus room and board, a figure that rose to $35 at another ranch in Alberta. Consequently, they demanded an increase in wages. Matthew Cochrane was being pressed between the aspirations of his shepherds and the moneymaking priorities of his associates. To complicate matters, the British American Ranche's foreman had lost confidence in one of the key shepherds, Alexander Stuart, who was in charge of a band of at least two thousand sheep.[46] The situation led to a dispute over management between Stuart and the foreman. Stuart was independent enough to indicate that he hoped for an amicable settlement rather than the disruption of operations. But the British American Ranche's owners, unwilling to seek a compromise, blamed the dispute on Stuart and dismissed him in April 1888. With the talented Stuart out of the picture, the sheep raising concern was not in a position to make much progress.

In addition to facing labour difficulties at the Big Hill, the British American Ranche found itself in an increasingly bitter contest with settlers for access to the grasses of the open range. Some farmers simply moved onto the ranch's vast lease, occupying the land of their choice as squatters. Others sought to enter into an arrangement with the ranch's owners or its resident manager to begin farming 160 or 240 or 320 acres of the lease and grazing their livestock on it.[47] Matthew Cochrane was unalterably opposed to such arrangements. His goal was twofold: to ensure the British American Ranche of the grass it needed, and to deny its use to all settlers. From time to time, Cochrane visited the Big Hill to control his pasturelands, but he was acutely conscious that the settlers were making serious inroads on them. The development of the large ranch was expensive and required a long-term commitment. Cochrane was reluctant to make the necessary investments of capital and time; between 1887 and 1890, the British American Ranche ceased to exist as he gave up the lease and sold the sheep and horses.[48]

By contrast, outside the Bow Valley, Cochrane learned about successful cattle ranching practices and the lessons paid off not only

Chapter 7: Building the Ranching Community

with reference to his personal wealth but also with respect to his impact on the development of the Alberta economy. He spent large sums of money on and gave considerable time to the improvement of his cattle at the Cochrane Ranche on the Belly and Waterton rivers, and this helped to make that cattle-raising enterprise a success.

Quorn Ranche Company

While the growth of ranching in the Bow Valley in the mid-1880s owed something to raising sheep on the British American Ranche, the creation and development of the big cattle ranches had most to do with it, especially those that had strong links to Great Britain. In the case of one of the most famous of these ranches, the Quorn Ranche Company, the story unfolded at a place that spread south from Sheep Creek – it lay west of Okotoks, near the Big Rock, the glacial boulder that later became a provincial historic site. Charles W. Martin of Quorn Place, County of Leicester, England was the initial guiding force in the company that came to be called the Quorn Ranche Company.[49] Martin's visit to the Sheep Creek area in 1884 set the stage for his entrance into the ranching industry. Greatly impressed by the area's potential for cattle raising, he established the Sheep Creek Ranche Co. Joining him as a partner was James S. Moore, a businessman who then lived in Ireland and two years later came to the Bow Valley to become more involved in running the ranch and to back his wife Elizabeth as she developed her private bank, Lafferty & Moore, in Calgary. With Ottawa remaining an important factor in big business opportunity in the Bow Valley, the federal government leased Martin and Moore a tract of 125,000 acres on Sheep Creek. Before long, they hired Irish-born John J. Barter, a former employee of the Hudson's Bay Company and a competent stockman, as resident manager of the Sheep Creek Ranche.[50]

Martin derived much of the support for the founding of the Sheep Creek Ranche from family and friends in England. In securing the starting capital, personal trust was essential. Martin, his family, and his fellow members of the Quorn Hunt Club of Leicestershire accounted for a substantial part of the financing.[51] However, even with the support of these people, the Sheep Creek Ranche began operations short of money, a weakness revealed by unexpected events in the late 1880s.

Chapter 7: Building the Ranching Community

Brood mares on the Quorn Ranche, c. 1893. (Courtesy of Glenbow Archives, NA-2084-1).

In the meantime, Martin, Moore, and Barter led the Sheep Creek Ranche into a period of considerable growth. The ranch's strategy – a strong emphasis on quality livestock – resulted in substantial sales and an expanding enterprise. In August 1884, Barter, the able resident manager, brought in 760 head of cattle from Montana.[52] By March 1886, there were fifteen hundred head of cattle grazing on the open range at the Sheep Creek Ranche, including about ninety head of purebred Polled Angus cattle from central Canada.[53] Although beef was their main product, the ranch's owners diversified by moving into raising horses, the number being five hundred at this time.[54] John Ware, an African-American cowboy from Texas who later went on to establish his own ranch on Sheep Creek, was recruited to look after the horse herd and break broncos.[55] Ware had nerve, took pride in his great strength, was an excellent rider, and proved himself trustworthy and reliable at the Sheep Creek Ranche.

To build up their herd of cattle, Martin and Moore purchased "large numbers" of cattle in the fall of 1886.[56] Like the other big ranchers in Alberta, they put up very little hay for their cattle, relying instead on the grasses on the open range to fatten them for market. For the Sheep Creek Ranche Co., which was still trying to establish itself in the cattle-raising business, the results of the terrible winter of 1886-1887 were almost disastrous. The fierce snowstorms killed nearly all the cattle acquired a few months before.[57] By the spring of 1887, the Sheep Creek Ranche teetered on the brink of failure.

Chapter 7: Building the Ranching Community

These problems soon brought changes to the company. Completely discouraged, James S. Moore dropped out of the partnership, which was reorganized on 4 May 1887 as the Quorn Ranche Company.[58] A venture incorporated under England's general incorporation laws, the new company was formed by Charles W. Martin and other members of the Quorn Hunt Club of Leicestershire and capitalized at £70,000. The Quorn Hunt Club men at the corporation's head office in Leicester guided the company's development. Martin served as president, and George F. Farnham acted as secretary. But the Quorn Ranche Company was cash-poor. The Quorn Ranche's officers looked for someone to lend them money. In the spring of 1887, they borrowed $10,000 from John J. Barter, who was still the ranch's resident manager.[59]

In running their company, the executives at the Quorn failed in their attempt to balance a quest for growth with a desire to enjoy life in Leicester's high society. Despite this, they usually supported Barter's efforts to produce top-quality cattle and horses at the Quorn. Certainly, they appreciated his drive and commitment. Barter, who brought a long-term perspective to his job, worked hard and demonstrated that he understood the open-range system of ranching. In addition to rebuilding the herd of cattle by purchasing more bulls, heifers, and steers, he brought in a trainload of brood mares from Ireland in August 1887.[60] He fattened the cattle and horses on the grasses of the open range. Barter also fenced in some fields and irrigated them, put up considerable hay for winter-feeding, and erected cattle sheds and horse barns.

Over most of the next ten years, Imperial Bank of Canada helped finance the Quorn's operations. The directors of chartered banks such as the Imperial Bank of Canada were prudent men who wanted both safe progress and profits. Knowing that big ranches in the Bow Valley such as the Quorn were willing to offer thousands of head of cattle and horses as security, these directors felt that it was safe to lend this company large sums of money. Although the loans did not always work perfectly, the bank in the end still made substantial profits.

But Charles Martin's quest for the high society life affected the Quorn Ranche. For most of the year, he lived at Quorn Place in the County of Leicester and paid only partial attention to the Quorn's business affairs. Other Quorn executives emulated Martin, when they could, and sometimes they and their friends used the ranch as a summer playground. Like Martin, they were known as persons who

Chapter 7: Building the Ranching Community

enjoyed lavish hunting parties at the ranch. The Quorn's owners could not afford such a lifestyle, for the years of Martin's presidency were not ones of profits. Cattle and horse sales did not cover costs at the Quorn Ranch. There was another problem: in 1889, James S. Moore claimed that Charles Martin owed him a huge sum of money from their earlier business dealings. When Martin refused to pay, Moore sued him. The Supreme Court of the Northwest Territories in Calgary ruled against Martin, awarding Moore damages in the amount of $55,897.[61] The decision obviously forced Martin to pay his debts, and this greatly impaired his ability to offer the Quorn the financial support it required.

The Quorn needed all the help it could get. When Barter died in 1890, Quorn's executives borrowed $20,000 from his widow Lizzie to stay afloat.[62] It became difficult to find a resident manager as talented as Barter to look after the Quorn's herd of five thousand head of cattle and its herd of 1,250 horses.[63] After awhile, Edward J. Swann, one of the existing English stockholders, stepped forward to become resident manager. Swann had no prior experience in ranching, but he soon learned the ropes. To secure funds for the development of the Quorn, he drove many of its cattle and horses along the Macleod Trail to the Canadian Pacific Stockyards in Calgary, selling some of the animals in the local market, shipping others to British markets, and selling a number of horses to the Moore & McDowall Company in Prince Albert for $2,000.[64]

Meanwhile, the Quorn had fallen behind in payments on its loans from the Imperial Bank of Canada. The loans totalled $33,698 and were secured by chattel mortgages on the Quorn's livestock. In January 1892, the bank obtained an injunction from the Supreme Court of the Northwest Territories in Calgary forbidding the Quorn to sell any more cattle and horses.[65] Over the next four years, Quorn's executives sent money from England, paying off some the ranch's debts to the Imperial Bank of Canada.

By the mid-1890s, the bank permitted the Quorn to make limited cattle and horse sales in return for cash payments. During the year ending 15 November 1895, the Quorn loaded 62 head of cattle and 215 horses onto Calgary and Edmonton cars at the railway's siding in Okotoks for shipment to the Canadian Pacific Stockyards in Calgary. The sale of these animals in local, national, British markets allowed the Quorn to meet some of its obligations. Irrigation ditches valued at $750 played an important part in the

Table 7. Ranching Statistics for the Bow Valley, 1891-1901

Year	1891	1901
Number of Big Ranches	2	2
Number of Small Ranches	176	458

Source: Manuscript Census of 1891 for Calgary, Canmore, Gleichen, High River, Davisburg, Fish Creek, Pine Creek, Namaka, and Morley; Manuscript Census of 1901 for Calgary, Canmore, Gleichen, High River, Davisburg, Pine Creek, Morley, Queenstown, Shepard, Nose Creek, Springbank, Cochrane, Jumping Pound, Okotoks, Millarville, Priddis, and Pekisko.

production of hay and oats for the livestock. Numerous fields surrounded by barbed-wire fences were devoted to controlling grass and water for the cattle and horses.

But by this time, little growth had occurred. In the previous twelve months, 250 calves and 125 foals had been branded. Yet the ranch's total number of cattle had plummeted to 1,330 head; its herd of horses had dropped to 890 mares and geldings and 9 stallions.[66] The Quorn was considered a bit safer than four years before, but it still did not have sufficient capital to carry on its business. Edward J. Swann and Lizzie Barter helped rescue the ranch. In June 1896, they guaranteed the Quorn's notes as the Imperial Bank of Canada made a loan of $3,000 to it.[67] Even so, the business was struggling simply to survive. Despite the lack of adequate financial resources, the high quality of its cattle and horses continued to give the Quorn access to markets and helped it to maintain its operations through the remainder of the decade and a few years into the twentieth century.

Small Ranches

When we look at the ranching industry in the Bow Valley in the late nineteenth century, we are apt to see only the big ranches on which thousands of head of cattle grazed to produce the region's beef. To be sure, the large ranch was an essential part of the story, but that part should not be mistaken for the whole. Table 7 shows that between 1891 and 1901, while two big ranches existed in the Bow Valley, the number of small ranches increased from 176 to 458, most of which had fewer than three hundred head of cattle.[68]

The continual appearance of new ranching businesses was a testament to the resilience of the small ranching sector even during

Chapter 7: Building the Ranching Community

the Bow Valley's worst economic depressions. In the late nineteenth century, small ranchers pioneered significant livestock operations in the region. The typical cattle raiser was a small rancher, who usually secured a 160-acre homestead as a headquarters for his ranch near a river, creek, or fine springs. A piece of legislation that made a tremendous impact on the Bow Valley was the Dominion Lands Act of 1872. Designed to promote the spread of family farms across the prairie West, this Act also greatly benefited settlers who became small ranchers. It offered a quarter section of homestead land, 160 acres, to a settler for a $10 filing fee.[69] The settlers had to live on their homesteads at least six months each year for three years, and during this period they had to break thirty acres and put twenty acres into crop. After this prove-up period, the homesteaders acquired full title to their farms or ranches.

Many of the ranch families owned between twenty-five and two hundred cattle and some horses. The principal markets for cattle raised on small ranches, like those produced on big ranches, in the Bow Valley were Calgary and Alberta, central Canada, and Great Britain. Small livestock raisers used their savings, as well as loans from extended-family members and friends, private banks, and, in some cases, chartered banks, to establish their small ranches. In most cases, they proved to be reliable borrowers. Included among the ranch families who raised cattle for market were the Malcolm T. Millar family at Millarville, the Samuel T. Mayhood family in the Nose Creek district, and the Joseph Bassett family at Mitford.[70]

On the small cattle ranches – most of the units in the Bow Valley operated on a small scale by the last half of the 1890s – the owners and their families themselves worked in the fields and on the open range. Even if they could afford cowboys, they worked alongside them. Small ranching businesses competed successfully throughout the late nineteenth century with the much larger cattle companies in the Bow Valley by remaining resilient. Many small ranches owed their resilience especially to the wide range of their owners' livestock raising skills, including their ability to deal with the health problems of their cattle if they did not have easy access to veterinarian services. Most small ranching enterprises adjusted better than the big companies to misfortune and change. Their resilience allowed many of them to survive and expand even during the hard times of the mid-1880s and mid-1890s.

Osborne E. Brown
Elbow River Rancher

One of the important figures in the small ranching industry was Osborne E. Brown, a settler who hailed from Great Britain. Brown was a son from an established family who wanted to prove himself. Born in 1867 in Lancashire, England, he was educated at a local school.[71] When Osborne Brown was a young boy, his father, an Anglican minister, died, but his mother and the man appointed as his guardian were both very supportive. Many years later, his stepson Glen Macdougall recalled that Osborne Brown "talked with a great deal of affection about his old guardian."[72] Osborne Brown took a job with Lloyd's of London; still a teenager, he travelled by train to work every day. But within a few weeks, he quit his job with Lloyd's to take up ranching in Alberta.

Brown had read the Canadian Pacific Railway's advertisements of the day about possibilities available to settlers in Alberta and, with his facility for mathematics, he calculated the riches from raising cattle. He wanted to seize the opportunities offered by agricultural progress and economic expansion in the Bow Valley. In 1885, barely eighteen years old, he joined other English immigrants in a trip across the Atlantic and Canada to Calgary.[73]

Some ranchers in the Calgary area lived a rough life among men of diverse backgrounds, and there were those whose adventures ended in failure. But with the confidence and energy of early manhood, the teenaged Brown set out to claim his fortune in ranching. In August 1886, he selected his 160-acre homestead on the Elbow River directly beside Sam Livingston's farm. Brown had brought with him some money from his family in England, and with this capital he developed his homestead. By June 1890, after breaking eighteen acres of rich sod, he had been harvesting crops of grain for three years. Other improvements included a log cabin, a barn, corrals, a well, and fences surrounding the fields, the total value of which amounted to $600. Brown's livestock consisted of four beef cattle and eight horses.[74]

Cold weather sometimes taxed Brown's shelter facilities and brought tragedy to his neighbours. On one occasion, during a severe cold spell, his log cabin was not warm enough for him. Glen Macdougall recalled that Brown, who had a mare and a colt, told

Chapter 7: Building the Ranching Community

Interior of Osborne E. Brown's log ranch house on the Elbow River, c. 1890. (Courtesy of Glenbow Archives, NA-3913-1).

him that "he used to bring the colt into the cabin at night, not to keep it warm but to keep himself warm." Another story, a tragic one, that came down to Glen Macdougall from Brown was:

> the still moonlight night, probably about thirty below zero, when Brown heard a horse come into the yard, a saddle horse. Brown got up and went out. There was a horse with a man on it, and Brown walked over to him and said, "Come on, put your horse in the barn and come in and get warm." The horse followed him down to the barn, but the man was dead, frozen stiff on the horse.[75]

Around 1892, while continuing to devote most of his energies to his ranch, Osborne Brown diversified by moving into the restaurant business in Calgary. He formed a partnership with the three English-born Critichley brothers, Oswald and Harry, both of whom were ranchers in the Bow Valley, and Thomas, to acquire the Criterion Restaurant on Stephen Avenue. From the outset, Brown and his partners sought to make it a first-class licensed restaurant. An entrepreneurial response to the needs of the male business community, the Criterion Restaurant became one of the sights of Calgary, accommodating prominent men from the town and the surrounding area in the dining hall and bar. The dining hall and bar, imitating aspects of the Criterion in London, England, gave citizens in Calgary and the Bow Valley an opportunity to do business over liquor or lunch or dinner. But the economic depression of the mid-1890s hurt the Criterion Restaurant, and by 1894 Brown and his associates had sold it, no doubt for a smaller sum than the $8,500 the Merchants Bank of Canada paid for the building in 1903.[76]

As the years passed, Osborne Brown acquired more land and expanded his cattle-raising operations. Growth was made possible through retained profits and loans from the Bank of Montreal in Calgary. The loans he obtained from this bank were protected by the small herd of cattle he offered as collateral, and had no trouble spots. Brown made the most of his profits by purchasing cattle in Calgary and Bow Valley markets, fattening them on grass, and selling them throughout Alberta. By the late 1890s, he was running about a hundred head of cattle on his ranch.[77] Like numerous other ranchers, he benefited from allowing his cattle to grow fat on free grass on the open range. He had many friends and business contacts, including neighbours with whom he shared the work of the round-up of cattle between the Bow and Elbow rivers each spring, and meat packer Pat Burns, who purchased cattle from him.[78] An ardent polo player, Brown again diversified by raising polo ponies for customers in Calgary and the Bow Valley.[79] By this time, too, he had a family. Around 1894, he married English-born Annie Patterson, daughter of local rancher George Patterson. Osborne and Annie had two sons: Richard was born in 1895; Frank arrived five years later. By the start of the next decade, the Brown household, which included two cowboys born in England, was focused on plans for further improvements on the ranch.[80] Now that Osborne Brown had accumulated the small fortune he had always dreamed about, he spared no expense in transforming the ranch into one of the showplaces in the Bow Valley.

Brown valued the ranch for the long-term security it provided for him and his family. Glen Macdougall remembered that

> Brown had a beautiful house, big and rambling. He was a great lover of gardens and his place was known for its fine lawns and flowerbeds. There was a big barn, with a concrete

Chapter 7: Building the Ranching Community

foundation and a loft. Also, there were corrals and various sheds, all well painted and well kept up.[81]

Brown, usually seen wearing "a Stetson hat, a silk handkerchief around his neck, a tweed jacket, corduroy trousers, and riding boots," was a familiar figure in the Bow Valley and Calgary. "He was very good, very quiet, with horses. I never saw him abuse or knock a horse around. He could make a horse do almost anything. He was a good judge of horses. Quite often, they used to get him to serve as a judge at horse shows," recalled Glen Macdougall.[82] Osborne Brown was "one of the very fine type of Englishmen who constituted the vanguard of young ranchers in Alberta. He was a kindly, cultured, fine type of man," said Harold Riley.[83]

Arthur G. Wolley-Dod
Pine Creek Rancher

Like Osborne Brown, Arthur G. Wolley-Dod, another Bow Valley rancher, came from England. Born in 1860 in Eton, Arthur Wolley-Dod was the son of the headmaster of Eton College.[84] Arthur was educated in a private school in Brighton. He then attended Eton, where his love of books was evident from the start. After Wolley-Dod graduated, he worked as an apprentice mechanical engineer at the Crew Works in England for nearly five years.[85]

At the end of this period, finding that he could get no job as a mechanical engineer, he wanted to become a farmer. One of the joys of his boyhood had been to ride horses on the family place in Cheshire. In 1882, Wolley-Dod, together with thirty-four other young men under the leadership of a clergyman, travelled to Minnesota to learn how to farm. Once the men reached the state, however, the original arrangement to have their leader place them on various farms was abandoned due to poor organization, and each was free to seek farm work on his own. As it turned out, Wolley-Dod's first job was to take the census of the town of Rochester, Minnesota. He then went to Winona on the Mississippi River, where he worked for a farmer for a year and a half before returning to England.[86] Wolley-Dod purchased a dairy farm in Cheshire and became deeply involved in making cheese.

Chapter 7: Building the Ranching Community

The ambition to better himself led to his decision to sell his farm after about four years. It became Wolley-Dod's dream to make his fortune in ranching in the Canadian West. In the spring of 1887, he left home to go abroad. A ship carried him to Canada. In Montreal, he boarded a train for Vancouver. Then it was back eastward into the interior of British Columbia. He stopped often; and wherever he stopped, he searched for land suitable for ranching. Finally, in the summer he headed for Calgary. Arriving by train, he parked his luggage at a hotel near the Canadian Pacific station, rented a team and wagon, and drove out into the country looking for land. Wolley-Dod purchased eight hundred acres of fertile prairie land from the Canadian Pacific Railway southeast of Midnapore, on the Bow River in the Pine Creek area.[87]

Arthur G. Wolley-Dod in middle age, rancher on Pine Creek. (Courtesy of Glenbow Archives, NA-3620-1).

Later that summer, Arthur Wolley-Dod returned to England to marry Annie Frances Brown, a woman of Scottish descent who had been born in India into a British military officer's family.[88] Following their honeymoon in Devonshire, the couple boarded a train for London. Before long, Arthur and Annie were crossing the Atlantic to Canada. On 15 October 1887, they arrived at their ranch site in the Pine Creek area. Now Arthur Wolley-Dod began to develop the ranch that he hoped to own and operate for a long time. This was one form of the Canadian dream, and for Wolley-Dod, living the dream, it had an aura of surprise. There was astonishment not only at his good fortune, but also at the back-breaking labour required to profit from it.

Like other Bow Valley livestock raisers, Arthur Wolley-Dod faced the ceaseless problems of how to pay for current ranching operations and how to finance development in the future. To a large degree, he relied on his savings and family wealth.[89] Money

Chapter 7: Building the Ranching Community

from his family in England allowed him to erect a house and a barn, acquire machinery, break the prairie sod, fence his fields, put in crops of wheat and oats, and purchase cattle and horses. No neighbour welcomed Arthur and Annie more warmly than Edwin Winterbottom, who invited them to stay in his house while theirs was being built.[90]

For a number of years, they bought most of their supplies from I. G. Baker & Co.'s store in Calgary. Like other cattle operators in the late nineteenth century, Arthur Wolley-Dod depended to a considerable extent on open-range herding. While he enclosed some of his pastures with barbed-wire fences and put up hay to hand-feed his cattle during the cold winter months, he often kept down production costs by fattening them on free grass on unfenced, unclaimed pasturelands. But he also made important choices about the disposition of earnings from the sale of cattle to cattle dealers like William Roper Hull in Calgary. Wolley-Dod retained significant amounts of money for reinvestment. This permitted him to focus on the long-term good of the ranch.

By the early 1890s, however, there were not enough funds to finance development. In these years the drought, combined with prairie fires, hurt the ranch.[91] Mortgage loans, therefore, became vital to growth.[92] In April 1890, Wolley-Dod borrowed $200 from James L. Wilson, the Calgary architect, at an 18 percent annual interest rate. The loan, with a ten-month maturity, was secured by a mortgage on Wolley-Dod's ranch implements. In October of the same year, Wolley-Dod obtained a $500 loan of four months at 15 percent interest from William Roper Hull. A mortgage on Wolley-Dod's ranch, as well as one on his cattle, horses, and implements, served as collateral for this loan.

The demand for Arthur Wolley-Dod's cattle grew, and the earnings from cattle sales permitted him to pay off his loans and expand his herd. By 1893, he was running about thirty head of cattle on his ranch.[93] Everyone agreed that he was an outstanding horseman. He spent much time on his saddle horse, giving his cattle a great deal of attention. Arthur's brother Hova came to work for him in 1893 and toiled on the ranch for five years before he went to Scotland to learn the business of farming.[94] Eleven years younger than Arthur, Hova was a practical and spirited man, caught up in his brother's effort to develop the ranch. The success of their ranching operations allowed Arthur and Annie Wolley-Dod to raise and feed their growing family, using some of their land for a garden. By 1893, they had three children: Ethel, aged five; Marjorie, four; and William, who was a few months old.[95] Annie balanced her various domestic responsibilities, caring for the infants, cooking meals, and doing the laundry.

In many respects, a co-operative spirit informed the Wolley-Dod household. Among other things, Arthur enjoyed helping Annie tend their vegetable and flower garden. ""Father was a great gardener," recalled daughter Marjorie many years later.[96] The Wolley-Dods, who loved to experiment, were also active in the Fish Creek Agricultural Society, of which Arthur became a vice-president. At the society's fair in July 1893, Arthur won second prize for the best year-old cattle, while Annie took prizes for her collections of petunias and cut garden flowers.[97] Later, in 1899, 1900, and 1903, Arthur was president of the Calgary Agricultural Society's fair.[98]

During the economic depression in the mid-1890s, however, things began to tighten up in the ranching business. With little cash flow, Arthur Wolley-Dod was in trouble. He fell behind in his payments to the Hudson's Bay Company store in Calgary for goods he had purchased there on credit. In November 1895, when he owed the store $657, it demanded security and got from him a mortgage on his implements, cattle, and horses. A year later, with $463 of his debt still unpaid, Wolley-Dod re-mortgaged his cattle, horses, and implements to the Hudson's Bay Company store.[99]

In this difficult period, Arthur Wolley-Dod continued to be a source of support and encouragement for his family. As his children reached school age, he recruited a governess to teach them on the ranch. The product of his upbringing, he was a man of many friendships and represented the neighbourliness of pioneer Bow Valley. One of the activities that called forth his qualities was polo, a game he mastered and worked to popularize in the Pine Creek area. By 1895, Arthur was secretary of the Pine Creek Polo Club.[100] The Wolley-Dod children absorbed their father's love of competition, enthusiasm for learning, optimism in trying circumstances, and willingness to work hard. They also appreciated the opportunity their father and mother gave them to continue their education in England. Marjorie attended a private girls' school in Bexley, Kent, and William studied at Haileybury College.[101]

Annie Wolley-Dod, who toiled at her husband's side on the ranch from the beginning, played an important role in its success. It

Chapter 7: Building the Ranching Community

was particularly fitting that she should later share with her Calgary friends some lofty thoughts to lift their spirits:

> The study of art, literature and music should be encouraged. No nation that ever amounted to anything has been without its men and women who had visions, dreams, and ideas to lead them on. We cannot command genius, but we can do our best to make the people of the Northwest a truly cultured and noble-minded people. For then we do not lose sight of reward of our efforts or feel that we have lived in vain.[102]

The revival of the national, Calgary, and Bow Valley economies in the late 1890s renewed the demand for Arthur Wolley-Dod's cattle. His troubles of the mid-1890s seemed increasingly remote as orders for his cattle flowed in to augment his earnings. Under his watchful eye, the herd on his ranch grew at the turn of the century. Work exchanges occurred between Arthur and his brother Hova, who operated a small ranch on Pine Creek for about eleven years before the outbreak of World War I. Both being superb gardeners, they also shared their knowledge of vegetables, flowers, shrubs, and trees. But just as Arthur's income was rising, the expansion of farming and the proliferation of barbed-wire fences in the Bow Valley closed the open range and brought an end to free grass. As he told a reporter for the *Albertan*, "the encroachment of wire fences" on the open-range country caused him to sell his small ranch and move to the Elbow Park district in Calgary in 1909.[103] Calgary became the beneficiary of his interest in gardening, as he developed a magnificent garden at his home in the city. A founding member of the Calgary Horticultural Society, Wolley-Dod became its president in the 1920s.[104]

John Quirk and his Medium-Sized Ranch

One additional development in the Bow Valley ranching industry is worthy of notice. A few medium-sized ranches sprang up and flourished, and these also promoted the economic growth of Calgary and the Bow Valley. The willingness of their owners to use their savings to establish themselves, combined with their access to loans from friends and banks, helped these ranches to prosper. The story

Chapter 7: Building the Ranching Community

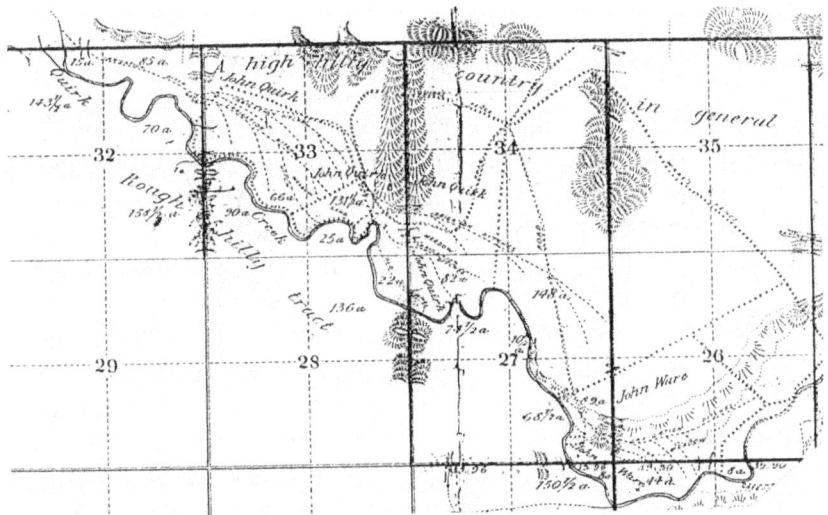

Map 4. Township 20 Range 4 W5M in 1894. John Quirk's homestead and ranch land near to John Ware's homestead and ranch land on what came to be called the North Fork of Sheep Creek. This map also shows the irrigation ditches that run through Quirk's land and Ware's land. (Courtesy of National Archives of Canada).

of John Quirk illustrates the importance of medium-sized ranches to the development of livestock raising. Born in 1838 in southern Ireland, Quirk owed much of his success to what he learned in the ranching business in Montana during the late 1870s and early 1880s. In the Missoula district, he discovered how to handle cattle and horses on his ranch by observing Montana ranchers at work. Quirk borrowed the techniques of Montanans and, as he moved with his wife Kate to his homestead at High River in 1882, brought with him not only 650 head of cattle but also the American open-range approach to cattle raising.[105] When he chose a new location for his operations on the North Fork of Sheep Creek in the Millarville area during 1887, he continued to use the range-herding technique. At the same time, he enclosed some of his pastures with barbed wire, irrigated them in dry years, made hay for winter-feeding, and used the enclosures to improve the bloodlines in his herds. Quirk's livestock raising business grew, and by 1893 there were 750 head of cattle and 100 horses grazing on his Millarville ranch.[106]

As a medium-sized rancher, Quirk generally held his own with large ranches in livestock raising and even came to regard the big rancher as a friend. Making progress in ranching on the open range

Chapter 7: Building the Ranching Community

in the Bow Valley often meant co-operating with big ranchers and, at a time when large ranchers dominated the livestock raising industry in the region, business success frequently meant success through co-operation. In 1888, Quirk joined other ranchers, both big and medium-sized, in the Bow Valley and Alberta to establish the Alberta Stock Growers' Association.[107] Eight years later, in 1896, at a gathering of livestock raisers in Calgary, Quirk emerged as an important figure in organizing the Western Stock Growers' Association in the southwestern prairies.[108] These associations, linking Bow Valley ranchers with livestock raisers in other parts of Alberta and the prairies, helped create a registry of brands, organized co-operative spring and fall round-ups, and worked together to protect themselves against the risk of losing their cattle to rustlers, wolves, prairie fires, and diseases such as mange. They gained political influence in the territorial and federal arenas and, in doing so, sought to secure better control over sources of water and to set up effective marketing systems.

In the Bow Valley, the large and medium-sized ranchers generally had much more political power at local, regional, and national levels than small ranchers and farmers. But there were exceptions. For example, in part because of his connections at the Ranchmen's Club, Arthur G. Wolley-Dod, a small rancher, also had influence in political circles. In the political arena, the top priority of all ranchers was to form organizations and to push for legislation that would help them to create and maintain profitable ranching businesses. In this way, they also made a significant contribution to the growth of the Calgary and Bow Valley economies.

The Ranchmen's Club, established in 1891 in Calgary, reinforced ties among big, medium-sized, and small livestock raisers. Club membership blended individual self-interest and collective well-being of ranchers. Included among the Club's members by the early twentieth century were big ranchers such as Pat Burns, medium-sized livestock raisers such as A. E. Cross, and small ranchers such as Henry R. Middleton of Okotoks.[109] They considered membership in the Club as a way to get ahead economically, as much as a way of creating and preserving social relationships. In the settlement period, these members' goals of sharing social activities such as lawn tennis, billiards, ping-pong, and polo complemented the development of their ranches.[110]

Most ranchers, whether big, medium-sized, or small, were part of well-developed neighbourhoods in the Bow Valley in the late nineteenth century. Neighbourhood was more than a geographic designation – it meant a set of economic and social relations. Ranch people created informal neighbourhoods in several ways: exchanging work, exchanging products, and visiting. Like cattle round-ups, the construction of new ranch buildings often demanded important work exchanges. Big, small, and medium-sized ranchers exchanged not only work, but also the products of their toil. While they frequently sold their cattle in larger, more impersonal markets, they at times exchanged them for cash through community networks in the Bow Valley. Visiting helped to integrate economic and social life in the region. The Western Stock Growers' Association and the Ranchmen's Club encouraged ranchers not only to become part of a web of community ties that connected ranches and families in rural neighbourhoods, but also to make economic and social links with other livestock raisers that went beyond geographic proximity. Overall, neighbourhood strategies of co-operation proved especially vital for maintaining the Bow Valley ranching society.

Improving the Canadian Pacific Stockyards

An important railway centre that was still a frontier city in the mid-1890s, Calgary was always filled with people passing through: merchants, ranchers, farmers, commercial travellers, immigrants, and tourists. At the Canadian Pacific Stockyards, there was an ever-changing mixture of ranchers, farmers, cattle dealers, and butchers, all of whom were either selling or purchasing livestock. In 1895, the Canadian Pacific shipped 325 carloads of cattle, 61 carloads of horses, and 13 carloads of sheep from the stockyards to external markets. In the same year, the railway's stockyards received for various people 50 carloads of cattle, 9 carloads of hogs, 4 carloads of horses, and one carload of sheep.[111]

Booster literature on Calgary portrayed it as a place where ranchers and farmers were well served. But there was a problem – in 1895, people began complaining that the Canadian Pacific Stockyards' hand pump for watering livestock was miserably inadequate in light of the heavy traffic. Finally, in March of the following year, J. N. Niblock, Canadian Pacific's assistant

Chapter 7: Building the Ranching Community

superintendent in the Calgary district, wrote to William Whyte, the railway's general superintendent of its western lines:

> I really think [that our] facilities for watering stock at Calgary should be [upgraded] as our cattle business appears to be improving and very much on the increase. We should do all we can to make things as pleasant as possible for our patrons and give them the least room we can to find fault.[112]

Whyte agreed and made significant changes. When the stockyards' new facilities for watering livestock were completed, they consisted of a steel windmill, a five-thousand-gallon tank, and a hundred feet of troughs. The Canadian Pacific Stockyards now had a water-supply system that met the needs of livestock raisers.

The improved stockyards helped to tighten Calgary's ties to ranching and farming in the Bow Valley. If the town was to become a truly important city, it had to encourage and support farmers and ranchers. The ranching and farming industries, combined with the Canadian Pacific, made possible Calgary's growth in the late nineteenth century.

8

Maintaining the Family Farm

In the first week of October 1885, a reporter for the *Calgary Tribune* returned to Calgary from a visit to the Davisburg area south of the town to file a story about the early homesteaders who were pioneering farms there. "Albert E. Banister," he reported,

> ... came from England last fall. He has 20 acres broken, a part of which he has under oats and barley which ripened early. His potatoes and vegetables are a splendid crop. He has 200 head of sheep, 37 pigs, and a few cattle. He expects his family to join him in the spring. His location on the Bow River bottom is very pretty indeed.[1]

The Banister Family Farm at Davisburg

Albert E. Banister, a veterinary surgeon, boarded a ship in Bridport, England bound for Canada. He was forty-two and the year was 1884. With his four oldest sons, Bertram, Albert, William, and Harold, he made the Atlantic crossing to Quebec City. There they paused, and then continued their journey by train to Owen Sound, by steamboat to Port Arthur, by train to Calgary, and finally by team and wagon to Davisburg. Settlers named the area Davisburg in honour of D. W. Davis, manager of I. G. Baker & Co.'s store in Fort Macleod, who was the area's first elected representative in the House of Commons.

The twenty-three-year story of the Banister farm at Davisburg had its roots in that 1880s odyssey, which brings to mind some of

Chapter 8: Maintaining the Family Farm

Albert E. Banister and his wife, Helen, in 1894. (Courtesy of Glenbow Archives, NA-66-1, NA-66-2).

history's remarkable adventures. A part of Albert Banister's family – his wife Helen and eight of their thirteen children – left England and joined him at the fertile family farm on Bow River Bottom in 1887. By this time, Banister and his four sons had erected a two-storey house on the five hundred acres he purchased from the Canadian Pacific Railway. The Banisters' eldest daughter, Fanny, arrived three years later.

Albert Banister built up and maintained the family farm by using family help and by developing neighbourhood ties with other Davisburg farmers. Already in the early years, before Helen and the rest of the family came, neighbouring played a vital role in sustaining the farm. For instance, Flora Andrews, wife of Tom Andrews, homesteaders who lived nearby, "used to mend for the boys," wrote Audrey Banister Bolin, a granddaughter of Albert and Helen Banister. Son "Harold was supposed to be the cook but neighbours were all very good at helping the bachelors."[2] While Albert Banister, as a veterinary surgeon, received cash income for providing medical treatment to his neighbours' horses and cattle, he also was often involved in economic exchanges with local farmers, such as trading a mare for a cow.[3] Banister's story reverberates with his vision of progressive farming fostered by expanding the farm to 820 acres through the acquisition of a 160-acre homestead and the purchase of an adjoining quarter section under pre-emption rights, buying new technology, increasing the cultivated acreage, rotating crops, fallowing land, constructing an irrigation system, and protecting the health of his livestock through veterinary care.

Business and family connections with people in Calgary also aided Albert and Helen Banister in developing their farm. In 1890, they speeded the work of harvesting their crops by purchasing a Massey binder from Joseph Maw, manager of the Toronto-based Massey Manufacturing Company dealership in Calgary.[4] They were able to profit from selling their fattened sheep and cattle to William Roper Hull, the prominent Calgary meat packer and rancher. When their daughter Emmeline married Hull, family ties reinforced their economic links to Calgary. In some years during the late 1880s and 1890s, drought, sharp frosts, and heavy rains created a harsh environment for Albert and Helen Banister's farm, but they persevered and continued to receive a return for their labour and their capital investment.

They could not, however, afford to give their younger children – Eva, born in 1880, and Ida, born two years later – any spending money. As granddaughter Audrey Banister Bolin wrote,

> Aunt Eva and Aunt Ida used to tell the story of a sickly calf that was given to them as no one thought the animal would live. Through the girls' tender loving care, it survived and they sold it. The money they got for it was the first either had ever had. They were allowed to go to Calgary for the first time, to spend it, and they bought presents for every member of the family. That trip was the highlight of their young lives.[5]

After keeping the family farm going for twenty-three years, Albert and Helen Banister sold it to someone outside the family and moved to Victoria, British Columbia in 1907. Albert was now sixty-five, and Helen sixty-three. Although the original Banister family farm was no longer in the family's hands, its family farming tradition continued in Alberta, especially in the career of son Stephen, who married Ida Miller. Stephen and Ida Banister became farmers, selecting a 160-acre homestead at Nose Hills west of Coronation in 1907, a family farm that they developed and which existed in the Nose Hills area for more than half a century.

Farming businesses developed concurrently with the growth of ranching in the Bow Valley. Farms were not latecomers to the agricultural scene; their evolution was an essential part of the expansion of agriculture in the region in the late nineteenth century. In at least one neighbourhood, agricultural work brought farmers and ranchers together in a formal organization. A group of small livestock raisers and farmers met at Davisburg in December 1888 to form the Davisburg Ranchers Society, of which Albert E. Banister was elected president.[6] In the first year of the Society's operations, a total of nineteen farmers and ranchers signed on as charter members. Under Banister's leadership, they aimed at protecting their interests through education. At their meetings, members read well-researched papers on topics such as the feeding and fattening of cattle for the market; the origin, prevention, and cure of blackleg, a disease that afflicted especially young cattle; and the raising of purebred cattle, including Polled Angus and Herefords.[7] Information sharing was not just an academic exercise, but was an economic survival strategy that farm and ranch people consciously chose to pursue. Of those who lived in the Davisburg area, most were farmers and they, like the ranchers, benefited a great deal from these exchanges.

From the mid-1870s onward, farms became increasingly important to the Bow Valley economy and, as in other forms of business endeavour such as the general store industry, the growth of the farming industry was based on family businesses. The founders of these pioneer family farms raised a variety of crops, including wheat, oats, barley, and rye. Crop rotation and fallowing were some of the traditions brought to the Bow Valley by settlers born in central and eastern Canada, Great Britain, and the United States. Ideally, a field was cropped for two years and then often fallowed for one year. The sustained economic progress that engendered capitalism in the Bow Valley came especially from the rising productivity of agriculture, including the grain and livestock-based farm economy.

Farm Protest Movement in the Bow Valley

From the beginning, the Bow Valley farmer was politically articulate. He did not stand by silently as the big ranchers tried to deny him access to the ranges claimed by them. The farmlands in the region were a fertile breeding ground for agrarian protest. A step to organize settlers was taken on 5 April 1885, on the occasion of a demonstration at John Glenn's farm on Fish Creek south of Calgary to coincide with the outbreak of the Saskatchewan Rebellion. Sam Livingston presided at a meeting of about fifty farmers, at which was formed the Alberta Settlers' Rights Association. The protest in the Bow Valley emanated from a relatively prosperous area where an immediate crisis – lack of titles to their land – threatened to deprive farmers of the property they claimed. Most outspoken among the settlers were Livingston and Glenn. Both had behind them a number of years of experience in successful farming in the region. "I defend my claim, as my neighbours do, behind my Winchester," declared Livingston. Glenn stated "that he would hold his claim with a shot gun." But no acts of violence marred the peaceful progress of the meeting. George Murdoch, mayor of Calgary, was present and defended the demonstration: "He was," reported the *Calgary Herald*, "in full sympathy with the settlers and hoped they would get their rights. The town of Calgary depended upon the settlers."[8]

The upshot of the settlers' meeting was a series of resolutions forwarded to Prime Minister John A. Macdonald, including time-worn panaceas such as the opportunity for a farmer to acquire secure title to land, cancellation of the leases of ranchers who engaged in land speculation and the opening of these tracts for settlement, and a request that townships 23 and 24 in the Calgary area be opened to homesteaders. On 20 April Macdonald, alarmed by the farm protest movement in the Bow Valley and the problem of leased ranch land in southwestern Alberta held by speculators, gave clear instructions to David L. Macpherson, minister of the interior: "the ranches should be inspected and all the leases cancelled without mercy where there has been a substantial breach of the conditions. Those who have bone fide endeavoured to stock their ranches should be of course protected."[9] By May, the federal government had opened townships 23 and 24 in the vicinity of Calgary for homesteading.[10] But the farm movement in the Bow Valley was not strong enough to garner for the farmer the immediate benefit of being free to head for significantly more unplowed land. Only gradually, over the next decade and a half, did relations with the big ranchers become less wary and combative as the federal government made life for land-seeking farmers easier by opening more townships in the region to settlement.

Chapter 8: Maintaining the Family Farm

Emergence of the Calgary Market

The emergence of Calgary as an important market for farmers' products stimulated the development of farming in the Bow Valley. Farmers were often so pressed for ready cash to pay store bills, instalments on machinery, interest, and taxes that they had to sell their products as quickly as possible. The establishment of the Alberta Roller Flour Mill by Donald McLean in Calgary in 1892 provided them with a convenient outlet for their wheat. Born in 1851 in Stormont County, Ontario, McLean attended the local public school and worked on his family's farm. He became very interested in flour milling and, at the age of eighteen, began a six-year apprenticeship at a mill in Lakefield. He then went into the flour milling business on his own account, first at Kinmount, Victoria County, and later at Young's Point on Stoney Lake, as well as at Lakefield. McLean spent the early months of 1892 seeking a new location for flour milling, choosing Calgary by March of that year. Wesley F. Orr, a Calgary real estate entrepreneur and chairman of the town council's public works committee, entered into correspondence with him and convinced him to visit the town.

Calgary possessed an important asset: business and civic leaders eager to attract McLean's mill and willing to provide McLean with financial assistance. Through their co-operative efforts, he won the backing of Calgary ratepayers, who supported a by-law granting him a bonus of $3,000 and exemption from taxes for ten years. By October 1892, McLean had built his three-storey stone flour mill with a capacity of 125 barrels per day. Much of its machinery was driven by a seventy-five-horsepower Brown engine that local people considered one of the marvels of the age. A reporter for the *Calgary Tribune* ran a story of the mill under the headline "The Flouring Mill":

> The whole of the machinery is of the latest improved styles, and is manufactured by the North American Milling Co. of Stratford, Ontario, which has the reputation of being the leading flour mill building company in Canada.[11]

There was a large hopper scale, with a capacity of sixty bushels, for receiving grain from farmers' wagons. The farmers in the Bow Valley benefited from Calgary's participation in financing the Alberta

Roller Flour Mill, which sharpened concerns about co-operation between people in the town and the countryside. By January 1893, Bow Valley farmers had sold ten thousand bushels of wheat to McLean's flour mill.[12]

Many settlers outside Calgary were scattered on outlying homesteads, but small market centres did appear to supply the needs of local people by the late 1880s. Most of these settlements appeared on rivers and creeks and near stopping points on the trails in and out of Calgary, as business between the town and its region grew. For instance, High River, on the Highwood River south of Calgary, began as an agricultural community of ranchers and farmers. The Macleod Trail became the most important road leading to Calgary from High River and other parts of southern Alberta.

By 1892, the Calgary and Edmonton Railway had penetrated the Bow Valley. Livestock and grain trading for the whole Bow Valley centred increasingly in Calgary as it grew to become the rail hub of the region. The railways also stimulated the development of Calgary's agricultural hinterland. Farmers from central and eastern Canada, Great Britain, and the United States were attracted to the fertile Bow Valley made more accessible by improved transportation.

William "Barney" Toole, born in Curracloe, Wexford County, Ireland in 1871, became the Canadian Pacific Railway's district land agent in Calgary in 1895 at the age of twenty-four, accepting responsibility for selling the company's lands in Alberta and for encouraging the inflow of immigrants.[13] In Calgary, the energetic and genial Barney Toole "met the trains," recalled his daughter Barbra.

> When the immigrants first came out here, he met every train and helped them to find some place to stay overnight, and to become located on a farm. In greeting immigrants from Germany, for example, he knew enough German to be able to speak to them in their own language and make them feel at home.[14]

Using his local contacts and relying on his broad knowledge of agriculture, Barney Toole thus played a vital role in helping newcomers to become established on family farms in the Calgary region and beyond. Barney Toole, who later became a partner in Toole Peet, a successful Calgary real estate business that has lasted for more than a century, understood a great deal about what kinds

Chapter 8: Maintaining the Family Farm

Table 8. Farming Statistics for the Bow Valley, 1891-1901

Year	1891	1901
Number of Farms	478	270

Source: Manuscript Census of 1891 for Calgary, Canmore, Gleichen, High River, Davisburg, Fish Creek, Pine Creek, Namaka, and Morley; Manuscript Census of 1901 for Calgary, Canmore, Gleichen, High River, Davisburg, Pine Creek, Morley, Queenstown, Shepard, Nose Creek, Springbank, Cochrane, Jumping Pound, Okotoks, Millarville, Priddis, and Pekisko

of priorities mattered most to farmers, and he saw how the city would benefit from the further development of agriculture. At the same time, Calgary's rising population in the late 1890s provided an expanding market for fresh agricultural produce from family farms and contributed to their growth.

Shattered and Fulfilled Dreams

Dreams of preserving the family farm were often shattered by falling grain and livestock prices, perpetual indebtedness through farm mortgages, the disruptive effects of illness and untimely deaths in the family, and economic distress caused by the depression in the mid-1890s. In addition to plant diseases such as rust that devastated crops, there were weather-related disasters such as droughts, frosts, and rain and hailstorms. Even a few of these factors, particularly the droughts and the economic depression, were enough to drive many settlers out of farming, and to discourage scores of newcomers from starting to farm. It is plain that in certain communities, such as High River and Pine Creek, the decline in the number of farms and the increase in the number of ranches were very pronounced, largely because settlers learned that their environment was more suited to ranching than farming. In the process, some farmers transformed their holdings into ranches, while others left the community to farm elsewhere or to go into another line of business, sometimes in Calgary or Vancouver or California.

Table 8 shows that between 1891 and 1901, the number of farms in the Bow Valley plummeted from 478 to 270.[15] While many Bow Valley farms did not survive beyond the first generation, a substantial number of farms in the region grew and remained within the family for two or three or more generations. Hundreds of settlers dreamed of developing viable farming businesses and ultimately passing them on to their children, and in many cases their dreams were fulfilled.

Chapter 8: Maintaining the Family Farm

Making a living on Bow Valley farms during the late nineteenth century was usually a collective effort, with husbands, wives, and children all making significant contributions to the development of family farms through hard work. Rural society in the Bow Valley was characterized by practices of mutuality and interdependence. Far from being isolated, many family farms were part of a network of community ties that linked farms and families in the region in circles of mutual need and mutual benefit.

Robert Findlay
Homesteader at High River

In the late nineteenth century, the farming frontier in the Bow Valley advanced as new homesteaders settled the region. Robert Findlay's case was typical of one kind of homesteading, where a web of family members who began together on a farm would eventually settle on individual homesteads but close to one another. Born in 1837 in Scotland, Findlay moved to Canada and became a general storekeeper in Manotick, Ontario. Robert Findlay and his wife Mary made a respectable living from their store, selling a variety of goods. By the early 1880s, however, they had five sons and one daughter and needed more income to support their family. When news of exciting opportunities to engage in farming in the Bow Valley reached them, they decided to go to the region. Canada was, after all, the land of starting again, of the second chance. Leaving Manotick in the fall of 1883, Robert and their eldest son, Alexander, travelled by the Canadian Pacific to Calgary. Setting the stage for future success, they chose a 160-acre homestead beside the Macleod Trail, three miles north of High River near Tongue Creek.[16]

Before long, Robert Findlay returned to Manotick and made plans to move with his family to his High River homestead. In the spring of 1884, he sold the family store, and so had some capital for his Alberta venture. With his wife and children helping him, Robert put settlers' supplies, six Shorthorn cows, and a purebred bull into a railway car and set out to journey to the Bow Valley.[17] When they arrived in Calgary, Mary and the younger children squashed into a tent in the town and stayed there for three months until their cabin on the homestead had been built. Each morning, the children left the

Chapter 8: Maintaining the Family Farm

Robert Findlay in late middle age, homesteader at High River. (Courtesy of Glenbow Archives, NB-9-49).

tent to attend the school near the Canadian Pacific station. To their dismay, the Findlays discovered that they had lost several boxes of bedding, dishes, and family pictures on their trip across Canada.[18] Other families might have been crestfallen, but the Findlays were the sort of people who only grew more determined with trouble.

Leaving Calgary for his homestead on his wagon drawn by his two-horse team, Robert Findlay ran into heavy rain that drenched his clothes as well as his matches. This made it impossible for him to light a fire at the homestead until he obtained some matches from his neighbour Dick Wallace. Securing the matches cost Findlay a night's sleep, however, because he got lost in the darkness, fell into Tongue Creek, and wandered around for hours before he found his homestead again. Despite such problems, Robert and his son Alexander were able to complete the construction of the family's cabin. The entire move west was eased by Mary's brother William Pollock, a bachelor who entered an adjacent homestead, and new Calgary and High River friends, all of whom helped settle the Findlay family in their new home.

Living conditions on the prairies in the High River area were primitive as they faced insufficient transportation and broad spaces with few people, but Robert and Mary Findlay saw their early years as a temporary experience. Coming with the expectation of remaining long after they had proved up their homestead and gained title, they sought to make the farm their permanent home. Their younger children played a significant role in this process, immediately aiding the family by doing things such as "picking wild cotton balls to make pillows."[19] A skilled hunter, Robert Jr. did not indulge in a mindless, wasteful slaughter of wildlife. Instead, he carefully limited his killing of wildlife to meet economic need, bringing home a few wild ducks, geese, and prairie chickens, as

Chapter 8: Maintaining the Family Farm

well as some fish from Tongue Creek, thereby helping the family to put food on the table. His efforts were almost thwarted on one occasion, however, when a lynx attacked him and killed his dog, and he himself barely escaped with his life.

Using their farm as a focus for the family and coping with the rigours of country life, Robert Sr. and Mary eventually helped to locate their sons George, Robert, and Gavin on their own homesteads in the High River area. On the original Findlay homestead, the team spirit was very much alive. Father and sons erected buildings, broke the sod with a walking plough and horses, planted crops of oats, wheat, and barley, and fenced the fields, while mother and daughter Nellie prepared meals, washed and ironed clothes, did the sewing and mending, cared for the poultry, and looked after the gardening. In the fall of 1888, a reporter for the *Calgary Herald* visited the Findlays' farm and wrote that they had splendid crops on their forty acres, with the stalks of wheat measuring four feet six inches and the stalks of barley four feet.[20] Grain prices were falling, however. Farming was a struggle – the Findlays had to try to make the farm pay their expenses.

Adjusting to economic difficulty, the Findlays decided to diversify into dairying. The whole family co-operated in the daily task of milking the herd of twenty cows, morning and evening. Each day Robert and Mary skimmed and cooled the milk. Using a home-made barrel-churn, the children churned the cream into butter by hand every day of the week except Sunday. Then the butter was packed in wooden tubs and picked up for distribution by Richard N. Brodrick, who operated a pack train. Butter sales, especially to the Canadian Pacific construction crews and the Hudson's Bay Company store in Calgary, became an important source of cash for the Findlays while at the same time stimulating the urban growth of Calgary.

From time to time, Robert Findlay also helped to accelerate Calgary's development by personally delivering butter to its businesses, including the Hudson's Bay Company, in exchange for supplies. Using the Macleod Trail on his trips by team and wagon to Calgary, he became an important force in opening Bow Valley markets. But the Macleod Trail, which crossed streams such as Sheep Creek, did not offer reliable year-round travel. One spring day, Findlay travelled north to Calgary, safely crossing Sheep Creek on ice; after purchasing supplies in the town he returned two days later, only to find the creek swollen with swiftly flowing icy water.

Chapter 8: Maintaining the Family Farm

He was left with no choice but to try to ford the creek with his wagon and horses. Although Findlay, together with his team and the front half of the running gear, managed to get across the creek, the torrent swept away the rest of the wagon and his supplies.[21] Still, the old Macleod Trail remained an important road, providing vital commercial connections between Calgary and the farms and ranches to the south. These economic contacts proved a mutually profitable arrangement for Findlay and the town.

By the late 1880s, the Findlay farm had expanded through the pre-emption and purchase of an adjoining quarter section, and 250 acres had been broken. One key element in the progress Findlay made was his successful use of new farm equipment technologies. Having acquired a steel plough, Robert Findlay could more easily open up for cultivation the rich prairie soil. Cultivating larger fields required better harvesting equipment. The tools and implements in use on the farm included a scythe and a flail at first, and later, a second-hand mechanical reaper drawn by a team of horses, for threshing grain.[22] The mechanical reaper that Robert Findlay bought from Orville A. Smith, a local rancher, could harvest about three to five acres per day more than the traditional implements that were operated by hand. In the early 1890s, Robert Findlay joined his neighbour Jim Monkman in purchasing a second-hand, horse-powered threshing machine. Soon Robert Findlay and his sons acquired their own steam-powered threshing outfit, which they used not only to harvest their own crops but also to custom thresh those of their neighbours. With improved equipment, the operations on the Findlay farm became more efficient.

Robert Findlay hoped that an improvement in High River's transportation corridor would make his products more profitable in the Calgary market. With the arrival of the Calgary and Edmonton Railway in High River in 1892, the whistle of the train that signified High River's links to Calgary and more distant places punctuated daily rhythms on the Findlay farm. From this time forward, the farm's threshing machine and the railway worked in a complementary manner. All the threshed grain Robert Findlay and his sons sent by rail to Calgary became a feeder for the town. The threshing machine gave the Findlays the technology they needed to gain wealth from the fertile Bow Valley, and by the mid-1890s that Bow Valley prosperity had helped Calgary to become an important grain centre.

Chapter 8: Maintaining the Family Farm

Before the coming of the railway to High River, all of the Findlay family's farm products destined for Calgary arrived in that town by wagon. Calgary's rail line into the High River area changed all this. The railway carried the grain, butter, and other products of the Findlays and other farmers rapidly, safely, and in large quantities. By the middle of the decade, it outstripped the traffic in farm products of wagons, with most of Calgary's farm produce shipments arriving in the cars of the Calgary and Edmonton. This tremendous increase in grain traffic created a great need for warehouses and elevators and an efficient way of storing and marketing it. Here flour millers, grain dealers, and the railway took the initiative. Initially, Robert Findlay and his sons piled their sacks of grain on the Calgary and Edmonton's siding at High River, from where the railway's cars took them to the warehouse of Donald McLean's Alberta Roller Flour Mill in Calgary.[23] By 1905, the Winnipeg-based Nicholas Bawlf Company's grain elevator on the Canadian Pacific in High River was handling the Findlay family's grain.

In its tremendous drive for markets and resources, Calgary helped create an integrated city-country system that included small centres such as High River. During the 1890s, Robert Findlay and his sons began to take some of their farm products, such as butter and oats, to the newly organized High River Trading Company in High River in exchange for supplies. This company usually relied on wholesale merchants in Calgary for its goods. Farmers like the Findlays, the High River Trading Company, and Calgary wholesale merchants were bound together in an interdependent exchange system that greatly increased the market for Calgary businesses.

Always willing to devote much time and energy to the farming operations, son Alexander was his father's right-hand man on the farm, a position he occupied until his death from an abscess on his leg in February 1891.[24] During the months Alexander was confined to bed, brother George brought the local medical doctor to his bedside each day, but all efforts to restore his health failed in the end. For the Findlay family, the funeral service for Alexander provided an important emotional link in the chain of experiences and memories that deepened the family's western identity.

Gavin lived and worked alongside his father on the home place while proving up his own homestead a little to the north. The practice of father and son labouring together remained a conspicuous feature of the Findlay family farm. Yet Robert Findlay Sr. had

Chapter 8: Maintaining the Family Farm

Gavin Findlay and his wife, Caroline, and their son, Tom. (Courtesy of Bobbi Scarlett).

to face difficulties and expenses which increased the costs of his operations. Drought presented a major challenge in the last half of the 1880s and the first half of the 1890s. Insufficient rain and hot winds added to debt difficulties by cutting into crop yields. Despite these problems, there were crops of wheat, oats, and barley each year. While Findlay sold a portion of these crops in Calgary and High River, he also used them for feeding his growing herd of cows.[25] He thus practised diversified, mixed farming. At the same time, the demand for dairy products encouraged him to continue engaging in the production of butter.

Inheritance arrangements helped to maintain the Findlay farm and keep it within the family as it was transferred from the first to the second generation in the early 1920s, and to the third generation in the early 1950s.[26] From the beginning, Robert and his wife Mary looked to the future and pursued their goal of strengthening their family at High River. They sought to make the home farm the centre of a network of Findlay farms spread across the High River area. Within this network of related households, they maintained regular contacts with their children and their families through the sharing of resources. Long before his death in 1923 at the age of eighty-six, Robert through his will made provision to pass on the family farm to his youngest son Thomas and give Mary a life interest in the house and the land.[27] Thomas ran the sixteen-hundred-acre farm, while Robert and Mary continued to live on it for a number of years. Operating the farm successfully, Thomas was able to care for his widowed mother from 1923 until her death in 1927. The family farm that Thomas bequeathed at his death in 1952 to his only living son Clair was an outstanding farm, and it represented what he had inherited. But it was only a fraction of the

Chapter 8: Maintaining the Family Farm

The Findlay farm at High River. (Courtesy of Bobbi Scarlett).

farming business that Robert Findlay had helped create. He gave land to his other sons as well, including Gavin, who together with his wife Caroline built up another Findlay family farm, which their son Tom inherited when they died in 1953. A farmer of excellent reputation, Tom exemplified the Findlay tradition of working hard to keep a prosperous farm within the family.

The Andrews Family Farm at Davisburg

Like Robert and Mary Findlay, William James Andrews and his wife Catherine ("Kate") of Inverness, Quebec re-enacted the fundamental Canadian rite of setting out in search of new opportunity. In the mid-1880s, a number of settlers from Quebec were moving excitedly into frontier areas of the prairie West. The construction of the Canadian Pacific Railway lured many settlers into the region. In June 1885, William and Kate Andrews, tired of trying to scratch out a living from hardscrabble farming in Quebec, packed their belongings – farm implements, oxen, cows, two hens, a rooster, and lumber – into a Canadian Pacific car and headed toward the sparsely settled Calgary area. For about two weeks, they travelled along the main line of the railway, riding through Canadian Shield forests and prairie lands. Many years later, Kate recalled that "the railway people were very good to us. When we arrived in Calgary they side-tracked our car and allowed us to continue living in it until we could make

Chapter 8: Maintaining the Family Farm

William J. Andrews and his Clydesdale stallion near his original barn, c. 1917. (Courtesy of Russell Martin).

other arrangements."²⁸ They were evidently in urgent need of money, and so Kate worked at the Royal Hotel in Calgary for a while.

As William and Kate on a wagon finally approached their destination – the Davisburg area south of Calgary and spreading west from the Bow River and north from the Highwood River, which William's brother Thomas had discovered the year before – the last twenty-three miles proved especially arduous, and the oxen negotiated Fish Creek and Pine Creek with difficulty. Thomas, together with his own family and other relatives, now accompanied William and Kate to Davisburg. Like Thomas and the other newcomers, William Andrews selected a homestead in the Davisburg district, but he and Kate had to work part-time for Colonel James F. Macleod in Fort Macleod in order to make ends meet. With William serving as groomsman and Kate as cook in the Colonel Macleod household for about two years, they were able to save enough money to become full-time farmers. Still far from flush with cash at the time, William built a small house for himself and Kate, with a lean-to for their livestock.

For all the fertile soil on the Andrews homestead at Davisburg, the farming prospects were momentarily bleak. A prairie fire swept from the Bow River toward their homestead, devouring all the grass in its path, and they feared that they might lose everything. Fortunately for the family, William had already taken the precaution of making a firebreak – ploughed land intended to check a grass fire. But his neighbour, Joseph Hogge, had no such protection. William saw the need not only to protect his own homestead but also to place his neighbour beyond danger. "Our father," William's daughter Cora later said, "ran one and a half miles to Joe Hogge's, to warn him of the fire as he had lumber piled up for a home and no fireguard. They got busy with the plough and the fire went by."²⁹

Though times were tough, William Andrews set out with no modest ambition to transform his raw homestead into a farm that would soon depend on new technology. As William's daughter Ethel later wrote, "I remember my father walking and broadcasting

Chapter 8: Maintaining the Family Farm

Kate Andrews (centre), her daughter Laura (far left), and a neighbour lady and child (far right) in front of the Andrews farm house at Davisburg, c. 1902. (Courtesy of Russell Martin).

grain from a leather apron, in the fall cutting it with a scythe and finally threshing on a flailing board. Progress came fast, soon binders were used."[30] Water for the Andrews and their livestock was scarce, however. To overcome this difficulty, William and Kate "carried water from a spring over a mile to the south. In time a well was dug and the young couple acquired horses, cattle and poultry."[31] Engaged as he was in mixed farming, William Andrews raised Clydesdale horses and Aberdeen Angus cattle and grew oats and barley, and his successful farming venture provided his family with a secure life. William and Kate's eldest children, Ethel and Norman, twins, were born in May 1890, but Norman died of pneumonia thirteen months later.[32] Laura arrived in May 1892, and Cora was born in September

Chapter 8: Maintaining the Family Farm

1896. The positive feelings Ethel, Laura, and Cora expressed in later years about their parents were sincere and heartfelt. As generally happened in Davisburg farm households, the eldest daughter Ethel spent much time and energy helping her mother with her siblings.

The three daughters remembered their parents as having great respect for education – as witnessed by their enrolment in the one-room Melrose School. William donated the land for the school from his homestead in 1890. "At the age of six, I started at this school and walked across the homestead usually with Dinah, William and Spearman Kenney and Fred Bates," recalled Ethel.[33] Ethel went on to attend the Okotoks High School and then, after teaching in the Allan School on a permit for one year, the Calgary Normal School. She eventually became the teacher at the Melrose School, as had her cousins Emma, daughter of Thomas Andrews, and Eva, daughter of George Andrews, before her. Like her sisters Ethel and Laura, Cora Andrews attended the Melrose School. Four years later, Cora graduated from the Central Collegiate Institute in Calgary. William and Kate Andrews sustained their relationship with the nearby Melrose School over the years, for its teachers always boarded in their home; for many years, William also served as a trustee for the school. As well, initially this school building was used for church meetings by the Andrews family and other homesteaders. Kate Andrews, a devout Baptist, was the first to establish in her daughters' minds an enduring equation between Christian religion and good character.[34]

With the passage of time, William and Kate Andrews steadily improved their farm at Davisburg. They took much pride in producing high-quality products. Calgary was most appreciative of their achievements: in September 1888, the town's Agricultural Hall welcomed them to the Calgary Agricultural Society's third annual fall exhibition. They heard warm greetings from Amos Rowe, the Society's president, and James A. Lougheed. William Andrews received second prizes for his cheese and butter, while Kate won first prize for her home-made bread.[35] Their displays, like those of other exhibitors, were arranged to demonstrate the exciting notion of the era, the idea of progress. The *Calgary Herald* reporter who covered the exhibition expressed the idea well. Walking through the Agricultural Hall, he noted that "a visit to the Fall Fair … was a perfect revelation of the progress and development of Alberta.… The display of grain, butter, cheese … would do credit to any country in the world."[36] The crowds that entered the Agricultural Hall saw more than dazzling entertainment. The exhibition transported them to the agricultural world of the Bow Valley, to which Calgary merchants had close ties.

William and Kate Andrews also displayed their farm products at other fairs. At the Davisburg Agricultural Society's first annual show in October 1892, William won first prize for his two-year-old gelding, second prize for the best colt, first prize for his bull, and first prize for a sheaf of grain, while Kate received first prize for her fancy pin cushion.[37] By this time, William was breeding Clydesdale horses with his purebred stallion. In July 1893, he won first prize for his barley at the Fish Creek Agricultural Society's show.[38] By 1894, he had become a director of the Davisburg Agricultural Society. At the Society's fall fair in that year, William exhibited his prize-winning oats and gelding; Kate received a prize for twenty pounds of butter she had made and another one for her three loaves of home-made bread.[39]

The farm products of William and Kate Andrews and other Davisburg farm families – oats, barley, wheat, butter – were fed into Calgary by wagon on the Blackfoot Trail in the late 1880s and early 1890s. But even when they could raise sufficient crops, William and Kate suffered for the lack of bridges and a good road to carry their produce to market. Consequently, they eagerly looked forward to an improvement in Davisburg's transportation corridor. By 1893, they often took their farm products to the Calgary and Edmonton siding at DeWinton, from where they were shipped by the railway to Calgary. While William kept most of his oats and barley to feed his livestock, he sold some of these crops, along with much of his butter, to Calgary merchants in exchange for supplies. Especially the Calgary and Edmonton Railway that made this possible tightened the economic bond between the Davisburg area and Calgary, with both places benefiting from the relationship.

Early on, the Andrews family regularly interacted with nearby relatives and neighbours in a network of economic and social contacts in the Davisburg district.[40] William Andrews employed Bill Kenney, a young man, to help with the farm work. Extremely skilful and fast with knitting needles, Kate Andrews knitted socks and mittens for the Kenney family children in exchange for fish that they caught in the Bow River. Kate also became a part of a more distant network, which she maintained primarily by letters, that reached back to Quebec and beyond to Lowell, Massachusetts, where her

Chapter 8: Maintaining the Family Farm

younger brother George Blackwood had settled. At Davisburg, the neighbourly bonds established by social relations were deepened as Kate provided support to neighbours who began to have their own families. In the 1890s, Kate as a midwife was present and aided the mothers in the Maxwell, Grant, Blackwood – Isabella Blackwood was Kate's younger sister – Kenney, Grierson, and Robinson families with the births of their children. Thus, although they resided on a somewhat isolated frontier, William and Kate Andrews also lived, through the intertwining of local support, the presence of relations, the exchange of goods, and visits back and forth, within a broader regional economic and social support network.

This network, reliant on the willingness of friends and relatives to co-operate, also aided William and Kate Andrews in expanding their farming operations. Increasingly, William's brother Hugh, who had recently moved to a nearby farm at Davisburg, played a significant role in shaping their support network. One autumn William turned to Hugh for help in bringing in coal from west of Black Diamond for the winter months. When Hugh later decided to return to Quebec, William Andrews purchased his 160-acre farm.[41] William also bought another nearby quarter section, "a fine piece of land on which there was a stream" and a spring of fresh water "from which" he and Kate "had taken their water at first."[42] Possessing this quarter section gave them an enormous advantage, for they now controlled a continuous supply of excellent water. The Andrews family brought new acres under cultivation as they expanded in the Davisburg area, contracting substantial debts in doing so.

Their hopes of a secure future in the Davisburg district were realized. In 1900, William and Kate Andrews and their children – Ethel, Laura, and Cora – moved their house and its contents from its old site

> ... to a pleasant spot near the spring. The kitchen and living room were moved in two parts. When they moved the kitchen, the fire was burning in the stove. A space was left between the two parts when they were settled on their new site. The space between was boarded up and used for storing grain at first. Later it became the dining room and the upstairs was finished as bedrooms.[43]

Chapter 8: Maintaining the Family Farm

Stacking oats sheaves in preparation for threshing just west of the Andrews farm buildings, c. 1903. Left to right: Frank Matthews (hired man); William J. Andrews, his younger brother Hugh, his daughter Laura, and his daughter Cora. (Courtesy of Russell Martin and DeWinton and District Historical Committee).

By this time, the Andrews family had about eight Clydesdale horses and some thirty head of Aberdeen Angus cattle.[44] Using logs that he had hauled with oxen from Priddis to the new location, William built a solid, new barn that required no nails. Fortified by a circle of local relations and friends upon whom they could rely for help in trying to establish their farm, William and Kate's efforts met with success. As they grew older, Kate's daughters provided more and more assistance in cleaning, cooking, canning, making soap, and sewing clothes, thereby helping her to endure the privations of frontier life.

Kate Andrews joined her husband William in helping to preserve the family farm, laying the foundation for a successful enterprise that has remained in the family to the present time.[45] In the second generation, Cora, who married Melvin Martin, a native of Manitoba and a local farmer, inherited the home place in 1945 when Kate died. William and Kate left a part of the family farm to Laura, who married Howard Norris, another Davisburg farmer. Ethel, who also married a local farmer, Hillyerd Oneil, inherited some family property – the DeWinton general store. Cora and Melvin Martin planned to pass on the family farm to their two sons, Russell, who married Marion Cameron, and George, who married Marion Downs. When Cora died in 1975, the family farm was divided, with part of it going to Russell and the other part to George, both of whom, together with their wives and children, still run their farms, with the touch of a master hand. Recognizing that

Chapter 8: Maintaining the Family Farm

co-operation in the past had given the family farm important advantages, these families in the Bow Valley often work together, while still maintaining their autonomy and viability.

James F. McKevitt
Midnapore Farmer

An important component of the Bow Valley society was a core of settlers tied to the Midnapore area some nine miles south of Calgary and spreading south from Fish Creek. They arrived singly or in families and often had extensive contacts with each other. James F. McKevitt came to the area in 1884. Born in 1863 on a farm at Carrickmacross, County Monaghan, Ireland, McKevitt failed to find work in his home community and moved to Toronto in 1883 at the age of twenty.[46] After doing odd jobs in Toronto for about a year, he headed for Alberta in search of better prospects. In 1884, McKevitt chose a 160-acre homestead four miles west of Midnapore near Red Deer Lake.[47] When he arrived at the place, he sensed why settlers liked the area. The land itself was very fertile, gently rolling, and partly covered with willow brush. Due west of the new quarter were the Rocky Mountains. Gazing upon the willow brush, the young man realized that the new quarter would gradually have to be cleared.

McKevitt could not clear and cultivate enough land to feed himself, however. How could he make his fortune in such a community? McKevitt was perceptive about the future – he was optimistic and decided to make the best of the situation. For more than a year, he spent some months on the homestead and the rest of his time working on a survey crew for the Canadian Pacific Railway between Banff and Field, performing miscellaneous tasks such as carrying water and peeling potatoes for the cookhouse.[48] The money he earned on this job allowed him to purchase two horses, a walking plough, harrows, and an axe in Calgary. McKevitt worked long hours, clearing a few acres by felling the willow brush with his axe and removing the stumps with his horses. As he ploughed his first furrows, harrowed them, and put in some oats and wheat on the homestead, he hoped for excellent crops. The crops, which he cut with a scythe and threshed with a flail, were good enough to encourage him to continue clearing and breaking land, in addition

Chapter 8: Maintaining the Family Farm

James Francis and Julia McKevitt family, c. 1920. Back row left to right: Edward (son), Julie (mother), Joe (son), James Francis (father), Nellie (daughter). Middle row left to right: Bernard (son), Albert (son), James (son), Anna (daughter), Tom (son). Front row left to right: Pat (son), Catherine (daughter), Charlie (son). (Courtesy of James Frederick McKevitt).

to erecting a cabin and barn, digging a well, and building fences.

When James McKevitt took his produce to market in Calgary, he had the good fortune to meet Julia Kiely, who was working as a maid in the home of Charles B. Rouleau, judge of the Supreme Court of the Northwest Territories in the town. To escape looming poverty in the small town of Lismire, County Cork, Ireland, where she was born in 1870, Julia had sought a better life by immigrating to Calgary in 1888. "At that time there was a man in High River … and he used to go back to Ireland and bring out some of these young women who wanted to get positions" in Canada. "He brought my mother … when she was about eighteen," recalled her daughter Anna many years later.[49] Perhaps the thought of marrying a homesteader thrilled Julia; she likely conceived of work in a farm household as something she could do. The situation was ideal for romance, and a courtship soon developed. James and Julia married in 1890 and settled on his homestead at Midnapore.

Chapter 8: Maintaining the Family Farm

James and Julia McKevitt were competent farmers, and they lost little time in planting a garden and making use of prairie grasses for feeding their cows as well as for beautifying their home. At the Fish Creek Agricultural Society's show in July 1893, James won first prize for both his long and short beets, while Julia received a prize for the best bouquet of native grass.[50]

Before long, James and Julia began establishing a family. Two children, Edward and Anna, were born between 1892 and 1893. By the early twentieth century, nine more children had arrived. Anna remembered a great deal about her early upbringing. She enjoyed going for a visit to judge Rouleau's place in Calgary to see the trees that her uncle Bernard McKevitt, a bachelor who had settled on a homestead adjacent to her parents' farm, had planted: "I was just a little kid." The trees were "just five or six feet tall. Of course, they did grow to immense trees."[51]

James and Julia McKevitt were perfect settlers for Midnapore, but their farm of 160 acres was not adequate to feed, house, and clothe a large family. To solve this problem, they expanded by purchasing an adjoining quarter from the Canadian Pacific for $3 per acre in 1897.[52] James McKevitt's strategy was to build up equity by improving the farm with new clearings, new cultivated acres, new buildings, and new fences. Every expansion of fields increased the supply of food for the McKevitt family as well as the produce they could take to the market in Calgary. There was a limit to what James could do with only two horses, however. "He just made a living," recalled Anna. "He was so happy when he was able to afford four horses. I can remember when he had just two for everything. Two is what he had to pull the machinery, two is what he hitched on the wagon to go to town to get provisions, and the same two horses did the work on the land, with the harrows and that kind of thing."[53]

At the turn of the century, there was still little mechanization on the McKevitt family farm. In clearing more land, James cut down more willow brush, picked the roots, and gathered the stones by hand. He also carried water from the well to the troughs for the cattle and horses.[54] Anna had vivid memories of her father working in the fields:

> He walked behind the one-furrow plough and held the handles and went around the field. Besides that when he was seeding grain, he would put a basket affair with two ropes

around his shoulders and it fitted in against his body. He put his grain in there, a couple of big pailsful, two bushels. Then he would walk along with one hand going this way and one hand going that way. I saw him seed fifteen acres like that.[55]

James McKevitt unquestionably did much work with his hands, spending many hours each day to make his farm productive and support his family.

Success on James and Julia McKevitt's farm was measured largely in oats, wheat, potatoes, and cream, and in the 1890s they earned a reputation for developing great skill at co-ordinating production and marketing. The experience James gained in assisting his parents in growing potatoes back home in Ireland helps explain his emphasis on potatoes on his Midnapore farm. He also brought with him from Ireland knowledge of feeding oats to milk cows for the production of cream. On his farm there was a small creek, where he cooled his cream in the summer months.[56] The growing of wheat also played an important part in his operations. James and Julia's work load, which revolved around planting and caring for their crops, as well as managing their small dairy herd, kept them busy every day of the year.

Even as he was producing crops, James McKevitt established close contacts with a number of people in Calgary who needed his products. Daughter Anna remembered that her father, as a market gardener, travelled by team and wagon or by the Calgary and Edmonton train from the Midnapore siding to Calgary "to trade potatoes for groceries. He used to grow potatoes, a lot of them, and then he would sack the potatoes and take them to the town."[57] McKevitt often took not only his potatoes but also his cream and some of his oats and hay to John A. Nolan, a native of Sweden who operated a general store in Calgary.[58] "We used to come to town," said Anna, "and outside the store there would be all these sacks of grain, sacks of potatoes, or sacks of oats. I can remember walking by there and men would be sitting, chatting and talking."[59] In the fall, the sale of McKevitt's wheat to the Alberta Roller Flour Mill in Calgary provided an infusion of cash that permitted the family to buy clothing and shoes for the following year.

James McKevitt, together with his family, also benefited from the opportunity to sell his farm products and his labour to the Sacred Heart Convent in Calgary. As daughter Anna, who eventually

Chapter 8: Maintaining the Family Farm

became a student at the convent, recalled, her father "used to bring in grain to feed the cows. At that time the convent kept cows. Dad used to come in and plough the convent garden and put their potatoes in for them and some of this would help to pay my board. Without this, I would not have had the education that I got."[60]

Of necessity, there was a great deal of sharing of work in the Midnapore area between James McKevitt, his older brother Bernard, and other neighbours like Sam Livingston and Daniel Patton.[61] The threshing of grain was a major activity, not to be undertaken without the help of neighbours and Sam Livingston's threshing outfit. The threshing outfit was one of the few machines that appeared on McKevitt's farm in the 1890s. Mixed farming on his land still depended largely on hand labour. Feeding and looking after the milk cows and horses all required intensive work. James McKevitt also banded together with his neighbours to load railway cars at the Midnapore siding with grain and other farm products by hand.

James and Julia McKevitt exemplify the Bow Valley farm family tradition of keeping the farm within the family. Four years before his death in 1931, James McKevitt sold a quarter section of the home place for $4,800 to his son Joseph, who had married Helen Birney.[62] Joseph and Helen McKevitt had three children, one of whom was James Frederick. They weathered the Great Depression of the 1930s, and their hard work was rewarded. At her death in 1969, Helen McKevitt owned eighty acres. Helen and Joseph's strategy for the continuation of family farm was spelled out in their discussions with their family. James Frederick McKevitt, a highly competent farmer who had married Dorothy Lunn, inherited his mother's eighty acres in 1969, which ensured that the family farm operation survived for another generation.[63]

Farming at Davisburg

The David Suitor Family

The desire for family continuity on the farm in the Bow Valley was also illustrated by the career of David Suitor. When the Bow Valley was opened for settlement, the Canadian Pacific Railway issued pamphlets touting the "free homesteads" of the Calgary district as constituting thousands of quarter sections of fertile land in an area where "heavy crops" of wheat, oats, and barley were produced.[64] Such publicity could grab attention. Certainly it worked its magic upon David Suitor, who was farming at Leeds, Quebec. Born in 1830 in County Antrim, Ireland, Suitor as a boy moved with his parents to the Leeds area. He became a farmer and married Mary McKeage, who came from a United Empire Loyalist family. During their years on their farm at Leeds, David and Mary had fourteen children, five of whom died of diphtheria in infancy. They supported themselves and their remaining five sons and four daughters by raising grain and livestock. But their long-term economic prospects were almost totally bleak, because their place "was the stoniest farm you could see in Quebec."[65]

Like many other Leeds farmers of their time, David and Mary Suitor yearned for greater opportunities. For them, their choice to "go west" promised to deliver them and their sons and daughters from an economic situation that left much to be desired. The adventure began in 1889, when David and his two sons, Jack and William, travelled west by rail to look at the Calgary district for themselves. Encouraged by the fine land he saw, the fact that the new Alberta environment gave him instant relief from asthma, and the success his son David Jr. had been having as a blacksmith in Calgary since 1883, David Suitor filed claim to a 160-acre homestead in the Davisburg area in 1889 and made plans to bring his family from Quebec to his new place.[66]

Landing at their new homestead in 1890, together with their farm equipment and livestock from Quebec, David and Mary Suitor and their sons and daughters were ready at once to enter the new world of homesteading. After all, they had plenty of experience with farm life. But this was not farmland of the marginal kind at Leeds, Quebec. Understanding the basic necessities, such as the need for settling close to a water source, David had chosen a homestead on the Highwood River. The land here had rich, black topsoil. David's first real shock was the discovery that there was a squatter on his 160 acres. The process of settling the matter was an expense for David; it was a drain on his meagre resources.[67] Eventually the squatter left.

A strong man and accustomed to heavy work for many years, David Suitor at sixty was well prepared for the labour required to make the family homestead habitable: erecting a house and barn, breaking the prairie sod with horses and a one-furrow plough, fencing the fields, sowing, and reaping.[68] He knew as much as there

Chapter 8: Maintaining the Family Farm

Albert and Blanche Herr's original homestead and farm at Davisburg, c. 1925. (Courtesy of Doris Herr).

was to know about horses and cattle and used his animals effectively to develop the new farm. Desiring to expand his herds, he raised Clydesdale horses and Shorthorn cows. Excellent crops of oats and barley from his newly broken fields and abundant hay from his pastures allowed him to feed his livestock. At first, there was not sufficient money to dig a well deep enough to reach water near the house and barn. From the Highwood River, David hauled water in a barrel on a stoneboat drawn by two horses for use in the house, as well as in the barnyard for the animals. In the winter, the thick ice on the river had to be broken to get at the water.[69]

In order to support their fairly large family, David and Mary Suitor expanded by purchasing ninety acres at $2 per acre on the Highwood River from Edward Quinn. Besides helping their parents build up their farm, sons Jack and William claimed their own homesteads in the Davisburg area. When Jack left to file claim to a new homestead in the Gladys district, David and Mary took over his 160 acres.[70] By making the home place the centre of an economic and social network of Suitor farms in the Bow Valley, they maintained regular contacts with their sons and their families. When their daughters Jane, Maggie, Elizabeth, and Martha married Bow Valley farmers and had their own families, they also were drawn into this circle of mutual support. In October 1894, the Suitors as successful farmers were quite visible at the Davisburg fall fair, where David won third prize for his two-year-old heifer and fourth prize for his dairy cow and son Jack received third prize for his brood mare and foal.[71]

While most of David and Mary Suitor's time was spent in a close-knit rural neighbourhood, David made occasional trips by

Chapter 8: Maintaining the Family Farm

Albert and Blanche Herr's sons Forest, Cliff, Bill, Harold, and Doug hauling grain from the farm to the elevators in DeWinton, c. 1925. (Courtesy of Doris Herr).

team and wagon along the Blackfoot Trail or by the Calgary and Edmonton train from DeWinton to Calgary to fetch supplies and sell the butter and dressed poultry which he, Mary, and their children produced. In Calgary, David, an experienced horse breeder, also sold Clydesdale horses to farmers and lighter driving and riding horses to the Mounted Police. At other moments, David or son Jack or son William called David Jr., the blacksmith from Calgary, to repair their implements or make some new tools for them: "David, could you come out and do something for me on the machinery?" As a relative recalled, David Jr. "used to go out and spend a week or two, maybe a month, making things for them for their farms."[72] In this way, the Suitor families acquired new farm equipment technologies.

Living on a homestead in the Davisburg area also provided David and Mary Suitor with opportunities to mingle with Native Canadians. North of their farm was the Dunbow Industrial School and, from time to time, David hired teenage Native boys from this institution to help him with tasks such as stooking, making hay, and driving horses. Like other Davisburg farmers, David and Mary loved to go to band concerts, ball games, and hockey games at the school.[73] Their eyes would light up with excitement when they talked about these wonderful times at the institution that provided a wider horizon. The Sisters of Charity at the school, one of whom helped the Suitors in times of sickness, were held in high regard by these homesteaders for their kindness and for their knowledge of the liberal arts.[74]

David and Mary Suitor had much in common with the many Bow Valley homesteaders who sought to keep the family farm

Chapter 8: Maintaining the Family Farm

within the family. Among other things, they, like numerous other farmers in the region, made arrangements for orderly inheritance and succession. Around 1910, their son James, who had married Violet Bolton, took over the home place as they retired and went to live with one of their daughters and her family. In the 1930's, James and Violet's only child, James Jr., who had married Grace Welch, took over the family farm. For some time, James Jr. and his wife Grace lived and worked together with his parents on the home place. At the present time, Grace Suitor, a widow, still owns and lives on the family farm she did so much to help build; her grandson Glenn Groeneveld runs it from his own farm in the Gladys district.[75]

Informal Economic Networks

Beyond inheritance, farmers found other ways to build and maintain family farms in the Bow Valley in the late nineteenth century. They sometimes worked together informally in an attempt to develop their farms. In many cases, they created informal economic networks through co-operative efforts. For example, Robert Findlay, his sons, and his son-in-law William C. MacDougall, a homesteader who had married his daughter Nellie, joined forces with their neighbour Dick Wallace to construct an irrigation ditch that ran from the Highwood River through their farms.[76] Some of their crops and hay lands were irrigated when water in the river was plentiful, although in times of drought they received insufficient river water.

Every year Robert Findlay co-operated with several neighbours in the High River area in threshing, as well as in slaughtering beef. In the Davisburg district, Ontario-born John Alexander Irving, who filed claim to a homestead two miles west of David and Mary Suitor's place in 1887, joined four to six of his neighbours in the mid- and late 1890s to haul grain by wagon to the Calgary and Edmonton siding at DeWinton, where they filled a car with about two thousand bushels for shipment to Calgary.[77] By uniting to ship grain by the carload, they brought down the cost of freight on the railway. By 1899, this co-operative effort included Albert Herr, a successful farmer from Ontario who had married Irving's daughter Blanche.[78] Later, in the 1920s, Albert and Blanche Herr's sons hauled grain by wagon from the family farm at Davisburg to the elevators in DeWinton. Henry Inglis Thomson, a native of Saint John, New Brunswick who entered his homestead on Sheep Creek near Black Diamond in 1898, used his threshing outfit to harvest not only his own crops but also those of his neighbours, Bob and Joe Price.[79] And then there was James Hogg, who came from Aberdeen, Scotland to farm at Longview in 1904. Before long, he was exchanging labour with local farmers during the threshing season.[80] Such economic networks helped to keep farm costs down, increased the resources available to each family farm, and played an important role in the survival and growth of farming enterprises in the Bow Valley.

The ability of economic family networks to create bonds of assistance among farm neighbours is further illustrated in the ways John V. Thomson maintained community ties with relatives and friends, particularly those in the Gladys district. Born in County Ayr, Scotland, Thomson began on his homestead at Gladys in the late 1880s.[81] Together with his wife Elizabeth, he developed the farm, raising cattle, horses, hogs, and poultry and growing wheat, oats, barley, and rye. He dug a thirty-foot well by hand to secure fresh water and lined it with sandstone. No one in the community could ignore the well's importance, for it continued to provide water for the farm for more than a century. Thomson built connections with his brother Tom, who farmed nearby, as well as with other neighbours into support networks. Joint endeavours included putting out prairie fires, threshing, erecting farm buildings, and aiding neighbours struggling to survive disasters such as hailstorms, house fires, and snowstorms.

Agricultural Societies and Fairs

Agricultural societies complemented informal family networks in the Bow Valley. From the mid-1880s, interest in agricultural societies in Calgary and the surrounding area grew rapidly. Their officers and members were concerned about agricultural problems and devoted a great deal of time to improving farm and ranch practices and to the activities of their organizations. By 1894, there were agricultural societies in Calgary, Pine Creek, Davisburg, Fish Creek, Springbank, and Sheep Creek. In these organizations, farmers and ranchers set aside any differences they might have to work on matters of common interest.

Chapter 8: Maintaining the Family Farm

The agricultural societies in the Bow Valley promoted education by organizing agricultural fairs. James Walker, the Calgary lumber manufacturer, farmer and rancher, played an important role in starting the movement for fairs in the city and its region. Having begun the growing of grain and vegetables, he was eager to have local and regional fairs at which his products and those of other progressive farmers and ranchers could be exhibited. The Calgary District Agricultural Society's fair, which first met in October 1886, was a promising beginning.[82] In part through Walker's efforts, the territorial government in Regina and the federal government provided funds to aid prairie agricultural societies in offering prizes at their fairs. Merchants and manufacturers in Calgary also supported the fairs, as they did the agricultural societies.

The fair in Calgary came to be seen as a time when farmers and ranchers could come to the city to observe high-quality cattle, horses, sheep, dogs, pigs, chickens and grains, new techniques, and new implements while their wives examined superior vegetables, flowers, butter, cheese, knitted and embroidered goods, and paintings.[83] But even at the height of its educational emphasis, the Calgary fair was a social occasion to which everyone looked forward. Most settlers and city people saw the fair as both a learning experience and social event. For many settlers, it was one of the important ways to overcome loneliness and isolation during the frontier era. The fair allowed visitors to take a break from their work routine, talk with old friends and meet new ones, and compete for awards and prizes.

Davisburg's first venture began as an agricultural "show" in October 1892. It was so successful that the next year it was enlarged and called the "second annual fall fair." Besides "a large attendance from the whole countryside" at the 1893 fair, "there was a large attendance from Calgary of businessmen and others, and nearly all were astonished at the products exhibited, few believing that the like was in the country," wrote a reporter for the *Calgary Tribune*.[84] The exhibition was the "best Fall Fair that has so far been held in Southern Alberta," he declared, with more space for displays of purebred bulls, heavy draught horses, drivers, saddle horses, top-quality butter and bread, and the added attraction of a baby show. With sufficient funds available, the fair harmoniously blended farmers, ranchers, cowboys, and Calgary people.

Like Davisburg's fair, the fair at Fish Creek in July 1893 drew support from many farmers and ranchers as well as numerous

Calgary merchants. Prize-winning exhibits included Felix A. McHugh's purebred stallion, R. Hamilton's Polled Angus bull, Duncan McArthur's Fife wheat, Miss J. E. Bernard's oil and water colour paintings, and Annie Wolley-Dod's garden flowers.[85] The Fish Creek fair succeeded in financing more than one hundred prizes for the best showing of animals, grains, vegetables, bread, flowers, paintings, and plain and fancy needlework. Funding was a concern; however, by 1899 the Fish Creek people had solved this problem by combining their efforts with those of Calgarians in support of the city's fair.[86]

Community leaders hoped that fairs would educate farmers and ranchers about scientific agriculture and improved standards of living. In an attempt to complement the work at fairs, the Canadian government occasionally provided speakers from the Central Experimental Farm in Ottawa for educational talks on new scientific methods of farming at agricultural societies' meetings in the Bow Valley.[87] Contests at fairs in the region introduced exhibitors and fairgoers to local and regional experts' criteria for judging products such as improved seeds and purebred livestock.

The late nineteenth century was remarkable for its great North American fairs, with expositions in Philadelphia (the Centennial Exposition in 1876), Chicago (the Columbian Exposition in 1893), and Toronto (1894), where fairgoers were impressed by the advances western civilization had made and thrilled by the promises of future times.[88] Fairs in the Bow Valley became small-scale expositions showing progress in agriculture and some of the latest inventions and products. At these fairs merchants, manufacturers, ranchers, and farmers tried to emulate what they knew was occurring in the national and international arenas. Certainly, people in the region were very much aware of what was happening in the rest of North America. After receiving the first prize at the Toronto Industrial Exhibition in 1890, the Elbow Park Ranche's imported Irish purebred stallion Faughaballaugh twice carried away the top prize from the Calgary fair in the next few years.[89] The Calgary manufacturers Robert J. Hutchings and William J. Riley won a gold medal for their saddles and harnesses at the world's fair in Chicago in 1893.[90] Mingling with visitors at the large fairs in big cities gave Bow Valley people an opportunity to appreciate the importance of new inventions, new agricultural practices, and new products of their age.

Chapter 8: Maintaining the Family Farm

Dairy farming became an important agricultural business in the Bow Valley. In June 1892, farmers at Springbank responded eagerly to the opportunity to ship their milk to the Young Bros.' newly opened cheese factory in the community.[91] The cheese factory's output was sold locally, across the prairie West, and in Calgary, with a substantial share going to the Hudson's Bay Company store. By the end of the year, a creamery had been established at the Behan Ranch in Springbank.[92] The creamery, which offered high-quality butter to customers, provided farmers with another choice for selling their milk.

Voluntary Associations in the Bow Valley

A complex network of voluntary associations in the Bow Valley, including churches, fraternal lodges, and literary societies, helped to spread new ideas on agriculture, technology, and commerce. When agricultural society organizers came calling, important forms of association and community-building already existed, as did links between friends and neighbours to facilitate recruitment into a new organization. These voluntary networks, coupled with the strong commitment most people had to the wider community, also eased tensions between farmers and ranchers in the countryside and conflicts between Conservatives and Liberals in the political culture. Nearly all citizens sought to avoid antagonizing others in their neighbourhood. Inspired by a lively community spirit, most people were willing to co-operate and anxious to play down divisive issues. Calgary merchants and manufacturers recognized that they shared with ranchers and farmers the desire for the improvement of transportation and communication throughout the Bow Valley, for their products to sell profitably, and for the region to prosper.

Neighbourly and kinship ties were augmented and reinforced by voluntary associations such as churches in the predominantly Anglo-Saxon, Victorian culture in the Bow Valley. Churches were numerous and formally organized with national affiliations, but seldom deeply divided by ethnicity and fundamental beliefs. During the 1880s and 1890s, the region had Anglican, Roman Catholic, Methodist, Presbyterian, and Baptist churches. Besides the congregations in Calgary, these churches had congregations in the countryside. Activities such as Bible studies, raising money to furnish the churches and sustain mission work, and musical programs for the whole community enhanced the image of congregations and strengthened the ties of members. Fraternal lodges, based on voluntary association, were tremendously popular in the Bow Valley and Canada during this period. Merchants, manufacturers, unskilled and skilled workers, as well as ranchers and farmers, were well represented in lodges such as the Masons and Oddfellows – all of them recognized that membership in these lodges was good for business. The Masonic lodge, with its women's auxiliary, the Order of the Eastern Star, was organized in Calgary in 1884. Within a few years, the Oddfellows lodge, with its women's auxiliary, the Rebekahs, had been established in the town.[93] The lodges provided benefits for their members and members' families in times of sickness or impoverishment and for funerals. Members who lived in the countryside often travelled many miles on horseback or in horse-drawn vehicles to attend meetings in Calgary. Literary societies – in Calgary, Pine Creek, and Springbank – also gave neighbours a place to meet and a common cultural forum that could overcome differences.[94] Despite economic distinctions and many divisions, most long-time residents of the Bow Valley valued unity and commitment to the well-being of the community.

Farmers and the Natural Environment

Some Bow Valley farmers, aware of the availability of good land elsewhere in Alberta, disregarded the need for soil conservation. Pioneers knew that Bow Valley's soil was very fertile, which led some to take it for granted and misuse it. At the same time, many farmers thought of leaving productive land to their children and avoided careless use of the soil. To prevent soil exhaustion, they rotated crops, used manure, planted alfalfa or clover, and fallowed. On numerous farms, the productivity of the land never declined sharply in the late nineteenth century.

For ages before farmers came to the Bow Valley, annual prairie fires had killed grasses, trees, bushes, and other vegetation. Widespread ploughing resulting from settlement checked raging prairie blazes. Creating firebreaks by ploughing in strategic places also helped to check fires that blackened billowing prairie grasses. Farmers enhanced the natural environment by planting trees and

Chapter 8: Maintaining the Family Farm

bushes around houses and between fields. With the appearance of various new bushes, trees, and flowers, settlers' farms became garden spots in the Bow Valley, providing beauty and variety and softening life. This imported vegetation also provided new habitats for songbirds and other birds natural to prairies.

Financial Problems

Commercial agrarian society in the Bow Valley faced major financial problems in Canada's emerging industrial economy. Offering land as security, many early farmers had to take out loans to develop their farms and sustain their families in the 1880s and 1890s. Globally, agricultural production was rising as more land was opened to farming. With the increase in supplies, wheat prices fell, but Bow Valley farmers grew ever-larger crops in order to pay their debts. When their land could no longer be mortgaged, they sometimes borrowed money on chattels.[95] Consequently, during bad years many farm families could not leave Alberta because their cattle, horses, and farm equipment were mortgaged and could not be removed from the district.

Kenneth Cameron
Okotoks Farmer

The experience of Kenneth Cameron, an Okotoks farmer, illustrates how hard times exacerbated his financial problems. Born in the town of Beauly near Inverness, Scotland, Cameron immigrated to Canada and became a farmer in Bruce County, Ontario.[96] He married Edinburgh-born Elizabeth Mary Carstairs and began to raise a family. But the Camerons were not having much success as farmers. Hoping that his wife and seven children would have a better life, in 1877 Kenneth alone left Bruce County for the Gladstone area of Manitoba. But the hardships of the next three years on his farm here discouraged him. He decided to move farther west to the Calgary region. In 1880, the journey took several months by wagon and oxen, with the traveller's spirits improving as he settled on land on Sheep Creek at Okotoks, beside the Macleod

Chapter 8: Maintaining the Family Farm

Trail, in section 29, township 20, range 29, west of the fourth, first entering it as a squatter and then filing a homestead claim on the northeast quarter.[97]

Before long, Kenneth Cameron expanded his farm by purchasing an adjoining quarter section under the pre-emption law. The business started operations on a shoestring. In July 1881, Cameron borrowed $1,000 from the Winnipeg-based Manitoba and Northwest Loan Company at an interest rate of 9 percent per annum.[98] The loan, with a five-year maturity, was secured by a mortgage on a portion of his land. He used most of this money to buy farm implements, a few horses, some cows, seed grain, and materials to erect a house and a barn on his homestead.

Cameron was proud of his business accomplishments. But the farmer's ebullience proved short-lived. Despite the sale of some grain, by the spring of 1883 the business was short of operating capital. In the depressed economy at this time, credit was tight. Cameron owed the Manitoba and Northwest Loan Company $188 in interest charges.[99] He pushed himself hard, working long hours on the farm. He managed to finance the most pressing debts, including a payment to the Canadian Pacific Railway in the fall of that year for bringing his wife and children to Calgary so that they could join him on the farm at Okotoks.

Occasional discouragement did not smother Cameron's business imagination. He had long known that success in the farming business depended on co-operation. To be effective, he exchanged work during the harvest season and at other times with his sons-in-law, Alexander McRae and Norman McInnis, neighbouring farmers who had married his daughters Anne and Marion respectively. As a director of the Sheep Creek Agricultural Society, Cameron joined other local farmers in promoting the development of farming in the community.[100] But he worried about how to finance his ongoing operations on the farm. Because of the urgent need for cash, in March 1887 he borrowed $500 from Gillies Bros. in the Ottawa area.[101] Cameron also sold the two lots he owned in Calgary.

But in June 1887, the Manitoba and Northwest Loan Company brought suit against Kenneth Cameron in the Supreme Court of the Northwest Territories in Calgary. This case involved a claim for damages arising from Cameron's failure to make any payment on the loan from the company. Besides having taken a mortgage on his land, the company had accepted a chattel mortgage on his cattle,

Chapter 8: Maintaining the Family Farm

horses, and wagon. Sheriff Peter W. King had already seized some of Cameron's horses and cattle. The trial of the case, in which he spoke in his own defence without the aid of lawyer, resulted in a damage award of $1,992, a large amount in those days.[102] Cameron faced the prospect of bankruptcy. Rather than let him fail, the company apparently decided to give extra time to him.

Kenneth Cameron did not relinquish his interest in the farm, but he soon resolved to devote more of his energies to the stopping house that he had set up on it earlier. Taken together, the next six years were busy ones for Kenneth and his wife Elizabeth and those of their daughters who were still at home. He and his family were determined to harness the opportunities presented by the growing demand for good meals and a comfortable bed. Well located on the Macleod Trail, the stopping house attracted numerous travellers and freighters. Keen to capitalize on the reputation for service Kenneth had already established, Elizabeth, an industrious woman, was supportive of her husband's ambitions and became involved in many of his decisions in the business. Kenneth Cameron died in 1893, leaving Elizabeth, not a big fortune, but a stopping house that was holding its own.[103]

Politics and Progress

While a number of Bow Valley farmers were in trouble, many of them were appalled by what they saw as the federal government's favouring of central Canadian industrial interests through a high tariff on manufactured goods and large subsidies to the Canadian Pacific Railway. Farm incomes failed to keep pace with the great advances being made in central Canadian industry. The political instruments through which the distressed farmers tried to find solutions to their financial problems were the Conservative and Liberal parties, but these traditional parties did not do enough to satisfy agrarian interests. For years, the financial question continued to roil Bow Valley agrarian politics and established a base on which the United Farmers of Alberta movement of the first decade of the twentieth century was to be built.[104]

Despite these impediments to progress, no part of southern Alberta had been so transformed into farming country by 1900 as the Bow Valley. There was still fertile land outside the ranching community in the valley that was neither settled nor farmed. But the grain belt was beginning to take shape, with emphasis on the production of wheat, oats, barley, and rye and the feeding of livestock for the market. Capital investments in prairie and foothills land, improvements, and farm implements were high, mortgage indebtedness was becoming heavier, and hundreds of farmers were prospering. The prosperity was halted by the economic depression of the mid-nineties and the consequent decline in land values and in dollar returns from grain and livestock, but farmers continued to make improvements, their farms grew, and the Bow Valley was soon ready for another era of development.

9

From Town to City

A Promising Place

As the Bow Valley began to fill up with homesteaders who broke the prairie sod with steel ploughs and put in crops of grain, Calgary continued to serve as the region's main shipping and supply centre. Horse-drawn wagons arrived with cash crops – wheat, oats, and barley – and left with lumber, harnesses, saddles, cookstoves, groceries, and ready-made-clothing. Pioneers in the town and the surrounding area associated salient events such as the appearance of important visitors with growth and overall progress. By 1886, Calgary's population was fifteen hundred, and when John A. Macdonald came into the town by the Canadian Pacific Railway in July of that year, the Prime Minister saw it as a promising place. He predicted that "Calgary would yet be a large metropolitan city."[1]

To promote and give direction to the town's growing economy, merchants and manufacturers continued to support the Calgary board of trade. At a special general meeting of the board in the town hall on 6 March 1886, the members agreed to raise the annual membership fees to $10.[2] Already Calgary had been launched as the largest livestock market in Alberta. Recognizing this, the board called for the establishment of a new road – "a trail between the southern ranches and Calgary for the purpose of driving cattle to this market as the best and most centrally located town in the province."[3]

However, Calgary "is decidedly the most unfinished town I have yet found in the Canadian Northwest," a visitor from London, England wrote. "The streets are strewn, and in some cases almost blockaded, with building materials…. The town … has grown so rapidly that they have not time either to pave the streets or to

Chapter 9: From Town to City

construct sidewalks."[4] Nor were there any sewers. To make matters worse, there was no drainage. From time to time, rainwater collected in rancid puddles on the streets, where it was fed by waste runoff from business establishments, overflowing backyard privies, and barns. The obnoxious character of the streets included swirling clouds of dust during dry, windy spells in the summer. At night, people had to use lanterns to negotiate the cluttered, disorderly streets.

In the spring, roads and trails in and around the town remained almost impassable for weeks, threatening to bring business to a standstill. Fortunately for Calgarians and the people in the surrounding area, the original prairie trails were generally passable during most of the year. But there were problems. As the *Calgary Herald* wrote,

> ... since settlement has commenced and fields and quarter sections, even sections, of land are being enclosed, the original trails have been in a great many places interfered with, and the distant settler who has to plod his way to Calgary headquarters has to take round about ways, and dismount to open bars and gates as they happen to be erected by the proprietor who has formed these barricades.[5]

This was the situation along the Macleod Trail, from Calgary to Sheep Creek and beyond. Settlers found it difficult to reach the town with their wagons because of the numerous fences that had been built across the trail; nearby sloughs of water prevented them from making detours. Retail merchants feared that the lack of good roads would hurt their trade.

Calgary's single most important asset was the people who were drawn to it – youthful, visionary, inventive, and assertive residents, many of them from central Canada, the maritime provinces, and Great Britain, as well as more than a few from the United States. Most of them arrived by railway; some, after visiting the land titles office in Calgary, headed out by team and wagon to unseen homesteads in the Bow Valley. But a goodly number of them, their hopes raised by the young town's confident air, obtained jobs or opened businesses and settled down.

Chapter 9: From Town to City

Calgary
Southern Alberta's Railway Hub

Travellers visiting Calgary in early 1886 found it a small town in a big hurry, filled with restless activity that focused on improving transportation. A group of the town's leaders, including James A. Lougheed, met at James D. Lafferty's home on 19 February.[6] Many of them were members of the board of trade. These were the men who promoted the town; their town's future, they agreed, was with railway development. They envisioned a line running north from Calgary to Edmonton, as well as a line stretching south to Fort Macleod. They believed that these tracks would boost Calgary, extend its hinterland, and help settle the Bow Valley and other parts of Alberta. Their ideas and actions concerning improved transportation helped assure Calgary's place as southern Alberta's railway hub.

Lougheed and his fellow townsmen applied to the Canadian government for charter rights to build a railway from Calgary south through Fort Macleod to the Montana border and north to Edmonton. Acting as solicitor for the Calgary group, Lougheed submitted the application to Prime Minister John A. Macdonald.[7] Calgary was served by the Canadian Pacific and eagerly awaited branch line track.

Macdonald, however, rejected the application in order to maintain the Canadian Pacific Railway's monopoly in the southern Canadian prairies.[8] The monopoly of the railway foiled Lougheed's dream of branch lines for about two years. The Canadian Pacific's charter of 1881 contained a monopoly clause that prohibited for twenty years the construction of any competing line between the main line of the Canadian Pacific and the American boundary.[9] In the first instance, this clause was designed to prevent American railroads, especially the Northern Pacific, from pushing branch lines into Canadian Pacific territory. Its effect, however, was to deny entrepreneurs such as Lougheed and his associates the opportunity to provide any alternative route to shippers of livestock and grain from the southern prairies. Thus, the Canadian Pacific's freight rates were not competitive rates. In February 1888, Lougheed and his colleagues took up the fight against the monopoly clause by petitioning the Macdonald government to cancel it.[10] But it was in Manitoba that the public revulsion against monopolies gained the greatest force, producing an anti-monopoly provincial government that condemned the Canadian Pacific charter's monopoly clause. With the Canadian Pacific being thrust into the foreground of anti-monopoly indictments, the Macdonald government cancelled this clause in the railway's contract in the spring of 1888.

Developments over the next few years virtually guaranteed Calgary's place as the railway centre of southern Alberta. If individual leaders such as Lougheed shaped railway policy in Calgary, he did not do so alone. He had the support of the town council as well as the board of trade. In March 1889, a group of men including Mayor Arthur E. Shelton and John L. Bowen as well as Fort Macleod leaders D. W. Davis, local I. G. Baker & Co. manager and member of the House of Commons for Alberta, and John Cowdry, a private banker, secured a charter for the Calgary, Alberta, and Montana Railway.[11] The road was to run from Calgary north to Edmonton and south through Fort Macleod to the Montana border.

But Calgary entrepreneurs and their Fort Macleod allies did not make Calgary a major railway hub without the Canadian Pacific's considerable help. As small-town businessmen, filled with enthusiasm and respected locally but undercapitalized, they took the plunge into railroading without fully calculating the risks and problems that lay ahead. Developmental railroading, intended to service the local economy, was difficult in a region so sparsely populated, with very little capital. Unable to raise sufficient money in Calgary and Fort Macleod, in the spring of 1890 the Calgary, Alberta, and Montana Railway sold its interests to the newly incorporated Calgary and Edmonton Railway, which functioned as a subsidiary of the Canadian Pacific.[12]

Edmund B. Osler from Toronto, an influential Canadian Pacific director and senior partner in the Toronto and Winnipeg firm Osler, Hammond & Nanton, financiers and stockbrokers, was a principal director of the Calgary and Edmonton. Seeing the Calgary and Edmonton as the key to the future of Alberta, Osler played an important role in persuading the Macdonald government to grant Dominion lands to the Calgary and Edmonton to help pay for the construction of the railway that was to run from the Canadian Pacific's main line in Calgary north to Edmonton and south to Fort Macleod.[13] This was part of Osler's nationalistic vision of a great rail system that would bind together large sections of Canada. In response to public opinion in Calgary, which had grand dreams, the *Calgary Herald* wrote: "the building of the Calgary and Edmonton railway will make our town the most important railway centre, now existent, or that ever will be, in Canada west of Winnipeg."[14]

In Osler, Hammond & Nanton, the partners – Edmund Osler, Herbert C. Hammond, and Augustus Meredith Nanton – had the knowledge, contacts, prestige and also the sense of timing needed to raise capital by attracting British investors into new, untried ventures in the prairie West.[15] As significant figures in the Anglo-Canadian financial establishment, they were major entrepreneurs in the business universe. Their abilities often gained investors a return in prairie railways. A new railway, whose future was still uncertain, could usually not reach investors directly; it needed endorsement from a reliable financial firm with a good credit rating before either institutional or individual investors would provide money. In the early 1890s, Osler and his partners became the chief conduit for British capital that helped finance the Calgary and Edmonton. Taking huge risks, they greased the wheels of international finance and achieved increasingly more power in the process. They profited, but so did Calgary and Fort Macleod, both hungry for branch line transportation. Osler and his colleagues played a crucial role in developing a north-south Alberta rail and economic system that reinforced Calgary's place as a regional railway centre.

The 295-mile Calgary and Edmonton road, ultimately transformed into a branch line of the Canadian Pacific, became an important trans-Alberta railway centred in Calgary. Construction began in Calgary in July 1890 and, twelve months later, trains operated between Calgary and Strathcona on the south bank of the North Saskatchewan River opposite Edmonton. The rails reached Fort Macleod in November 1892.[16] Cayley, on the southern segment of the Calgary and Edmonton, possessed substantial stockyards and became a principal centre for the shipment of cattle destined for markets in Calgary, other parts of Canada, and abroad.[17]

First, however, a consistent source of long-term capital was needed. Therefore, in the summer of 1890, Osler travelled to London, England, where he relied heavily on Morton, Rose & Co., a major Anglo-American private banking firm. The late Sir John Rose, who had been a partner in this firm headed by the American banker Levi P. Morton, had been Osler's friend and the Dominion of Canada's second finance minister. Osler negotiated the sale of $5 million in Calgary and Edmonton bonds to Morton, Rose & Co. Others shared the risk, however. Osler himself bought 4 percent of the original bond issue of $5,400,000, that is $200,000. James Ross from Montreal, a director of the Calgary and Edmonton as well as of the Canadian Pacific who together with William Mackenzie and Donald D. Mann built the Calgary and Edmonton, also purchased $200,000 in bonds. From the start, the Canadian Pacific ran the Calgary and Edmonton under a leasing arrangement, for this was one of the conditions on which Morton, Rose & Co. had agreed to buy $5 million worth of Calgary and Edmonton bonds.[18] Thus, the Canadian Pacific bore responsibility for the future of the line. Calgarians welcomed British and central Canadian bondholders, who brought much-needed capital.

But more capital was needed as the Calgary and Edmonton was building from Calgary to Strathcona and to Fort Macleod, capital that British investors would provide only if they had a shrewd man on the spot to watch over their interests. In Osler, Hammond & Nanton's Winnipeg office, Augustus Nanton served in this role; his task essentially was to oversee the sale of the Calgary and Edmonton's lands in Alberta. In 1891, this railway transferred its federal land grant of 6,400 acres per mile of rail line, a total of 1,888,000 acres, to the Calgary and Edmonton Land Company, a British-chartered corporation organized in London in May of that year. Capitalized at £270,000, the company had several directors. The three directors in London included merchant Charles D. Rose, who acted as chairman, while those in Canada were Edmund Osler and James Ross.[19]

People in Calgary and other parts of Alberta appreciated Augustus Nanton's efforts to make the Calgary and Edmonton Land Company's lands available to settlers. In April 1892, he sent his older brother Harry W. Nanton, a graduate of Upper Canada College, to Osler, Hammond & Nanton's newly opened branch office in Calgary to manage the sale of the company's lands in Alberta.[20] When Harry Nanton moved from Osler, Hammond & Nanton's office in Winnipeg to Calgary, it was an auspicious time for him. Settlers in search of land were streaming into Alberta, and Harry Nanton was ready for them. For instance, in the spring of 1893, he sold land to eighty-one settlers from Nebraska in the Olds district. At Olds, he provided temporary accommodation for them at the hotel built by the Calgary and Edmonton Railway and the immigrant shed erected by Osler, Hammond & Nanton.[21]

Chapter 9: From Town to City

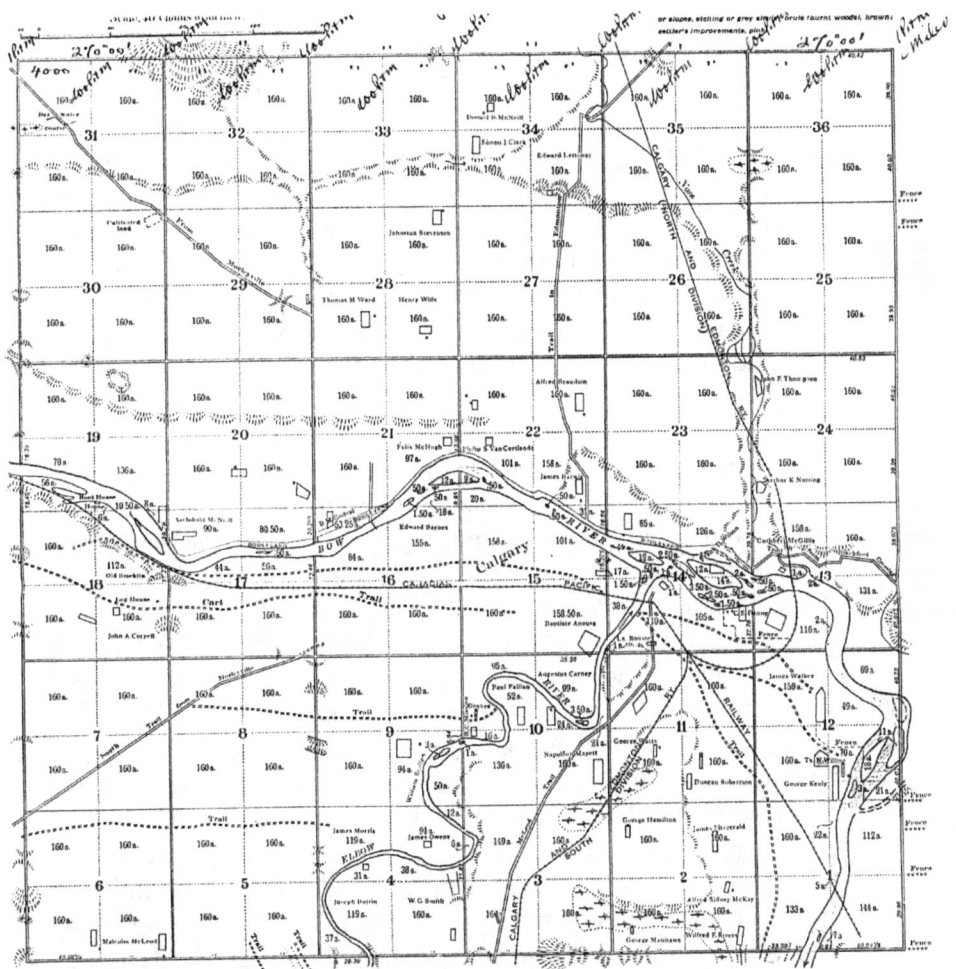

Map 5. Township 24 Range 1 W5M in 1895. Most of the names given on various tracts of land are those of homesteaders who started farms or ranches. (Courtesy of National Archives of Canada).

The nationwide economic depression in Canada in the mid-1890s shattered hopes for further rapid land sales.

Nevertheless, by 1894, settlers in the Calgary area had acquired some of the Calgary and Edmonton Land Company's lands and were making progress in their farming operations. Calgary added inducements to attract settlers. For example, it provided Ratcliffe Bros. with a bonus of $6,000 to aid them in establishing a creamery and cold storage plant at the junction of the Calgary and Edmonton and the Canadian Pacific near the city limits.[22] By 1898, Harry

Nanton had returned to Osler, Hammond & Nanton's Winnipeg office, and Charles S. Lott, a Calgary broker and insurance agent who had been born in London, England, had replaced him in Calgary. Like Harry Nanton before him, Charles Lott, who had earlier worked as a draughtsman in the Canadian Pacific's Winnipeg land office, was a successful land salesman.[23]

By the end of 1900, as the directors reported to the shareholders, Augustus Nanton had sold a total of 187,090 acres for the Calgary and Edmonton Land Company.[24] A great deal of this land was located in the Alberta foothills region, from near Innisfail south to the Montana border. Even by 1894, an increasing number of settlers were entering the region to acquire land, and towns such as Olds, Innisfail, and Red Deer along the Calgary and Edmonton were growing rapidly. Along the southern segment of its line, the Calgary and Edmonton also was responsible for spurring settlement and the development of many towns, including Okotoks, High River, and Nanton, which was named after Augustus Nanton. Intimately associated with the southern segment of the Calgary and Edmonton as well were the growth of the cattle industry and the rise of meat processing in Calgary. As early as the end of November 1892, the Cold Meat Storage Company's slaughterhouses in Calgary received a shipment of three carloads of cattle from the Cochrane Ranche south of Fort Macleod.[25] Transportation sped up all along the Calgary and Edmonton route. Mails that had spent days in transit by stagecoach now arrived overnight. By the beginning of the twentieth century, the Calgary and Edmonton was benefiting from an overpowering combination: an upturn in the business cycle, a flood of settlers, and hard-driving management of the railway.

The Calgary and Edmonton wedded ranches, farms, hamlets, and villages to Calgary. More than ever before, economic functions became interconnected in complex ways. Bow Valley people and others fed farm and ranch products into Calgary, purchased goods from Calgary, and serviced the tracks connecting local communities to the rising city. It was a significant milestone, one reflecting Calgary's lengthening and broadening economic reach. Calgary tapped ever-growing hinterlands, drawing from them livestock, grain, and dairy products. Lumber, saddles, harnesses, processed meats, and other goods from Calgary's industrial establishments sped by rail into expanding Bow Valley markets.

Sometimes, railway accidents marred the new transportation route, inflicting death on wandering cattle. For the most part, however, the Calgary and Edmonton affected the Bow Valley in positive ways. The road helped to hoist land values and to bring new land under cultivation. Besides gradually eliminating stagecoach travel, it reduced wagon traffic. Many farmers and ranchers remote from tracks still moved cargo by wagon, but a goodly number could make use of the trains, which clicked along at sustained speeds of forty or more miles per hour. Wagons lumbered along at about three miles per hour, and stagecoach speeds were about six miles per hour for long trips from Calgary to Edmonton or Fort Macleod. The railway helped to reduce frontier isolation, increasing social contact between rural and urban communities.

In August 1901, Augustus Nanton visited Calgary to evaluate the Calgary and Edmonton, its finances and prospects. "The prospects for business on C. & E. were never better.... It is only a question of a short time when the C.P.R., in its own interest, will have to get hold of the railway," Nanton wrote to Edmund Osler.[26] The Calgary and Edmonton showed modest profits a year later. In 1903, the Canadian Pacific, having considerable resources, purchased the railway and began overhauling it. The improvements, such as rebuilding bridges and tracks and renewing freight and passenger cars, involved hundreds of workers, including those who lived in Calgary. Here was progress, and the Canadian Pacific continued to foster it by gaining access to downtown Edmonton from Strathcona via the Edmonton, Yukon, and Pacific Railway across the North Saskatchewan River.[27] At last, Calgary had a rail connection with Edmonton, a major agricultural and marketing centre in the north. By 1900, the Canadian Pacific had carried out its ambitious program of branch-line acquisition and construction from Medicine Hat through Lethbridge, Fort Macleod, and the Crow's Nest Pass to Cranbrook, British Columbia. In October 1903, the Calgary board of trade announced that it had persuaded the Canadian Pacific to substantially reduce its freight rates on shipments by wholesalers in Calgary to retailers in the vast area spreading north to Edmonton, south and west to Fort Macleod, Cranbrook and Revelstoke, and south and east to Lethbridge and Medicine Hat.[28] All this made it possible for Calgary to strengthen its position in the traffic of Alberta and southeastern British Columbia.

Chapter 9: From Town to City

Making Funds Available to Settlers

Augustus Nanton's contribution to the growth of Calgary and Alberta included making funds available to settlers to develop their farms. By the early 1890s, it was clear that the opening of the region to settlement required far more capital than the sums that were needed for the railways that already were transforming economic life. Settlers found credit very difficult to obtain during their early, frequently uncertain years. Nanton was prepared to help fill this need, most notably by serving at Osler, Hammond & Nanton as an agent for the North of Scotland Canadian Mortgage Company in Aberdeen, Scotland, which involved itself in land mortgages. During the late nineteenth and early twentieth centuries, Augustus Nanton played an important role in the export of Scottish capital to the Alberta economy, and particularly to one of its dynamic components, the farms. Nevertheless, he needed someone in Alberta to offer to lend Scottish money to settlers.

Augustus Nanton's chance for financing Alberta settlers came in 1892, when his brother Harry took charge of Osler, Hammond & Nanton's office in Calgary.[29] Usually, bank loans of from thirty to ninety days were too short to help finance farm expansion in land or equipment, or to produce and market a crop. Consequently, farmers, especially in frontier regions like the Bow Valley, often had to rely for credit on merchants, implement dealers, or loan companies. Thus, an opportunity presented itself to Harry Nanton. He loaned some North of Scotland Canadian Mortgage Company money on mortgage to Alberta farm owners on a long-term basis.

Charles S. Lott, Harry Nanton's successor in Osler, Hammond & Nanton's Calgary office, continued to invest the company's money in mortgages on farms. For instance, in May 1900, Lott lent $500 to Joseph Hope, a farmer at Midnapore. The five-year loan, secured by a mortgage on Hope's 320-acre farm, carried an annual interest rate of 9 percent.[30] Lott played a significant role in opening up the Bow Valley, not only by lending North of Scotland Canadian Mortgage Company money to farmers, but also by selling Calgary and Edmonton Railway as well as Canadian Pacific Railway lands to them.[31]

Lott and other early Calgary entrepreneurs had a clear understanding of the city's symbiotic relationship with its surrounding area. Calgary and its tributary region – the Bow Valley – created each other and depended on each other for survival. In its drive for resources and markets, Calgary helped establish an interconnected city-country economic system. At the same time that Lott was getting ahead personally by building up the farm mortgage business for the North of Scotland Canadian Mortgage Company, settlers with credit were making progress by ploughing up prairie sod. As Calgary transformed the Bow Valley, this valley in turn transformed the city, with the rail network as the main agency for both changes.

The Great Fire

Before Calgary gained Calgary and Edmonton Railway service, it was a town with few modern amenities beyond a board of trade, a courthouse, the beginnings of electrical lighting, and a small telephone exchange. It had no adequate sewage system. The town also lacked an adequate fire department.

On the eve of the great fire of 1886, Calgarians feared for their families and property as the almost entirely dry summer and fall of that year turned their cheaply built town of wood into a mass of highly flammable material. On Monday evening, 6 September, about thirty citizens met at Boynton Hall to discuss the need for fire protection. James Reilly, part owner of the Royal Hotel, warned that the inaction of the town councillors "allowed the town to run the risk of being burnt out."[32] Outside the main business district, nearly every building was made of wood, while the few stone or brick structures downtown had wooden signs on their fronts.[33] All of them had wooden roofs covered with shingles or tar. The substantial commercial buildings were surrounded by flimsy frame shanties and saloons. To protect themselves against fire loss, the owners of a number of business establishments depended on some insurance coverage, not solid construction. Repeatedly, Calgary's fire department had recommended that the town construct deeper wells, acquire a reliable fire engine, and organize a proper hook and ladder company, but the town government had failed to act on these recommendations. By the beginning of November, this town of wood had been dried out by a severe drought. Only a little rain had fallen between 16 June and 6 November. Further increasing the danger, large amounts of combustible material were lying around in yards or stored in the homes of Calgarians. With

Chapter 9: *From Town to City*

Great Fire of 7 November 1886. (Courtesy of Glenbow Archives, NA-298-3).

winter approaching, sheds and household barns were filled with hay to feed horses or cattle. Guarding the whole town of fifteen hundred people was a fire department of only a handful of firefighters with a tiny supply of water and a small, inadequate fire engine.

On Sunday morning, 7 November, around 5:30 a.m., a fire broke out in the centre of the town in the lean-to at the rear of S. Parrish & Son's flour and feed store on the corner of McTavish Street and Atlantic Avenue. A great deal of baled hay and other flammable material was stored in the lean-to. Someone spotted flames licking up the lean-to and spreading to J. L. Lamont's tin shop and the Massey Manufacturing Co.'s warehouse. Within minutes, the Church of England bell began booming its alarm over the sleeping town, but it was a full quarter of an hour before two dozen people arrived on the scene.[34] Aided by a strong wind off the prairie, the fire turned into a 4½-hour blaze that consumed part of the town's core, leaving many people homeless. In the first hours of the fire, a rumour spread that it was started by an arsonist.[35] No one was ever able to substantiate this, but the arson story went through Calgary and out to the world.

The fire ripped through a number of buildings in an hour, but it might have been contained as a small fire had it not been for the wind, which picked up considerably before long. It was a terrifying spectacle for the citizens of Calgary. As men and women and the Mounted Police with pails of water and wet blankets lined up to block and fight the inferno in front of them, sparks and burning cinders flew over them, creating new fires behind them. Within two hours, hotels and saloons were on fire, and then stores, including those of I. G. Baker & Co. and Chipman Bros. & Co., began burning from top to bottom. At 7:00 a.m., James Thomson, manager of the local Hudson's Bay Company store, wired Joseph Wrigley, the company's chief commissioner in Winnipeg:

> Serious fire in Calgary this morning. Stores totally destroyed: Baker, Parrish, Massey, Chipman and others smaller. Our buildings safe.... No clue has yet been obtained as to how the fire originated but a suspicion exists that it has been the work of an incendiary.[36]

When the fire reached George Murdoch's harness shop, George C. King, the general merchant who had been elected mayor of Calgary in the municipal election a few days before, and the Mounted Police were sure that they could prevent it from spreading to other buildings by demolishing the shop and thus creating a firebreak. That evening Murdoch wrote in his diary:

> Woke by fire alarm about 5:30. My block on fire. Saved all the wall goods but was turned out before I could get the shelf goods. House tried to be blown up by the Police but was torn down by order of the Mayor.[37]

To help check the flames, Murdoch assisted the Mounted Police and his fellow citizens in tearing down his shop and carrying away the pieces. For Murdoch, it was a vivid reminder of the Great Fire in Chicago in 1871, when he had allowed his house and harness shop in that city to be "blown up there to save others."[38]

The rescue of Charles Sparrow was one of the sensational stories of the fire. A bookkeeper for A. C. Sparrow & Co., butchers, Sparrow also served as the town's treasurer. He kept the treasurer's books and papers in his home, behind the Athletic Saloon. E. R. Rogers of Rogers & Grant, hardware merchants, helped Sparrow put out the flames on his house with a Babcock fire extinguisher.

Chapter 9: From Town to City

Sparrow was able to save everything in his home, although it was "much scorched and blackened."[39]

By about 10:00 a.m., the fire had run its course. It was the greatest catastrophe in Calgary's history. The first business now was the assessment of the damage. Property worth $103,200 was destroyed – twenty-six buildings in downtown Calgary between Atlantic Avenue and Stephen Avenue – with insurance covering $24,500. No people died in the fire, but "a few parties got their faces and hands a little scorched."[40] In the first week after the fire, there were reports in the newspapers of looting and arson. That Sunday afternoon, the town council appointed six men as special constables to guard the ruins of stores, dwelling houses, and other buildings for forty-eight hours. For a time, Mayor King placed Calgary under full Mounted Police law, entrusting their local commanding officer, Colonel W. M. Herchmer, with the good order and safety of the town. Herchmer told King that "any persons who were rendered homeless could have tents from the barracks till they could procure suitable dwelling places."[41]

I. G. Baker & Co., owner of the largest store in Calgary, was the biggest loser that Sunday morning. Just the day before, the firm had received three carloads of new winter stock. Almost all of it was reduced to ashes.[42] The total loss on the stock alone at Baker & Co., apart from its buildings, was estimated to be $50,000. Only $15,000 of this amount was covered by insurance. The firm did not, however, accept defeat in the town. Calgary would rise again, and so would Baker & Co. John L. Bowen, the firm's manager, remained in the town directing the work of reconstruction through the snow that soon began to fall.

Not everyone, however, was hurt by Calgary's fire. T. C. Power & Bro.'s general store in the town escaped the flames. As Daniel W. Marsh, the store's manager, wrote, "The fire reached within 150 ft. of us and it looked for awhile as though we would go, but as we were pretty well covered by insurance were but little frightened." Nor was Marsh moved by the plight of his competitor, Baker & Co.

He added: "The losses in published statement [in the *Calgary Tribune*] are somewhat exaggerated, particularly in IGB & Co.'s case. Presume they do not lose over $10,000 and to offset that they get rid of a lot of trash and old stock."[43]

As Arthur D. Braithwaite, manager of the Bank of Montreal's Calgary branch, looked over the wreckage of the town, he focused on only one group of fire victims, ignoring the others. "The fire has cleaned out a number of shanties and low grog shops, has really hurt no one," Braithwaite reported to Wentworth Buchanan, the bank's general manager in Montreal.[44]

But there were plenty of people who were hurting, among them George Murdoch. On the morning after the day of the fire, he was up at daybreak, inspecting his property. He had lost almost everything in his harness and saddle business, except for some stock and the ground on which he had built his shop in Calgary. After spending several days helping hired men build a new shop on the old site, Murdoch brought the stock he had saved back into the building and prepared to make harnesses and saddles again. But "at stock taking," he found $600 worth of stock "missing and spoiled." On 16 November, he wrote in his diary that the "insurance man will not allow me for lost stock, only a trifle on what he can see is damaged."[45] Despite his losses, Murdoch gradually recovered from the disaster and expanded his harness and saddle manufacturing enterprise.

That Sunday morning at ten o'clock, the day of the fire, Mayor King called a special meeting of the town council. Representing the progressive spirit of Calgary, he immediately initiated a number of public improvements, including proposals for fire protection. The council passed motions providing for the deepening of the town wells to secure more water, the organization of a reliable hook and ladder company, and the acquisition of an adequate fire engine – three needs made obvious by the fire.[46]

King recognized how badly the fire had hurt Calgary. Because the conflagration had been fed by dozens of wooden buildings, on 8 November he led the town council in passing a by-law that prohibited the construction of frame structures in the central business area bounded on the west by Barclay Street, on the east by Drinkwater Street, on the north by McIntyre Avenue, and on the south by Atlantic Avenue.[47] Calgarians wanted buildings that would not succumb to another fire. Within the boundaries of this area, the walls of all new buildings had to be constructed of brick, stone, brick veneer, or plaster, and the roofs had to be of tin, galvanized iron, felt covered with gravel, or shingles laid in two inches of mortar. The ban within these limits, however, did not provide for the removal of any existing wooden structures. The erection of new wooden sheds no higher than twelve feet was also tolerated. Still, Calgary was beginning to meet the need for more public control over construction practices. In December, the town government continued to show regard for fire safety by contracting with Michael O'Keefe, a building contractor, to erect a fire hall and construct a large water tank.[48]

Postfire Calgary's Builders

Postfire Calgary's builders were entrepreneurs, architects, and engineers who met the challenges and needs of many customers and ordinary citizens. Six years after part of the town was consumed by the firestorm, it had a population of over four thousand people and an infrastructure of urban services that was remarkable – a telephone system, three thousand five hundred street lamps powered by electricity, a well equipped fire department, a waterworks with six miles of mains, ten miles of sewers, over fifty acres of island parks, and a number of fine stone buildings.[49]

Calgary's reconstruction occurred in two stages. The first phase lasted three years and led to the rebuilding of the burned-out area and the revitalization of the town's economy. Beginning around 1890, the second act of the postfire drama lasted until the creation of the city of Calgary and the onset of the economic depression in the mid-1890s.

Although it levelled a portion of the business district, the fire spared vital parts of Calgary's economy – Canadian Pacific tracks linking the town to the nation, the stockyards, meat packing facilities, lumberyards and mills on the Bow River, and commercial banks. In reality, Calgary's economy grew at a faster pace in the year after the fire than it had in the previous year, stimulated by the development of the Canadian Pacific. In 1887, the railway's stockyards in the town handled a growing number of cattle.[50] Made possible by the Canadian Pacific, this uninterrupted prosperity underwrote the town's recovery.

By November 1887, Calgary had a significant frontage of sandstone and brick buildings and dozens of smaller frame buildings completed or under construction despite the previous winter, which had been unusually severe.[51] When the new sandstone Presbyterian Church was dedicated with a splendid celebration near the first anniversary of the fire, the downtown area was almost entirely rebuilt. The building went ahead with even more energy during the following two years, when the town gradually improved its streets

Chapter 9: From Town to City

T. C. Power & Bro. (at far right) on Stephen Avenue in 1888. From George Henry Ham, *The New West*. (Courtesy of Glenbow Library).

as well. On Stephen Avenue, the Bank of Montreal constructed a handsome sandstone office. Designed by local architects and engineers James T. Child and James L. Wilson, the new office was one of the most striking symbols of the recent recovery.[52] Calgary's business core of December 1889 resembled the downtown of 1886, except that it was larger and higher.

A great deal of the capital for the construction and expansion of the business core came from existing industries and commercial institutions. Many of the materials for the construction of the new buildings came from local sandstone quarries, brickyards, and saw mills. In the late 1880s, Calgary continued to grow as southern Alberta's greatest distribution and manufacturing centre. The main architects of the new town were a combination of the designers of the old one and a number of new architects. The town also expanded in numbers, almost doubling in size. New office blocks, hotels, department stores, and homes were built. But the old, compact walking town remained, still held together by tracks that led to the train station. When the Canadian Pacific freight and passenger train roared into the downtown business section, newspaper reporters noted the travellers who stepped down into a scene of urban activity and the goods that were unloaded onto waiting freight wagons.

Chapter 9: From Town to City

Canadian Pacific Station

The beating pulse of bustling Calgary could best be felt at the Canadian Pacific station on Atlantic Avenue. Completed in early 1884, it was a wooden, two-storey building that, like Canadian Pacific stations in most small prairie towns, was not one of the wonders of the age. But the structure with its distinctive feature – three chimneys – was the emblem of the triumph of railways, the coming and dominance of the new mode of transportation. The basic elements of the station consisted of the platform for the trains, the office for the issue of tickets and sending telegrams, rooms for the accommodation of the stationmaster, and a waiting room for passengers.

By 1887, outgoing and incoming passengers found the station too small and lacklustre in appearance, however. William Whyte, general superintendent of the Canadian Pacific's western division, supported by the citizens of Calgary, began requesting a larger station, one made of sandstone, but the railway's top executives did not act on his request until 1893.[53]

Already in the mid- and late 1880s, however, the train station was one of the hubs of town life, a centre of news, advice, and gossip, and the home of the telegraph office and the ticket office. The Calgary station was truly fascinating, a gateway through which people passed in an endless stream hungry for the town's excitements and opportunities, a place of parting and reunion, joy and sadness, important comings and goings. This was where merchants, manufacturers, ranchers, and farmers mingled, where the mail, groceries, ready-made clothing, and farm implements arrived, where newspapers and magazines were delivered, where Canadian-born people and immigrants crossed paths. As well, here was the gateway to the country, to the Bow Valley, to the national and international world. "There has been a perfect boom of freight business at the C.P.R. station for the last few days," wrote a reporter for the Calgary *Herald* in June 1889.[54]

Chapter 9: From Town to City

Business and Hotels

Visiting the Royal Hotel at the corner of Stephen Avenue and McTavish Street one block from the railway station, that same *Calgary Herald* reporter came upon a scene the following day nearly as lively with business energy as the place he had left the day before. As the reporter noted, D. W. Bole, wholesale druggist from Regina, was but one of the many businessmen "registered at the Royal Hotel."[55] In Calgary, a hotel was much more than a place in which to eat and sleep; here men met to discuss commercial and political questions of great importance. A three-storey, brick building, 50 by 130 feet, the Royal Hotel had sixty rooms. For a desperate hour or so, it had been in danger of falling prey to the fire of 1886, but the tremendous efforts of Calgary citizens and the Mounted Police had saved it. "The taste with which it is decorated, the newness and the cleanliness of the rooms, and last, but not least, the sumptuousness of its table, has placed the Royal Hotel in the front rank of first-class houses," wrote George Henry Ham in his 1888 book, *The New West*.[56] The dining room was often swarming with businessmen who filled the air with trade talk hour after hour. James Reilly, part owner of the Royal Hotel, was a power in the Liberal party and made his hostelry a centre for the party's meetings and a place where Liberals and local men of affairs could make connections.

The hotel of the Conservatives, and of some of the town's and Bow Valley's leading businessmen and ranchers, was the even grander three-storey Alberta Hotel at the corner of Stephen Avenue and Scarth Street, one of the first buildings made of sandstone in postfire Calgary.[57] Built in 1889 and run by one of its owners, H. A. Perley, it represented, more than any other hotel in the town, the intimate Calgary connection between Canadian Pacific trains, the railway station, ranching, and important hotels. Child and Wilson were the architects for this building.[58] "The Alberta Hotel ... is the best hotel in Manitoba and the Northwest and is run in a strictly first-class manner," wrote the Toronto *Globe* reporter in 1891. "The building is of stone and is heated throughout with water.... The incandescent system of electric lighting is used. The table is all that could be desired, and the service perfect.... Travellers all speak in the highest terms of the Alberta."[59]

Chapter 9: From Town to City

Alberta Hotel in 1890. (Courtesy of Glenbow Archives, NA-205-2).

Sandstone City

The Alberta Hotel and the Royal Hotel were Calgary's pre-eminent examples of conspicuous display and architectural celebration, proclaiming the town's rise from both the fire and its crude frontier beginnings. Coming to fire-ruined Calgary five years after the conflagration, the *Globe* reporter did not know what to expect. But he found that the town had risen up, phoenix-like, out of its own ashes, more attractive than ever:

> Calgary is almost a model town. The high hills surrounding it are underlaid with a very superior quality of sandstone, easily worked, and which hardens when exposed to the air.... This stone is being largely utilised in building up the town, and Calgary will doubtless yet be called The Sandstone City.[60]

People actually did begin calling it the Sandstone City. Ontario writers, especially, saw this unfinished town, with its surging business energy, as the Sandstone City, the "Coming Northwest Metropolis." Most prairie towns were conscious of their physical limitations, but not Calgary, the striking product of Canadian expansionism. This was the confident spirit of Canada, but it also was the spirit of youth, for Calgary remained a town of young men and women. Postfire Calgary was a place where a young person could go and participate

Chapter 9: From Town to City

Alexander Block, c. 1890s. (Courtesy of Glenbow Archives, NA-1100-2).

in an attempt to rebuild the town. Entrepreneurs and architects rose to the opportunity, co-operating in an effort to remake Calgary.

Turning Business Ideas into Business Organizations

The big ideas of Calgary were business ideas, and the town had a number of important industries and commercial institutions. The office block, the meat packing plant, the sawmill, and the saddle and harness making shop reflected Calgary ideas and the promoters of these ideas. George Alexander, William Roper Hull, Peter Anthony Prince, Robert John Hutchings, and William James Riley turned these ideas into business organizations that comprised major parts of Calgary's commercial and industrial engine, powering the town's recovery from the fire, building the new downtown business district, and giving the town the Calgary and Edmonton Railway in 1891. Indeed, far from being merely ivory-tower theorists, these men drew their ideas on business from pragmatic philosophy and played a pivotal role in pioneering dynamic businesses in commerce and production.

Calgary was, of course, much more than a commercial and

Chapter 9: From Town to City

industrial engine, but to know how the Calgary machine was reconstructed after the fire and how it operated is to comprehend Calgary in the year of the coming of the Calgary and Edmonton Railway. An understanding of 1891 Calgary and the Calgary machine is impossible without insight into the lives of the entrepreneurs who projected themselves so powerfully in these important businesses.

George Alexander and the Alexander Block

As the Toronto *Globe* reporter approached the Alexander Block on the corner of Scarth Street and Stephen Avenue, he was greatly impressed. "The present building is designed to be the finest stone business block between Ontario and the Pacific, and it is invested with a particular value and interest from the fact that the whole of the materials and labour employed in its erection are furnished by the town of Calgary," wrote the reporter. Designed by Child and Wilson and run by George Alexander, the Irish-born owner, the Alexander Block was built in 1891.

> The building is designed in the Romanesque style which is adapted to show the beautiful Calgary freestone with the best effect, the entire design and characteristic corner turret harmonising with the other buildings around to form a general impression of architectural beauty which is the first object of admiration to the visitor to Calgary.[61]

For years one of the town's prominent entrepreneurs, George Alexander was president of the Calgary Gas & Water Works Co., as well as part owner of the Two Dot Ranch in the Nanton area, on which fifteen hundred head of cattle and some horses were grazing.[62] It was prosperous times in the Bow Valley and southern Alberta during the late 1880s and early 1890s that opened the way for the establishment of office blocks in Calgary. Included among the businesses that occupied offices under a lease in the Alexander Block were the Molson's Bank, Osler, Hammond & Nanton, and Child & Wilson. In addition, there was on the upper floor,

> ... a large public hall with seating accommodation for over three hundred people and designed to secure the highest

excellence in acoustic properties, thereby supplying a want hitherto much felt in Calgary. There are also on this floor some suites of bedrooms and sitting rooms with bathrooms for the accommodation of bachelors and others who require a home, yet do not care to undertake the responsibilities of a householder.[63]

From his office in the Alexander Block, George Alexander ran not only the block but also his ranch and the Calgary Gas & Water Works Co. Alexander's ascent was in part attributable to his entrepreneurial energy, but he had one significant advantage. He came to Calgary at a time ideal for men with substantial projects. Local and national conditions were ripe for a historic jump forward in urban development and ranching. Alexander was a very able organizer, and organization was extremely important in the world of business in the early 1890s. Though fairly large in size, his business empire was not an impersonal organization. It was a family concern, with ownership and decision making resting firmly in family hands.

William Roper Hull

Meat Packer and Rancher

When the reporter for the Toronto *Globe* reached the town in 1891 to do stories on leading Calgary figures, he asked people to suggest persons who best represented western life and ability. The replies he received included the name William Roper Hull. On his tour of Hull's establishment on the corner of Stephen Avenue and McTavish Street, the reporter retained one main impression, that of a "very extensive firm of butchers and ranchers."[64]

Hull liked to tell stories about his British origins. In 1873, at the age of seventeen, he left his family's home in Devonshire, England for the ranching country in the interior of British Columbia.[65] He went with his brother John, and they made it to Kamloops via Panama, San Francisco, and Victoria. William and John Hull began raising cattle and horses at Kamloops, saving considerable money over the next decade. In 1886, the Hull brothers and their partner W. P. Trounce set up a butchering business in Calgary known as Hull, Trounce and Co. William Hull and Trounce moved to Calgary

Chapter 9: From Town to City

Hull Bros. & Co. float in Calgary parade on Stephen Avenue in 1901. (Courtesy of Glenbow Archives, NA-1173-2).

to run the business, while John Hull remained in Kamloops. When Trounce withdrew from the partnership around 1890, William and John established Hull Bros.& Co.

Natural ability played an important part in William Roper Hull's rise, but so did good luck. He arrived when Calgary was the place where money could be made virtually on the ground floor. In May 1887, Hull's company obtained the lucrative contract for supplying beef on the Pacific division of the Canadian Pacific Railway.[66] By the following year, his company, with its head office in Calgary, had branch butcher shops at Banff, Donald, Revelstoke, and Kamloops. The size and complexity of the company compelled its founders to delegate authority to salaried managers. H. B. Brown became the manager of the company's Calgary butcher shop. It would be a mistake, however, to view Hull Bros. & Co. of the 1890s as an impersonal organization. In 1891, Hull Bros. & Co. was largely William and John. It was a family affair, and the two brothers kept it that way.

Chapter 9: From Town to City

William Roper Hull ran the largest butchering establishment in Calgary in 1891 from his company's stone block on the corner of Stephen Avenue and McTavish Street. This block, measuring 130 by 50 feet and built at a cost of $15,000 two years before, filled "about the last gap made by the great fire of November 1886," wrote the *Calgary Herald* in 1889.[67] At the very corner of the building was the company's Pioneer Meat Market. William Roper Hull was the founder of the modern meat packing industry in Calgary. The entire operation, from his slaughterhouse on the Bow River to the refrigerated facilities – chilling rooms and cold-storage area – in his meat market in downtown Calgary, was quick and efficient. Skilled butchers, assisted by unskilled workers, did almost all the work. The raw materials – cattle, hogs, sheep, deer, antelope, turkeys, geese, ducks, chickens, and fish – varied considerably in size, shape, and weight, and so the killing and cutting-up process required a great deal of hand labour.[68] In disassembling a steer, the technology was partially mechanized: once stunned and killed, the animal was raised by a steam hoist, put on an iron rail, and sent down the line to a number of men, each of whom performed a part of the cutting-up process. Meat packing became an assembly-line industry, in which the division of human labour and technology were used as a way of reducing production time and costs at Hull Bros. &Co. in Calgary.

In 1891, much of the meat was sold in Calgary to individual homes, hotels, boarding houses, and general stores, while a substantial part of it was sent directly to Canadian Pacific refrigerator cars, bound for Hull Bros. & Co.'s butcher shops and dinner tables in Canmore, Anthracite, Banff, Field, Golden, Donald, and Revelstoke. The technology of refrigerated cars and storage rooms at the company's facilities permitted it to become involved in year-round production of perishable products and expand its dressed meat trade. Meat also was delivered as steaks and roasts to the railway's dining cars. Beyond this, some meat was shipped to wholesale butchers in other centres, who, in turn, supplied retail grocers and meat shops in their communities. William Roper Hull's profit strategy in the dressed meat trade was to charge low prices, which allowed only small margins per pound but made possible significantly increased total profits through high volume.[69] When the competition became fierce, Hull sometimes dropped his prices below cost, market share being the most important thing for him.

Hull's meat market in Calgary was closely linked to his company's

Chapter 9: From Town to City

four-thousand-acre cattle ranch on Fish Creek, the Bow Valley Ranche, which served as a major source of beef supply. He had purchased the land on which this ranch was located from Senator Theodore Robitaille of New Carlisle, Quebec, who had bought the land from the Canadian government after the old Government Farm on it was closed. Hull constructed irrigation ditches across the Bow Valley Ranche, producing excellent crops of oats on the irrigated fields to feed his cattle.[70] Visitors to the ranch were impressed by the herd of some one thousand head of cattle grazing in its pastures. Power derived from rationally organized beef production helps to explain Hull's success as a modern meat packer. The entire operation was vertically integrated, production and distribution nicely complementing each other. Indeed, Hull established Calgary's first major vertically integrated meat packing business, a well managed, medium-sized firm that reached out to control the supply, production, and distribution of its products, from the acquisition of western cattle to their delivery as roasts and steaks to customers.

Hull's system was the most efficient production and distribution network in Calgary in the early 1890s. At his desk in his office, he received letters and telegrams from all over western Canada as well as the American West providing him with information on changing prices of beef, pork, and mutton. When the demand for his products exceeded local supplies, he brought in cattle, hogs, and sheep from places like Manitoba, British Columbia, Montana, and Washington.[71] A hard-bargaining entrepreneur, he made a reputation as an astute meat packer, and he won the admiration of the editor of the Toronto *Globe*, who wrote, "we may expect Hull to develop into the [Philip] Armour of the Northwest. He is a man of fine physique, of genial manner, and of unusual business capacity."[72] To compete, other meat packers like Pat Burns had little choice but to follow Hull's strategy. By the late 1890s, Burns had turned to a vertically integrated organization to co-ordinate the flow of meat from his ranches through his packing plant in Calgary to local and regional markets.[73]

Beef was a city-forming material. The beef supplies of the Bow Valley and southern Alberta helped make possible Calgary's significant commercial and industrial growth in the late 1880s and early 1890s. In October 1893, Wesley F. Orr, chairman of Calgary's Public Works Committee, told Augustus M. Nanton that "one tenth of the export of cattle from the whole Dominion this year is from Calgary and district."[74] Beef helped to induce many businesses to locate in Calgary, including the Calgary and Edmonton Railway, which brought cattle to the Canadian Pacific's stockyards in the town for local consumption and, most importantly, for shipment to other parts of Canada and abroad.

Beef attracted two types of businesses to Calgary: those, like butcher shops and meat markets, that processed meat, and those, like hotels and boardinghouses, that used it to feed people. Beef also aided Calgary in making the transition from town to city in early 1894 by contributing to the development of an industrial economy. Calgary was the largest manufacturing centre in Alberta by this time, surpassing Edmonton in total value of goods produced, although still trailing well behind Winnipeg. Processing local and regional resources, Calgary's factories pioneered early forms of mass production based on skilled and unskilled labour and governed by owner-managers or salaried managers assisted by clerks. "There are two large saw mills, sash and door factory and planing mill, sandstone quarry, brick kiln, cold storage warehouses, roller flour mill, tannery, and soap factory" in Calgary, *Henderson's Manitoba and Northwest Territories Gazetteer and Directory* announced in 1893, in a terse but accurate report.[75]

Peter A. Prince and the Eau Claire & Bow River Lumber Co.

The growth of Calgary's industries spurred the exploitation of regional timber and coal, accelerated the expansion and improvements of transportation services, extended the reach of the town, and attracted newcomers. By the early 1890s, the pace of industrialization had increased. Manufacturing tightened Calgary's ties to its hinterland – the Bow Valley and southern Alberta. The Eau Claire & Bow River Lumber Co. and James Walker's Bow River Lumber Mills sent out thousands of feet of lumber to ranchers and farmers all over the countryside.

By this time, Calgary entrepreneurs were moving to control the supply as well as the distribution of lumber in the town and the Bow Valley. Most prominent of these was Peter A. Prince, general manager of the Eau Claire & Bow River Lumber Co. Born in 1836 near Three Rivers, Quebec, he was the son of an Eau Claire, Wisconsin millwright. Prince followed in his father's footsteps, becoming a millwright in Eau Claire and gaining much experience in

Chapter 9: From Town to City

Peter A. Prince, c. 1918, manager of Eau Claire & Bow River Lumber Co. (Courtesy of Glenbow Archives, NA-1360-1).

lumbering there over twenty years. During his vacation in Alberta in 1885, he became convinced of the possibilities of lumbering in Calgary. In 1886, Prince became general manager of the newly formed, Wisconsin-based Eau Claire & Bow River Lumber Co., a medium-sized firm which had obtained cutting rights from the Canadian government on sixty-four thousand acres of Dominion timber on the Bow, Kananaskis, and Spray rivers west of Calgary.[76] The company's experience well illustrates the growing role of the United States as a source of foreign direct investment in Calgary and the Bow Valley.

The Eau Claire & Bow River Lumber Co. story includes the significant work of Isaac K. Kerr, the company's president, who helped run it from his office in Eau Claire, Wisconsin. Kerr was born in 1840 near Ottawa, Ontario. As a teenager, he went to work for Frederick Weyerhauser in Wisconsin, an important figure in the history of lumbering. In 1883, just after the coming of the Canadian Pacific Railway to Calgary, Kerr examined the timber on the Bow, Kananaskis, and Spray rivers.[77] By the time he became president of the Eau Claire & Bow River Lumber Co. in 1886, he had over two decades of experience in the lumber business. While Kerr remained in Eau Claire, Wisconsin until around 1908, when he moved to Calgary, Prince was in Calgary from the company's inception and played a major role in formulating company policy and in running it. Peter Prince's son John, an engineer and assistant manager of the company, was also active in Calgary from the beginning.

Peter Prince planned the company's strategy with great care and carried it out with considerable speed. As general manager, he understood that what was needed was a transfer of sawmill technology from Eau Claire, Wisconsin to Calgary. Bringing in the machinery as well as an experienced workforce from Eau Claire

Chapter 9: From Town to City

Eau Claire & Bow River Lumber Co. in 1899. (Courtesy of Glenbow Archives, NA-806-1).

by the Canadian Pacific, Peter Prince and his son John built a steam-powered sawmill measuring thirty-two by one hundred feet, a planing mill, a lumber yard, and a mill workers' village on the south bank of the Bow in Calgary, near Prince's Island.[78] The office staff included Will Olson, the company's bookkeeper.[79] Among the men in the workforce were Bernt Thorp, a millwright; Conrad Anderson, a teamster; and Lemsley Carr, a millwright.[80] Tragedy struck when Lemsley Carr and several other men drowned in icy water in the Kananaskis country during a log drive. But within two years, Peter and John Prince were manufacturing for the Calgary and Bow Valley markets over two million feet of lumber annually.[81] The sawmill "is most admirably located, being built on the Bow River, having a large frontage and splendid harbour," wrote George Henry Ham, author of *The New West*.[82]

The pine and spruce trees Peter Prince's lumbermen cut in the winter harvesting season were hauled on horse-drawn sleds over snow to the Bow River. On the swollen stream in the spring, they were then floated in log rafts down to the sawmill in Calgary with men riding the logs or running alongside them, employing long

Chapter 9: From Town to City

hooks or poles to drive them onward. "Prince came down from the mountains Sunday. He has been superintending the drive of logs for his mill here.... He represents the river as being the easiest to drive he has ever seen.... A little cutting and clearing along its banks had to be done," observed a reporter for the *Calgary Tribune* in June 1887.[83] After being transformed into lumber – boards of standard lengths and dimensions – the wood was carried by horse-drawn wagons to building contractors in Calgary and to settlements in the Bow Valley.

Prince was a well-built man, full of energy and spirit. In his long and fruitful life of business, he reflected a strong current of innovation and improvement. Prince helped Calgary to enter the age of electricity. In 1889, he organized the Calgary Water Power Company and became its managing director, ready to compete with the Calgary Electric Lighting Company formed two years earlier.[84] A reporter for the Toronto *Globe* wrote that "the rivalry between the two companies gives the townspeople probably the cheapest electric lighting in Canada."[85] Prince constructed the Calgary Water Power Company's electric light plant on his sawmill site. Powered by a new hundred-horse-power Corliss steam engine purchased by Prince in Toronto, the plant provided electric lighting for the Eau Claire & Bow River Lumber Co., the Canadian Pacific Railway grounds, and many business establishments and private residences including Prince's home. At the same time, Prince enlarged the sawmill. By 1891, the Eau Claire & Bow River Lumber Co. produced for the Calgary and Bow Valley markets over four million feet of lumber annually.[86] The company's history spanned almost seventy years of manufacturing lumber. Investing for the long term in Calgary became an Eau Claire & Bow River Lumber Co. hallmark.

The builders of postfire Calgary included entrepreneurs like Peter Prince, who provided much of the lumber that was still needed for the construction of many buildings in the town. He contributed to Calgary's image as a town made possible by substantial economic projects with commitment to community. The biggest town in Alberta in 1891, Calgary was capable of doing important things, and this became part of its enduring reputation.

Hutchings & Riley
Harness and Saddle Makers

Like lumber and electricity, harnesses and saddles were products of Calgary's evolving economy. By the end of 1889, Hutchings & Riley was the town's leading firm in the production of saddles and harnesses. The entrepreneurs who created this enterprise were Robert John Hutchings and his partner, William James Riley. Significant builders of postfire Calgary, they owned and managed Hutchings & Riley. The story of Robert Hutchings is that of a man living at a time of change in the history of Bow Valley capitalism. During his career, manufacturing became much more important in the region's economic structure. While agriculture and commerce continued to grow, industrial production increased.

Robert Hutchings was born in 1866 in Newboro, Leeds County, Ontario. The son of Elijah and Harriet Hutchings, he was educated in the local elementary and high schools. Leaving Newboro at the age of sixteen, in 1882 Robert began to serve an apprenticeship as a saddle and harness maker in the firm of his older brother Elisha, the E. F. Hutchings Saddlery Company, in Winnipeg.[87] Distinguished by his ability to use hand tools and sewing machines, as well as by his business qualities, Robert set out to make his way in the saddle and harness making trade. Around 1887, after completing his apprenticeship, he became a junior partner in the company. The enterprise was a fast-growing business. More than anyone else in the firm, Robert saw Calgary as a key to further expansion. He felt that "Calgary was where the future was," recalled his daughter Blanche.[88] In February 1889, Robert Hutchings moved to Calgary where he opened a branch of the company.

In setting up the Calgary branch, the E. F. Hutchings Saddlery Company purchased George Murdoch's stock of harnesses and saddles in his small shop in the Murdoch Block on Atlantic Avenue between Osler and McTavish streets.[89] The company rented the shop from George Murdoch. During the next few months Robert Hutchings, using hand tools and sewing machines, became one of the most successful and respected saddle and harness makers in Calgary. Robert "just loved leather, loved to look at it, smell and feel it, and he really knew it," remembered his daughter Blanche.[90] "Already" the Hutchings Saddlery Company "is doing a big business," wrote the *Calgary Herald* in mid-March.[91]

Chapter 9: From Town to City

Bringing in a steady stream of tanned leather from Winnipeg and Toronto by rail, the company's shop in Calgary turned out a growing number of saddles and harnesses. Several specialty goods dominated the shop's product line: an assortment of saddles, including the sidesaddle for women, and complete cowboy outfits. In the late 1880s and 1890s, ranching and farming were rapidly expanding in the Bow Valley. Consequently, the region's livestock raisers required many saddles for themselves and their cowboys, and their cowboys also needed outfits including chaps and lariats. Although saddles and cowboy outfits were the shop's leading products, Robert Hutchings followed a policy of diversified production and sales from the beginning. In addition to saddles and cowboy outfits, he manufactured the Concord harness for heavy draught horses and the light driving harness.[92] Light driving harnesses for a team sold for $30. Ranchers, farmers, and many Calgary business firms needed harnesses. Most of the shop's sales occurred through word-of-mouth to prospective customers in Calgary and the Bow Valley. But success did not come to Robert Hutchings without hard work and long hours. "In those early days, he had to be his own drayman, carrying his leather on his back from the [Canadian Pacific] station to the saddlery, and working long and late at his craft," reported the *Calgary Herald*.[93]

In early May 1889, Ontario-born William J. Riley, an experienced local harness maker, became Robert Hutchings's partner in manufacturing harnesses and saddles. At the same time, the new firm, known as Hutchings & Riley, bought the stock in the Murdoch Block from the Hutchings Saddlery Company for $3,715.[94] In a business that depended on the production of both harnesses and saddles, the two partners brought complementary talents to the enterprise: Hutchings, twenty-four years old, was admired especially for his skill as a saddler, and Riley, aged thirty-four, gained recognition particularly as a harness maker.[95]

Theirs was a relatively small business, founded in an area of the Bow Valley that was beginning to industrialize and in which there was an increasing demand for the technology of saddle and harness production. Employing a handful of skilled men, Hutchings & Riley was largely self-financed through the reinvestment of profits and stood in the central business district of Calgary. Responsible for the firm's daily management, Robert Hutchings and William Riley personally worked with tanned leather and handled finished goods.

The market for harnesses and saddles was growing, and Hutchings

Chapter 9: From Town to City

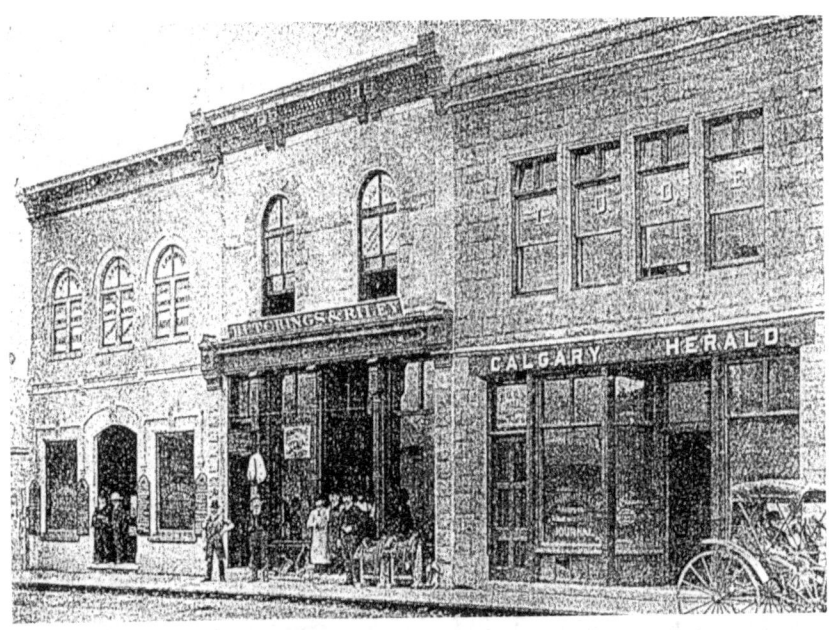

Hutchings & Riley (centre) in 1890, with *Calgary Herald* to the right and Smith & West law office to the left. From *The Dominion Illustrated*, Calgary Special, 28 June 1890. (Courtesy of Glenbow Library).

& Riley was able to sell not only to Bow Valley ranchers and farmers and Calgary businesses but also to the Mounted Police stationed in the town. Rising sales allowed the firm to become prosperous. Prosperity brought changes to Hutchings & Riley. In early November 1889, the firm moved out of its small shop in the Murdoch Block to larger rented quarters in the Lineham Block on Stephen Avenue.[96] As it grew, Hutchings & Riley began to expand its distribution system, selling its products in southeastern British Columbia.[97]

The early 1890s were also prosperous years for the firm. Despite strong competition from Carson & Shore, another local harness and saddle maker, Hutchings & Riley's sales increased. Observers thought that Hutchings & Riley had a bright future. In January 1890, a credit correspondent from R. G. Dun & Co. reported that the firm was worth between $5,000 and $10,000. Three and a half years later, the correspondent noted that Hutchings & Riley's worth had increased to between $10,000 and $20,000.[98]

As craftsmen, Robert Hutchings and William Riley were knowledgeable in all the steps in making saddles and harnesses. They personally approved the quality of each harness and each

Chapter 9: From Town to City

saddle before selling them and continued to spend most of their time on the shop floor. Hutchings and Riley knew their employees by name. Constantly ensuring that their products were of the highest possible quality, they tried to meet customers' needs. Hutchings & Riley's exhibit at the 1893 World's Fair in Chicago was designed to show the high quality of their firm's saddles and harnesses. The two partners won a gold medal for their exhibit.[99] Two years later, in 1895, Robert Hutchings was in charge of their exhibit at the Territorial Fair in Regina. It consisted of "two plain stock saddles for practical use, a full stamp and highly ornamented stock saddle, a very handsome lady's ranche saddle, a cowboy bridle, chaps, lariat and general outfit." Hutchings & Riley's exhibit in Regina "took first prizes in every line."[100]

As Hutchings & Riley grew, it added apprentices to its workforce in Calgary. Sometimes apprentices stayed at the firm only a relatively short time and then struck out on their own elsewhere in the Bow Valley. For instance, Levi and John Bradley, two Ontario-born brothers who apprenticed at Hutchings & Riley in 1898, transferred the technology of saddle and harness production from Calgary to High River, a rising agriculture service centre. In 1900, John opened a harness and saddle making shop in High River, and Levi bought him out two years later.[101] Using hand tools, as well as Pearson sewing machines imported from England, Levi Bradley made harnesses, saddles, whips, and other leather goods and built up a thriving business in High River over the next five and a half decades.[102]

By the late 1890s, Hutchings & Riley had emerged as one of the most successful saddle and harness firms in Calgary, the Bow Valley, and the Canadian West. Expanding by opening a branch store in Maple Creek, Saskatchewan in 1897, the firm was part of a rapidly growing industry.[103] As it developed, Hutchings & Riley competed with Carson & Shore, as well as with the E. F. Hutchings Saddlery Company in Winnipeg, which was controlled by Robert Hutchings's brother Elisha. Seeking to limit competition, these three firms began to consider co-operation. In July 1899, the firms' owners joined forces to arrange the merger of the E. F. Hutchings concern, Carson & Shore, and Hutchings & Riley, forming a new corporation called the Great West Saddlery Company to manufacture saddles and harnesses.[104] While the head office of the new company was in Winnipeg, its leading branch office was in Calgary. As vice-president of the company, Robert Hutchings, like his brother Elisha, who became president, made the necessary investments of money and time to develop the concern as a whole as well as its parts. At this time, the Great West Saddlery Company's medium-sized Calgary plant employed about sixty men. From the beginning, the plant depended on Robert Hutchings for business planning and strategic thinking. His financial support helped to keep the plant alive and improve its long-term competitive position. The company's history forcefully demonstrated sustained commitment to the city – its corporate life in Calgary spanned more than half a century. As the years passed, Robert Hutchings decided to include some skilled Native Canadians in the work force at the Calgary plant. "The best leather toolers always came from the Reserve, about twelve Indians," recalled Robert's daughter Blanche Hutchings.[105]

Environmental Problems

While rapid, unregulated growth made Calgary a place of great economic opportunity, it also generated health and environmental problems. In trying to solve these problems while continuing to expand, Calgary revealed both its strengths and weaknesses.

From the beginning, Calgary had drainage and waste-disposal problems. With the passage of time, the lack of a sewage system led to health problems and raised environmental concerns. In the fall of 1890, cholera hit the growing town with considerable force. "We are hearing a great deal of cholera infantum these days in our town, and the wisest heads are fearful of further consequences should a continuance of the present well and closet system be continued," wrote the *Calgary Herald*.[106] Filthy water and exposed sewage, many people believed, caused cholera.

Human waste was deposited in outdoor privy vaults which were frequently located near shallow wells, a situation that resulted in the pollution of the drinking water. In addition, garbage, water, and animal dung accumulated in the streets.

Many of the town's residents could not get away from stagnant water, garbage, and the stench of damp and unhealthy ground. Prevailing winds crossed Calgary from the northwest. Sharp northwesterly winds swept the streets, blowing smoke from manufacturing establishments, smells from horses and other animals, odours from butchering, and dust downwind into homes and stores.

To meet the problem of waste disposal, the local authorities employed the firm Child & Wilson as town engineers in September 1890 to develop a plan to save Calgary from a health crisis.[107] Child & Wilson, visionary engineers with a strong sense of civic duty and an ability to plan major public projects, carried through the construction of a comprehensive sewage system in the town. Although many Calgary homes did not immediately use the new sewers, a start had been made on alleviating the sewage problem.[108]

Alexander Lucas and Alberta's First City

Alexander Lucas, Calgary's mayor in 1892 and 1893 and a partner in Fitzgerald & Lucas, financial, insurance, and Canadian Pacific land agents, dreamed of big things for the development of the Bow Valley and urban growth. Recognizing that irrigation in the Bow Valley was an economic boon for Calgary, on 7 October 1893 Lucas visited a major irrigation project ten miles west of the town on the Bow. Here George Alexander, president of the newly incorporated Calgary Hydraulic Co., was building irrigation works for several ranches, including his own ranch. As mayor of Calgary, Lucas had an appreciation for the process by which western cities often evolved. After viewing the irrigation project, he praised Alexander, whom he saw as one of the makers of the city of Calgary, for inducing "the investment of so much capital into Calgary and vicinity, particularly that expended in the waterworks scheme, magnificent buildings in Calgary, and now in one of the most important schemes for the benefit of the lands around Calgary."[109]

Nine days later, on 16 October, Lucas, supported by nearly all the ratepayers of the town, received a charter from the legislative assembly of the Northwest Territories for the city of Calgary, which allowed him to improve the fire hall and other services as well as to raise public funds to provide bonuses to the flour mill and the tannery.[110] An aggressive business and civic leader, Lucas as mayor continued to press for urban improvement and witnessed the birth of the city of Calgary on 1 January 1894, Alberta's first city. Although he did not seek another term as mayor, he entered the election for a seat on the new city council in mid-January and won.[111]

Wesley F. Orr and a Young and Ambitious City

Calgary's new mayor, Wesley F. Orr, real estate entrepreneur and correspondent for the American credit reporting firm R. G. Dun & Company, took direct action to deal with the problems facing the city during the depression of the mid-1890s. Deeply affected by the economic downturn, Calgary saw its population shrink, had difficulty in attracting new people, and faced an uncertain future. Under Orr's direction, the city council sought economies at every turn: it ordered cuts wherever possible, including the reduction of the annual salary of I. S. Cowan, city treasurer, from $300 to $200.[112]

A strong leader in the businessman-mayor tradition, Wesley Orr helped maintain a partnership between city council and the private business community as well as a relationship between the city and settlers in the Bow Valley. Convinced that the economic health of Calgary and its region had to be the first priority, Orr used his influence and power as mayor to attract settlers to the surrounding area and to provide them with economic services.[113] Agriculture remained essential to Calgary. The city's importance was reinforced by an increase in ranching and farming activity. Location, rail connections, and abundant farm and ranch products, Orr boasted, made the city an excellent place for the profitable investment of capital.

In addition to emphasizing the positive impact of agricultural development on urban growth, Orr also focused on giving the central business district a face-lift. He was confident that he could help to alter the old image of Calgary as a crude frontier town by encouraging the construction of sandstone buildings. Sandstone buildings raised urban values. The great fire of 1886 temporarily postponed the building of sandstone structures in Calgary, but local architecture actually benefited from the delay. Sandstone Calgary was constructed building by building, one after another rising out of the old town, in a process of ongoing demolition and construction that made downtown Calgary look attractive to visitors. One of the most thrilling sights to Orr was the new two-storey, sandstone Canadian Pacific station. Looking forward to William C. Van Horne's first visit to Calgary after it became a city, Orr wrote to the president of the Canadian Pacific in May 1894:

> This young and ambitious city extends to you a most hearty welcome. It affords us much pleasure to enjoy this privilege of thanking you for the beautiful and substantial station and

Chapter 9: From Town to City

dining hall, which your company has erected in the centre of the city, built entirely of Calgary's freestone and covered with Westminster slate. We are pleased to note the interest your company is taking in our city by beautifying the grounds around your station.[114]

The new Canadian Pacific station in Calgary was, the *Calgary Herald* reporter believed, handsome and practical:

> The building ... contains on the ground floor a dining room 32 by 27, a lunch bar 30 ft. long, hall, kitchen and pantry, while upstairs are six large bedrooms to be used by the employees. The whole is finished in B. C. cedar and white pine. The station contains a general waiting room with ladies' and gentlemen's rooms and ticket office in connection. Each room has a handsome tiled open fireplace and mantelpiece. Lavatories with all the modern appliances are in connection. In the centre of the building is the baggage room and on the right is the express office. Upstairs is the commercial telegraph office, a room for the use of the express messengers, of whom no less than fourteen run into Calgary, and two spare rooms.

The reporter's hope was that the work of beautifying Calgary would continue so as to rid it of the unsightly wood shanties near the station. "If," he wrote, "some of the miserable hovels that disgrace Atlantic Avenue were now to be removed, the efforts of the railway company in beautifying their side of the roadway would be considerably furthered."[115] Despite the crude buildings on Atlantic Avenue, the train station remained a place of hope and unquenchable humanity.

Sandstone Calgary was built in an age of civic pride by entrepreneurs and visionaries driven by the resolve to transform their city into beautiful a place. The sandstone buildings were houses of economic faith, where members of the business community gathered to do business. In the city and the Bow Valley there was a promising market for household goods. During the years immediately after the great fire, one kind of business more than any other capitalized on this situation to create something new – the sandstone department store. Reaching out to city and country homes with its goods, I. G. Baker & Co. made Calgary the department store capital of the Bow Valley and southern Alberta.

10

Department Stores and Mass Distribution

Recovering from the Great Fire

The great Calgary Fire of 1886 provided I. G. Baker & Co.'s owners with an opportunity to go forward with their plans to transform their general store into a department store – the first of the mass distributors in the city. With the passage of time, other department stores appeared – the Hudson's Bay Company and Glanville & Robertson. But Baker & Co. laid the foundation for the department store business in Calgary, allowing consumers' range of choices to become greater. The Fort Benton-based firm pioneered an organization that could serve as an alternative to the traditional general store. In the process, Calgary absorbed an increasing foreign direct investment outflow from the United States. By mid-November, a week after the fire, the immediate feeling of helplessness that often follows such disasters had given way at Baker & Co. to a fight for survival and an effort to rebuild on a grander scale. No firm in Calgary recovered from the calamity as quickly or spectacularly as Baker & Co. did.

In the first hour of the fire, John L. Bowen, manager of Baker & Co.'s store on the corner of Stephen Avenue and McTavish Street in Calgary, made sure that that firm's books, business records, paper money, and gold watches were secure in the safe. Although the books and records "were charred to some extent," they were "quite legible" and were recovered from the burnt-out store, as was the money and some of the watches.[1] These valuable possessions formed the basis for the new and larger Baker & Co. store, built with

Chapter 10: Department Stores and Mass Distribution

I. G. Baker & Co. department store in 1888. (Courtesy of Glenbow Archives, NA-419-2).

the help of thousands of dollars in loans that owners William and Charles Conrad and I. G. Baker secured on their reputation. When the Conrads in Fort Benton and I. G. Baker in St. Louis, Missouri received the news about the fire, they immediately decided to rebuild their Calgary store on the same site but on a larger scale. By this time, Baker & Co. had become a Calgary legend for its role in local and regional development, and it continued to be effective at managing and expanding its business.

Mass Distribution in Fort Benton

Within a few days, the Conrads sent D. W. Davis, manager of Baker & Co.'s Fort Macleod store and the company's general manager in Alberta, to Calgary to assist Bowen in planning the construction of a department store.[2] In keeping with the Conrads' character, the new store was to express tremendous commercial energy. The decades after the Civil War were extremely fertile in American and Montana history for dreamers. As Civil War veterans, Charles and William

Conrad had earlier turned to private life with great zest. Envious of the overnight wealth of young entrepreneurs like John D. Rockefeller in the oil industry, many returning soldiers sought to emulate their big fortunes. The triumph of the North accelerated economic development, promoting urbanization and industrial capitalism, creating a new world of mass production and mass distribution, and opening up the American Great Plains.

Fort Benton had no tradition of mass distribution, but the potential money to be made in one type of mass distribution – the department store – was irresistible to the Conrads. Fascinated by the dynamic business they had seen at Marshall Field's big department store in Chicago, they opened a relatively small department store in Fort Benton in 1879. Before long, William and Charles Conrad prospered in their department store business south of the border. Now, in November 1886, as they scanned the field of enterprise, their target of opportunity lay farther from home: in Calgary.

Calgary's First Department Store: I. G. Baker & Co.

In Calgary, John Bowen directed workers as they pulled down ruined walls and began erecting a new store – Calgary's and Alberta's first department store. By mid-January 1887, the store was nearing completion. "Mr. Bowen is rapidly getting I. G. Baker & Co.'s new store into shape for a complete opening," wrote the *Calgary Tribune*. "The finishing touches are being put on, and when finished the store, both inside and outside, will be perhaps the finest in the Northwest."[3] One hundred feet long and thirty feet wide, it was a handsome, two-storey building facing Stephen Avenue. Behind a heavy sandstone façade, the two floors were roomy and airy, drawing sunlight from rows of plate-glass windows.[4] Magnificent British Columbia cedar heightened the beauty of the interior. "The immense business is thoroughly organised under different departments ... and in these departments can probably be found more goods suited to the wants of the people in this section of the country than can be found under any one roof in the Northwest," observed George Henry Ham.[5]

William and Charles Conrad, with the assistance of John Bowen, planned that the opening of their new store in April 1887 would be an event that Calgarians and Bow Valley people would not forget.

Chapter 10: Department Stores and Mass Distribution

Customers found that the store featured a variety of departments: ladies' clothing, men's clothing, boots and shoes, crockery and glassware, carpets and oilcloths, and groceries. They also discovered that shopping could be a pleasure in this attractive atmosphere. The first floor was devoted to ladies' clothing, men's clothing, and boots and shoes. To the second floor, customers could go either by the elevator or by the stairway to see the crockery and glassware as well as the carpets and oilcloths. If they chose to do so, they could descend to the basement by the elevator to shop for groceries.[6] The opening itself became a remarkable event, because to all these departments had been brought large quantities of new goods that Bowen had purchased on his buying trip to Toronto, Montreal, Chicago, and New York City more than a month before.[7] His knowledge of product lines, their strengths and weaknesses, was vital. He had great respect for the tastes of consumers, paying much attention to what they wanted.

Beginning with the recruitment of H. B. Andrews as head of the men's clothing department, Charles and William Conrad had assembled a team of able, congenial department heads who helped build the Calgary store into Alberta's strongest retail outlet. Both William and Charles had quick minds for numbers and great skill with balance sheets. Neither was satisfied with modest success, and they were both ready to go as fast and as far as the marketplace permitted. Over the next year or so, their department heads and clerks included Sadie Dye, a capable dressmaker, Jennie Flemming, Charles Thornton, and John Bowen's brother, Herbert. In keeping with the Conrads' emphasis on accurate records, they hired the competent P. J. Mount as their bookkeeper.[8] Charles and William Conrad were tied by a common business dream, lived close to each other in Fort Benton, and shared the task of writing letters and paying visits to their Calgary store.[9] They were tough-minded administrators, who made their wishes known to John Bowen, reserving the right to approve all major commitments of funds.

The grand opening of I. G. Baker & Co.'s department store in Calgary was to a large degree a retail show designed to attract especially ladies in a town and its region where women were starting to catch up to men numerically. Bowen spared no effort to win and keep female customers. Right at the top of his big newspaper advertisement was a warm welcome: "We extend a most cordial invitation to the Ladies of Calgary and surrounding country to visit our Dry Goods Emporium."[10] Goods that promised to attract the ladies' attention were dresses, millinery trimmings, laces, corsets, gloves, and hosiery.

But Baker & Co.'s sparkling department store did not cater exclusively to women. It also offered a great deal to men. Any man who entered the men's clothing department was reminded by its head, H. B. Andrews, of the words in the advertisement, "We can make a gentleman or a cowboy out of you in no time. We have a large stock of Ready-made Clothing, and can take your measure for the same if you wish."[11] Andrews also created one part of an eye-catching window display, which was aimed at men in need of clothing. A reporter for the *Calgary Tribune* described it as "a model of good taste. It is extremely handsome, the tints of colors being brought together in a most harmonious blending."[12]

Credit and Cash Sales

Baker & Co. also carried an assortment of goods that brought farmers to the store to exchange their farm produce for supplies. The public announcement of this came in an advertisement at the time of the grand inauguration: "All kinds of farmers' produce bought and sold, and special attention given to our country patrons."[13] To do business with farmers, most of whom could not pay for their purchases until their crops came in, it was often imperative to offer generous financing. Using business methods established by Charles and William Conrad, Bowen was prepared to provide liberal credit to reliable farmers.

Baker & Co.'s store was something of a cross between a mercantile enterprise and a private bank. If it was devoted primarily to selling manufactured goods, it also typified the old-fashioned private bank where deals with Calgarians, ranchers, and farmers were sealed with a handshake. For the most part, security such as a promissory note or a chattel mortgage was not required to obtain credit. By December 1887, for instance, Bowen had sold $1,762 worth of goods to James Votier, a Midnapore farmer, on book credit without security. Beneath a genial air, Bowen was concerned about this account. He now pressed Voiter to pay his bills. For security he accepted a chattel mortgage for $1,762 from Votier, who offered his livestock and his wagon as collateral and promised to pay off the

Chapter 10: Department Stores and Mass Distribution

debt in a year plus interest at the rate of 12 percent per annum. For a variety of reasons, however, Voiter could not meet his obligations. Creditors differed in their patience, but Bowen agreed to renew the loan at least three times before Voiter had paid his debt in full.[14]

While William and Charles Conrad frequently competed on their ability to furnish credit, they were determined to sell their goods in the Calgary store for cash whenever possible. Rather than seeking compensation for the failure of some customers to pay their bills through steep markups and high interest rates on credit, they tried to increase their trade by cutting prices. "The low prices" in our store, they told their long-time and prospective customers, "will astonish the people."[15] By eliminating credit when circumstances allowed them to do so, the Conrads reduced risk. Scarcely dreaming that Bowen could do business on a cash-only basis, they still were pleased to learn about the progress he was making in cash sales. Even Bowen's small sale of $7.60 worth of groceries and kitchen equipment for cash to one customer in April 1887 deserved notice, for it was a step in the right direction.[16]

In an era of money shortages, however, Bowen needed to scrounge to find customers who were able to pay cash for the goods at Baker & Co.'s Calgary store. In January 1888, to attract cash purchasers, Bowen's advertisement trumpeted to prospective customers that

> ... we have decided for the next month, and until our buyer leaves to visit the eastern markets to purchase spring goods, to hold a grand 20 percent Discount Cash Sale on our magnificent stock of Dry Goods, Clothing, Furs, and Boots and Shoes, and will give to Every Lady purchasing a Dress one of McColl's perfect fitting New York Bazaar Patterns.[17]

Bowen made the Baker & Co. store the fashion centre for women. Customers were encouraged to browse without pressure to buy goods. In the words of Bowen's April 1888 advertisement, "No trouble to show goods and no offence if you don't buy."[18] The department heads and clerks were expected to know the names of every important customer. As soon as a lady finished making her purchases, they apparently offered to deliver them to her home.

Wholesale Division

The wholesale division of Baker & Co.'s store in Calgary beautifully complemented its retail division.[19] A substantial portion of the goods sold over the retail counters came from the wholesale division, located in the firm's warehouse behind the store. This advantage gave the retail division a dependable source of supply. Careful buying in large quantities directly from manufacturers in Montreal, Toronto, Chicago, and New York City allowed John Bowen to secure low-cost stocks of merchandise and undergirded the store's low-price policy. Low prices attracted not only bargain-hunting retail customers in Calgary and the Bow Valley, but also wholesale customers such as John H. Kerr, a Calgary merchant tailor; F. D. Moulton, a Banff hotelkeeper; and Neelin & Wilkinson, general merchants in Anthracite, all of whom were searching for volume bargains.[20]

Retail Division

Retail sales constituted the most important part of Baker & Co.'s business in Calgary, however. Bowen, the department heads, and the clerks welcomed both men and women, but they looked forward especially to the frequent visits of ladies to the firm's department store, for they accounted for the majority of the retail purchases. One such customer was Mrs. M. A. Johnson, the wife of architect H. D. Johnson, who was the superintendent of Dominion Public Works in Calgary.[21] She shopped for herself and infant daughter Ellen, as well as for the family as a whole when it came to things such as groceries and other household items. Other women provided other business opportunities. For instance, Rozella Smith, an unmarried woman, sold her horse and phaeton to Baker & Co.'s store for $150, which the firm probably turned over at a profit.[22]

Baker & Co.'s retail business also depended upon a flow of customers from various sections of the agricultural community in the Bow Valley. As a major enterprise in Calgary, the firm's store was strategically positioned to profit from agricultural development, and during the late 1880s and early 1890s it marched in lockstep with the progress of ranchers and farmers. The success of ranchers accelerated the Bow Valley's economic growth, creating a demand for a variety of goods from the store.

Chapter 10: Department Stores and Mass Distribution

Before long, John Bowen was extending credit without security to a number of ranchers, including W. D. Kerfoot, who had a ranch in the Grand Valley district. Kerfoot was a product of the credit-based society in the Bow Valley and owed Baker & Co.'s store $525 for the goods he had purchased by April 1888. At this juncture, for security Bowen accepted a chattel mortgage for this amount from Kerfoot, who offered eight horses as collateral and agreed to pay off his debt in six months plus interest at the rate of 8 percent per annum.[23] He promptly repaid the loan. Equally prompt in repaying his loan of $600 for purchases on credit at Baker & Co.'s store was Leo Slattery, a Midnapore farmer, who offered fifty head of cattle as collateral on the chattel mortgage the store accepted from him.[24]

Baker & Co.'s store in Calgary extended credit to many other customers but often encountered problems that seemed insuperable. The loans the store made to some customers were very risky, nothing short of gambling. For example, by January 1889 Bowen had provided $707 without security to a rancher in the High River area. Having decided that the rancher had reached the permissible limit, Bowen at this point demanded and obtained from him a chattel mortgage for this amount. The rancher was now borrowing on the collateral of his twenty-five steers, and he promised to repay the loan in six months plus interest at the rate of 12 percent per annum. Bowen was clearly worried as he struggled to collect loans from this and other debtors in order to pay off the Baker & Co. store's own debts to suppliers. After making a few small payments, the rancher defaulted.[25]

Despite these problems, under Charles and William Conrad's direction Bowen kept Baker & Co.'s store in Calgary going in good times and bad by staying close to customers through the provision of personal services such as credit. When possible, Bowen carried the customers over until the loans could be repaid, or he assumed all of the collateral if he judged that the customers could not pay back the loans. Many ranchers and farmers in the Bow Valley expanded their operations as demand for foodstuffs grew during the late 1880s and early 1890s, often using loans backed by mortgages on their livestock. The Conrads and Bowen sought to circumvent credit problems by emphasizing the cash business at the Calgary store, but in the year 1889, the credit system dominated the picture – the credit sales totalled $86,179 while the cash sales came to $66,128.[26]

William and Charles Conrad reinvested most of the store's earnings in their Calgary enterprise, building what became in the late 1880s and early 1890s the most up-to-date department store in Alberta. Yet in 1889 they made only a slender net profit at the store – $4,026, or 3 percent on total sales.[27] Given the careful record keeping at the store, the Conrads could nevertheless easily co-ordinate a wide array of data. The ledger book enabled them to monitor both individual transactions and the business as a whole in Calgary. Numbers gave them an objective yardstick, making it possible for them to keep track of their far-flung operations in Montana and Alberta. Even so, loan losses at Baker & Co.'s store in Calgary were substantial.

Competition

Whereas a favourable external environment, especially the growth of agriculture in the Bow Valley, aided the development of Baker & Co.'s Calgary store, this environment became more hostile with the rise of local competition from general stores such as the Hudson's Bay Company and G. C. King & Co. Baker & Co. did not fall behind these firms in selling women's clothing, men's clothing, boots and shoes, crockery and glassware, carpets and oilcloths, and groceries, but it was making considerably more money in its large cattle ranching venture at Queenstown than in its department store business in Calgary.

Part of the problem at the Calgary store was that its credit operations brought financial woes: there were not enough safe loans to ensure that it would avoid excessive risk. In generously stoking the Bow Valley economy with credit, the store had assumed many risky loans. Charles and William Conrad, the principal owners of the store, were not men to dawdle in a concern that seemed to face a bleak future. Their careers had few wasted steps, and they rarely wavered when the moment for advancement came. Thus, they decided to go out of the department store trade and expand their cattle ranching business in Alberta.

Sale of I. G. Baker & Co.'s Stores

In May 1890, William Conrad wrote to Donald A. Smith, offering to sell Baker & Co.'s stores in Calgary, Fort Macleod, and Lethbridge to the Hudson's Bay Company. Conrad's offer included an invitation to the Hudson's Bay Company to examine Baker & Co.'s books and its merchandise. As a director and a major shareholder in the Hudson's Bay Company, Smith was receptive to Conrad's sales pitch, and persuaded the other directors to consider the offer. In August 1890, he instructed the company's chief commissioner Joseph Wrigley in Winnipeg to obtain all the information he could on Baker & Co.'s mercantile enterprises in Alberta.[28] It took Wrigley only a few days to dispatch his experienced assistants, W. H. Adams and E. K. Beeston, to Alberta to examine Baker & Co.'s businesses and their history.

Even before Adams and Beeston submitted their report to Wrigley, his Winnipeg office received comments on Baker & Co.'s stores from E. F. Gigot, manager of the Hudson's Bay Company store in Fort Macleod. "I. G. Baker & Co.," wrote Gigot,

> ... are certainly not doing well, or else they would not wish to get out of business.... They are getting sick of it, but they can not shut down on their credits, and collect, and at the same time carry on their business. If they manage to sell out, or for any other reason close up and commence to press their debtors, nine tenths of the people of the vicinity would be ruined for years, and would be a mighty poor community for any other merchant who might succeed them to make money out of.

Gigot concluded by saying that

> ... the whole thing looks to me like this. For some fifteen years I. G. Baker & Co. have skimmed all the cream off this part of the country, and lived on it and grew fat. Now, that the cow is getting somewhat dry, cream rises but sparingly, there are other spoons in the dish, and I. G. B. & Co.'s share is getting small.[29]

Chapter 10: Department Stores and Mass Distribution

When Adams and Beeston had carefully looked over the books of I. G. Baker & Co. in Calgary, Fort Macleod, and Lethbridge and had a good idea of the business and of the methods by which it was done, they had a different story to tell. Although they could see that the enterprise was marred by constant headaches over the credit operations, in early October 1890 Adams and Beeston told Wrigley that

> ...on the whole ... the offer of Messrs. Baker & Co. would seem well worth entertaining. ... the business [in Calgary] is the least desirable of the three.... At the same time, however, if the amount of the *good* business only done by Messrs. Baker & Co. [at Calgary] can be added to the [Hudson's Bay Company's] present business [there], it would form a very valuable addition. The sales [in Calgary] for the 8 months of the present year show an increase of about $2,000."[30]

The Hudson's Bay Company assumed a higher profile in Alberta in early 1891, when it acquired I. G. Baker & Co.'s stores in Calgary, Fort Macleod, and Lethbridge. Charles and William Conrad made the deal attractive to the Hudson's Bay Company by selling their stocks of merchandise to the company at 25 percent below cost and by accepting responsibility for collecting the debts on their books. "I think there can be no doubt that the bargain in itself is an advantageous one for the Company. The success of the investment, however, must mainly depend upon the prosperity of the country and the management of the business," wrote Joseph Wrigley.[31]

But in Calgary a latent tension now strained relations between Baker & Co. manager John L. Bowen and James Thomson, manager of the old Hudson's Bay Company store. One day in late January, Bowen told Thomson that the transfer in Calgary would take place in March. At the same time, there was a rumour that Bowen was underselling the Hudson's Bay Company by offering goods to his customers at cost. Upset by the rumour, Thomson reported to his boss, Joseph Wrigley in Winnipeg, that

> ... since the purchase became publicly known customers of I. G. Baker & Co. have been informed that goods will be sold at cost until 1 March. I do not imagine that this action has been inspired from headquarters [in Fort Benton] but it is scarcely

carrying out the spirit of the agreement. If persisted in, it will operate very naturally to our disadvantage.... We could not ask more for goods than the price they had been offered at by I. G. Baker & Co.[32]

The Hudson's Bay Company's lawyer, James A. Lougheed, "was aware goods were being sold below retail prices" at Baker & Co.'s store, said Thomson a few days later. Thomson went on to tell Wrigley that

> I have not mentioned the matter of underselling to Mr. Bowen. I am satisfied he would not act on any suggestions or instructions from me. We are on most friendly terms but his promise would be no guarantee of justice to the [Hudson's Bay] Company."[33]

Thomson could not remain silent, however, passively awaiting the outcome. When he learned that "large quantities of goods have been disposed of" at Baker & Co.'s store "since Saturday morning far below retail prices if not below cost," Thomson took a tougher approach to the thorny problem. "Today I felt obliged to call Mr. Bowen's attention to the matter. It will not be repeated tomorrow," Thomson wrote Wrigley on 2 February.[34] Wrigley fully backed Thomson, immediately firing off a telegram to Charles Conrad asking him to put a "stop" to "this."[35] Charles Conrad responded positively to the telegram, closing Baker & Co.'s Calgary store on 3 February and instructing Bowen to begin taking stock the next day.

Whatever prices he had been marketing the store's goods at, Bowen immediately started the process of stocktaking and worked to help complete the transfer. "We finished up every thing with the H. B. Co. here some three weeks since," he reported to William Conrad at his winter home in White Post, Virginia on 26 March. Charles Conrad had come up from Fort Benton on 2 March to assist Bowen with the transfer and then had gone to Winnipeg to see Joseph Wrigley about the deal. Many customers, however, had failed to pay off their debts at Baker & Co.'s Calgary store. For Bowen, this was a pressing concern. It was his task to pry loose the money from the debtors. "Trying to collect up. Doing tolerably well. Taking notes when I cannot get the cash," Bowen wrote to William Conrad.[36] Three weeks later, in mid-April, Bowen had worse news for William: "Slow collecting, but we are getting a good many notes. It is a bad time of the year to collect. I am doing my best."[37] Bowen also asked the collection agency in Calgary, Fitzgerald & Lucas, to collect payments from some debtors.[38] But in the end, many debts on Baker & Co.'s books remained unpaid.

The future for Baker & Co. in Alberta was in the growth of its cattle ranch at Queenstown. In selling its stores in Calgary, Fort Macleod, and Lethbridge, the firm cut down on its losses in Alberta and had more resources with which to expand its ranching business. "I think it is well we got rid of those stores as soon as we did. They only lost money and were liable to get us into serious trouble," William Conrad wrote his brother Charles.[39]

A New Era in the Department Store Business

Hudson's Bay Company

Joseph Wrigley, however, was convinced that a new era in department store business was dawning in Calgary. His great hope was that doubters within the Hudson's Bay Company, such as James Thomson, would come to share his view. Before long, Thomson agreed with Wrigley that the purchase of Baker & Co.'s store in Calgary would help to open the way for the Hudson's Bay Company's entry into the promising department store trade in the town. "Although I felt somewhat opposed to the purchase when I heard last September that negotiations had been entered into, no effort shall now be spared to make the transaction profitable to the Hudson's Bay Company," Thomson told Wrigley.[40]

If Thomson entered the department store business in Calgary with some reservations, he now embraced it as a big opportunity to become involved in mass distribution. As always, Thomson enjoyed cordial relations with Wrigley and worked well under his direction. Far from seeing the potential of the department store in a sudden revelatory flash, in his thinking Wrigley had made a gradual transition from the general store to the department store in 1890 and the beginning of 1891. Wrigley's visionary leadership, as well as his capacity to think in strategic terms, influenced Thomson to become enthusiastic about the department store trade. Thomson knew something of this business from observing the operations

Chapter 10: Department Stores and Mass Distribution

of Baker & Co.'s department store in Calgary. Able to use the old Baker & Co. store from early March 1891 onward, Thomson plunged headlong into the business. Eager not to miss an important opportunity, Thomson and Wrigley belonged to a new breed of people in the emerging department store trade who purchased and distributed a wide range of products in Calgary and the Bow Valley.

Grand Opening

The date chosen for the grand opening of the old Baker & Co. department store under Hudson's Bay Company ownership and management was Thursday, 5 March. In the days leading up to this event, the fair-minded Charles Conrad was present and Thomson found him most helpful in making final arrangements for the transfer. "On Mr. Conrad's arrival ... the goods ... were examined and on talking the matter over he accepted our valuation. I think he was satisfied our valuation was fair. He was very agreeable and did not wish to place any obstacles in the way of a settlement," Thomson wrote Wrigley on 4 March. "The store will be opened tomorrow and I expect a big rush. Advertisements have been put temporarily in both the local newspapers."[41] Thomson's advertisement in the *Calgary Herald* and the *Calgary Tribune* announced that "stock, comprising dry goods, clothing, boots & shoes, groceries, crockery and glassware will be sold at GREATLY REDUCED PRICES. Come early and secure the best bargains ever offered in Calgary."[42]

While Joseph Wrigley always determined the Hudson's Bay Company's overall strategy for its department store in Calgary, that strategy was implemented by James Thomson. Wrigley's basic objective was to achieve a high-volume, high-turnover flow of trade by selling at low prices and low margins, and Thomson agreed. Volume, not markup, was to produce profits. With a number of sales people making hundreds of sales, it was logical for Wrigley and Thomson to adopt a one-price policy. They also followed the policy of clear and accurate descriptions of goods in the store with money-back guarantees if customers were dissatisfied with their purchases. In the evening of 5 March, at the close of the store's first full day of operations, Thomson reported to Wrigley that "the store was opened this morning and the sales having been fully what I expected – the cash sales amounting to $325.10. Remnants and damaged goods are being cleared off at a good profit."⁴³ Three days later, Thomson wrote that "so far the business has been a great success," with total cash and credit sales reaching $2,067.⁴⁴

The pressure from customers for credit was great and, consequently, Thomson conducted business in the department store in Calgary on both a cash and credit basis. His preference for short-term and safe credits arose from his determination to avoid the well-known problems associated with I. G. Baker & Co.'s liberal credit policy. From the very start, Thomson recognized that a safe policy for one customer might not be safe for another. He also understood that to refuse credit to some customers was to refuse important business. As he told Wrigley,

> When I. G. Baker & Co.'s books show accounts to have been satisfactory, credit will not now be refused. When given there will be a distinct understanding as to date and manner of payment. Losses may, and no doubt will, arise, but keeping Messrs. Baker's experience in view every precaution will be taken to have as small losses as possible.

Thomson courted "all former customers of I. G. Baker & Co.," mailing out letters to each one. He was pleased to report that "there seems to be every disposition on the part of customers to patronise and continue with the [Hudson's Bay] Company."⁴⁵

When the Hudson's Bay Company opened the old Baker & Co. store, the number of employees, including Thomson, was nine: Edmund Taylor served as accountant; Henry Atkinson and A. Vaux were dry goods salesmen; David Kerr, C. H. Parlow, and F. A. Jenner served as grocery salesmen; Miss M. Trimble was cashier; and George Greenwood served as porter. All the members of the staff knew one another. Informality characterized the management style at the Hudson's Bay Company store in Calgary at this time. In the early 1890s, the store's operations were small enough to be run without a managerial hierarchy. Business was usually conducted on a personal, face-to-face basis in this family atmosphere. When Thomson needed to purchase additional dry goods in March 1891, he had an informal talk with Henry Atkinson, after which he bought the goods.⁴⁶ The store continued to enjoy success in the summer of 1891. "At Calgary, business continues very satisfactory, and the sales are good," reported W. T. Livock, a senior Hudson's Bay Company officer.⁴⁷

Chapter 10: Department Stores and Mass Distribution

New Sandstone Department Store

Entry into the field of the department store trade had been foremost among Joseph Wrigley's plans for the growth of the Hudson's Bay Company's business in Calgary for some time. Already in 1890, he had persuaded the company's board in London, England to build a new store in the Alberta town. James Thomson was enthusiastic about Wrigley's plans to transform the existing general store into a department store. Instead of remaining on a familiar path, Thomson and Wrigley wanted to risk the company's fortune and its future in Calgary on a new and untried venture. As early as December 1889, Thomson wrote to Wrigley, pointing out that the company's general store had fallen far behind other stores in the town and recommending a new approach to merchandising: "When merchants here and others coming in show varied and attractive stocks in large handsome shops, they can only be opposed successfully by similar display."[48]

Thomson did not misjudge his audience, for Wrigley showed great interest. As Wrigley wrote the Hudson's Bay Company's London board,

> The present store at Calgary is a wooden building and is very inferior to the stone stores which surround it. In Mr. Thomson's opinion the company loses trade from want of suitable premises. He estimates the cost of a suitable building of stone at $15,000.... He believes that progress will continue to be made surely if slowly, having confidence in the natural advantages of Calgary and the resources of the large fertile country tributary to it.... I believe what Mr. Thomson says is correct, and if the Board see no objection to the investment as suggested, I think it ought to prove remunerative for the cost stated.[49]

The company's London board thought Wrigley and Thomson's idea had commercial possibilities, and in June 1890 it authorized Wrigley to proceed with the construction of a new department store in Calgary. Osborne Wickenden, the Nova Scotia-born architect who had been asked to prepare plans for the proposed sandstone store, estimated that the cost of the entire work would be about $17,500.[50] Before long the Calgary contractor, W. H. Cushing, had been engaged, and construction of the new building on the northwest corner of Stephen Avenue and McTavish Street began on 1 August.[51]

Harrison Young, one of the company's senior officers, predicted

> ... that by 1 August 1891 we will occupy premises second to none west of Winnipeg, which will be a credit to the town, and convince our customers that we are fully awake to their needs, and do not intend to get left in the race by any of our opponents. It is a standing custom of all opponents of our company to state that we are slow and old fashioned and not up to the times. I think the proposed store at Calgary will offer a most substantial argument against their assertion.

Young went on to link the future of the store to the development of farming in the Bow Valley.

> During the year a large number of settlers took up land in the vicinity of Calgary, and they were as a rule of a good class with moderate means. Past experience has shown that ranching on a large scale will not pay, but that mixed farming will. The country around Calgary is admirably filled for this, and I think that at no distant day we will reap the benefit of the trade of the farmers.[52]

Thomson and Wrigley understood that building a new department store in Calgary was financially risky. A serious miscalculation in construction could place the entire project in jeopardy. Wrigley and Thomson thus had strong incentives to develop a risk reduction strategy. In an effort to avoid missteps, the thirty-year-old Thomson studied the architect's plans carefully, discussed the construction of store with contractor W. H. Cushing, and kept Wrigley fully informed about work on the project. Hudson's Bay Company officer E. K. Beeston wrote that Thomson was "a very energetic and reliable man, possessing good judgement and business ability."[53] Although building operations were suspended during the winter of 1891, they were resumed in March of that year. Wrigley reported:

Chapter 10: Department Stores and Mass Distribution

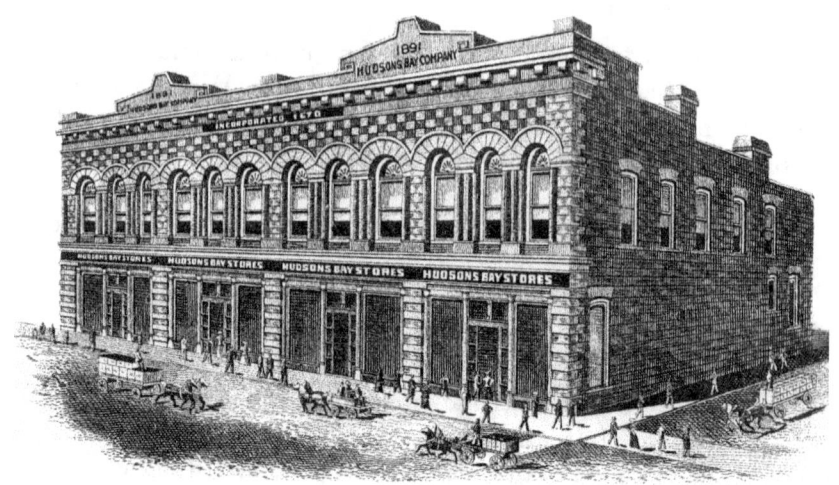

Hudson's Bay Company department store, c. 1904. (Courtesy of Glenbow Archives, NA-419-1).

As far as can be seen the new building will have a good appearance and seems substantially built. It will be necessary to carry on the spring trade in Messrs. Bakers' store, as the new building will not be ready until July, in good time for the autumn trade. There appears to be an air of prosperity about the town of Calgary. So far as can be seen there is a prospect of the town making gradual progress. The winter has been very mild and favourable for ranching.[54]

When Clarence C. Chipman succeeded the ailing Joseph Wrigley as the Hudson's Bay Company's chief commissioner in Winnipeg in June 1891, the future of its department store business in Baker & Co.'s store in Calgary looked bright. The venture in mass distribution was now an established enterprise and certainly anticipated continued growth. Clarence Chipman played an important role in its development. Born in 1856 in Amherst, Nova Scotia, Chipman was the son of the postmaster in the local post office. He attended school in Amherst. In 1882, Chipman served as private secretary to Sir Charles Tupper, a native of Amherst and minister of railways and canals in John A. Macdonald's government. A year later, when Tupper became high commissioner for Canada in London, England, Chipman accompanied him to the imperial capital as his secretary.[55] As a member of the high commissioner's staff, Chipman's tasks included organizing and directing the Canadian exhibit at the exhibition in Antwerp in 1885, as well as organizing and supervising the Canadian section of the exhibition in London the following year. London, the site of the Hudson's Bay Company's head office, was where Chipman was appointed as the corporation's chief commissioner in Winnipeg.

Chipman was an important addition to the Hudson's Bay Company's management. A bundle of energy, he developed a good relationship with James Thomson. Described by *The Beaver* as a man whose "tact and diplomacy often stood him in good stead," Chipman was an able leader.[56] On his visits to Thomson in Calgary, Chipman became familiar with the company's position in the town, and the two men stayed in close touch with each other through regular correspondence. Chipman reported:

> I am altogether well pleased with the state of our affairs at Calgary, and it is not too much to anticipate that this will be one of our most profitable sales shop businesses in a very short time. The clerk in charge, Mr. James Thomson, is careful, painstaking, intelligent, and industrious; and I may mention that we are also fortunate at this place in our staff generally.[57]

On 19 September 1891, ten days before the opening of the Hudson's Bay Company's new department store in downtown Calgary, Chipman gave his impression of it from his recent visit to the town:

> Our new store at Calgary was approaching completion, and it appeared to be a substantial and well built structure. The contractor has evidently done his work efficiently, and we have, without a doubt, the best building for a store in Calgary. We have been most fortunate in the situation of this building, and from appearances I should not be at all surprised if it proved to be in the near future too small for our requirements.[58]

Chipman's plan was to move all the merchandise into the new store and then sell the old Baker & Co. store.

Thomson hoped that the opening of the new, two-storey sandstone store on the northwest corner of Stephen Avenue and

Chapter 10: Department Stores and Mass Distribution

McTavish Street on 29 September would be an event that people in Calgary and the Bow Valley would remember. He had made enormous strides in the short time since beginning in the department store trade. He clearly wanted this magnificent new store not only to be a sign of past growth and the need for a bigger building but also, by its very grandeur, an indication of greater things in the future. Having become the leading store in the town, it had to maintain its standing. Without staying ahead in the realm of new ideas and accommodations, it could not continue to be the leader in sales.

Consequently, the move involved careful preparations. Thomson paid special attention to fitting up the interior of the store in the most attractive way. A reporter for the *Calgary Tribune* noted that "the interior is finished throughout in British Columbia cedar and white pine, the ceilings, the shelving, the counters and in fact all the woodwork presents a rich and elegant appearance, [and] the taste, too, displayed in the arrangements does much credit to those who have this work in hand."[59] The big job of transporting the large retail and wholesale stocks by team and wagon along Stephen Avenue from the old Baker store to the new store was nearing completion.

Up the steam freight elevator to the second floor was taken everything for several departments: carpets and house furnishings, ready-made clothing, and crockery and glassware. While one room served as a bedroom for accountant Edmund Taylor, two rooms were devoted to dressmaking, one for sewing and the other for fitting. On the first floor were placed goods for three departments: dry goods, groceries, and boots and shoes. There were five large plate glass show windows, four in the front facing Stephen Avenue and one on the McTavish Street side. "One of the noticeable features of the store is the magnificent office accommodation. In this respect, it is ahead of anything outside of the large cities of the east," wrote the *Calgary Tribune* reporter.[60] In front of the office, "the cash girl's stand," which made use of Whiting's cash railway system, was installed by Peddie and Erskine of Winnipeg.[61] When the doors were opened Tuesday morning, 29 September, people poured into the building. All came to see what for that era was a gorgeous array of merchandise and offered "at remarkably low prices."[62] "Business in the new store has been very satisfactory," reported Thomson two days later.[63]

Thomson could offer goods at low prices because of the Hudson's Bay Company's ability to buy with cash large lots at lowest market prices directly from manufacturers, in Montreal and Toronto as well as in Great Britain, France, and Germany.⁶⁴ Whether in Canada or abroad, every manufacturer knew that sales to the company meant a volume purchase and ready money in hand. To secure this kind of business, manufacturers were often willing to bid low. The Canadian Pacific Railway played a direct role in transporting products to the Hudson's Bay Company store on their way to the consumer. Orders for a wide variety of goods from manufacturers were brought to Calgary in carload lots, thereby helping to keep a steady stream of low-priced, up-to-date merchandise flowing toward the company's store by rail.⁶⁵

As part of his duties as manager, Thomson was expected to make a record of his awareness of new business opportunities and contribute suggestions for seizing them. The end of prohibition in the Northwest Territories in the early 1890s seemed to hold the promise of new business in the liquor trade. Thomson was a keen-eyed observer of the first stages of the liquor trade, and he believed that money could be made in this business. Additional space would be required, however. So, in October 1891, Thomson recommended to Chipman that the old Baker & Co. store be sold to the Imperial Bank of Canada and that the Hudson's Bay Company diversify by opening a wholesale liquor department in a part of the building that the bank did not need for its services. "The trade here would be an important source of revenue and it is desirable that the Company should be in a position to handle it," Thomson wrote Chipman.⁶⁶ With the sale of the old Baker & Co. store to the Imperial Bank of Canada for $15,000, Thomson established a wholesale liquor department there and ran it from the Hudson's Bay Company's store. In his advertisement in the *Calgary Tribune*, Thomson offered "special inducements to Cash customers, Retail men, and Hotels."⁶⁷

Labour Relations

As the diversified operations of the Hudson's Bay Company's store in Calgary expanded, labour relations at the store became more complex. Executives in Winnipeg combined a commitment to employee rewards with opposition to quick wage increases for everyone on the staff. If Chipman considered employees hard-working and worthy, he sometimes increased their wages. When Edmund Taylor, accountant, and David Kerr, grocery salesman and

Chapter 10: Department Stores and Mass Distribution

stockkeeper, asked for higher remuneration in September 1891, their monthly wage was upped by $10.[68] Wages for the lower ranks of the company's employees remained relatively low, however.

At the company's Calgary store, labour relations were still informal. Paternalistic, personal relations were the norm, something that was intended to help create a loyal workforce. Weekend outings were usually well attended by local management and other employees alike. For instance, one Sunday in July 1892 James Thomson and his staff paid a visit to D. M. Ratcliffe's dairy farm at Big Hill Springs, whose creamery supplied the company's store with fresh butter. A reporter for the *Calgary Tribune* wrote:

> The day was as fine as could be desired, and an early start enabled the party to arrive at their destination at 10 o'clock in the morning. The 25 miles of trail between Calgary and the Big Hill runs for the most part through cattle and horse ranches, and at points a most extensive view of the country stretching clear to the base of the mountains is obtained. On arriving at the Springs a most cordial welcome was extended to the party by both Mr. and Mrs. Ratcliffe, and after lunch had been served Mr. Ratcliffe proceeded to show his guests the sights of the Big Hill.[69]

Rewarding James Thomson

Promotion was the way the Hudson's Bay Company rewarded the performance of managers, and this contributed to good results. It was James Thomson's growing sales at the Calgary store and by mail to rural customers in the Bow Valley, as well as his self-confidence, that led Chipman to groom him for larger responsibilities. In March 1893, after Thomson and his wife Helen and their infant son Eric had vacationed at his old home in the Orkneys for some time, he was promoted to manager of the company's store in Vancouver.[70]

It was enormously important to James Thomson that Chipman and business people in Calgary see him as trustworthy. The personal and collective relationship Thomson had established with the citizens of Calgary during his eight years in the town held a special significance for him. Thirty-five prominent Calgarians acknowledged the contributions James and Helen had made to

Chapter 10: Department Stores and Mass Distribution

Calgary's development, when they gathered one evening for a farewell at the Alberta Hotel and presented a silver tea service with tray to Helen and read an address to James:

> The business interests of the town owe much to you. Representing an ancient and conservative corporation, you have so administered its affairs during a period of rapidly changing circumstances that it has continued in every sense the pioneer establishment of Calgary.... By your integrity and courtesy you have gained the esteem of all with whom you have come in contact, and the friendship of those closely associated with you, and this esteem and friendship Mrs. Thomson has shared in an equal degree with yourself amongst all those who have had the pleasure of her acquaintance.[71]

The good labour relations in the Hudson's Bay Company's store in Calgary were reflected in the farewell gift, a framed photograph of the entire staff, presented to James Thomson by those who had worked under him.[72]

Edmund Taylor

New Manager

Chipman looked within the Hudson's Bay Company's Calgary store for a new manager. One of Thomson's strengths, Chipman realized, was his willingness and ability to groom a successor. One internal prospect was Edmund Taylor, the store's accountant, and Chipman picked him. Business and personal connections influenced his choice. He was personally acquainted with Taylor through his visits to the store. Chipman took a liking to Taylor, and the two men became friends. But more than friendship was involved in Chipman's decision. He knew Taylor as an able accountant.

Born in May 1871 in Manitoba, Edmund Taylor was the son of Thomas and Elizabeth Margaret Kennedy Taylor, both of leading Hudson's Bay Company families. After attending local schools in Manitoba, Edmund Taylor went on to study at Emmanuel College in Prince Albert, a Church of England institution. He joined the Hudson's Bay Company as an apprentice clerk in 1885 and, during

Chapter 10: Department Stores and Mass Distribution

the next few years, served at several of its fur trading posts in the Northwest Territories.[73] Between June 1889 and January 1891, Taylor was accountant at the company's post in Edmonton. In February 1891, he was transferred to the company's store in Calgary to serve as accountant. When he joined the Calgary store, Taylor was described as "a good accountant being careful and accurate" by James Thomson. "Mr. Taylor is an exceptionally clever and morally good young man."[74] Taylor was delighted with his position in the Hudson's Bay Company's store in Calgary. "He is a very steady young man and a competent accountant," reported Thomson five months later.[75]

Taylor's background in accounting at the Hudson's Bay Company appealed to Clarence Chipman. Also important in determining Chipman's choice was his perception of Taylor's character and leadership abilities. He saw Taylor as a strong leader, a take-charge manager at the company's Calgary store. For Chipman, Taylor typified the sound store manager whose word was his bond.

From the beginning, Taylor brought forceful, imaginative leadership to the store. He spent his first few weeks visiting the store's departments and talking with heads about their operations. He was active and visible, an energetic man who stayed in touch with the needs of the growing departments through regular meetings with the heads. The management set-up in the store was flexible, giving enough authority over day-to-day decisions to department heads.

Then, too, Taylor got along well with Chipman, his boss. Besides keeping him fully informed about the store's business, he sought his approval before making major capital expenditures. For instance, after Chipman agreed to the necessity of building a new vault in the Calgary store, Taylor went ahead with the project in the spring of 1893.[76] With Chipman's blessing, Taylor also renovated the crockery and glassware department in the summer of that year.[77] He expanded on the basis of the store's strengths, which lay partly in the marketing of crockery and glassware. In particular, goods such as handsome china dinner sets in this department were targeted for growth, for it was expected that Calgary and Bow Valley women would be eager to see and buy them. A factor that made shopping in this department attractive to customers during the opening week was Taylor's decision to serve tea, hot or iced, free of charge to them as they browsed and dreamed without pressure to buy in the unhurried atmosphere.[78]

Table 9. Sales and Profits at the Hudson's Bay Company's Calgary Store, 1892-1894

Year	1892	1894
Sales	$159,701	$140,243
Profits	$8,670	$4,602

Source: HBCA, D32/4, f. 202, Abstracts of Balance Sheets, 1892-1894

But the instability of the national economy and increasing local competition, both of which hurt the Hudson's Bay Company's Calgary store, amplified in the mid-1890s. Table 9 shows that as business in Calgary and the Bow Valley languished, purchases of the store's goods fell, pulling its total sales down from $159,701 in 1892 to $140, 243 in 1894.[79] In the same period, profits plunged from $8,670 to $4,602. The operations at the store, however, were still profitable under Edmund Taylor's direction. He still provided able leadership and helped to maintain a high level of morale among the employees under him.

Expansion

Chipman still viewed the Calgary store, and its place in the Hudson's Bay Company, favourably. In fact, he wanted to continue the store's development and asked the London board for its approval to expand by constructing an addition to the building. "In view of the comparatively good results of Calgary Post and the present prospects of trade there, I would beg to recommend for the approval of the Board the appropriation of the further sum needed for the completion of this building," Chipman wrote in October 1894.[80] The total estimated cost of the addition was $12,364.

The London board committed this sum to the construction of an addition to the company's Calgary store. When the construction of the enlarged store was finished in September 1895, the *Calgary Tribune* wrote that the Hudson's Bay Company "have now at Calgary the largest and most complete mercantile establishment between Winnipeg and the Coast."[81]

On a fall afternoon, a few days before the formal opening of the completed store, a reporter for the *Calgary Tribune* visited the enterprise. His assignment: to file a story on the greatest urban merchandising concern in Alberta in the late nineteenth century. The store he entered, through its doors on Stephen Avenue, was a symbol of Calgary's postfire pride and prosperity. Billed as "The Best Place to Patronise in Calgary," it employed fifteen people, including two dressmakers, the new accountant A. Dyson, who had previously worked for the Hudson's Bay Company in its store in Qu'Appelle, and delivery wagon driver James Grant.

No store in Calgary grew faster in the mid- and late 1890s or was more stunningly alive than the Hudson's Bay Company's store, where customers went to see the shape of the future. When he entered the dry goods department on the first floor together with his host Edmund Taylor, the *Calgary Tribune* reporter "began to cast his eyes about him and for the first time realised what it means to conduct a modern retail dry goods establishment. Truly every country in the civilised world is represented within the walls of this sightly emporium."[82]

Taking his guest to the ladies' dress goods section, Taylor remarked: "these are what we call China silks. It will not be difficult for you to imagine what the effect will be when they have passed through the hands of the dressmaker and appear on the floor of the ballroom." What surprised the *Calgary Tribune* correspondent was that the price of the China silks was only forty-five cents. Upon reaching the chenille curtains in the carpet department on the second floor of the store with his guest, Taylor said "these are positively the best value we have ever had in these goods. Can you imagine how such a conglomeration of skill, art, and material can be produced for $3.50 a pair?" After returning to the first floor and coming to the men's furnishing department, "the reporter was actually talked into investing in a suit, which, while costing only $15, even an expert could not decide but that it was the production of a fashionable west-end London tailoring establishment."[83]

Taylor's relatively low prices encouraged customers to make purchases in the Hudson's Bay Company's Calgary store. Before the *Calgary Tribune* reporter left the store that afternoon, Taylor said: "I wish you would just step into the grocery department again and get one of our price lists. I cannot deny that I have heard it said that the prices at the Hudson's Bay Company store are high and I want to satisfy you that this is not the case." As on the price list, the prices on the groceries were clearly marked. "From a perusal of the price list, the reporter concluded that the charge was unfair," wrote the *Calgary Tribune* correspondent.⁸⁴ The *Calgary Tribune's* endorsement clearly helped the business.

For the most part, Taylor's strategy – low prices on a wide range of fresh goods with a strong emphasis on quality and service – resulted in growing profits and expanding operations. The gradual recovery of the Calgary and Bow Valley economies after 1895 contributed to his success. By 1899, total annual sales at the Hudson's Bay Company's Calgary store had climbed to $182,044, and total annual profits had risen to $9,472.⁸⁵ If reliable customers wanted to purchase goods on credit, they were usually able to do so. Despite Taylor's close credit policy, in most years sales to charge customers exceeded cash sales and were always an essential part of the business. As usual, in 1899 the store's credit sales were most important, accounting for 67 percent of all its sales. In the mid-1890's, Taylor's major charge customers included William James Halliday, a Calgary baker; Elizabeth Coulter Clarke, who together with her husband Simon owned the Queen's Hotel in the city; and Felix A. and John J. McHugh, owners of the Bow River Park Ranche just west of the Blackfoot reserve on the south bank of the Bow.⁸⁶

But problems continued to plague the store, especially the problem of intense competition. By 1899, there were dozens of retailers in Calgary, some engaged in general merchandising and others specializing in dry goods or men's furnishings or groceries, as well as the department store Glanville & Robertson, owned and run by J. F. Glanville and William Robertson. In this competitive situation, Taylor struggled in the department store business. To help meet competition and foster high-volume selling, he continued to stress low prices, and he increasingly made price as well as guaranteed satisfaction the focus of his advertising in local newspapers. After diversifying by opening a new department for safety bicycles in 1896, Taylor invited readers of his advertisement to the Hudson's Bay Company's store to see the "high class wheel The Chief Factor for $100.00. Discount for cash, 10 percent, or at the low net price of $90.00. Special prices for clubs of not less than five members on application. N. B. Every machine guaranteed by the Hudson's Bay Company."⁸⁷ By this time, safety bicycles had replaced the older ordinary bicycles with high front wheels. The bicycle craze in Calgary in the mid-1890s created a demand for safety bicycles, and Taylor responded effectively to this demand at the company's store. His decision to advertise and sell the Calgary

Chapter 10: Department Stores and Mass Distribution

Table 10. Sales and Profits at the Hudson's Bay Company's Calgary Store, 1899-1903

Year	1899	1903
Sales	$182,044	$223,494
Profits	$9,472	$14,915

Source: HBCA, D32/4, f. 202, Abstracts of Balance Sheets, 1899-1903

Brewing and Malting Co.'s popular beer reaffirmed his policy to keep the store diversified so that it would not rely too much on a few products for its sales and profits.[88]

Taylor also developed the Calgary store's mail-order business. As early as April 1893, he had told readers of his advertisements that "mail orders shall receive strict attention."[89] Sitting in their homes, by 1896 rural and small-town customers in the Bow Valley could page through a copy of the Hudson's Bay Company's latest catalogue and send orders for goods to the store.[90] Taylor offered to sell by mail a generous assortment of merchandise, from ready-to-wear Sunday dresses to boots and shoes, making federal postal employees into part of the company's sales force.[91] He treated customers in the Bow Valley, as well as in Calgary, as his friends, asking them to write to him about their merchandise needs if they could not visit the store personally.[92] Taylor became a symbol of trust to urban and rural people alike, promptly carrying out his promise to ship goods to customers in the countryside by rail and to deliver them to those in the city by the company's express wagons.[93]

When Edmund Taylor was promoted to general manager of the stores department in the Hudson's Bay Company's Winnipeg office in October 1899, George A. Sharpe was chosen as the new manager of the company's Calgary store.[94] Sharpe, who had previously worked for the company at its small store in Vernon, British Columbia, welcomed the chance to run an expanding department store in Calgary. Under Sharpe's leadership, the Calgary store remained committed to low prices and high-quality goods as a way of meeting growing competition in merchandise. Table 10 shows that between 1899 and 1903, as the Calgary and Bow Valley economies continued to recover from the depression in the mid-1890s, total sales at the company's store in the city rose from $182,044 to $223,494, and total profits increased from $9,472 to $14,915.[95] In many respects, the developments that took place at the company's department store in Calgary resembled those that occurred in its stores at Fort Macleod, Lethbridge, Pincher Creek, and Edmonton, but the Calgary store's operations were considerably larger than those of the others.

As the Hudson's Bay Company's store in Calgary grew, expanded its sales, and looked toward its future, its management remained focused on the demands of customers. The men and women at the store understood that they were part of a dynamic merchandising venture responding to business opportunities and providing important products and services.

In the 1890s, the number of female shoppers at the Hudson's Bay Company store grew steadily. But relatively few women created and maintained business enterprises in Calgary and the Bow Valley at this time. They nevertheless entered into business activities, taking risks, making investments in the local and regional economies, and selling goods and services.

11

Women in Business

As business people, women in Calgary and the Bow Valley had a history of entrepreneurship, beginning in the mid-1880s. Although most enterprises owned by women were small, undercapitalized, and constantly in danger of insolvency, progress occurred in the late nineteenth century. By the year 1900, about 15 percent of all retail purchases in the region were being made by women, and since 1890 their power as consumers had grown steadily. So had their influence as employees.[1] But women did not secure an equal economic footing with men, in either 1890 or 1900. While the intervening decade opened up some business opportunities for women, they did not make big strides in closing the gap between female and male business owners. Settlers brought their belief system with respect to appropriate roles for men and women to Calgary and the Bow Valley. Men entered economic life outside the household and worked in the home, while most women worked in the household-based economy and raised the children.

Even so, some women pioneered business enterprises in Calgary and the Bow Valley and achieved success in business outside the home without neglecting the home as their first priority. Catering to the needs and likes of their own group, most women-owned businesses targeted female consumers. The modest success of their ventures reinforced their faith in capitalism, with its emphasis on entrepreneurial opportunity. Money, then as now, knew no gender. Like men-owned businesses, women-owned enterprises were capitalistic, resting on the notion that economic growth is desirable and possible, for men and women, families, business firms, as well as an entire nation.

Chapter 11: Women in Business

Table 11. Women in the Out-Of-Home Workforce in Calgary and the Bow Valley, 1891-1901

Year	1891	1901
Women with Paying Jobs	145	158

Source: Manuscript Census of 1891 for Calgary, Canmore, Gleichen, High River, Davisburg, Fish Creek, Pine Creek, Namaka, and Morley; Manuscript Census of 1901 for Calgary, Canmore, Gleichen, High River, Davisburg, Pine Creek, Morley, Queenstown, Shepard, Nose Creek, Springbank, Cochrane, Jumping Pound, Okotoks, Millarville, Priddis, and Pekisko.

Gender and Workforce

A relatively free labour market is one of the essential conditions of a dynamic economy, even of capitalism. Women, like men, should have some control over whom they will work for. At the same time, they must be able to keep most of their wages to meet their own needs and those of their families. Table 11 shows that between 1891 and 1901, the number of women in the out-of-home workforce in Calgary and the Bow Valley who had paying jobs increased from 145 to 158.[2] Women thus entered the labour market and the business community in a small way, but fairly early in the story. During the late nineteenth century, their status in business, like their numbers, advanced slowly.

Between the mid-1880s and the early 1890s, women's jobs in Calgary and the Bow Valley were concentrated in several areas: domestic service, teaching, nursing, cooking, and products and services for other women, such as dressmaking and millinery. By the turn of the century, some women were also working in business offices. Table 12 shows that as early as 1901, women made up 11 percent of the region's clerical workforce, as compared to only 0.8 percent in 1891.[3] This change stemmed in part from the use of the modern-keyboard typewriter and the telephone, invented in 1872 and 1876 respectively, as instruments of business, as well as from growth in office staffs of firms. Letters were still written by hand in many offices, but typewriters were increasingly used in firms that required more letter writing. By 1901, over 62 percent of all stenographers and typists and 20 percent of all bookkeepers were female.[4]

Table 12. Women in Clerical Workforce in Calgary and the Bow Valley, 1891-1901

Year	1891	1901
% Women in Clerical Workforce	0.8%	11%

Source: Manuscript Census of 1891 for Calgary, Canmore, Gleichen, High River, Davisburg, Fish Creek, Pine Creek, Namaka, and Morley; Manuscript Census of 1901 for Calgary, Canmore, Gleichen, High River, Davisburg, Pine Creek, Morley, Queenstown, Shepard, Nose Creek, Springbank, Cochrane, Jumping Pound, Okotoks, Millarville, Priddis, and Pekisko.

While many men still worked in offices as bookkeepers and stenographers, some of them moved into the more highly paid profession of accounting. But as office work expanded in growing firms, more women were hired as stenographers and bookkeepers. Some women in Calgary and the Bow Valley also took new office jobs as telephone operators and telegraph operators. Around 1900, office jobs were among the best jobs available to most women in the region. It made sound economic sense to try to secure office work. Despite its limits for women, office work could open the way to more education and, perhaps, better paying jobs in successful, forward-looking companies. Work for women covered a wide range of salaries, often with the possibility of making more money as time passed. In Calgary and the Bow Valley, as in other parts of Canada such as Ontario and in American cities such as Chicago, most female office workers were young, unmarried women from relatively modest economic backgrounds.[5]

At the Hudson's Bay Company department store in Calgary, job opportunities for women were expanded in the 1890s and in the first decade of the next century. In 1896, Miss M. Trimble, formerly the store's cashier, worked in the establishment as a stenographer; Miss Miller as a dressmaker; Miss Kinnisten as a dry goods saleswoman; and sixteen-year-old Helen Macleod, eldest daughter of Colonel James F. Macleod, who had died two years before, as cashier.[6] By 1898, Helen Macleod had been promoted to assistant accountant in the store.[7]

Like most female workers, Helen Macleod expected to marry and quit her job. In 1899, she married A. E. Cross, Calgary brewer and owner of the A7 Ranch, and left the employ of the Hudson's Bay Company store. By 1906, all the female members of the staff had been replaced by new women and two had been added, bringing the total to six. Among those women who now filled jobs at

Chapter 11: Women in Business

Helen Rothney Macleod in 1899, in her wedding dress for her marriage to A.E. Cross. Prior to this, Helen worked first as a cashier and then as an assistant accountant at the Hudson's Bay Company store. (Courtesy of Glenbow Archives, NA-2536-4).

the store were Miss L. Passmore, head of the mantles department, with a monthly salary of $50; Miss Fletcher, cashier, who was paid $25 a month; and Miss E. Draper, head of the crockery department, with a monthly salary of $20.[8] Differences in salary among these women meant that they, like other women workers, had available considerably different levels of resources for meeting their needs.

One of the women on the store's staff in 1906 was Colonel James F. Macleod's daughter Jean, a graduate of Central School in Calgary who had begun four years before as cashier for $15 a month at age sixteen.[9] She had followed her sister Roma, who had started at the store as cashier in 1900 and by the following year had been promoted to assistant bookkeeper.[10] By 1906, Jean Macleod had taken a shorthand and typing course in the evenings for about two months and had risen to become a stenographer at the Hudson's Bay Company store with a monthly salary of $35.[11] But Jean always felt obliged to contribute significantly to the support of her widowed mother Mary Macleod – who had been left with almost no money by her husband's death – and the family. "I don't think [Jean] ever saw a pay cheque. It just went to the family account," recalled her daughter Rothney Montgomery-Bell many years later. "There were very long hours [at the store]. I think she worked until six o'clock every night and on Saturday it was until ten. I don't think she got a half day off, just Sunday," added Rothney.[12]

The size and gendered composition of the office workforce in Calgary and the Bow Valley was gradually changing in the late nineteenth and early twentieth centuries. The number of clerical workers in the region steadily increased. Typing and stenography often turned into women's jobs as some men moved on to become accountants, business administrators, and personnel managers. Like typing, stenography and shorthand required special training. Susan Harris, one of the earliest Calgary stenographers, was trained after office hours by Miss McMillan, a stenographer who worked for William B. Barwis, an insurance agent.[13] Born in 1882 in Birtle, Manitoba, Susan Harris was the daughter of Helen and Michael Harris. Her father, a civil engineer, and her mother hoped that Susan would do well in Central School. They were delighted with her ability to learn quickly. When Susan went to work as a stenographer for John Sharples, a retail and wholesale grocer and grain merchant on Stephen Avenue between the Royal Hotel and the Post Office, she was a happy seventeen-year-old:[14]

Mrs. R. S. Knight (Susan Harris), in 1911. Before she was married, Susan Harris worked as a stenographer for John Sharples, a Calgary retail and wholesale grocer and grain merchant. (Courtesy of Glenbow Archives, NA-2788-41).

> I began at $15 a month and before long I got $40. That was a good salary for girls at that time. I did the bookkeeping. Mr. Sharples dictated letters to me. He was a nice Englishman. I had a typewriter, typed letters, and wrote out the accounts. I also looked after the banking. I worked from 9:00 a.m. to 6:00 p.m., six days a week. When I left Mr. Sharples' store in 1903 to get married [to Reginald S. Knight, Sharples] hired a new girl. One girl in the office was sufficient.[15]

Stenographers in Calgary by 1900-1901 included Vivian Dawson at the real estate firm Ellis & Grogan, Emily O'Connor at the law firm McCarthy & Stuart, and Madge Macfarlane at the brokerage firm Charles S. Lott.[16] Other office work was also available to young women in the Bow Valley. As early as 1891, twenty-year-old Mary Pennock was working as a telegraph operator in the Canadian Pacific Railway station in Gleichen.[17] Mary probably contributed to the support of her widowed mother, Mrs. E. Pennock, and the family.

By 1905, women could aspire to become office workers in banks. For instance, by this time Miss Gertrude Martin had a job as a stenographer in the Bank of Montreal's Calgary branch. "I beg to say Miss Martin has become a useful member of our Staff," wrote the branch's manager W. H. Hogg to general manager Edward

Chapter 11: Women in Business

Clouston. "I think she should now be paid a better salary, & I should be glad if you would authorize an increase to $50 a month, to enable her to live in reasonable comfort."[18] The all-male bank office of the late nineteenth century in the city became, by the early twentieth century, a place where women comprised a small part of the clerical workforce.

A business culture that included women developed rapidly. By the turn of the century, women and men could study shorthand, typing, stenography, and English at the Calgary Business College, established in 1899.[19] In 1904, when Miss A. Parsons was a student at the college, W. H. Coupland was the principal. "When I finished, Mr. Coupland asked me to stay in the college to teach the beginners and do the commercial work. There were businessmen who did not have enough work to employ a stenographer, but they came in to get letters written there and that was good experience for me," remembered Miss A. Parsons, who before long got a job as a stenographer in the city clerk's office.[20]

Later, between 1912 and 1914, Miss Pansy L. Pue had a similar experience at Garbutt Business College, founded in Calgary in 1907:

> I took a course there and at the end of that course I went on staff. I taught typing, stenography, bookkeeping, and business administration. I started at $60 a month and that was considered a fair salary at that time. A little later my salary was increased to $75. Some of the students came from the country, many from the city. Their ages were from fifteen to twenty or over and they were mostly preparing to be stenographers and bookkeepers. The college certainly kept in touch with business firms and was generally ready to provide a bookkeeper or a stenographer for firms that were looking for these office workers."[21]

While some teenagers learned commercial skills in high school, business college training was becoming an important complement to public schooling in Calgary and the Bow Valley. Besides being schools for young men and women, business colleges were employment agencies.

Table 13. Women-Owned Businesses in Calgary and the Bow Valley, 1891-1901

Year	1891	1901
No. of Women-Owned Bus.	45	49
% Women-Owned Bus.	6.3%	4.9%

Source: Manuscript Census of 1891 for Calgary, Canmore, Gleichen, High River, Davisburg, Fish Creek, Pine Creek, Namaka, and Morley; Manuscript Census of 1901 for Calgary, Canmore, Gleichen, High River, Davisburg, Pine Creek, Morley, Queenstown, Shepard, Nose Creek, Springbank, Cochrane, Jumping Pound, Okotoks, Millarville, Priddis, and Pekisko.

Entrepreneurship

In the late nineteenth century, there were more female entrepreneurs in Calgary and the Bow Valley than is commonly thought. What stood out was that women operated businesses catering to other women. Table 13 shows that at the same time, female business owners comprised only 4.9 percent of all business owners across the region in 1901, as compared to 6.3 percent in 1891.[22] The actual number of women-owned businesses rose slowly during the decade, from forty-five to forty-nine. Most female entrepreneurs were single, either unmarried or widowed.

By 1901, dressmakers and milliners made up 40.8 percent of all female entrepreneurs in Calgary and the Bow Valley, with women in the dressmaking trade numbering sixteen and women in the millinery business four.[23] Together, they comprised the most important entrepreneurial category of women, in 1901 and in 1891. While fourteen dressmakers operated businesses in Calgary in 1901, there was one dressmaking shop in Cochrane and one in Jumping Pound. Calgary was home to all four milliners. Not surprisingly, already in 1891 dressmakers and milliners tended to congregate in Calgary, but in that year there also were two dressmakers in Morley.

Seeing the production of women's clothing as an art and believing that women were naturally blessed with garment-making skills, most dressmaking shop owners in Calgary and the Bow Valley did not perform the mechanical work without emphasizing beauty in dress. They were involved in a variety of tasks, including cutting garments from the cloth, sewing dresses together with a sewing machine and by hand, and taking responsibility for the final fitting. They produced individualized and unique dresses, usually selling them

Chapter 11: Women in Business

Women working at typewriters in the Canadian Pacific Railway land department, Calgary, in 1915. (Courtesy of Glenbow Archives, NA-5055-1).

directly to customers in local and regional markets. Most shops were quite small, often simply a room in a home in which a dressmaker lived. Because customers served nicely as walking advertisements, dressmakers did not have to spend money on expensive displays of the clothing they made. Dressmakers, however, faced increasing competition from other dressmakers and ready-to-wear clothing available in local and regional stores during the 1890s.

By and large, dressmakers in Calgary and the Bow Valley were unmarried women. In running their businesses, most of them depended on their own efforts, offering their products for sale from a room they rented in a private home. They were entrepreneurial in outlook, seeking gain for themselves as individuals and for other family members. Unmarried dressmakers often put the subsistence needs of the families they belonged to ahead of short-run profit maximization. More often than not, they owned no property. In 1891, nineteen-year-old Kate Bruce, a Morley dressmaker who lived with her parents, fell into this category, as did twenty-one-year-old Eva Harris, a Calgary dressmaker who lived in a local merchant's home. In Calgary, dressmaker Annie Clegg, aged twenty-five, lived in the home of Julia Malloy, who operated a fancy goods business and who likely bought and sold some of Annie's products.[24]

Janet Dewar and Dressmaking

One of Calgary's best-known dressmakers in the early and mid-1890s was Ontario-born Janet Dewar. Janet served an apprenticeship as a dressmaker in a dressmaking concern in Winchester, Ontario. In 1891, at age thirty-five, she moved to Calgary to set up her own dressmaking shop. Being a boarder in building contractor Thomas Underwood's home, Janet established her dressmaking business in her room in the house. A key development in her shop's three-year history was that ladies in well-to-do families became her customers. For example, she sold some of her dresses to Mrs. Kate Underwood for $3 apiece. By 1894, the year Janet Dewar married local farmer Thomas Beveridge, she had built a thriving enterprise in dresses. "Janet made fairly good money," remembered her daughter, Miss B. Beveridge.[25]

Mary Macleod

Dressmaker

Another prominent dressmaker in Calgary was Mary Macleod, widow of Colonel James F. Macleod, former commissioner of the Mounted Police. Mary Macleod was about as independent as a woman could be. She was a strong personality, and many Calgarians viewed her as fervently engaged in trying to improve her family's condition. While briefly accepting help from her friends and neighbours following the death of her husband in 1894, Mary, at age forty-two, became a dressmaker to support herself and her family.[26] "After my grandfather died, my grandmother was left with five children. Things were

Mary Macleod, c. 1880s. After the death of her husband, James F. Macleod, in 1894, Mary became well known as a dressmaker. (Courtesy of Glenbow Archives, NA-2536-1).

not very rosy for Mounted Police families at that time. Pensions were not established. So my grandmother had a really rough time making ends meet. It was pretty rough at first, but they got into better shape afterwards when all the kids went off to work," recalled her granddaughter Rothney Montgomery-Bell.[27]

Mary Macleod became an inspirational figure, in part because as a dressmaker she succeeded in running a viable business and meeting the needs of her children. She "sewed constantly for the numerous balls" in Calgary, "training her daughters Mary, Roma and Jean as her assistants," wrote historian Sherrill MacLaren.[28] Against heavy odds, Mary Macleod as widow, mother, and dressmaker won a victory in her fight to maintain her home.

Margaret Leishman

Milliner

Like women who made dresses, Margaret Leishman as a milliner believed that hatmaking was an art. A craftswoman at heart, Margaret was a hatmaker who owned and managed one of Calgary's earliest millinery shops. Born in 1861 in Ontario, she lived with her mother Clementine, a widow, and her sister Minnie in Calgary.[29] Margaret Leishman emerged as an entrepreneur in her own right. By 1890, at age twenty-nine, she was running her own millinery establishment on Stephen Avenue. Possibly twenty-three-year-old Minnie, who was an experienced hatmaker, worked for her. Named after sellers of fancy goods in sixteenth-century Milan, Italy, the millinery trade attracted a number of craftswomen in Canada. In her shop, Margaret Leishman carried about $1,500 worth of goods by 1893.[30]

Margaret Leishman's millinery business was largely self-financed through reinvested profits. But in her hatmaking trade, she also depended on credit from suppliers, who provided her with raw materials such as fabrics, lace, ribbons, flowers, and feathers. At her grand opening on 31 March and 1 April 1893, Leishman offered a variety of hats.[31] Among her customers were Calgary women, as well as ranch and farm women in the Bow Valley. In July 1893, Leishman's hatmaking shop was worth between $1,000 and $2,000 and her credit was good, reported the R. G. Dun & Company credit correspondent.[32]

Annie A. Milner and the Millinery Trade

In September 1893, Margaret Leishman sold her millinery shop on Stephen Avenue to Mrs. Annie A. Milner and moved to British Columbia. Annie's husband, William, was in failing health at the time and died several years later, leaving her with one infant daughter. Born in 1868 in Ontario, Annie Milner began learning the millinery craft in her native province. She worked for Margaret Leishman for a few months in the summer of 1893 before buying her shop. Included in the purchase were goods worth $600 for which Annie Milner paid cash.[33]

It was not an easy business. During the economic depression in the mid-1890s, sales of hats were not booming, and it was clear that the small millinery shop on Stephen Avenue was struggling to survive. Annie Milner's assets were worth less than $1,000 and her credit was limited, noted the credit reporter for R. G. Dun & Company in 1895 and 1896.[34] But Milner was a resourceful woman. By the fall of 1896, she was diversifying by moving into fancy goods and children's wear. She also opened a mail-order service for customers in rural Bow Valley and beyond.[35] Annie Milner's sales efforts proved only partially successful. Sales rebounded as economic recovery occurred in the late 1890s, but not as quickly as those of her major competitors such as the Hudson's Bay Company and A. Allan & Co. More dressmaking shops had also come into existence, such as the one on Northcote Avenue established by Miss Eliza Nichols, a fashionable dress and mantle maker who had recently come from Detroit to Calgary, thus increasing competition in the industry.[36] Still, by 1899 Milner's assets had grown to between $2,000 and $3,000, reported the R. G. Dun & Company credit correspondent.[37] By this time, too, Annie Milner's shop was doing well enough for her to hire Miss Alma Bell, an experienced milliner, to run the millinery department.[38] In part, employing Alma Bell was designed to allow Annie Milner as a widow both to maintain her millinery shop and to give her infant daughter Mary the care and supervision she needed.

Frances Marie Carr

Boardinghousekeeper

Frances Marie Carr was an excellent example of those women in Calgary who succeeded in business as boardinghousekeepers. Between 1891 and 1901, the number of women who ran boardinghouses in the city increased slightly from six to seven.[39] Frances Carr opened a boardinghouse in Calgary in 1889, the year her husband Lemsley, a millwright who worked for the Eau Claire & Bow River Lumber Co. and lived with his family in a rented company house near the sawmill, drowned in swirling icy water in the Kananaskis River area during a log drive. "My grandfather hung on to a rock for three or four hours, but eventually the cold water just grabbed him and drowned him," remembered his granddaughter, Helen Carr McCormick.[40]

Born in New Brunswick, Frances Carr started her boardinghouse in the Eau Claire district shortly after becoming a widow at age thirty-three.[41] "My grandmother was on her own, three thousand miles from any relatives, and she had two children. So she opened a boardinghouse and raised her children," recalled her granddaughter, Helen Carr McCormick.[42] To her children, Sadie age eleven and Charles ten, Frances Carr as a widow proved to be a good provider. Concerned for their well-being, she made it possible for them to continue their studies at Central School.

Running a household required a constant supply of money, and Frances Carr began earning it with a great deal of energy, converting the house the family continued to rent from the Eau Claire & Bow River Lumber Co. into a boardinghouse with four bedrooms for unmarried male boarders who worked for the company. From their cash wages, they paid Frances Carr for room and board. It was regular income for her. But "life was hard and rugged," remembered Helen Carr McCormick.[43] Frances Carr toiled incessantly, preparing meals, doing the laundry, and keeping the house clean and tidy. In what spare time they had, her children helped her as much as they could. By 1901, Sadie had become a dressmaker and Charles had taken a job as a teamster at the Eau Claire & Bow River Lumber Co.[44] Charles and Sadie probably handed over a large part of their earnings to their mother. Boardinghousekeepers like Frances Carr required working capital, and her children helped supply some of it. Working capital was necessary to purchase food, bedding, and fuel.

Agnes K. Bedingfeld
Pekisko Rancher

In yet other cases, women in the Bow Valley became ranchers. One was Agnes Katherine Bedingfeld, a widow. Born in 1846 in Norfolk, England, Agnes very likely derived some income from the estate of her late husband, Captain George L. Bedingfeld, who had served in the British army in India.[45] These funds must have helped Agnes start her ranch in the Pekisko area, about twenty-six miles southwest of High River.[46] In August 1883, at age thirty-eight, she settled as a squatter on the land that was to become her homestead, living in a tent with her seventeen-year-old, English-born son Frank, who was her only dependant.[47] Nine months later, in May 1884, Agnes filed claim to a 160-acre homestead, the NW¼ in section 1, township 17, range 3, west of the fifth meridian, on Pekisko Creek about two and a half miles upstream from the North West Cattle Company's Bar U Ranch.[48] Agnes Bedingfeld was an able rancher, and her capital was vital to the ranch's success, but more was still needed. Before too long, Agnes arranged a partnership with her son Frank, who chose a homestead adjacent to hers, the NE¼ in section 1.

Agnes Bedingfeld plunged headlong into the ranching industry, and her enthusiasm overflowed into her partnership with Frank. Sharing the house on her homestead with her son for more than twenty-five years, she always expressed her confidence in him. Both believed in the long-term prospects of the business, never regarding it as a mirage that would soon vanish. From the beginning, Agnes was willing to dirty her hands with ranch work. Assisted by her enterprising son, she established the ranch headquarters on her homestead. By mid-May 1884, they occupied a small, plain log house, built by Frank, and by the end of that year Agnes had acquired twelve horses and six head of cattle.[49] Word-of-mouth advertising was used to generate cattle and horse sales in Calgary and the Bow Valley.

The meadows on Agnes Bedingfeld's property became pastures for the livestock. Spattered with willow brush, they also provided shelter for the animals. These natural advantages, combined with Pekisko Creek, converged to promote the ranch's growth. To supplement income from the ranch, Agnes for a time devoted some of her energies to toiling as a cook at the Bar U, while Frank spent some of his working as a cowboy there.[50] In 1886, Frank began

Chapter 11: Women in Business

Agnes K. Bedingfeld, c. early 1900s, standing inside the fence at her ranch house. (Courtesy of Glenbow Archives, NA-2467-3).

breaking the land on his mother's homestead, and immediately brought part of it under cultivation to grow oats for winter-feeding.[51] Despite some cattle losses in the severe winter of 1886-1887, by 1889 Agnes and Frank were running twenty head of cattle and thirty Clydesdale horses on the ranch.[52] The cattle they produced were mostly Herefords, but they also had Shorthorns, as well as a blend of Herefords and Shorthorns.[53]

Agnes and Frank Bedingfeld made a good team, and they applied the team concept to every aspect of the ranch's operations. Agnes operated her ranch largely as a family enterprise, grooming her son to inherit her business. While Agnes controlled most of the capital in the ranch, Frank's percentage of ownership increased gradually. By 1893, they had thirteen acres in crops on Agnes's homestead. The original log house on it had been enlarged and improved, measuring sixty by twenty-one feet and valued at $1,000. A log structure, twenty by ten feet, housed the chickens. Fencing valued at $350 surrounded the fields and pastures.[54] On Frank's homestead, conveniently near the house on Agnes's property, there were three stables, one shed, and three fenced feeding yards for the livestock, the total value of which was $500. By this time, sixty horses and a number of head of cattle were grazing on Agnes and Frank's holdings.[55]

Because Agnes and Frank Bedingfeld saw themselves as a part of the well-developed Pekisko neighbourhood, they emphasized the

Chapter 11: Women in Business

Agnes K. Bedingfeld, left, and her son Frank, on their horses at their ranch, c. early 1900s. (Courtesy of Glenbow Archives, NA-2467-12).

importance of community. They knew all their neighbours, including George Emerson, founder of the Rocking P Ranch, George Lane, foreman of the Bar U, A7 Ranch owner A. E. Cross, and rancher Joseph Harrison Brown, and benefited from their relationships with them. These neighbours were supportive as Agnes and Frank expanded and secured their holdings. In 1899, when Agnes Bedingfeld applied to the department of the interior for a clear title to a quarter section adjoining her homestead, the SW¼ in section 1, which she had purchased under pre-emption law, A. E. Cross and George Emerson wrote statements in support of her successful application.[56] Similarly, Joseph Harrison Brown and George Lane supported Frank Bedingfeld's successful application for a clear title to his homestead, the NE¼ in section 1.[57]

Known by many people as "Seven U Brown," Irish-born Joseph Harrison Brown rose at the Bar U in the mid-1880s to become head of the cowboys, one of whom was Frank Bedingfeld.[58] By 1891, Brown was residing on Agnes Bedingfeld's homestead with her and Frank and had formed a partnership with Frank. By 1900, Frank Bedingfeld and Brown were running a herd of more than fifty horses on the open range, north of the Highwood River.[59]

Chapter 11: Women in Business

Agnes Bedingfeld was at the centre of Frank and Brown's home life, making the meals and performing other household tasks.

At the Bedingfeld ranch, Agnes remained the major owner. As such, she was well positioned to profit from the business, and for many years her career marched in lockstep with the progress of the ranching industry in the Bow Valley. By 1899, after surviving the economic depression in middle of that decade, Agnes and Frank had 150 Clydesdale horses and sixty head of cattle.[60] But for Agnes Bedingfeld, ranching was not mainly an opportunity to pile up riches. While Agnes's home looked small in comparison to towering Calgary mansions owned by men such as Pat Burns, in time she rebuilt it into a substantial two-storey log and frame structure with a shingle roof, a verandah, and a fireplace in the living room, its lawn, shrubbery and garden providing a parklike atmosphere.[61] Rather than seeking to parade her wealth, Agnes tried to blend into the picturesque landscape. Famous for making the ranch an inviting place, she was extraordinarily adept at building and maintaining friendships in the Pekisko ranching community. "This kindly old lady was known as a sort of godmother to the cowboys of this section, and she is still remembered by them for the Christmas parties to which she invited them from far and wide, and none who sought shelter under her roof was ever turned away," wrote the *Calgary Herald* later.[62]

In a natural division of labour, Agnes Bedingfeld was in charge of the housework while Frank tended the livestock. But during the summers of 1898 and 1899, when Frank was prospecting for gold in the Yukon, Agnes ran the ranch at Pekisko.[63] The gold fever was so infectious in Calgary and the Bow Valley that other men from the region also rushed to the Yukon. Each time he came back, Frank had great tales to tell, but he harvested no fortune from gold. Agnes's ability to keep the ranch going during these periods shows the close mesh of housekeeping and livestock work in parts of her career. A talented businesswoman with considerable skill in handling cattle and horses, she won recognition among Bow Valley livestock raisers as a remarkable rancher.

Agnes and Frank Bedingfeld were interested in modest success, and they both continued to work hard to build up their small ranch.[64] They produced high-quality livestock and sold some cattle and horses each year at the best possible prices. Their policy of ploughing most of their profits back into the business allowed them to expand their herds. They had numerous business contacts in

Calgary and the Bow Valley. One of these was Eneas McCormick, a Calgary saddler who supplied them with saddles and harnesses. In April 1905, the Bedingfeld ranch was prosperous enough to allow Agnes to lend Eneas McCormick $400 at an interest rate of 8 percent a year.[65] Many ranches were dragged down by the very cold winter of 1906-1907, a terrifying experience for a generation of Bow Valley ranchers. But the Bedingfeld ranch survived the gloomy days of that winter. By the end of 1909, besides having fifty acres in crops, Agnes and Frank Bedingfeld were running a hundred head of cattle and a hundred horses in their pastures.[66] In 1910, Frank married English-born Josephine Maitland, whom he had first met after returning from his second visit to the Yukon.[67] Frank and Josephine Bedingfeld then took over the reins at the ranch.

During the first half of 1911, Agnes Bedingfeld, now aged sixty-five, moved to Calgary, where she resided in a house she had purchased from William G. Hunt for $10,500.[68] During World War I, Agnes was still living in the city, and some of her income came from moneylending. In September 1916, she lent $1,600 to James A. Ferguson, a commercial traveller based in Calgary. The three-year loan carried an annual interest rate of 8 percent.[69]

The ranch at Pekisko, where a hundred horses and a hundred head of cattle were still grazing in 1915, flourished during the war.[70] Frank and Josephine Bedingfeld were making money, especially from the sale of horses to the army.[71] But the Bedingfelds also found their lives disrupted by the war, the last two years of which saw Frank serving as an ambulance driver overseas while Josephine ran the ranch at home. Returning to Pekisko after the conflict in poor health, Frank was unable to continue in the ranching business.[72] In October 1919, he sold the ranch to Edward, Prince of Wales, who operated it as the E. P. Ranch.[73] "Recalling a recent visit to the Bedingfeld Ranch and the impression made on us, we can to some extent appreciate the Prince's decision, for it is naturally one of the finest locations in the country. At that time a profusion of flowers and shrubs surrounded the ranch house and the deep green of the grain fields made it a beauty spot long to be remembered," wrote the *High River Times*.[74] "This fine property carried with it about four hundred or five hundred extra well bred Clydesdale horses, which have been bred on this ranch for over thirty years. They have also a nice bunch of range cattle numbering approximately one hundred and fifty to two hundred head," added the newspaper.[75]

Chapter 11: Women in Business

Like Agnes Bedingfeld, who had gone back to England by this time, Frank soon returned to his native country, taking his wife and their daughter Josephine Mabel with him.[76] Spending his last days in a nursing home in Hertfordshire, Frank died in 1920.[77] Agnes Bedingfield also died in England. Agnes's granddaughter, Josephine Mabel, married Alberta-born rancher Richard W. Gardner in 1939 in Redburn, Hertfordshire and returned with him to the Mount Sentinel Ranch, nine miles south of the E. P. Ranch.

In some respects, Agnes Bedingfeld's story is nothing less than the history of Bow Valley ranching itself. For more than two decades, her ranch was an important part of the small ranching scene in the region. It weathered the hard winter of 1886-1887, the economic depression in the mid-1890s, and the terrible winter of 1906-1907. Like other female ranchers such as Jessie H. Huggard, widow Margaret McDonald, and Ann Laycock in the Nose Creek district and widow Annie Dowling, Mary Reilly, and widow Margaret Moore in the Priddis area, and like countless male ranchers across the Bow Valley, Agnes Bedingfeld developed a small-scale ranch.[78] Although these female and male ranchers did not roll up fabulous fortunes, they made effective use of scarce capital. To the outside world, women ranchers often were invisible. But at home, they were recognized for performing significant ranching tasks and for operating as co-equals of men ranchers. Just as Agnes Bedingfeld ran her ranch while her son Frank was in the Yukon, so Sarah Gardner was in charge of the Mount Sentinel Ranch while her husband William C. Gardner, the ranch's founder and Richard's father, served overseas with the British Navy during World War I.[79]

Adela Cochrane

Mitford Entrepreneur

Like most businesses elsewhere in Canada, Bow Valley businesses were usually family enterprises in the late nineteenth century. Bow Valley business people relied heavily upon family members, who served in a variety of capacities. In many business ventures, wives played an important role, assisting their husbands and strengthening their families. Among such wives was Lady Adela C. Cochrane, whose husband Thomas depended increasingly upon her. Founders of Mitford, Thomas and Adela became possessed of a great vision of the hamlet's future. In defiance of the difficult approach to frontier Mitford that the Canadian Pacific Railway saw, the Cochranes found it a fine place on the Bow River west of Calgary surrounded by a beautiful expanse of grassland and forest. Creative entrepreneurs, they pioneered several new businesses in the Bow Valley.

Born in England, Lady Adela was the daughter of the Earl of Stradbroke. Adela married Thomas Belhaven Henry Cochrane, son of Admiral Sir Thomas Cochrane and a Lieutenant in the Royal Navy.[80] A woman of wealth and privilege, Adela conceived of herself as an entrepreneur who could join her husband in creating and developing business enterprises. Thomas and Adela Cochrane settled in the High River area in 1883. In 1884, they participated in organizing the Little Bow Cattle Company on Mosquito Creek, a ranch that ran cattle and horses on a 55,000-acre lease.[81] Thomas Cochrane obtained the lease from the Canadian government in his own name.[82] The actual shareholders in the company were Thomas Cochrane, Hugh Graham, Ted and Frank Jenkins, and Cochrane's cousin William "Billie" E. Cochrane. Billie Cochrane was the ranch's resident manager. This medium-sized new ranch required a great deal of capital. Adela, who probably had brought money into their marriage, helped Thomas meet his financial obligations. To develop the ranch, Thomas Cochrane borrowed $10,000 from the private bank Lafferty & Smith in mid-November 1885. Carrying an annual interest rate of 12 percent, the two-month loan was secured by the ranch's thousand head of cattle and sixty horses. Thomas Cochrane realized that reputation and image were important in obtaining funds to finance the ranch's operations. Like other ranchers, he needed to project a good image. He established a high credit rating at Lafferty & Smith by promptly repaying the entire loan on 8 January 1886.[83]

Adela Cochrane, c. 1890s, Mitford entrepreneur. (Courtesy of Glenbow Archives, NA-18-11).

Because of the severe winter of 1886-1887, however, the Little Bow Cattle Company suffered large cattle losses. Ted and Frank Jenkins dropped out of the company, leaving Thomas Cochrane, Hugh Graham, and Billie Cochrane to rebuild the cattle herd.[84] These three remaining partners had equal investments in the ranch.[85] By the end of 1887, the company's financial statement revealed a surplus of $50,000. This fine showing allowed the partners to borrow $1,000 from the Imperial Bank of Canada's Calgary branch to help finance the expansion of their ranch on Mosquito Creek.[86] Throughout this early stage of the ranch's growth, Adela worked closely with Thomas, providing him with additional capital and thereby making their business more financially viable.

Thomas and Adela Cochrane, meanwhile, became involved in lumber and other businesses outside the Little Bow Cattle Company. In 1885, they diversified into lumber production at Mitford on the Bow River and on the Canadian Pacific Railway's main line, twenty-six miles west of Calgary. Originally, the place was named Saw Mill, but Adela changed that. As time passed, it was called Mitford after Adela's niece in England, Mrs. Percy Mitford, the first Earl of Egerton's sister.[87] "We quite agree with you," Adela wrote Canadian Pacific vice-president William C. Van Horne,

> ... that Saw Mill is not a pretty name. I think that if this place were called Mitford it would be much better. We have long been wishing to make a change, but as the name would be that of a great friend of ours I am now writing to England to ask if she has any objections. But as I am quite certain she will not refuse, don't you think we might start in at once and call this Mitford?[88]

Van Horne agreed.

In 1885, Thomas Cochrane set up the partnership Calgary Lumber Company to manufacture various kinds of lumber at Mitford.[89] Joining him as active partners were Hugh Graham; Frank White, a Mitford sheep rancher; Archibald W. McVittie, a Dominion land surveyor in Calgary; and Andrew Henderson, a Calgary medical doctor. Vigorous efforts on the part of Thomas Cochrane to raise operating funds were successful. At the beginning of December 1885, he secured a $10,000 loan from Lafferty & Smith, using the Calgary Lumber Company's sawmill and its

Chapter 11: Women in Business

leasehold interests in Dominion timber lands, covering thirty-three square miles in the Grand Valley and on Dog Pound Creek, as collateral.[90] The company's mortgage to Lafferty & Smith was paid off on 15 March 1886. Thomas Cochrane derived additional support for the founding of the Calgary Lumber Company from family fortunes and friends. His wife Adela likely accounted for a significant part of the financing. All this helped the company to establish its credit.

The Calgary Lumber Company began operations at its sawmill in Mitford in the spring of 1886.[91] Located near the Canadian Pacific's main line and on the north side of the Bow River in the SE¼, section 8, township 26, range 4, west of the fifth meridian, the sawmill site provided the firm with the space and water needed to start work.[92] The company cut timber in the Grand Valley and on Dog Pound Creek which was then hauled to the sawmill by its own short railway. Before long, fifty men, each paid from $20 to $30 a month, toiled at the sawmill, manufacturing lumber which was carried by the company's horse-drawn wagons to the Canadian Pacific and shipped to Calgary and other centres on the line.[93] Thomas and Adela Cochrane constructed durable, well-insulated bunkhouses for the men.[94] By November 1886, Thomas Cochrane had purchased Frank White and Archibald McVittie's interest in the company.[95] Among the company's Bow Valley customers was the ranching firm Smith & More, owned and run by the Reverend E. Paske Smith and Bentley More.[96] Soon the Calgary Lumber Company became more aggressive in turning out and pushing its products.

But even as they expanded production at the sawmill, Lady Adela and Thomas Cochrane had reason to expect that the next few years would be a rough ride. The Calgary Lumber Company did not keep up with its counterparts in Calgary, the Eau Claire & Bow River Lumber Co. and the Bow River Mills, in producing lumber. It was not that the Calgary Lumber Company failed to manufacture quality lumber, but it did not have as desirable a location as did its competitors. Although Mitford had a railway connection to regional and national markets for finished goods, it was able to secure only a Canadian Pacific flag station partly because of the arduous approach to the hamlet. Initially, William C. Van Horne was inclined to grant Thomas and Adela Cochrane's request for a full-fledged station where the line would provide scheduled service. "I think the enterprise" Thomas Cochrane "has shown" at Mitford "deserves

Chapter 11: Women in Business

recognition to the extent of giving him the station.... A considerable industry has developed" there "through Mr. Cochrane's enterprise," Van Horne told William Whyte, general superintendent of the Canadian Pacific's western division, in May 1888.[97] But Whyte's emphasis on the lack of a good approach for the railway to Mitford ultimately changed Van Horne's mind. "There are draw backs to making Mitford a regular station as it stands on a grade. The line rises east from Mitford for the distance of a mile on a 34-foot grade," Whyte wrote Van Horne.[98] In addition, the Mitford area did not have abundant timber resources.

To complicate matters, the Calgary Lumber Company did not have enough capital to carry on its business, a situation that led Thomas Cochrane to take the initiative in transforming the partnership into a North West Territories-chartered corporation, the Calgary Lumber Company, in August 1887. Capitalized at $85,000, the company had three stockholders: Thomas Cochrane, Hugh Graham, and Billie Cochrane.[99] With its promise of limited liability to investors, the corporate form of organization potentially became a means to obtain more capital. In fact, the capitalization of the new corporation was raised to $175,000 by the beginning of 1890. By this time, too, the stockholders had paid for all the shares.[100]

Even before the capitalization of the company was increased, Thomas and Adela Cochrane had worked hard to build up Mitford as a hamlet. By mid-1888, they had erected a general store, a hotel, and a livery stable. Over the next year, they opened a post office, while a medical doctor came to the hamlet to set up his practice and construct a drug store.[101] The Cochranes themselves lived in a "nice little house," said Mrs. Algernon St. Maur, their friend from England who visited them in the summer of 1888.[102] Adela and Thomas Cochrane had a number of ponies and horses, possessed two cows and two pigs, raised chickens, and grew vegetables such as cabbages, lettuce, carrots, beans, cauliflower, and beets in the rich soil in their garden.[103] Thomas and Adela Cochrane emerge from Mrs. St. Maur's chronicle of events as energetic, enterprising, and responsible people. Natural leaders, they made their home a resort for men and women in trouble or in need of company. Adela performed tasks like planting the garden and looking after the poultry, while Thomas did other jobs around the home such as building a garden fence and erecting a new hen house.

In the Mitford area, as in other parts of the Bow Valley, ownership of land really mattered. Like most other settlers in the community, the Cochranes became landowners, with Thomas filing claim to a 160-acre homestead: the SW¼ in section 4, township 26, range 4, west of the fifth meridian, and Adela purchasing 160 acres: the NE¼ in section 5.[104] Thomas, together with his friend from England the Earl of Norbury, bought additional land, sections 8 and 19. The Cochranes used the land, especially section 8 as well as Adela's quarter and Thomas's homestead, to establish the Calgary Lumber Company in the lumber trade, to build a home and graze their horses, ponies, and cows, and to develop the hamlet of Mitford. The lands backing onto Mitford and nearby creeks made perfect ranches, where ranchers such as William D. Kerfoot helped to create a rural neighbourhood and shared work with the Cochranes as owners of livestock.[105] Adela and Thomas Cochrane and Kerfoot understood that they were part of a common neighbourhood, and they exchanged work in breaking horses and ponies.

Careful not to make themselves too dependent on the lumber market, Thomas and Adela Cochrane began manufacturing bricks at Mitford in the late 1880s. More importantly, they diversified into coal mining at the hamlet. In mid-1888, they purchased a local coal mine from J. W. Vaughan and soon formed the Canada North-West Coal & Lumber Co.[106] Thomas Cochrane was the new company's managing director. By July 1890, the company had expanded its coal mining operations to Canmore, where the quality of coal was much better.[107] In Calgary, the company sold its Canmore coal to customers at $5.50 a ton.[108] The firm also was able to sell a fair amount of coal to the Canadian Pacific. Fortunately for Adela and Thomas Cochrane, the expansion of the company's operations at Canmore brought more coal sales to the railway. "I am very glad that you are increasing your output of coal at Canmore. I have no doubt the [Canadian Pacific] Company will be able to take about all you can turn out if the prices are satisfactory," Van Horne, by now the railway's president, told Thomas Cochrane.[109]

But for the patience of the banks Thomas and Lady Adela Cochrane might have lost their company and much more. As part of the financing for the old firm, the Calgary Lumber Company, Thomas had borrowed $3,752 from the Bank of Montreal's Calgary branch. In June 1891, this debt had still not been repaid.[110] A year later, Thomas and Adela Cochrane personally and individually endorsed the notes of the Canada North-West Coal & Lumber

Chapter 11: Women in Business

Co. to the Imperial Bank of Canada's Calgary branch to a total of $4,700, a move that helped the company reestablish its credit.[111]

Adela helped manage their finances and was resourceful. She also provided entrepreneurial direction, raising funds in England for their business enterprises. Thomas often ran out of money, and without Adela's financial resources, they would not have been able to meet their obligations. Adela managed their businesses during Thomas's trips to England. They frequently mentioned each other in their letters to Van Horne. Adela met Thomas on equal ground as a friend and confidant. Their ideal hamlet was the kind they imagined Mitford would be with a regular Canadian Pacific station, a place that would attract more businesses and grow into a town. Under their leadership, a school was erected in the community, to serve the families in the hamlet as well as the ranching families in the surrounding area. As members of the Church of England, Adela and Thomas built All Saints' Anglican Church complete with a churchyard as a burial place in Mitford in 1892. The church received various gifts, "including a fine linen cloth, worked with gold lace, valued at $500, the gift of Adela Cochrane, and a communion set, offered by Mrs. Mitford," wrote the *Calgary Tribune*.[112]

As a shareholder in the Canadian Pacific, Lady Adela Cochrane continued to press the railway's officers to upgrade the flag station at the hamlet to a regular station. In May 1893, she arrived in Montreal from England and immediately went to Van Horne's office. Learning from his secretary that he was out of town, Adela wrote to him from the railway's Windsor Hotel before leaving for Mitford by train: "When in England I talked over with Lord Mount Stephen," the Canadian Pacific's first president and still a director, "the possibilities of a station at Mitford, & he most kindly offered to write to you on the subject. Naturally if you find it practicable I shall consider it a personal as well as general benefit to that part of the world. As you know I am building a bridge across the Bow River at Mitford, & as a shareholder in the C.P.R., it seems to me that the placing of a station there would materially help local business on the railway to a large degree by the traffic North & South of that District."[113] Van Horne himself had already visited Mitford, but what he had seen there in regard to the difficult approach for the Canadian Pacific did not make Adela's ideas about the place and her concept of a regular station come alive for him. Instead, he continued to favour the development of the railway's regular station three miles to the east, at Cochrane, which the railway could enter easily and where the flourishing cattle trade guaranteed it more business.

Van Horne, nevertheless, continued to maintain the flag station at Mitford, thereby contributing to the survival of Adela and Thomas Cochrane's lumber, coal, and brick enterprises at the hamlet, at least for the time being. Between May 1892 and April 1893, the large bulk of the Canadian Pacific's considerable freight business at Mitford consisted of the ties the railway purchased from the Cochranes. Other important freight that came from Thomas and Adela Cochrane at the hamlet included coal, bricks, wood, and fence posts.[114] Opportunities for the sale of the Canada North-West Coal & Lumber Co.'s products became more abundant as the Cochranes appointed agents across the Canadian West: Stanley Mitchell in Calgary; W. F. Buchanan in Winnipeg; Smith & Ferguson Co. in Regina; and J. M. Buxton in Vancouver.[115] But the Canada North-West Coal & Lumber Co.'s coal mine project at Mitford proved a costly business disappointment. The coal was not satisfactory for use in the Canadian Pacific's locomotives. Although a substantial lumber manufacturer, the lumber company was not an especially successful business.

Despite the disappointment with the coal and lumber business at Mitford, Thomas and Adela Cochrane pursued the ranching business on Mosquito Creek full force. Perhaps they hoped that the development of the Little Bow Cattle Co. would offset the problems at Mitford in the last half of the 1880s and the 1890s. They certainly wanted to make profits quickly in their Mosquito Creek ranching venture, which was still managed by Billie Cochrane. Their hopes were only partly realized. Although Thomas Cochrane had relinquished the 55,000-acre lease in May 1888, the Little Bow Cattle Co. had acquired enough land on Mosquito Creek to continue its substantial operations.[116] In 1890, there were eight hundred head of cattle and forty horses grazing in the company's pastures.[117] By blending Galloways and Herefords, Billie Cochrane was able to produce high-quality cattle.[118] But constructing irrigation ditches on the ranch, during the dry years between the late 1880s and mid-1890s, proved more difficult than had been anticipated.[119] At times, the lack of capital hindered progress. The $4,000 loan Thomas Cochrane secured from the Imperial Bank of Canada's Calgary branch in October 1896 helped ease the situation for the Little Bow Cattle Co.[120] As a founding member of the Western

Stock Growers' Association, Thomas Cochrane looked to this organization as one way to bolster cattle prices and stabilize the company's business.[121] But ongoing difficulties at Mitford led Adela and Thomas Cochrane to sell all their business enterprises at the hamlet and return to England in the late 1890s.[122] Thomas became the Isle of Wight's deputy governor, a position Lady Adela helped him obtain.[123] By this time, the Little Bow Cattle Co. had one thousand head of cattle and thirty horses, and its operations were profitable, more so than the Cochranes' ventures at Mitford, a hamlet that soon faded.[124]

Agnes Carroll and the Holy Cross Hospital

On 30 January 1891, a nurse named Agnes Carroll arrived in Calgary, eager to establish the Holy Cross Hospital. Carroll was a harbinger of the coming of organized health care to the town, a development that gave the place its second hospital. An opportunity to help organize health care prompted local business people to donate money to the institution. Carroll's arrival in Calgary was a significant event in the town's business history because she combined the education and managerial skills that were needed to found and maintain a hospital.

Born in 1854 in Birr, County Offaly, Ireland, Agnes Margaret Carroll was educated in a local school. After moving to Montreal, Carroll studied the French language in a school there, became fluent in French, and exemplified the social ties bilingual people built between English-speaking and French-speaking cultures. In 1871, she entered the order of the Sisters of Charity of the General Hospital in Montreal, commonly called the Grey Nuns. Agnes Carroll professed in 1874, and in the next year the Grey Nuns, a well-established charitable and hospital order, sent her to work in the Roman Catholic mission in Lac La Biche, Alberta. In September 1890, she returned to Montreal to receive instructions from Mother Superior of the General Hospital to open a hospital in Calgary. At this time, Mother Superior appointed Agnes Carroll as Superior of the Holy Cross Hospital in the town.[125]

There is in the life of any important institution a moment when it becomes conscious of its special place in history. For the Holy Cross Hospital, that moment was 2:30 a.m., 30 January 1891.[126] In that early morning hour, Sister Agnes Carroll, aged thirty-six, and three

Chapter 11: Women in Business

Agnes Carroll, c. 1890s, founder of the Holy Cross Hospital. (Courtesy of Glenbow Archives, NA-2900-3).

other Grey Nuns stepped down from the train into the extremely cold air in Calgary to begin the hospital project. As Superior of the hospital, Carroll played a key role not only in the medical and spiritual life of the institution, but also served as its business manager. In the day-to-day conduct of the Holy Cross Hospital's business affairs, she managed its finances and supervised its nursing staff under the direction of Mother Superior in Montreal. Carroll received hospital revenues, paid the bills, and made a cash book of all transactions a tool of managerial control. In her letters to Mother Superior, she reported financial transactions, described the care of the ill, and commented on the relationship between the hospital and the people in Calgary and the surrounding area.

After finding a temporary room in the Sacred Heart Convent in Calgary's Roman Catholic Mission District, Agnes Carroll witnessed the construction of the Holy Cross Hospital in this district. Writing to Mother Superior, she said that

> ... after a few hours rest, we arose, took a good dinner which had been prepared by the kind Sisters, and then went to visit our *hospital*. On entering our future residence a feeling of dismay came over me, and I had to use great efforts to restrain my tears – A house 2 stories high, and 20 feet square, separated by a partition in the middle, neither lathed nor plastered, with chinks and holes in every corner, through which the cold wind blew freely. There was only one small stove which was hardly sufficient to heat the apartment where the men were working.... [There were] six iron bedsteads, some old dirty looking mattresses, three old washing stands which needed a good scrubbing, and other bedroom necessities, all second hand articles purchased at an auction.... If the trial of beginning in such a house seemed

too hard for the Grey Nuns who are so rich now, I manifested my surprise that the house was not more advanced.[127]

But Agnes Carroll immediately set a remarkable example in leadership, behaviour, and loyalty. A woman sensitive to the needs of other people, she treated the small group of Grey Nuns working under her supervision with respect. Carroll praised the accomplishments of Sisters Olivia Beauchemin, Elizabeth Valiquette, and Madeleine Beemer Gertrude, set high standards for health care, and built an esprit de corps. "Seeing there was no remedy for our present position," Carroll told Mother Superior,

> ... we set to work at once, put up 4 beds, washed the old furniture which was indispensable, and placed all in one side of the upper story which we call *a dormitory*.... We got up a cooking stove on Saturday, so we were able to prepare a frugal supper in our own home.... I have already become acquainted with some of the principal ladies in town, and these have sent donations – blankets, quilts, towels, etc. We will certainly have to suffer for some time but there are good prospects for the future.[128]

In early April 1891, about half a year after the General Hospital was established in Calgary, the first patient was admitted to the Holy Cross Hospital.[129] The new Holy Cross Hospital was a public, non-sectarian hospital from the start. Most patients were expected to pay for the care they received. But as a charitable institution, the hospital also cared for the sick poor without demanding payment for its services. "We have to admit some from whom we cannot expect any retribution on account of their poverty, but I have never reason to regret an act of charity of this kind," Agnes Carroll wrote Mother Superior. In mid-October 1891 Carroll reported that

> I have spent $200.00 to get water in, to have the sick rooms ventilated, to have a veranda, porch, and fence put up. I am now getting a water closet for the sick, and double windows for the front part of the house which is towards the North, so very cold. These will cost a good sum of money, I know, but they are indispensable.[130]

Chapter 11: Women in Business

Holy Cross Hospital on the Elbow River as it appeared on a postcard, c. early 1900s. (Courtesy of Glenbow Archives, NA-4092-1).

By the end of October, the hospital had cared for a total of fifty-six patients. The problem was that those known as paying patients sometimes neglected to meet their obligations. This led to cash shortages at the Holy Cross Hospital. "It is sometimes very hard to get paid. All sorts of fine promises are made when a patient enters the hospital, but after recovery they seem to forget to pay their expenses. Then I have to write, solicit, urge for payment," said Agnes Carroll.[131]

Because of the shortage of money to run the Holy Cross Hospital, Sister Carroll often seized opportunities to raise funds. In doing so, she became an effective fund-raiser, using her entrepreneurial skills to promote the hospital. Friends and the congregation of St. Patrick's Parish in Montreal had given the hospital $209.75, but after paying for the train fares for herself and the other three Grey Nuns, Carroll had only $73.75 left when they arrived in Calgary. So, in addition to collecting $300 from Canadian Pacific construction workers as she travelled along the railway's branch line between Calgary and Edmonton, Carroll canvassed the area from Calgary to Fort Macleod and Pincher Creek for donations to the Holy Cross Hospital.[132] She could look upon her accomplishments at the end of November 1891 with satisfaction. "When I consider the state of our affairs," Carroll told Mother Superior, "I am filled with hopes for the future. We have $700.00 on hand, over a hundred due to the hospital, no debts, and besides I have spent 250 getting

Chapter 11: Women in Business

indispensable improvements made on this house."[133]

Plans to construct a new hospital dominated Agnes Carroll's thoughts as the year 1891 drew to a close. Her willingness to oversee the building project served the Holy Cross Hospital well. Carroll's efforts to secure the co-operation of Calgary's Protestant medical doctors also proved successful. "If the Protestant doctors continue to patronize our hospital as they have done up to the present," Carroll wrote Mother Superior, "I think we can hope. If we were dependent exclusively on Catholics, we would not have many paying patients to register."[134] The new Holy Cross Hospital, a three-storey stone and brick structure complete with plumbing, hot and cold running water, baths, an operating room, up-to-date medical equipment, electricity, telephone, and accommodation for twenty-five to thirty patients, opened its doors in November 1892 on Hamilton Street, between Doucet and Rouleau avenues, in the Roman Catholic Mission District.[135] Located just west of the Elbow River, the site, chosen by Agnes Carroll, gave the hospital the space needed to provide medical services. "Everything about the hospital," reported the *Calgary Herald*, "is very clean and the rooms present a particularly bright appearance."[136] A Calgary resident wrote that "the location is perfect for hospital purposes, being especially favored with pure air and fresh breezes."[137] To finance the construction of the hospital, Carroll borrowed $6,000 from the Grey Nuns' Mother House in Montreal and used generous donations from Calgarians and from Sister Devins, a Montreal Grey Nun whose deceased brother, R. J. Devins, had left the hospital a large sum of money, as well as a grant of $75 from the Northwest Territories Executive Council.[138] Working day and night to make sure that everything was protected adequately, Carroll took out an insurance policy on the hospital.[139]

Agnes Carroll and her colleagues learned how to combat the spread of highly infectious diseases in Calgary. During the smallpox epidemic in the town in the summer of 1892, isolation procedures in makeshift quarters on Nose Creek staffed by Sisters Beauchemin and Valiquette helped save lives. In August 1893, during the outbreak of diphtheria, Carroll and the other Grey Nuns gave up their own rooms on the new hospital's second floor to establish a contagious disease unit there, and lived on the unfinished third floor while caring for diphtheria patients as well as other patients.[140]

The economic depression in the mid-1890s deeply affected the Holy Cross Hospital. As local businesses suffered from the downturn in the economy, Carroll found it more difficult to raise funds for the institution among potential donors in Calgary. "We hear of failures and insolvencies every day. There seems to be no money in the country, and no employment for the laborer," Carroll told Mother Superior.[141] The hospital, nevertheless, continued to receive donations from Calgarians, including lawyer C. C. McCaul, a recent patient who wrote to Sister Carroll:

> I only returned from Macleod yesterday when I found your memorandum of my indebtedness to the Hospital awaiting me. I enclose you my cheque for the amount, to which I have added $5.00 – the sinner's mite – as a small contribution to the good work you and the Sisters with you are doing.[142]

Carroll's budget in the Holy Cross Hospital remained tight, however. Her problem was not unusual. Calgary's General Hospital also was hard hit by the depression. Some relief for the Holy Cross Hospital came when it received a grant of $500 from the federal government to help meet the cost of providing care for poor immigrant patients.[143]

Despite its successful weathering of the depression, the Holy Cross Hospital remained cash-strapped. Agnes Carroll saw no alternative but to continue to raise funds through donations. Considerable economic recovery in the late 1890s brought more contributions from people in Calgary, some of the largest gifts coming from men such as Pat Burns. On 30 December 1899, Burns wrote to Sister Carroll:

> I beg to hand you herewith a contribution toward your Hospital which I trust you will accept with my best wishes for yourself and co-workers. Also with the hope that the coming new year will be a happy one for you and be crowned with success in your work.[144]

The donation from Pat Burns consisted of a cheque for $100.

Between 1900 and 1907, the year she rose to become Mother

Vicar, in charge of all Grey Nuns' institutions in Alberta as well as some in northern Saskatchewan, Agnes Carroll continued to build services of high caliber at the Holy Cross Hospital in Calgary.[145] She distinguished herself by developing a modern health program, complete with a school, begun in 1899, to train Grey Nuns to become nurses. Her humanity and kindness toward patients, nurses, students, and doctors were matched by her broad knowledge of medicine, her insightful analyses of financial problems related to enlarging and maintaining the hospital, and her method of driving home a point with a touch of appropriate humour.[146] Partly because she set a pattern of ability and devotion, the hospital's services worked effectively. Agnes Carroll was closely linked with laying the foundation for the opening of the Holy Cross School of Nursing in 1907. In the fall of that year, she stepped down as Superior of the hospital. As medical head of the institution and as its business manager, Carroll was a tremendous success by any standard of measurement.

Annie and Jean Mollison and Braemar Lodge

The growth of Calgary at the turn of the century provided new opportunities for capitalists to start hotel enterprises. Some became experts in hosting the travelling public as well as in finance. Notable among these entrepreneurs were two sisters, Annie and Jean Mollison, who founded what would become one of the city's leading hotels in the early twentieth century: Braemar Lodge.

Born in Inverness, Scotland, Annie and Jean Mollison moved to the Canadian West with their father, two brothers, and two sisters in the late 1880s. Their father, James W. Mollison, who learned the farming business as manager of the Elgin Estates in Scotland, became general manager of Sir John Lister Kaye's farms in Alberta and Assiniboia. In 1889, James Mollison acquired a ranch on Willow Creek in the Fort Macleod area, which he operated for a number of years with the help of his sons and daughters. After assisting their father on the ranch called The Willows for some time, Jean and Annie worked for the Canadian Pacific Railway, managing its mountain hotels in Banff, Laggan (later Lake Louise), and Field.[147] Earlier, back in Inverness, Scotland, their father had spent liberally on their education, recognizing that they had inherited his business instincts.

Chapter 11: Women in Business

Braemar Lodge, founded by Annie and Jean Mollison, as it appeared on a postcard, c. 1910. (Courtesy of Glenbow Archives, NA-3506-8).

In 1904, Annie and Jean Mollison, unmarried and needing a broader outlet for their creative and managerial talents, opened Braemar Lodge at 215 – 4th Avenue S.W. in Calgary. The building they had secured for their hotel had been built in 1892 by Daniel Webster Marsh for Anglican Bishop Cyprian Pinkham.[148] Used by Pinkham as a residence for himself and his family, the handsome structure, designed from plans by a New York City architect and measuring fifty by fifty feet, had five rooms on the ground floor and eight bedrooms, as well as other rooms on the second floor and in the attic, all quite spacious, with high ceilings and well lit and ventilated. Amenities in the house included baths and plumbing. In the interval, the building had passed into the hands of Marsh, who now sold it to the Mollison sisters for $8,500, with Annie and Jean each having a 50 percent interest in it.[149] Annie was manager of Braemar Lodge and Jean assisted her in running it.

Braemar Lodge was a hotel located in downtown Calgary, not far from the Canadian Pacific station. Symbolizing the height of the city's social sophistication, it anchored Calgary's fashionable 4th Avenue. Adjacent to Braemar Lodge stood Daniel Webster Marsh's splendid home.[150] Constructed on expensive land, the hotel reflected Calgary's growing prosperity and self-confidence. In the early 1900s, downtown hotels like Jean and Annie Mollison's Braemar

Chapter 11: Women in Business

Lodge dominated the city's lodging industry. Their diligence, sound management, and reputation for cleanliness and cordial hospitality won them acceptance among those business people responsible for Calgary's vigorous economic development.

Conscious of the need to excel, the Mollison sisters soon decided to upgrade their hotel. In 1906, they enlarged and remodeled Braemar Lodge, making it a grander structure at a cost of $25,000. The building contractor selected for the project was Thomas McCaffery.[151] With its attractive stone and brick façade, the reconstructed three-storey hotel was quickly recognized as a landmark in downtown Calgary. The careful attention paid to the outward appearance of the building was also given to its interior. Jean and Annie Mollison wanted a hotel that would provide the most up-to-date facilities for lodging and include the most comfortable accommodation available. Intelligent investment and excellent service were the hallmarks of these two hotel entrepreneurs.

To finance the construction project and the acquisition of new furnishings for Braemar Lodge, Annie and Jean Mollison secured a $30,000 loan from the Imperial Bank of Canada's Calgary branch, using the hotel and their interest in The Willows Ranch at Fort Macleod as collateral. They were well connected to Calgary's business leaders, especially William Roper Hull and Pat Burns, who agreed to endorse their notes to the bank in February 1906.[152] The Mollison sisters' ability to mobilize these funds obviously derived in part from their interest in The Willows Ranch, which they had inherited from their father, who had died in October 1905.[153] James W. Mollison had his own ideas about what constituted a good business, and he was happy with the way his daughters were running Braemar Lodge. He also showed his confidence in them by making them the executrixes of his will.[154] For some time prior to his death, he lived with them in Braemar Lodge. For Annie and Jean, there were last things to be done, and they cared for their father, who was in poor health during his stay with them.[155]

Jean and Annie Mollison worked hard to develop a distinctive personality for their hotel. Braemar Lodge focused on the upscale segment of the hospitality market. It featured well-groomed grounds, hitching posts, a spacious lobby, immaculate, bright rooms, comfortable mattresses, baths, and a restaurant, among other things.[156] From the beginning, the image of respectability was fundamental. The hotel appealed to value-conscious customers, especially business and leisure travellers, both men and women, Bow Valley ranchers, and government officials.

Under the Mollison sisters' management, guest accommodations and food services at the hotel were presented with extraordinary quality and panache to lodgers. Through positive word-of-mouth communications, the flow of travellers to the hotel gradually increased. It thrived on rising passenger rail traffic. Between late 1906 and mid-1907, guests at Braemar Lodge included Alfred E. Whiffen from Medicine Hat; W. H. Rowley, president of the E. B. Eddy Co. and brother of C. W. Rowley, manager of the Canadian Bank of Commerce's Calgary branch; R. E. Speakman from Doddington, Cheshire, England; Mrs. Grogan from Port-of-Spain, Trinidad; T. L. Beiseker from Fessenden, North Dakota; Isaac K. Kerr and his wife from Eau Claire, Wisconsin; Miss E. E. Babcock from Vancouver; G. E. Goddard, manager of the Bow River Horse Ranch; Mrs. and W. C. A. Hamilton from Montreal; and William Saunders, director of the Experimental Farms Branch of the Dominion Department of Agriculture in Ottawa.[157] Certainly, Braemar Lodge catered to both male and female tastes.

The success of Braemar Lodge encouraged the Mollison sisters to continue to pursue their dream of transforming their hotel into a superior product. Invariably, lodgers were looking for convenience and comfort, and Annie and Jean sought to offer these qualities in the most efficient manner. To finance further development, they borrowed $25,000 from Richard Gregg, a gentleman in Davenport, England, in November 1907.[158] The following month, they obtained an $8,000 loan from William Roper Hull and Pat Burns, who had relatively large sums of cash available for lending. Both loans carried an annual interest rate of 9 percent. Because Jean and Annie Mollison were usually prompt in repaying their debts, credit remained available to them.

Around this time, Jean moved to Vancouver, while Annie continued to reside in Calgary managing Braemar Lodge. Both remained owners of the hotel, but they needed bank credit to operate effectively. More than two years later, in January 1910, the Mollison sisters secured a $15,000 loan from the Canadian Bank of Commerce's Calgary branch against the hotel for improving the facility. William Roper Hull and Pat Burns endorsed their notes to the bank.[159] Braemar Lodge's owners, like those of other local hotels such as the Alberta, "are efficient hosts and aid their patrons all they can," wrote the *Albertan* in 1911.[160] In December 1914, Jean Mollison sold her entire interest in Braemar Lodge to Annie. The value of the sixty-eight-room hotel and the land on which it stood was now $30,750.[161] As sole owner-manager, Annie Mollison displayed the persistence as well as the willingness to take risks that helped maintain the hotel for fifteen more years. In one respect, however, the next decade was somewhat bleak for Braemar Lodge, given the cash-flow problems it faced as a result of the coming of prohibition in 1915. A partial solution came within a year, when Annie Mollison transformed the establishment into a temperance hotel on a temporary basis, which allowed her to sell customers what was called temperance beer.[162] But the main targeted markets still were, and remained until Annie's death in 1929, business as well as leisure travellers who wanted a comfortable, functional room and a relaxing, secure environment.

Upon examination of the first twenty-five years of its history, when it was owned and managed first by Annie and Jean Mollison and then by Annie alone, Braemar Lodge stands out as one of the most important hotels in the history of Calgary's hospitality industry. During the decade before World War I, facing a rising demand for lodging from travellers crossing the nation by train, the city's hotel industry was ripe for well-organized and well-financed growth. In 1904, Annie and Jean Mollison, who were already experienced hotel managers, became tied into Calgary's world of money and marketing and accepted the challenge. For many years, they guaranteed every guest, including Agnes Bedingfeld, top-quality lodging and a superb restaurant.[163] Braemar Lodge's early history also has significance beyond the spheres of lodging and meals. Located two blocks north of the Grand Theatre, the hotel was a classic example of an enduring link between business and cultural development. Guests at Braemar Lodge, where Annie Mollison was recognized as a wonderful pianist and a collector of art and antique furniture, often enjoyed an evening at the theatre.[164]

In the economic arena, the late nineteenth and early twentieth centuries can be interpreted as a period when the Canadian dream of business achievement succeeded in the eyes of numerous dreamers in various walks of life in Calgary and the Bow Valley. It was the story of individual accomplishment and its triumph over obstacles, an ongoing theme of Canadian enterprise. In the city and the surrounding area, the process was far from an automatic one. How to obtain credit to finance their dreams became an overriding concern for many business people.

12

Financing the Canadian Dream

The Canadian Dream

The relatively high standard of living that many people in Calgary and the Bow Valley were able to achieve in the late nineteenth century owed much to Canadian democracy. The wealth of the city and its region was created by its people because they were free to work, save, and invest. They enjoyed the freedom to do these things because they and others in the nation believed in freedom. Although many individuals tried to avoid debt, there was general agreement that credit was frequently needed to secure the Canadian dream of a higher standard of living.

Even as people in Calgary and the Bow Valley sought upward mobility and economic security, they worked to obtain the funds required to gain these rewards. Though economic and social benefits derived from numerous sources, of key importance were savings and access to credit. The evolution of the financing of the Canadian dream of advancement occurred against the background of developments in the city and the surrounding area. Between the 1870s and 1890s, government and business leaders encouraged people to work hard to get ahead, thereby helping to shape conditions readily receptive to economic growth and prosperity. Calgary and the Bow Valley favoured rapid settlement for its effects on business, land values, and access to central Canadian markets. But for many people, especially the relatively weak and powerless, the economic depression of the mid-1890s brought an end to hopes for expected returns on investments in the city and its region. The

Chapter 12: Financing the Canadian Dream

depression, far from being unique to Calgary, revealed the city's links to the wider, battered national and international economies. Rather than receiving income from their investments, individuals in the city were suddenly faced with growing pressure to meet interest payments on debts incurred to finance improvements in their business enterprises. Even the fairly comfortable world that substantial companies had created in the late 1880s and early 1890s was shaken to its foundations by the depression. Some companies teetered on the brink of bankruptcy. Competition was more brutal, consumers were more demanding and choosier, and tough economic conditions squeezed profit margins. Overall, however, in the late nineteenth century the growing railway network combined with the increasing population movement to Calgary and the Bow Valley to speed the extension and integration of local, regional and national markets, the development of commercialized agriculture, the rise in land values, and the formation of capital.

Calgary and Bow Valley residents partook of the entrepreneurial spirit. In pursuing market forces, they embraced diversification, entering commerce, agriculture, manufacturing, and services. They thus established the kind of diversified economic base that was essential for the region's long-term prosperity. Raising the money needed for the development of their enterprises, urban and rural builders created the positive business climate that made Calgary and its region attractive.

Many businesses in the city and the country grew in strength, marrying efficiency and social responsibility. They provided stable, fairly well-paid jobs, supported charities, culture, and the arts, and in general shared the fruits of their success with the larger society. Institutions such as the Holy Cross Hospital and the General Hospital in Calgary often benefited from businesses' substantial contributions to local social-development programs.[1] Business enterprises frequently beautified their hometowns in the Bow Valley through the construction of handsome buildings. Calgary businessmen also helped create a more beautiful environment by encouraging the development of Island Park.[2] In the city and rural and small-town communities, business leaders not only sought to earn as large a profit as possible for themselves but also used their resources to pursue a variety of social goals.

Contrary to conventional wisdom, it is possible for individuals to have an important impact on history. James A. Lougheed – later Sir

Chapter 12: Financing the Canadian Dream

James A. Lougheed – Christina Kinnisten, Luey Dofoo, Samuel and Helen Shaw, Sandy Watson, Meopham Gardner, James C. Linton, William Hanson Boorne, James S. Mackie, and Ernest D. Adams are just a few individuals who helped shape the late nineteenth century in Calgary and the Bow Valley. They were visionaries with historic reach. The most significant measure of their influence was their contribution to modern prosperity, for they pioneered businesses that helped create the highest standard of living the city and its region had ever seen.

James A. Lougheed: Lawyer, Real Estate Entrepreneur, and Senator

James A. Lougheed – a pioneer of entrepreneurial capitalism and a personable, talented man who was born in 1854 in Brampton, Ontario, practised law briefly in Toronto, and by the late 1890s had become Calgary's most important lawyer – offers a good illustration of how lawyers financed the Canadian dream. When Lougheed began his career in Calgary in October 1883, its streets were prairie mud and the houses were wooden structures without sewers.[3] Operating on an increasingly larger scale as the years passed, he wanted as a lawyer and businessman not simply to get and spend, but to elevate Calgary to a city of power and significance. He also intended to transform it into a wonderful place to live. From the very beginning, he had a strong sense of public duty, demonstrated in his generous contributions to Calgary's charities and its cultural institutions. To him, giving meant more than the signing of a cheque when asked for help. Often he was an active force in the charitable and cultural institutions he supported. In January 1885, as a member and trustee of the Methodist Church in Calgary, he joined the other trustees in borrowing $400 from a local farmer to erect a church building and, like them, he personally accepted responsibility for repaying the loan.[4] In addition to providing financial support for the Calgary General Hospital and the Calgary volunteers in the Boer War, Lougheed played a major part in founding the Lyric Theatre in the city in 1905.[5]

As a young man in the 1880s and early 1890s, Lougheed was one of Calgary's leading land speculators, but in a way he also sought to check the town's acquisitive spirit, warning his clients against falling into the trap of overextending themselves in land speculation. Certainly, he was careful not to overextend himself in the land

Chapter 12: Financing the Canadian Dream

Sir James A. Lougheed, c. 1890s, who became a member of the Canadian Senate in 1889. (Courtesy of Glenbow Archives, NA-3232-7).

business. The main source of his relatively small income was his fledgling law practice. By serving as solicitor for the Canadian Pacific Railway and the Hudson's Bay Company in Calgary, he augmented his earnings. Like most small, struggling businesses, Lougheed's had to finance its initial growth through retained profits. Still considered a shaky venture in the mid-1880's, his law practice experienced difficulties in securing funds from outside sources. Only in the 1890s was his firm's financial base broadened through several substantial loans from the Hamilton, Ontario-based Canada Life Assurance Company.

Retained profits accounted for most of Lougheed's expansion. Five lots on Stephen Avenue, in what became downtown Calgary, were bought at $300 apiece with his firm's current income in 1883.[6] Whereas some people came to Calgary merely to gamble on rising land prices, Lougheed was interested in making permanent improvements on land he purchased and sold, adding to its value and increasing the attractiveness of the town. In 1884, earnings funded a new sixteen by twenty-four feet frame building for his law office on Stephen Avenue in the town's centre close to the Canadian Pacific station, as well as the acquisition of his small log house nearby, where he kept a cow and a horse.[7] In the same year, James Lougheed married Isabella "Belle" Hardisty, niece of Richard Hardisty and of Donald A. Smith of the Hudson's Bay Company. Before long, Lougheed's earnings allowed him to enlarge the house. Here, James and Belle began to raise a growing family, using some of their land for a garden. By the end of the decade, they had two sons; Clarence was born in 1885, and Norman arrived four years later. Family ties were reinforced by the business connection between James Lougheed and Belle's uncle, Richard Hardisty. For a while in the mid-1880s, Lougheed and Hardisty were apparently partners in a small cattle-ranching operation in the Calgary area.[8]

Growth in Lougheed's law firm occurred in January 1886,

when Peter McCarthy, a native of St. Catharines, Ontario, joined him as a partner.[9] Having met Lougheed before in Winnipeg, he was evidently invited into the firm to increase its capital. With McCarthy's arrival, the new partnership was styled Lougheed & McCarthy. Lougheed was thirty-two; McCarthy was forty-seven. Despite the difference in age, the partners divided equally the fees they received. Although McCarthy probably had more experience, he realized that Lougheed had established the firm. And so they agreed to divide the income from the law practice equally.[10]

In February of that year, Lougheed received his diploma as advocate in the Northwest Territories under a new ordinance, the first Calgary lawyer to obtain one.[11] Never did he have any doubts about his ability to perform the routine work of the office, such as writing deeds or drafting wills. He welcomed clients, listened to their complaints, and advised what he considered an appropriate course of action. Undeniably, he became an effective courtroom lawyer, demonstrating considerable skill as a cross-examiner.[12] He fully mastered the forms and procedures of litigation. In representing clients such as I. G. Baker & Co. in the Supreme Court of the Northwest Territories in Calgary, Lougheed made declarations that were models of clarity. By 1889, with Nicholas D. Beck having become a partner, the firm had evolved into Lougheed, McCarthy & Beck. But both McCarthy and Beck entered the partnership only in connection with Lougheed's law practice. Lougheed shrewdly kept his extensive real estate holdings segregated from his stake in the law firm.

Even in the late 1880s, Lougheed's method of financing the growth of his real estate business through retained profits persisted. The numerous additional lots he acquired in downtown Calgary were paid for mostly from his real estate earnings.[13] Mortgages on his lots in 1887, one for $1,500 to the Glasgow-based North British Canadian Investment Company and another for $1,100 to Matthew Dunn, a Calgary area rancher, provided almost the only source of funds, other than retained profits, available for Lougheed's real estate development needs.[14] As was typical of small businesses, Lougheed favoured a program of internally generated expansion. The rapid advance of land values helped some Calgary businessmen to become wealthy. By 1887, the total value of Lougheed's property in Calgary was $12,175; by 1889, its value had reached $75,000, making him one of the town's largest landowners.[15]

Chapter 12: Financing the Canadian Dream

By the summer of 1890, James Lougheed had enough money to complete the construction of the two-storey Lougheed Block on Stephen Avenue. "It ... is one of the handsomest suites of offices and stores in the town, composed entirely of sandstone quarried within a few miles of Calgary," wrote a reporter for *The Dominion Illustrated*.[16] In the Lougheed Block, Lougheed's law firm, the Canadian Agricultural, Coal and Colonization Company, Bown & Cayley's law firm, and H. J. Curley, an English-born architect and surveyor, occupied the offices. Lougheed demonstrated that a business block could be built and operated profitably.

Lougheed's income had already increased in 1889, when Senator Richard Hardisty was accidentally killed on a wagon in Saskatchewan and the Conservative James Lougheed was appointed by Prime Minister John A. Macdonald to the Canadian Senate seat left vacant by Hardisty's death. From the outset, Lougheed turned his Senate salary of $1,000 over to the firm Lougheed, McCarthy & Beck to aid it in its development. Lougheed actively participated in the work of the Senate in Ottawa for about three and a half months each year, the entire period during which Parliament met. But he spent much more time in his Calgary law office, carefully advising various corporate clients, in some of whose businesses he invested. In particular, he had an investment interest in the Calgary Gas & Water Works Company and the Herald Publishing Company, among others.[17] By spending the bulk of his time in his law office, he was in a better position to understand his clients' needs. He had a well-earned reputation as a superb corporate lawyer, for he often was able to advise his clients as to the most effective, least expensive, and most profitable way to pursue business opportunities.

In the beginning, Lougheed enjoyed cordial relations with McCarthy. Eventually, however, crosscurrents ruffled his relationship with McCarthy, whom he thought envious of his success in the real estate business. Every year Lougheed banked solid profits in land transactions. According to a later lawsuit, he had an unfailing knack of knowing who would help him in his career.[18] McCarthy became so embittered toward Lougheed that he accused him, quite unjustly, of wrongfully refusing to turn his Senate travel allowance of about $425 per annum over to their firm and of secretly profiting from a real estate deal in Calgary.

Contrary to McCarthy's allegation, there was nothing in the verbal agreement between the two partners that obligated Lougheed to pass on his Senate travel allowance to the firm. Although Lougheed had the benefit of a free Canadian Pacific pass as he journeyed by rail to and from Ottawa, his travel and living expenses together actually exceeded the travel allowance. As for the real estate deal, McCarthy could have audited it, for information on it was available in the partnership's books in the office. Lougheed's business connections with George C. Marsh, a local real estate agent, and A. E. Cross, owner of the A7 Ranch west of Nanton, helped to shape the deal. In November 1889, Lougheed used the partnership's name to borrow $2,500 from A. E. Cross's father, judge Alexander Cross in Montreal, to purchase three valuable lots in Calgary through Marsh. About a year later, Lougheed and Marsh sold these lots, each making a profit of $1,000. In the battle over money, Lougheed's partnership with McCarthy began to crumble and was dissolved in April 1893.[19]

Within a short time, however, Lougheed brought his life back under control. Even before parting company with McCarthy, he took a major step toward saving his law practice by taking George S. McCarter into the partnership.[20] From the start, the Lougheed & McCarter office on Stephen Avenue had numerous clients. The list included long-time clients such as the Canadian Pacific, the Hudson's Bay Company, and the Bank of Montreal, as well as new ones, such as the North British Canadian Investment Company, the Toronto-based Canada Permanent Loan & Savings Company, and the town of Calgary. But during the economic depression of the mid-1890s Lougheed did not make a great deal of money, even though he probably received one-half of the fees.

Back in 1891, however, his income, especially from real estate business, was so good that Lougheed and his family could afford to leave their crowded small house and move into their newly built sandstone mansion on the corner of Thirteenth Avenue and Ninth Street, south of the Canadian Pacific tracks.[21] Located on the southwestern edge of Calgary, Beaulieu, as it was called, was one of the most imposing private houses in the town. With a few other Calgarians of status and means, Lougheed had a magnificent home that stood on spacious grounds, soon to be laid out in walks and flower beds, all of which indicated a family of substance able to create a residential place of privilege. A man who loved open spaces, he chose the Thirteenth Avenue house for its large, high-ceilinged rooms, which included a billiard room in the basement, a drawing

Chapter 12: Financing the Canadian Dream

The Clarence Block on Stephen Avenue, c. 1890s, built by Sir James A. Lougheed in 1892 and named for his eldest son Clarence. (Courtesy of Glenbow Archives, NA-64-3).

room, and a dining room on the first floor, four bedrooms on the second floor, plus a sewing room and servants' rooms on the third floor, all lit with electricity. Behind the house, Lougheed built a stone stable. Thirty feet square and one and a half storeys high, it had two box stalls and one single stall for horses, as well as harness and carriage rooms and a hay loft. In their grand home, James and Belle Lougheed hosted the most-talked about parties in Calgary.

If there was merriment in the Lougheeds' house when they entertained guests, it also came from the playful moments they provided for their two infant sons, Clarence and Norman. Two years after they moved to Thirteenth Avenue, another son, Edgar, was born. Like Belle, James Lougheed could be a lively companion for their children. Both parents encouraged their sons' talents.

Driven by his faith in his family's and Calgary's future, Lougheed conceived a master plan for enterprise that would appear on Stephen Avenue, with sandstone business blocks named for his sons dotting the avenue – a vision he realized over a number of years. The Clarence Block was built in 1892, followed by the construction of the Norman Block in 1900.[22] Later, the Lougheed Block was renamed the Edgar Block. Each time James Lougheed erected a business block on Stephen Avenue, it opened more office space to business development, triggering economic growth in the city.

As always when inspired by the development ethos, Lougheed ran up bills that taxed even his large fortune. Rental income and retained earnings helped pay some of the bills. Measuring eighty by thirty feet, the Lougheed Block had tenants such as William Carroll's tailoring shop, W. H. Asselstine's jewellery store, J. B. Eshleman's musical instruments shop, W. E. Wing's photo studio, A. E. Waldon & Co.'s drugstore, and an Oddfellows Hall.[23] With a frontage of over a hundred feet, the two-storey Clarence Block also had a number of tenants.[24]

Chapter 12: Financing the Canadian Dream

But more than rental income and retained earnings were needed to meet Lougheed's expenditures. Mortgages on his property supplied a principal source of funds. Initially, much of the capital he required came from business friends. In October 1892, Lougheed borrowed $13,000 at a 6¾ percent annual interest rate from Nellie Graham, wife of John A. Graham, Winnipeg-based paymaster for the Canadian Pacific's western lines.[25] But by the end of the next two years, with the onset of the economic depression in the mid-1890s, no payments had been made on the original mortgage to Nellie Graham. At Lougheed's request, she extended the mortgage for another two years at 7 percent interest on the loan.[26] By 1897, the mortgage was paid off.

Compelled by the need for more capital to fund his real estate development, however, Lougheed modified the financing of his real estate projects. Retained profits continued to be a mainstay in the development of his financial base, but he increasingly obtained funds from outside sources, especially financial institutions, through mortgages on his Calgary property. After advancing Lougheed a substantial sum of money in September 1892, the Imperial Bank of Canada provided him with another sizeable loan three and a half years later.[27] In August 1895, Lougheed borrowed $13,000 from the Canada Life Assurance Company at a 6 percent annual interest rate.[28] Between 1896 and 1899, he continued to depend upon loans from the company, securing a total of $14,500, to take care of his real estate development needs.[29] In 1897, Lougheed raised additional operating funds for his real estate ventures through a $5,710 loan from the Bank of Montreal.[30]

As Calgary grew, so too did Lougheed's real estate business. In 1900, after the city had begun to recover from the economic depression, he erected the $20,000, two-storey Norman Block directly adjacent to the Clarence Block on Stephen Avenue. One of the largest tenants in the Norman Block was Glanville & Robertson, a small department store. By the end of 1900, Lougheed had also spent $25,000 in building two other sandstone blocks in the city, one for the Great West Saddlery and the other for the Union Bank of Canada.[31] Lougheed could well afford such moves, for the years 1899 and 1900 were ones of growth and profit. The market for business blocks was expanding, but Lougheed still needed money from outside sources, and in 1900 he obtained a $32,000 loan from the Waterloo, Ontario-based Mutual Life Assurance Company

Chapter 12: Financing the Canadian Dream

of Canada at five and one-eighth percent interest for real-estate development purposes.[32]

At about two-thirty on Christmas morning 1900, however, a tremendous fire swept through the Clarence Block and the Norman Block. Around ten minutes past two, George Robinson, manager of the Calgary Clothing Company store in the Clarence Block, heard a woman screaming in the block. Running into the hall, he found the building filled with smoke and immediately called the fire department. Within minutes, the fire engine arrived, but there was a delay in getting a big stream of water on the fire and soon the Clarence Block was in flames. "The firemen were working tooth and nail to prevent the flames from spreading to the Norman Block," a reporter for the *Calgary Herald* wrote, but a high wind swiftly carried them forward. With their walls made of heavy stone, Lougheed's buildings seemed invulnerable. But in less than an hour, the flames turned them into raging furnaces. "Eventually towards the morning the fire was got in hand but, not until [the Clarence Block] was in ruins and [the Norman Block] gutted."[33]

The tenants, including the Calgary Clothing Company, Watt & Co.'s tobacco store, and the Alberta Music Company, sustained large losses, and a number of people were left homeless. But the disaster fell most heavily on James A. Lougheed. The next morning, he was up at daybreak inspecting what remained of his properties. His business blocks worth $50,000 were destroyed; insurance covered two-thirds of this amount. In the Clarence Block, Lougheed's valuable law library and office furnishings and business records were reduced to ashes. But "Senator Lougheed ... is taking the most philosophical view of the situation possible," observed the *Calgary Herald* reporter. "The Senator is not discouraged. [He will] start building operations almost immediately."[34] Before long, the Clarence Block and the Norman Block were rebuilt and were again providing much-needed space for businesses and other tenants.

Encouraged by the endorsements he received from friends such as the *Calgary Herald* reporter, Lougheed planned to continue building his real estate business while, at the same time, nurturing his law practice with his new partner of four years, R. B. Bennett, and pursuing his Senate career. All three elements of Lougheed's work – law, real estate, and the Senate – had a future for the ambitious Calgarian. As always, retained earnings remained important in developing his financial base, but large loans from financial institutions continued to be essential to fund his real estate projects.

By the beginning of the twentieth century, few Calgary entrepreneurs served as a better model of business management and its role in fostering economic prosperity and social stability than did James A. Lougheed. He pioneered a number of businesses in Calgary. For him, good business management was a strategic priority. Beginning in the early 1880s, as he consolidated his holdings in the city, he saw responsible governance as his principal means of winning public acceptance of a network of business enterprises controlled by him. In Alberta business circles, Lougheed's name receded after World War II, but it never entirely disappeared. His work remained an important touchstone for his grandson, Peter Lougheed, throughout his life. It continues to be written about by business historians.

Christina Kinnisten

Calgary Confectioner

Christina Grant Kinnisten may be one of the most obscure of the early Calgary entrepreneurs. Yet in her day she was a successful business woman and gained the respect of the leading pioneers of entrepreneurial capitalism, among them Murney Morris, manager of the Imperial Bank of Canada's Calgary branch.

In the city, the female entrepreneurial universe encompassed owners of confectionery stores. Christina Kinnisten assumed ownership and managerial control of a confectionery store in the city when her Ontario-born, thirty-eight-year-old husband, William Hugh Kinnisten, died suddenly of congestion of the lungs and intestate in March 1898 after running the family business since 1884.[35] The Supreme Court of the Northwest Territories in Calgary confirmed the inheritance of the family property by Christina Kinnisten and their two children, Cecil and Marion. Born in 1865 in Scotland, Christina, now thirty-three, found the books of the confectionery store up to date and in order. A careful examination of the books showed a healthy surplus.[36] The business might still have collapsed had it not been for the leadership of Christina, a

Chapter 12: Financing the Canadian Dream

resourceful and courageous woman whose dream of the long-term security of her family continued to inspire her.

During the five years that Christina Kinnisten ran the confectionery store, selling fruit, tobacco, and other goods, it competed successfully with other mercantile enterprises and served both the Calgary and Bow Valley markets. She saw the business as a vital institution of democracy, with complex responsibilities to a number of constituencies, including her children, customers, and the community. In 1903, her store was worth between $10,000 and $20,000, noted the R. G. Dun & Company credit reporter.[37] The store's growth was in part self-financed through retained profits. Christina also relied on credit, from the Molson's Bank's Calgary branch, as well as from the Imperial Bank of Canada's branch in the city.[38] In addition, Christina Kinnisten raised funds for the expansion of her confectionery store by making loans carrying 7 to 9 percent interest to individuals such as Hiram G. Worden, a Calgary baker and confectioner, and Abraham Code, a farmer in the Olds area.[39]

Christina Kinnisten's success in business had a profound effect on her family and the community. She sensed the constructive force of her store, and sought to bring growth to the business. Her unquestioning loyalty to her children enhanced her judgment when it came to finding solutions to business problems. Overall, her view of the human side of the enterprise served to increase the trust between herself and her customers and contributed to prosperity in Calgary and the Bow Valley.

Luey Dofoo and the Restaurant Business

Luey Dofoo provides an excellent case study of the energetic owner of a firm who, looking for new challenges, had a great deal to offer in the restaurant business in Calgary. As an entrepreneur, he carried out effectively his role in making strategic decisions in the enterprise.

Born in 1880 in the village of Sunhong, Kwangtung, China, Dofoo was the son of a hardscrabble farmer. The eldest of eight children, he attended a local school for three years, all the while toiling in the rice fields on the family farm. He then worked for a linen manufacturer, who told him that "everyone is pleased with your performance."[40]

Chapter 12: Financing the Canadian Dream

When word reached him from his cousin Luey Nuey in Calgary of opportunities to get ahead in Alberta, Dofoo began to dream of a new life in Canada. More than perhaps many other immigrants of the late nineteenth century, his work exhibited both the progress and the pain that mark periods of rapid economic development. Finding a ship in Canton to cross the Pacific Ocean was not easy, but on 5 June 1899 he landed in Vancouver and paid the required $50 federal head tax. After roaming the city in search of work, Dofoo found a job in the home of a local family. He cleaned house, sawed wood, and did other chores for $3 a month. Within a short time, he quit that job and doubled his wage by accepting an offer to work in the kitchen of another home in the city.[41]

Luey Dofoo in late middle age. (Courtesy of Paul Dofoo).

Canada was a good place to make money, provided a person was diligent and enterprising. The industrious Dofoo also relied on friends and relatives for financial assistance. Having received a Canadian Pacific passenger ticket from Luey Nuey, he took the train to Calgary to work as a cook in his cousin's Prince of Wales Restaurant. Dofoo, aged twenty, arrived on 5 March 1900. It was a fortunate move, for he was now paid $30 a month. When his cousin died within a few years, however, Dofoo found a job as a cook on a ranch in the Bragg Creek area. After a two-year stint on the ranch, he returned to Calgary to work as a cook in a boardinghouse, a job that again lasted for two years. From the beginning, he used a Chinese-English Dictionary to help him to learn to speak and write English. With his pay continuing at $30 a month, he was able to save enough money over six years to travel to China to get married to Ho Eng, but not enough to bring his wife back with him.[42]

Dofoo returned from China with only $5 in his pocket, but he was eager to strike out on his own. In 1906, he borrowed $150 from a friend and purchased the equipment in the Sunlight Restaurant

Chapter 12: Financing the Canadian Dream

at 311 – 8th Avenue S.E. in Calgary from a bankrupt relative. He paid $35 a month rent for the building that housed the restaurant. Immediately, the situation in the enterprise began to turn around. "As soon as I took the restaurant over my business went up every day. I was kept pretty busy. I made good money in those days," recalled Luey Dofoo.[43] Growing profits allowed Dofoo to pay off his debt to his friend, to make the monthly rental payments, and to hire a dishwasher and some waiters.

Within a year or so, Dofoo's Sunlight Restaurant was self-financed through reinvested profits. Doing all the cooking himself, he provided delicious Canadian food, with each full meal priced at twenty-five cents. Word-of-mouth advertising brought an increasing number of customers for breakfast, lunch, and supper. "I fed all the C.P.R. men: engineers, brakemen, firemen, and the men working in the freight sheds, all those fellows. They liked my cooking," remembered Dofoo.[44] He planned for the future by deciding to continue to offer quality food and to grow by ploughing profits back into the enterprise.

The demand for Dofoo's meals outstripped his capacity in several years. Soon his brother Luey You became his partner in the restaurant, which was reorganized as Luey Brothers Café. As the senior partner, Luey Dofoo continued to bring his cooking talent, his entrepreneurial skills, and his social grace to bear on the enterprise. In 1912, the restaurant business was booming, and Luey Dofoo was able to pay for the passage of his wife Ho to Calgary. To make it possible for her to enter Canada, he also paid the head tax, which by this time had increased to $500.[45]

In 1913, the couple's son, Paul, was born in Calgary. Luey Dofoo imbued his family and his brother in the restaurant with a sense of common purpose. In the 1920s, a meal ticket for twenty-one meals could be purchased at the Luey Brothers Café for $4.[46] The café continued to prosper. During the hard times of the early 1930s, Luey Dofoo phased out his restaurant business and, in partnership with son Paul, opened the Midwest Delicatessen at 1203 – 1st Street S.W. Luey and Paul's dream was modest: they would make a variety of foods and build a small, successful business. The firm grew slowly. Especially popular were their meat pies, which they sold for five cents apiece during the Great Depression and the early years of the Second World War.[47]

The most important testament to the power of Luey Dofoo's

Chapter 12: Financing the Canadian Dream

personality was that despite his humble beginnings, he had a profound impact on a number of Calgary and Bow Valley business people, encouraging them to become prosperous. These included his family, particularly Paul. He played a pivotal role in fostering his son's personality and ambitions. Many could not explain that great charm of his, but it worked with almost everybody. It was a charm that enabled Luey Dofoo to influence countless individuals in Calgary and the Bow Valley.

Samuel and Helen Shaw
Midnapore Entrepreneurs

Samuel William and Helen Maria Shaw, together with their eight children, immigrated to Canada from Rochester, Kent, England in the spring of 1883, and the family settled in Midnapore. Helen was thirty-six and Samuel forty-three.[48] Dreaming of farming and other business opportunities in the Canadian West, they had decided to try their luck in the Bow Valley. Both were well educated. Samuel learned to speak seven languages, and Helen studied at a convent in France.[49] Their lives were a tangible proof of the Canadian dream, the ability of enterprising immigrants both to do well in their adopted country and to reinvent themselves.

The Shaws brought with them from England food supplies, bolts of linen, flannel, and cotton, geese, hens, machinery for a woollen mill, and two hired men They also brought telegraph instruments, materials for a telephone, a photography outfit, and a splendid library. Before leaving Winnipeg on the Canadian Pacific for Swift Current, the end of track, they purchased cattle, horses, wagons, a plow, a binder, and a rake. Their four prairie schooners, pulled by oxen, carried two cars of effects the rest of the way to Midnapore.[50] Samuel Shaw spent some time in the summer of 1883 searching for a location for farming, eventually choosing a homestead on Fish Creek: the SE¼ in section 4, township 23, range 1, west of the fifth principal meridian. Here Samuel and Helen Shaw established their farm.[51] "At first we lived in a tent, a huge marquee we had brought from England. Then we built a log house. With the coming of the railroad, the country soon began to be settled, and with such fine people too. Visitors would come along at any hour of the day or

Chapter 12: Financing the Canadian Dream

Samuel and Helen Shaw, c. early 1880s, Midnapore entrepreneurs. (Courtesy of Glenbow Archives, NA-64-5, NA-225-3).

night, and they always brought their blankets. Food and shelter they knew they would get," recalled Helen Shaw.[52]

But the Bow Valley was deeply chastened by the economic depression in the mid-1880s. In these hard formative years on their farm, Samuel and Helen Shaw were tough and adaptive. They relied on information supplied by neighbours like John Glenn to determine how they should attempt to survive the depression and build up the farm. For the Shaw family, accustomed to working together, the difficult times accentuated the need for co-operation. Samuel and Helen gave an example to their children by their hard work and personal responsibility for the family's well-being. Samuel toiled in the fields, while Helen contributed substantially to the development of the farm by feeding the family, looking after the garden, and caring for the chickens and geese. In early September 1884, Samuel wrote:

> ... the soil is all that a farmer can desire, for both grain growing, sheep or stock raising. My experience is confined to the sod, on which I have about five acres of oats, and a similar piece of barley. The oats are well headed and about four and a half feet high, and probably thresh out about 45 bushels

to the acre – these were sown in May, on land ploughed the end of April. The barley was sown June 15, on land ploughed June 10, and is now ripe. As regards vegetables, I have some very good potatoes, turnips, carrots, and also beans which are doing well.[53]

Soon the Shaws engaged in mixed farming, producing mostly grain but also some cattle, horses, and poultry.

Realizing the limited area of their 160-acre homestead, the Shaws pressed ahead over the next few years with the acquisition of more land, purchasing a quarter section under pre-emption law adjacent to their homestead, as well as two nearby sections from the Canadian Pacific and the Hudson's Bay Company.[54] In addition, in 1893 Helen bought 320 acres from the Isaac Robinson estate.[55] As early as 1888, Samuel joined several other Midnapore farmers in reporting that for a number of years they "had invariably grown good crops of wheat, oats, barley, potatoes, beets, carrots, turnips, and peas."[56] At Calgary's agricultural show in October 1889, Samuel exhibited the Shaw family's prize-winning oats, cabbages, and onions.[57] The local and regional markets were significant outlets for the Shaws' farm products. Besides producing cash crops, they obtained income from the general store they established in Midnapore as they started to diversify. Samuel was Midnapore's first postmaster, and his salary helped increase the family earnings.[58]

The Shaws' farm and store profits were small, but the growth of their store and farm was still financed in part through retained profits. Debt was nevertheless at the financial core of the development of their mercantile and farming businesses. Borrowing money from friends, as well as from the Bank of Montreal's Calgary branch, was especially important in making it possible for Samuel and Helen Shaw to acquire more land, to pay for seed, tools, and labour before the harvest, and to conduct commerce at their store.[59]

As industrialization began to unfold in the Bow Valley, the Shaws diversified still further by setting up a woollen mill on their homestead in Midnapore. Samuel and Helen provide an instructive example of creative entrepreneurship. In December 1889, they opened the Midnapore Woollen Mills, the first wool making factory in the Canadian West, with a bit of fanfare.[60] In a letter published in the *Calgary Herald*, Samuel Shaw wrote of the importance of the new facility.[61] Measuring thirty by sixty feet, employing a handful of

Chapter 12: Financing the Canadian Dream

Midnapore Woollen Mills, c. 1896, built in 1889. (Courtesy of Glenbow Archives, NC-12-6).

workers, and costing about $5,000, the two-storey factory was one of the largest plants to open in the Calgary area in the last half of the 1880s.[62] The factory was within easy reach of the wool produced by sheep ranchers in the Bow Valley and elsewhere in Alberta. By the summer of 1890, the facility was operating at its full capacity, producing many blankets and bolts of flannel and tweed per day.[63] Midnapore was located a few miles south of Calgary, the largest and fastest-growing market for woollen goods in the Bow Valley.

Initially, the factory used I. G. Baker & Co.'s store in Calgary as a retail outlet for its finished products, but soon the Shaws exploited this market more fully by opening their own retail store and tailor shop on Stephen Avenue, two doors east of the Alexander Block. While Samuel ran the plant, Helen, who was a fine seamstress and, like her husband, a very competent business person, was in charge of the salesroom and tailor shop in Calgary.[64] Besides offering blankets and bolts of tweed and flannel, Helen sold tailor-made clothing, including men's grey, woollen shirts which proved to be very warm. The Shaws' strategy was to manufacture high-quality products and provide good service.

To finance their Midnapore Woollen Mills and their Calgary operations, it became necessary for Samuel and Helen Shaw to take on debt. Already in September 1889, they had obtained a ninety-day, $3,300 loan from the private bank Lafferty & Moore to purchase wool.[65] In mid-October 1891, the Shaws borrowed $2,622 from Daniel Webster Marsh. At the end of the same month, they approached F. W. Pettit and Albert J. Ellis, Calgary insurance and real estate agents, and returned to them again in 1892, in the two years securing in loans $7,000.[66] Pettit and Ellis also became investors in the Shaw enterprises for which they provided credit.[67] As the Bow Valley economy slipped into the doldrums in the mid-1890s, however, the Shaws worried about repayment and raising more cash.

Economic recovery in the late 1890s made credit easier and safer to obtain for entrepreneurial purposes. In March 1898, Helen Shaw became head of the Midnapore Woollen Mills, and within a year and a half she borrowed $2,500 from Calgary lawyer Michael C. Bernard and Innisfail medical doctor Henry George, as trustees of a friend's estate, to improve the factory.[68] The Shaws' son Maltman worked as engineer in the plant. The Midnapore Woollen Mills was a more diversified and complex firm than ever before, with the increasing demand for supplies among gold seekers destined for the Yukon. Continuing to use Alberta wool, Helen Shaw manufactured and sold not only blankets, bolts of flannel and tweed, and shirts, but also mackinaw suits. Advertising and sales strategy quickly shifted in part to this new gold rush market. In addition, Helen broadened the product line to include men's and ladies' dressing gowns, ladies' skirts, and boys' knickerbockers.[69]

All this brought growth and profitability to the Shaws' wool business. By 1903, the *Northwestern Journal of Progress* could write in its pamphlet on Calgary that "their high class goods and standard methods have made the Midnapore Woollen Mills widely known as an excellent and reliable concern."[70] But 1907, with its economic depression, was a difficult year for the factory, as it was for Bow Valley businesses generally. Around this time, Helen and Samuel Shaw sold the Midnapore Woollen Mills.[71] They continued, however, to operate their general store and farm for many years. Even at the age of seventy-four in 1921, after her husband had been dead for two years, Helen Shaw was still the classic hands-on entrepreneur, who ran almost every detail of the business from her office in Midnapore.[72]

Samuel and Helen Shaw's lives and worldview were emblematic of the business spirit in Calgary and the Bow Valley at the turn of the century and helped to define relatively small business enterprise

Chapter 12: Financing the Canadian Dream

as we know it today. Self-assured innovators, they were completely at home with the technology of industrialization and its challenges. Their effort to develop a woollen factory won them legitimacy in the industrial arena and contributed to prosperity. Besides bringing a sound financial orientation to their business, Helen and Samuel had a perfect feel for their products. They saw the factory, not as an impersonal machine, but as an economic and social institution. To them, social interaction, including teamwork and co-operation within the family, was the key to managing the relationships within the enterprise.

Sandy Watson

Pine Creek Farmer

The story of Saunders "Sandy" Watson, a farmer in the Bow Valley, illustrates how farmers financed the Canadian dream. For many years, Sandy Watson enjoyed considerable success in the valley, and his growing farming venture provided his family with a secure life. Around 1883, at the age of forty-six, he brought his family to the Pine Creek area. Born in Ontario, he came to this frontier community with his wife Eliza and their two sons and four daughters. He chose a 160-acre homestead on Pine Creek, directly beside the Macleod Trail.[73] Watson did not begin homestead life with enormous resources, but he was determined to make the best possible use of the little capital he possessed. Within a few years, he made his mixed farm productive by breaking the thick prairie sod with a plough, putting in crops of wheat, oats, and barley, and raising some cattle and horses. Seeing the need to have more land to meet his family's needs, he expanded his holding by purchasing one quarter section adjacent to the homestead. He now owned a small family farm complete with log buildings – a house and a barn – and fenced fields, and became part of an established farm neighbourhood at Pine Creek.

Sandy Watson regularly exchanged work with his son Harry, who selected his own homestead about four miles from the home place in 1886.[74] By exchanging work at breaking new land, haying, and threshing, father and son increased their labour force without adding the cost of a hired man. By 1888, Harry

Chapter 12: Financing the Canadian Dream

was cultivating fifteen acres on his farm. Sandy Watson also participated in a work exchange with John Owens, a nearby Ontario-born homesteader.

In 1886, Sandy Watson diversified by remodelling and enlarging his farmhouse, thereby allowing him to use it not only as a family home but also as a stopping house.[75] He looked upon

Sandy Watson's stopping house on his farm on Macleod Trail, c. 1920, built by him, c. 1886. (Courtesy of Ruth Lynch).

the $1,500 he spent on construction of the frame building as a good investment.[76] The first possible stop south of Calgary on the Macleod Trail, the stopping house, known as the Watson House by 1889, offered food, drink, and sleeping arrangements for travellers and fodder and water for their horses and oxen.[77] The trail was heavily used before the coming of the Calgary and Edmonton Railway in 1892, and even after that year it continued to contribute toward meeting the needs of farmers, ranchers, merchants, and freighters. Eliza Watson was an excellent cook, and her fine meals brought many a weary traveller to her door. Certainly, Sandy and Eliza Watson's establishment was a welcome refuge for all people who passed along the old trail, permitting them to eat or rest or both.

To finance improvements at their stopping house and farm, Sandy and Eliza Watson usually relied on retained earnings, but they also had to borrow money from time to time. They raised the necessary funds with chattel and land mortgages at private banks in Calgary.[78] In April 1889, Sandy Watson obtained an $850 loan of six months from Le Jeune, Smith & Co. at an 18 percent annual interest rate. The loan was secured by a mortgage on Watson's horses and farm implements. Unable to pay off the mortgage promptly, he was granted a renewal by the bank. By the end of a year, the debt had been repaid. In August 1890, Lafferty & Moore provided a $664 loan of ninety days at 18 percent interest to Sandy and Eliza Watson, accepting for collateral a mortgage on their horses and wagons as well as a mortgage on their 320-acre farm. These loans helped the Watsons to maintain a productive farming operation at Pine Creek. By this time, the meadow on their farm yielded from seventy-five to a hundred tons of hay per year.[79]

Productive uses of borrowed money alone did not ensure the

Chapter 12: Financing the Canadian Dream

persistence of their family farm. Instead, endurance also came from neighbouring in the early and mid-1890s. The Watsons continued to build networks of economic and social ties with family members and neighbours. Work exchanges with their son Harry reaffirmed family connections and integrated social life.[80] The work demands of farming blended with visiting, for exchanging labour during the daily routines of farm life might include a social visit. Neighbouring went beyond obligations of kinship to sharing religious ties. The Watsons shared membership in the Anglican Church with some of their neighbours, and their stopping house came to be used for Anglican services.[81] Their community was quite stable. Even when Sandy and Eliza Watson sold their farm to their neighbour Robert Pratt in the late 1890s, the process of neighbourhood formation continued as he brought in relatives from Scotland to settle nearby.[82]

Sandy Watson's effort to develop a farm and a stopping house had a significant impact on the Pine Creek community. His pioneering work helped bring about prosperity in the settlement era. Decades later, the main trends in mixed farming sped along the tracks that Watson laid. His son Harry's farm was, in fact, a logical extension of Watson's efforts to carry out farming tasks effectively. Sandy Watson's belief in the importance of economic and social networks in a modern democracy was perfectly in tune with the pioneer years in the Bow Valley. To this day, his ideas echo in the work of people in the Pine Creek district.

Meopham Gardner
Ranching in the Bragg Creek Area

Picture another scene. A young clerk is bored by the lack of challenge at Lloyd's of London and quits after some time on the job. He dreams of a rewarding life in ranching in the Canadian prairies, almost gets killed in the Saskatchewan Rebellion, and ultimately succeeds as a cattle rancher in Alberta. This story, which in its details stretches over long distances, is the true-life story of Meopham Gardner.

Born into a well-to-do family in 1852 in Nickleham, Surrey, England, Meopham Gardner attended a local school, became fond of horses, and loved riding and fox-hunting as a youngster. "He was well educated," recalled his granddaughter Audrey

Macdougall.⁸³ Upon graduation, Gardner decided he wanted to join the Imperial Army but was unable to do so. Eventually, he went to work as a clerk for Lloyd's of London. Some time later, however, Gardner left Lloyd's, partly because clerking there had no excitement for him and partly because of his dream of a better life in the Canadian prairies.

In 1879, at the age of twenty-seven, Meopham Gardner immigrated to Russell, Manitoba to engage in ranching. He filed claim to a homestead, but the problem was finding some financing for the purchase of cattle. Fortunately for him, he inherited a substantial amount of money from his father; he also borrowed from him.⁸⁴ With his financing lined up, Gardner bought cattle and began developing his ranch. In 1883, he married Margaret Esam, a native of York, Yorkshire, England and daughter of a solicitor.⁸⁵ Meopham and Margaret's first child, Edward, was born in November 1884. Gardner's ranching career was interrupted a few months later, in the spring of 1885, when he joined Colonel C. A. Boulton's Scouts as a captain to fight in the Saskatchewan Rebellion. Riding his trusted horse, Gardner was seriously wounded in the battle of Fish Creek.⁸⁶ After some weeks' convalescence for his bullet-torn body, he was finally ready to go home. Back on the ranch at Russell, he was happy to be again with Margaret, who gave birth to their second son, Clem, in December 1885.

Meopham Gardner, c. 1901, carrying water with a yoke on his ranch in the Bragg Creek area. (Courtesy of Glenbow Archives, NA-1942-2).

But since his recent bout with asthma and the deterioration of his health, looking after his cattle had been difficult for Meopham Gardner. He now planned to conquer his infirmity by moving to the Bragg Creek area in Alberta, where he hoped that the dry and sunny climate would be beneficial to him. So in the spring of 1886, he and Margaret and their two infant sons left Russell, journeying about six hundred miles in a covered wagon to their destination and bringing their hundred head of cattle with them.⁸⁷

Chapter 12: Financing the Canadian Dream

Clem Gardner roping a steer, Calgary Stampede, in 1919. (Courtesy of Glenbow Archives, NA-1942-15).

Once in the Bragg Creek area, Gardner's health improved. In July 1886, he chose his 160-acre homestead on the Elbow River and started ranching again. Using money he borrowed or inherited from his father, Meopham Gardner was soon hard at work developing his ranch, only to suffer the loss of a number of his cattle in the terrible winter of 1886-1887. But he was quick to rebuild his herd, and by 1890 his ranch had ninety head of cattle and six horses.[88] The two gardens on the homestead provided the family with fresh vegetables. Apart from Gardner's livestock, his two log cabins, four barns, one corral, and fences around the fields were valued at $2,600. By this time, he had also bought a quarter section adjacent to his homestead. Before long, he increased his holding by purchasing more land nearby, so that he soon owned two and a half sections on which he grazed his cattle and saddle horses.[89] Like other ranchers, he also grazed his cattle on the open range, where they had access to free grass. Producing quality cattle and horses, he travelled regularly to sell them in Calgary and its region. Gardner's numerous friends and business contacts included Pat Burns, who bought his cattle, and the Elbow River Polo Team, of which he was a member, as well as other Bow Valley polo players, some of whom purchased and rode the saddle horses he raised.[90]

By the early 1890s, the popularity of Gardner's cattle and horses in the Calgary and Bow Valley markets was growing. His ranching operation was largely self-financed, from the money he had inherited and through reinvested profits. To help fatten his cattle, he grew crops of oats and timothy grass in his fenced fields, using them as feed in the winter months. But like other livestock raisers, Captain Gardner, as he was known, faced the problem of drought. To solve this problem, he constructed two irrigation ditches in 1893. "Captain Gardner, rancher, on the Elbow River near Calgary, has put in two ditches this present year – one a mile in length, the other three-fourths of a mile. Twenty acres of oats and timothy were watered this season with most satisfactory returns, the timothy measuring 3 ft. 6 in. at time of cutting. Two hundred acres will be irrigated in all," wrote the *Calgary Tribune*.[91]

The organization of work at Gardner's ranch required the recruitment of cowboys. Among the cowboys who worked for him in the late 1880s, 1890s, and beyond were: John Bateman, who was born in Cork, Ireland; Arthur Norman, a native of Northampton, England who first met Gardner in the Yale Hotel in Calgary; Frank and Bruce Long, two brothers who came from Haldimand County, Ontario; and a few English-born Barnardo Homes orphan boys.[92] Inspired by the orphan boys, Meopham Gardner could be found giving financial support to the Barnardo Homes for many years.[93] The gifted Margaret Gardner, besides making meals for the cowboys and her family and writing articles on flowers and plants for the *Family Herald* and *Weekly Star*, was busy raising her children, numbering five by 1901 – Edward, aged sixteen; Clem, fifteen; Edith, fourteen; Minnie, thirteen; and Ruby, ten.

Because of the lack of a nearby school, Margaret and Meopham Gardner decided to hire governesses to provide their children with an education during their early years. At the turn of the century, the governess in the Gardner household was Grace Somerville, a native of Bryson, Quebec who later married Millarville rancher Thomas Jameson; the couple's youngest daughter, Sheilagh Jameson, in time became a well-known archivist and historian. Grace Somerville was an important member of the Gardner household, and one of her duties was to teach Clem Gardner, a fast learner, in the home classroom. Observing that Grace Somerville "came from a good family and was well brought up," Audrey Macdougall, Clem Gardner's daughter, believed that her father had the benefit of a fine education.[94]

The history of the second generation Gardner venture began in the early twentieth century, when Clem Gardner took over the small

Chapter 12: Financing the Canadian Dream

family ranch his father had established in 1886. Reinvesting profits, he gradually transformed it into a larger enterprise producing high-grade cattle. "Clem Gardner was a tremendous worker, he was a good businessman, and he had tremendous drive," said Audrey Macdougall. "He won the champion all-round Canadian cowboy title" at the 1912 Calgary Stampede.[95] Meopham Gardner, who was sixty years old by this time, gave his son the chance to demonstrate the full range of his amazing talents.

Meopham Gardner's initiatives in ranching were designed to remove the uncertainties that often characterized the lives of Bow Valley livestock raisers. A pioneer rancher and one of the most forward-thinking livestock raisers of his time, Gardner became a great influence on his children, including Clem, and the wider Alberta society. Optimism prevailed and many ranchers became prosperous. Having observed his father's success, Clem was prepared to mold his life around Meopham's, just as Clem's brother Edward had. Meopham poured his energies into both his work on the ranch and a wide-ranging network of friendships in Calgary and the Bow Valley. Similarly, Clem Gardner used his commitment to his ranch, his income from raising cattle and horses, and his ties to Calgary's and its region's business leaders to make his own mark on life in the city and the nation and beyond. "I remember your father in 1912. I was at the Stampede in 1912. My greatest ambition was to be able to ride like him," said Stuart Taylor Wood, Royal Canadian Mounted Police Commissioner, as he was speaking with Audrey Macdougall in Ottawa during World War II.[96] Clem Gardner, like his father, supported the Barnardo Homes for decades, until his death in 1963. "I know at Christmas he always sent off a cheque to the Barnardo Homes," recalled Audrey Macdougall.

James C. Linton and Books

As in the case of Meopham Gardner, the lure of opportunity in the West was irresistible to James Campbell Linton, a Calgary bookseller. Born in 1858 in Chatham, Ontario, James Linton attended the local school.[97] As a young man, he heard about the social changes that accompanied the opening of the West to settlement. He was particularly struck by how fast money could be made and lost in the frontier environment. Dreaming of making

Chapter 12: Financing the Canadian Dream

Linton's Book Store on Stephen Avenue in 1884. James C. Linton is standing in the doorway. (Courtesy of Glenbow Archives, NA-2656-1).

his fortune by selling books, he entered the bookstore business in partnership with his brother Thomas in Rat Portage, Manitoba in 1883. Early in the following year, James Linton learned of an opportunity to go into the book selling business in Calgary.

In April 1884, while Thomas remained at the Rat Portage store, James went to Calgary to establish the firm's second bookstore.[98] The twenty-six-year-old James Linton who descended from the train in Calgary had reason to be optimistic. Gazing up and down dusty Stephen Avenue, he realized that the place was larger than Rat Portage. He believed that he could make a living in Calgary, a town of a thousand people.

Opening the bookstore on Stephen Avenue, two doors east of the Royal Hotel, Linton began with stock worth $1,500, all of which he had purchased on credit from suppliers in cities such as Winnipeg, Toronto, Montreal, New York, and London, England.[99] He himself had little capital. In his Calgary store, he offered a wide assortment of goods, including especially schoolbooks authorized for use in the Northwest Territories, but also professional and technical reference

Chapter 12: Financing the Canadian Dream

books, histories, biographies, novels, magazines, and the latest newspapers. Although books were his leading products, Linton followed a policy of diversified sales. In addition to useful and interesting reading materials, he sold stationery, fancy goods, wall paper, toys, musical instruments, sporting goods, and tobacco.[100] Linton's enterprise was in a good position to meet competition from its rival, Thomson Bros.' bookstore.

From the start, Linton's primary focus was the Calgary market. He also sought a growing demand for his goods in the Bow Valley among ranchers and farmers. He financed his venture through ongoing credit from suppliers and by reinvesting profits. Perhaps he also borrowed money from friends and relatives. In 1886, Linton purchased a $2,000 life insurance policy from the Toronto-based Confederation Life Insurance Company, which he probably offered as security for loans.[101] He needed funds in that year to pay for his new frame residence, built at a cost of $1,100.[102]

Despite the growth of its business, James Linton's bookstore remained short of funds, a situation that led to managerial changes. He looked for more capital. His brother Thomas helped rescue the partnership. In 1886, after Thomas and James Linton had sold their Rat Portage store, Thomas moved to Calgary and brought with him the desired additional money.[103] The partnership in Calgary was reorganized as Linton Bros., with James and Thomas as active partners. All these changes did a great deal to improve the firm's finances. "Linton Bros. possess business qualities of a high order, and are honoured and respected by all who know them, for their strict integrity and high character," wrote George Henry Ham, author of *The New West*, in 1888.[104] In July 1889, James Linton married Edith Maude Van Wart.[105] Edith, a native of Fredericton, New Brunswick and daughter of Calgary merchant John G. Van Wart, likely brought some money into the marriage. By 1890, Linton Bros.' capital had grown to between $2,000 and $5,000.[106]

The demand for Linton Bros.' goods – especially books and stationery – soon outstripped their store's capacity. In 1891, James and Thomas moved their operations to larger quarters in the Imperial Bank of Canada building on Stephen Avenue. When these rented premises became too small for their trade in 1893, they borrowed $6,000 from the Confederation Life Insurance Company to help them purchase the more spacious Freeze Block on Stephen Avenue and moved their business there.[107] They acquired the Freeze

Block at a cost of $11,000. By this time, Linton Bros. were worth between $5,000 and $10,000, reported the R. G. Dun & Company credit correspondent.[108] The harsh economic climate of the mid-1890s bit into Linton Bros.' profits. But with James and Thomas's persistent entrepreneurship, the partnership survived the hard times and expanded in the early twentieth century to become a regional firm of considerable repute.

The impact of James C. Linton's work is best illustrated by the influence the bookstore had on many readers, both in Calgary and in the Bow Valley. As a bookseller, his greatest strength was his ability to recognize and foster interesting and useful information, much of which contributed to prosperity in the region. For numerous readers, the books and magazines in the store opened up a new world. For instance, Isaac and Evelyn Freeze, who were James C. Linton's neighbours in the city and who had brought dozens of books with them from New Brunswick, found that the books they purchased from him provided them with new, exciting knowledge.[109] Always fond of history and newspapers, Ontario-born John Mosley, owner of the Dominion Hotel in Calgary, probably enjoyed visiting the bookstore.[110] Frequent visits to James C. Linton's store, especially its magazine section, helped open Clara Christie's eyes to the tremendous opportunities in medicine. Born in Winchester, Ontario, Clara Christie, who taught school in Calgary during World War I and studied medicine at McGill University and obstetrics and gynecology at Yale University, began practising as a medical doctor in Calgary in 1927.[111] By 1937, the year she married lawyer Orrin Might, Clara Christie had won recognition as an excellent obstetrician.

William Hanson Boorne and the Rise of his Photography Studio

In some respects, William Hanson Boorne, or Hanson Boorne as he was called, resembled Calgary entrepreneurs such as James C. Linton. Like Linton, Hanson Boorne, a photographer, was future-oriented and willing to take risks in the area of his choice – Calgary and the Bow Valley. With his self-confidence and optimism, Boorne personified the boosterism that pervaded Calgary's business community in the late nineteenth century. Like most other local entrepreneurs, he conducted business on a small scale and was always seeking more capital to finance his operations.

Chapter 12: Financing the Canadian Dream

William Hanson Boorne in 1884, who ran the most important photography establishment in Calgary in the late nineteenth century. (Courtesy of Glenbow Archives, NA-33-1).

Born in 1859 in Bristol, England, Boorne attended a local school. He studied pharmacy and found a hobby in photography. Lured by enticing Canadian Pacific Railway advertising and low homestead prices, in 1884 he decided to immigrate to Canada. At Bird's Hill near Winnipeg, Boorne filed claim to a 160-acre homestead. While working on his farm, he took pictures of activities such as harvesting. In the spring of 1885, he spent a few months in Calgary, getting snaps of the growing town. Boorne's talents as a photographer inevitably attracted attention. Admired by those around him, he began to dream of starting a photography business in the place. Leaving his homestead some time later, he opened a photography studio in Calgary in 1886.[112]

James C. Linton, who displayed a collection of pictures Boorne had taken in England in his bookstore window, aided Boorne, a portrait and landscape photographer. A newspaper reporter, after interviewing the photographer, wrote: "Mr. Boorne has favoured us with an inspection of some of his work as an amateur in the old country, and all we can say is that if he succeeds as well here as a professional he ought to receive considerable patronage."[113] This display gave the Boorne photographs a high-quality image.

As a pioneer in the photography business in Calgary, Hanson Boorne put a great deal of energy into trying to attract clients from the town and the surrounding area. Offering his services as photographer in the studio on the corner of McTavish Street and Angus Avenue as well as at Calgarians' homes and businesses and at ranches and farms in the Bow Valley, he was constantly on the move with his camera, capturing views and scenes on glass negatives. In April 1887, Boorne's English-born cousin, Ernest G. May, became his partner.[114] May worked as darkroom technician in the studio, moving glass negatives into the darkroom and finished photographs out. In this production environment, May was an important asset. Profits were small – there was little to reinvest in Boorne & May, but the business was finally on its way.

Most of the money Boorne infused into the partnership came from family and friends. With his experience in photography, he understood the promotional power of pictures but lacked the capital to build the business. Besides paying rent for the office that housed the studio, by the end of 1886 he had spent $600 on the construction of a frame residence on Northcote Avenue for himself and his wife May Woolridge Hichens Boorne.[115] To carry out his vision of developing a photography business that could compete with other Calgary photographers such as A. J. Ross, Hanson Boorne needed more funds. In June 1887, he borrowed $1,736 from Charles Boorne in Bristol, England, possibly his brother, at an interest rate of 5 percent per annum. The loan, with a fourteen-year maturity, was secured by a mortgage on Hanson Boorne's property in Calgary.[116]

Using these funds, Hanson Boorne expanded by developing the photography business in fields he had already entered, including pictures of Calgary businesses and homes, the Rocky Mountains, and Natives for sale to interested buyers. As a portrait and landscape photographer, he understood that he had to be selective in his approach. "The difficulty of photographing in the Far West," Boorne wrote later,

> ... arises not so much from a dearth of subjects, as in making a selection which would be likely to prove interesting to your Eastern as well as Western readers. A landscape photographer who covers this enormous Western country of ours in the course of a few years is likely to see not only very different varieties of country, from the flat and rolling prairies to the noble, towering Rockies, but to meet with many incidents and scenes which are totally different from anything to be found in more densely populated districts. For instance, the Indians with which our neighbourhood abounds – although not exactly up to the standards of the "noble red man" of Fenimore Cooper – are very interesting [and] well worth a visit from any knight of the camera.[117]

Boorne was so imbued with the magic of photographic technology,

Chapter 12: Financing the Canadian Dream

so caught up in the concept of fascinating western landscapes, that he succeeded in selling many of his pictures. One of the outlets for his "Calgary, Mountain and Indian Photos" was Linton's bookstore.[118]

It was George Henry Ham who best described Boorne's photographs in 1888:

> Pictures taken by the most modern processes of photography, by which the features of the very young and aged are easily caught with the most surprising life-like rapidity." Boorne & May "make a specialty of landscapes, sceneries (embracing a fine collection of mountain views along the C.P.R.), buildings, interiors, machinery, architecture; also groups of societies, clubs and parties, their work being among the most perfect in the city.[119]

During the late 1880s and early 1890s, the photography business continued to grow under Boorne's guidance. In Calgary, he rented a large office on the ground floor of the Barber Block on Stephen Avenue for his studio. He also opened branch studios in Banff, Edmonton, and Montreal, as well as in Glacier and Victoria, British Columbia.[120] The Calgary photographer was recognized for his work across Canada. But Boorne's reputation grew more rapidly than his resources. He needed help not only to finance nation-wide growth, but also to raise money he required to buy out Ernest May, who withdrew from the partnership in December 1889.[121] In September 1889, Hanson Boorne obtained a $3,000 loan from Richard S. Hichins, possibly May Woolridge Hichens Boorne's brother, and William P. Harvey in County Cornwall, England at a 5 percent annual interest rate. The next year, Hanson Boorne borrowed $682 from Edmund Cave, a Calgary lawyer, at 12 percent interest. In April 1891, Boorne obtained a $1,400 loan at a rate of 12 percent from Charles A. Miner of Eastbourne, County Sussex, England. Two and a half years later, in October 1893, Boorne borrowed $4,000 from Harold E. Forster in Hamilton, Ontario, for which the rate was 9 percent.[122]

Throughout this period, Boorne continued to operate under the valuable name Boorne & May, in keeping with an understanding he had reached with his former partner Ernest May, who had become a farmer in the Fish Creek area. But in December 1891, the chronic need for capital prompted Hanson Boorne to transform his firm into a corporation, the Boorne & May Company. Capitalized at

$15,000, the company had two stockholders in addition to Boorne: Henry A. Perley, part owner of the Alberta Hotel; and Robert H. M. Rawlinson, a Calgary area rancher.[123] With sufficient money to expand his business, toward the end of 1892 Boorne opened a new art store filled largely with his own products in the Barber Block. The store had "a fine show of curios, photographs, pictures, and art and fancy goods of all descriptions," wrote a reporter for the *Calgary Herald*.[124]

In the fall of 1893, Boorne recruited J. M. Loundes, a photographer formerly with the English firm Heath & Sons, "Royal Photographers, " to assist him in the studio.[125] By this time Boorne & May was worth between $5,000 and $10,000, reported the R. G. Dun & Company credit correspondent.[126] Boorne advertised his photographs heavily, placing interesting advertisements in Calgary newspapers. He also promoted his offerings through a free catalogue, which had "over 1000 Rocky Mountain, Indian, and Ranching Scenes."[127] In August 1893, Wesley F. Orr told R. G. Dun & Company that Boorne was a "good steady fellow," but he also reported that "there have been rumours that something was going to happen to Boorne & May.... I do not think Boorne & May deserve a high financial rating at all."[128] Although financial problems led Boorne to sell his photography business in 1894, to many people in Calgary, the Bow Valley, and Canada he had become a leading figure in the photography world.

For almost a decade, Boorne's operations achieved tremendous visibility. Admiring the work of the photographer and entrepreneur, people from Calgary and all parts of the Bow Valley came to his studio to have their pictures taken. Customers in Edmonton, Banff, Montreal, Victoria, and Glacier obtained photographs of themselves in his branch studios. Through catalogue sales of Canadian views and scenes, Boorne's national influence extended beyond his studios' distribution.[129] Boorne's photographs, with their remarkable clarity and detail, became a major feature of the Montreal-based *Dominion Illustrated*, Calgary Special, a June 1890 issue that focused on the histories of important commercial, ranching, farming, industrial, and banking businesses in the city and the surrounding area.[130] This helped to create a positive image of the region, which, in turn, made a contribution to prosperity. Over the next century and beyond, business and social historians were happy to shine a light on the work of Hanson Boorne in their publications.

Chapter 12: Financing the Canadian Dream

James S. Mackie

Gunsmith and Bookseller

Another prominent entrepreneur was James S. Mackie, a Calgary gunsmith. Born in 1860 in Westminster, London, England, Mackie was the son of parents who came from Ayrshire, Scotland. After attending the local school, he became a newspaper reporter in London, where George Bernard Shaw belonged to his circle of friends.[131] An avid reader in this imperial environment, Mackie profited in a variety of ways from the work of numerous authors, including Shaw and Charles Dickens, as well as those who had written histories of Great Britain and the British Empire. From this atmosphere of information came Mackie's dream of taking advantage of new business opportunities in the Canadian West.

Believing that his financial prospects were greater in Canada than in London, in 1882 James Mackie immigrated to Winnipeg to learn the gunsmithing trade at the Hingston Smith Arms Company.[132] After three years of apprenticeship, during which time he acquired the necessary technical skills to turn out an assortment of guns, in 1885 Mackie returned to London to work there for a while. Planning to open a gun establishment in Calgary, in 1886 he boarded a ship for Canada. It was on board this ship that he met his future wife, Grace MacMillan Forgan, a native of Bo'ness, near Edinburgh, Scotland, who was heading with her family to Omaha, Nebraska, where her father, a prominent banker, would open a bank. Mackie talked with Grace, and they agreed to write to each other. Upon his arrival in Calgary later that same year, Mackie joined Walter Mackay, a taxidermist, in setting up a gun, sporting goods, and fur shop on the corner of Stephen Avenue and Osler Street.[133] The partnership of Mackie & Mackay was short-lived. By early 1887, Mackie had taken a new partner, Joseph W. Cockle, a taxidermist who had started his own business in Calgary two years before.[134]

At the beginning of their Calgary careers, Mackie and Cockle were men of relatively few financial assets. A substantial loan eased these constraints. In July 1887, Mackie and Cockle borrowed $750 from the North British Canadian Investment Company at a 10 percent annual interest rate. Their Calgary lot secured the loan, with a two-year maturity.[135] They turned these funds to good account, but by the early months of 1888 the partnership of Mackie & Cockle had been dissolved. As each went into business on his own, James Mackie established himself as an independent gunsmith while Joseph Cockle became an independent taxidermist in the town.

In his metalworking establishment, Mackie toiled long hours, using his skills to produce breach-loading guns, revolvers, and ammunition. As a firearm manufacturer in the small-arms industry, he encouraged potential customers in Calgary and the Bow Valley to visit his shop and examine his products. Reluctant to tie his firm's future too closely to a few goods, he expanded its scope of production by moving into manufacturing other items: fishing tackle, cutlery, and a wide range of sporting goods. The young entrepreneur's sales of firearms, as well as sporting goods, fishing tackle, and cutlery, rose steadily. George Henry Ham wrote of Mackie in 1888:

James S. Mackie in 1901, a prominent gunsmith in Calgary's early history. (Courtesy of Glenbow Archives, NA-3885-14).

> Being a thoroughly practical mechanic, perfectly conversant with his business and its details, being also energetic and enterprising, it cannot be wondered at that his trade has steadily increased. The reputation of his goods stands high, both for workmanship and reliability. Those who have occasion to deal with him will always be treated with courtesy and dealt with in the most upright manner.... [Mackie] fills all orders entrusted to him promptly, giving each and every article turned out of his concern his personal attention and supervision. This is the largest gun establishment in the Northwest.[136]

Mackie diversified his operation further by trying his hand at preparing, stuffing, and mounting the skins of birds. By 1890, the stuffed birds he made provided him with additional income and caught the attention of the reporter for *The Dominion Illustrated*: "Mr. Mackie, who is a gunsmith, is also something of a naturalist, enough, at least, to make him a respectable taxidermist."[137]

James Mackie found time to travel to Omaha, Nebraska in 1891 to visit Grace Forgan, and in February of the following year he married her.[138] As the daughter of a successful banker, Grace helped to solidify James's social and economic position in Calgary. "J. S. Mackie, gunsmith and general ammunition and arms dealer, is a young married man. Very steady and industrious, he ... is no doubt making some money all the time. He owns the lot and shop in which he has business worth $3,000 to $4,000. He also has 3 very nice residence lots on which he has built a snug house, in which he lives, worth $1,500," wrote Wesley F. Orr to R. G. Dun & Company in June 1893.[139]

In his spare time, James Mackie was often drawn to the splendid library in his house.[140] One of his most striking traits remained a pronounced interest in books written by great authors, not only Dickens and Shaw but also others such as William Shakespeare. From the beginning of his business career, intellectual curiosity had driven him to read. Besides deriving personal enjoyment from books, he loved to read to his children after dinner.[141] To fulfil his dream of becoming a bookseller, in November 1899 Mackie sold his gunmaking establishment and purchased Thomson Bros.' bookstore on Stephen Avenue for $6,866. Mackie was able to pay $2,000 of the price in cash, because he borrowed this amount from the A. M. Austin estate at Pine Creek. A mortgage on the books in the store to Thomson Bros. allowed Mackie to pay them the balance of $4,866 in instalments.[142]

The early 1900s were prosperous years for James Mackie's bookstore. Although books and stationery dominated the goods he offered to customers in Calgary and the Bow Valley, he pursued a policy of diversified sales. In addition to books and stationery, he sold Kodak cameras and supplies, artists' materials, and Karn pianos and organs.[143] As his fledgling enterprise grew, Mackie also came to play an increasingly important role in civic politics. He ran successfully for Calgary mayor in December 1900.[144] In his term as mayor, Mackie initiated several public improvements, including the extension of the city boundaries to include Victoria Park. At the end of Mackie's year in office, the *Calgary Herald* wrote: "J. S. Mackie, the retiring mayor of Calgary, deserves great credit for his work during the past year.

While in office he has often at considerable personal sacrifice devoted much time to municipal affairs."[145] Mackie's bookstore nonetheless continued to flourish under his guidance. By 1903, a credit reporter for R. G. Dun & Company noted that his firm was worth between $10,000 and $15,000.[146]

In many respects, James S. Mackie's approach to the bookstore business was a recipe of the best practices of modern management. His people skills had a profound impact on the shape of the management legacy that he passed on to the Calgary and Bow Valley business world. He understood that a great deal of the creative potential of a business rests on co-operation within the enterprise and on ties to informal economic and social networks. His ideas found practical expression in the Mackie Block he built in the city on 8th Avenue West in 1908, as well as in the Lancaster Building he erected at the corner of 8th Avenue and 2nd Street West several years later. Mackie also recognized the historical importance of office blocks and buildings. For him, the history of these businesses was a most interesting chapter in the history of the city, and illustrated the force of entrepreneurs. They were symbols of entrepreneurial capitalism. The raising of each of these structures from the city's pavement became a great civic event. Both the Mackie Block and the Lancaster Building, with their surging commercial energy, encouraged young people to come to the city and take part in an effort to make it prosperous.

Service Businesses

Visitors found Calgarians enterprising and confident. In Calgary, the Canadian go-ahead spirit, the urge to press forward, was evident everywhere. It was the confident spirit of Canada, but it was also the spirit of youth, for Calgary remained, as ever, a city of young people. It was much easier for young men and women to rise to positions of influence in the Calgary business world in the late nineteenth and early twentieth centuries than in Toronto, Montreal, or Halifax.

The development of service businesses, such as insurance companies, brokerage houses, and accountancy firms, was an essential part of the evolution of Calgary's business system in this period. While branches of insurance companies like the Winnipeg-based Great West Life Assurance Company grew rapidly in Calgary, there was only one accountancy firm and one brokerage house in the city by 1900.¹⁴⁷ The appearance of more brokerage houses and accountancy firms lay in the future. But full-time accountants were already employed in businesses like the Hudson's Bay Company, P. Burns & Co., and the chartered banks as these enterprises grew in size and complexity. The first brokerage firm appeared in Calgary in 1898, when entrepreneur Charles S. Lott opened his brokerage house. He also sold real estate, insurance, and coal, and lent British money to Calgary and Bow Valley businesses.

With the expansion of his business operations, Lott recruited as a clerk around 1900 Ernest D. Adams, who proved that he could succeed in more than one field.¹⁴⁸ Born in 1868 in Bombay, India, the son of a British military officer, Ernest Adams attended school in London, England. In 1884, at the age of sixteen, he immigrated with his family from England to Winnipeg to become an apprentice clerk in the Hudson's Bay Company store at nearby Lower Fort Garry. After working for the company for eight years, he invested his savings in a homestead he selected on the North Fork of Sheep Creek in the Millarville area and formed a ranching partnership with a neighbouring livestock raiser William H. King in 1892.¹⁴⁹ Adams and King raised some thoroughbred horses, which they purchased from the Quorn Ranche, and some Galloway cattle and financed their small operation with reinvested profits from the sale of their livestock.¹⁵⁰ As time progressed, they exchanged work with their neighbour Walter Phillips, a small rancher, at haying time.

Selling his interest in the ranch to his partner King around 1900, Ernest Adams then pursued his dream of becoming a financier by starting to clerk in Charles Lott's brokerage firm in Calgary.¹⁵¹ Lott had a profound impact on Adams, teaching him everything he needed to know about the brokerage business, insurance, real estate, coal, and money lending, and, with this training, Adams contributed significantly to the firm's growth. His relations with Lott were harmonious. As a securities broker, Lott acted as an intermediary in arranging trades of securities, including stocks and bonds, and Adams assisted him in this work. In 1901, Adams married Carrie McCarthy, daughter of Peter McCarthy. Before long, the couple had children: Peter, Evelyn, Margaret, and William.

With his fairly modest salary, Adams supported his family and made a sensible investment in raising thoroughbred horses, some of which he sold to the Pacific Cartage Co. in Calgary, owned by

Chapter 12: Financing the Canadian Dream

Charles Lott.[152] In the process, Adams the astute entrepreneur lifted his household from working-class to middle-class status, moving his family from a small house in Calgary to a larger and more comfortable home in the city's Elbow Park district in 1911. While Lott financed the development of the brokerage business and the Pacific Cartage Co. through reinvested profits and substantial loans from the Imperial Bank of Canada, Adams borrowed $4,500 from Lott at an annual interest rate of 6 percent to help fund his horse raising venture.[153] All the while, Adams proved his worth in the thriving brokerage house. When Lott died in 1914, Ernest Adams, named as one of the executors in Lott's will, assisted in the administration of his estate and purchased an interest in the brokerage firm which continued to prosper under his management.[154]

All business enterprises, in whatever industry, shared a basic problem: how to finance the dreams of their owners. The businesses built by Ernest D. Adams, Charles S. Lott, James S. Mackie, William Hanson Boorne, James C. Linton, Margaret Leishman, Christina Kinnisten, Luey Dofoo, Sandy Watson, Meopham Gardner, James A. Lougheed and others depended on reinvested profits and credit. They were of great importance to the development of the Calgary and Bow Valley economies and to the improvement in the standard of living in the region. The Canadian dream of a higher standard of living certainly did not come true for everyone, but it materialized for enough people in Calgary and the Bow Valley so that many others were encouraged to try. Even though numerous individuals lacked the money to develop their enterprises, businesses with access to credit often grew. As business owners' financial power increased, more and more people flourished.

Conclusion

Themes of an Era, 1870–1900

New Technologies in Tranportation and Communication

Improved transportation and communication was one of the most newsworthy business trends in Calgary and the Bow Valley in the late nineteenth century. As new railways spread across the region, so did new telegraph lines. Enhanced transportation and communication through railway and telegraph technologies spurred settlement and facilitated the development of business enterprises. The impact of these technologies on the Calgary and Bow Valley economies is one of the central themes in the exploration of the history of business in the city and its region. Railways speeded the carriage of mail and funnelled people, commerce, agriculture, industry and banking into the area. The advent of the telegraph made communication almost instantaneous, even over long distances, permitting railway managers to schedule the movement of trains. With a few strokes of the telegraph key, the telegraph operator could deliver fresh information from many other business people to particular individuals within the business system.

For a period of over ten years, from about 1870 to 1883, the technology that best symbolized the transportation system in Calgary and the Bow Valley was the wagon. The wagon came to be regarded as a necessity, just as the railway would be later. Each in its time came to rank near such things as food and shelter as a perceived essential of life in the settlement era. The partial replacement of an old method of transportation by a new one happened rapidly. During less than one decade, from 1883 to 1892, about 150 miles of new railway tracks were introduced into the Bow Valley, linking Calgary to Montreal and Vancouver, as well as to Edmonton and Fort Macleod.

The gains in transportation technology allowed people to buy a greater variety of goods and services than dreamers in an earlier age would have thought possible. The period from 1870 to 1900 was a relatively short time – about half the lifespan of the average Canadian then. Yet, our ancestors in Calgary and the Bow Valley in 1900 lived very differently from the way they did three decades before. Important changes were already underway in 1900, but numerous daily routines were much like those of 1870. A number of people in 1900 were experiencing the excitement of journeying by train, but many still travelled by horse-drawn wagon. Obviously, nobody in 1900 had an automobile. Numerous shoppers were purchasing branded goods such as Levi Strauss overalls; but many families were still sewing their own clothing. In 1901, as automobiles first appeared on the scene, Calgary and the Bow Valley were becoming richer markets, and they were growing fast.

New Goods for Consumers

An apparently unlimited array of new goods was offered to consumers in Calgary and the Bow Valley by the end of the nineteenth century. By the 1890s, dozens of new products per year appeared in the local and regional markets. Every year, new items were put out for sale in department stores, general stores, saddle and harness shops, hardware stores, meat markets, grocery stores, implement shops, drugstores, boot and shoe shops, dry goods stores, jewellery stores, bookstores, millinery shops, furniture stores, and confectionery stores.

The market in Calgary and the Bow Valley changed as the needs and wants of consumers evolved. A number of new products proved unsatisfactory. Consequently, manufacturers had opportunities to develop new goods. Receiving messages from advertisers in the newspapers day after day, consumers tended to try out new products. As consumers made choices in the marketplace, they played an important role in the success of various items.

By 1900, over 150 commercial and industrial firms were doing business in the city of Calgary and in Bow Valley hamlets and villages, selling goods and services to consumers. With the exception of the Canadian Pacific Railway and the chartered banks, none of these firms was very large. All the city and regional firms began small. Most of them originated as entrepreneurial start-ups and remained relatively small; a few became medium-sized enterprises. By the 1890s, the small to medium-sized department store was not only offering the broadest range of consumer goods, but also selling them at the lowest prices. In their approach to business, general stores and most other small firms operated on one basic principle. They stressed high margins on a low volume of transactions – this was the key to their success. In contrast, the department store followed a policy of handling a high volume of business at low margins and created a mass market for a variety of merchandise. However, like the department store, many other firms, including the general store, offered a diverse set of goods to consumers. Diversification is a theme that pervades the entire history of business in Calgary and the Bow Valley in the late nineteenth century.

Business by Economic Sector

In addition to diversification, several other themes stand out in the thirty-year period from 1870 to 1900.

The field of sales, especially retailing, presented a mixed picture for businesses in Calgary and the Bow Valley. Challenged by department stores, small retailers also faced growing competition from other small retail outlets in the late 1880s and 1890s. New competitive pressures made the task of management at the small retail stores more difficult. In these years, the number of small retailers grew faster than the region's population as a whole. Nevertheless, although there were more competitors in the market, small retail outlets often survived by catering to consumers' preferences.

Agriculture, a growing segment of the Bow Valley economy, became a stronghold of small ranching and farming businesses. From the early 1880s into the 1890s, the number of small family ranches in the Bow Valley was rising. Initially, big corporate ranches dominated the production of livestock. But by the late 1890s, the number of small to medium-sized ranching businesses had more than doubled. The most important social institution enabling small ranches to grow was the family. Virtually all family ranchers had an entrepreneurial outlook; many of them were resilient. Small ranch resilience depended heavily on a broad range of livestock raising

Conclusion: Themes of an Era, 1870–1900

skills. Capable of recovering from shock, many founders proved successful as owner-managers of small-scale ranching businesses. The ability of small ranches to adjust to misfortune or economic change helps to explain their growing importance.

Between the 1870s and 1890s, the small, owner-occupied family farm was the norm in the Bow Valley. In the region, there were no bonanza farms organized as corporations and designed to earn quick profits for their shareholders. Although the number of farms declined, many family farmers added some land to their 160-acre homestead and made significant improvements. The majority of the farmers were entrepreneurially motivated. They engaged in diversified agriculture, producing enough food for their own family needs, but usually also raising crops and livestock for markets in the Bow Valley, Calgary, other parts of Canada, and abroad. Far from being isolated, most family farms were part of a network of economic and social ties that linked farms and families in rural communities.

In banking services, branches of chartered banks were of increasing importance in the Calgary and the Bow Valley. Credit networks existed in an informal manner in the late nineteenth century, as merchants loaned funds to ranchers and farmers and to other members of their communities. In 1885, private bankers began providing credit services for merchants, ranchers, farmers, and manufacturers. Branches of chartered banks soon followed, always established by chartered banks in central Canada seeking profitable forms of investment. By the early 1890s, people in Calgary and the Bow Valley often depended on chartered banks' branches to meet their financial needs.

Versatility and small to medium size were the hallmarks of most Calgary industrial firms in the late nineteenth century. With skilled workforces and up-to-date machinery, the manufacturers could rapidly switch to various kinds of products as markets altered. For the most part, the owner-managers of the manufacturing establishments remained close to their work. Although Calgary was not immune to labour unrest, ties binding workers and owners moderated disagreements. Owners and workers knew each other personally through work on the plant floor and through membership in the same social organizations in the city. Their flexibility permitted most Calgary manufacturing businesses to prosper even during the economic turmoil of the mid-1890s. Owners identified personally with their business enterprises, which they frequently saw as parts of their families. In the 1890s, the experiences of Calgary manufacturers illustrate the ongoing opportunities for small business people in the field of manufacturing.

Conclusion: Themes of an Era, 1870–1900

Between the years 1870 and 1900, Calgarians and rural people in the Bow Valley generally embraced the capitalist system, which offered opportunities for independent-minded individuals with the initiative to start a business. Merchants, ranchers, farmers, manufacturers, and bankers played an important role in the economic success of the region. Many Bow Valley citizens endured hard times, along with people in other parts of North America. As the business cycle moved up and down, the Bow Valley economy, like capitalist economies elsewhere, suffered depressions – in the mid-1870s, the mid-1880s, and the mid-1890s. Business firms prospered, floundered, went bankrupt, and in some cases recovered. Individuals made and lost fortunes. Although many small firms had a lifespan of five years or less, the late 1890s saw the flowering of small businesses. Calgary owed its resilience to considerable diversification of its economic activities, the breadth of its business skills, and its ability to create new jobs by attracting new and growing enterprises.

By 1900, the Canadian family had become increasingly important as a haven from economic storms in Calgary and the Bow Valley. In the last three decades of the nineteenth century, a shift occurred in the balance between the rights of the individual and the needs of the married couple, as the nuclear family became the norm in the region. Of children born to married parents, most could anticipate that the marriage would last until death took either the mother or the father. Mutual responsibilities that were traditionally inherent in certain relationships, like those between husband and wife and parent and child, grew even stronger as these relationships became more solid. Although the rights of the individual were stressed, there was a growing emphasis on responsibilities and the needs of the family and community.

In the late Victorian world, many people in Calgary and the Bow Valley saved and sought economic independence. They went into business – in farming, ranching, commerce, industry and banking. Businesses were involved in social activities that benefited the broader society, with their leaders playing a significant role in the cultural and charitable undertakings in Calgary and rural communities. What remained remarkable was their optimism about the future. Several of the successful business founders ran businesses that grew and persisted beyond ten years into the twentieth century, making a strong impact upon their family and community, as well as upon the local, regional, and national economies.

Chronology

1870 Transfer of Rupert's Land from the Hudson's Bay Company to the Dominion of Canada, which left the federal government in full control of the region.
1871 John J. Healy and Alfred B. Hamilton set up a trading post in Calgary.
1872 The Canadian Parliament passed the Dominion Lands Act.
1873 John McDougall started a mission, a general store, and a cattle ranch in Morley.
1875 The Northwest Territories Act passed by the Canadian Parliament.
1875 Sam Livingston established his farm on Fish Creek in the spring.
1875 John Glenn started his farm in Midnapore in July.
1875 North West Mounted Police arrived in Calgary in August.
1875 I. G. Baker & Co.'s general store opened in Calgary mid-September.
1875 I. G. Baker & Co. established its cattle ranch in the Calgary area.
1875 Hudson's Bay Company's general store set up in Calgary end of September.
1876 I. G. Baker & Co. obtained a permit from the U.S. government to ship buffalo robes and furs from the Canadian prairies through Fort Benton to Montreal or London, England in bond.
1877 Treaty 7, covering Blackfoot, Stoney, Sarcee, Blood, and Peigan land in Southern Alberta, signed at the Blackfoot Crossing 22 September.
1879 Disappearance of the buffalo from Alberta.
1880 Okotoks founded as a hamlet (incorporated as a village in 1899).
1880 Kenneth Cameron established his farm in Okotoks in September.
1881 Cochrane Ranch Company incorporated 5 May (first herd of cattle arrived at the ranch west of Calgary in the fall).
1881 High River founded as a hamlet (incorporated as a village in 1901).
1882 Order in Council approved by the Canadian Parliament dividing the Northwest Territories into districts: Alberta, Saskatchewan, Assiniboia, and Athabaska.
1882 Benton & St. Louis Cattle Co. formed in Fort Benton, Montana.
1883 Gleichen founded as a hamlet.

Chronology

1883 George Murdoch set up his harness and saddle shop in Calgary in May.
1883 Victor J. Beaupré opened his general store in Gleichen in the summer.
1883 Hudson's Bay Company moved the headquarters of its Alberta trade from Edmonton to Calgary in July.
1883 Canadian Pacific Railway arrived in Calgary 11 August.
1883 Agnes K. Bedingfeld established her ranch on Pekisko Creek in August.
1883 Canadian Pacific Railway reached Morley in September.
1883 Robert Findlay entered his homestead in the High River area in the fall.
1883 James A. Lougheed opened his law office in Calgary in October.
1884 James C. Linton set up his bookstore in Calgary in April.
1884 Canadian Pacific Railway arrived in Canmore in May.
1884 Calgary incorporated as a town 7 November.
1884 Canmore founded as a hamlet (incorporated as a village in 1965).
1884 Sheep Creek Ranche established (reorganized as Quorn Ranche in 1887).
1884 James F. McKevitt entered his homestead in the Midnapore area.
1885 Lafferty & Smith, private bank, set up its Calgary branch in March.
1885 Farm Protest Movement in the Bow Valley began 5 April.
1885 William James Andrews entered his homestead in the Davisburg area in the fall.
1885 Sacred Heart Convent was opened in Calgary.
1886 Benton & St. Louis Cattle Co. established its ranch in the Kipp area in the spring.
1886 The Canadian Parliament granted representation to the Northwest Territories, with the district of Alberta receiving one seat in the House of Commons.
1886 William Hanson Boorne opened his photography studio in Calgary.
1886 Meopham Gardner established his ranch in the Bragg Creek area in July.
1886 Great Fire in Calgary 7 November.
1886 Hull, Trounce & Co. started its butchering business in Calgary.
1886 The Eau Claire & Bow River Lumber Co. began operations in Calgary.
1887 The Central School opened in Calgary.
1887 Arthur G. Wolley-Dod started his ranch in the Pine Creek area.
1887 The opening of Calgary's first department store: I. G. Baker & Co., in April.
1888 The Canadian Parliament established a legislative assembly for the Northwest Territories in Regina, to which the Calgary electoral district elected two of Alberta's six members.
1888 James S. Mackie became an independent gunsmith in Calgary.
1889 LeJeune, Smith & Co. bought Lafferty & Smith's Calgary business 23 February.
1889 Lafferty & Moore, first women-owned bank, formed in Calgary 23 February.
1889 Frances Marie Carr opened her boardinghouse in Calgary.
1889 Hutchings & Riley, manufacturers of harnesses and saddles, began operations in Calgary.

Chronology

1889 Samuel and Helen Shaw opened the Midnapore Woollen Mills in December.
1890 The Calgary and Edmonton Railway, a subsidiary of the Canadian Pacific, began construction in Calgary in July (the rails reached Strathcona on the south bank of the North Saskatchewan River opposite Edmonton in July 1891 and Fort Macleod in November 1892).
1890 The General Hospital opened in Calgary.
1891 Agnes Carroll established the Holy Cross Hospital in Calgary 30 January.
1891 Sale of I. G. Baker & Co.'s department store in Calgary to the Hudson's Bay Company in February.
1891 Grand opening of the Hudson's Bay Company's department store in Calgary 5 March
1891 George Alexander built the Alexander Block in Calgary.
1891 Janet Dewar set up her dressmaking shop in Calgary.
1893 The Circle Ranch was established in the Queenstown area.
1893 Hutchings & Riley won a gold medal for their saddles and harnesses at the World's Fair in Chicago.
1894 Calgary incorporated as a city 1 January.
1894 Mary Macleod started her dressmaking business in Calgary.
1897 The Canadian Parliament passed a law that gave the Northwest Territories responsible government.
1898 Christina Grant Kinnisten became the owner and manager of a confectionery store in Calgary in March.
1898 Charles S. Lott opened his brokerage house in Calgary.
1899 The Calgary Business College was established.
1903 Cochrane incorporated as a village.
1903 Western Canada College was established in Calgary.
1904 Annie and Jean Mollison opened Braemar Lodge in Calgary.
1904 St. Hilda's Ladies' College was established in Calgary.
1906 Luey Dofoo became the owner and manager of the Sunlight Restaurant in Calgary.

Notes

Note to Preface

1. Thomas K. McCraw, ed., *Creating Modern Capitalism: How Entrepreneurs, Companies, and Countries Triumphed in Three Industrial Revolutions* (Cambridge, Mass.: Harvard University Press, 1997), 4.

Notes to Introduction

1. W. L. Morton, *Manitoba: A History* (Toronto: University of Toronto Press, 1967), 152, 157–59; Carroll Van West, *Capitalism on the Frontier Billings and the Yellowstone Valley in the Nineteenth Century* (Lincoln: University of Nebraska Press, 1993), 89-95, 192–93.
2. National Archives of Canada (hereafter NAC), Department of the Interior Records, RG15, vol. 664, file 290709, statement on Calgary Town Council stationery, 5 April 1892.
3. Alfred D. Chandler, Jr., *The Visible Hand: The Managerial Revolution in American Business* (Cambridge, Mass.: Harvard University Press, 1977), 79. On railroad construction and the expansion of the frontier in the American West during the late nineteenth century, see C. Knick Harley, "Transportation, the World Wheat Trade, and the Kuznets Cycle, 1850–1913," *Explorations in Economic History* 17 (July 1980), 218–50. For a misleading account about the issue of the importance of the railroad, see Robert Fogel's quantitative argument that the railroads were not indispensable to American economic growth in the nineteenth century: Robert William Fogel, *Railroads and American Economic Growth: Essays in Econometric History* (Baltimore: Johns Hopkins University Press, 1964). The interested reader is invited to pursue the great significance of railroads to economic growth in the United States further in a recent work, Albro Martin, *Railroads Triumphant: The Growth, Rejection & Rebirth of a Vital American Force* (New York: Oxford University Press, 1992).
4. On the Canadian Pacific Railway and the economic development of the Canadian West, see John A. Eagle, *The Canadian Pacific Railway and the Development of Western Canada, 1896-1914* (Montreal: McGill-Queen's University Press, 1989); J. C. Herbert Emery and Kenneth J. McKenzie,

"Damned if you do, damned if you don't: an option value approach to evaluating the subsidy of the CPR mainline," *Canadian Journal of Economics* 29 (May 1996), 255–70.
5. Robert M. Stamp, "The Response to Urban Growth: The Bureaucratization of Public Education in Calgary, 1884–1914," in Anthony W. Rasporich and Henry C. Klassen, eds., *Frontier Calgary Town, City, Region 1875-1914* (Calgary: McClelland and Stewart West, 1975), 153–68; Douglas Coats, "Calgary: The Private Schools, 1900-16," in Rasporich and Klassen, eds., *Frontier Calgary*, 141–52; *Calgary Herald*, 26 January 1933.
6. Margaret Morton Fahrni and W. L. Morton, *Third Crossing A History of the First Quarter Century of the Town and District of Gladstone in the Province of Manitoba* (Winnipeg: Advocate Printers Limited, 1946), 1-2, 7-20; C. Robert Haywood, *Cowtown Lawyers Dodge City and Its Attorneys, 1876-1886* (Norman: University of Oklahoma Press, 1988), 17.
7. *Calgary Herald*, 7 November 1888.
8. W. T. Easterbrook and Hugh G. J. Aitken, *Canadian Economic History* (Toronto: Macmillan Company of Canada, 1967), 417–35; McCraw, ed., *Creating Modern Capitalism*, 310–16. See also James Willard Hurst, *Law and the Conditions of Freedom in the Ninteteenth-Century United States*. (Madison: University of Wisconsin Press, 1956).

Notes to Chapter 1
The Meeting Place

1. Hugh A. Dempsey, *Calgary: Spirit of the West* (Saskatoon: Fifth House, 1994), 4–5.
2. Paul F. Sharp, *Whoop-Up Country: The Canadian-American West, 1865–1885* (Norman: University of Oklahoma Press, 1978), 38–50.
3. Joel Overholser, *Fort Benton, World's Innermost Port* (Fort Benton: Joel Overholser, 1987), 75; James E. Murphy, *Half Interest in a Silver Dollar: The Saga of Charles E. Conrad* (Missoula: Mountain Press Publishing Company, 1983), 30.
4. Overholser, *Fort Benton*, 75.
5. National Archives of Canada (hereafter NAC), RG18, Royal Canadian Mounted Police Records (hereafter RCMP Records), vol. 4, file 98-75, statement made by I. G. Baker of Fort Benton, Montana, 25 February 1875.
6. Quoted in Dempsey, *Calgary*, 11.
7. NAC, RCMP Records, vol. 4, file 98-75, statement made by I. G. Baker, 25 February 1875.
8. Ibid.
9. Dempsey, *Calgary*, 12–13.
10. Glenbow-Alberta Institute Archives (hereafter GAIA), D. W. Davis Papers, file 1, Eloise Davis, "Biography of D. W. Davis."
11. *Dawson News*, 8 June 1906.
12. Lewis O. Saum, "From Vermont to Whoop-Up Country: Some Letters of D. W. Davis, 1867–1878," *Montana: The Magazine of Western History*, 35 (Summer 1985), 62, 9 June 1867, D. W. Davis to Daniel Davis.

13. *Calgary Herald*, 8 June 1957.
14. Ibid.
15. Saum, "From Vermont to Whoop-Up Country," 67, Fort Hamilton, 28 June 1873, D. W. Davis to Daniel Davis.
16. *Calgary Herald*, 8 June 1957.
17. Saum, "From Vermont to Whoop-Up Country," 67, Fort Hamilton, 28 June 1873, D. W. Davis to Daniel Davis.
18. *Calgary Herald*, 8 June 1957.
19. GAIA, Richard Hardisty Papers, box 3, Bow River, 21 December 1874, John Bunn to Richard Hardisty; Provincial Archives of Manitoba, Hudson's Bay Company Archives (hereafter HBCA), D20/3, ff. 547-547d, Edmonton, 24 December 1875, Rober Hamilton to James A. Grahame; NAC, Department of the Interior Records, vol. 320, file 74920, Ottawa, 19 March 1883, statement made by D. W. Davis.
20. Hartwell Bowsfield, ed., *The Letters of Charles John Brydges 1879–1882: Hudson's Bay Company Land Commissioner*. With an Introduction by Alan Wilson. (Winnipeg: Hudson's Bay Record Society, 1977), 264, Winnipeg, 28 September 1882, C. J. Brydges to W. Armit.

Notes to Chapter 2
I. G. Baker & Co.

1. *Globe-Democrat*, 6 April 1904.
2. Missouri Historical Society Archives, P. Chouteau Maffitt Collection, Fort Benton, 29 August 1864, I. G. Baker to P. Chouteau Jr. & Co.
3. Baker Library, Graduate School of Business Administration, Harvard University, R. G. Dun & Co. Collection, Montana, vol. 1, 236.
4. National Archives, Washington, D.C. (hereafter NA), RG75, Office of Indian Affairs Records, reel 498, file B1285, Washington, D.C., 30 October 1874, George A. Baker to E. P. Smith.
5. James E. Murphy, *Half Interest in a Silver Dollar: The Saga of Charles E. Conrad* (Missoula: Mountain Press Publishing Company, 1983), 20.
6. NA, Office of Indian Affairs Records, reel 498, file B1285, Washington, D.C., 30 October 1874, George A. Baker to E. P. Smith.
7. NA, Office of Indian Affairs Records, reel 498, file B935, Fort Benton, 29 July 1874, I. G. Baker & Co. to E. P. Smith.
8. NA, Office of Indian Affairs Records, reel 490, file S872, statement made by W. B. Pease, 6 August 1870.
9. NA, Office of Indian Affairs Records, reel 490, file not recorded, statement made by J. A. Viall, 6 December 1870.
10. NA, Office of Indian Affairs Records, reel 498, file B1285, Washington, D.C., 30 October 1874, G. A. Baker to E. P. Smith.
11. NA, RG39, Secretary of the Treasury Records, vol. 5, payment, 26 September 1870.
12. NAC, RG18, RCMP Records, vol. 4, file 98/75, statement made by I. G. Baker, 25 February 1875.
13. *Great Falls Tribune*, 28 November 1902.

14. Hugh A. Dempsey, ed., *R. B. Nevitt: A Winter at Fort Macleod* (Calgary: McClelland and Stewart West, 1974), 19.
15. *Fort Benton Record*, 16 August 1878.
16. NAC, RCMP Records, vol. 4, file 88/75, Fort Macleod, 10 January 1875, James F. Macleod to Hewitt Bernard.
17. Canada, *Sessional Papers*, 1879, no. 188, North West Mounted Police Expenditure, 1879.
18. Dempsey, *R. B. Nevitt*, 30–31; *Fort Benton Record*, 19 June 1875.
19. NAC, RG15, Department of the Interior Records, vol. 320, file 74920, statement made by D. W. Davis, 19 March 1883.
20. Canada, *Sessional Papers*, 1879, no. 188, statement of payments made to I. G. Baker & Co., 1875–1876.
21. GAIA, Richard Hardisty Papers, Fort Benton, 30 June 1874, I. G. Baker & Co. to McDougall Bros.
22. NAC, RCMP Records, vol. 4, file 98/75, statement made by I. G. Baker, 25 February 1875.
23. *Scarlet and Gold*, vol. 5, 69.
24. Richard Hardisty Papers, Bow River, 14 December 1875, John Bunn to Richard Hardisty; Spitsea, 15 December 1875, Wm. Leslie Wood to Richard Hardisty.
25. *Fort Benton Record*, 24 July 1875; 5 May 1876.
26. HBCA, D20/7, ff. 229–30, Montreal, 7 September 1877, James Bissett to James A. Grahame; D20/14, ff. 26–27, Montreal, 3 September 1879, James Bissett to James A. Grahame.
27. *Fort Benton Record*, 15 February 1878.
28. NAC, RCMP Records, vol. 11, file 248/76, Ottawa, 13 November 1876, Fred White to Secretary of State.
29. NAC, RCMP Records, vol. 10, file 170/76, St. Louis, 20 May 1876, I. G. Baker to Hugh Richardson.
30. NAC, RCMP Records, vol. 10, file 170/76, Fort Benton, 30 April 1876, W. G. Conrad to Hugh Richardson.
31. NAC, RCMP Records, vol. 11, file 248/76, Ottawa, 13 November 1876, Fred White to Secretary of State.
32. Canada, *Sessional Papers*, 1879, no. 188, statement of vouchers for pay to the Mounted Police.
33. Howard Palmer, with Tamara Palmer, *Alberta: A New History* (Edmonton: Hurtig Publishers, 1990), 41–42.
34. Sarah Carter, *Aboriginal People and Colonizers of Western Canada to 1900* (Toronto: University of Toronto Press, 1999), 121–27; R. Douglas Francis, Richard Jones, and Donald B. Smith, *Destinies: Canadian History Since Confederation*, Third Edition (Toronto: Harcourt Brace & Company Canada, 1996), 59–62; Sarah Carter, *Lost Harvests: Prairie Indian Reserves Farmers and Government Policy* (Montreal: McGill-Queen's University Press, 1990); Treaty Elders and Tribal Council, with Walter Hildebrandt, Sarah Carter, and Dorothy First Rider, *The True Spirit and Original Intent of Treaty 7* (Montreal: McGill-Queen's University Press, 1996).

35. NAC, RG10, Department of Indian Affairs Records, vol. 3632, file 6260, Ottawa, 15 April 1876, I. G. Baker to David Laird.
36. NAC, Department of Indian Affairs Records, vol. 3632, file 6260, Ottawa, 15 April 1876, David Laird to I. G. Baker & Co.
37. NAC, Department of Indian Affairs Records, vol. 3632, file 6260, St. Louis, 21 August 1876, I. G. Baker & Co. to David Laird.
38. Sir Cecil E. Denny, *The Law Marches West* (Toronto: J.M. Dent and Sons, 1972), 114.
39. *Fort Benton Record*, 25 May 1877; Canada, *Sessional Papers*, 1879, no. 7, report of the Deputy Superintendent General of Indian Affairs.
40. The amount of sales to Indians and settlers is not known, but for sales to the Mounted Police see Canada, *Sessional Papers*, 1879, no. 188, payments made to I. G. Baker & Co., 1875–1876.
41. *Albertan*, 22 March 1909.
42. R. G. Dun & Co. Collection, R. G. Dun, Missouri, vol. 45, 136.
43. Provincial Archives of Alberta (hereafter PAA), accession no. 79.266, Supreme Court of the Northwest Territories, Calgary, Civil Cases, file 2160, *I. G. Baker & Co. v Helen Maria Gouin* (1889).
44. GAIA, North West Mounted Police, letterbook, 23 November 1876, James Macleod to I. G. Baker & Co.
45. NAC, Department of the Interior Records, vol. 320, file 74920, statement made by W. G. Conrad, 30 January 1883.
46. Montana Historical Society Archives, T. C. Power Papers, box 273, file 28, Agreement between I. G. Baker & Co. and T. C. Power & Bro., 18 January 1881.
47. K. Ross Toole Archives, University of Montana Library, Missoula, C. E. Conrad Papers, Fort Macleod, 24 October 1881, Mary I. Macleod to Alicia Conrad; *River Press*, 5 January 1881.
48. C. E. Conrad Papers, Fort Macleod, 5 January 1881, James F. Macleod to C. E. Conrad.
49. T. C. Power Papers, box 273, file 28, agreement between I. G. Baker & Co. and T. C. Power & Bro., 12 September 1881; box 274, file 2, agreement between I. G. Baker & Co. and T. C. Power & Bro., 14 February 1883.
50. NA, RG101, Comptroller of the Currency Records, Organizational Papers, file 2476, Articles of Association of the First National Bank of Fort Benton, 24 April 1880.
51. NA, Comptroller of the Currency Records, Organizational Papers, file 2476, First National Bank of Fort Benton, list of stockholders.
52. Montana Historical Society Archives, S. T. Hauser Papers, box 7, file 10, St. Louis, 12 February 1882, W.G. Conrad to S. T. Hauser.
53. Sharp, *Whoop-Up Country*, 221–22.
54. S. T. Hauser Papers, box 48, file 3, First National Bank of Fort Benton, individual balances, 23 September 1884, I. G. Baker & Co.
55. *Fort Benton Record*, 7 November 1879.
56. *Fort Benton Record*, 9 July 1880.
57. *Fort Benton Record*, 14 May 1880.

Notes to pp. 33–44

58. *Fort Benton Record*, 22 October 1880.
59. *Fort Benton Record*, 13 July 1882.
60. HBCA, D20/63, f. 222, results taken from I. G. Baker & Co.'s books.
61. *Macleod Gazette*, 4 September 1882.
62. *Macleod Gazette*, 1 July 1882.
63. *Macleod Gazette*, 14 September 1882.
64. Ibid.; *Lethbridge Herald*, 25 April 1949.
65. GAIA, Frank M. Crosby Papers, Calgary, 30 September 1882, Frank Crosby to his father.
66. PAA, accession no. 66.21, Calgary Court House, chattel mortgages, 1883–1890.
67. C. E. Conrad Papers, letterpress book, Ottawa, 25 April 1883, C. E. Conrad to Tees, Costigan & Wilson.
68. *Macleod Gazette*, 1 July 1882; 14 September 1882.
69. PAA, Calgary Court House, chattel mortgages, 1883–1890.
70. NAC, Department of the Interior Records, vol. 1182, file 1107, statement showing livestock imported into Alberta from the United States, 1 June 1880–30 January 1885.
71. State of Montana, Helena, Secretary of State, Corporation Bureau, file B188, Articles of Incorporation of Benton & St. Louis Cattle Co., 25 May 1882.
72. *Fort Benton Record*, 25 May 1882; Henry C. Klassen, "The Conrads in the Alberta Cattle Business, 1875–1911," *Agricultural History*, 64 (Summer 1990), 39.
73. *River Press*, 8 March 1882.
74. GAIA, Diary of Frank White, agreement between I. G. Baker & Co. and the Cochrane Ranche Company, 5 September 1882.
75. NAC, Department of the Interior Records, vol. 320, file 74920, statement made by D. W. Davis, 19 March 1883.
76. Montana Historical Society Archives, I. G. Baker Papers, St. Louis, 13 February 1883, I. G. Baker to C. E. & W. G. Conrad.

Notes to Chapter 3
Hudson's Bay Company

1. Michael Bliss, *Northern Enterprise: Five Centuries of Canadian Business* (Toronto: McClelland & Stewart, 1987), 79–102; Ann M. Carlos and Jill L. Van Stone, "Stock Transfer Patterns in the Hudson's Bay Company: A Study of the English Capital Market in Operation, 1670–1730," *Business History*, 38 (April 1996), 15–18.
2. J. G. Nelson, *The Last Refuge* (Montreal: Harvest House, 1973), 78–83; J. G. MacGregor, *John Rowand, Czar of the Prairies* (Saskatoon: Western Producer Prairie Books, 1978), 92–97.
3. GAIA, Richard Hardisty Papers, Bow River, 14 December 1875, John Bunn to Richard Hardisty.
4. HBCA, D20/7, ff. 215-215d, Montreal, 1 September 1877, James Bissett to James A. Grahame.

5. Richard Hardisty Papers, Bow River, 14 December 1875, John Bunn to Richard Hardisty.
6. Shirlee Anne Smith, "Richard Charles Hardisty," *Dictionary of Canadian Biography*, Vol. 11, *1881 to 1890* (Toronto: University of Toronto Press, 1982), 383–84.
7. HBCA, D20/4, ff. 10-10d, 11-11d, Edmonton, 4 January 1876, Richard Hardisty to James A. Grahame.
8. A. A. den Otter, "The Hudson's Bay Company's Prairie Transportation Problem, 1870–1885," in John E. Foster, ed., *The Developing West: Essays on Canadian History in Honor of Lewis H. Thomas* (Edmonton: University of Alberta Press, 1983), 27–31.
9. Richard Hardisty Papers, Fort Calgary, 24 November 1876, John Bunn to Richard Hardisty.
10. HBCA, D20/3, f. 549d, Edmonton, 24 December 1875, Robert Hamilton to James A. Grahame.
11. Richard Hardisty Papers, Bow River, 9 September 1875, John Bunn to Richard Hardisty.
12. HBCA, D20/3, f. 549, Edmonton, 24 December 1875, Robert Hamilton to James A. Grahame.
13. HBCA, D20/4, f. 10d, Edmonton, 4 January 1876, Richard Hardisty to James A. Grahame.
14. HBCA, A12/16, f. 106, Carlton House, 22 June 1874, Richard Hardisty to James A. Grahame.
15. HBCA, D20/3, ff. 548-548d, Edmonton, 24 December 1875, Robert Hamilton to James A. Grahame.
16. HBCA, D20/3, f. 548d, Edmonton, 24 December 1875, Robert Hamilton to James A. Grahame.
17. HBCA, D20/3, f. 549d, Edmonton, 24 December 1875, Robert Hamilton to James A. Grahame.
18. Richard Hardisty Papers, Fort Calgary, 24 November 1876, John Bunn to Richard Hardisty.
19. PAA, accession no. 74.32, Homestead Records, reel 2000, file 43503, statement made by Samuel Livingston, 15 September 1883.
20. Richard Hardisty Papers, Elbow Post, 8 February 1877, John Bunn to Richard Hardisty.
21. Ibid., Bow River, 16 June 1877, John Bunn to Richard Hardisty.
22. Ibid., Bow River, 2 July 1877, John Bunn to Richard Hardisty.
23. Ibid., Elbow Post, 1 November 1877, John Bunn to Richard Hardisty.
24. Ibid., Elbow Post, 1 November 1877, John Bunn to Richard Hardisty.
25. Ibid., Elbow Post, 23 July 1877, John Bunn to Richard Hardisty.
26. Ibid., Bow River, 16 June 1877, John Bunn to Richard Hardisty.
27. HBCA, A12/17, f. 333, Fort Garry, 15 November 1876, James A. Grahame to William Armit.
28. HBCA, A12/17, ff. 537–38, Fort Garry, 30 May 1877, James A. Grahame to William Armit.
29. Richard Hardisty Papers, Elbow Post, November 1877, John Bunn to Richard Hardisty.

30. Homestead Records, reel 2001, file 86890, statement made by Angus Fraser, 20 February 1885.
31. HBCA, D20/23, f. 161d, Edmonton, 20 June 1882, Richard Hardisty to James A. Grahame.
32. HBCA, D20/10, ff. 159-159d, Edmonton, 5 June 1878, Richard Hardisty to James A. Grahame.
33. Hartwell Bowsfield, ed., *The Letters of Charles John Brydges 1879–1882: Hudson's Bay Company Land Commissioner*. With an Introduction by Alan Wilson. (Winnipeg: Hudson's Bay Company Record Society, 1977), xxxvii-xl; Alan Wilson and R.A. Hotchkiss, "Charles John Brydges," *Dictionary of Canadian Biography*, Vol. 11, *1881–1890* (Toronto: University of Toronto Press, 1982), 121–25.
34. HBCA, D20/16, ff. 152-152d, Winnipeg, 10 May 1880, C. J. Brydges to James A. Grahame.
35. HBCA, D20/18, f. 181d, Fort Garry, 10 February 1881, J. H. McTavish to James A. Grahame.
36. HBCA, D20/22, ff. 276-276d, Edmonton, 6 March 1882, Richard Hardisty to James A. Grahame.
37. HBCA, D20/22, f. 276d, Edmonton, 6 March 1882, Richard Hardisty to James A. Grahame.
38. HBCA, D20/22, f. 276d, Edmonton, 6 March 1882, Richard Hardisty to James A. Grahame.
39. Homestead Records, reel 2001, file 86890, statement made by Angus Fraser, 20 February 1885.
40. Homestead Records, reel 2001, file 44770, statement made by James Walker, 22 December 1882; Interview by the author with Ruth Walker, 6 January 1975; HBCA, D20/19, f. 210d, Edmonton, 26 May 1881, Richard Hardisty to James A. Grahame; Grant MacEwan, *Colonel James Walker, Man of the Western Frontier* (Saskatoon: Western Producer Prairie Books, 1989), 102–09.
41. HBCA, D20/24, ff. 309-309d, Fort Edmonton, 4 September 1882, Wm. McKay to Laurence Clarke.
42. Bowsfield, ed., *The Letters of Charles John Brydges*, 264–65, Winnipeg, 28 September 1882, C. J. Brydges to William Armit.
43. Ibid., 265, Winnipeg, 28 September 1882, C. J. Brydges to William Armit.
44. Ibid.
45. Ibid.
46. HBCA, D20/22, f. 44, Montreal, 11 January 1882, C. J. Brydges to James A. Grahame.
47. Homestead Records, reel 2000, file 43503, Montreal, 21 October 1883, C. J. Brydges to L. Russell.

Notes to Chapter 4
Rails and Marketing

1. J. Lorne McDougall, *Canadian Pacific: A Brief History* (Montreal: McGill-Queen's University Press, 1968), 21–25.
2. Ibid., 51.
3. Omer Lavallee, *Van Horne's Road: An illustrated account of the construction and first years of operation of the Canadian Pacific transcontinental railway* (Montreal: Railway Enterprises, 1974), 77.
4. HBCA, D20/23, ff. 161-161d, Edmonton, 20 June 1882, Richard Hardisty to James A. Grahame.
5. Lavallee, *Van Horne's Road*, 77.
6. HBCA, D20/24, f. 310, Fort Edmonton, 4 September 1882, Wm. McKay to Laurence Clarke.
7. Lavallee, *Van Horne's Road*, 83.
8. HBCA, D20/25, f. 158, Edmonton, 22 February 1883, Richard Hardisty to James A. Grahame.
9. HBCA, D20/26, f. 85, Edmonton, 19 June 1883, Richard Hardisty to James A. Grahame.
10. K. Ross Toole Archives, University of Montana Library, Missoula, C. E. Conrad Papers, letterpress book, Ottawa, 24 March 1883, C. E. Conrad to W. G. Conrad; Ottawa, 9 May 1883, I. G. Baker & Co. to Fred White.
11. *Macleod Gazette*, 14 June 1883.
12. *Macleod Gazette*, 4, 14, 24 July 1883; 24 August 1883.
13. *Macleod Gazette*, 4 June 1883; 4 August 1883.
14. NAC, Department of the Interior Records, vol. 320, file 74920, Ottawa, 27 March 1882, I. G. Baker & Co. to John A. Macdonald.
15. GAIA, Edgar Dewdney Papers, Fort Benton, 1 January 1883, W. G. Conrad to Edgar Dewdney.
16. NAC, Department of the Interior Records, vol. 320, file 74920, Ottawa, 29 March 1883, C. E. Conrad to John A. Macdonald.
17. PAA, Homestead Records, reel 2000, file 43503, Ottawa, 14 April 1884, A. M. Burgess to D. L. Macpherson; NAC, RG15, vol. 320, file 74920, Ottawa, 30 May 1892, L. Pereira to W. Pearce.
18. Canadian Pacific Archives, Montreal, Van Horne Correspondence, Winnipeg, 1 August 1883, John M. Egan to W. C. Van Horne.
19. GAIA, Canada Northwest Land Company Papers, box 2, file 33, Calgary townsite, deed of sale, 22 August 1884; Max Foran, "The CPR and the Urban West, 1881–1930," in Hugh A. Dempsey, ed., *The CPR West: The Iron Road and the Making of a Nation* (Vancouver: Douglas & McIntyre, 1984), 91.
20. *Calgary Herald*, 2 November 1883.
21. Calgary Land Titles Office, Calgary townsite plans.
22. *Calgary Herald*, 16 January 1884; Burns & Elliott, eds., *Calgary, Alberta: Her Industries & Resources* (Calgary: Burns & Elliott, 1885), 33.
23. Calgary Land Titles Office, Calgary townsite plans.
24. *Calgary Herald*, 5 March 1884.
25. *Calgary Herald*, 4 June 1884.

26. C. E. Conrad Papers, letterpress book, Ottawa, 23 March 1883, C. E. Conrad to W. G. Conrad.
27. NAC, RCMP Records, vol. 1006, file 235, Ottawa, 30 March 1883, I. G. Baker & Co. to Fred White; vol. 1009, file 519, Ottawa, 13 October 1883, Fred White to A. G. Irvine; *Macleod Gazette*, 4 August 1883.
28. HBCA, A12/51, ff. 257–58, Winnipeg, 2 August 1883, James A. Grahame to W. Armit.
29. HBCA, D20/26, f. 339, Calgary, 15 August 1883, Richard Hardisty to James A. Grahame.
30. HBCA, D20/27, ff. 48–50, Calgary, 18 September 1883, Richard Hardisty to James A. Grahame.
31. HBCA, D20/27, f. 136, Calgary, 24 October 1883, Richard Hardisty to James A. Grahame.
32. HBCA, D20/27, f. 136, Calgary, 24 October 1883, Richard Hardisty to James A. Grahame.
33. HBCA, D20/28, ff. 111–12, Calgary, 13 February 1884, Richard Hardisty to James A. Grahame.
34. *Calgary Herald*, 20, 27 February 1884.
35. HBCA, D20/29, f. 84, 15 May 1884, Richard Hardisty to James A. Grahame.
36. HBCA, A12/27, f. 4, Winnipeg, 25 August 1884, J. Wrigley to W. Armit.
37. *Calgary Herald*, 5 March 1884.
38. HBCA, D20/29, ff. 84–85, Calgary, 15 May 1884, Richard Hardisty to James A. Grahame.
39. HBCA, D20/32, f. 115, St. Louis, 21 August 1884, I. G. Baker & Co. to the Hudson's Bay Company.
40. HBCA, D20/32, ff. 115–17, St. Louis, 21 August 1884, I. G. Baker & Co. to the Hudson's Bay Company.
41. HBCA, D20/32, f. 107, London, 9 September 1884, W. Armit to I. G. Baker & Co.
42. Eleanor Stardom, *A Stranger to the Fur Trade: Joseph Wrigley and the Transformation of the Hudson's Bay Company, 1884–1891* (Winnipeg: University of Winnipeg Rupert's Land Research Centre, 1995), 21.
43. HBCA, D20/30, f. 56, Winnipeg, 14 August 1884, Richard Hardisty to Joseph Wrigley.
44. HBCA, A12/27, f. 4, Winnipeg, 25 August 1884, J. Wrigley to W. Armit.
45. HBCA, D20/30, ff. 202–03, Calgary, 30 September 1884, Richard Hardisty to Joseph Wrigley.
46. HBCA, A12/27, f. 54, Winnipeg, 6 October 1884, Joseph Wrigley to W. Armit.
47. HBCA, D20/30, f. 235, Calgary, 11 October 1884, Richard Hardisty to Joseph Wrigley.
48. HBCA, D20/30, ff. 105–06, Millwood, Clarke County, Virginia, 21 January 1885, W. G. Conrad to Joseph Wrigley.
49. HBCA, A12/53, f. 82, Montreal, 10 March 1885, Donald A. Smith to W. Armit.

50. HBCA, A12/27, ff. 233-233d, Winnipeg, 19 March 1885, Joseph Wrigley to W. Armit.
51. C. E. Conrad Papers, letterpress book, Ottawa, 20 March 1883, C. E. Conrad to J. E. Chipman.
52. *Calgary Herald*, 12 November 1884.
53. Ibid.
54. Ibid..
55. *Calgary Herald*, 12 February 1885.
56. *Calgary Herald*, 4 June 1885.
57. Canada, *Sessional Papers*, 1886, no. 6A, report upon the Suppression of the Rebellion in the Northwest Territories and Matters in Connection therewith in 1885 (hereafter Rebellion Report), 165–66; *Macleod Gazette*, 11 April 1885.
58. Rebellion Report, 166; Montreal Star, 28 May 1885.
59. *Macleod Gazette*, 21 July 1885.
60. HBCA, D20/33, f. 233, Calgary, 17 April 1885, Richard Hardisty to Joseph Wrigley.
61. HBCA, D20/33, ff. 243–44, Calgary, 17 April 1885, Richard Hardisty to Joseph Wrigley.
62. HBCA, D20/33, f. 244, Calgary, 17 April 1885, Richard Hardisty to Joseph Wrigley.
63. HBCA, D20/34, f. 191, Calgary, 4 June 1885, Richard Hardisty to Joseph Wrigley.
64. HBCA, D20/34, ff. 190–92, Calgary, 4 June 1885, Richard Hardisty to Joseph Wrigley.
65. HBCA, D20/33, ff. 201–02, Calgary, 10 April 1885, Richard Hardisty to Joseph Wrigley.
66. HBCA, D20/36, ff. 97-97d, Calgary, 17 September 1885, James Thomson to Joseph Wrigley.
67. HBCA, D20/36, f. 97d, Calgary, 17 September 1885, James Thomson to Joseph Wrigley.
68. HBCA, D20/36, f. 127, Calgary, 22 September 1885, James Thomson to Joseph Wrigley.
69. Canada, *Sessional Papers*, 1886, no. 6, report of the Department of Indian Affairs for the year ending 31 December 1886.
70. Ibid.
71. *Macleod Gazette*, 14 June, 1885; 6 October 1885.
72. *Calgary Herald*, 16 September 1885; 18 November 1885.
73. *Calgary Herald*, 15 July 1885.
74. *Macleod Gazette*, 13 June 1885.
75. Canada, *House of Commons Debates*, vol. 22, 5 May 1886, 1076.
76. *Macleod Gazette*, 13 June 1885.

Notes to Chapter 5
The Emergence of the Town of Calgary

1. Stephen Lyons, Canadian Pacific Archives, Montreal, to the author, 16 March 1998; NAC, John A. Macdonald Papers, vol. 402, Calgary, 23 April 1884, George B. Elliott to John A. Macdonald.
2. *Nor'Wester*, 29 April 1884.
3. *Calgary Herald*, 31 August 1883.
4. Burns & Elliott, eds., *Calgary, Alberta: Her Industries & Resources* (Calgary: Burns & Elliott, 1885), 33; James G. MacGregor, *Vision of an Ordered Land: The Story of the Dominion Land Survey* (Saskatoon: Western Producer Prairie Books, 1981), 82.
5. *Calgary Herald*, 25 July 1895.
6. Ibid., 8 February 1936.
7. Max Foran, "George Murdoch," *Dictionary of Canadian Biography*, Vol. 13, *1901 to 1910* (Toronto: University of Toronto Press, 1994), 747; Dick Cunniffe, "George Murdoch, Mayor 1884–1885," in *Good Morning, Your Worship, Mayors of Calgary, 1884–1975* (Calgary: Century Calgary Publications, 1975), 9.
8. GAIA, George Murdoch Papers, George Murdoch's Diary, 13 May 1883.
9. George Murdoch's Diary, 15 May 1883.
10. Ibid., 14 May 1883.
11. Ibid., 16 May 1883.
12. Ibid., 19, 27 October 1883.
13. Ibid., 14 January 1884.
14. Ibid., 25 March 1884.
15. Ibid., 4 March 1884.
16. Ibid., 7 July 1883; 13 October 1883; 24 September 1883; 8 September 1884; 24 February 1885.
17. Ibid., 19 August 1883; 4 November 1883.
18. Desmond Morton and Reginald H. Roy, eds., *Telegrams of the Northwest Campaign 1885* (Toronto: The Champlain Society, 1972), 32–33; George Murdoch's Diary, 7 April 1885.
19. George Murdoch's Diary, 16 April 1885.
20. Ibid., 19 April 1885; Morton and Roy, eds., *Telegrams of the Northwest Campaign 1885*, 36.
21. George Murdoch's Diary, 24 April 1884; 25 May 1884; 7 September 1884.
22. Ibid., 24 February 1885; 30 April 1885.
23. Ibid., 5 June 1885; 21 August 1885.
24. Ibid., 8 September 1885.
25. Ibid., 23 January 1886.
26. GAIA, I. S. Freeze Papers, Foreword by Audrey Pettigrew, 15 May 1978.
27. Interview by the author with Edith A. Durkee, 3 November 1973.
28. *Calgary Herald*, 13 January 1921.
29. Freeze Papers, Calgary, 16 June 1883, I. S. Freeze to Evelyn Freeze.
30. Ibid., Pense, 29 June 1883, I. S. Freeze to Evelyn Freeze.

31. Ibid., Calgary, 5 August 1883, I. S. Freeze to Evelyn Freeze.
32. Ibid., Calgary, 12 August 1883, I. S. Freeze to Evelyn Freeze.
33. Ibid., Calgary, 2 September 1883, I. S. Freeze to Evelyn Freeze.
34. Ibid., Calgary, 29 September 1883, I. S. Freeze to Evelyn Freeze.
35. *Calgary Herald*, 2 November 1883.
36. Freeze Papers, Calgary, 24 October 1883, I. S. Freeze to Evelyn Freeze.
37. Ibid., Calgary, 24 October 1883, I. S. Freeze to Evelyn Freeze.
38. Ibid., Calgary, 25 November 1883, I. S. Freeze to Evelyn Freeze.
39. Ibid., Calgary, n.d., I. S. Freeze to Evelyn Freeze.
40. Ibid., Calgary, 5 January 1884, I. S. Freeze to Evelyn Freeze.
41. Ibid., Calgary, 9 March 1884, I. S. Freeze to Evelyn Freeze.
42. Burns & Elliott, eds., *Calgary*, 42.
43. *Calgary Herald*, 23 April 1884.
44. Freeze Papers, Calgary, 26 January 1884, I. S. Freeze to Evelyn Freeze.
45. Ibid., Calgary, n.d., I. S. Freeze to Evelyn Freeze.
46. Calgary Land Titles Office, land mortgage records, 1883–1885.
47. Edith A. Durkee interview, 3 November 1973.
48. Ibid.
49. Burns & Elliott, eds., *Calgary*, 42.
50. *Calgary Herald*, 15 July, 16 September, 1885.
51. Edith A. Durkee interview, 3 November 1973.
52. Burns & Elliott, eds., *Calgary*, 21, 23, 67.
53. Calgary Public Library, Manuscript Census of 1891 for Calgary.
54. *Calgary Herald*, 4 September 1927; Manuscript Census of 1891 for Calgary.
55. Interview by the author with Ida Graves, 19 October 1973; *Calgary Tribune*, 5 November 1886.
56. *Calgary Herald*, 4 September 1927.
57. Burns & Elliott, eds., *Calgary*, 67.
58. Toronto *Globe*, 17 October 1891.
59. *Calgary Herald*, 30 July, 1884; 27 August 1884; 15 October 1884; 12 November 1884.
60. Ibid., 5 March 1885.
61. Ida Graves interview, 19 October 1973.
62. Burns & Elliott, eds., *Calgary*, 67.
63. *Calgary Herald*, 7 May 1885.
64. Ibid., 7 October 1885; 18 November 1885.
65. *The Dominion Illustrated*, Calgary Special, 28 June 1890; Max Foran, "Land Speculation and Urban Development: Calgary 1884–1912," in A. W. Rasporich and Henry C. Klassen, eds., *Frontier Calgary Town, City, and Region 1875–1914* (Calgary: McClelland and Stewart West, 1975), 207.
66. GAIA, Wesley F. Orr Papers, letterbook, 3, Calgary, 28 June 1893, W. F. Orr to Adam C. Orr.
67. *Calgary Herald*, 5 March 1884.
68. Ibid., 16 January 1884; Interview by the author with Ruth Walker, 6 January 1975.
69. George Murdoch's Diary, 24 January 1884.
70. *Nor'Wester*, 13 May 1884.

71. GAIA, George Murdoch Papers, petition to Edgar Dewdney, 25 January 1884.
72. *Calgary Herald*, 25 June 1884.
73. *Nor'Wester*, 15 July 1884.
74. *Calgary Herald*, 12 November 1884.
75. Ibid., 3 December 1884.
76. *Dominion Illustrated*, Calgary Special, 28 June 1890.
77. *Calgary Herald*, 26 February 1885.
78. Ibid., 17 December 1884.
79. GAIA, Calgary town council minutes, 10 January 1885.
80. *Calgary Herald*, 25 December 1884; Calgary town council minutes, 14 January 1885.
81. *Calgary Herald*, 22 January 1885.
82. George Murdoch Papers, miscellaneous memorandum, George Murdoch.
83. *Calgary Herald*, 26 February 1885.
84. Ibid., 15 January 1885.
85. Ibid., 22 January 1885.
86. Calgary town council minutes, 4 March 1885.
87. *Calgary Herald*, 19 February 1885.
88. Ibid., 8 January 1885.
89. Ibid., 8 July 1885; 2 September 1885.
90. Calgary town council minutes, 7 October 1885.
91. *Calgary Herald*, 15 July 1885.
92. Ibid., 26 February 1885; 4 September 1886; Calgary town council minutes, 19 January 1887; 7 April 1887.
93. *Calgary Herald*, 15 July 1885.
94. Ibid., 21 October 1885.
95. Hugh A. Dempsey, *Calgary: Spirit of the West* (Saskatoon: Fifth House Publishers, 1994), 20.
96. Frederick Hunter, "Why is the early Stoney settlement west of Calgary called Morley?" in *Chinook Country Historical Society Newsletter*, March/April 2000.
97. Edna Appleby, *Canmore: The Story Of An Era* (Canmore: Edna Appleby, 1975), 26–44, 145–46.
98. Canadian Pacific Archives, Van Horne Correspondence, Winnipeg, 2 January 1894, W. Whyte to J. Niblock; Manuscript Census of 1891 for Canmore; A. A. den Otter, "Bondage of Steam: The CPR and Western Canadian Coal," in Hugh A. Dempsey, ed., *The CPR West: The Iron Road and the Making of a Nation* (Vancouver: Douglas & McIntyre, 1984), 194.
99. *Trails to Little Corner: A Story of Namaka and Surrounding Districts* (Calgary: Namaka Community Historical Committee, 1983), 23–25; PAA, Homestead Records, reel 2001, file 68024, statement made by Thomas Bland Strange, 23 June 1886.
100. *The Gleichen Call: A History of Gleichen and the Surrounding Areas 1877 to 1968* (Calgary: Gleichen United Church Women, 1968), 58.
101. Homestead Records, reel 2002, file 86751, statement made by Samuel H. Livingston, 8 May 1885; *Calgary Herald*, 9 April 1885.
102. *Calgary Herald*, 15 May 1930; 13 June 1959.

103. Homestead Records, reel 2002, file 86751, statement made by Samuel H. Livingston, 8 May 1885.
104. Sheilagh S. Jameson, "John Glenn," *Dictionary of Canadian Biography*, Vol. 11, *1881 to 1890* (Toronto: University of Toronto Press, 1982), 354–55.
105. *Calgary Herald*, 15 July 1966.
106. *Macleod Gazette*, 4 August 1883.
107. *Calgary Herald*, 10 September 1884.
108. Homestead Records, reel 2002, file 89165, statement made by John Glenn, 8 May 1885.
109. *Sodbusting to Subdivision* (DeWinton: DeWinton & District Historical Committee, 1978), 309–13; *Calgary Herald*, 26 January 1933; *Albertan*, 16 April 1941.
110. *Calgary Herald*, 10 September 1884.
111. *A Century of Memories 1883–1983: Okotoks and District* (Okotoks: Okotoks and District Historical Society, 1983), 6, 148.
112. Homestead Records, reel 2016, file 267213, statement made by Hannibal Clark, 5 May 1891.
113. *Calgary Herald*, 3 September 1884.
114. Henry C. Klassen, "John Lineham," in *Dictionary of Canadian Biography*, Vol. 14, *1911–1920* (Toronto: University of Toronto Press, 1998), 657–58.
115. Homestead Records, reel 2002, file 86064, statement made by John D. Norrish, 2 February 1885; *Leaves From the Medicine Tree* (High River: Pioneers' and Old Timers' Association, 1960), 437–39; Lillian Knupp, *Life and Legends: A History of the Town of High River* (Calgary: Sandstone Publishing, 1982), 11.
116. Homestead Records, reel 2014, file 22835, statement made by James McDonough, 2 September 1886.
117. Canadian Pacific Archives, Van Horne Correspondence, Cochrane, October 1890, E. G. Jenkins and others to W. C. Van Horne.
118. Van Horne Correspondence, Medicine Hat, 6 June 1888, J. Niblock to W. Whyte.

Notes to Chapter 6
Creating Banking Services

1. NAC, Bank of Montreal, Minute Book of the Board of Directors, 2 June 1884.
2. PAA, Calgary Court House, chattel mortgages, 1883–1885; PAA, accession no. 79.266, Supreme Court of the Northwest Territories, Calgary, Civil Cases, *Mount Royal Ranche Co. v. I. G. Baker & Co.*, 29 January 1890.
3. Calgary Land Titles Office, land mortgage records, 1883–1885; PAA, Calgary Court House, chattel mortgages, 1883–1885.
4. *Calgary Herald*, 30 April 1885.
5. *Calgary Tribune*, 10 July 1889; Cecil C. Tannahill, *Private – Chartered Banks in the Territories of Assiniboia and Saskatchewan and the Province of Saskatchewan 1880–1936* (Regina: Cecil C. Tannahill, 1986), 98–104.

Notes to pp. 122–130

6. *Albertan*, 30 July 1920; Tannahill, *Private – Chartered Banks*, 104.
7. *Calgary Tribune*, 16 December 1885.
8. *Regina Leader*, 10 March 1885; 21 April 1885.
9. Burns & Elliott, eds., *Calgary, Alberta: Her Industries & Resources* (Calgary: Burns & Elliott, 1885), 52; *Albertan*, 13 August 1930.
10. *Albertan*, 6 December 1940.
11. *Calgary Tribune*, 16 December 1885.
12. PAA, Calgary Court House, chattel mortgages, 1885–1889.
13. *Calgary Tribune*, 21 October 1885.
14. Bank of Montreal Archives (hereafter BMA), Montreal, Bank of Montreal, letterbook, Calgary, 20 April 1887, A. D. Braithwaite to the General Manager.
15. George Henry Ham, *The New West: Extending from the Great Lakes across Plain and Mountain to the Golden Shores of the Pacific* (Winnipeg: Canadian Historical Publishing Co., 1888), 131.
16. *Calgary Herald*, 9, 23 October 1886.
17. Henry C. Klassen, "Cowdry Brothers: Private Bankers in Southwestern Alberta, 1886–1905," *Alberta History*, 37 (Winter 1989), 9–22.
18. *Regina Leader*, 21 April 1885; *Calgary Herald*, 30 April 1885.
19. University of Calgary Library, *Dun & Bradstreet Reference Book*, July 1887, 593.
20. BMA, Bank of Montreal, letterbook, Calgary, 20 April 1887, A. D. Braithwaite to the General Manager.
21. Ibid.
22. David H. Breen, *The Canadian Prairie West and the Ranching Frontier 1874–1924* (Toronto: University of Toronto Press, 1983), 66.
23. *Calgary Tribune*, 30 January 1886.
24. PAA, Calgary Court House, chattel mortgages, 1885–1886; PAA, accession no. 68.96, Fort Macleod Court House, chattel mortgages, 1885.
25. PAA, Calgary Court House, chattel mortgages, 1886.
26. PAA, Calgary Court House, chattel mortgages, 1885–1886.
27. Ibid.
28. Bank of Montreal, letterbook, Calgary, 19 May 1887, A. D. Braithwaite to the General Manager.
29. PAA, Calgary Court House, chattel mortgages, 1887.
30. *Calgary Tribune*, 12 June 1886.
31. *Calgary Tribune*, 5 November 1886.
32. *Regina Leader*, 21 June 1887; Tannahill, *Private – Chartered Banks*, 99, 106.
33. PAA, Calgary Court House, chattel mortgages, 1887–1889.
34. Bank of Montreal, letterbook, Calgary, 22 January 1889, A. D. Braithwaite to the General Manager.
35. *Calgary Herald*, 1 May 1889.
36. PAA, Calgary Court House, chattel mortgages, 1889.
37. *Calgary Tribune*, 10 July 1889.
38. Calgary Court House, Surrogate Division, Estate of Frederick G. Smith file, 9 July 1889.
39. Tannahill, *Private -- Chartered Banks*, 105–06.
40. *Calgary Herald*, 7 August 1889.
41. PAA, Calgary Court House, chattel mortgages, 1889–1891.
42. Bank of Montreal, letterbook, Calgary, 22 January 1889, A. D. Braithwaite to the General Manager.

Notes to pp. 131–141

43. Tannahill, *Private – Chartered Banks*, 101–03.
44. *Dun & Bradstreet Reference Book*, January 1890, 622.
45. *Calgary Herald*, 5 June 1891.
46. *Regina Leader*, 9 June 1885.
47. PAA, Calgary Court House, chattel mortgages, 1889–1891.
48. *Albertan*, 13 August 1930.
49. Calgary Land Titles Office, land mortgage records, 1893–1894; Tannahill, *Private – Chartered Banks*, 103.
50. *Calgary Herald*, 16 January 1884; Canada, *Journals of the House of Commons*, 19 March 1884, 253.
51. *Calgary Herald*, 13 October 1923.
52. Canadian Imperial Bank of Commerce Archives, Toronto (hereafter CIBCA), Imperial Bank of Canada, Minute Book of the Board of Directors, vol. 3, 7 October 1886, 305.
53. *Monetary Times*, 31 December 1886.
54. CIBCA, Imperial Bank of Canada, Minute Book of Board of Directors, vol. 3, 30 September 1886, 303.
55. *Calgary Tribune*, 9 October 1886.
56. *Monetary Times*, 17 December 1880.
57. *Canadian Annual Review*, 1911, Special Historical Supplement, 67.
58. *Monetary Times*, 10 December 1886, 654.
59. *Calgary Tribune*, 21 December 1892.
60. *Monetary Times*, 10 December 1886; Victor Ross, *A History of The Canadian Bank of Commerce*, Vol. 2 (Toronto: Oxford University Press, 1922), 310.
61. Imperial Bank of Canada, Minute Book of the Board of Directors, vol. 3, 24 March 1887, 365; 29 December 1887, 483; 1 March 1888, 510; 27 March 1888, 525; 25 October 1888, 598; vol. 4, 4 September 1890, 165.
62. PAA, Calgary Court House, chattel mortgages, 1890; Calgary Land Titles Office, land mortgage records, 1890.
63. Imperial Bank of Canada, Minute Book of the Board of Directors, vol. 3, 13 January 1887, 340; 23 February 1888, 508–09; 5 July 1888, 566; 13 June 1889, 693; vol. 4, 27 February 1890, 77; 6 March 1890, 80; 6 August 1891, 309; 29 September 1892, 492.
64. Imperial Bank of Canada, Minute Book of the Board of Directors, vol. 4, 25 July 1892, 466.
65. *Monetary Times*, 24 September 1886.
66. Merrill Denison, *Canada's First Bank: A History of the Bank of Montreal*, Vol. 2 (Toronto: McClelland & Stewart, 1967), 410–11, 419.
67. Ibid., 208, 247, 409–10, 419–20.
68. *Calgary Tribune*, 16 October 1886.
69. NAC, Bank of Montreal, Minute Book of the Board of Directors, 7 September 1886.
70. NAC, Bank of Montreal, Minute Book of the Board of Directors, 1 October 1886.
71. *Albertan*, 12 April 1934.
72. BMA, Bank of Montreal, letterbook, Calgary, 26 October 1886, A. D. Braithwaite to the General Manager.

73. Imperial Bank of Canada, Minute Book of the Board of Directors, vol. 3, 14 October 1886, 307.
74. Bank of Montreal, letterbook, Calgary, 28 October 1886, A. D. Braithwaite to the General Manager.
75. Bank of Montreal, letterbook, Calgary, 29 October 1886, A. D. Braithwaite to the General Manager.
76. Calgary Land Titles Office, land mortgage records, 1887.
77. Bank of Montreal, letterbook, Calgary, 22 December 1886, A .D. Braithwaite to the General Manager.
78. Ibid.
79. Toronto *Globe*, 17 October 1891; *Calgary Herald*, 9 July 1890.
80. Bank of Montreal, letterbook, Calgary, 10 September 1890, A. D. Braithwaite to the General Manager.
81. Bank of Montreal, letterbook, Calgary, 17 September 1890, A. D. Braithwaite to the General Manager.
82. Bank of Montreal, letterbook, Calgary, 26 February 1887, A. D. Braithwaite to the General Manager.
83. *The Commercial*, 10 February 1890.
84. Calgary Land Titles Office, land mortgage records, 1890.
85. Ibid.
86. Toronto *Globe*, 17 October 1891.
87. *Calgary Herald*, 9 December 1889.
88. NAC, Bank of Montreal, Minute Book of the Board of Directors, 27 September 1892.
89. *Calgary Herald*, 29 September 1892.
90. Henry C. Klassen, "Entrepreneurship in the Canadian West: The Enterprises of A. E. Cross, 1886–1920," *Western Historical Quarterly*, 22 (August 1991), 326.
91. Bank of Montreal, letterbook, Calgary, 11 September 1893, W. B. Graveley to the General Manager.
92. Bank of Montreal, letterbook, Calgary, 10 November 1886, A. D. Braithwaite to the General Manager.
93. *Calgary Tribune*, 19 November, 3 December 1886.
94. Bank of Montreal, letterbook, Calgary, 26 February 1887, A. D. Braithwaite to the General Manager.
95. Ibid., Calgary, 20 January 1888, A. D. Braithwaite to the General Manager.
96. CIBCA, Imperial Bank of Canada, Minute Book of the Board of Directors, vol. 3, 12 April 1888, 530.
97. Bank of Montreal, letterbook, Calgary, 1 March 1892, A. D. Braithwaite to the General Manager.
98. Calgary Land Titles Office, land mortgage records, 1886–1887; Henry C. Klassen, "Scottish Capital on the Canadian Frontier, 1876–1920," *Scottish Tradition*, 16 (1990/91), 56–75.

Notes to Chapter 7
Building the Ranching Community

1. Canadian Pacific Archives, Van Horne Correspondence, Winnipeg, 27 May 1886, J. M. Egan to W. C. Van Horne.
2. Montana Hisorical Society Archives, T. C. Power Papers, box 129, file 3, Calgary, 16 June 1884, D. W. Marsh to T. C. Power.
3. *Calgary Tribune*, 19, 26 November 1886; 3 December 1886.
4. Van Horne Correspondence, Winnipeg, 6 October 1887, W. Whyte to W. C. Van Horne; *Calgary Tribune*, 14 January 1887; 27 May 1887; Max Foran and Heather MacEwan Foran, *Calgary, Canada's Frontier Metropolis: An Illustrated History* (Windsor Publications, 1982), 100–01.
5. *Calgary Herald*, 8 August 1888.
6. David H. Breen, *The Canadian Prairie West and the Ranching Frontier 1874–1924* (Toronto: University of Toronto Press, 1983), 18.
7. Henry C. Klassen, "Entrepreneurship in the Canadian West: The Enterprises of A.E. Cross, 1886–1920," *The Western Historical Quarterly*, 22 (August 1991), 320–22.
8. Quoted in Sheilagh Jameson, *Ranchers, Cowboys and Characters: Birth of Alberta's Western Heritage* (Calgary: Glenbow-Alberta Institute, 1987), 8.
9. Manuscript Census of 1891 for Calgary, Canmore, Gleichen, High River, Davisburg, Fish Creek, Pine Creek, Namaka, and Morley; Manuscript Census of 1901 for Calgary, Canmore, Gleichen, High River, Davisburg, Pine Creek, Morley, Queenstown, Shepard, Nose Creek, Springbank, Cochrane, Jumping Pound, Okotoks, Millarville, Priddis, and Pekisko.
10. *Calgary Tribune*, 18 March 1887.
11. NAC, Department of the Interior Records, vol. 320, file 74920, statement made by W. G. Conrad, 30 January 1883.
12. Ibid., statement made by D. W. Davis, 19 March 1883.
13. Ibid., Ottawa, 2 January 1892, A. Chisholm to John R. Hall.
14. Calgary Land Titles Office, land transfers, 1896–1902; *Canadian Cattlemen* (March 1943), 164–65, 168.
15. Saskatchewan Archives Board, Regina, Department of Provincial Secretary, Companies Branch, Old Companies Files, Conrad Circle Cattle Co. file.
16. John Harris Papers, Marjorie Gray Collection, Highwood, Montana, St. Louis, 9 March 1898, I. G. Baker to John Harris.
17. Interview by the author with Lillian McMorris, Queenstown, 10 July 1988; PAA, Homestead Records, reel 2022, Calgary, 5 February 1902, Lougheed & Bennett to P. G. Keyes.
18. Henry C. Klassen, "The Conrads in the Alberta Cattle Business, 1875–1911," *Agricultural History*, 64 (Summer 1990), 54–57.
19. Klassen, "The Conrads in the Alberta Cattle Business, 1875–1911," 42–56.
20. Saskatchewan Archives Board, Regina, Department of Provincial Secretary, Companies Branch, Old Companies Files, Conrad Investment Co. file.
21. Alberta Registries, Corporate Registry, Edmonton, Cochrane Ranche Company file.
22. Ibid.

23. Grant MacEwan, *Colonel James Walker, Man of the Western Frontier* (Saskatoon: Western Producer Prairie Books, 1989), 95–97.
24. *Canadian Cattlemen* (June 1939), 219,223; Jameson, *Ranchers, Cowboys and Characters*, 20–22.
25. Saskatchewan Archives Board, Regina, Department of Provincial Secretary, Companies Branch, Old Companies Files, Cochrane Ranche Company file.
26. PAA, Supreme Court of the Northwest Territories, Calgary, Civil Cases, file 467, *Alexander Stuart v. the British American Ranche Company*, statement made by Matthew H. Cochrane, 8 October 1890.
27. Calgary Court House, Surrogate Division, Estate of William Duncan Kerfoot file, 5 August 1909.
28. PAA, Supreme Court of the Northwest Territories, Calgary, Civil Cases, file 2031, *W. D. Kerfoot v. the British American Ranche Company*, statement made by John M. Browning, 29 June 1887.
29. *Calgary Herald*, 24 September 1884.
30. Klassen, "Entrepreneurship in the Canadian West," 315–16.
31. *W. D. Kerfoot v. the British American Ranche Company*, Calgary, 19 October 1885, W. D. Kerfoot to J.M. Browning.
32. *W. D. Kerfoot v. the British American Ranche Company*, Calgary, 15 May 1885, W. D. Kerfoot to J.M. Browning.
33. Catholic Pastoral Centre Archives, Sparrow Papers, "Materials for a History of the Sparrow Family," typescript copy, 2; *Calgary Herald*, 27 February 1884.
34. *W. D. Kerfoot v. the British American Ranche Company*, Cochrane, 17 September 1886, W. D. Kerfoot to J. M. Browning.
35. *W. D. Kerfoot v. the British American Ranche Company*, statement made by John M. Browning, 29 June 1887.
36. *W. D. Kerfoot v. the British American Ranche Company*, Hillhurst, 30 March 1885, Matthew H. Cochrane to W. D. Kerfoot.
37. *W. D. Kerfoot v. the British American Ranche Company*, Calgary, 19 October 1885, W. D. Kerfoot to J. M. Browning.
38. *Macleod Gazette*, 31 August 1886; *W. D. Kerfoot v. the British American Ranche Company*, Montreal, 10 September 1886, J. M. Browning to W. D. Kerfoot.
39. *W. D. Kerfoot v. the British American Ranche Company*, Cochrane, 17 September 1886, W. D. Kerfoot to J. M. Browning.
40. *W. D. Kerfoot v. the British American Ranche Company*, Calgary, 28 October 1886, M. H. Cochrane to W. D. Kerfoot.
41. *W. D. Kerfoot v. the British American Ranche Company*, judgment made by Charles B. Rouleau, 13 April 1888; Edward Brado, *Cattle Kingdom: Early Ranching in Alberta* (Vancouver: Douglas & McIntyre, 1984), 76–77; Ted Byfield, ed., *The Great West Before 1900*, Vol. 1 (Edmonton: United Western Communications, 1991), 195.
42. *Calgary Tribune*, 20 March 1886.
43. PAA, Supreme Court of the Northwest Territories, Calgary, Civil Cases, file 467, *Alexander Stuart v. the British American Ranche Company*, statement made by Lougheed & McCarthy, 10 September 1888.
44. *Calgary Herald*, 6 November 1886.

45. *Alexander Stuart v. the British American Ranche Company*, Aberdeen, 6 November 1888, George Bruce to Bleecker & Smith.
46. *Alexander Stuart v. the British American Ranche Company*, statement made by Alexander Stuart, 12 November 1889.
47. *W. D. Kerfoot v. the British American Ranche Company*, Montreal, 8 December 1885, J. M. Browning to W. D. Kerfoot.
48. *Calgary Herald*, 5 December 1888.
49. PAA, accession no. 76.266, box 1, file 2958, agreement between John J. Barter and Charles W. Martin, 14 March 1887.
50. *Macleod Gazette*, 30 May 1885.
51. Saskatchewan Archives Board, Regina, Department of Provincial Secretary, Companies Branch, Old Companies Files, Quorn Ranche Company file.
52. NAC, Department of the Interior Records, vol. 1182, file 1107, District of Alberta, statement of cattle imports, 9 August 1884.
53. *Calgary Tribune*, 20 March 1886; Jameson, *Ranchers, Cowboys and Characters*, 28;
54. Brado, *Cattle Kingdom*, 146.
55. *Leaves From the Medicine Tree* (High River: High River Pioneers' and Old Timers' Association, 1960), 370.
56. L.V. Kelly, *The Range Men, 75th Anniversary Edition* (High River: Willow Creek Publishing, 1988), 100.
57. Ibid.
58. Saskatchewan Archives Board, Quorn Ranche Company file.
59. PAA, accession no. 76.266, box 1, file 2958, agreement between John J. Barter and Charles W. Martin, 14 March 1887.
60. *Calgary Tribune*, 26 August 1887.
61. PAA, Supreme Court of the Northwest Territories, Calgary, Civil Cases, unnumbered box, file 539, *James Stewart Moore v. Charles William Martin*.
62. PAA, accession no. 79.266, box 21, file 2958, agreement between the Quorn Ranche Company, Charles W. Martin, and Lizzie M. Barter, 13 December 1890.
63. NAC, Department of the Interior Records, vol. 1220, file 192192, Ottawa, 5 February 1890, Lyndwode Pereira to William Pearce.
64. PAA, accession no. 79.266, unnumbered box, file 567, *Samuel Barber and the Imperial Bank of Canada v. the Quorn Ranche Company*.
65. Ibid.
66. PAA, Supreme Court of the Northwest Territories, Calgary, Civil Cases, box 21, file 2958, Quorn Ranche accounts, 15 November 1895.
67. CIBCA, Imperial Bank of Canada, Minute Book of Board of Directors, vol. 5, 4 June 1896, 257.
68. Manuscript Census of 1891 for Calgary, Canmore, Gleichen, High River, Davisburg, Fish Creek, Pine Creek, Namaka, and Morley; Manuscript Census of 1901 for Calgary, Canmore, Gleichen, High River, Davisburg, Pine Creek, Morley, Queenstown, Shepard, Nose Creek, Springbank, Cochrane, Jumping Pound, Okotoks, Millarville, Priddis, and Pekisko.
69. Gerald Friesen, *The Canadian Prairies: A History* (Toronto: University of Toronto Press, 1984), 182–85.

70. Homestead Records, reel 2019, file 330119, statement made by Malcolm T. Millar, 27 April 1893; reel 2049, file 481853, statement made by Samuel H. Mayhood, 23 May 1898; reel 2040, file 434107, statement made by Joseph Bassett.
71. *Albertan*, 29 September 1941.
72. Interview by the author with Glen Macdougall, 6 May 1974.
73. Ibid.
74. Homestead Records, reel 2014, file 238886, statement made by Osborne E. Brown, 20 June 1890.
75. Glen Macdougall interview, 6 May 1974.
76. Glen Macdougall interview, 6 May 1974; Manuscript Census of 1891 for Calgary; *Dun & Bradstreet Reference Book*, July 1893, 644; *Albertan*, 7 December 1901; *Calgary Herald*, 2 May 1895; 11 December 1899; 5, 24 December 1901; Homestead Records, reel 2016, file 266717, statement made by William Herbert Heald, 11 April 1891; NAC, Merchants Bank of Canada, Minute Book of the Board of Directors, 7 April 1903.
77. Glen Macdougall interview, 6 May 1974.
78. *Alberta Tribune*, 19 June 1897.
79. *Albertan*, 29 September 1941.
80. Manuscript Censuses of 1891 and 1901 for Calgary.
81. Glen Macdougall interview, 6 May 1974.
82. Ibid.
83. *Calgary Herald*, 29 September 1941.
84. Interview by the author with Marjorie Swann, 30 June 1976.
85. *Calgary News Telegram*, 27 April 1912.
86. *Albertan*, 31 August 1929.
87. Ibid.
88. Interviews by the author with William A. Wolley-Dod, 22, 25 January 2000.
89. Marjorie Swann interview, 30 June 1976.
90. *Calgary News Telegram*, 27 April 1912.
91. *Albertan*, 8 November 1913.
92. PAA, Calgary Court House, chattel mortgages, 1890; Calgary Land Titles Office, land mortgage loans, 1890.
93. Marjorie Swann interview, 30 June 1976.
94. William A. Wolley-Dod interviews, 22, 25 January 2000.
95. Manuscript Census of 1901 for Pine Creek.
96. Marjorie Swann interview, 30 June 1976.
97. *Calgary Tribune*, 25 January 1893; 12 July 1893.
98. William A. Wolley-Dod interviews, 22, 25 January 2000; *Alberta Tribune*, 3 June 1899.
99. PAA, Calgary Court House, chattel mortgages, 1895–1896.
100. *Alberta Tribune*, 2 July 1895.
101. Interview by the author with William R. Wolley-Dod, 12 October 1973; Marjorie Swann interview, 30 June 1976.
102. *Albertan*, 8 November 1913.
103. Ibid., 31 August 1929.

104. William A. Wolley-Dod interviews, 22, 25 January 2000.
105. *Our Foothills*, 196–97; *Leaves From the Medicine Tree*, 39–41.
106. NAC, Department of the Interior Records, T12440, vol. 710, file 362780, statement made by John Quirk, 23 January 1893.
107. *Henderson's Northwest Ranchers' Directory and Brand Book 1888*, 6.
108. *Alberta Tribune*, 18 April 1896.
109. GAIA, A. E. Cross Papers, box 1, file 6, organizational meeting of the Ranchmen's Club, 27 November 1891; Calgary Brewing & Malting Co. Papers, box 58, file 461, Ranchmen's Club, list of members, 21 November 1904; Ranchmen's Club Papers, Calgary, minute book, 1891–1913, report of the committee of management for the year ending 30 April 1892; statement of expenditure and revenue from 1 May 1893 to 30 April 1894.
110. Calgary Brewing & Malting Co. Papers, box 58, file 461, Ranchmen's Club, report of the committee of management for the year ending 30 April 1905.
111. Canadian Pacific Archives, Van Horne Correspondence, Calgary, 19 March 1896, G. Hillier to W. Whyte.
112. Van Horne Correspondence, Medicine Hat, 13 March 1896, J. N. Niblock to W. Whyte.

Notes to Chapter 8
Maintaining the Family Farm

1. *Calgary Tribune*, 7 October 1885.
2. Audrey Banister Bolin, "Albert Edward and Helen Mary Banister," in *Sodbusting to Subdivision* (DeWinton: DeWinton & District Historical Committee, 1978), 146.
3. GAIA, Ledger of Records of A. E. Banister, 50.
4. Ledger of Records of A. E. Banister, 66.
5. Bolin, "Albert Edward and Helen Mary Banister," 147.
6. GAIA, Mrs. Lavinia Hunter Collection, Davisburg Ranchers Society, minutebook, 1888–1889, n. p.
7. Davisburg Ranchers Society, minutebook.
8. *Calgary Herald*, 9 April 1885.
9. NAC, Department of the Interior Records, T13060, vol. 340, file 87776, Ottawa, 20 April 1885, John A. Macdonald to David L. Macpherson.
10. Ibid., T13060, vol. 340, file 87776, Ottawa, May 1885, A. M. Burgess to Sam Livingston.
11. *Calgary Tribune*, 21 September 1892.
12. Ibid., 11 January 1893; GAIA, Wesley F. Orr Papers, letterbook, vol. 2, Calgary, 11 February 1892, W. F. Orr to D. McLean; GAIA, Calgary town council minutes, 20 January 1892, 4 October 1892; William Cochrane, *The Canadian Album Men of Canada* (Brantford, Ont.: Bradley, Garretson & Co., 1894), 74.
13. Interview by the author with Barbra Connelly, 21 May 1974; Tyler Trafford, *Toole Peet 1897–1997: An Enduring Partnership* (Calgary: Toole, Peet & Co. Limited, 1997), 6–7.

14. Barbra Connelly interview, 21 May 1974.
15. Manuscript Census of 1891 for Calgary, Canmore, Gleichen, High River, Davisburg, Fish Creek, Pine Creek, Namaka, and Morley; Manuscript Census of 1901 for Calgary, Canmore, Gleichen, High River, Davisburg, Pine Creek, Morley, Queenstown, Shepard, Nose Creek, Springbank, Cochrane, Jumping Pound, Okotoks, Millarville, Priddis, and Pekisko.
16. Interviews by the author with Tom A. Findlay, 16 May 1991, 27 May 1999.
17. Ibid.
18. *Leaves From the Medicine Tree*, 235.
19. Ibid.
20. *Calgary Herald*, 8 August, 27 September 1888.
21. *Leaves From the Medicine Tree*, 235.
22. Tom A. Findlay interviews, 16 May 1991, 27 May 1999.
23. *Calgary Tribune*, 11 January, 1 March 1893.
24. Tom A. Findlay interviews, 16 May 1991, 27 May 1999.
25. *Leaves From the Medicine Tree*, 236.
26. Tom A. Findlay interviews, 16 May 1991, 27 May 1999.
27. Calgary Court House, Surrogate Division, Estate of Robert Findlay file, 8 September, 1916.
28. Quoted in *Sodbusting to Subdivision* (DeWinton: DeWinton & District Historical Committee, 1978), 213.
29. Quoted in *Sodbusting to Subdivision*, 213–14.
30. Quoted in *Sodbusting to Subdivision*, 212.
31. *Sodbusting to Subdivision*, 214.
32. Interviews by the author with Russell and Marion Martin, 10, 28 September 1999.
33. Quoted in *Sodbusting to Subdivision*, 212.
34. Russell and Marion Martin interviews, 10, 28 September 1999.
35. *Calgary Herald*, 26 September 1888.
36. Ibid.
37. *Calgary Tribune*, 5 October 1892.
38. Ibid., 12 July 1893.
39. Ibid., 10 October 1894.
40. Russell and Marion Martin interviews, 10, 28 September 1999.
41. *Sodbusting to Subdivision*, 214.
42. Ibid.
43. Ibid.
44. Russell and Marion Martin interviews, 10, 28 September 1999.
45. Ibid.
46. Interview by the author with Anna English, 21 January 1974.
47. Interview by the author with James F. McKevitt, 28 October 1999.
48. Ibid.
49. Anna English interview, 21 January 1974.
50. *Calgary Tribune*, 12 July 1893.
51. Anna English interview, 21 January 1974.
52. Ibid.
53. Ibid.
54. *Sodbusting to Subdivision*, 456.

55. Anna English interview, 21 January 1974.
56. James F. McKevitt interview, 28 October 1999.
57. Anna English interview, 21 January 1974.
58. Interview by the author with Lillian Soley, 3 December 1974; James F. McKevitt interview, 28 October 1999.
59. Anna English interview, 21 January 1974.
60. Ibid.
61. James F. McKevitt interview, 28 October 1999.
62. *Sodbusting to Subdivision*, 457.
63. James F. McKevitt interview, 28 October 1999.
64. *Alberta: The Calgary District Harvest News 1890* (1890), n. p.
65. Interview by the author with Grace Suitor, 5 October 1999.
66. Ibid.
67. Ibid.
68. *Sodbusting to Subdivision*, 182.
69. Grace Suitor interview, 5 October 1999.
70. *Sodbusting to Subdivision*, 182.
71. *Calgary Tribune*, 10 October 1894.
72. Interview by the author with William E. Suitor, 22 April 1975.
73. *Sodbusting to Subdivision*, 182.
74. Grace Suitor interview, 5 October 1999.
75. Ibid.
76. Tom A. Findlay interviews, 16 May 1991, 27 May 1999.
77. Interview by the author with Ernest W. Irving, 5 October 1999; *Sodbusting to Subdivision*, 164–68.
78. Interview by the author with Doris Herr, 11 October 1999.
79. Interview by the author with Harry Thomson, 27 May 1999.
80. Interview by the author with Bill Hogg, 7 September 1999.
81. Interview by the author with Glen and Jean Morrison, 27 May 1999.
82. *Calgary Tribune*, 11 September, 16 October 1886; Grant MacEwan, *Colonel James Walker, Man of the Western Frontier* (Saskatoon: Western Producer Prairie Books, 1989), 126–39.
83. *Calgary Herald*, 23 October 1889.
84. *Calgary Tribune*, 4 October 1893.
85. Ibid., 12 July 1893.
86. *Alberta Tribune*, 3 June 1899.
87. *Calgary Herald*, 10 September 1890.
88. Keith Walden, *Becoming Modern in Toronto: The Industrial Exhibition and the Shaping of a Late Victorian Culture* (Toronto: University of Toronto Press, 1997); Dave Walter, *Today Then: America's Best Minds Look 100 Years into the Future on the Occasion of the 1893 World's Columbian Exposition* (Helena: American & World Geographic Publishing, 1992).
89. *Alberta Tribune*, 4 April 1896.
90. Ibid., 20 August 1895.
91. *Calgary Tribune*, 22 June 1892.
92. Ibid., 2 November 1892.
93. *Calgary Herald*, 7 May 1884; *Calgary Tribune*, 14 March 1888.

94. *Calgary Herald*, 30 January 1884, 11 December 1889; *Calgary Tribune*, 27 April 1892.
95. Calgary Land Titles Office, land mortgage records, 1884–1900; PAA, Calgary Court House, chattel mortgages, 1883–1900.
96. *A Century of Memories 1883–1893: Okotoks and District* (Okotoks: Okotoks and District Historical Society, 1983), 148–49.
97. PAA, Supreme Court of the Northwest Territories, Calgary, Civil Cases, file 2071, *The Manitoba and North West Loan Company v. Kenneth Cameron*, statement made by Kenneth Cameron, 25 June 1887.
98. *The Manitoba and North West Loan Company v. Kenneth Cameron*, statement made by Peter McCarthy, 10 May 1887.
99. Ibid.
100. *Calgary Tribune*, 26 August 1887.
101. Calgary Land Titles Office, land mortgage records, 1887.
102. *The Manitoba and North West Loan Company v. Kenneth Cameron*, statement made by clerk of the court, H. A. L. Dundas, 25 June 1887.
103. *Calgary Tribune*, 25 January 1893; *Henderson's Manitoba and Northwest Territories Gazetteer and Directory for 1892*, 348; *Henderson's Manitoba and Northwest Territories Gazetteer and Directory for 1895*, 489.
104. W. L. Morton, *The Progressive Party in Canada* (Toronto: University of Toronto Press, 1950), 10–11.

Notes to Chapter 9
From Town to City

1. *Calgary Herald*, 24 July 1886.
2. *Calgary Tribune*, 13 March 1886.
3. Ibid.
4. *Calgary Herald*, 13 November 1886.
5. Ibid., 24 July 1886.
6. *Calgary Tribune*, 20 February 1886.
7. Ibid., 20 February 1886.
8. Ibid., 22 May 1886.
9. J. Lorne McDougall, *Canadian Pacific: A Brief History* (Montreal: McGill University Press, 1968), 39–41.
10. *Calgary Tribune*, 1, 8 February 1888; *Calgary Herald*, 21 March 1888.
11. Canada, *Statutes of Canada*, 52 Victoria, cap. 51, 20 March 1889.
12. Ibid., 53 Victoria, cap. 84, 24 April 1890; A. A. den Otter, *Civilizing the West: The Galts and the development of western Canada* (Edmonton: University of Alberta Press, 1982), 184–86.
13. Chester Martin, *Dominion Lands Policy*. Edited and with an Introduction by Lewis H. Thomas (Toronto: McClelland and Stewart, 1973), 63–65, 76, 89–91.
14. *Calgary Herald*, 22 July 1890.
15. R. G. MacBeth, *Sir Augustus Nanton: A Biography* (Toronto: Macmillan of Canada, 1931), 9–18; Paul Nanton, "A. M. Nanton's 41 Years in Winnipeg,

1883–1926," *Manitoba History*, 6 (Fall 1983), 15–16; W. A. Craick, *A Short Sketch of the Osler Family 1837–1913* (Toronto: Wm. Tyrrell & Co., 1938), 15–16; Joseph Schull, *100 Years of Banking in Canada: A History of the Toronto-Dominion Bank* (Toronto: Copp Clark, 1958), 86.
16. *Calgary Herald*, 22 July 1890; *Macleod Gazette*, 1 December 1892.
17. *Leaves From the Medicine Tree*, 275–76.
18. Canada, *House of Commons, Debates*, 17 February 1898; 3 September 1903; 10 May 1904; Raymond Andrew Christenson, "The Calgary and Edmonton Railway and the Edmonton Bulletin," M. A. Thesis, University of Alberta, 1967, 75–103.
19. Saskatchewan Archives Board, Regina, Department of the Provincial Secretary, Companies Branch, Old Company Files, Calgary and Edmonton Land Company file; Kirk N. Lambrecht and John Gilpin, "The Land Grant to the Calgary and Edmonton Railway Company," *Alberta Law Review*, 32 (No. 1 1994), 72–79.
20. *Calgary Tribune*, 27 April 1892.
21. *Calgary Herald*, 8 April 1893.
22. Canada, *Sessional Papers*, 1895, No. 13, report of Amos Rowe, 175.
23. GAIA, A. E. Cox Family Papers, file 38, Calgary, 5 March 1903, C. S. Lott to A. E. Cox; *Calgary Herald*, 31 March 1914.
24. Saskatchewan Archives Board, Regina, Department of Provincial Secretary, Companies Branch, Old Company Files, Calgary and Edmonton Land Company file.
25. *Macleod Gazette*, 1 December 1892.
26. Quoted in John A. Eagle, *The Canadian Pacific Railway and the Development of Western Canada, 1896–1914* (Kingston: McGill-Queen's University Press, 1989), 86.
27. Eagle, *The Canadian Pacific Railway and the Development of Western Canada*, 86; T. D. Regehr, *The Canadian Northern Railway: Pioneer Road of the Northern Prairies 1895–1918* (Toronto: Macmillan of Canada, 1976), 164–67.
28. *Calgary Herald*, 24 October 1903.
29. *Calgary Tribune*, 27 April 1892.
30. Calgary Land Titles Office, land mortgage loans, 1900; *Calgary Herald*, 26 March 1898.
31. Canadian Pacific Archives, Shaughnessy Correspondence, Denver, 24 April 1902, E. B. Osler to the directors of the North of Scotland Canadian Mortgage Company.
32. *Calgary Tribune*, 11 September 1886.
33. *Calgary Herald*, 13 August 1886; *Calgary Tribune*, 5 November 1886.
34. *Calgary Herald*, 13 November 1886.
35. *Calgary Tribune*, 12 November 1886.
36. HBCA, D20/43, f. 34, Calgary, 7 November 1886, J. Thomson to J. Wrigley.
37. GAIA, George Murdoch's Diary, 7 November 1886.
38. *Calgary Herald*, 13 November 1886.
39. Ibid.
40. *Calgary Tribune*, 12 November 1886.
41. Ibid.
42. *Calgary Herald*, 13 November 1886.

43. Montana Historical Society Archives, T. C. Power Papers, box 129, file 6, Calgary, 9 November 1886, D. W. Marsh to T. C. Power.
44. BMA, Bank of Montreal, letterbook, Calgary, 10 November 1886, A. D. Braithwaite to W. J. Buchanan.
45. George Murdoch's Diary, 8, 15, 16 November 1886.
46. GAIA, Calgary town council minutes, 7 November 1886.
47. *Calgary Tribune*, 12 November 1886.
48. Calgary town council minutes, 24 December 1886.
49. *Calgary Tribune*, 24 February 1892.
50. Canadian Pacific Archives, Van Horne Correspondence, Winnipeg, 6 October 1887, W. Whyte to W. C. Van Horne.
51. *Calgary Tribune*, 18, 25 November 1887.
52. *Calgary Herald*, 18 December 1889; HBCA, D20/58, ff. 253–54, Calgary, 28 January 1890, Child & Wilson to J. Wrigley.
53. Van Horne Correspondence, Winnipeg, 17 June 1889, W. Whyte to W. C. Van Horne; *Calgary Herald*, 17 May 1890.
54. *Calgary Herald*, 12 June 1889.
55. Ibid.
56. George Henry Ham, *The New West: Extending from the Great Lakes across Plain and Mountain to the Golden Shores of the Pacific* (Winnipeg: Canadian Historical Publishing Co., 1888), 131–32.
57. *Calgary Tribune*, 7 August 1889.
58. HBCA, D20/58, ff. 253–54, Calgary, 28 January 1890, Child & Wilson to J. Wrigley.
59. Toronto *Globe*, 17 October 1891.
60. Ibid.; Janice Dickin McGinnis, "Birth to Boom to Bust: Building in Calgary, 1875–1914," in A. W. Rasporich and Henry Klassen, eds., *Frontier Calgary: Town, City, and Region 1875–1914* (Calgary: McClelland and Stewart West, 1975), 11–12.
61. Toronto *Globe*, 17 October 1891.
62. *Leaves From the Medicine Tree*, 445–46.
63. Toronto *Globe*, 17 October 1891.
64. Ibid.
65. *Calgary News Telegram*, 11 January 1913.
66. *The Commercial*, 10 May 1887.
67. *Calgary Herald*, 13 February 1889.
68. Ibid., 3 March 1891.
69. Ibid.
70. Calgary Land Titles Office, land mortgage records, 1892; *Calgary Tribune*, 11 October 1893.
71. *Calgary Herald*, 6 February 1889; 29 September 1893; 13 October 1893.
72. *Alberta Tribune*, 28 September 1895.
73. *Calgary Herald*, 22 November 1899.
74. GAIA, Wesley F. Orr Papers, letterbook, 3, Calgary, 20 October 1893, Wesley F. Orr to A. M. Nanton.
75. *Henderson's Manitoba and Northwest Territories Gazetteer and Directory for 1893*, 272.

Notes to pp. 252–260

76. *Calgary Tribune*, 12 June 1886; Alberta Registries, Corporate Registry, Eau Claire & Bow River Lumber Co. file; GAIA, Eau Claire & Bow River Lumber Co. Papers, Agreement to organize the Eau Claire & Bow River Lumber Co., 25 June 1883.
77. *Calgary Herald*, 3 December 1929; *Albertan*, 4 December 1929.
78. Interview by the author with Anton Anderson, 11 March 1974.
79. Interview by the author with Helga Olson, 11 March 1974.
80. Interview by the author with Lillian Jacques, 14 January 1974; Anton Anderson interview, 11 March 1974; Interview by the author with Helen Carr McCormick, 24 October 1973.
81. *Calgary Tribune*, 27 May 1887.
82. Ham, *The New West*, 131.
83. *Calgary Tribune*, 10 June 1887.
84. *Calgary Tribune*, 24 July 1889; W. E. Hawkins, *Electrifying Calgary: A Century of Public & Private Power* (Calgary: University of Calgary Press, 1987), 3–7.
85. Toronto *Globe*, 17 October 1891.
86. Ibid.
87. *Albertan*, 13 February 1937.
88. Interview by the author with Blanche Ross, 22 May 1974.
89. *Calgary Herald*, 20 February 1889.
90. Blanche Ross interview, 22 May 1974.
91. *Calgary Herald*, 13 March 1889.
92. Ibid., 20 February 1889; 13 March 1889.
93. Ibid., 12 March 1932.
94. PAA, Calgary Court House, bills of sale, 1889; *Calgary Herald*, 8, 29 May 1889.
95. Calgary Public Library, Manuscript Census of 1891 for Calgary.
96. *Calgary Herald*, 6 November 1889.
97. Ibid., 27 November 1889.
98. University of Calgary Library, *Dun & Bradstreet Reference Book*, January 1890, 622; *Dun & Bradstreet Reference Book*, July 1893, 645.
99. *Alberta Tribune*, 20 August 1895.
100. Ibid.
101. Interview by the author with Lou R. Bradley, 30 April 1991.
102. Lou R. Bradley interview, 30 April 1991; *High River Times*, 1 May 1975; Lillian Knupp, *Harness, Boots & Saddles* (High River: Sandstone Publishing Co., n. d.), 4–8.
103. *Alberta Tribune*, 1 May 1897.
104. Alberta Registries, Corporate Registry, Great West Saddlery Company file; *Calgary Herald*, 12 April 1899; *Albertan*, 13 February 1937.
105. Blanche Ross interview, 22 May 1974.
106. *Calgary Herald*, 2 September 1890.
107. Ibid., 24 September 1890.
108. Ibid., 5 April 1893.
109. *Calgary Tribune*, 11 October 1893.
110. *Calgary Herald*, 17 October 1893; 9 January 1894; Hugh A. Dempsey, *Calgary: Spirit of the West* (Saskatoon: Fifth House Publishers, 1994), 65–68.

111. *Calgary Herald*, 12 January 1894; *Calgary Tribune*, 10 January 1894.
112. GAIA, Wesley F. Orr Papers, letterbook, 3, Calgary, 11 February 1894, Wesley F. Orr to James E. Orr.
113. Wesley F. Orr Papers, letterbook, 3, Calgary, 2 April 1894, Wesley F. Orr to E. A. Pfettscher.
114. Canadian Pacific Archives, Van Horne Correspondence, 1 May 1894, Wesley F. Orr to W. C. Van Horne.
115. *Calgary Herald*, 26 September 1893.

Notes to Chapter 10
Department Stores and Mass Distribution

1. *Calgary Tribune*, 12 November 1886.
2. *Calgary Herald*, 13 November 1886.
3. *Calgary Tribune*, 14 January 1887.
4. *Calgary Herald*, 4 April 1888.
5. George Henry Ham, *The New West*, 129.
6. *Calgary Tribune*, 15 April 1887.
7. Ibid., 8 April 1887.
8. *Henderson's Gazetteer and Directory of British Columbia, N. W. T., Manitoba, and Northwest Ontario, including a complete classified Business Directory for the year 1889*, 548–49, 552–53, 558, 560.
9. *Calgary Tribune*, 6 May 1887.
10. Ibid., 15 April 1887.
11. Ibid.
12. *Calgary Tribune*, 23 April 1887.
13. Ibid., 15 April 1887.
14. PAA, Calgary Court House, chattel mortgages, 1887–1891.
15. *Calgary Tribune*, 15 April 1887.
16. GAIA, Edward M. H. Parlby Collection, I. G. Baker & Co., receipts and invoices, 1887–1889.
17. *Calgary Herald*, 25 January 1888.
18. Ibid., 4 April 1888.
19. *Calgary Tribune*, 27 June 1888.
20. PAA, Calgary Court House, chattel mortgages, 1887–1889; *Calgary Herald*, 14 March 1890.
21. *Calgary Herald*, 7 November 1888.
22. PAA, accession no. 66.21, Calgary Court House, bills of sale, 1888.
23. PAA, Calgary Court House, chattel mortgages, 1888.
24. Ibid., chattel mortgages, 1889.
25. Ibid., chattel mortgages, 1889–1890.
26. HBCA, D20/63, ff. 207–21, 230, Winnipeg, 30 October 1890, W. H. Adams and E. K. Beeston to J. Wrigley.
27. Ibid.
28. HBCA, D20/62, f. 210, London, 6 August 1890, Donald A. Smith to W. G. Conrad.

29. HBCA, D20/63, ff. 140–44, Fort Macleod, 2 September 1890, E. F. Gigot to W. Clark.
30. HBCA, D20/63, ff. 207–32, Winnipeg, 3 October 1890, W. H. Adams and E. K. Beeston to J. Wrigley.
31. HBCA, A12/33, ff. 16–18, Winnipeg, 12 January 1891, J. Wrigley to W. Armit.
32. HBCA, D20/65, ff. 244–45, Calgary, 26 January 1891, J. Thomson to J. Wrigley.
33. HBCA, D20/65, ff. 263–64, Calgary, 30 January 1891, J. Thomson to J. Wrigley.
34. HBCA, D20/65, ff. 278–80, Calgary, 2 February 1891, J. Thomson to J. Wrigley.
35. HBCA, A12/33, f. 78, Winnipeg, 2 February 1891, J. Wrigley to W. Armit.
36. K. Ross Toole Archives, University of Montana Library, Missoula, C. E. Conrad Papers, Calgary, 26 March 1891, J. L. Bowen to W. G. Conrad.
37. Ibid., Calgary, 17 April 1891. J. L. Bowen to W. G. Conrad.
38. Ibid., Calgary, 12 May 1892, Fitzgerald & Lucas to Conrad Bros.
39. Ibid., White Post, Virginia, 1 April 1891, W. G. Conrad to C. E. Conrad.
40. HBCA, D20/65, ff. 176–77, Calgary, 17 January 1891, J. Thomson to J. Wrigley.
41. HBCA, D20/66, ff. 36–38, Calgary, 4 March 1891, J. Thomson to J. Wrigley.
42. *Calgary Herald*, 9 March 1891; *Calgary Tribune*, 4 March 1891.
43. HBCA, D20/66, ff. 45–49, Calgary, 5 March 1891, J. Thomson to J. Wrigley.
44. HBCA, D20/66, ff. 88–90, Calgary, 9 March 1891, J. Thomson to J. Wrigley.
45. Ibid.
46. HBCA, D20/66, ff. 45–49, Calgary, 5 March 1891, J. Thomson to J. Wrigley.
47. HBCA, D20/67, ff. 179–81, Calgary, 22 July 1891, W. T. Livock to C. C. Chipman.
48. HBCA, D20/57, ff. 298–302, Calgary, 5 December 1889, J. Thomson to J. Wrigley.
49. HBCA, D12/30, ff. 461–62, Calgary, 9 December 1889, J. Wrigley to W. Armit.
50. HBCA, A12/31, f. 205, Calgary, 9 April 1890, C. Osborne Wickenden to J. Wrigley.
51. *Calgary Herald*, 28 September 1891.
52. HBCA, D20/62, ff. 211–14, Edmonton, 22 August 1890, Harrison J. Young to J. Wrigley.
53. HBCA, D25/10, ff. 93–116, Inspection report by E. K. Beeston, 28 April-1 May 1891.
54. HBCA, A12/33, f. 74, Winnipeg, 2 February 1891, J. Wrigley to W. Armit.
55. *Canadian Who's Who for 1898*, 184; *The Beaver* 4 (March 1924), 218–19.
56. *The Beaver* 4 (March 1924), 218–19.
57. HBCA, A12/5, 509/1, ff. 5–7, Winnipeg, 19 September 1891, C. C. Chipman to W. Armit.
58. Ibid.
59. *Calgary Tribune*, 30 September 1891.
60. Ibid.
61. *Calgary Herald*, 28 September 1891.

62. *Calgary Tribune*, 9 September 1891.
63. HBCA, D20/68, f. 233, Calgary, 1 October 1891, J. Thomson to C. C. Chipman.
64. *Calgary Tribune*, 9 September 1891.
65. Ibid., 14 September 1892.
66. HBCA, D20/68, f. 312A, Calgary, 26 October 1891, J. Thomson to C. C. Chipman; A12/S, 509/1, f. 10, Winnipeg, 20 November 1891, C. C. Chipman to W. Armit.
67. *Calgary Tribune*, 4 May, 14 September 1892.
68. HBCA, D20/68, f. 123, Calgary, 15 September 1891, J. Thomson to C. C. Chipman.
69. *Calgary Tribune*, 20 July 1892.
70. Ibid., 10 August 1892.
71. Ibid., 29 march 1893.
72. Ibid., 5 April 1893.
73. *The Beaver*, 9 (December 1929), 350; *Calgary Herald*, 3 October 1929.
74. HBCA, D20/66, ff. 140–43, Calgary, 16 March 1891, J. Thomson to J. Wrigley.
75. HBCA, D20/67, ff. 457–59, Calgary, 31 August 1891, J. Thomson to C. C. Chipman.
76. *Calgary Tribune*, 17 May 1893.
77. Ibid., 5 July 1893.
78. Ibid., 13 September 1893.
79. HBCA, D32/4, f. 202, Abstracts of Balance Sheets, 1892–1894.
80. HBCA, A12/S, 509/1, ff. 11–12, Winnipeg, 15 October 1894, C. C. Chipman to W. Ware.
81. *Calgary Tribune*, 28 September 1895.
82. Ibid., 5 October 1895.
83. Ibid.
84. Ibid.
85. HBCA, D32/4, f. 202, Abstracts of Balance Sheets, 1895–1899.
86. Calgary Land Titles Office, land mortgage loans, 1894–1895.
87. *Alberta Tribune*, 21 March 1896.
88. Ibid., 6 March 1897.
89. *Calgary Tribune*, 19 April 1893.
90. *Alberta Tribune*, 21 March 1896.
91. Ibid., 18 February 1899.
92. *Calgary Tribune*, 19 July 1893.
93. Ibid., 5 September 1894; *Calgary Herald*, 7 July 1898.
94. *Alberta Tribune*, 14 October 1899; *Calgary Herald*, 5 March 1900, 3 October 1929.
95. HBCA, D32/4, f. 202, Abstracts of Balance Sheets, 1899–1903.

Notes to Chapter 11
Women in Business

1. Manuscript Census of 1891 for Calgary, Canmore, Gleichen, High River, Davisburg, Fish Creek, Pine Creek, Namaka, and Morley; Manuscript Census of 1901 for Calgary, Canmore, Gleichen, High River, Davisburg, Pine Creek, Morley, Queenstown, Shepard, Nose Creek, Springbank, Cochrane, Jumping Pound, Okotoks, Millarville, Priddis, and Pekisko.
2. Ibid.
3. Ibid.
4. Ibid.
5. Marjorie Griffin Cohen, *Women's Work, Markets, and Economic Development in Nineteenth-Century Ontario* (Toronto: University of Toronto Press, 1988), 126–34, 146–51; Lisa M. Fine, *The Souls of the Skyscraper: Female Clerical Workers in Chicago, 1870–1930* (Philadelphia: Temple University Press, 1990), 17–50; Sharon Hartman Strom, *Beyond The Typewriter: Gender, Class, and the Origins of Modern American Office Work, 1900–1930* (Urbana: University of Illinois Press, 1992), 172–226; Claudia Goldin, *Understanding the Gender Gap: An Economic History of American Women* (New York: Oxford University Press, 1990), 4–15, 54–55.
6. GAIA, photographic department, file NA-5304-1, Hudson's Bay Company staff at Calgary in 1896.
7. Sherrill MacLaren, *Braehead: Three Founding Families in Nineteenth Century Canada* (Toronto: McClelland & Stewart, 1986), 269, 288.
8. HBCA, A12/S, 509/1, ff. 96–100, Inspection report by J. S. Braidwood on Calgary sales shop, 31 March 1906.
9. Interview by the author with Rothney Montgomery-Bell, 19 January 1974.
10. *Henderson's Manitoba, Northwest Territories and Western Ontario Gazetteer and Directory for 1900*, 56; *Lovell's Directory of Manitoba and Northwest Territories for 1900–1901*, 365.
11. Rothney Montgomery-Bell interview, 19 January 1974; HBCA, A12/S, 509/1, ff. 96–100, Inspection Report by J. S. Braidwood on Calgary sales shop, 31 March 1906.
12. Rothney Montgomery-Bell interview, 19 January 1974.
13. Interview by the author with Mrs. R. S. Knight, whose maiden name was Susan Harris, 18 October 1973.
14. *Calgary Herald*, 24 December 1901.
15. Mrs. R. S. Knight interview, 18 October 1973.
16. *Lovell's Directory of Manitoba and Northwest Territories for 1900–1901*, 360, 365, 368.
17. Manuscript Census of 1891 for Gleichen.
18. BMA, Bank of Montreal, letterbook, Calgary, 17 October 1905, W. H. Hogg to the General Manager; *Henderson's City of Calgary Directory for 1908*, 256.
19. *Henderson's Manitoba and Northwest Gazetteer and Directory for 1905*, 178
20. Interview by the author with Mrs. S. P. Barth, whose maiden name was A. Parsons, 7 May 1974.
21. Interview by the author with Pansy L. Pue, 11 October 1973.

Notes to pp. 299–306

22. Manuscript Census of 1891 for Calgary, Canmore, Gleichen, High River, Davisburg, Fish Creek, Pine Creek, Namaka, and Morley; Manuscript Census of 1901 for Calgary, Canmore, Gleichen, High River, Davisburg, Pine Creek, Morley, Queenstown, Shepard, Nose Creek, Springbank, Cochrane, Jumping Pound, Okotoks, Millarville, Priddis, and Pekisko.
23. Ibid.
24. Manuscript Census of 1891 for Morley and Calgary.
25. Interview by the author with B. Beveridge, 19 November 1973.
26. Manuscript Census of 1901 for Calgary.
27. Rothney Montgomery-Bell interview, 19 January 1974.
28. MacLaren, *Braehead*, 270.
29. Manuscript Census of 1891 for Calgary.
30. GAIA, Wesley F. Orr Papers, letterbook, 3, Calgary, 3 October 1893, W. F. Orr to E. W. Matthews.
31. *Calgary Herald*, 29 March 1893.
32. *Dun & Bradstreet Reference Book*, July 1893, 645.
33. Wesley F. Orr Papers, letterbook, 3, Calgary, 31 July 1893, W. F. Orr to E. W. Matthews; Calgary, 3 October 1893, W. F. Orr to E. W. Matthews.
34. *Dun & Bradstreet Reference Book*, September 1895, 369; September 1896, 373.
35. *Alberta Tribune*, 31 October 1896.
36. *Calgary Herald*, 6 April 1898.
37. *Dun & Bradstreet Reference Book*, September 1899, 678.
38. *Calgary Herald*, 14 October 1899.
39. Manuscript Census of 1891 and 1901 for Calgary.
40. Interview by the author with Helen Carr McCormick, 24 October 1973.
41. Manuscript Census of 1891 for Calgary.
42. Helen Carr McCormick interview, 24 October 1973.
43. Ibid.
44. Manuscript Census of 1901 for Calgary.
45. Manuscript Census of 1891 for High River; Manuscript Census of 1901 for Pekisko; *Leaves From the Medicine Tree*, 71.
46. *High River Times*, 16 October 1919.
47. PAA, accession no. 74.32, Homestead Records, reel 2053, file 513196, statement made by Agnes K. Bedingfeld, 17 March 1899.
48. Ibid.; Interview by the author with Richard W. Gardner, 16 December 2000.
49. Homestead Records, reel 2053, file 513196, statement made by Agnes K. Bedingfeld, 17 March 1899.
50. Simon Evans, *Prince Charming Goes West: The Story of the E. P. Ranch* (Calgary: University of Calgary Press, 1993), 51.
51. Homestead Records, reel 2053, file 513196, statement made by Agnes K. Bedingfeld, 17 March 1899.
52. Ibid.
53. Richard W. Gardner interview, 16 December 2000.
54. Homestead Records, reel 2057, file 535111, statement made by Agnes K. Bedingfeld, 11 June 1893.
55. Homestead Records, reel 2057, file 535111, statement made by Frank Bedingfeld, 11 June 1893.

Notes to pp. 307–312

56. Homestead Records, reel 2053, file 513196, statement made by A. E. Cross, 17 March 1899; statement made by George Emerson, 30 March 1899.
57. Homestead Records, reel 2057, file 535111, statement made by Joseph H. Brown, 10 January 1906; statement made by George Lane, 12 August 1911.
58. Richard W. Gardner interview, 16 December 2000.
59. Ibid.
60. Homestead Records, reel 2053, file 513196, statement made by Agnes K. Bedingfeld, 17 March 1899.
61. Homestead Records, reel 2057, file 535111, statement made by Agnes K. Bedingfeld, 11 June 1893; Evans, *Prince Charming Goes West*, 52; Harry A. Tatro, *A Survey of Historic Ranches*, Vol. 2 (Ottawa: Historic Sites and Monuments Board of Canada, 1973), 192–93.
62. *Calgary Herald*, 25 September 1923.
63. Homestead Records, reel 2057, file 535111, statement made by Frank Bedingfeld, 15 September 1905; Richard W. Gardner interview, 16 December 2000.
64. Homestead Records, reel 2752, file 1208837, statement made by Agnes K. Bedingfeld, 15 September 1905.
65. Calgary Land Titles Office, mortgage loans, 1905.
66. Homestead Records, reel 2057, file 535111, statement made by Frank Bedingfeld, 27 December 1909.
67. Richard W. Gardner interview, 16 December 2000.
68. Calgary Land Titles Office, land transfers, 1911.
69. Calgary Land Titles Office, mortgage loans, 1916.
70. Homestead Records, reel 2057, file 535111, statement made by Frank Bedingfeld, 3 November 1915.
71. *Leaves From the Medicine Tree*, 72.
72. Richard W. Gardner interview, 16 December 2000.
73. *High River Times*, 16 October 1919.
74. Ibid.
75. Ibid.
76. Richard W. Gardner interview, 16 December 2000.
77. Ibid.
78. Manuscript Census of 1901 for Nose Creek and Priddis.
79. Richard W. Gardner interview, 16 December 2000.
80. Calgary Land Titles Office, land transfers, 1886; *Calgary Herald*, 28 November 1964.
81. *Leaves From the Medicine Tree*, 446.
82. Homestead Records, reel 2038, file 430090, Ottawa, department of the interior, memorandum, 22 September 1891.
83. PAA, accession no. 68.96, Macleod Court House, chattel mortgages, 1885–1886.
84. *Leaves From the Medicine Tree*, 446.
85. Homestead Records, reel 2038, file 430090, statement made by Hugh Graham, 3 July 1888.
86. CIBCA, Imperial Bank of Canada, Minute Book of the Board of Directors, vol. 3, 3 November 1887, 460.

87. *Colonist*, 28 October 1962.
88. Canadian Pacific Archives, Van Horne Correspondence, Saw Mill, n. d., Adela Cochrane to W. C. Van Horne.
89. *Dun & Bradstreet Reference Book*, July 1887, 592.
90. Calgary Land Titles Office, mortgage loans and land transfers, 1885–1886.
91. Calgary Land Titles Office, land transfers, 1885–1886; Donald Edward Brown, "A History of the Cochrane Area," M. A. Thesis, University of Alberta, 1951, 38–39.
92. Calgary Land Titles Office, land transfers, 1885–1886.
93. Mrs. Algernon St. Maur, *Impressions of a Tenderfoot During a Journey of Sport in the Far West* (London: John Murray, 1890), 37.
94. *Colonist*, 28 October 1962.
95. Calgary Land Titles Office, land transfers, 1885–1886.
96. Calgary Land Titles Office, mortgage loans and assignments in trust, 1888.
97. Canadian Pacific Archives, Van Horne Correspondence, Montreal, 8 May 1888, W. C. Van Horne to W. Whyte.
98. Canadian Pacific Archives, Van Horne Correspondence, Winnipeg, 29 October 1890, W. Whyte to W. C. Van Horne.
99. *Report of the Territorial Secretary of the North-West Territories for 1901*, 13.
100. *Dun & Bradstreet Reference Book*, January 1890, 621.
101. Brown, "A History of the Cochrane Area," 42–43.
102. St. Maur, *Impressions of a Tenderfoot*, 36.
103. Ibid., 37, 45–46.
104. Canadian Pacific Archives, Van Horne Correspondence, Mitford, 15 March 1892, T. B. H. Cochrane to W. C. Van Horne; *Big Hill Country Cochrane and Area* (Calgary: Cochrane and Area Historical Society, 1977), 799; Brown, "A History of the Cochrane Area," 180.
105. St. Maur, *Impressions Of A Tenderfoot*, 37.
106. Canadian Pacific Archives, Van Horne Correspondence, Cochrane, 10 July 1888, T. B. H. Cochrane to W. C. Van Horne.
107. Canadian Pacific Archives, Van Horne Correspondence, Mitford, 13 July 1890, T. B. H. Cochrane to W. C. Van Horne.
108. *Calgary Herald*, 4 July 1890.
109. Canadian Pacific Archives, Van Horne Correspondence, Montreal, 24 July 1890, W. C. Van Horne to T. B. H. Cochrane.
110. BMA, Bank of Montreal, letterbook, Calgary, 29 June 1891, A. D. Braithwaite to the General Manager.
111. CIBCA, Imperial Bank of Canada, Minute Book of the Board of Directors, vol. 4, 21 July 1892, 463.
112. *Calgary Tribune*, 2 November 1892.
113. Canadian Pacific Archives, Van Horne Correspondence, Montreal, 2 May 1893, Adela Cochrane to W. C. Van Horne.
114. Canadian Pacific Archives, Van Horne Correspondence, Winnipeg, 14 June 1893, W. Whyte to W. C. Van Horne.
115. Canadian Pacific Archives, Van Horne Correspondence, Mitford, 29 March 1892, T. B. H. Cochrane to W. C. Van Horne.
116. Homestead Records, reel 2038, file 430090, Ottawa, department of the interior, memorandum, 22 September 1891.

Notes to pp. 317–323

117. NAC, RG15, Department of the Interior Records, vol. 1220, file 192192, Calgary, 15 January 1890, W. Pearce to the Secretary, department of the interior.
118. *Calgary Tribune*, 8 June 1892.
119. Homestead Records, reel 2038, file 430090, Calgary, 20 July 1898, W. E. Cochrane to W. Pearce.
120. PAA, accession no. 66.21, Calgary Court House, chattel mortgages, 1896; accession no. 68.96, Macleod Court House, chattel mortgages, 1896.
121. *Alberta Tribune*, 18 April 1896.
122. Canadian Pacific Archives, Van Horne Correspondence, Henham, Wangford, 29 October 1897, T. B. H. Cochrane to W. C. Van Horne; RG2AA, file 52727, Quarr Abbey, Ryde, Isle of Wight, 28 November 1898, Adela Cochrane to T. Shaughnessy.
123. *Colonist*, 28 October 1962.
124. Homestead Records, reel 2038, file 430090, statement made by William E. Cochrane, 13 November 1901.
125. Grey Nuns of Montreal Archives, Holy Cross Hospital Correspondence, circular no. 12, 1911–1912, 39–42.
126. Grey Nuns of Montreal Archives, Holy Cross Hospital Correspondence, *Western Catholic*, vol. 9, no. 13, 28 March 1929.
127. Grey Nuns of Montreal Archives, Holy Cross Hospital Correspondence, Calgary, 3 February 1891, Agnes Carroll to Mother Superior.
128. Ibid.
129. *Calgary Herald*, 24 October 1890.
130. Grey Nuns of Montreal Archives, Holy Cross Hospital Correspondence, Calgary, 19 October 1891, Agnes Carroll to Mother Superior.
131. Grey Nuns of Montreal Archives, Holy Cross Hospital Correspondence, Calgary, 30 October 1891, Agnes Carroll to Mother Superior.
132. Barbara Kwasny, ed., *Nuns and Nightingales: A History of the Holy Cross School of Nursing 1907–1979* (Calgary: The Alumnae Association of the Holy Cross School of Nursing, 1982), 14–15.
133. Grey Nuns of Montreal Archives, Holy Cross Hospital Correspondence, Calgary, 22 November 1891, Agnes Carroll to Mother Superior.
134. Ibid.
135. *Calgary Herald*, 5 December 1892.
136. Ibid.
137. Grey Nuns of Montreal Archives, Holy Cross Hospital Correspondence, "Historical Sketch Holy Cross Hospital, Calgary," by a Calgarian.
138. Grey Nuns of Montreal Archives, Holy Cross Hospital Correspondence, Calgary, July 1892, Agnes Carroll to assistant to Mother Superior.
139. Grey Nuns of Montreal Archives, Holy Cross Hospital Correspondence, Calgary, 23 November 1892, Agnes Carroll to Mother Superior.
140. Kwasny, *Nuns and Nightingales*, 16.
141. Grey Nuns of Montreal Archives, Holy Cross Hospital Correspondence, Calgary, 14 February 1895, Agnes Carroll to Mother Superior.
142. Grey Nuns Regional Centre Archives, Edmonton, Holy Cross Hospital Papers, Calgary, 22 April 1895, C. C. McCaul to Agnes Carroll.

143. Grey Nuns Regional Centre Archives, Holy Cross Hospital Papers, Calgary, 26 March 1895, Agnes Carroll to the Secretary, Department of the Interior.
144. Grey Nuns Regional Centre Archives, Holy Cross Hospital Papers, Calgary, 30 December 1899, P. Burns to Agnes Carroll.
145. Kwasny, *Nuns and Nightingales*, 17.
146. Grey Nuns Regional Centre Archives, Holy Cross Hospital Papers, Calgary, 19 July 1905, Agnes Carroll to Sister McKenna; Grey Nuns of Montreal Archives, Holy Cross Hospital Correspondence, Calgary, 12 July 1907, Agnes Carroll to Sister McKenna.
147. *Calgary Herald*, 16 October 1889; *Calgary Tribune*, 9 August 1893; *Calgary Herald*, 22 July 1929.
148. *Calgary Herald*, 29 March 1892.
149. Calgary Land Titles Office, land transfers, 1904.
150. *Calgary Herald*, 5 November 1964.
151. Calgary Land Titles Office, mechanics' liens, 1906–1907.
152. Calgary Land Titles Office, mortgage loans, 1906; CIBCA, Canadian Bank of Commerce, Minute Book of the Board of Directors, vol. 11, 1 May 1906, 507.
153. *Macleod Gazette*, 19 October 1905.
154. Calgary Land Titles Office, land transfers, 1907.
155. *Macleod Gazette*, 19 October 1905.
156. *Calgary Herald*, 11 October 1934; *Albertan*, 25 April 1973.
157. GAIA, M1606, Braemar Lodge Records, register, vol. 1, 17 October 1906 – 10 August 1907.
158. Calgary Land Titles Office, mortgage loans, 1907.
159. CIBCA, Canadian Bank of Commerce, Minute Book of the Board of Directors, vol. 13, 28 January 1910, 168.
160. *Albertan*, 28 February 1911.
161. Calgary Land Titles Office, land transfers, 1914.
162. *Dun and Bradstreet Reference Book*, September 1916, 12.
163. Braemar Lodge Records, register, vol. 3, 10 April 1911.
164. *Calgary Herald*, 7 March 1918; *Calgary Herald*, 22 July 1929; *Albertan*, 25 April 1973.

Notes to Chapter 12
Financing the Canadian Dream

1. Grey Nuns Regional Centre Archives, Edmonton, Donations in Aid of Holy Cross Hospital in Calgary in 1891; Grey Nuns of Montreal Archives, Holy Cross Hospital correspondence, Calgary, 22 November 1891, Sister Carroll to Mother Superior; *Calgary Tribune*, 25 January 1893; *Calgary Herald*, 29 September 1893.
2. *Alberta Tribune*, 23 November 1895.
3. *The Dominion Illustrated*, Calgary Special, 28 June 1890.
4. Calgary Land Titles Office, land mortgage loans, 1885.
5. *Alberta Tribune*, 31 October 1896; *Calgary Herald*, 4 January 1900; Leishman McNeill, *The Calgary Herald's Tales Of The Old Town* (Calgary: Calgary Herald, 1966), 32.

6. Marian C. McKenna, "Sir James Alexander Lougheed: Calgary's First Senator and City Builder," in Max Foran and Sheilagh Jameson, eds., *Citymakers: Calgarians After The Frontier* (Calgary: The Historical Society of Alberta, Chinook Country Chapter, 1987), 99.
7. *Calgary Herald*, 26 March 1884; McNeill, *The Calgary Herald's Tales Of The Old Town*, 26.
8. *Calgary Tribune*, 16 January 1886.
9. Ibid.
10. PAA, Supreme Court of the Northwest Territories, Calgary, Civil Cases, file 2302, *Peter McCarthy v. James A. Lougheed*, 15 January 1895.
11. *Calgary Tribune*, 27 February 1886.
12. Ibid.; *Calgary Herald*, 6 August 1886.
13. PAA, Homestead Records, reel 2000, file 443503, statement, 12 September 1885.
14. Calgary Land Titles Office, land mortgage loans, 1887.
15. City of Calgary Archives, Town of Calgary, assessment roll for 1887; PAA, Supreme Court of the Northwest Territories, Calgary, Civil Cases, file 2302, *Peter McCarthy v. James A. Lougheed*, 15 January 1895.
16. *The Dominion Illustrated*, Calgary Special, 28 June 1890.
17. *Report of the Territorial Secretary of the Northwest Territories for 1901* (Regina, 1902), 14.
18. PAA, *Peter McCarthy v. James A. Lougheed*, 15 January 1895.
19. Ibid.
20. GAIA, Calgary Brewing & Malting Company Papers, box 1, file 4, Calgary, 21 September 1892, P. McCarthy to A. E. Cross; *Henderson's Manitoba and Northwest Territories Gazetteer and Directory for 1893*, 279.
21. *Calgary Herald*, 16 January 1892.
22. Ibid., 27 June 1892; 4 January 1893; 13 December 1900.
23. Ibid., 21 November 1892.
24. Ibid., 4 January 1893.
25. Calgary Land Titles Office, land mortgage loans, 1892.
26. Ibid., land mortgage loans, 1895; Henry C. Klassen, "Lawyers, Finance and Economic Development in Southwestern Alberta, 1884–1920," in Carol Wilton, ed., *Beyond the Law: Lawyers and Business in Canada 1830 to 1930* (Toronto: The Osgoode Society, 1990), 304.
27. CIBCA, Imperial Bank of Canada, Minute Book of the Board of Directors, vol. 4, 22 September 1892, 486; vol. 5, 8 May 1896, 246.
28. Calgary Land Titles Office, land mortgage loans, 1895.
29. Ibid., land mortgage loans, 1896–1899.
30. BMA, Bank of Montreal, letterbook, Calgary, 16 November 1897, W. B. Graveley to the General Manager.
31. *Calgary Herald*, 13 December 1900.
32. Calgary Land Titles Office, land mortgage loans, 1900.
33. *Calgary Herald*, 26 December 1900.
34. Ibid.
35. *Calgary Herald*, 10 March 1898.
36. Calgary Court House, Surrogate Division, Estate of W. H. Kinnisten file, 19 December 1898.

37. *Dun & Bradstreet Reference Book*, July 1903, 392.
38. Estate of W. H. Kinnisten file, 19 December 1898.
39. Calgary Land Titles Office, mortgage loans, 1899.
40. Interview by the author with Luey Dofoo, 15 October 1973.
41. Ibid.
42. Ibid.
43. Ibid.
44. Ibid.; See also J. Brian Dawson, "The Chinese Experience in Frontier Calgary: 1885–1910," in A. W. Rasporich and Henry C. Klassen, eds., *Frontier Calgary: Town, City, and Region 1875–1914* (Calgary: McClelland and Stewart West, 1975), 124–40.
45. Interview by the author with Paul Dofoo, 1 May 2000.
46. Ibid.
47. Ibid.
48. Manuscript Census of 1891 for Fish Creek; *Albertan*, 14 August 1939.
49. Interview by the author with Mrs. Leslie Douglass, 6 November 1973; *Albertan*, 16 April 1941.
50. Interview by the author with Mrs. W. Woodall, 19 October 1973; *Calgary Herald*, 15 January 1930; *Albertan*, 17 January 1931.
51. *Calgary Herald*, 22 February 1888.
52. Ibid., 15 January 1930.
53. Ibid., 10 September 1884.
54. *Albertan*, 17 January 1931.
55. GAIA, S. W. Shaw Family Fonds, land transfer, J. J. Robinson, executor of the Isaac Robinson estate, to Helen Maria Shaw, 12 May 1893.
56. *Calgary Herald*, 22 February 1888.
57. Ibid., 23 October 1889.
58. *Albertan*, 17 January 1931.
59. S. W. Shaw Family Fonds, Midnapore Supply Company, letterbook, Midnapore, 7 October 1916, Helen Shaw to the Manager, Bank of Montreal.
60. *Calgary Herald*, 11 December 1889.
61. Ibid.
62. S. W. Shaw Family Fonds, land transfer, J. J. Robinson, executor of the Isaac Robinson estate, to Helen Maria Shaw, 12 May 1893; Midnapore Supply Company, letterbook, Midnapore, 27 April 1920, Helen Shaw to R. T. Stephenson.
63. *Calgary Herald*, 14 March 1890; 14 July 1890.
64. *Calgary Tribune*, 16 March 1892.
65. PAA, accession no. 66.21, Calgary Court House, chattel mortgages, 1889.
66. Calgary Land Titles Office, mortgage loans, 1891–1892.
67. S. W. Shaw Family Fonds, Midnapore Woollen Mills letterhead.
68. PAA, accession no. 87.89, Index to Partnerships in Calgary, Helen Shaw, Midnapore Woollen Mills, 7 March 1898; Calgary Land Titles Office, mortgage loans, 1899.
69. *Calgary Herald*, 13 June 1898; 18 March 1899.
70. *Calgary, Alberta* (Winnipeg: Northwestern Journal of Progress, 1903), 23.
71. *Dun and Bradstreet Reference Book*, July 1906, 5.

72. S. W. Shaw Family Fonds, Midnapore Supply Company, letterbook, Midnapore, 22 August 1921, Helen Shaw to J. J. McCabe; Midnapore, 17 October 1921, Helen Shaw to James Duff.
73. Interview by the author with Ruth Lynch, 5 January 2000.
74. PAA, Homestead Records, reel 2018, file 287250, statement made by Henry Alexander Watson, 11 April 1895.
75. *Sodbusting to Subdivision* (DeWinton: DeWinton & District Historical Committee, 1978), 412–13.
76. *Calgary Tribune*, 5 November 1886.
77. *Calgary Herald*, 26 June 1889.
78. PAA, Calgary Court House, chattel mortgages, 1889–1890; Calgary Land Titles Office, land mortgage loans, 1890.
79. *Calgary Herald*, 1 October 1890.
80. Homestead Records, reel 2018, file 287250, statement made by Henry Alexander Watson, 11 April 1895.
81. *Alberta Tribune*, 16 January 1897.
82. Ruth Lynch interview, 5 January 2000.
83. Interview by the author with Audrey Macdougall, 6 May 1974.
84. Ibid.
85. Ibid.
86. *Albertan*, 17 April 1944.
87. Audrey Macdougall interview, 6 May 1974.
88. PAA, Homestead Records, reel 2014, file 238666, statement made by Meopham Gardner, 3 June 1890.
89. Audrey Macdougall interview, 6 May 1974.
90. Ibid.
91. *Calgary Tribune*, 11 October 1893.
92. *Chaps and Chinooks: A History West of Calgary*, Vol. 1 (Calgary: Foothills Historical Society, 1976), 219–20, 256, 301, 315. Manuscript Census 1901 for Springbank.
93. Audrey Macdougall interview, 6 May 1974.
94. Audrey Macdougall interview, 6 May 1974; *Our Foothills* (Calgary: Millarville, Kew, Priddis, and Bragg Creek Historical Society, 1975), 143.
95. Audrey Macdougall interview, 6 May 1974; *Calgary Herald*, 10 July 1939.
96. Audrey Macdougall interview, 6 May 1974.
97. *Albertan*, 21 December 1942.
98. Burns & Elliott, eds., *Calgary, Alberta: Her Industries & Resources* (Calgary: Burns & Elliott, 1885), 22, 53.
99. PAA, accession no. 85.268, bankruptcy records, box 1, file 559, Estate of James C. Linton, 24 September 1927.
100. *Calgary Herald*, 10 September 1884.
101. PAA, bankruptcy records, box 1, file 559, Estate of James C. Linton, 24 September 1927.
102. *Calgary Tribune*, 5 November 1886.
103. George Henry Ham, *The New West* (Winnipeg: Canadian Historical Publishing Co., 1888), 134.
104. Ibid.

105. *Calgary Tribune*, 24 July 1889; *Calgary Herald*, 14 May 1920.
106. *Dun & Bradstreet Reference Book*, January 1890, 622.
107. *Calgary Herald*, 4 July 1925; PAA, accession no. 87.89, Index to Partnerships in Calgary, 17 May 1892; Calgary Land Titles Office, land mortgage loans, 1893.
108. *Dun & Bradstreet Reference Book*, July 1893, 645.
109. Interview by the author with Edith A. Durkee, 3 November 1973.
110. Interview by the author with Lillian Hughes, 26 November 1973.
111. Interview by the author with Mrs. Clara Might, whose maiden name and professional name was Clara Christie, 22 November 1973; *Calgary Herald*, 14 January 1937, 14 March 1959, 9 October 1987.
112. *Farm and Ranch Review*, October 1960, 18.
113. Quoted in ibid., 19.
114. PAA, Index to Partnerships, Calgary, 30 April 1887.
115. *Calgary Tribune*, 5 November 1886.
116. Calgary Land Titles Office, land mortgage loans, 1887.
117. W. Hanson Boorne, "With the Savages in the Far West," *The Canadian Photographic Journal*, Christmas 1893, 372.
118. *Calgary Tribune*, 11 November 1887.
119. Ham, *The New West*, 137.
120. *Calgary Herald*, 31 December 1891; 5 December 1892; 17 October 1893.
121. PAA, Index to Partnerships, Calgary, 3 December 1889.
122. Calgary Land Titles Office, land mortgage loans, 1889–1893.
123. *Report of the Territorial Secretary of the Northwest Territories for 1901*, 23.
124. *Calgary Herald*, 5 December 1892.
125. Ibid., 17 October 1893.
126. *Dun & Bradstreet Reference Book*, July 1893, 644.
127. *Calgary Tribune*, 27 April 1892.
128. Wesley F. Orr Papers, letterbook, 3, Calgary, 16 August 1893, Wesley F. Orr to E. W. Matthews.
129. *Calgary Herald*, 17 October 1893.
130. The *Dominion Illustrated*, Calgary Special, 28 June 1890.
131. Interview by the author with Norman S. Mackie, 26 October 1973.
132. *Calgary Herald*, 21 January 1949.
133. Norman S. Mackie interview, 26 October 1973.
134. Ham, *The New West*, 138.
135. Calgary Land Title Office, land mortgage loans, 1887.
136. Ham, *The New West*, 138.
137. *The Dominion Illustrated*, Calgary Special, 28 June 1890.
138. Norman S. Mackie interview, 26 October 1973; *Albertan*, 1 August 1956.
139. Wesley F. Orr Papers, letterbook, 3, Calgary, 15 June 1893, Wesley F. Orr to E. W. Matthews.
140. Norman S. Mackie interview, 26 October 1973.
141. Ibid.
142. PAA, Calgary Court House, chattel mortgages, 1899; Calgary Land Titles Office, land mortgage loans, 1899.
143. *Calgary Herald*, 15 March 1900; 30 June 1900.

144. *Albertan*, 4 December 1900.
145. *Calgary Herald*, 24 December 1901.
146. *Dun & Bradstreet Reference Book*, July 1903, 392.
147. *Henderson's Manitoba, Northwest Territories and Western Ontario Gazetteer and Directory for 1900*, 45–63.
148. Interview by the author with C. W. Adams, 25 March 1974.
149. Ibid.; *Our Foothills*, 73–74.
150. C.W. Adams interview, 25 March 1975.
151. Ibid.
152. Ibid.
153. CIBCA, Imperial Bank of Canada, Minute Book of the Board of Directors, vol. 8, 26 March 1907; vol. 9, 18 March 1908; vol. 10, 18 June, 1909; Calgary Court House, Surrogate Division, Estate of C. S. Lott file, 15 May 1914.
154. C.W. Adams interview, 25 March 1974; Calgary Court House, Estate of C. S. Lott file, 15 May 1914; *Calgary Herald*, 31 March 1914.

Bibliography

Primary Sources

Manuscript Collections

Alberta Registries, Corporate Registry, Edmonton
  Cochrane Ranche Company file
  Eau Claire & Bow River Lumber Co. file
  Great West Saddlery Company file

Baker Library, Graduate School of Business Administration, Harvard University
  R. G. Dun & Co. Collection

Bank of Montreal Archives, Montreal
  Bank of Montreal, letterbook

Calgary Court House, Surrogate Division, Records
  Estate of Robert Findlay file
  Estate of William Duncan Kerfoot file
  Estate of W. H. Kinnisten file
  Estate of Frederick G. Smith file

Calgary Land Titles Office
  Land Mortgage records
  Calgary townsite plans

Canadian Pacific Archives, Montreal
  Shaughnessy correspondence
  Van Horne correspondence

Bibliography

Canadian Imperial Bank of Commerce Archives, Toronto
Imperial Bank of Canada, Minute Book of the Board of Directors

Catholic Pastoral Centre Archives, Calgary
Sparrow Papers

City of Calgary Archives
Assessment Roll of 1887 for Calgary

City of Calgary Public Library
Manuscript Census of 1891 for Calgary, Canmore, Gleichen, High River, Davisburg, Fish Creek, Pine Creek, Namaka, Morley.

Manuscript Census of 1901 for Calgary, Canmore, Gleichen, High River, Davisburg, Pine Creek, Morley, Queenstown, Shepard, Nose Creek, Springbank, Cochrane, Jumping Pound, Okotoks, Millarville, Priddis, and Pekisko.

Duke University Library
W. G. Conrad Papers

Glenbow-Alberta Institute Archives
A. E. Cox Family Papers
A. E. Cross Papers
Braemar Lodge Records, Registers
Calgary Brewing & Malting Co. Papers
Calgary Town Council Minutes
Canada Northwest Land Company Papers
Diary of Frank White
D. W. Davis Papers
Eau Claire & Bow River Lumber Co. Papers
Edgar Dewdney Papers
Edward M. H. Parlby Collection
Elizabeth Bailey Price Manuscript & Clippings
Frank M. Crosby Papers
George Murdoch Papers
I. S. Freeze Papers
Ledger of Records of A. E. Banister
Mrs. Lavinia Hunter Collection, Davisburg Ranchers Society, minutebook
North West Mounted Police, letterbook
Ranchmen's Club Papers, minute book
Richard Hardisty Papers
S. W. Shaw Family Fonds
Wesley F. Orr Papers

Grey Nuns of Montreal Archives, Montreal
Holy Cross Hospital correspondence

Bibliography

Grey Nuns Regional Centre Archives, Edmonton
Holy Cross Hospital Papers

K. Ross Toole Archives, University of Montana Library, Missoula
C. E. Conrad Papers

Marjorie Gray Collection, Highwood, Montana
John Harris Papers

Missouri Historical Society Archives
P. Chouteau Maffitt Collection

Montana Historical Society Archives, Helena
I. G. Baker Papers
S. T. Hauser Papers
T. C. Power Papers

National Archives of Canada, Ottawa
Bank of Montreal, Minute Book of the Board of Directors
Department of Indian Affairs Records
Department of the Interior Records
John A. Macdonald Papers
Merchants Bank of Canada, Minute Book of the Board of Directors
Molson's Bank, Minute Book of the Board of Directors
Royal Canadian Mounted Police Records

National Archives, Washington, D. C.
Comptroller of the Currency Records
Office of Indian Affairs Records
Secretary of the Treasury Records

Provincial Archives of Alberta
Bankruptcy Records
Calgary Court House, Chattel Mortgage Records
Homestead Records
Index to Partnerships in Calgary
Macleod Court House, Chattel Mortgage Records
Supreme Court of the Northwest Territories, Calgary, Civil Cases Files
W. D. Kerfoot v. the British American Ranche Company, 1888
I. G. Baker & Co. v. Helen Maria Gouin, 1889
Alexander Stuart v. the British American Ranche Company, 1890
The Mount Royal Ranche Company v. I. G. Baker & Co, 1890
James Stewart Moore v. Charles William Martin, 1891
I. G. Baker & Co. v. S. Watson, 1891
Samuel Barber and the Imperial Bank of Canada v. the Quorn Ranche Company, 1892
Peter McCarthy v. James A. Lougheed, 1895

Bibliography

Provincial Archives of Manitoba
Hudson's Bay Company Archives, Hudson's Bay Company Papers

Royal Bank of Canada Archives, Montreal
B. Jamieson, "Union Bank of Canada, 1865-1925," Montreal: typescript copy, 1957.

Saskatchewan Archives Board, Regina, Department of Provincial Secretary, Companies Branch, Old Companies Files
Calgary and Edmonton Land Co. file
Cochrane Ranche Company file
Conrad Circle Cattle Co. file
Conrad Investment Co. file
Quorn Ranche Company file

State of Montana, Helena
Secretary of State, Corporation Bureau Records, Benton & St. Louis Cattle Co. file

University of Calgary Library
Dun & Bradstreet Reference Books

Interviews by the Author
Anton Anderson, 11 March 1974
Mrs. S. P. Barth, 7 May 1974
B. Beveridge, 19 November 1973
Lou R. Bradley, 30 April 1991
Barbra Connelly, 21 May 1974
Luey Dofoo, 15 October 1973
Paul Dofoo, 1 May 2000
Mrs. Leslie Douglass, 6 November 1973
Edith A. Durkee, 3 November 1973
Anna English, 21 January 1974
Tom A. Findlay, 16 May 1991; 27 May 1999
Richard W. Gardner, 16 December 2000
Ida Graves, 19 October 1973
Doris Herr, 11 October 1999
Bill Hogg, 7 September 1999
Ernest W. Irving, 5 October 1999
Lillian Jacques, 14 January 1974
Mrs. R.S. Knight, 18 October 1973
Ruth Lynch, 5 January 2000
Audrey Macdougall, 6 May 1974
Glen Macdougall, 6 May 1974
Norman S. Mackie, 26 October 1973
Russell and Marion Martin, 10, 28 September 1999
Helen Carr McCormick, 24 October 1973

Bibliography

James F. McKevitt, 28 October 1999
Lillian McMorris, 10 July 1988
Clara Might, 22 November 1973
Rothney Montgomery-Bell, 19 January 1974
Glen and Jean Morrison, 27 May 1999
Helga Olson, 11 March 1974
Pansy L. Pue, 11 October 1973
Blanche Ross, 22 May 1974
Lillian Soley, 3 December 1974
Grace Suitor, 5 October 1999
William E. Suitor, 22 April 1975
Marjorie Swann, 30 June 1976
Ruth Walker, 6 January 1975
William A. Wolley-Dod, 22, 25 January 2000
William R. Wolley-Dod, 12 October 1973
Mrs. W. Woodall, 19 October 1973

Newspapers

Alberta Tribune
Albertan
Calgary Herald
Calgary News Telegram
Calgary Tribune
Colonist
Dawson News
Fort Benton Record
Globe-Democrat
Great Falls Tribune
High River Times
Lethbridge Herald
Macleod Gazette
Nor'Wester
Regina Leader
River Press
Toronto Globe

Business Magazines

Canadian Cattlemen
The Commercial
Monetary Times
Farm and Ranch Review

Bibliography

Magazines

Scarlet and Gold
The Dominion Illustrated
The Beaver

Directories and Pamphlets

Alberta: The Calgary District Harvest News 1890
Calgary, Alberta
Henderson's City of Calgary Directory for 1908
Henderson's Gazetteer and Directory of British Columbia, N.W.T., Manitoba, and Northwest Ontario, including a complete classified Business Directory for the year 1889
Henderson's Manitoba, Northwest Territories and Western Ontario Gazetteer and Directory for 1900
Henderson's Manitoba and Northwest Territories Gazetteer and Directory for 1893
Henderson's Manitoba and Northwest Gazetteer and Directory for 1905
Henderson's Manitoba and Northwestern Ontario and Northwest Towns and City of Winnipeg Directory for 1886–87
Henderson's Northwest Ranchers Directory and Brand Book
Lovell's Directory of Manitoba and Northwest Territories for 1900–1901

Government Documents

Canada, *House of Commons Debates*, 1870–1900.
Canada, *Journals of the House of Commons*, 1870–1900.
Canada, *Sessional Papers*, 1879, no. 7, report of the Deputy Superintendent General of Indian Affairs.
Canada, *Sessional Papers*, 1879, no. 188, statement of payments made to I. G. Baker & Co., 1875–1876; North West Mounted Police Expenditure, 1879; statement of vouchers for pay to the North West Mounted Police.
Canada, *Sessional Papers*, Department of Indian Affairs, Annual Reports, 1884–1886.
Canada, *Sessional Papers*, 1886, no. 6, report of the Department of Indian Affairs for the year ending 31 December 1886.
Canada, *Sessional Papers*, 1886, No. 6A, report upon the Suppression of the Rebellion in the Northwest Territories and Matters in Connection therewith in 1885.
Canada, *Sessional Papers*, 1895, No. 13, report of Amos Rowe.
Canadian Annual Review
Report of the Territorial Secretary of the North-West Territories for 1901

Secondary Sources
Books

A Century of Memories 1883–1983: Okotoks and District. Okotoks: Okotoks and District Historical Society, 1983.

Appleby, Edna, *Canmore: The Story of an Era*. Canmore: Edna Appleby, 1975.

Big Hill Country: Cochrane and Area. Calgary: Cochrane and Area Historical Society, 1977.

Bliss, Michael, *Northern Enterprise: Five Centuries of Canadian Business*. Toronto: McClelland and Stewart, 1987.

Bowsfield, Hartwell, ed., *The Letters of Charles John Brydges 1879–1882: Hudson's Bay Company Land Commissioner*. With an Introduction by Alan Wilson. Winnipeg: Hudson's Bay Record Society, 1977.

Brado, Edward, *Cattle Kingdom: Early Ranching in Alberta*. Vancouver: Douglas & McIntyre, 1984.

Breen, David H., *The Canadian Prairie West and the Ranching Frontier 1874–1924*. Toronto: University of Toronto Press, 1983.

Buenger, Walter L., and Joseph A. Pratt, *But Also Good Business: Texas Commerce, Banks and the Financing of Houston and Texas, 1886–1986*. College Station: Texas A & M University Press, 1986.

Burns & Elliott, eds., *Calgary, Alberta: Her Industries and Resources*. Calgary: Burns & Elliott, 1885.

Byfield, Ted, ed., *The Great West Before 1900*. Vol. 1. Edmonton: United Western Communications, 1991.

Canadian Who's Who for 1898.

Carter, Sarah, *Aboriginal People and Colonizers of Western Canada to 1900*. Toronto: University of Toronto Press, 1999.

Carter, Sarah, *Lost Harvests: Prairie Indian Reserve Farmers and Government Policy*. Montreal: McGill-Queen's University Press, 1990.

Chandler, Alfred D. Jr., *The Visible Hand: The Managerial Revolution in American Business*. Cambridge, Mass.: Harvard University Press, 1977.

Chaps and Chinooks: A History West of Calgary. Vol. 1. Calgary: Foothills Historical Society, 1976.

Cochrane, William, *The Canadian Album Men of Canada*. Brantford, Ont.: Bradley, Garretson & Co., 1894.

Cohen, Marjorie Griffin, *Women's Work, Markets, and Economic Development in Nineteenth-Century Ontario*. Toronto: University of Toronto Press, 1988.

Craick, W. A., *A Short Sketch of the Osler Family 1837–1913*. Toronto: Wm. Tyrrell & Co., 1938.

Dempsey, Hugh A., ed., *Calgary: Spirit of the West*. Saskatoon: Fifth House Publishers, 1994.

Dempsey, Hugh A., ed., *R. B. Nevitt: A Winter at Fort Macleod*. Calgary: McClelland and Stewart West, 1974.

Dempsey, Hugh A., ed., *The CPR West: The Iron Road and the Making of a Nation*. Vancouver: Douglas & McIntyre, 1984.

den Otter, A. A., *Civilizing the West: The Galts and the Development of Western Canada*. Edmonton: University of Alberta Press, 1982.

Denison, Merrill, *Canada's First Bank: A History of the Bank of Montreal*. Vol. 2. Toronto: McClelland and Stewart, 1967.

Denny, Sir Cecil E., *The Law Marches West*. Toronto: J. M. Dent and Sons, 1972.

Eagle, John A., *The Canadian Pacific Railway and the Development of Western Canada, 1896–1914*. Montreal: McGill-Queen's University Press, 1989.

Easterbrook, W. T., and Hugh G. J. Aitken, *Canadian Economic History*. Toronto: Macmillan Company of Canada, 1967.

Elofson, Warren M., *Cowboys, Gentlemen and Cattle Thieves: Ranching on the Western Frontier*. Montreal: McGill-Queen's University Press, 2000.

Evans, Simon, Sarah Carter, and Bill Yeo, eds., *Cowboys, Ranchers and the Cattle Business: Cross-Border Perspectives on Ranching History*. Calgary: University of Calgary Press, 2000.

Evans, Simon M., *Prince Charming Goes West: The Story of the E. P. Ranch*. Calgary: University of Calgary Press, 1993.

Fahrni, Margaret Morton, and W. L. Morton, *Third Crossing: A History of the First Century of the Town and District of Gladstone in the Province of Manitoba*. Winnipeg: Advocate Printers Limited, 1946.

Fine, Lisa M., *The Souls of the Skyscraper: Female Clerical Workers in Chicago, 1870–1930*. Philadelphia: Temple University Press, 1990.

Fogel, Robert William, *Railroads and American Economic Growth: Essays in Econometric History*. Baltimore: Johns Hopkins University Press, 1964.

Foran, Max, *Calgary: An Illustrated History*. Toronto: James Lorimer & Company, 1978.

Foran, Max, and Heather MacEwan Foran, *Calgary Canada's Frontier Metropolis: An Illustrated History*. Toronto: Windsor Publications, 1982.

Francis, R. Douglas, Richard Jones, and Donald B. Smith, *Destinies: Canadian History Since Confederation*. Third Edition. Toronto: Harcourt Brace & Company Canada, 1996.

Friesen, Gerald, *The Canadian Prairies: A History*. Toronto: University of Toronto Press, 1984.

Goldin, Claudia, *Understanding the Gender Gap: An Economic History of American Women*. New York: Oxford University Press, 1990.

Ham, George Henry, *The New West: Extending from the Great Lakes across Plain and Mountain to the Golden Shores of the Pacific*. Winnipeg: Canadian Historical Publishing Co., 1888.

Hawkins, W. E., *Electrifying Calgary: A Century of Public and Private Power*. Calgary: University of Calgary Press, 1987.

Haywood, C. Robert, *Cowtown Lawyers: Dodge City and its Attorneys 1876–1886*. Norman: University of Oklahoma Press, 1988.

Hildebrandt, Walter, *Views from Fort Battleford: Constructed Visions of an Anglo-Canadian West*. Regina: Canadian Plains Research Center, 1994.

Hildebrandt, Walter, and Brian Hubner, *The Cypress Hills: The Land and its People*. Saskatoon: Purich, 1994.

Hurst, James Willard, *Law and the Conditions of Freedom in the Nineteenth-Century United States*. Madison: University of Wisconsin Press, 1956.

Jameson, Sheilagh, *Ranchers Cowboys and Characters: Birth of Alberta's Western Heritage*. Calgary: Glenbow-Alberta Institute, 1987.

Kelly, L. V., *The Range Men: 75th Anniversary Edition*. High River: Willow Creek Publishing, 1988.

Knupp, Lillian, *Harness, Boots & Saddles*. High River: Sandstone Publishing Co., n.d.

Knupp, Lillian, *Life and Legends: A History of the Town of High River*. Calgary: Sandstone Publishing, 1982.

Kwasny, Barbara, ed., *Nuns and Nightingales: A History of the Holy Cross School of Nursing*. Calgary: The Alumnae Association of the Holy Cross School of Nursing, 1982.

Lavallee, Omer, *Van Horne's Road: An Illustrated Account of the Construction and First Years of Operation of the Canadian Pacific Transcontinental Railway*. Montreal: Railway Enterprises, 1974.

Leaves from the Medicine Tree. High River: The High River Pioneers' and Old Timers' Association, 1960.

MacBeth, R. G., *Sir Augustus Nanton: A Biography*. Toronto: Macmillan of Canada, 1931.

Martin, Albro, *Railroads Triumphant: The Growth, Rejection & Rebirth of a Vital American Force*. New York: Oxford University Press, 1992.

Martin, Chester, *Dominion Lands Policy*. Edited and with an Introduction by Lewis H. Thomas. Toronto: McClelland and Stewart, 1973.

MacEwan, Grant, *Colonel James Walker, Man of the Western Frontier*. Saskatoon: Western Producer Prairie Books, 1989.

MacGregor, J. G., *John Rowand, Czar of the Prairies*. Saskatoon: Western Producer Prairie Books, 1978.

MacGregor, James, G., *Vision of an Ordered Land: The Story of the Dominion Land Survey*. Saskatoon: Western Producer Prairie Books, 1981.

MacLaren, Sherrill, *Braehead: Three Founding Families in Nineteenth Century Canada*. Toronto: McClelland & Stewart, 1986.

McCraw, Thomas K., *Creating Modern Capitalism: How Entrepreneurs, Companies, and Countries Triumphed in Three Industrial Revolutions*. Cambridge, Mass.: Harvard University Press, 1997.

McDougall, J. Lorne, *Canadian Pacific: A Brief History*. Montreal: McGill-Queen's University Press, 1968.

McNeill, Leishman, *The Calgary Herald's Tales of the Old Town*. Calgary: Calgary Herald, 1966.

Morton, Desmond, and Reginald H. Roy, eds., *Telegrams of the North-West Campaign 1885*. Toronto: The Champlain Society, 1972.

Morton, W. L., *Manitoba: A History*. Toronto: University of Toronto Press, 1967.

Morton, W. L., *The Progressive Party in Canada*. Toronto: University of Toronto Press, 1950.

Murphy, James E., *Half Interest in a Silver Dollar: The Saga of Charles E. Conrad*. Missoula: Mountain Press Publishing Company, 1983.

Bibliography

Nelson, J. G., *The Last Refuge*. Montreal: Harvest House, 1973.

Overholser, Joel, *Fort Benton: World's Innermost Port*. Fort Benton: Joel Overholser, 1987.

Our Foothills. Calgary: Millarville, Kew, Priddis, and Bragg Creek Historical Society, 1975.

Palmer, Howard, with Tamara Palmer, *Alberta: A New History*. Edmonton: Hurtig Publishers, 1990.

Rees, Tony, *Polo, The Galloping Game: An Illustrated History of Polo in the Canadian West*. Cochrane: Western Heritage Centre Society, 2000.

Regehr, T. D., *The Canadian Northern Railway Pioneer Road of the Northern Prairies 1895–1918*. Toronto: Macmillan of Canada, 1976.

Rennie, Bradford James, *The Rise of Agrarian Democracy: The United Farmers and Farm Women of Alberta, 1909-1921*. Toronto: University of Toronto Press, 2000.

Report of the Territorial Secretary of the NorthWest Territories for 1901.

Ross, Victor, *A History of the Canadian Bank of Commerce*. Vol. 2. Toronto: Oxford University Press, 1922.

Sanders, Harry M., *Watermarks: One Hundred Years of Calgary Waterworks*. Calgary: The City of Calgary, 2000.

Schull, Joseph, *100 Years of Banking in Canada: A History of the Toronto-Dominion Bank*. Toronto: Copp Clark, 1958.

Schumpeter, Joseph A., *Capitalism, Socialism and Democracy*. With a new introduction by Tom Bottomore. New York: Harper Torchbooks, 1976.

Sharp, Paul F., *Whoop-Up Country: The Canadian-American West, 1865–1885*. Norman: University of Oklahoma Press, 1978.

Smith, Donald, ed., *Centennial City: Calgary 1894–1994*. Calgary: University of Calgary Press, 1994.

Sodbusting to Subdivision. DeWinton: DeWinton & District Historical Committee, 1978.

Sparks, Susie, ed., *Calgary: A Living Heritage*. Calgary: Junior League of Calgary, 1984.

St. Maur, Mrs. Algernon, *Impressions of a Tenderfoot during a Journey of Sport in the Far West*. London: John Murray, 1890.

Stardom, Eleanor, *A Stranger to the Fur Trade: Joseph Wrigley and the Transformation of the Hudson's Bay Company, 1884–1891*. Winnipeg: University of Winnipeg Rupert's Land Research Centre, 1995.

Strom, Sharon Hartman, *Beyond the Typewriter: Gender, Class, and the Origins of Modern American Office Work, 1900–1930*. Urbana: University of Illinois Press, 1992.

Tannahill, Cecil C., *Private – Chartered Banks in the Territories of Assiniboia and Saskatchewan and the Province of Saskatchewan 1880–1936*. Regina: Cecil C. Tannahill, 1986.

Tatro, Harry A., *A Survey of Historic Ranches*. Vol. 2. Ottawa: Historic Sites and Monuments Board of Canada, 1973.

The Gleichen Call: A History of Gleichen and the Surrounding Areas 1877 to 1968. Calgary: Gleichen United Church Women, 1968.

Trafford, Tyler, *Toole Peet 1897–1997: An Enduring Partnership*. Calgary: Toole, Peet & Co. Limited, 1997.

Trails to Little Corner: A Story of Namaka and Surrounding Districts. Calgary: Namaka Community Historical Committee, 1983.

Treaty 7 Elders and Tribal Council, *The True Spirit and Original Intent of Treaty 7*. With Walter Hildebrandt, Sarah Carter, and Dorothy First Rider. Montreal: McGill-Queen's University Press, 1996.

Van West, Carroll, *Capitalism on the Frontier: Billings and the Yellowstone Valley in the Nineteenth Century*. Lincoln: University of Nebraska Press, 1993.

Walden, Keith, *Becoming Modern in Toronto: The Industrial Exhibition and the Shaping of a Late Victorian Culture*. Toronto: University of Toronto Press, 1997.

Walter, Dave, *Today Then: America's Best Minds Look 100 Years into the Future on the Occasion of the 1893 World's Columbian Exposition*. Helena: American & World Geographic Publishing, 1992.

Articles

Benoit, Jean, "Andrew Thomson," *Dictionary of Canadian Biography*, Vol. 13, *1901–1910*. Toronto: University of Toronto Press, 1994, 1027–30.

Boorne, W. Hanson, "With the Savages in the Far West," *The Canadian Photographic Journal*. (Christmas 1893), 272–73.

Carlos, Ann M., and Jill L. Van Stone, "Stock Transfer Patterns in the Hudson's Bay Company: A Study of the English Capital Market in Operation, 1670–1730," *Business History 38* (April 1996), 15–39.

Carter, Sarah, " 'He Country in Pants' No Longer – Diversifying Ranching History," in Simon Evans, Sarah Carter, and Bill Yeo, eds., *Cowboys, Ranchers and the Cattle Business: Cross-Border Perspectives on Ranching History*. Calgary: University of Calgary Press, 2000, 155–66.

Coats, Douglas, "Calgary: The Private Schools, 1900–16," in Anthony W. Rasporich and Henry C. Klassen, eds., *Frontier Calgary: Town, City, and Region, 1875–1914*. Calgary: McClelland and Stewart West, 1975, 141–52.

Cunniffe, Dick, "George Murdoch, Mayor 1884–1885," in *Good Morning, Your Worship, Mayors of Calgary, 1884–1975*. Calgary: Century Calgary Publications, 1975, 9–11.

Dawson, J. Brian, "The Chinese Experience in Frontier Calgary: 1885–1910," in A. W. Rasporich and Henry Klassen, eds., *Frontier Calgary: Town, City, and Region 1875–1914*. Calgary: McClelland and Stewart West, 1975, 124–40.

den Otter, A. A., "Bondage of Steam: The CPR and Western Canadian Coal," in Hugh A. Dempsey, ed., *The CPR West: The Iron Road and the Making of a Nation*. Vancouver: Douglas & McIntyre, 1984, 191–207.

den Otter, A. A., "The Hudson's Bay Company's Prairie Transportation Problem, 1870–85," in John E. Foster, ed., *The Developing West: Essays on Canadian History in Honor of Lewis H. Thomas*. Edmonton: University of Alberta Press, 1983, 25–47.

Elofson, W. M., "Adapting to the Frontier Environment: The Ranching Industry in Western Canada, 1881–1914," in Donald H. Akenson, ed., *Canadian Papers in Rural History*, Vol. 8. Gananoque, Ontario: Langdale Press, 1992.

Elofson, Warren M., "The Untamed Canadian Ranching Frontier, 1874–1914," in Simon Evans, Sarah Carter, and Bill Yeo, eds., *Cowboys, Ranchers and the Cattle Business: Cross-Border Perspectives on Ranching History*. Calgary: University of Calgary Press, 2000, 81–99.

Emery, J.C. Herbert, and Kenneth J. McKenzie, "Damned if you do, damned if you don't: an option value approach to evaluating the subsidy of the CPR mainline," *Canadian Journal of Economics* 29 (May 1996), 255–70.

Evans, Simon M., "Tenderfoot to Rider: Learning 'Cowboying' on the Canadian Ranching Frontier during the 1880s," in Simon Evans, Sarah Carter, and Bill Yeo, eds., *Cowboys, Ranchers and the Cattle Business: Cross-Border Perspectives on Ranching History*. Calgary: University of Calgary Press, 2000, 61–80.

Foran, Max, "George Murdoch," *Dictionary of Canadian Biography*, Vol. 13, *1901–1900*. Toronto: University of Toronto Press, 1994, 747–48.

Foran, Max, "Land Speculation and Urban Development: Calgary 1884–1912," in A. W. Rasporich and H. C. Klassen, eds., *Frontier Calgary: Town, City, and Region 1875–1914*. Calgary: McClelland and Stewart West, 1975, 203–20.

Foran, Max, "The CPR and the Urban West, 1881–1930," in Hugh A. Dempsey, ed., *The CPR West: The Iron Road and the Making of a Nation*. Vancouver: Douglas & McIntyre, 1984, 89–106.

Harley, C. Knick, "Transportation, the World Wheat Trade, and the Kuznets Cycle, 1850–1913," *Explorations in Economic History* 17 (July 1980), 218–50.

Jameson, Sheilagh S., "John Glenn," *Dictionary of Canadian Biography*, Vol. 11, *1881 to 1890*. Toronto: University of Toronto Press, 1982, 354–55.

Klassen, Henry C., "Cowdry Brothers: Private Bankers in Southwestern Alberta, 1886–1905," *Alberta History* 37 (Winter 1989), 9–22.

Klassen, Henry C., "Entrepreneurship in the Canadian West: The Enterprises of A. E. Cross, 1860–1920," *Western Historical Quarterly* 22 (August 1991), 313–33.

Klassen, Henry C., "International Enterprise: The House of T. C. Power & Bro. in the Cypress Hills Trade, 1875–1893," *Saskatchewan History* 43 (Spring 1991), 57–71.

Klassen, Henry C., "Lawyers, Finance and Economic Development in Southwestern Alberta, 1884–1920" in Carol Wilton, ed., *Beyond the Law: Lawyers and Business in Canada 1830 to 1930*. Toronto: The Osgoode Society, 1990, 299–319.

Klassen, Henry C., "The Conrads in the Alberta Cattle Business, 1875–1911," *Agricultural History* 64 (Summer 1990), 31–59.

Lambrecht, Kirk N., and John Gilpin, "The Land Grant to the Calgary and Edmonton Railway Company," *Alberta Law Review* 32 (No. 1 1994), 71–92.
McGinnis, Janice Dickin, "Birth to Boom to Bust: Building in Calgary, 1875–1914," in A. W. Rasporich and Henry Klassen, eds., *Frontier Calgary: Town, City, and Region 1875–1914*. Calgary: McClelland and Stewart West, 1975, 6–19.
McKenna, Marian C., "Sir James Alexander Lougheed Calgary's First Senator and City Builder," in Max Foran and Sheilagh Jameson, eds., *Citymakers: Calgarians after the Frontier*. Calgary: Historical Society of Alberta, Chinook Country Chapter, 1987, 95–116.
Nanton, Paul, "A. M. Nanton's 41 Years in Winnipeg, 1883–1926," *Manitoba History* 6 (Fall 1983), 15–20.
Saum, Lewis O., "From Vermont to Whoop-Up Country: Some Letters of D. W. Davis, 1867–1878," *Montana: The Magazine of Western History* 35 (Summer 1985), 56–71.
Smith, Shirlee Anne, "Richard Charles Hardisty," *Dictionary of Canadian Biography*, Vol. 11, *1881 to 1890*. Toronto: University of Toronto Press, 1982, 383–84.
Stamp, Robert M., "The Response to Urban Growth: The Bureaucratization of Public Education in Calgary 1884–1914," in Anthony W. Rasporich and Henry C. Klassen, eds., *Frontier Calgary: Town, City, Region, 1875–1914*. Calgary: McClelland and Stewart West, 1975, 153–68.
Wilson, Alan, and R. A. Hotchkiss, "Charles John Brydges," *Dictionary of Canadian Biography*, Vol. 11, *1881–1890*. Toronto: University of Toronto Press, 1982.

Theses

Brown, Donald Edward, "A History of the Cochrane Area," M.A. thesis, University of Alberta, 1951.
Christenson, Raymond Andrew, "The Calgary and Edmonton Railway and the Edmonton Bulletin," M.A. thesis, University of Alberta, 1967.
English, Linda Christine, "The Calgary Exhibition and Stampedes: Culture, Context and Controversy, 1884-1923," M.A. thesis, University of Calgary, 1999.
Foran, M. L., "The Calgary Town Council, 1884–1895: A Study of Local Government in a Frontier Environment," M.A. thesis, University of Calgary, 1970.

Index

A. Allan & Co., 303
A. C. Sparrow & Co., 237–38
Aberdeen Angus cattle, 201, 205
accountancy firms, 365–66
Adams, Ernest, 331, 366–67
Adams, W. H., 272–73
advertising, 104, 276; Boorne, 361;
    Bowen, 90, 268; Canadian Pacific
    Railway, 93, 173, 210, 358;
    newspaper, 127, 276, 283;
    Rankin and Allan, 106
Agricultural societies: education,
    215–16
agriculture, xxviii, 371; change, 126;
    commercialized, 330;
    development, 105; expansion,
    xxvii; fairs, 216; jobs, 22; new
    ideas, 217–18; scientific, 217
Alberta: formation, xxxiv
Alberta Hotel, 243, 285
Alberta Music Company, 338
Alberta Roller Flour Mill, 190–91,
    197, 209
Alberta Stock Growers' Association,
    182
Alexander, George, 143, 245–46, 260;
    family business, 247
Alexander, Henry B., 142
Alexander Block, 246–47, 376
Allan, Alexander, 95, 105
Allan, Hugh, 67
American railroads. *See* railways

Anderson, Conrad, 253
Andrews, Cora, 200–02; inherited
    home farm, 205
Andrews, Ethel, 200–02; inherited
    DeWinton general store, 205
Andrews, Flora, 186
Andrews, H. B., 266–67
Andrews, Hugh, 204
Andrews, Kate, 199, 201, 205; fairs,
    202; as midwife, 204; worked at
    Royal Hotel, 200; worked for
    Colonel Macleod, 200
Andrews, Laura, 201–2; inherited part
    of family farm, 205
Andrews, Thomas, 200
Andrews, William James, 199, 202,
    204–5, 375; firebreak, 200;
    homestead, 200; worked for
    Colonel Macleod, 200
Anglican Church, 218, 316, 350
Annouse, Baptiste, 19
Armstrong, Frank H., 132
Atkinson, Henry, 277

Babcock, E. E., 327
Babcock fire extinguisher, 236–37
Baker, George, 12, 31–32
Baker, Isaac G., xvii, 2, 9, 21, 82,
    264; Benton & St. Louis Cattle
    Co., 35; bonded commerce, 23;

435

Index

contract to supply Mounted Police, 17; as entrepreneur, 22, 36; expansion in Montana, 13; First National Bank of Fort Benton, 31–32; fur trade, 27; Great Plains pioneer merchant, 11; knowledge of operations, 28; Native supply contracts, 25–26; offer to sell, 79; ranching, 155, 157; ties with North West Mounted Police, 15; Victorian character, 15; whiskey trade, 3
Baker & Brother. *See* I. G. Baker & Brother
Baker & Co. *See* I. G. Baker & Co.
Banff, 248
Banister, Albert, 185–86, 188; business and family connections, 187
Banister, Helen, 186–87
Banister, Ida (Miller), 187
Banister, Stephen, 187
Bank Act, 134, 137
Bank of Hamilton, 134
Bank of Montreal, 119–20, 125, 127–28, 131, 133, 138–46, 241, 337; British American Ranche Company, 162; Calgary branch opened, 140–41; Calgary town account, 146–47; capital stock, 139; federal government, 141; Hudson's Bay Co, 141; I. G. Baker & Co., 24, 141; James Lougheed's client, 335; Lafferty & Moore, 130, 132; Lafferty & Smith, 124–25, 127, 132, 141; land titles office, 141; loans to ranchers, 146; Mounted Police detachment, 141; new building, 145; Osborne Brown, 175; post office, 141; Shaw family, 345; staff, 145, 297; Thomas and Adela Cochrane, 315; ties with Canadian Pacific, 68, 139; women employees, 297
Bank of Nova Scotia, 104
banking, xxi, xxvi, 31–32, 119–48, 373; branches of chartered banks, 372;
deposits and loans, 127, 129, 135, 138, 141, 147; federal legislation, xxviii; women employees, 297–98
Baptist Church, 218
Bar U, 307; Agnes Bedingfeld at, 305
barbed-wire fencing, 154, 156, 158, 171, 178, 181
Barber, Samuel, 134–36, 138, 147
Barnardo Homes, 354; orphans employed by Meopham Gardner, 353
Barter, John, 167–70
Barter, Lizzie, 170–71
Barwis, James, 98
Barwis, William B, 297
Bateman, John, 353
Beauchemin, Sister Olivia, 320, 322
Beaupré, Victor, 114, 120, 375
beaver, 40
The Beaver, 281
Beck, Nicholas D., 333
Bedingfeld, Agnes, xvii, 310, 328, 375; family enterprise, 306–7; home life, 308; income from late husband, 305; moneylending, 309; reinvesting profits, 308; squatter, 305; supportive neighbours, 307
Bedingfeld, Frank, 306; as cowboy, 305, 307; married Josephine Maitland, 309; prospecting for gold, 308; sale of horses to army, 309
Bedingfeld, Josephine (Maitland), 309
Bedingfield, Josephine Mabel, 310
beef, 65, 89. *See also* meat production and distribution; Calgary's transition to city, 250–51; Montana, 35; Mounted Police and Native supply contracts, 25, 31, 35–36, 89; prices, 151; for railway's construction crews, 149
Beeston, E. K., 272–73, 279
Behan Ranch: creamery, 218
Beiseker, T. L., 327
Bell, Alma, 303
Bennett, R. B., 157, 338

Index

Benton & St. Louis Cattle Co., 35, 374–75; leased land from Canadian government, 156; winter, 1886–87, 156
Bernard, Hewitt, 17
Bernard, M. C., 138
Bernard, Michael, 347
Beveridge, Thomas, 301
big ranchers, 151; leases for, 159
Bissett, James, 53
Blackfoot, xxviii, 6, 20, 98; Baker & Co., 7, 50, 59, 155; blankets, 88; horse breeding, 21; horses and repeating rifles, 44, 53; Hudson's Bay Co., 7, 43–45, 49–50, 53–55, 59, 77, 88–89; supply contracts, 26; Treaty 7, 25, 374; whiskey trade, 2–4
Blackfoot Confederacy, 1
Blackfoot Crossing, 2
Blackfoot reserve, 25, 157, 374
Blackfoot Trail, 213
blacksmiths, 211
Blackwood, George, 204
bloodlines. *See under* breeding programs
Bloods, xxviii, 1, 7, 26, 88–89, 374; reserve, 25
boardinghouses, 304
Bole, D. W., 243
Bolin, Audrey Banister, 186–87
bonded commerce, 23, 34, 44
bookkeepers, 295
booksellers, 354–55, 357, 364
Boorne, May Woodridge Hichens, 359
Boorne, (William) Hanson, 331, 367, 375; advertisements, 361; boosterism, 357; branch studios, 360; capital, 357; leading figure in photography, 361; loans, 360; money from family and friends, 359; photography studio opened, 358
Boorne & May, 360–61
boosterism, xxx, 108, 110, 112, 138, 145, 183, 357
borrowing. *See* credit

Botterell, Albert E., 130
Bow River, xxi, xxix; navigability, 47; water for irrigating, xxx
Bow River Mills, 251, 313
Bow Valley, 93–94; agricultural development, xix, xxi; cattle economy, 151; cultural homogeneity, xxxii; ethnic makeup, xxxii, xxxiii; foreign direct investment, 9; immigrant groups, xxxii; natural environment, 154; population, xx, xxxii; population by age and gender, xxxiii; schools, xxxii; settlement, xx; symbiotic relationship with Calgary, xix, xxii, xxx, 126, 197, 232, 234–35; urban and rural connections, xix; Victorian culture, xxxi; villages and settlers, 113–18
Bow Valley Ranche, 250
Bowen, Herbert, 266
Bowen, John, 72, 264–66, 268, 273; advertising, 90; barter, 35; Calgary Board of Trade, 113; charter, Calgary, Alberta, and Montana Railway, 228; credit to customers, 35, 268, 270; credit to farmers, 267; diversified sales, 75; great fire, 238, 263; low price policy, 269; new manager, Baker & Co., 33–34; price war, 83
Braemar Lodge, 324–27, 376; cultural development and, 328; prohibition, 328; as temperance hotel, 328
Bragg Creek area, 351–52
Braithwaite, Arthur, 125, 140–47, 238; on Great Fire, 239
Bredin, William F., 130
breeding programs, 158; bloodlines, 154, 181; horse breeders, 203, 213; purebred cattle, 188
Brett, Robert G., 98
Brisebois, Ephrem, 24
British American Ranche, 161; horses to Canadian troops, 164; labour

437

Index

relations, 165–66; sheep raising, 162; shepherds, 163, 165–66
brokerage houses, 365–67, 376
Brown, Annie Frances. *See* Wolley-Dod, Annie Frances (Brown)
Brown, Annie (Patterson), 175
Brown, H. B., 248
Brown, Joseph Harrison, 307–8
Brown, Osborne, 173, 176; capital, 173; restaurant business, 174–75; retained profits and loans, 175
Brown & Cayley, 334
Browning, John M., 160, 165
Browning, M., 162
Bruce, Kate, 300
Brunskill, Dr., 97
Brydges, Charles, 7, 55, 60–61; ties with Indian Affairs, Mounted Police, 57
Buchanan, Wentworth, 139–40, 142, 144, 147
buffalo: decline, 27–28; disappearance, 57, 374
buffalo robes, 1–2, 4, 6, 14, 21, 23, 43, 45, 47, 49–50, 53–55
Buie, Archibald, 132
Bunce, Thomas, 132
Bunn, John: business beyond Native trade, 49; on horses and rifles, 53–54; supply shortage, 44, 50–51; trading post at Calgary, 6–7, 43; transportation difficulties, 46–47
Burns, Pat, 105, 138, 175, 182, 250, 326, 352; donations to Holy Cross, 323; loan to Mollison sisters, 327
Burns, T. S., 104, 106
business ethos, xxi
business leaders: cultural and charitable activities, xxxvi, 323, 328, 330–31; social activities, 373
business offices: women employees, 294
butter, 213; William Andrews, 203
butter sales: Findlays, 198
Byers, William, 148

C. H. Field & Co., 98
Calgary, 7, 93–118, 213; access to central Canada, 71; banking, xxx, 119, 146; banking, competition for, 147; became city, xix, 251, 260; Board of Trade, 113, 225, 228; booster literature, 183; business ethos, xxi; business ideas, 245; business system, 6; businessmen, 128, 136; by-laws, 110, 239; C. Brydges' description, 62; capital for reconstruction, 241; city of young people, xxxiii, 226, 244, 365; Civic Committee, 108–9; civic expenditures, 111; connections with outside world, 66; culture, xxviii; depressions, 79, 110, 261; diversification, 373; drainage and waste-disposal, 226, 259; economy, 10; entrepreneurs, xxx, 234, 251; essential hub, 11; fire department, 107, 109, 112, 235–36, 240; fire protection, 108, 110, 239; foreign direct investment (U.S.), 9, 149; as grain centre, 196; great fire, 146, 235–40, 261, 263, 375; grid design, 75, 94–95; growth, 65, 234; growth of ranching and, xxx, 126; health and environmental issues, 94, 259; import and export, xxx; incorporation, 107–10, 375–76; inducement to settlers, 231; industrialism and consumerism, xx; infrastructure, 240; integrated city-country system, 197; island community, 65; island parks, 240; lack of modern amenities, 235; land speculation, 107–8; links to Native communities, 7; livestock market, 225; manufacturing and distribution, 97, 241, 251; market, 208; as market, 190, 192; meeting place, xxvi, 1, 4, 6; money supply, xxx; natural

438

Index

advantages, 93–94; police service, 107, 110; population, xx, 11, 76, 109, 225, 240; property and licence taxes, 110–11; railway hub, 191, 227–29; rapid development, 65; real estate values, xxv, 67, 107–8; reconstruction (postfire), 240, 254–55; resilience, 373; saloons, xxxi; sanitary regulations, 110; selection of townsite, 74; sewage system, 107, 226, 260; supply centre, 84–85, 225; telephone system, 240; town council, 228, 239; town government, 110, 112, 235; town hall, 112; trading, 39, 155, 191; transportation and communication, xxx, 68, 77–78; waterworks, 143, 240; as whiskey post, 3–4, 6; "Wild West" frontier town, xxxi

Calgary, Alberta, and Montana railway, 228

Calgary Agricultural Society, 179, 202

Calgary and Bow Valley: cattle economy, 151; ethnic makeup, xxxii, xxxiii; foreign direct investment, 9; population by age and gender, xxxiii; schools, xxxii; symbiotic relationship, xix, xxii, xxx, 126, 197, 232, 234–35; urban and rural connections, xix, xxii; Victorianism, xxxi, xxxii

Calgary and Edmonton Land Company, 230, 232; depression 1890s, 231

Calgary and Edmonton Railway, xxxi, 71, 191, 203, 213, 227, 229, 234, 245–46, 251, 376; arrival in High River, 196–97; bonds, 230; capital, 230; cattle industry, 232; Dominion lands, 228; purchased by Canadian Pacific, 233

Calgary Brewing & Malting Co., 145–46, 290

Calgary Business College, 298, 376

Calgary Clothing Company, 338

Calgary Electric Lighting Company, 254

Calgary fair, 217, 345; educational emphasis, 216; social occasion, 216

Calgary Gas & Water Works Co., 143, 246–47, 334

Calgary General Hospital. *See* General Hospital

Calgary Herald: advertisements, 90, 104, 276; on Agnes Bedingfeld, 308; on Atlantic Ave. fire, 112; on Boorne's art store, 361; boosterism, 108; on business in Calgary, 83; on Calgary & Edmonton Railway building, 229; on Calgary as distribution centre, 94; on Calgary fair, 202; on Canadian Pacific Station, 242, 262; on Canadian Pacific stockyards, 150; on cholera, 259; on Clarence Block fire, 338; on farm protest, 189; on Findlay farm, 195; on Holy Cross Hospital, 323; on Hutchings Saddlery Co., 255–56.; on incorporation of Calgary, 109; on Mayor Mackie, 364; on Mayor Murdoch, 111; on Midnapore Woollen Mills, 345; on new Bank of Montreal, 145; on Royal Hotel, 243; on William Roper Hull, 249

Calgary Horticultural Society, 180

Calgary Hydraulic company, 260

Calgary Lumber Company, 126, 312–13, 315; capital, 314

Calgary Stampede, 354

Calgary Tribune: advertisements, 276, 283; on All Saint's Anglican Church, 316; on Davisburg fair, 216; on Davisburg homesteaders, 185; on Gardner's irrigation, 353; on Hudson's Bay Co. department store, 282, 287–89; on I. G. Baker department store, 265, 267; on McLean's mill, 190; on

Prince's Sawmill, 254; on winter of 86/87, 154
Calgary Water Power Company, 254
Cameron, Elizabeth, 221
Cameron, Elizabeth Mary (Carstairs), 220, 222
Cameron, John, 132
Cameron, Kenneth, 117, 220, 374; stopping house, 221; trial, 222
Cameron, Marion, 205
Canada Life Assurance Company, 332, 337
Canada North-West Coal & Lumber Co., 315
Canada Northwest Land Company, 74–75, 107, 177, 234
Canada Permanent Loan & Savings Company, 335
Canadian Agricultural, Coal and Colonization Company, 334
Canadian Bank of Commerce: banker for Cochrane Ranche, 160; loan to Mollison sisters, 327
Canadian bonded goods. *See* bonded commerce
Canadian go-ahead spirit, 365
Canadian government. *See* federal government
Canadian Pacific Railway, xxvi, xxviii, xxx, 66, 98, 104–5, 122, 186, 221, 375; advantage to Calgary, xvii, 65, 75–76, 94, 97, 125, 240; advertisements, 93, 173, 210; big ranch companies, 151; branch lines, 71, 227, 233; British American Ranche, 164; Calgary and Edmonton bonds, 230; Canada North-West Coal & Lumber Co., 315; Canmore, 114; chartered banks and, 133; Cochrane, 118; construction crews, 195; Eau Claire & Bow River Lumber Co., 252–53; flag station at Mitford, 316; freight rates, 227; funding, 67–68; government subsidy and land grant, xxviii, 67; grounds, 254;

hotels, 324; Hudson's Bay Co., 63, 70, 283; I. G. Baker & Co., 71–73; I. G. Baker and, 91; I. S. Freeze and, 100–01; James Lougheed's client, 332, 335; James Thomson, 88; Maple Creek, Saskatchewan, 69; and military payroll funds, 86; Mitford station, 316; monopoly, 227–28; Montreal to Vancouver, 65; Morley, 113; Pembina-Winnipeg branch line, 71; purchased Calgary and Edmonton, 233; Richard Hardisty on, 70; role in marketing and distribution, 66–67; settlers in prairie West, 199; station, 74–75, 242, 261–62; subsidiaries, 74; success of, 76; survey crew, 206; ties to Montreal, xxx, 139; west of Winnipeg, 69
Canadian Pacific Railway land. *See* Canada Northwest Land Company
Canadian Pacific Stockyards, 149, 157, 170, 183, 240, 251; pollution, 150; water-supply system, 184
Canmore, xxx, xxxi, 113–14, 315, 375
capitalism, xvii, xxv; and agriculture, xxvii, 188; British business experience, 41; industrial, 66; livestock, 151; mixed economy, xxxv; natural resources, xxvii; negative elements, xxvi; Northwest Territories Act and, xxxiv; second industrial revolution, 119
Carr, Charles, 304
Carr, Frances Marie, 304, 375
Carr, Lemsley, 253
Carr, Sadie, 304
Carroll, Henry J., 120
Carroll, Sister Agnes, 318, 376; became Mother Vicar, 323–24; borrowed from Grey Nuns' Mother House, 322; business manager, 319, 324;

Index

construction of Holy Cross Hospital, 320; fundraising, 321–23
Carroll, William, 132
Carson & Shore, 257–58
Cassils, William, 162
cattle drives, 161
cattle round-ups, 183
Cave, Edmund, 360
Cayley stockyard, 229
Centennial Exposition (Philadelphia), 217
central Canadian companies: influence, xxx
Central Collegiate Institute in Calgary, 202
Central Experimental Farm in Ottawa, 217
Central School, xxxii, 297, 304, 375
change, xvii, xviii, 49
charities. *See* culture and charities
chartered banks, 119, 121, 125, 131, 133–48, 172; branch banking, 139
chattel mortgages. *See* mortgages, chattel
Chenier, Joseph, 114
Child, James T., 241
Child & Wilson, 243, 246, 260
Chipman, Clarence, 280–81, 283–87
Chipman, J. E., 82
Chipman Bros. & Co. store, 237
cholera, 259
Christie, A. E., 128
Christie, Clara, 357
Christie, Thomas, 123–24, 127–30, 132
churches, 218
Circle Ranch, 157–58, 271, 275, 376
Civil War, 13, 116, 264
Clarence Block, 336–37; fire, 338
Clark, Hannibal, 117
Clark, S. J., 109
Clarke, Elizabeth Coulter, 289
Claxton, Frank J., 126
Clegg, Annie, 300
closed-range ranching, 154

Clouston, Edward, 143, 146, 298
Clute, Jim, 99
Clydesdale horses, 201, 203, 205, 212–13, 308–9
co-operative efforts, 206, 221; Samuel and Helen Shaw family, 344; shipping grain, 214
coal, xxxvi
coal mining, 114
Cochrane, Adela, 310, 314; capital, 311–13; fund raising, 316; managing of finances, 316
Cochrane, Billie, 311–12, 314, 317
Cochrane, Ernest B., 165
Cochrane, James A., 160
Cochrane, Matthew, 159, 161–63, 165–66; influence in Ottawa, 160, 164
Cochrane, Thomas, xxxi, 118, 314, 376; coal mining, 315; credit rating, 311; family fortunes and friends, 313; Lafferty & Smith, 126, 312–13; lease from Canadian government, 311; loan from Imperial Bank of Canada, 317; lumber business, 312; manufacturing bricks, 315; ranching business, 317–18
Cochrane Ranche Company, 36, 167, 232, 374; financial losses, 161; lease, 159; management, 160–61
Cockle, Joseph W., 362
Code, Abraham, 340
Cold Meat Storage Company, 232
Colonel Macleod (steamboat), 16, 33
Columbian Exposition (Chicago), 217
communication, xvii, xx, xxx, xxxvi, 10, 54, 66, 125–26, 151, 369; telegraph, xvii, xxvi, 66, 71, 295, 297, 369; telephone, 294–95
confectionery stores, 339–40
Confederation Life Insurance Company, 356
Conrad, Charles, 12, 28–29, 34, 82, 155, 158, 264–73; applied for homestead, 73; business methods, 267; Canadian Pacific

441

Index

and, 71; cattle raising, 35; charm, 13; closing of Baker & Co.'s Calgary store, 274, 276; credit, 268, 270; as entrepreneur, 9, 22, 36; leases, 156; manager of Fort Macleod store, 17; married Alicia Stanford, 30; Queenston Ranch, 158; reinvested profits, 271; at signing of Treaty 7, 26; ties with Mounted Police, 15–16

Conrad, William, 12, 16, 28–29, 32–34, 73, 82, 155, 158, 264–66, 268, 270, 272; business methods, 266–68; business with Canadian government, 32; cattle raising, 35; on closing of Calgary store, 275; effort to sell Calgary business, 81, 272–73; as entrepreneur, 9, 22, 36; First National Bank of Fort Benton, 31; leases, 156; office work, 13; Queenston Ranch, 158

Conroy, James, 114
Conservative Party, 67, 218, 221–22, 243
consumer goods, 370–71
Coupland, W. H., 298
Cowan, I. S., 261
cowboys, 168, 172, 353; demography, 152–53, 155
Cowdry, John, 228
Cranbrook, 233
creative destruction, xviii, xix
credit, xxv. *See also* loans; Baker & Co. store, 35, 267–68, 270, 277, 289; bank, 119, 139, 340; Canada North-West Coal & Lumber Co., 317; Canadian dream and, 329, 367; economic recovery and, 347; farmers, 136, 148, 221; Hudson's Bay store, 277; Margaret Leishman, 302; Mollison sisters, 327; private, xxi, 119–21, 372; ranchers, 126, 148; settlers, 234–35; short-term, xxvii, 126, 133, 142
Cree, 25–26

Criterion Restaurant, 174–75
crop rotation, 188
Crosby, Frank, 34
Cross, A. E., 145–46, 151, 163, 182, 307, 335
Crowfoot, Chief, 3
Crow's Nest Pass, 233
culture and charities, 330; Barnardo Homes, 354; business leaders' contribution, xxxvi, 328, 331
Cummings, J. H., 98
Curley, H. J., 334
currency, 135
Cushing, William H., 128, 279

dairy farming, 218
Davis, D. W., 18–19, 28, 34, 90, 185, 264; acceptance by Mounted Police, Natives, settlers, 20, 22; member for Alberta, 228
Davis, Donald Watson: at Fort Whoop-Up, 6; whiskey trading, 4
Davis, J. C., 126
Davisburg, xxxi, 185, 200, 202, 210, 214; economic bond with Calgary, 203; neighbourly bonds, 204
Davisburg Agricultural Society, 203
Davisburg fair, 212, 216
Davisburg Ranchers Society, 188
Dawson, E. C., 130
Dawson, Vivian, 297
debts, 192, 204, 329
democracy, 329, 340, 350
department stores, xxvi, 263–91. *See also* Hudson's Bay Company; I. G. Baker & Co.; high volume, 371
depressions, 172, 210, 373; (1873–79), xxvi, 22, 28, 56, 67; (1883–88), xxvi, 78–79, 110, 120, 140, 192, 261; (1893–97), xxvi, 108, 120, 231, 303, 308, 323, 329–30, 335
Dewar, Janet, 301, 376

442

Index

Dewdney, Edgar, 73, 108–9; shares in first National Bank of Fort Benton, 32
DeWinton, 213–15
DeWinton, Colonel Francis, 98
diptheria, 322
diversification, xxvii, 330, 371, 373
Dofoo, Luey, 331, 340, 367, 376; financial assistance from friends and relatives, 341; married Ho Eng, 341; reinvested profits, 342
Dofoo, Paul, 342–43
Dominion Illustrated, 334, 361, 364
Dominion Immigration House, 100
Dominion lands, 155, 228
Dominion Lands Act, 59, 374; family farms and small ranchers, 172
Dominion notes, 135
Dominion of Canada: creation of, 43
double-entry bookkeeping, 29, 34
Douglas, J. S., 138
Dowling, Annie, 310
Downs, Marion, 205
Draper, Miss E., 296
dressmakers and dressmaking, 294, 299–301, 304, 376
Dunbow Industrial School, 213
Dunn, Mathew, 333
Dunn & Lineham Block, 134, 140–41
duty free Canadian goods, 23
Dye, Sadie, 266
Dyson, A., 288

E. F. Hutchings Saddlery Company, 255, 258
Eau Claire & Bow River Lumber Co., 138, 142, 251, 254, 313, 375; machinery and workforce, 252
Edgar block, 336
Edmonton, 40
Edmonton Trail, 10, 43, 45, 49, 62, 72
education, xxxii, 188, 202, 210, 216, 353; belief in, xxxi; business college training, 298; governesses, 353

educational and religious organizations, 116
Edward, Prince of Wales, 309
Egan, John M., 73
Elbow Bridge, 112
Elbow River whiskey post, 2–3
electricity, 66, 254
Elliott, George B., 104–5, 108
Ellis & Grogan, 297
Emerson, George Washington, 49, 307
enclosed fields, 154, 169, 171, 181
entrepreneurship, xxv, xxvi, xxxvi, 142, 227–29, 240, 245, 261; Calgary Board of Trade, 113; Canadian Pacific Railway, 65; capitalism, xviii, 36, 39, 339, 365; chartered banks, 120, 139; creative destruction, xviii, xix, 36; I. G. Baker & Co., 9; individual, xxvii, 41; women, xxviii, 130, 299, 324
E. P. Ranch, 309

F. G. Smith & Co., 122
fairs, 203, 216; education, 217; funding, 217; scientific management, 217
fallowing, 187–88, 219
family: importance of, 373; nuclear, 373; security, xxxvi; small ranches and, 371
family enterprises, xxxv, 9, 248, 306, 310
family farms, 172, 188, 192–93, 195, 198, 205–6, 210, 213–14; co-operation, 206, 344; inheritance and succession, xxvi, 185, 198, 213–14; network of economic and social ties, 372; teamwork, 195, 348
Farm Protest Movement, 188–89, 375
farmers and farming, 11, 93–94, 104, 115, 117, 124, 126, 128, 190, 373; credit, 148; dairy, 180; evolution, 188; expansion of, 180; as family business, 188; family farms, xxvi, 172, 185,

188, 192–93, 195, 205–6, 210, 213–14; farm mortgage business, 235; finance, 348; financial problems, 220; incomes, 222; irrigated farms, 116; limited access to credit, 141; loans (long-term), 234; mixed farming, 198, 201, 210; owner occupied family farms, 372; short-term loans, 126; small farming, 371; tension with ranchers, 89; tree planting, 219
Farnham, George F., 169
Faughaballaugh (stallion), 217
federal government, 164, 167; aid for Langevin Bridge, 112; banking regulations, 137; Canadian Pacific Railway monopoly, 227–28; Canadian Pacific Railway subsidies, xxviii, 67, 222; favouring of central Canadian industrial interests, 222; grants to Holy Cross Hospital, 323; land grants to railways, xxxv; land policy, 157; leases, 151, 154, 156–57, 159, 167, 189, 311; legislation of banking, xxviii; squatters, 155; supply contracts, 25–26, 28, 30, 33, 52, 56–57, 76; tariffs, xxviii, 222
fenced-in fields. *See* enclosed fields
Ferland, A., 113
Findlay, Alexander, 193–94, 197
Findlay, Clair, 198
Findlay, Gavin, 195, 197–99
Findlay, George, 195, 197
Findlay, Mary, 193–95, 198
Findlay, Robert, 193–95, 197–99, 214, 375; diversified, mixed farming, 198; inheritance arrangements, 198; tools and implements, 196
Findlay, Robert Jr., 194–95
Findlay, Thomas, 198–99
Findlay farms: network of, 198
firearm manufacturers, 363
firebreaks, 200, 219
fires, 112, 200; Clarence and Norman Blocks, 338; great fire, 146, 235–40, 261, 263, 375; prairie fires, 215, 219
First National Bank of Fort Benton, 31; depository for Canadian Mounted Police and Native funds, 32
Fish Creek Agricultural Society, 179, 203, 208
Fish Creek fair, 216–17
Fitzgerald & Lucas, 260
Flemming, Jennie, 266
Fletcher, Miss, 296
Flood, Margaret. *See* Murdoch, Margaret (Flood)
foreign direct investment, 9, 149, 155, 252, 263
Forgan, Grace MacMillan. *See* Mackie, Grace MacMillan (Forgan)
Forster, Harold E., 360
Fort Benton, 2–4, 9, 39
Fort Calgary, 18
Fort Hamilton. *See* Fort Whoop-Up
Fort Macleod, 10, 16–17, 227–28, 233, 272–73; railway, 229; store, 26
Fort Walsh, 10
Fort Whoop-Up, 2–4, 6, 14
Fraser, Angus, 54, 58–62, 76–77, 87–88
Fraser, George L., 120
fraternal lodges, 218–19
freedom, 329
freemarket economy, 95
Freeze, Evelyn, 357
Freeze, Isaac, 95, 100–02, 105, 109, 113, 357; advertising, 104; credit accounts to customers, 104; credit at Bank of Nova Scotia, 104; moved his store, 103
Freeze Block, 105, 356
freight rates, 227, 233
freighters and wagoners, xx
French, George, 15
French Canadians, xxxii
Frith, F. W., 130
fur regions: Lac La Biche, 40
fur trade, 14, 40–42; free traders, 42, 48; Hudson's Bay monopoly, 43

Index

G. C. King & Co., 82–83, 271; bankruptcy, 82, 144; private credit, 120; ties with Bank of Montreal, 143
Galloway cattle, 366
Garbutt Business College, 298
gardening, 179–80, 208, 220
Gardner, Clem, 351, 353; champion cowboy, Calgary Stampede, 354; reinvesting profits, 354
Gardner, Edward, 351
Gardner, Margaret, 353
Gardner, Meopham, 331, 350, 354, 367, 375; health improved, 352; inherited and borrowed from father, 351–52; married Margaret Esam, 351; reinvested profits, 353
Gardner, Richard, 310
Gardner, Sarah, 310
Gardner, William C., 310
General Hospital, xxi, 320, 323, 330, 376; James Lougheed's support, 331
general store business, 100, 103, 116, 120
George, Henry, 347
Gertrude, Sister Madeleine Beemer, 320
Gibb, J.S., 138
Gigot, E. F., 272
Gillies Bros, 221
Gladys district, xxxi, 212, 215
Glanville, J. F, 289
Glanville & Robertson, 263, 289, 337
Gleichen, xxx, xxxi, 114–15, 374
Glengarry Ranche, 136
Glenn, John, 19, 49, 116–17, 189, 344, 374; farm, 21
Goddard, G. E., 118, 327
gold standard, 135
Golden Mining & Smelting Co. of Canada, 142
government supply contracts (Mounted Police and Natives), 25, 30, 33, 52; cattle, 26, 57, 76
Graham, Hugh, 311–12, 314

Graham, Nellie, 337
Grahame, James A., 44–45, 46–47, 49, 51, 62, 68–70, 76–77; conservative outlook, 53, 80; lack of vision, 52
Grand Trunk Railway, 56, 69, 71
Grant, Archibald, 109, 138
Grant, James, 288
Gravely, W. B., 145–46
Gray, P. G., 131
great fire, 146, 235, 239–40, 261, 375; arson theory, 236–37; and department stores, 263; looting and arson, 238
Great West Life Assurance Company, 365
Great West Saddlery Company, 258–59, 337
Great Western Railway, 56
Greenwood, George, 277
Greer, Albert A., 132
Gregg, Richard, 327
Grey Nuns, 318, 322
Groeneveld, Glenn: runs Suitor farm, 214
grog shops, 239
Grogan, Mrs., 327

H. W. McNeill & Co., 114
Hailand, P. S., 126
Halliday, William James, 289
Ham, George Henry, 124, 243, 253, 265, 356, 360, 363
Hamilton, Alfred B., 3, 374
Hamilton, Robert, 2, 45, 46; call for mercantile program, 48; conflict with Richard Hardisty, 47; dream of middlemen, 48
Hamilton, W. C. A., 327
Hammond, Herbert, 229
hard work, xviii, xxi, 193, 210
Hardisty, Richard, 44–46, 50–51, 53–54, 58–59, 68, 70, 76–78, 80–81, 86–89, 332; on Baker & Co. competition, 55; Canadian

445

Index

Pacific and, 68–69; conflict with Robert Hamilton, 47–48; death, 334; diversification of products, 68; management skill, 85; strategy, 70
harness and saddle making, 66, 95–99, 110, 239, 255–59, 375
Harriott, John Edward, 42
Harris, Charles F., 128
Harris, Eva, 300
Harris, Howell, 158–59
Harris, John, 156–57
Harris, Susan, 297
Hatton, Major George W., 99
Haultain, Frederick, xxxiv
Hauser, S. T., 31–32
hay, 154, 168–69, 171, 178, 181
head tax, 341–42
Healey, John J., 2–3, 6
health: Alberta's atmosphere and, 211, 351–52
Healy, John J., 374
Henderson, Anderson, 113
Henderson, Andrew, 312
Henderson's Manitoba and Northwest Territories Gazetteer and Directory, 251
Hepburn, Irwin & Smith, 122
Herald Publishing company, 334
Herr, Albert, 214
Hichins, Richard S., 360
High River, xxxi, 117–18, 191–92, 194, 196, 232, 258, 374; rail line to, 197
High River Times, 309
High River Trading Company, 197
Highwood River, 2, 117
Hingston Smith Arms Company, 362
Hogg, James, 215
Hogg, S. J., 109, 113
Hogg, W. H., 145, 297
Holy Cross Hospital, xxi, 318–19, 330, 376; budget, 323; cash shortages, 321; construction of, 319; depression in 1890s, 323; Protestant doctors, 322
Holy Cross School of Nursing, 323

homesteading, 185, 189, 193–94, 206, 211. *See also* farmers and farming; settlers; Bow Valley, 225; free homesteads, 210
Hope, Joseph, 234
hotels, 324. *See also* stopping houses; downtown, 326; James Conroy's, 114
Howland, H. S., 134
Hudson's Bay Company, xxvi, xxix, 20, 23, 31, 36–37, 39–63, 67–68, 141; acquired Baker & Co.'s stores, 273; and American traders, 47; Baker & Co.'s offer, 79–82; British investors, 40; and Canadian traders from Montreal, 41; Charles Brydges as land commissioner, 55–57; competition, 41–42, 55, 57; Edmonton House, 1; government supply contracts, 57–58, 89; James Lougheed's client, 332, 335; Manitoba traders, 48; merged with Northwest Company, 41; new store at Battle River, 78; offices, 73; outposts, 47; payroll funds for military, 85–86; Peigan post, 41–42; relocation from Edmonton to Calgary, 76–77, 375; store at Battle River, 78; trade monopoly, 40, 42–43
Hudson's Bay Company Calgary store, 46, 54, 69, 179, 195, 218, 237, 271–72, 374; business problems, 44; business with Mounted Police, 49; decline of, 53; old Baker & Co. department store, 276–77, 280; Saskatchewan Rebellion, 85–87; shaky existence, 58; shortage of goods, 45, 49–51, 53, 59–62, 69–70; transportation problems, 45, 47, 62
Hudson's Bay Company Department store, 278–82, 285–86, 289, 291, 303, 376; addition, 287;

446

Index

competition, 287, 289; employees, 288; labour relations, 283–85; low prices, 282–83; mail order business, 290; office accommodation, 282; volume sales, 276; women employees, 295; women shoppers, 285
Hudson's Bay Company trading post (Calgary), 7, 9
Huggard, Jessie H., 310
Hull, John, 248
Hull, Trounce & Co., 247, 375
Hull, William Roper, xxxi, 178, 187, 245, 247–48, 326; butchering establishment, 249; entrepreneur, 250; loan to Mollison sisters, 327; vertically integrated operation, 250
Hull Bros. & Co., 249; branch butcher shops, 248; contract for beef to Canadian Pacific, 248; family affair, 248
Hunt, William G., 309
Hutchings, Blanche, 255, 259
Hutchings, E. J., 98
Hutchings, Robert, xxxvi, 217, 245, 255–59
Hutchings & Riley, 255, 375–76
Hutchings and Riley: diversified products and sales, 256; exhibit at World's Fair, 258; exhibit in Regina, 258; prosperity, 257
Hutchings Saddlery Company, 256
Hutchinson, Henry, 99

I. G. Baker & Brother, 12–13
I. G. Baker & Co., xxvi, 6–7, 13, 39, 44–45, 50–51, 54, 57, 60–61, 89, 91, 95, 141, 155, 178, 238, 262, 333; agreements with Power & Bro., 31; banking, 24, 26, 31–32, 119; Blackfoot and, 59; bonded commerce, 23; branch stores, 32; buffalo robes, 14; Calgary store built, 18; Canadian criticism, 55; Canadian government and, 24–25, 30, 156; Canadian Pacific and, 71–73, 82; capital, 55; cattle, 26; competition, 30–31, 83; contracts with Canadian government, 17, 33, 35–36, 76, 82; depression in mid-1880s, 78, 82; as entrepreneurial or family enterprise, 9; expansion into Canada, 10, 14; fur trade, 14; general store, 18, 21, 374; good relations with Alberta's settlers, 91; goods on credit, 121; government supply contracts, 16, 25–26, 28, 90; growth, 67; growth strategy, 14; import and export business, 24; international trade, 9; mail service, 18–19; markets, 155; merchandise sales, 32; monopoly on water and grass, 155; in Montana, 14; Mounted Police business, 53; Mounted Police payroll, 24; Native trade, 23; offer to sell to Hudson's Bay Co., 79, 81; private credit, 120; purchases in Central Canada, 23; ranch, 21, 89, 271, 374; recovery from great fire, 263–64; retail outlet for woollen mill, 346; sales at Calgary, 76; Saskatchewan Rebellion, 83–84; squatter, 72; steamboats, 16–17, 33; store in Fort Macleod, 17, 32; supplies from Calgary to Edmonton, 84; ties to Mounted Police, 30; ties to Native people, 25; ties with farmers and ranchers, 121; transportation costs, 82; treaty money to Natives, 26; whiskey trade, 14
I. G. Baker & Co. Calgary store, 32, 34, 237, 281; Blackfoot, Sarcees, and Stoneys, 26; buffalo robe trade, 23; credit, 35; double-entry bookkeeping, 29, 34; hay for Mounted Police, 29; leading products, 22; management, 33;

447

Index

as meeting place, 19; Montreal suppliers and, 75; newspaper advertising, 90; personal trust, 34; prosperity, 28; sold to Imperial Bank of Canada, 283

I. G. Baker & Co. department store, 265, 276, 375–76; bad debts, 274–75; cash business, 270–71; credit, 267–68; credit problems, 270–71; farmers' produce, 267; grand opening, 266; low price policy, 268–69; offer to sell, 272; ranchers, 270; sold to Hudson's Bay Company, 273–74; wholesale division, 269; women customers, 266–68

Imperial Bank of Canada, 119–20, 124–25, 127–28, 131, 133–34, 137–38, 141, 326, 337, 367; Calgary branch, 135, 138, 312, 317, 339–40; Calgary town account, 147; credit for Calgary businessmen, 135; credit for ranchers, 135; farmers and, 136; notes, 135; Quorn Ranche Co., 169–71; staff, 138; Winnipeg branch established, 135

Indians. *See* Native people

industrialization, xxxvi, 66, 119, 251, 255, 345

informal credit networks, 119–21

informal economic networks, 214–15

Innisfail, 232

insurance, 235, 238, 338, 356; Holy Cross Hospital, 322

insurance companies, 365

international finance, 229

international trade, 9

investment, xx, 95; American, 152, 229; British, xxxv, 152, 229–30; foreign direct, 9, 149, 155, 252, 263

irrigation, 116, 158, 169, 181, 187, 260, 317; ditches, 170, 214, 250, 353

Irving, John Alexander, 214

Island Park, 95, 330

Jameson, Sheilagh, 353

Jameson, Thomas, 353
Jarrett, S. N., 109
Jenkins, E. G., 118
Jenkins, Ted and Frank, 311–12
Jenner, F. A., 277
John A. Macdonald's government, 30, 159, 280
Johnson, James, 118
Johnson, Mrs. M. A., 269
Johnston, W. N., 98
joint-stock companies, xxxv, 133

Kanouse, Fred, 4
Kerfoot, William, 162–64, 270, 315; dismissed from British American Ranche, 165
Kerr, David, 277, 283
Kerr, Isaac K., 252, 327
Kerr, John H., 269
Kiely, Julia, 207
King, George, 49, 98, 108, 143–45; at Baker & Co., 28, 33–34; as mayor, 146, 237–39
King, Sheriff Peter W., 222
King, W.F., 94
King, William H, 366
Kinghorn, Mr., 19
Kinnisten, Christina, 295, 331, 367, 376; credit, 340; inheritance, 339; retained profits, 340

Lac La Biche, 40, 318
Lafferty, James, 122–23, 125, 127–28, 130, 227
Lafferty, Jessie, 123, 125, 127–28, 130–32
Lafferty, T. B., 132
Lafferty & Moore, 121, 130, 167, 375; Calgary business people, 132; farmers, 132; Shaw family, 347; small ranchers, 132
Lafferty & Smith, 121–23, 125, 128, 141, 311–13, 375; diversification,

448

124; link to ranching industry, 126; loans to businessmen, 129; loans to farmers, 126, 129; loans to ranchers, 126, 129; loans to small borrowers, 126; newspaper advertising, 127
Laird, David, 25–26
Lambert, James, 99
Lamont, J. L.: tin shop, 236
land leases. *See* leases
land speculation, 107–8, 189, 331. *See also* real estate
land values, 330; Calgary and Edmonton Railway, 233
Lane, George, 146, 307
Langevin Bridge, 112
law and order, 6, 15; lawlessness, 4; rule of law, xxv, 41
Lawford, C. A., 145
Lawson, Henry C., 130
Lay, J. M., 138
Laycock, Ann, 310
Le Jeune, Smith & C0., 349
leases, 151, 154, 156, 159, 167, 189, 311
leather, 66
Leishman, Margaret, 303, 367; credit, 302
LeJeune, Henry, 127–28
LeJeune, Smith & Co., 121, 128–32, 375; deposits from Calgary businessmen, 129; deposits from ranchers, 129; loans to Calgary businessmen and small ranchers, 130
Lethbridge, 233, 272–73
Lewis, Evelyn, 100
Liberal government of Alexander Mackenzie, 24, 67
Liberal Party, 218, 221–22, 243
limited liability, xxxv, 314
Lindsay, Neville James, 109
Lineham, John, 117
Lineham Block, 117
Linton, James, 331, 354, 367, 375; capital, 355–56; credit from suppliers, 355–56; diversified sales, 356; information service, 357; money from marriage, 356; partnership with brother Thomas, 355; photographic display, 358; reinvesting profit, 356
Linton, Thomas, 356
Linton Bros. Bookstore, 356–57, 360
liquor trade, 283
literary societies, 218–19
Little Bow Cattle Co., 136, 318; losses, 312; need for capital, 311
Livingston, Sam, 49, 115, 189, 374; farm, 21; threshing outfit, 210
Livock, W. T., 277
loan companies, 148
loans, 120–21. *See also* credit; to ranching businesses, 136, 138, 172, 180; to small borrowers, 126
Lott, Charles, 232, 234–35, 297, 376; opened brokerage firm, 366; reinvested profits and loans, 367
Lougheed, Belle, 336
Lougheed, James, xvii, 157, 202, 274, 330, 367, 375; appointed to Senate, 334; Calgary Board of Trade, 113; fire, 338; home life and children, 335–36; as Kerfoot's lawyer, 165; land speculator, 331; land values, 333; loans, 332, 337; long-term clients, 335; married Isabella "Belle" Hardisty, 332; model of business management, 339; railway policy and, 227–28; real estate business, 337–38; relations with McCarthy, 334–35; retained profits, 332–33, 337–38; Supreme Court of the Northwest Territories, 333
Lougheed, McCarthy & Beck, 333–34
Lougheed, Peter, 339
Lougheed & McCarthy, 333
Lougheed Block, 334; tenants, 336
Lucas, Alexander, 260
Luey Brothers Café, 342
lumber, 66, 312; yards and mills, 240, 252–53

Index

Lynch, J. D., 130
Lynch, Thomas, 126, 148
Lyric Theatre, 331

Macdonald, John A., 56–57, 72–73, 160, 334; on Calgary's future, 225; Canadian Pacific subsidy, 67; Canadian Pacific's monopoly, 227–28; on foreign ownership, 90; lease system, 151, 159, 189
Macdougall, Audrey, 351, 353–54
Macdougall, Glen, 173–76
MacDougall, William C., 214
Macfarlane, Madge, 297
Mackay, Walter, 362
Mackenzie, Alexander, 24, 67
Mackenzie, William, 230
Mackie, Grace MacMillan (Forgan), 362
Mackie, James, 331, 367, 375; bookseller, 364–65; diversified sales, 364; firearm manufacturer, 363; gun, sporting goods and fur shop, 362; married Grace Forgan, 364; mayor of Calgary, 364; modern management, 365; partner, Joseph W. Cockle, 362; taxidermist, 364
Mackie Block, 365
MacLaren, Sherrill, 302
Maclay, Edgar G., 31–32
Macleod, Colonel James F., 15–17, 26, 29–31, 49, 200; Victorian lifestyle, 16
Macleod, Helen, 295
Macleod, Jean, 296
Macleod, Mary, 296, 301–2, 376
Macleod, Neil, 104
Macleod, Norman, 34
Macleod Gazette, 72, 90–91
Macleod Trail, 10, 72, 191, 195, 222, 226, 348
Macpherson, David L., 189
mail, 76, 232, 369
Mallette, Joe, 49

Malloy, Julia, 300
Manitoba, xxix; anti-monopoly government, 228; outlet for wheat, 67
Manitoba and Northwest Loan Company, 221
Manitoba traders, 48
Mann, Donald D., 230
manufacturing, 251, 255, 372–73
Maple Creek, Saskatchewan, 70
market economy, xxv
market share, 249
marketing systems, 182
markets: British and American, 126; central Canadian, 329; national and international, xxxi
Marsh, Daniel Webster, 149, 238, 325
Marsh, George C., 335
Martin, Charles, 167–68; high society life, 169; sued by Moore, 170
Martin, George: inherited part of family farm, 205
Martin, Gertrude, 297
Martin, Melvin, 205
Martin, Russell: inherited part of family farm, 205
Martin, William, 165–66
Masons, 219
mass distribution, 265, 275, 280; in Fort Benton, 264
mass market, 371
Massey Manufacturing Co., 236; binder, 236
Matthias, E. H., 132
Maw, Joseph, 187
May, Ernest, 358, 360
McArthur, Duncan, 132, 217
McCaffery, Thomas, 326
McCallum, John G., 138
McCarter, George S., 335
McCarthy, Peter, 134, 142, 333–35
McCarthy & Stuart, 297
McCaul, C. C., 323
McCormick, Eneas, 309
McCormick, Helen Carr, 304
McDonald, Margaret, 310
McDonough, James, 118

Index

McDougall, David, 19, 88, 98
McDougall, John, 49, 113, 155, 374
McEachran, Duncan, 160–61
McHugh, Felix A., 115, 217, 289
McHugh, John J., 289
McHugh, Thomas P., 157
McHugh Bros., 136–37
McInnes, M., 117
McInnis, John F., 126
McKay, William, 59–60, 70
McKevitt, Anna, 209
McKevitt, Bernard, 208, 210
McKevitt, Helen (Birney), 210
McKevitt, James Frederick, 206, 375; hand labour, 210; keeping farm in family, 210; market gardener, 209; married Julia Kiely, 207; mixed farming, 210; purchased more land from Canadian Pacific, 208; success, 209
McKevitt, Joseph, 210
McKevitt, Julia, 208–9; keeping farm in family, 210
McLean, Donald, 190, 197
McMillan, Miss, 297
McNeill, H. W., 114
McPherson, Addison, 136
McTavish, John H., 58
McVittie, Archibald W., 74, 109, 312–13
meat production and distribution, xxxi, 66, 214, 232, 240, 245, 247. *See also* beef; slaughtering, 214
mechanical reapers, 115, 196
mechanization: lack of, 208
Medicine Hat, 233
medium-sized ranches, 151, 180–81
Melrose School, 202
Merchants Bank of Canada, 127, 175
Mernard, J. E., 217
Methodist Church, 218, 331
Middleton, Henry R., 182
Midnapore, xxxi, 21, 116, 207, 209, 234, 343, 345–46; settlers, 206, 208
Midnapore School, xxxii
Midnapore Woollen Mills, 345–47, 376

Midwest Delicatessen, 342
Miles, Joseph A., 130
Military Colonization Ranch Company, 114
mill workers' village, 253
Millarville, xxxi, 172
Miller, Miss, 295
milliners, 294, 299, 302–3
Millward, J. H., 109
Milner, Annie: credit, 303; mail-order service, 303
Miner, Charles A., 360
Mission Bridge, 113
Mitford, 172, 312–15, 318; school, 316
mixed economy, xxxv
mixed farming, 198, 201, 210
Mollison, Annie, 324–26, 376; credit, 327; cultural life, 328; loan from Imperial Bank of Canada, 326; as sole owner-manager, 328
Mollison, James W., 324, 326
Mollison, Jean, 324, 327–28, 376
Molson's Bank, 131, 133, 135, 246, 340
monopolies, 41, 227–28
Monroe, John, 19
Montana: as source for beef, 35
Montana ranching techniques, 159
Montana whiskey traders, 2, 4, 6
Montgomery-Bell, Rothney, 302
Montreal, 106; as central terminus for Canadian Pacific, 68; groceries from, 71; wholesalers, 121
Montrose School, xxxii
Moore, Elizabeth, 130–32, 167
Moore, James Stewart, 130, 167–70
Moore, Margaret, 310
Moore & McDowall Company, 170
Moose Jaw, Saskatchewan, 69
More, Bentley, 313
Morley, xxxi, 113, 155
Morris, Murney, 138, 339
mortgages, 221, 223, 234, 364; chattel, 121, 126, 142, 267, 270, 349
Morton, Rose & Co., 229–30
Mosley, John, 357
Moulton, F. D., 269
Mount, P. J., 266

451

Index

Mount Royal Ranche, 120
Mount Sentinel Ranch, 310
Mounted Police, 10, 48, 50–51, 53, 73, 243, 257, 374; arrival in Alberta, 6, 43; Baker & Co., 19; business with, 49; Davis and, 20; demand for beef, 155–56; forts, xx; great fire, 237–38; horses for, 213; payroll, 24, 36, 52; post, 18; private property, 7; supply contracts, 28, 30, 52, 57, 76, 82, 89–90; whiskey trade and, 7, 15
Murdoch, George, 95, 375; bookkeeping system, 99; Civic Committee, 108; customers, 98; defended farm protest, 189; elected mayor, 109; financial support from wife Margarett, 97, 100; great fire, 239; harness shop, 237; learned harness and saddle making, 96; as mayor, 109, 111–12; retained earnings, 99; retained profits, 100; sold to E. F. Hutchings Saddlery, 255
Murdoch, Margaret (Flood), 96–97, 99
Mutual Life Assurance Company, 337

Namaka, xxxi, 114–15
Nanton, 232
Nanton, Augustus, 229–30, 232–34, 250
Nanton, Harry, 230, 232, 234
Native people, xxvi, xxviii, xxxii, 28, 30, 52, 76, 88, 104, 213; demand for beef, 155–57; difficulties on reserves, 26; Great West Saddlery Company, 259; horses and repeating rifles, 44; hunting and fishing, 28; as markets, xxxiii, 48–49; reliance on government annuities, 27; reserve system, 25–26, 33; trade, 6; trading, 1; Treaty 6, 26; Treaty 7, 25–26, 374; treaty payments, 36, 88; whiskey trade, 2

Native supply contracts, 57, 76, 82, 89; blankets, 88
Native trails, xxix
Native treaties, 25–26
Native treaty money, 36
natural resources, xxvii, 93; development of, xxvi; lumber, 66, 240, 252–53, 312; oil and gas reserves and coal, xxi; timber and coal, 251
Neelin & Wilkinson, 269
neighbouring, 186, 307, 350; Davisburg area, 204
neighbourly and kinship ties, 218
networks: of economic and social ties, 203, 350, 372
Nevitt, Richard, 15, 17
The New West (Ham), 124, 243, 253, 356
New York City, 106
Niblock, J. N., 118, 183
Nicholas Bawlf Company's grain elevator, 197
Nichols, Eliza, 303
Nolan, John A., 209
Norman, Arthur, 353
Norman Block, 336–37; fire, 338
Norris, Howard, 205
Norrish, John D., 117–18
North British Canadian Investment Company, 148, 335, 362
North of Scotland Canadian Mortgage Company, 234–35
North West Mounted Police. *See* Mounted Police
Northern Pacific Railroad, 16, 227
Northwest Company, 41
Northwest Territories: established, xxix; responsible government, 376
Northwest Territories Act, xxxiv, 374
Northwestern Journal of Progress, 347
Nor'Wester, 108
Nose Creek, xxxi, 172
Nose Hills, 187
Nuey, Luey, 341–42
nursing, 294

Oak Lake, Manitoba, 68
O'Connor, Emily, 297
Oddfellows, 219
Ogburn, Robert, 129
oil and gas reserves and coal, xxi
O'Keefe, Michael, 240
Okotoks, xxxi, 117, 167, 220–21, 232, 374
Okotoks High School, 202
Olding, James, 99
Olds, 230, 232
Olson, Will, 253
one-price policy, 276
Oneil, Hillyerd, 205
Ontario Bank, 123
open-range system, 152, 154–55, 169, 178, 181
Order of the Eastern Star, 219
Orr, Wesley F., 190, 250, 364; entrepreneur, 261
Osler, Edmund, 228–30, 233
Osler, Hammond & Nanton, 228–30, 232, 234, 246
Owens, John, 349

Pacific Cartage Co., 366–67
Parlow, C. H., 277
Parrish, Samuel, 128, 141; credit needs, 141–42
Parsons, Miss A., 298
Passmore, Miss L., 296
Patrick, W. H., 33
Patterson, Annie. *See* Brown, Annie (Patterson)
Patton, Daniel, 210
Peigans, xxviii, 1, 7, 20, 26, 88–89, 374; land, 25
Pekisko area, 305–6, 308–9
pemmican, 54
Perley, Henry A., 243, 361
photography, 357, 359; western landscapes, 360
Pickard, James W., 126
Pine Creek, xxxi, 117, 177, 192, 348–50

Pinkham, Bishop Cyprian, 325
Pioneer Meat Market, 249
planing mill, 253
ploughing, 219
Polled Angus, 188
Pollock, William, 194
polo, 179, 182, 352
polo ponies, 175
Portage la Prairie, xxvii
Power, T. C., 31–32
Power & Bro., 23, 149
prairie fires, 215, 219
prairie trails, 62, 66, 226
Pratt, Robert, 350
pre-emption law, 186, 196, 221
Presbyterian Church, 218, 240
price wars: Baker & Co. and G. C. King & Co., 83
Priddis School, xxxii
Prince, John, 252–53
Prince, Peter Anthony, 142, 245, 251, 253–54; mills, 253; technology from Eau Claire, Wis., 252
Prince of Wales Restaurant, 341
Prince's Island, 253
private bankers, 372
private banks, 119, 121–33, 172; and farming operations, 148
private credit networks, 119–21
private property, xxv, xxxiv, 7, 109
progress: belief in, xxxi
prohibition, 283, 328
promissory notes, 34, 142, 267
property rights, 41, 43
property taxes, 110
prosperity, 126, 339
Pue, Pansy L., 298

Queenstown ranch, xxxi, 157–59, 271, 275, 376
Quinn, Edward, 212
Quirk, John, 128, 180–82
Quorn Hunt Club, 167; high society, 169
Quorn Ranche Company, 136, 171,

Index

366; links to Great Britain, 167; loans, 169; owners' lifestyles, 170; starting capital from family and friends, 136

R. G. Dun & Co., 29, 125, 257, 261, 302–3, 340, 357, 361, 364–65
railways, xvii, xxxvi, 66, 226, 242, 369. *See also* Calgary and Edmonton Railway; Canadian Pacific Railway; transportation; accidents, 233; Chicago, Milwaukee & St. Paul Railroad, 69, 71; Chicago & North Western Railroad, 16; construction, xxxi; developmental railroading, 228; federal government financing, xxviii; and formation of capital, 330; rail network, 235; settlement and, xx; St. Paul, Minneapolis & Manitoba Railroad, 69, 71; St. Paul & Pacific Railroad, 67; U.S. railway network, xxxi, 16, 67, 69, 71, 227–28
Ramsay, W. T., 74, 107
ranchers and ranching, xxvi, 20, 115, 118, 149–84, 373; American influence, 152–53, 155, 159, 181; Baker & Co., 275; Bank of Montreal and, 143; barbed-wire fencing, 154, 156, 158, 171, 178; big ranchers, 159; Bragg Creek, 350–54; closed-range ranching, 154, 156, 171, 181; co-operation, 182; community, 151; credit, 148; and farming, 11, 21, 65, 188, 192, 218; financing, 146; Imperial Bank of Canada, 135–36, 138; Lafferty & Smith, 126, 128; medium-sized ranches, 151, 180–81; open-range system, 154–55, 169, 178, 180–81; small ranches, 151, 171–73, 310, 371–72; winter feed, 154, 156,

158, 178, 353; winter of 1886–87, 144, 153
Ranchers' Bank of Canada, 134
Ranchmen's Club, 182–83
Rankin, Andrew D., 95, 106, 113
Rankin & Allan, 105, 107, 138; advertising, 106
Rawlinson, Robert H. M., 361
real estate, 337–38. *See also* land speculation
Rebekahs, 219
Rebellion of 1885. *See* Saskatchewan Rebellion
Red Cloud (steamboat), 16, 33
Red Deer, 232
Reilly, James, 235, 243
Reilly, Mary, 310
reinvested profits, xxvii, 353–54, 367
religious ties, 350
responsible government, xxxiv, 339
restaurant business, 340
retained profits, 99–100, 175, 340, 345, 349; James Lougheed, 332–33
Riley, William James, xxxvi, 217, 245, 255–58
risk takers, xvii
risks, 229
Rivers, Wilfred F., 98
Roberts, W. R., 112
Robertson, William, 289
Robinson, George, 338
Robitaille, Senator Theodore, 250
Rockefeller, John D., 265
Rocking P. Ranch, 307
Rocky Mountains, xxix
Rogers, E. E., 126
Rogers, E. R., 113, 237
Rolls, John K., 132
Roman Catholic church, 218
Rose, Charles D., 230
Roselle, Louis, 49
Ross, A. J., 359
Ross, James, 230
rotating crops, 187, 219
Rouleau, Charles B., 165, 207
round-ups, 152, 175
Rowley, W. H., 327

Royal Canadian Bank, 123
Royal Hotel, 200, 243–44
rule of law, xxv, 41
Rupert's Land, xxix, 42, 374; transfer to Canada, 43; transferred to Dominion of Canada, 7
rural society, 175, 182–83, 193, 210. *See also* farmers and farming; ranchers and ranching; social activities, 182–83, 330; support networks, 186, 203–4, 215, 218, 350, 372; urban and rural connections, xix, xxii; work exchanges, 175, 180, 183, 210, 221, 315, 348, 350

S. J. Hogg & Co., 128
S. Parrish & Son, 236
Sacred Heart Convent, xxxii, 209, 375
saddle and harness making, 66, 217, 245
saloons: licence fees, 111
Samples, A. P., 44
Samuel T. Mayhood family, 172
sandstone, 240–41, 243–44, 261–62, 265, 278, 281, 334, 337
Sandstone Calgary, 262
Sandstone City, 244
Sanford, Vail & Co., 103
Sarcees, xxviii, 1, 7, 20, 26, 45, 89, 155, 157, 374; land, 25
Saskatchewan, xxxiv; formation, xxxiv
Saskatchewan Rebellion, xxxiv, 83, 86–87, 99, 134, 164, 189, 350–51
Saunders, William, 327
savings, 180, 329
sawmills, 245, 254; and lumber businesses, 117; steam-powered, 253
Schumpeter, Joseph, xviii
Second Industrial Revolution, xxxvi, 66, 119
self-finance, xxvii
settlement, xxix, 43, 329; and business development, xvii

settlers, 20, 115, 156, 172, 188–89, 191, 208, 232. *See also* farmers; homesteading; credit, 234–35; land available for, 230; open range and, 166; from Quebec, 199
shanties, 239, 262
sharing: social activities, 182–83, 330; of work, 175, 210
Sharpe, George A., 290
Sharples, John, 297
Shaw, Helen, 331, 343–44, 347
Shaw, Maltman, 347
Shaw, Samuel, 116, 132, 148, 331, 343, 376; debt, 345–46; general store, 345; loans, 347; Midnapore Woollen Mills, 345; mixed farming, 345; retained profits, 345
sheep, 117, 151, 162–66; drives, 163; wool and mutton, 164
Sheep Creek, 167
Sheep Creek Agricultural Society, 221
Sheep Creek Ranche, 375; diversified into horses, 168; starting capital from family and friends, 167; winter of 1886–87, 168
Shelton, Arthur E., 138, 147, 228
shopping as pleasure, 266
short-term credit. *See* credit
shorthand, 297
Shorthorn cows, 212
Sisters of Charity. *See* Grey Nuns
Slattery, Leo, 270
slaughtering. *See under* meat
Slideout, 2
small farming, 371–72
small ranches, 151, 171–73, 310, 371–72
small retailers, 371
smallpox, 322
Smith, Bruce, 129
Smith, Donald A., 68, 82, 139, 332
Smith, Frederick, 122–23, 125, 127–28; death, 129
Smith, Reverend E. Paske, 313
Smith, Rozella, 269

455

Index

Smith & More, 313
Smithers, Charles F., 139–40
social activities: sharing of, 182–83, 330
social relations, xxxvi, 348; ranching, 183
social responsibility, xxi, 330
social stability, 339
social structures, xxxiv
social support network, 204
soil conservation, 219
Somerville, Grace, 353
Soules, T. W., 113
Soules & McGinnes, 138
South Sea Bubble, 41
Spalding, Charles, 130
Spalding, John, 130
Sparrow, Angus C., 164
Sparrow, Charles, 237
Speakman, R. E., 327
Springbank, xxxi, 218
squatters, 58, 72–73, 155, 166, 211, 305
St. Hilda's Ladies' College, xxxii, 376
St. Paul, Minneapolis & Manitoba Railroad, 69, 71
St. Paul & Pacific Railroad, 67
standard of living, 329
Standoff, 2
Steele, Sam, 99
stenography, 295–97
Stephen, George, 68–69
Stephen Avenue, 74–75, 77
Stewart, Alexander P., 165–66
Stimson, Joseph, 144
stockyards, 149–50, 240, 251
Stoneys, xxviii, 1, 7, 20, 26, 45, 78, 89, 155, 157, 374; land, 25
stopping houses, 222, 349. *See also* hotels
Strachey, L., 145
Strange, Major-General Thomas B., 85, 114
Stuart, Alexander, 165–66; dismissed from British American Ranche, 166
Suitor, David, 210–11; horse breeder, 213
Suitor, David and Mary, 212–13

Suitor, David Jr., 211, 213
Suitor, Grace (Welch), 214
Suitor, Jack, 212
Suitor, James: took over home place, 214
Suitor, James Jr.: took over family farm in 1930s, 214
Suitor, Mary (McKeage), 211
Suitor, Violet (Bolton), 214
Suitor, William, 212
Suitor farms: network of, 212
Sunlight Restaurant, 341–42, 376
support networks, 215, 218; economic and social ties, 203, 350, 372; neighbouring, 186, 350
Supreme Court of the Northwest Territories, 170, 221, 333, 339
Swann, Edward J., 170–71

T. C. Power & Bro., 14, 30–31, 44, 238; stockyards, 149
Taylor, Edmund, 277, 283, 285–88, 290; low price strategy, 289
technology, 115, 196, 200, 213, 369; advances in, xxxvi; farming, 187; of industrialization, 348; meat packing, 249; mechanical reapers, 115, 196; from New Brunswick and Chicago, 96; new ideas, 218; photographic, 359; refrigerator cars, 249; sawmill technology, 252; threshing machines, 115, 196
Tees, Costigan & Wilson, 34, 71
telegraph, xvii, xxxvi, 66, 71; lines, 369; operators, 295, 297
telephone, xxxvi, 294; operators, 295
tension: farmers and ranchers, 218
territorial government: funds for agricultural societies, 216
territorial law, xxxv
Thompson, Arthur, 128
Thomson, Helen, 284–85
Thomson, Henry Inglis: threshing outfit, 215

Index

Thomson, James, 87, 89, 237, 273, 275–86; diversification, 88
Thomson, John V., 215
Thomson Bros. bookstore, 356, 364
Thornton, Charles, 266
Thorp, Bernt, 253
threshing, 210, 214–15; machines, 115, 196
timber and coal, 251
tobacco, 104
Toole, William "Barney," 191
Toole Peet, 191
Toronto *Globe*, 243–44, 246–47, 250, 254
Toronto Industrial Exhibition, 217
trails, 10; freighting roads, 11; influence, xx; prairie trails, 62, 66, 226
transportation, xx, 67, 151, 218. *See also* railways; Baker & Co., 33, 71, 83; Calgary and Edmonton Railway, 191, 196, 203, 227, 232; Calgary-Edmonton route, 39; costs, 52, 57; difficulties for Calgary store, 45–47, 62; Fort Benton-Calgary route, 39; freighters and wagoners, xx, 49; Great Plains, 16; high cost, 39; Hudson's Bay Co., 54, 61; improvements in, xxx, 125–26, 251, 369; revolution in, xvii, xxxvi, 66; stagecoach, 233; steamboats, 16, 59, 78; technical changes, 10; technology, 370; wagons, 10, 33, 233, 369
Trimble, Miss M., 277, 295
Trounce, W. P., 247–48
Tupper, Sir Charles, 280
Turf Club, 110
Two Dot Ranch, 246; loans to, 143
typing, 294, 296–97
Underwood, Kate, 301
Union Bank of Canada, 133, 135, 337
United Farmers of Alberta, 222
upward mobility, 329
urban and rural connections, xix, xxii

Valiquette, Sister Elizabeth, 320, 322
Van Horne, William, 69, 261, 312–16
Vanwart, John G., 100–02
Vaughan, J. W., 315
Vaux, A., 277
vertically integrated operations, 250
veterinary care, 187
Victorianism, xxxi, xxxii, 15–16, 218, 373
voluntary associations, 218–19
Votier, James, 267–68

wagons, 10, 33, 233, 369
Walker, James, 59, 108–9, 113, 138, 160–61, 216, 251
Wallace, Dick, 214
Ware, John, 151, 168
water, xxix, xxx, 94, 157, 171, 201, 208; distribution, 110; source, 211; system, 107; wells, 212, 215, 239; William Andrews' farm, 204
Watson, Eliza, 349
Watson, Harry, 348–50
Watson, Sandy, 331, 367; exchanged work, 348–49; loan from Le Jeune, Smith & Co., 349; mixed farming, 348, 350; retained earnings, 349; Watson House, 349
Watson House, 349
Watt & Co.'s tobacco store, 338
wells, 212, 215; Calgary, 239
Western Canada College, xxxii, 376
Western Stock Growers' Association, 182–83, 317–18
Weyerhauser, Frederick, 252
wheat, 190; national and international markets, xxxi
Whiffen, Alfred E., 327
whiskey related violence, 6
whiskey trade, 2–3, 7, 15
whiskey traders, 14–15; Alberta, 2; conflict with Native Canadians, 3–4, 6; life in Alberta, 3
White, Frank, 312–13

457

Index

White, Fred, 24
White Eagle, 4
Whitford, Willie, 49
wholesalers: goods on credit, 121
Whoop-Up Trail, 3–4, 11, 16
Whyte, William, 184, 242, 314
Wickenden, Osborne, 278
Widdicombe, John, 130
Wilkie, D. R., 135–36
Willow Creek Ranche, 146
Willows Ranch, 324; as collateral, 326
Wilson, James L., 178, 241
Wilson, Stephen, 129
Winder Ranche, 136
winter 1886–87, 153, 156, 168; Benton & St. Louis Cattle Co., 156; Little Bow Cattle Co., 312
winter feed, 154, 156, 158, 178, 353
Winterbottom, Edwin, 178
Wolley-Dod, Annie Frances (Brown), 177–79, 217
Wolley-Dod, Arthur G., 176, 178–79, 375; as gardener, 180; governess, 179; loans, 178; married Annie Frances Brown, 177; mortgages, 178–79; savings and family wealth, 177–78; work exchanges, 180
Wolley-Dod, Hova, 178, 180
women, xxviii; in banking, 130; in business, xxvi, 123, 293–328, 339–40; business training, 298; department store customers, xxviii, 107, 266–69, 286, 291; entrepreneurship, xxviii, 299; office work, 295–97; ranchers, 305–10; ratio of men and women, 102; roles, 293; salaries, 296; wives role in business ventures, 310; in workforce, 294–98
wool and mutton, 164
woollen mills, 116
Worden, Hiram G., 340
work exchanges, 175, 180, 183, 210, 221, 315, 348, 350; co-operative efforts, 214
working capital, 304
World's Fair, Chicago, 1893, xxxvi
Wright, Bryce, 128, 130
Wrigley, Joseph, 80–82, 86–89, 237, 272–73, 275–80
Wyllie, William B., 126

Young, Harrison, 279

www.ingramcontent.com/pod-product-compliance
Lightning Source LLC
Chambersburg PA
CBHW070746230426
43665CB00017B/2267